No Room for Mistakes

No Room for Mistakes

British and Allied Submarines in European Waters 1939–1940

Geirr H Haarr

Seaforth
PUBLISHING

To those still on patrol

Copyright © Geirr H Haarr 2015

First published in Great Britain in 2015 by
Seaforth Publishing,
Pen & Sword Books Ltd,
47 Church Street,
Barnsley S70 2AS

www.seaforthpublishing.com

British Library Cataloguing in Publication Data
A catalogue record for this book is available from the British Library
ISBN 978 1 84832 206 6

Maps by Peter Wilkinson
Typeset and designed by JCS Publishing Services Ltd, www.jcs-publishing.co.uk
Printed and bound in Great Britain by CPI Group (UK) Ltd, Croydon, CR0 4YY

Contents

Acknowledgements

MANY PEOPLE HAVE CONTRIBUTED to this book, some from a lifetime of their own research, others with a small but important detail. Their contributions are highly appreciated.

Above all, the selfless help and support from David Goodey is gratefully acknowledged. Were it not for him, this project would have been shelved a long time ago. Erling Skjold, Erik Ettrup, Stewart Clewlow, David Roberts and Andrew Smith are also thanked sincerely. Without their help and constant support nothing would have been achieved.

The nameless staffs of The National Archives at Kew, the Bundesarchiv in Koblenz and Freiburg, the Imperial War Museum in London and Riksarkivet in Oslo deserve thanks for patience and professional dedication.

The members of the Traditiekamer Onderzeedienst in Den Helder, Holland, Jouke Spoelstra and Frans Klut, are warmly thanked for great enthusiasm and superb assistance, together with Hans Jehee of the Werkgroep Kriegsmarine and Anselm van der Peet of the Netherlands Institute for Naval History.

Likewise, Horst Bredow and Peter Monte at the U-boot Archiv in Cuxhaven are also thanked for sharing their time and keenness with me and for letting me use their files and archives. Sadly I received the news that Horst Bredow had passed away as the manuscript of this book was being completed. He spent a lifetime dedicated to naval history and he will be deeply missed.

I owe George Malcomson at the Royal Navy Submarine Museum in Gosport great thanks for repeated support and assistance as well as Andrew Jeffrey and David Kett at Dundee International Submarine Memorial.

Basil Abbott, manager at Diss Museum in Norfolk is warmly thanked for his enthusiastic assistance.

Julian Mannering at Seaforth Publishing deserves many thanks for believing in me and giving me the deadlines I needed. Without his support the project might never have seen completion. The fine maps were made by Peter Wilkinson who has a patience beyond comprehension with my many demands and changes. Similarly, Steve Williamson has been fantastic in completing the manuscript.

My friends in RMHF, Øistein Berge, Atle Skarsten, Odin Leirvag, Tor Ødemotland, Erik Ettrup, Asbjørn Husebø and Hjalmar Sunde have been providing information, archive material and photos as well as historical and military rectifications.

Rick Harding, Reinhard Hoheisel-Huxmann, Olve Dybvig, Atle Wilmar, Paul Sedal, Ragnar Ulstein, Jac Baart, Robert Briggs, Andrzej Bartelski, Peter Kreutzer, Thorsten Reich, Tore Eggan and Ulf Larsstuvold all deserve acknowledgement.

Last, but not least, thanks to my beloved wife Gro, for accepting that my passion for her is shared with that for naval history, listening patiently when I needed to discuss some detail and skilfully distracting me when I needed to relax.

Geirr H Haarr
Sola, Stavanger, August 2015

There is no room for mistakes in submarines.
You are either alive or dead.

Vice-Admiral Max Horton

Introduction

Damned Un-English Vessels[1]

THE SUBMARINES OF THE late 1930s spent most of their time on the surface; they were really sea-going torpedo boats capable of operating underwater to hide from enemy predators. To be able to submerge, several fighting capabilities such as speed and observation had to be sacrificed, and going underwater was, early in WWII, largely a defensive or stealth measure. Its nature as a fighting vessel was very different from anything on the surface and required different thinking, training, tactics and strategies to function to its full potential; above all, the quality of the men and equipment, then as now, was what made a submarine work optimally.

In addition to the actual losses inflicted on enemy warships, transports and men, the threat of submarines in an area tied up vast resources dedicated to anti-submarine (A/S) measures. Inevitably, being a small vessel with relatively few men on board, each individual boat could be considered expendable by most naval strategists and could therefore be given riskier missions with less hope of coming back than other naval vessels. All the more so as it was a versatile weapon capable of delivering torpedoes and mines, performing reconnaissance and rescue missions, acting as a navigational beacon, and landing special units on enemy coastlines.

Above all, though, submarines were and are lethal threats to maritime supply lines and with Great Britain in particular being dependent on such, they were traditionally viewed with a certain distaste by the Royal Navy as well as the British public prior to WWII. The success of the German U-boats during the Great War did nothing to change this, even though British submarines were rather successful too, particularly in the Baltic and the Mediterranean. Quite to the contrary, the description of German U-boats and their submariners in British propaganda vastly overshadowed the exploits of the boats of the Royal Navy, which to some extent were toned down for political and intelligence reasons. In various disarmament conferences between the wars, British politicians actually sought to abolish the submarine as a weapon of war.

In early 1919 the Royal Navy could muster 122 submarines, 58 capital ships, 103 cruisers and 456 destroyers. Great Britain was the unchallenged master of the seas. Following WWI, widespread economic and social reforms were necessary and reduced military spending was inevitable. The British Navy would become almost insignificant within ten years and one by one, the shipbuilding and ordnance companies collapsed or merged, leaving a minimal workforce with relevant skills.

By September 1922, the number of submarines in commission with the Royal Navy had fallen to forty-four with eleven in reserve. A parallel plummeting of proficiency and understanding among the staffs in particular and naval officers in general, resulted in a British submarine policy that at best can be characterised as confused some years after WWI. Admiral Arthur Cheveson, C-in-C Far Eastern Fleet, inadvertently summed up the attitude of the Royal Navy in 1924 when he wrote in a memo: 'Until I have got a great number of destroyers on the station, I would not spend a shilling on submarines

. . . submarine thinking officers, as well as others, are beginning to admit that their capabilities in their pet line are a good deal over-rated.'[2]

The result was that the Admiralty saw the submarine as a tactical weapon, at best adding to the capability of a surface fleet. Two distinct concepts were pursued, both complete failures as it turned out: patrol submarines to replace the need for cruiser squadrons at far-flung imperial bases, particularly in the Far East, and the so-called fleet submarines to operate with battle groups of capital surface vessels. Attempting to develop such types of boats, contrary to the experience available to the strategists from WWI, strained the meagre technological and human resources available, tied up tonnage available to the Royal Navy through the treaties, and lulled commanders and tacticians of the surface fleet into believing that the general threat from submarines was manageable. Britain's own submarines were seen to have a limited role in the defence of the sea lanes and the submarines of potentially alien nations, it was believed, could be handled by the technology available to the Royal Navy.

Hence, the Submarine Service was not given much priority by the Admiralty between the wars. The boats built between 1918 and 1934 were large, slow and unreliable – not because the British shipbuilding industry could not build proper submarines, but because they were built as specified by the Admiralty. 'It has been apparent to many Submarine and other Officers that the new construction submarines built and delivered since the war are not nearly as well thought out as they should have been,' wrote George Villar, engineer captain at the staff of the Rear Admiral Submarines – RA(S) – in December 1934 in the foreword to his paper on British submarine design. Rather than facing up to the fact that the available technologies were inadequate and tactics outdated, the Royal Navy steadfastly held on to the concept that naval wars would be won by big guns.[3] This was a belief that would cost many submariners their lives.

One example of how casually some of the issues related to submarines were treated is their diving depth. The O-, P- and R-class boats were designed to withstand pressures normally found at 500 feet. Nevertheless, RA(S) laid down 300 feet as the maximum test diving depth of the boats and gave them a routine operational depth of 200 feet or less. In 1928, the director of tactical division (DTD) explained: 'The ability to dive to 500 feet was introduced principally in order that pressure hulls of these submarines should be more capable of withstanding the effect of the explosion of a depth charge. Submarine officers do not visualise any intentional diving to such depths as 500 feet though the ability to do so is an asset in the event of an involuntary deep dive which might cause the submarine to go much deeper than ever was intended.'[4] It has not been possible to find reference to an in-depth analysis of the tactical use of a submarine, its ways of avoiding an enemy or the weapons that may be used against it as a basis for such an analysis resulting in these rather arbitrary round numbers.

According to the terms of the Washington Treaty, the first new-built submarine after the armistice of WWI, *Oberon*, would reach her retirement age in the mid-1940s and would be quickly followed by the other O-, P- and R-class boats. Hence, new-builds were being forced on the Royal Navy. Further submarine restrictions were imposed by the 1930 London Naval Treaty, which sanctioned 52,700 tons for Britain.[5] The second London Naval Treaty signed in 1936 was in effect a failure, ending further attempts at regulating international naval armament.[6] Nevertheless, it would influence British submarine construction significantly. Stanley Baldwin's Conservative government, against the advice of the Admiralty, actually suggested abolishing all submarines or, failing that, limiting their size to 250 tons. Predictably, this was rejected and the numbers from the first treaty remained, adding an upper individual limit for each submarine of 2,000 tons. For all practical purposes the prospect of regulating naval shipbuilding was over but the internal discussions within the Royal Navy and the pressures from the government to abandon all use of submarines had made their mark. Boats with a displacement of about 1,000 tons were seen as a suitable compromise between size and functionality. Discrepancies as to their final design and armament between the director of naval construction (DNC) and RA(S) delayed the construction of the new boats by more than a year.[7]

On 1 May 1935 Admiral Reginald Henderson, Third Sea Lord and controller of the navy, called a meeting in the Admiralty. RA(S) attended, as did the assistant chief of the Naval Staff, director of naval construction, deputy engineer-in-chief, director of naval equipment and the director of electrical equipment. The subject of the meeting was the design of the new patrol submarine, what was to become the T-class, in light of the various treaty limitations and the experiences of the S-class boats, from the mid-1930s. A broad agreement was reached, and the formal staff requirement was drawn up following the meeting. Still, it would be December before tenders were invited from Cammell Laird, Vickers-Armstrongs and Scotts, and February 1936 before the design based on these received the final approval by the Admiralty Board. On 5 March 1936, the first boat of the class, *Triton*, was ordered from Vickers. Belatedly, the Royal Navy Submarine Service finally had a purpose.[8]

Along the way, however, just before the outbreak of WWII, an unlucky accident would illustrate the challenges facing the submariners as well as the incompetence and prejudice still existing in the Royal Navy against submarines. The lack of understanding in the traditional navy of what a submarine actually was, what conditions on board were like and, not least, how to deal with an emergency would all be tragically illustrated. To the public, the disaster would be all the more mystifying as the Royal Navy was supposed to be master of the seas with large warships providing stability and safety, not horrible deaths in home waters.

— 1 —

The Admiralty Regrets

'. . .has failed to surface'

THETIS, THE FIRST OF the new T-class submarines to be built at Cammell Laird's yard in Birkenhead, slid down the slipway into the river Mersey on 29 June 1938. Within months, officers and ratings assigned to her crew arrived at Birkenhead to familiarise themselves with their new boat and see her through the fitting-out and work-up period. *Thetis*'s commander, Lieutenant Commander Guy 'Sam' Bolus was among the first, as was Lieutenant Frederick Woods, the torpedo officer. He arrived in October 1938 to oversee the torpedo room assembly, including the tubes and their internal and external fittings.

The early trim and torpedo-firing tests were conducted in Cammell Laird's Wet Basin in March 1939. A number of minor items were logged for attention, including pipes and indicators that were found to be missing or had not been properly connected. Lieutenant Commander Bolus took *Thetis* to sea for the first time in late April. Prior to leaving the yard, *Thetis* had been declared seaworthy by Bolus, Principal Ship Overseer Lieutenant Albert Hill and some officials from Cammell Laird. Even so, the trial was a complete failure, embarrassing to the naval personnel as well as the shipbuilders. Firstly, when

Thetis in the wet-basin at Cammell Laird, testing trim and basic operations. (Author's Collection)

orders were given for port rudder, *Thetis* promptly swung to starboard: the steering mechanisms had been incorrectly fitted. Secondly, the forward hydroplanes jammed when tested. Bolus decided enough was enough and turned back. The fact that such faults could have escaped the yard's own quality control as well as the navy overseers seems to have been taken rather lightly.

While the repairs to the steering gear and rudder were effectuated, the insides of the six forward torpedo tubes were coated with bitumastic paint and enamel to prevent corrosion and ensure the torpedoes would run smoothly. This highly specialised work, which included liquidising the solution with a blow torch, had been sub-contracted to the Wailes Dove Bitumastic company. Upon completion, the job was supposedly inspected and approved by an assistant Admiralty overseer who, it seems, had no previous experience with this kind of work. How well this inspection was performed would later become an issue of contention among those involved and is still disputed today.[1]

Eventually, *Thetis* was declared ready and left Birkenhead for a second attempt at passing her diving trials on the morning of 1 June 1939. Unlike the first time, when the trials were to have been performed in the sheltered Gare Loch off the Clyde, Bolus this time intended to go no further than Liverpool Bay to save time. *Thetis* had not been commissioned and was technically still the property of Cammell Laird. The purpose of the sea trials was to verify that the ship had been built according to contract so that invoices from the yard could be honoured. According to Admiralty manuals, all trials 'shall be conducted at the risk and at the expense of the Contractors. [. . .] The diving, trimming and submergence trials shall be carried out by Naval Officers and crew. The contractors shall work the main and auxiliary machinery etc., and provide a pilot with attendant vessel.' The shipbuilders were not trained to work together as a team and the navy provided the crew to operate the submarine during the tests. Lieutenant Commander Bolus would be the connection between the two sets of men and no one had any doubt that he would hold sole command at sea. The whole trip was supposed to last for thirteen hours, of which three would be submerged.[2]

In addition to *Thetis*'s complement of fifty-one, a large number of Cammell Laird personnel, overseers and observers had embarked, making a total of 103 men on board. The extras were Henry Oram, Captain(S) of the 5th Submarine Flotilla at Gosport, nine other naval officers, six civilian Admiralty overseers, thirty-three employees of Cammell Laird and Vickers-Armstrongs, two employees of a catering firm and a pilot. The naval board of inquiry later concluded that at least a dozen of these should have disembarked before the test-dive commenced.[3] To escort *Thetis* and stand by on the surface during the trials, Cammell Laird's tug *Grebe Cock* under Master Alfred Godfrey had been chartered. Also on board the tug were Lieutenant Richard Coltart and telegraphist Victor Crosby. It was intended that personnel not strictly needed on board *Thetis* should transfer to *Grebe Cock* before the dive. At 13:30, though, some fifteen miles off Great Ormes Head, *Grebe Cock* was hailed and informed that nobody would disembark the submarine and that the dive was about to commence. Ten minutes later a signal was sent from *Thetis* to the 5th Submarine Flotilla operations centre at Fort Blockhouse, Gosport, with a copy to the Admiralty and C-in-C Portsmouth, informing them that the submarine was ready to begin its dive and would dive for up to three hours. Captain Oram later wrote:

Picture the Control Room crammed with people. Under normal conditions, the captain would have been surrounded by his First Lieutenant, Navigating Officer, two hydroplane operators, helmsman, asdic operator and his mate, the Electrical Artificer, the Outside ERA and his mate, the Control Room messenger and the signalman. That adds up to 'a ton of men' according to the old submarine saying. In *Thetis*' Control Room that day, we were nearly a ton-and-a-half, including the two other submarine captains, the Admiralty Constructor, Mr. Bailey, and myself. Conditions were undeniably cramped [. . .]. Bolus was standing at the periscope and I was somewhere near him just watching what was happening. [. . .] We made ourselves as inconspicuous as possible. Then came the command: 'Open up for diving'.[4]

At first, there was a rush of air from the submarine, clearly heard on board *Grebe Cock*, as Bolus ordered the main vents to be opened. Once the tanks had been filled, *Thetis* should have been at neutral buoyancy and able to dive using her hydroplanes, slowly and deliberately, to maintain control. To the surprise of those aboard the tug, though, *Thetis* did not submerge as expected, until, just before 15:00, she suddenly disappeared beneath the surface.[5]

When, at 14:00, Lieutenant Commander Bolus gave the order to take *Thetis* down, she was too light and unable to dive, even with the use of increased speed and hydroplanes, as well as additional water being taken into the auxiliary tanks. A check of all the tanks was instigated to verify that the amount of water on board corresponded with the 'trim chit'.[6] This included an inspection of whether the internal forward torpedo tubes (numbers five and six) had been filled with water, as they were supposed to have been before leaving the yard, effecting ballast in the absence of torpedoes.

On the inner rear door of each torpedo tube, a small-bore test-cock could be opened, allowing liquid to spill out in a controlled manner if the tube contained water. No water coming out of the test-cock would indicate it was empty, or nearly so, and therefore that the

Thetis leaving Birkenhead in the morning of 1 June 1939. (Wirral)

bow cap was closed. On this morning, with *Thetis* still on the surface, the torpedo officer Lieutenant Woods opened the test-cocks on tubes five and six to verify they contained water. Number six tube produced a small amount of water, indicating it was at least half full. From number five test cock, there was nothing – neither air nor water. Woods concluded that number six tube had some water in it and number five was empty or nearly so. He made his way to the control room and reported his findings to First Lieutenant Harold Chapman, asking if they were not meant to be full. To his surprise, he got conflicting answers. Chapman confirmed they should be full, while the supervisor from Cammell Laird, Arthur Robinson, said no, and that this had been changed from that on the trim chit and they were now empty. Lieutenant Chapman sent him back to check once more. Convinced that number five tube was empty, Woods this time checked only number six tube and, getting the same result, reported to the control room that this was half full.[7]

Unknown to all on board, during the painting and subsequent enamelling of the torpedo tubes, the inspection hole leading to number five test cock had been blocked, creating a stopper that now prevented water from the torpedo tube dripping out, thus unable to reveal the true status of the tube. This had not been discovered by the naval overseer Edward Grundy or the commissioned engineer Roy Glenn, neither of whom had examined the interior of the doors meticulously.

To verify that the inspection tubes were open and free of debris, a 10-centimetre (4-inch) brass pin, known as a rimer, was provided in a housing at each door, to clear any obstructions. Woods did not use the rimers, either the first time he checked the tubes or the second time, after coming back from the control room. He later stated that he believed the employees of Cammell Laird should have checked that the holes were clear in a new submarine and that he had not even noticed that there was a rimer fitted to the test cock. Neither did Woods check the inboard drain valves, which were meant to empty a tube flooded after firing a torpedo before loading a new one. Had he done so, this would unequivocally have revealed whether there was water in the tube. The report from the naval inquiry later concluded that the general safety instructions, as well as Woods's training on this point, had been inadequate.[8]

Having reported again the status of the torpedo tubes, as he believed them to be, Woods asked Chapman if he might be requested to fill the tubes. Receiving a confirmation to this, he started to prepare the necessary procedures to do so if requested. Woods then started to inspect the tubes to see if they were dry by opening the inner rear doors. Why this was necessary at this stage was never fully explained and it is incomprehensible that he would do so without the consent of Bolus or Chapman. If the two tubes had been flooded for ballast as intended, the water would have run into the bilges when the doors were opened, upsetting the trim even further. At the tribunal, Woods said that he:

> wished to inform the First Lieutenant of the state of the tubes and to see if they were dry myself [and] that the bow caps were not leaking. [. . .] I had information from a Cammell Laird official that the tube was not full. That, coupled of course with the use of the test cock, wiped out in my mind any idea that it was full.[9]

As part of the door-opening procedure, Woods ordered power to be put through to the telemotor bow-cap operating panel. Provided the bow-cap operating levers were in the 'shut' position, this should have resulted in all caps being shut, if they were not already so. It could not be ascertained later with absolute certainty that switching the power to the forward section had been fully effectuated in time. The operating levers were mounted on a small panel, outboard of the tubes. The levers of tubes one, three and five were on the starboard bulkhead, the other three on the port. In addition to 'open' and 'shut' the levers had a central 'neutral' position. It appears from several statements that when *Thetis* left port that morning the operating levers were at 'neutral' rather than 'shut' position, contrary to practice. If the lever was taken from 'open' directly to 'neutral' without being taken all the way over to the 'shut' position first, this may explain why number five tube was open. Woods insisted the operating levers were all reported in the 'shut' position, but admitted he had not checked himself that they were.

Instead, he maintained, he checked the mechanical bow-cap indicators to ascertain they were in the 'shut' position. These indicators were badly positioned and had a confused layout on the forward bulkhead, between the two vertical columns of rear doors. From top to bottom, the indicators were arranged in pairs, one mirroring the other so that what was read on one indicator appeared opposite to the way it was read on the one below. They had to be inspected from close up and could not all be seen at the same time. Number two was on top, followed by number one, four, three and six with number five at the base. Woods later said: 'I remember repeating in my mind, as I looked at each indicator, the words "shut", "shut", "shut", looking at number five first, then progressing upwards. I was satisfied at the time that it did show me "shut".[10]

Leading Seaman Walter Hambrook was assisting Lieutenant Woods. They had worked together on board the *Osiris*, where the forward lay-out was similar, and the two men knew each other and the routine they were about to perform well. It is difficult to believe that, even if the mechanics of the operations were cumbersome, both men should make coinciding mistakes or misreads in both the levers and the indicators at the same time. Satisfied that only number six tube contained water, the rear doors of tubes one to four were opened after testing that no water escaped from the cocks. Woods continued:

> I opened number five test-cock [once again] in the same manner and there was no sign of air or water. Then assisted by [Hambrook], I commenced to open number five rear door. I thought it was just a little that had not been drained away. I have seen this happen before.[11]

With the final movement of the rear-door lever, at about 15:10, water began to trickle from the bottom of the tube. Suddenly, the door was flung backward and a massive inrush of seawater almost knocked the men in the forward compartment off their feet. The bow cap of number five tube was open and now, with the inner door open too, water was pouring in at an alarming rate. Woods yelled, 'Get out of the compartment' and, turning to the petty officer at the telephone, shouted, 'Tell them to blow for Christ's sake.' As the indicators had shown all bow caps to be shut, his immediate thought was that there was a fracture in the tube, opening it to the outside. He later held that at no stage did it occur to him that the bow cap was open, adding that, had he realised, he might have been able to close it by using the operating lever.[12]

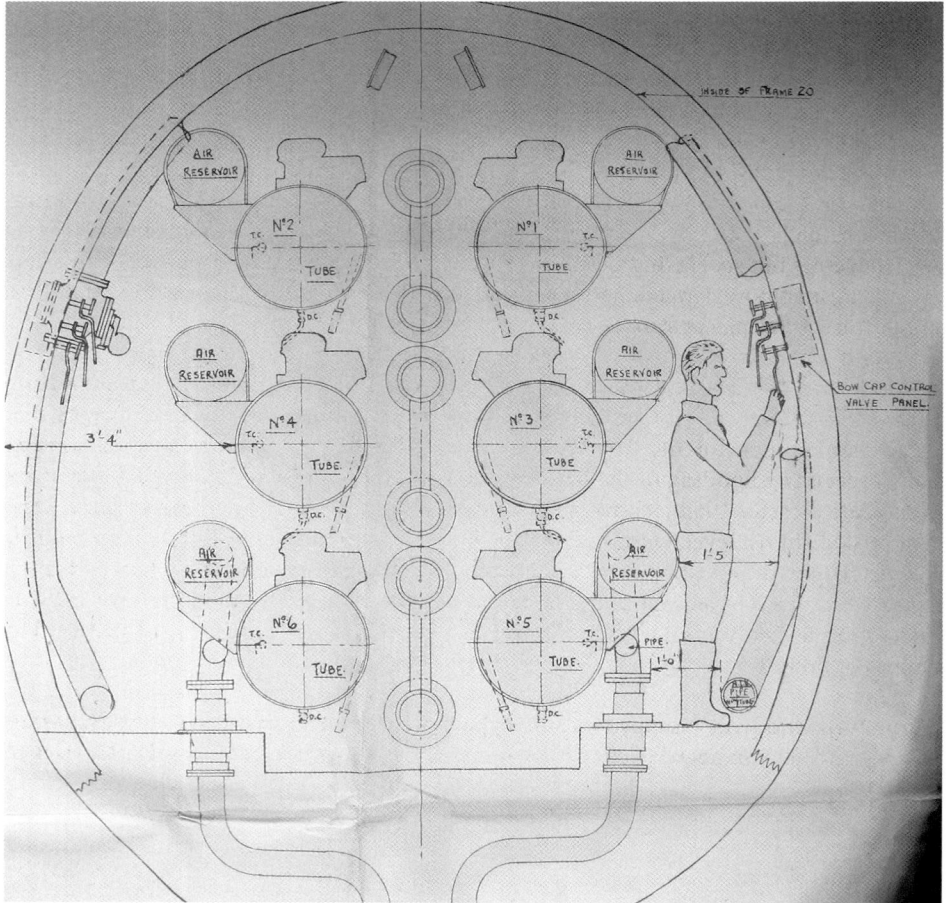

Sketch of the forward interior of the torpedo room of *Thetis*. This diagram was used at the public inquiry to describe the position of the bow cap control levers (left and right bulkhead) and indicators (between the torpedo tubes). Number five torpedo tube is lower right. (NA TS 32/112)

Oram did not need to be told something was wrong. The rush of air through the boat and sharp rise in air pressure indicated water was coming in and he immediately advised Bolus to blow the main tanks forward, which he did. For a while it seemed that *Thetis* was safe, but the inrush of water through the open torpedo tube was larger than the amount of water forced out of the tanks and slowly the bow tipped down, faster and faster as the incoming water gained weight. In less than ten seconds, some thirty tons of water had come inside the hull and the forward compartment was three-quarters full. Bolus realised he was wasting air by continuing to blow and gave the order to stop.

Woods and his men struggled out of the tube compartment and into the torpedo stowage compartment behind it. From there, they started to close the door in no. 25 bulkhead between the compartments in order to contain the water as far forward as possible.[13] In all, eighteen clips were welded to the door to ensure it would be completely watertight when shut. Some of the lower clips were hanging down, however, apparently becoming caught against the lower combing, preventing the door from being shut against the angle of the bow tilting downwards. The clips should have been secured in spring holders, actually made by Woods and not according to design specifications, but they were evidently not so. Having a door with a complicated closing mechanism as the main defence against bow damage had been questioned by several of those stationed in the compartment during construction.[14]

Now it was just not possible to close the door fully and the men had to give up before it was too late and move back to the next watertight door. They must have known that the submarine was not likely to ever surface again with water filling two of the forward compartments. The door leading to the third compartment was closed in time, preventing flooding of the battery stowage area, which would have led to a more immediate disaster. *Thetis*'s bow reached the seabed at 150 feet (46 metres). Slowly the boat settled almost level, with the bow down 6 degrees. Emergency lighting was rigged, the watertight doors that were not holding water opened again and two indicator buoys were released as well as a smoke flare. After an inspection of the forward end of the submarine, Bolus, Oram and senior personnel from Cammell Laird gathered to discuss options.[15]

When *Thetis* suddenly disappeared after apparently struggling to dive for the best part of an hour, the men on board *Grebe Cock* wondered if something was wrong, but the lack of

The tug *Grebe Cock*: not up to the assigned task. (Author's Collection)

any emergency signals meant that they took no action. Surprisingly, none of the smoke flares or indicator buoys released by *Thetis* after she went down was seen. Why this was so is one of the puzzling matters of this affair. It may be that the wire of the aft buoy got entangled and the forward one could have broken loose in the tide.

There was no firm knowledge on board the tug of when to expect the submarine back on the surface, but by 15:45 concern was growing and a signal was composed to Fort Blockhouse, the submarine headquarters at Gosport. In order not to raise any undue alarm, though, Coltart phrased it as a question: 'What was the duration of *Thetis* dive?' *Grebe Cock* was at the limit of the range of her radio set, however, and it took time until contact eventually was established with land and the telegram signal could be sent. Meanwhile, *Grebe Cock* was drifting in the strong tidal currents and Coltart and Godfrey no longer had any clear knowledge of *Thetis's* position. Master Godfrey was ordered to keep his position as best he could so that they had an idea of the vicinity where *Thetis* had dived. Due to the currents and water depth, however, it was 16:30 before anchoring was achieved, as *Grebe Cock's* two anchor cables had to be shackled together. The position in which the tug finally anchored was at least three miles west of *Thetis*, but nobody on board knew the extent of the drift with any certainty.[16]

The telegram was not marked with any urgency and therefore dispatched routinely through a number of signal stations on land, before being hand-delivered to Fort Blockhouse from the Gosport Post Office.[17] At Fort Blockhouse, the duty personnel were already on alert, as the signal from *Thetis* confirming that she had resurfaced was at least an hour overdue. The telegram from *Grebe Cock*, which finally arrived at 18:15, confirmed that something was indeed wrong. Hence, a 'Subsmash' alarm was issued and the Admiralty and RA(S) were alerted. However, instead of initiating an effective search-and-rescue operation, as intended, the system staggered into action and there appears to have been no immediate sense of urgency.

The nearest naval ship of relevance was the destroyer *Brazen*, returning from gunnery trials off Clyde and Lieutenant Commander Robert Mills was ordered to take her into Liverpool Bay to commence a search. Rather uncommon for a destroyer of her class at the time, *Brazen* was equipped with the asdic submarine detection system and so was well equipped for such a task.

During the evening, it was arranged with Cammell-Laird for the civilian tug *Vigilant* to head for the site as soon as possible with equipment and divers in case assistance was needed. *Vigilant* sailed at 21:45 – a very respectable achievement in isolation. Due to a series of misunderstandings, though, a request to the Liverpool and Glasgow Salvage Co. to arrange for more advanced equipment, such as air compressors, oxyacetylene cutting gear and a fore-hatch clamp, to be prepared was not actioned until regular working hours the next day.[18] The Royal Navy's specialised diving vessel *Tedworth*, a converted minesweeper, was ordered out from the Clyde at 19:25 as part of the early Subsmash initiatives. Being short of coal, however, she had to fill her holds from stores at Greenock and her experienced navy divers did not arrive until 03:00 on 3 June – far too late to influence events.[19] It appears that nobody thought of sending the divers and their equipment into Liverpool Bay on another ship to get their expertise to the scene of the accident. A request from the Admiralty to the Air Ministry at 18:35 as part of the Subsmash routine brought half a dozen Coastal Command aircraft into the search. As the first three did not get airborne until around 20:00, however, there was limited time for them to scan much before sunset.

Rear Admiral (Submarines) Bertram Watson was away sick and his Chief of Staff, Captain Ian Macintyre, was given overall command of the Subsmash operation. He, for unsatisfactorily explained reasons, chose to head for Liverpool Bay on board the duty destroyer *Winchelsea* rather than fly up. This meant he would not arrive for almost twenty-four hours, long after all hope had been lost, and he could not therefore play any significant role in the unfolding events.[20]

Arriving in Liverpool Bay shortly after 21:00, *Brazen* commenced an asdic search for *Thetis*, based on the position where the submarine was reported to have been seen last. She was nowhere to be found. Partly because the destroyer was given ambiguous information from *Grebe Cock*, and partly because time was wasted investigating a fishing buoy, mistaken for a marker by one of the aircraft in the fading light. On several occasions during the night, *Brazen* must have been very close to locating the submarine. There is no doubt that had *Grebe Cock* sighted any of the flares or buoys released by *Thetis*, or had *Brazen* located her earlier than she did, some men might have been able to escape during the night, leaving fewer individuals on board to share the dwindling oxygen reserves, and proper salvage gear might have arrived earlier.

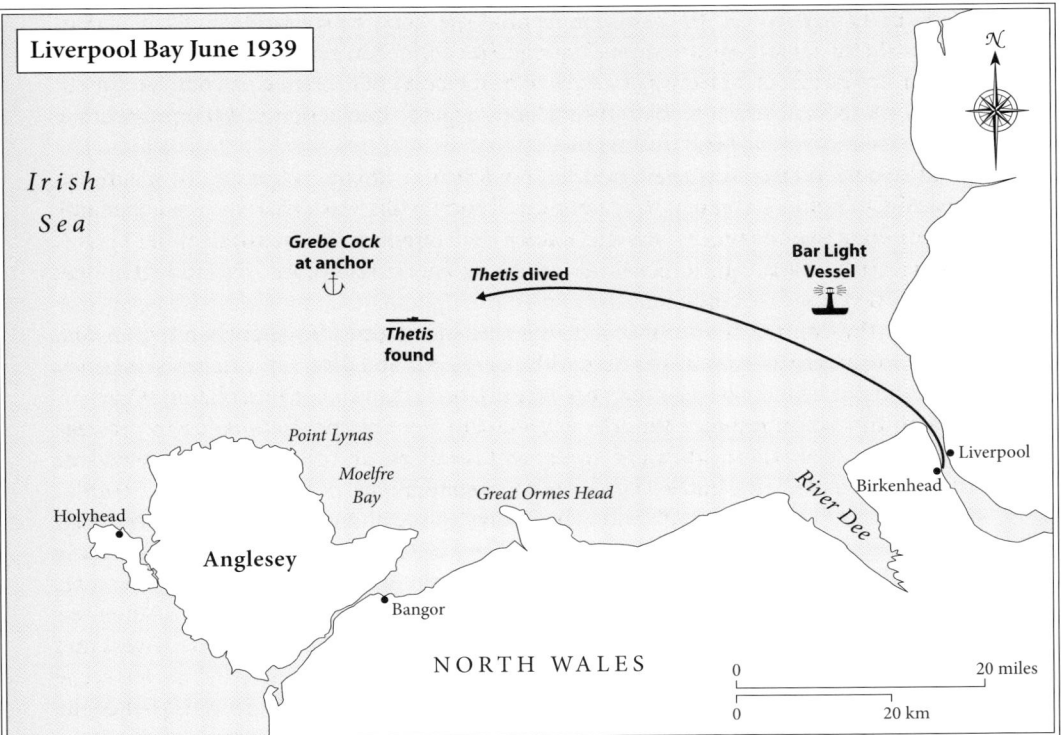

Liverpool Bay June 1939

Taken to the Surface

On board *Thetis*, blowing the water back out through the open torpedo tube was an obvious solution – had it not been for the hatch at the top of the stowage compartment. This was used for loading torpedoes into the boat and designed to take as much external pressure as the hull itself. It was only held down by the weight of the water above it, however, and, as there was no way to latch it down from the inside, increasing the pressure in the flooded compartments to push the water out might well lift the hatch, rendering the operation useless.

Instead, it was decided the only realistic option was to pump out the water. This would require number five torpedo rear door to be shut though, and somebody would have to pass back into the flooded compartments. *Thetis* was equipped with two escape chambers. The forward one was integrated into the bulkhead between the torpedo stowage compartment and the seamen's mess-deck, i.e. between the flooded and dry part of the submarine. It could therefore be used to re-enter the flooded compartment as it had two hatches, one opening into each part of the submarine.

First Officer Lieutenant Chapman volunteered to don his DSEA set and do the job.[21] Soon, however, overcome by claustrophobia and severe pains from the increased pressure when flooding the chamber quickly, he had to give up and signal to be let out again. Woods volunteered for a second attempt, accompanied by a petty officer, but they also had to give up. After some rest Woods, who had suffered only limited pains from the increased pressure, tried a third time with yet another volunteer, but failed once again. After this, Bolus said 'no more' and instead decided to rely on outside help and, if possible, the escape chambers. They were near the coast and *Grebe Cock* had seen them dive, so it would not be long before somebody would start looking for them and they would be found, he expected. It was decided that no attempts should be made to escape by DSEA until surface vessels arrived, unless forced to do so by conditions inside the submarine. If more men might have been saved had they started these escape procedures at once, taking their chance on the surface, we shall never know.[22]

In theory, there would be sufficient air for around thirty-six hours in a T-class submarine. *Thetis*, however, had twice the number of men usually aboard and it must have been clear to Lieutenant Commander Bolus that things would become critical long before that. The fact that many men were working hard, shifting water in buckets and rigging emergency pumps, did not help the oxygen reserves either. The reactions of any individual to carbon dioxide (CO_2) poisoning vary considerably. Usually, a concentration of about 10 per cent is lethal, but, depending on anxiety, age, health condition and general fitness, some will pass out sooner, while others will last longer. By midnight, conditions were getting 'stuffy' on board the submarine, though still manageable for most. Some of the less-fit men had started to feel the first symptoms of CO_2 poisoning – headaches, nausea and disorientation – during the night. It is perhaps also fair to assume that many more were struggling with increasing anxiety and claustrophobia. By morning, breathing had become difficult for most and the slightest effort resulted in panting, such as after heavy exercise. For some, this led to sickness and spasms; others drifted into a state of passiveness.[23]

Receiving no response to the indicator buoys and smoke signals dispensed, Lieutenant Commander Bolus decided to lighten the after-ship by dumping freshwater and fuel from the stern. *Thetis* was 84 metres long (275 feet) and lightening the stern sufficiently would raise it out of the water. Through re-coupling pipes and tanks during the night, some fifty tons were pumped out by 03:00 in the morning. The effect was that by first light, some 6 metres of the stern was out of the water. The resulting angle of the hull, however, made all movements even more strenuous, draining the meagre oxygen reserves even faster. Nevertheless, everybody on board was still alive and could still be saved. *Thetis* carried sufficient DSEA sets for all men on board, but these were not used at this stage as it was expected that they would be of better use later.

While the stern was lightened, Bolus gathered with Captain Oram and some of the other senior personnel to discuss what could be done from the outside, once they were found. They still believed the best would be to blow the water in the front compartments back out, with outside help, once the torpedo-loading hatch in the stowage compartment had been properly latched down by divers and high pressure hoses had been fitted to one of the two possible connection points. The men inside the submarine would be able to co-operate and open the necessary valves to allow the high-pressure air to be passed through no. 40 bulkhead. It was to be expected that divers on board the first vessels to arrive would not have much knowledge of submarines and, as time was becoming important, somebody from inside *Thetis* would have to provide the expertise.[24] Plans were drafted by hand onto pieces of paper and wrapped in plastic in order to be waterproof: the idea being to strap the package to the body of a volunteer and send him to the surface through the escape chamber, wearing a DSEA. Should he not survive, the plans would still be found on his body and the rescue operation could be initiated. The after escape hatch was only 6–7 metres below the surface and there was a good chance of getting out. Up until this point, it had been decided that no escape attempt should be made before they had been found, but now it was judged that this seemed like a risk worth taking. There had been no explosions from charges dropped by surface vessels to indicate they had been found, but it was nevertheless considered crucial to get the plans to the surface as daylight approached – preferably by somebody who had the experience and authority to cut through 'red tape' if necessary. Even a dead body at the surface would increase the chances for those trapped below, provided it was found. Oram stated at the public inquiry:

> We realised that it would take approximately 10 minutes to a quarter of an hour for each pair of men to escape from the after escape chamber and with the number of men we had onboard it was imperative that escaping should start as soon as possible, or have the grave danger that the last men would not have sufficient energy to be able to escape. I then felt it in my mind also that there might be a merchant ship or a fishing vessel standing by on the surface whilst we were needlessly delaying escape because we did not know she was there. I therefore offered to go to the surface with the plan. I asked for a volunteer and Lieutenant Chapman passed the word. I wanted to have somebody else with me so that it doubled the chances of us being found.[25]

Volunteers were called for. Lieutenant Woods and two seamen came forward. Woods argued that he would be able to convey the plans proficiently should he be rescued instead of Oram and this was accepted. Before they left for the escape chamber, Oram advised Bolus to carry on sending men up in pairs after he and Woods had gone: one sailor and

The stern escape chamber of submarine *Tribune*. This is modified compared to that of *Thetis*, but the size and general arrangement is similar. The forward chamber would have been similar and the door to the left would have been closed, holding the water in the forward part. The boxes below the door hold DSEA kits. (IWM A10930)

one civilian at a time. With dawn emerging, it was to be expected they would be found very soon. Sometime after 07:30, Oram and Woods were squeezed together inside the after escape chamber, wearing their DSEA sets and fighting the inescapable fear as the water was working its way up their bodies. Just at this time, everybody on board heard a series of distinct bangs from charges dropped by a vessel on the surface – *Thetis* had been located. When the chamber was filled, Woods opened the hatch and the two men shot to surface in a 'textbook' manner.[26]

At 04:15 on the 2nd, the first aircraft had taken off again to recommence the search over Liverpool Bay, but as the morning was hazy it took some time before one of the planes noticed a black object sticking out of the water. *Thetis* had finally been found. It was 07:50, almost eighteen hours after her initial attempts to dive. Minutes later, the stern of the submarine was sighted from *Brazen* and Lieutenant Commander Mills signalled for *Grebe Cock* and *Vigilant*, which had arrived during the night, to gather on him as he rushed across. To everybody's delight, shortly after lowering boats and dropping small charges near the tail sticking out of the water – the usual practice to signify they had arrived – two men shot up from the submarine. They were swiftly taken on board the destroyer for a hot bath and some dry clothes. A signal was sent from *Brazen* to the Admiralty and C-in-C Plymouth at 08:26. It was brief, saying that Oram and Woods were on board *Brazen* while 'the rest of the crew are alive in submarine and endeavouring to escape by DSEA'. The message was undoubtedly a relief to the chiefs at the Admiralty.

Oram, in spite of suffering from shock and CO_2 poisoning, produced the drawings and notes of the plan from their waterproof wrapping. Handing them to Mills and Lieutenant Coltart, who had come over from *Grebe Cock*, he gave instructions to ensure the right resources were urgently made available. He also told Mills to keep the destroyer at a distance and look out for men escaping from the submarine: in pairs about every twenty minutes. Thereafter, he literally collapsed for half an hour or so before recovering sufficiently to compose a signal to be sent to C-in-C Plymouth and his staff at Fort Blockhouse at 09:49. In it, he described the procedures for salvage and rescue that had been discussed before he left the submarine. After this, it appears his contribution, except from dictating a few signals, was limited due to his physical condition. Oram had done all that he possibly could.[27]

On board *Thetis*, the escape of Oram and Woods increased the hopes of all on board. The escape chamber had worked well and there was no reason not to continue getting men out, now there were ships above. When draining the chamber after the first escape, however, due to the angle of the boat, water flooded into the main engine's switchboard, sending thick white smoke into the already foul air from a short-circuit fire.

The smoke obviously increased the urgency for Lieutenant Chapman to get the men out and he ordered four men into the escape chamber. Hence, two sailors and two

Thetis has just been found in the morning of 2 June. (Author's Collection)

Cammell Laird workers squeezed into the cramped space, creating a disaster as panic ensued when the water started to rise. The four men struggled furiously to get out and, probably through trying to open the hatch too early, succumbed to a horrible fate. When the chamber eventually was drained down after quarter of an hour, three of the men were dead and the fourth was dying. Leading Stoker Walter Arnold told the board of inquiry:

> We dragged the three bodies back into the boat and helped the other chap out, and he was just about finished. Then Mr Glenn and Mr Jamison suggested sending two up, and they sent me and Shaw and said 'For God's sake try and get out and buck these lads up', because when we brought the three bodies back, it broke the morale of the men; you could see it in their faces.[28]

Derek Arnold, his son, told author David Roberts in an interview in 1998:

> My dad figured, well, I'm going to die, possibly, down here, I'd sooner die trying to escape rather than just waiting for it to come. By this time some of the older shipyard men were starting to look a bit the worse for wear, so he figured the end can't be far away. So I'm going to have a go, and if I'm killed then so be it. [. . .] The fittest guy there was Frank Shaw and dad said to Frank 'do you fancy having a go? . . . I'll do everything; you do nothing, just do exactly as I say'. They kitted up, went in the chamber and started flooding up. [. . .] As the chamber filled right up, father operated the mechanism to successfully open the hatch. [. . .] He pushed Shaw out first but noticed that the all-important valve was still closed, so as Shaw went up, my dad just held his foot, opened the valve for him and let him go. He shot up like a cork. Then he had to get out himself . . . he kicked free and he went to the top.[29]

Once the escape chamber had been readied again, it is fair to assume that a second pair climbed into it. It appears, however, that for some reason the chamber did not work any more and there would be no further escapes from *Thetis*.[30] By now, the effects of the CO_2 poisoning inside the boat, augmented by the setbacks from the failed escape attempts and the smoke from the short-circuit fire, almost certainly reached a critical level. Most men would have been panting heavily, lying down wherever they could, some probably drifting into unconsciousness, too exhausted to be concerned. This was unknown to those on the surface, however, and it was assumed that more men would follow through the escape chamber shortly – all the more so as Leading Stoker Arnold confirmed that this was the intent.

A Grasp of the Situation

During the morning of 2 June, at 10:30, *Tribal*-class destroyers of the 6th Destroyer Flotilla arrived on the scene. Captain D(6) Randolph Nicholson of *Somali* was senior to Lieutenant Commander Mills and assumed command, as per normal practice. Nicholson was a fine officer and would prove his competence many times over in the war to come. His knowledge of submarines in June 1939 was virtually non-existent, though, and he later admitted: 'I was trying to get a grasp of the situation. Having suddenly arrived up there, I did not know what steps had been taken or what had been done. What was going to be done, and what should be done now.'[31]

This was not the best of starting points and when Lieutenant Woods, having to a large extent recovered from his discomforts, expressed grave concern for those still on board the submarine as no further men came up, the pressure on Nicholson mounted. At this stage, there were no officers with submarine experience at the scene, except Coltart, Oram and Woods. Oram, the senior, was ill, suffering severely from the ordeal, while Coltart and Woods were possibly considered too junior by the decision-makers. Captain Macintyre was hours away on board *Winchelsea*. That there were a large number of experienced submariners in Birkenhead – on the boats being built next to *Thetis* (*Taku* and *Trident*) – seems not to have been considered.

There is no doubt that *Thetis*'s crew and the other men on board represented naval and technical skills that were extremely valuable to the Royal Navy. To the Admiralty, though, the Subsmash operation was based on the concept that the men trapped inside *Thetis* had the means to rescue themselves. The navy therefore supposedly just had to provide the best possible assistance on the surface and prepare for salvage of the boat once the crew was safe. The fact that Oram and Woods escaped, literally at the time that *Thetis* was found, was taken by those on the outside to show things were going according to plan. The DSEA sets apparently worked as they were supposed to, and Arnold and Shaw had shown that the civilians on board could also be brought to safety wearing one, in spite of never having tried them before. The fact that these special men had escaped through luck and audacity as much as training and routine, and that the men left inside the boat would not have the time to escape before being overcome by CO_2 poisoning, was overlooked. Saving a greater number of the men on board *Thetis* from the outside might have been possible, but would have needed a level of co-ordination that the pre-war Royal Navy was not prepared for.[32]

During the morning, *Vigilant* positioned itself close to the stern of *Thetis* and a diver was sent down when the tide slackened. Never having dived on a submarine before, he found neither the fore hatch nor the connection point where the high-pressure air hoses should be connected to the hull on his first dive. Before he could go down a second time, after a break, he received orders from *Somali* to stay out of the water. It had become known on board the destroyer that the tackle needed to secure the fore hatch would not arrive from Cammell Laird until late in the afternoon and it was feared the diver might be in the way of men escaping from the submarine.

Oram and Bolus's plan was disintegrating before it was even initiated. Instead it was decided to hold and perhaps raise *Thetis*'s stern further out of the water to allow a hole to be cut in the hull. A larger hole could then be cut later to let the men out. A wire was strung around the submarine's stern and *Vigilant* started a slow pull, assisted by two smaller tugs. This did bring the stern higher, but, being at an angle of over 50 degress, it also made the submarine more unstable as well as making life for those still alive inside even more difficult. At this stage, it appears that the rescue operation was led by men who did not understand what was going on, what needed to be done or the risks associated with the decisions being made. Above all, there seems to have been virtually no understanding of the urgency created by the dwindling air supply inside the boat as there was almost twice the normal complement of men on board. Later, when the wreck had been taken ashore, evidence was found that seemed to indicate that those onboard had prepared one last, desperate attempt at escape by flooding the engine room and the steerage compartment and leave the boat through the stern escape chamber with both inner and outer hatches opened at the same time. If this really was the case, why it failed cannot be fully ascertained.[33]

A signal from the Admiralty at 11:39 asked if conditions were suitable for making a hole in the stern to rescue the crew. The answer, twenty minutes later, was that the stern was not high enough for that. Captain Oram added in another signal at 12:35 that, when pontoons arrived, he would see to it that the stern was lifted 'with a view to cutting a hole'. At this stage, Oram was rather confused and was probably thinking in terms of a hole through which the crew could escape, not just to get air inside to prevent the men dying while the salvage equipment arrived.[34] It is clear from these signals that the Admiralty had no objections to drilling a hole in the hull as long as there was any chance at all that there were men alive inside the submarine. Oxyacetylene burning gear was on its way and arrived around 14:20. At that time, the stern was still above the surface, but the salvage personnel advised Nicholson that 'nothing can be done until the tide slackens at 18:00'.[35]

As an alternative, Wreck Master Charles Brock of *Vigilant* mounted *Thetis*'s stern in the early afternoon to see if it would be possible to open a pair of inspection plates that might give him access to the Z-tank, from where it should be possible to open a hole into the after compartment.[36] In Liverpool Bay in June, however, the tide is fierce, and just as Brock was about to open the plate, the tail of *Thetis* started to swing with the current and he had to jump clear.

In a desperate attempt to keep the stern above water, Nicholson, advised by one of the salvage specialists, had *Vigilant* and the assisting tugs hove in on the wire around the submarine's stern and start pulling it further up. Slowly, the stern rose, but inevitably the submarine became unstable and put too much strain on the wire which parted with a loud crack. *Thetis* slammed into *Vigilant*, turned around and disappeared below the surface for good. It was 15:10 on 2 June, some twenty-five hours after Lieutenant Commander Bolus gave the order to take *Thetis* down and seven hours after she had been found. To those still alive, tossed around inside the rolling hull among the dead and dying, any last hopes of getting out were shattered.

Nevertheless, divers heard faint tapping from the inside of *Thetis* after midnight on the 3rd, long after everybody should have succumbed, according to medical theory. When they reported this, it was decided to make one more attempt to get an air connection into the control room by drilling through the pressure hull at next slack water at 06:30. Tedworth arrived at 03:00 and her divers went down at slack tide a few hours later. Under the difficult conditions and short time available to them, they were unable to complete the work as planned, however, and reported that they would need several slack-tide periods to do so. Coupled with the fact that the tapping had ceased, it was concluded that no hope of saving further lives from *Thetis* remained. In a signal from the Admiralty at 13:02 on 3 June to RA(S), repeated to C-in-C Home Fleet and C-in-C Plymouth it was stated that:

> While Their Lordships appreciate your news in regard to the condition of the personnel in HMS *Thetis*, they feel however, that hope should not be abandoned until all efforts

Relatives of the men onboard *Thetis* waiting for news outside the gates of Cammell Laird. (Author's Collection)

to connect an air line combined with any immediate operations you consider possible to raise the vessel sufficiently to obtain access have proved unavailing. It is intended to salve HMS *Thetis*.[37]

At 16:49, Captain Nicholson concluded that, based on the information available, he considered there was 'very little hope of the men still on board being rescued alive'. Shortly after, a brief press release was issued from Whitehall: 'The Admiralty regrets there is now no longer justification for hope that any further lives can be saved from *Thetis*. Salvage work proceeds.' *Thetis* was lost, but the story of her misfortune would not go down with her.[38]

A Remarkable Combination of Errors

Less than a week after the disaster, a board was set up, led by Vice Admiral Robert Raikes, the previous Rear Admiral (Submarines), to hold a naval inquiry and explain how and why *Thetis* had been lost. A confidential report was issued by the end of the month. As *Thetis* had not been raised by the time, it was based solely on the evidence of the survivors and the rescue teams. The report concluded that although:

Lieutenant Woods carried out the inspection of the bow tubes by opening the rear doors on his own responsibility. Although there is no danger normally attached to opening the rear doors if the correct procedure is carried out [. . .]. The Commanding Officer would expect them to be closed before diving, especially under 'trial' conditions. We consider that in these circumstances, there was no adequate reason for Lieutenant Woods opening the rear tube doors and he was not justified in doing so without instruction. [It] would have involved a remarkable combination of errors, unlikely in the circumstances, that a mistake should have been made both in the case of the bow caps operating levers and the bow cap indicators. [. . .] To sum up, there must have been either a mechanical failure by which the bow cap indicator showed <u>shut</u> when in fact, the bow cap was open or else the position of this indicator was misread by Lieutenant Woods.[39]

The report thus went a long way towards blaming Lieutenant Woods for the disaster. It was also critical of Lieutenant Commander Bolus, who allowed an excessive number of unnecessary people on board with no specific duties. Later, the Admiralty added blame to the naval overseer Edward Grundy for not discovering the blocked test cock. For a number of reasons that might seem unjust today, though, the Admiralty chose to close ranks and not assign blame to any individual – thereby protecting themselves as well.

In June, a 'Naval Committee to investigate the Admiralty long term policy for the salvage of and the saving of life from submarines' led by Admiral Martin Dunbar-Nasmith was appointed. Furthermore, on the request of the government, a public tribunal was opened in July, to assess 'the circumstances attending the loss of His Majesty's Submarine *Thetis* and the subsequent attempts to save the lives of those in the ship'. For the tribunal, more or less the same people were summoned as at the naval inquiry, in addition to a number of additional expert witnesses.[40]

Left: Leading Stoker Walter Arnold (*left*) and Cammell Laird's Foreman Engineer Frank Shaw (*right*) arriving at the tribunal *Right*: Captain Henry Oram arriving at the tribunal, accompanied by his wife. (D Roberts' Collection; Author's Collection)

The survivors told their stories once more, under oath, along with most of those involved on the surface. Still, there was a feeling that the tribunal never explored sufficiently into the details of the tragedy. The report from the tribunal, published in January 1940, concluded that there were multiple causes for the accident, but the language used was carefully chosen not to put the blame anywhere specific. Nevertheless, the press were in attendance and reported in great detail every relevant statement given. Inevitably, the journalists and their readers would make their own conclusions and for many of those involved, the report was at best unsatisfactory.

Thetis was eventually salvaged and brought to shore on Traeth Bychan beach in Moelfre Bay, Anglesey on 3 September. From here, the remains of about sixty men were recovered to be identified and released for burial.[41] In November, *Thetis* was moved to Holyhead where the remaining bodies were removed and an inspection of the interior could be performed. The inspection team, representing the Admiralty, Cammell Laird and other interests, found, as expected, number five rear door open and fastened in its recess position while the other doors were firmly locked closed. To their surprise, though, as this was not what Lieutenant Woods had said at the inquiry, number five bow-cap indicator was in the 'fully open' position. This meant that either Woods had been more casual in his checks than he admitted, or something mechanical had gone wrong and the bow cap had been opened without a presumably competent crew recognising the fact.[42]

There are no doubts that Lieutenant Woods's actions were the root cause for the *Thetis* disaster. He opened the inner door of number five tube without satisfactorily conducting the checks that he, as torpedo officer, should have known he needed to do. Furthermore, he did so on his own initiative without seeking consent from his superiors, who were conducting a critical operation during a test dive. The fact that he did not have the complete drill off by heart, including the use of the rimers and test cocks, was later accepted by the board of the naval inquiry as being due to insufficient training. Why number five bow cap was open in the first place, however, was never fully explained and there is no report available today that unequivocally specifies a mechanical failure. It is

The wreck of *Thetis* on the beach at Moelfre Bay in September. (Author's Collection)

possible that some harbour debris had become stuck, preventing the cap from closing after the tubes had been filled, but no evidence to support this was ever found. In all likelihood, therefore, the position of the bow cap must be ascribed to the actions of one or more individuals, due to a misunderstanding or an error. Whether this was a civilian worker at the yard or a naval person onboard the submarine after leaving port, or both, will probably never be fully uncovered. Several people who worked with Woods later told that, although he outwardly continued to show a brave face, he apparently never got over the experiences of that disaster, and it is likely that he blamed himself for what happened in Liverpool Bay.

The blame for *Thetis* going down cannot be put solely on Woods though. Her loss and that of all but four of the men on board was the ultimate result of a tragic series of coincidental events. The poor job by the painter from Wailes Dove Bitumastic as well as negligence by inspectors and overseers, both from Cammell Laird and the navy, in not discovering this were underlying factors that Woods cannot be blamed for. Furthermore, the water filled two compartments due to a poorly constructed door-locking mechanism, not suitable for an emergency, and the hatch in the torpedo room was unable to take pressure from the inside without being closed from the outside by equipment that was not readily available.

Had *Thetis* been found earlier and had the escapes started earlier in an orderly manner by men not intoxicated by CO_2 poisoning, the loss of life would in all likelihood have been less. Lastly, the belief that the DSEA equipment allowed the submariners to save themselves meant that salvage operations were not initiated from the outside. Through a combination of faulty work, inadequate routines and plain bad luck, a series of events had led to the worst submarine accident the Royal Navy had faced in peacetime.[43]

For the survivors, life would never be the same. When dismissed from the hospital in Portsmouth, Leading Stoker Arnold was ordered by the Admiralty to say nothing to anybody outside the official inquiries as he was under the Official Secrets Act. The press could not interview him and should they try, he was duty bound to say nothing. On the other hand, the naval bureaucracy decided he would have to wait for a new paybook before being given his wages as the old one had been left inside *Thetis*: a process that took six months and during which time Arnold received nothing – except from his relatives – in spite of being responsible for his wife and their baby. Instead he was ordered to assist in the grim task of identifying the bodies recovered from *Thetis*. Arnold was eventually posted to *Spearfish*, but found he could no longer take the strain of serving underwater and applied for transfer to surface ships. He ended the war onboard the battleship *King George V* in the Pacific.[44]

Frank Shaw, who escaped with Arnold, was not bound by any naval code and received the enormous sum of £2,000 from the *Daily Express* for telling his story, in addition to a promotion and a house from Cammell Laird in compensation for his ordeal. Lieutenant Woods was awarded the DSC in August 1940 for bravery during the evacuation from Dunkirk, but he never served on submarines again. He died in a car accident in 1946. Captain Oram return briefly to Fort Blockhouse, but when the war broke out, he was given command of the cruiser *Cairo* and later *Hawkins*, looking after convoy traffic in the South Atlantic. From 1942 to his retirement in March 1946, Oram served with the Admiralty.

Left: Lieutenant Frederick Woods. A very burdened man. *Right*: The bow of *Thetis* after the wreck had been landed at Moelfre Bay. There is damage to most of the bow caps from the sea bed, but number five cap (lower starboard side) appears to be fully open. Note also that the forward hydroplanes are at a dive angle. (D Roberts' Collection; Author's Collection)

A *Thetis* fund was set up shortly after the disaster, partly through public support, but this was poorly managed and, at best, meant little to the families left behind.[45] Several court cases were brought against Cammell Laird, Lieutenant Woods, Leading Seaman Hambrook and Lieutenant Commander Bolus's wife Sybil for negligence. The Admiralty feared that a court decision against the navy personnel would fall back on them and the navy, and provided the necessary legal expertise to douse the cases. Eventually, after many bitter rounds in court, all claims were dismissed and the disaster befalling *Thetis* was officially declared 'a non-negligent accident'.

In February 1940 First Lord Winston Churchill summed up the disaster:

All interest in this tragedy has now been submerged by the war. I should deprecate any disciplinary actions unless some definite act can be traced to an individual. Indeed I should be glad if Lieut. Woods' mind could be set at rest. I think the Second, Fourth and Fifth Sea Lords should look into the matter and advise what the Admiralty should say and do. They should also advise on publication.[46]

By phrasing things in this manner he left his lesser Lords with no option but to leave *Thetis* to history and get on with the war. The official report that was eventually made public gave six main causes for the loss of *Thetis*: blocking of number five test-cock, opening of the rear-tube door, failure to close the watertight bulkhead door, failure of those on board to refloat *Thetis*, failure of assistance from the outside and failure of those on board to escape – but attached no blame to any one person or organisation. [47]

For the Submarine Service, the *Thetis* disaster came as a shock, dealing a heavy blow to morale. Most officers and men knew or had served with some of those who had perished and the inability to rescue those entrapped depressed the submariners, making them doubt if they were taken seriously by the rest of the navy. Still, heading for war, several improvements and recommendations were made by the various committees and boards looking at the disaster and there is no doubt that the British submarines became a safer place to be in general. Arthur Hezlet, first lieutenant on board *Trident* in 1939, later recounted:

We were, on the first trial [of *Trident*], very impressed with the boat. She dived in the Gareloch for the first time and she, I thought, handled beautifully. We were very happy with her. Mind you [. . .], we were the next submarine after the *Thetis* to do trials from Cammell Laird and there was apprehension, without any question, among the Cammell Laird's personnel, wondering whether this would go all right. We were extremely careful to make sure everything did go right, and it went perfectly. You could see the morale change after the first dive in the most remarkable way.[48]

In December 1940, nineteen months after her disastrous first dive, *Thetis* went to war as *Thunderbolt* (see chapter 28). This book covers this period and the transformation of the British Submarine Service from the 'ugly duckling' of the Royal Navy to a fully fledged instrument of war during that period.

— 2 —

The Thin Grey Line

Submarine Development

THE BRITISH SUBMARINE SERVICE was a rather mixed bag of vessels in September 1939. Some boats were of WWI design, others were brand-new designs, still struggling with flaws and defects to be ironed out. At least eight different classes were in service – ten of the O-, P- and R-classes are counted separately. This made maintenance, deployment and operations challenging, to say nothing of drill routines.

First of all, there was the L-class, a robust 891/1074-ton WWI design, incorporating lessons learned from that war.[1] In all, twenty-seven L-class boats were commissioned and the last of them, *L23*, was taken out of service in October 1945. Armament of the L-boats was four 21-inch bow tubes, two 18-inch beam tubes and one 4-inch gun. Normal complement was thirty-eight. The main engines of the L-class submarines were two twelve-cylinder diesels, giving a surface speed of slightly over 17 knots. Maximum submerged speed was around 10 knots. The official maximum diving depth for the L-class submarines in 1925 was 150 feet (46 metres). During WWII, however, depths of more than 250 feet (75 metres) were recorded and, except for minor leaks, withstood. The L-boats carried part of their fuel load, some 20 tons, in external tanks. These were lightly constructed and a dangerous concept in wartime when depth charges exploding nearby might create leaks that would tell the attackers on the surface where the boat was, unbeknown to the submariners.

Supplementing the L-class, a number of submarines were built at British yards to an American design, known as the H21-class. At first, motors and fittings were brought from the USA to speed up construction, but eventually all parts were made in Britain. The first of the 438/504-ton British-built H21-class boats entered service in January 1918 and the last, *H34*, was taken out of service in July 1945, almost twenty-eight years after she was laid down at Cammell Laird. Nimbler than the L-class boats, the H-class had significantly smaller engines and motors, giving them a maximum speed of only about 12 knots on the surface and 9 knots submerged. Armament was four 21-inch torpedo tubes with two reloads, but no gun. The normal complement was twenty-two.[2]

In May 1922, the first of a series of conferences was arranged by the Admiralty to discuss various aspects of the future design of British submarines. There was much to discuss and in February 1925 the assessments culminated in another conference discussing, 'The necessity for and use of various types of submarines' as a basis for the submarine section of the Ten Year Building Programme, a rolling conceptual plan of what ships the Admiralty believed the Royal Navy would need in the future. In attendance was the Deputy Chief of the Naval Staff (DCNS), Rear Admiral (Submarines) (RA(S)), and several other high-ranking staff officers, including the naval controller who was to be responsible for the finances of the final building programme. Discussions were extensive and opinions varied considerably,

Depot ship *Alecto* at Portland with the 6th Submarine Flotilla. *Left to right*: *H34*, *H44*, *H43*, *H32* and *H50*. At the time these were used as training boats, but all eventually went to war. (Author's Collection)

but most participants agreed that what the Royal Navy needed in terms of underwater vessels were fast, long-range overseas patrol submarines. Stern tubes were 'nice-to-have', but not at the expense of speed, while a 4-inch or 4.7-inch gun was considered essential. Mine-laying submarines, cruiser submarines and so-called fleet submarines were deferred until later. Even so, design programmes and studies of the tactical use of mine-laying submarines should be advanced to be ready for the next decision gate.

Based on these considerations, the first British submarines after WWI emerged as the O-class. For these, as for the subsequent P- and R-class boats, the primary specifications were speed, range and operational sustainability, making them large and unwieldy designs with poor underwater manoeuvrability and unreliable electrics. The prototype, *Oberon*, laid down in 1924, was a truly experimental design. She had much improved endurance and diving depth, compared with the 'L's and 'H's, but a 75 per cent increase in displacement made her slow and sluggish, both on the surface and submerged. In particular, a large number of topside fittings had a devastating effect on submerged speed. George Villar, engineer captain at the staff of RA(S), characterised *Oberon* as 'a mass of complication marking the start of the post war desire for mechanical gadgets', stating that she had never been satisfactory on account of unreliable engines and low operational speed.[3]

The two subsequent boats, *Oxley* and *Otway*, transferred to the Royal Australian Navy, had their engines upgraded but could still barely exceed 15 knots on the surface, which was quite insufficient compared to the requirements.[4]

Nevertheless, the orders for more overseas patrol submarines were confirmed. First, six boats of the *Odin*-class: *Odin*, *Oswald*, *Osiris*, *Otus*, *Olympus* and *Orpheus*, then six of the *Parthian*-class: *Parthian*, *Perseus*, *Poseidon*, *Proteus*, *Pandora* and *Phoenix* and finally, in 1928, six of the *Rainbow*-class: *Rainbow*, *Regent*, *Regulus*, *Rover*, *Rupert* and *Royalist*. The latter two were subsequently cancelled.

Thirteen feet longer than *Oberon*, to accommodate eight-cylinder diesel engines, the O-, P- and R-classes were otherwise similar in design – and in flaws. In particular, the engines were not up to the specifications, causing a lot of trouble and never giving the desired speeds. Above all, though, the riveted, external fuel tanks leaked to such an extent that they became a liability. Several attempts were made to overcome the leaks, but to no avail and the whole fuel-tank system had to be rebuilt in welded construction before the war. Of the seventeen overseas patrol submarines built, twelve were lost on active service in WWII. The last of these boats, *Otus*, was scuttled in 1946.[5]

There seems to have been very limited analysis and scenario-building exercises in the British Admiralty between the wars with reference to the efficiency of the German, and British, submarine warfare on commerce in WWI. Most British naval scenarios in the 1920s envisaged fast surface convoys relieving outposts like Singapore and Hong Kong during a crisis and the submarines holding the line until the full force of the Royal Navy could be deployed. The submarines were generally seen as part of the Fleet, shadowing and reporting enemy naval forces until the big guns could be brought to bear. Only then could they take part in the attack, if convenient, leading to a notion of large salvoes of torpedoes fired in straight shots at multiple targets.

These tactical concepts had several distinctive consequences for British submarine design. Firstly, in the size of the boats to accommodate machinery for speed. Secondly

Otus in dry dock, showing her starboard torpedo tubes and the huge bulges containing the riveted fuel tanks. (Author's Collection)

the desire for a large bow salvo gave rise to oval-shaped forward cross-sections to accommodate six torpedo tubes in two columns. Advantageous in many ways, this is a weaker structure than a circular shape, limiting diving depths, compared to contemporary German boats which had only three or four torpedo tubes in the bow. External bow tubes, added for the same reason, also caused challenges with large, visible bow waves and stability. Thirdly, the unsophisticated tactical concept of submarines as part of a fleet did not induce research into innovative torpedoes and fire-control systems. On the positive side though, this meant the British torpedoes in general were much more robust and reliable than the German or American ones during the early parts of the war.[6]

Ending the pause implied at the 1925 conference, the design of fleet submarines and minelayers was revisited in the early 1930s. Large, partially double-hulled boats intended for co-operation with surface fleets, the River-class submarines were equipped with two massive ten-cylinder 10,000-bhp diesel engines, giving them a record surface speed of 22.5 knots. This was fast, but not fast enough and *Thames*, *Severn* and *Clyde* fell significantly short of their specification. All the more so when submerged, as they could do no more than 10 knots. In addition, they had inherited the overloaded machinery and internal complexity of their predecessors, making them challenging to operate. In an attempt to keep down weight so as to obtain the required speed, the diving depth was reduced from 500 feet to 300 feet (152.5 to 91.5 metres) through reduced pressure-hull plating. As with the overseas patrol submarines, the River-class boats had external fuel tanks, but by now they were welded and the problem with leaks was largely eliminated, except inboard, where leaks occasionally occurred through rivets in the pressure-hull plating. Armament consisted of six 21-inch torpedo tubes in the bow with six reload torpedoes and one 4-inch gun. There were no torpedo tubes in the stern.

All three River-class boats were built at Barrow; *Thames* was completed in 1931 and the slightly larger *Severn* and *Clyde* in 1935. By then, capital ships with sustainable speeds

Thames in October 1932. (W&L)

of over 30 knots, supported by cruisers and aircraft carriers, had no tactical advantage from co-operation with submarines – quite the contrary. The Admiralty was forced to accept that the concept was misguided – the strength of submarines lay elsewhere than shackled to surface ships that they could not keep up with – and cancelled the twenty boats originally intended for the fleet submarine programme. Somewhat ironically, the River-class boats were never used operationally, as intended, with the Royal Navy's surface fleet.[7]

In parallel with the River-class, six double-hulled *Porpoise*-class mine-laying submarines were built and launched in 1936 and 1937. These were slightly smaller than the *River* boats, and included many of the same concepts and technologies, although they were in general a much more successful design. Up to fifty Mk XVI self-mooring contact mines could be carried in a full-length deck-casing above the pressure hull, giving them a characteristic, massive silhouette on the surface. The mines, running on four flanged wheels at the base of the sinkers, could be laid quickly by a chain-and-rack system through the hatch in the stern. Pressure tanks in the forward superstructure helped maintain level buoyancy as the mines were laid aft. As one mine was laid, the rest followed aft along the tramline rails in the floor of the casing and the right amount of water was taken into pressure-tight tanks forward to compensate for the shift of weight. The mines could be laid submerged or at the surface, the drill being similar. A full load of mines could be laid within less than ten minutes if all were placed in a single row. The speed at which the mines were laid was usually around 4 knots. If slower, it was found difficult to keep the mines in a straight line.[8]

The external fuel tanks of *Porpoise* were of 'non-leaking' welded construction, as in the River-class boats, although it was believed that leaks could occur if the tanks were damaged by depth charges. Hence, the hull shape of the next boat commissioned, *Grampus*, was changed by altering the pressure hull and extending the saddle tanks so that all fuel was carried internally. This also increased the main ballast water carried, improving stability and emergency buoyancy. *Grampus* and the five subsequent minelayers incorporating these modifications are hence also known as *Grampus*-class boats. The modified minelayers displaced 1,768 tons at the surface and 2,053 tons submerged with a full load of mines. They were fitted with two Admiralty-designed six-cylinder diesel engines generating 3,300 bhp. This gave a surface speed of around 16 knots, while tandem motors on each propeller shaft gave a submerged speed of up to 9 knots. In spite of the mine casing, the minelayers were operationally normal submarines once the mines had been placed, with six torpedo tubes in the bow. The boats were large, though, and difficult to manoeuvre, particularly in the shallow waters where the mines were usually laid. Of the six boats built, *Porpoise*, *Narwhal*, *Rorqual*, *Grampus*, *Seal* and *Cachalot*, only *Rorqual* survived the war to be decommissioned in April 1946.[9]

As part of the strategy for operating submarines in the Far East, the depot ship *Medway* was ordered from the Vickers-Armstrongs yard at Barrow-in-Furness. Completed in 1929, she was stationed at the China Station serving the O- and P-class submarines of the 4th Submarine Flotilla. In September 1939, she was at Singapore for refit and upon completion of this in early 1940 she was transferred to Alexandria, where she served the 1st Submarine Flotilla operating in the eastern Mediterranean.

Cachalot in September 1938. The tall, square casing above the waterline is the mine compartment. Note the off-centreline placement of the periscopes to allow them to move up and down outside the mine-rack. (W&L)

Medway was an instant success. She had large, useful workshops and excellent accommodation and was much liked by the submarine crews as well as her own complement of engineers, staff and support crews. The ability of *Medway* to sustain extensive submarine operations made the Royal Navy develop the concept and by the outbreak of the war, most flotillas had their own support vessel. The three modern depot ships, *Medway*, *Maidstone* and *Forth*, rotated between Hong Kong, Malta and the UK respectively, while the ancient *Alecto*, *Cyclops* and *Titania* were used in home waters, where the demand for mobility was less.[10] Stoker Sydney Hart of *Triad* wrote:

> Our depot ship, HMS *Forth* was a surface vessel of some 16,000 tons. *Forth*, although not going to sea herself, was the nerve-centre of activity. Aboard her, operations were planned by Staff Officers, officers who, in the First World War, had sailed their own submarines in these same waters in which we were about to operate. Our submarines would be supplied with fuel, food, torpedoes and spare parts from her and between her spacious decks would live, when in port, the crews of some twenty or more submarines.[11]

As would be shown later in the war, however, the depot ships were vulnerable should they be attacked by enemy aircraft or submarines.[12]

Having finally abandoned the fleet concept, the Admiralty in the early 1930s commenced a modernisation programme of the British Submarine Service that was to produce some of the finest boats of its time and eventually a very efficient wartime submarine force.

The S-class, designed for medium-range operations in the North Sea and other delimited waters, would be the first truly tactical submarines available to the Royal Navy. The combination of mechanical quality, reliability and ease of operation made the S-class boats very effective and, not least, safe – even if they maintained some of the complexity of the previous classes.

The 14,650-ton depot ship *Medway* as completed in May 1929. The depot ships were vulnerable when attacked by aircraft or submarines. (A Wilmar Collection)

There were three groups of S-class submarine. The boats of group one, *Swordfish*, *Sturgeon*, *Starfish* and *Seahorse*, were built at Chatham Dockyard between 1931 and 1933. Found to be a satisfactory construction, they were followed by eight more boats of group two: *Sealion*, *Salmon* and *Spearfish* built at Cammell Laird, *Shark*, *Snapper*, *Sunfish* and *Sterlet* built at Chatham and *Seawolf* built at Greenock, all between 1933 and 1938.

Table 1: Group one and group two S-class submarines of the pre-war programmes

	Cammell Laird	**Scotts** (Greenock)	**Chatham Dockyard**
Group one 1931–33			*Swordfish, Sturgeon, Seahorse, Starfish*
Group two 1933–38	*Sealion, Salmon, Spearfish*	*Seawolf*	*Shark, Snapper, Sunfish, Sterlet*

The group one S-class were able-looking boats displacing 640 tons on the surface and 930 tons submerged; they were reliable, easy to manoeuvre and quick to dive. There were six 21-inch torpedo tubes in the bow with one reload for each, giving a total of twelve torpedoes when leaving for patrol. Space was always an issue on board the early S-boats and the forty-odd men worked, slept, ate and lived in extremely confined quarters. The saddle-type fuel tanks were located inside the pressure hull, reducing the risk of leaks, but not doing much to improve space. The twin six-cylinder engines and 224 batteries powering the motors gave a maximum speed of around 13.5 knots on the surface and 10 knots submerged. At full speed submerged, the batteries only lasted an hour – compared to over 30 hours at 2 knots.

Sturgeon and *Swordfish*, the two first boats of group one, were fitted with a 'disappearing' gun, lowered into a forward extension of the base of the conning tower when diving. A great idea on paper, but subsequently raising the gun while the boat was surfacing caused alarming instability. As there were no measurable streamlining effects from the disappearing gun either, it was decided to rebuild the forward topside of the two submarines and give the succeeding boats a smooth foredeck with a fixed, deck-mounted 3-inch gun. Charles Anscomb, an experienced petty officer serving in many submarines before being assigned to *Sturgeon*, wrote:

> Smaller than the L boats, the S-class were an enormous improvement [. . .] but they had their teething troubles, like all new designs. *Sturgeon* was the first British submarine to be fitted with a disappearing gun. Diving was smooth enough. The steel casing opened up and the gun sank below out of sight in one very efficient mechanical operation. Surfacing, however, was tricky. When the gun was raised, with the ship still surfacing, the submarine took on some very alarming angles – so alarming and fraught with peril for us that the whole idea was scrapped for the time being and the gun removed. [. . .] We were glad to see it go; although Jones, our gunlayer, was thoroughly disgusted with the dummy wooden gun they gave us to preserve the streamline. Originally we had a very high fo'c'sle and a bow buoyancy tank as well as our jack-in-the-box gun. To make the ship lay head to wind while at anchor we had to hoist a sail aft. We were a very peculiar submarine for a long time. Then, when the high fo'c'sle and the gun were removed, *Sturgeon* began to behave more like a normal submersible.[13]

Spearfish launched at Cammell Laird on 11 December 1936. (Author's Collection)

There were considerable variations in design and several alterations as a result of the experience during the war. Teething troubles occurred in the group one boats, but most of these were ironed out through simplifications and modifications during the building of group two. Halfway through the series, for example, an extra two cylinders per engine added a knot to the surface speed while twin motors to each shaft improved the battery-charging capacity significantly. In particular, the lack of a stern torpedo tube was lamented, and eventually an external stern tube was added, bringing the number of tubes up to seven and the number of torpedoes carried to thirteen, although none of the boats with this improvement would be commissioned before the spring of 1942. In all, sixty-two S-class submarines were built over a period of fifteen years, making it the largest single group of submarines built for the Royal Navy. Losses were rather heavy, however, and in the North Sea alone, six of the class were lost in 1940.[14]

An even more successful design than the S-class was the 1,090-ton T-class ocean-going 'patrol submarines'. They were simple, efficient designs, easy to handle both above and below the surface, with relatively good diving characteristics. The first of the class, *Triton*, was confirmed as part of the 1935 programme, built at Vickers and commissioned in December 1938. The group one T-class boats were 83.8 metres long (275 feet). Their displacement was 1,327 tons at the surface and 1,527 tons submerged. The group two boats differed somewhat from those of group one externally, though their basic design remained similar.

Seahorse at Torquay in 1938: the Chatham-built group one boat was commissioned in October 1933. (Author's Collection)

Table 2: Group one and group two T-class submarines of the pre-war and early war programmes

	Vickers-Armstrongs	Cammell Laird	Scotts (Greenock)	Chatham Dockyard
Group one 1935	*Triton*			
1936	*Triumph*	*Thetis, Trident*	*Tribune*	
1937	*Thistle, Tarpon Triad, Truant*	*Taku*	*Tuna*	*Tigris*
1938	*Tetrarch*	*Talisman*		*Torbay*
Group two 1939	*Trusty Turbulent*	*Thrasher, Thorn Tempest*	*Traveller, Trooper*	

Thunderbolt, the rebuilt and renamed *Thetis* of group one, was in effect an eighth group two boat. *Trident* and *Torbay* had external fuel tanks retrofitted, which extended their range from 8,000 miles to 11,000 miles.

In spite of the principally sound design, wartime experience would reveal a handful of weaknesses in the first batch of T-class boats. One challenge was the need to ascend to between 28 and 30 feet with the periscope fully extended in order to see anything at all in even moderate seas. At this depth, the early T-class boats were difficult to handle and tended to break surface, unless the first officer was exceptionally competent. The most serious flaw, however, was the lack of surface speed due to limited engine capacity. Treaty-induced displacement limitations restricted the size of the T-class submarines and therefore the size of their engines. With a maximum of 2,500 hp surfaced and 1,450 hp submerged, the maximum surface speed of *Triton* and her companions was 9 knots submerged and a mere 15.25 knots on the surface. Maximum diving depth was set at 300 feet (91.5 metres).

On the positive side, the ten torpedo tubes, later increased to eleven, gave the T-boats an unprecedented sting. At first, these tubes, six internal and reloadable in the bow, two external over the bow and two external at the base of the conning tower, all faced forward, giving a fantastic 'shot-gun' effect, unmatched by any other submarine at the time. The lack of a stern tube, however, proved almost immediately to be a real disadvantage. Some argued that the inconvenience of the space taken up by stern tubes would not justify the added sternward firepower, but reports from crews returning from war patrols left no doubt as to the need for an urgent update.[15] During spells at the yard, *Taku, Tuna, Tigris, Thunderbolt, Torbay, Tribune, Trident* and *Truant* were eventually retrofitted with an eleventh torpedo tube installed on the centre-line, under the casing, facing aft. On the group two boats, in addition to this, tubes nine and ten were moved aft of the conning tower, facing astern. This resulted in eight forward-firing tubes and three firing aft, operationally a far more satisfying arrangement than the original concept. It was found, though, that the initial placement of the aft-facing tubes, angled 10 degrees off the centre-line, created an area of flat casing that affected the depth-keeping adversely. Hence, for

Triton, the first T-class boat on her first test run in Morecambe Bay in 1938, having been built at the Vickers-Armstrongs yard in Barrow-in-Furness. Note the forward-facing torpedo tube under the gun platform. (Author's Collection)

the two last boats of group two, *Traveller* and *Trooper*, the angle was reduced to 7 degrees, removing the problem. In addition to the torpedo tubes, a 4-inch gun was carried on deck, while three 0.303-inch machine guns could be brought up from below and fixed in removable mountings.

The group two boats had a slightly modified outer hull shape and, for most of the group, a welded rather than a riveted construction. The latter saved weight, increased diving limits and improved survivability during depth-charge attacks as well as enabling prefabricating of hull-sections away from the assembly yard. Removal of the bulbous bow casing lowered the bow wave which had hampered visibility and disrupted trim of the group one boats when running at periscope depth. At the outbreak of the war, fourteen T-class submarines were in commission and seven were at various stages of building or completion. The group three boats of the 1940 programme and onwards were further modified according to wartime experience and priorities, introducing such equipment as radar. All these boats were commissioned later in the war and destined for Far East service. In all, fifty-three T-class submarines were eventually built.[16]

The threat of war in 1939 naturally created an increase in all naval building programmes. With only three commercial yards having experience in building submarines outside the naval dockyards at Chatham, however, developing a new submarine force was not straightforward. All the more so as repairs and upgrades had to be accounted for as well. In early 1940, Vickers-Armstrongs became the main contractor for T-class submarines outside the navy yards at Portsmouth, Chatham and Devonport; Cammell Laird focused on S-class boats and Scotts later gave up on submarine construction altogether after suffering severe damage from German aerial bombing.[17]

During 1937, construction of three small submarines, *Undine*, *Unity* and *Ursula*, started at the Vickers-Armstrongs yard of Barrow-in-Furness. Originally the U-class were intended as simple and cost-efficient training and A/S target boats, but, due to the

Launch of *Ursula* at Vickers-Armstrongs, Barrow-in-Furness, 16 February 1938. (S Clewlow)

deteriorating international situation, it was decided to prepare them for war patrols. This included the addition of two external torpedo tubes to the four internal, reloadable tubes in the bow, giving a total payload of ten torpedoes. Furthermore, to allow for the installation of a 3-inch deck gun, the hull forward of the conning tower was reinforced, except for *Undine* and *Unity*, which were lost before there was time available in the yards. The U-class boats were initially not meant to have a gun and lacked a hatch for the gun crew. Hence, when attending the gun, the crew had to use the main conning tower hatch which turned out to be very inconvenient, especially if it became necessary to crash-dive.

Displacement of the U-class boats was 630 tons on the surface, increasing to 730 tons submerged. Single-hulled, they were not certified for more than 200 feet (61 metres) diving depth but their nimble size and quiet underwater operation made them difficult to track and therefore very suitable for inshore service.[18] The periscopes could only be raised some 12 feet (3.5 metres) above the top of the bridge casing. This meant that under certain conditions the shadow of the boat would be visible from the air when at periscope depth, which was only 27 feet (8.3 metres).

Propulsion for the U-class submarines was provided by a dual diesel-electric system. On the surface, the propellers were driven by the diesel engines, via two generators which also charged the batteries. When submerged, power for the electric motors was taken from the batteries, as usual. From their first sea trials, the three boats showed excellent handling and manoeuvrability, which, combined with ease of production and low cost, made the design particularly attractive. Accommodation was sparse though for the four officers and twenty-seven POs, artificers and ratings usually on board during wartime. Hence, the U-class boats were not suited for patrols of any length, particularly not in the rough seas of the northern part of the North Sea in winter time.

The two external torpedo tubes were quickly found to be a rather unfortunate idea. First of all, they gave a prominent bow wave, easily sighted, at the surface as well as at periscope depth, and made the boat difficult to control when just below the surface. Secondly, it was found that firing all six torpedoes in one salvo without losing control of the boat and breaking surface was only possible under the most favourable circumstances.[19]

At the start of the war, the Admiralty decided the U-class submarines were suitable for combat and a further twelve slightly modified boats were ordered under the 1939 supplementary programme. The first of these group two boats would become operational during the late summer of 1940. *Unique, Upright, Upholder* and *Utmost* had external tubes, but the tubes were removed from subsequent builds and the bow slightly extended. Apart from this, the group two boats were largely identical to those of group one. Under the 1940 and 1941 war programmes, a further forty-one U-class boats were ordered, of which thirty-four were eventually completed.

No Privacy

Life on board a submarine during WWII was quite unique. Apart from the daily challenge of living for an extended time in an overly confined space without access to even minimal levels of hygiene, privacy or comfort, there was the particular terror during depth-charge attacks. Stoker Hart of *Triad* held that a submarine patrol was '90 per cent boredom and 10 per cent cold fear'.[20] Not everyone could handle it and some – officers as well as ratings – had to be quietly transferred to other services.

In most boats, Axis or Allied, about half the crew lived in the bow compartment, among the torpedoes. Spare torpedoes were stored along the compartment walls or below the floorboards, while those in the tubes were repeatedly pulled back out, maintained and adjusted, with the help of a hoist attached to the roof. Space was a constant issue, but life became more comfortable with each torpedo fired.[21]

Privacy did not exist. Sharing a bunk with a mate on the opposite watch, each man tucked himself into a still-warm blanket vacated by a shipmate going on duty when he

Forward torpedo stowage compartment of *Tribune*. The photograph is probably taken just before departure as the crew's hammocks and kit bags still need to be organised. The doors forward lead to the torpedo room. (IWM A10909)

turned in. Only the captain would have the luxury of a tiny curtained-off area known as 'the cabin', usually close to the radio and hydrophone rooms, bearing no resemblance to similar areas on larger ships. In older boats like the British H-class used at the start of the war, there were no bunks, and the men slept on the battery boards. Soap was available but rarely used due to lack of water and beards were permitted for the same reason. Toilets existed, but were shared by many and, at the early stage of the war, could only be used when the boat was on the surface or at shallow depth. The smell of diesel, stale food and men soon permeated the clothes, which were damp most of the time, adding to the discomfort. Some of the engine-room crew hardly saw daylight during the mission, unless ordered on deck by a concerned captain. The storage of food was a significant challenge as few boats had specialised lockers for this, all nooks and crannies being used. After a few days on patrol, unprotected food was mouldy, and meals centred round tinned bully beef and sweet tea with condensed milk. There were no cooks on board the early boats and those least incompetent took in it turns to prepare whatever was to be eaten. Having a man on board who could make a decent meal was a real asset. Medical care existed only in the form of NCOs or men having attended a short course in basic first aid and taking time to study the boat's medical manual.

The fore end of all submarines held the torpedo room, with storage space for the reloads and the torpedo tubes proper. At the centre of the submarine was the control room, packed with wheels, valves, dials and gauges – most importantly, those related to the ballast tanks and diving controls. The periscopes were also found here, as was the ladder up to the main hatch and the conning tower. Most officers and petty officers had their quarters just forward of the central parts of the boats. Aft was the galley and the engine room. The clattering diesels first, then the electrical compartments.

On the surface, usually at night recharging the batteries, conditions on the bridge could vary from mysterious to miserable – usually the latter, as spray from the bow made the open area notoriously wet in anything but the calmest conditions. Below deck, the diesel engines were noisy and vibrating, their oil-stench creating seasickness and general misery that usually took several patrols getting used to.

Of the four to five officers on board, the captain and chief engineer were normally not included in the regular watch-keeping routines, but moved about as they saw fit and were called whenever needed. The others covered the boat in a regular system of watches, whether on the surface or at depth, with one officer in charge of each watch.

Torpedoes

The primary weapon of any submarine at the start of WWII was the unguided torpedo. Amongst the British submariners the torpedoes were known as 'fish', while the Germans knew theirs as 'aale', or 'eels'.

The Mk VIII 21-in (53.3-cm) diameter torpedo was the standard British torpedo at the time, first used in 1927 on board the O-class boats. It would remain more or less identical until long after the war. Similar designs were also in use by destroyers and motor torpedo boats (MTBs).[22] In the 1930s, design and test fabrication of British torpedoes was carried out at the Royal Naval Torpedo Factory (RNTF) in Greenock, Scotland, while production

Snapper loading practice torpedoes. They have a cold warhead, but otherwise are similar to the Mk VIII type – and as cumbersome to get into the boat. (IWM A1390)

was carried out in royal government factories or at the Vickers-Armstrongs (formerly Whitehead) works at Weymouth. In 1936 additional production was established at Alexandria, Dunbartonshire.[23]

The Mk VIII was the first British torpedo with a so-called burner-cycle propulsion. In the Brotherhood burner-cycle engine, pressurised air was heated to about 1,000°C (1,800°F) by burning a small amount of atomised kerosene-type fuel. This hot air–gas mixture was mixed with more fuel and fed into the engine, much like a semi-diesel. Electric motors for torpedoes were considered but rejected due to relatively poor performance and what was considered to be a relatively limited advantage of having no bubble-tracks.[24] The weight of the Mk VIII torpedo was 1,566 kg (3,452 lb), of which 340 kg (750 lb) was the TNT warhead. Its length was 6.6 metres (21.6 feet). Speed was a little over 40 knots and maximum range about 5,000 yards (4,500 metres). Most British torpedoes at the beginning of the war had contact pistols. The available magnetic pistol, known as a duplex coil rod (DCR) was unreliable and not much used.[25]

A much improved and modified torpedo, known as the Mk VIII**, was coming into service by the outbreak of the war, even if the older versions were still in use. The Mk VIII** had a warhead of 365 kg (805 lb) Torpex and two basic speed/range settings – 5,000 yards (4,500 metres) at 45.5 knots and 7,000 yards (6,400 metres) at 41 knots.[26] Hitting a target over 6 kilometres away was mainly down to serendipity, though.

The British Submarine Service went to war with an electromechanical torpedo-aiming director, rather primitive compared with that of an American or German boat. The British device, known as the 'fruit machine', would, based on input from the commanding officer (CO), calculate the boat's recommended course at the moment of attack through an intricate system of logarithmic scales. The submarine's own course was entered automatically from the gyrocompass, while all other data, including own speed and the target's speed, range, course and bearing, were entered manually by the torpedo officer, as reported by the CO at the periscope or on the bridge if on the surface.[27]

Based on this input, the fruit machine calculated the target's angle compared to the submarine and the two ships' relative positions, shown visually on the two rotating gauges in the centre of the device. In addition, the device would calculate traverse distance – i.e. the distance at which the target would pass in front of the submarine's bow, provided both maintained current courses – and give the 'aim-off' or distance ahead of the target that the aim-point should be in order to make the torpedo hit. The CO would then have to decide if he should fire his torpedoes from where he was or move to a different, better place. When at a satisfactory distance for an attack, the CO would have the fruit machine calculate the attack course, the course he would have to steer when firing the torpedoes, read this from the scale on the side of the device and pass it to the helmsman. After the submarine was on the correct course, the CO would be given the lead-angle from another scale, turn his periscope to that angle and wait for the target to enter the crosshairs of the periscope before giving the order to fire.

Simple, but for all practical purposes too simple. A large amount of data was gauged subjectively by the CO alone, increasing the risk of error. At each periscope observation, all numbers had to be reset. In combat conditions, there was often insufficient time for

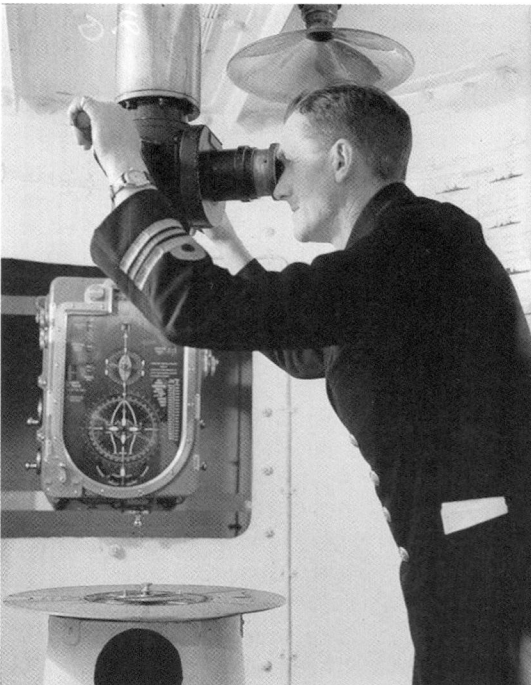

A lieutenant commander practising at the attack trainer at Blyth. Through the periscope he will see ship models moved about on rails. Beyond him is a 'fruit machine', identical to the one he would find in the control room of his submarine. Based on estimates of the target's speed, range and course, added to that of the submarine, the machine would calculate the amount of 'aim-off' to hit the target. (IWM A13861)

this and often the CO had to calculate solutions in his head without consulting the fruit machine. The torpedoes were fired in a straight line towards the place where the target was supposed to be when its course-line was intercepted and even a small error in the estimations had only one outcome – a miss.[28] Finally, the need to turn the boat onto a strictly determined attack course could take several minutes, not always affordable in combat. Should the target zigzag, the attack would in most cases have to be aborted and started all over again. Changes in the running depth of torpedoes had to be made by the torpedo operators via special devices installed on the tubes. Changing the torpedo's speed and thereby its range was not possible without pulling the torpedo out of its tube.

The ideal range to fire from was 600 to 1,500 metres. Beyond 2,000 metres, luck usually played an equal if not larger role than skill. Judging the distance, course and speed of a target through the periscope required substantial experience and the success of a single torpedo fired was rather remote. The answer was salvo firing, but as the torpedoes had no gyro-guiding mechanisms, it was only possible to fire straight shots at intervals as the target passed through the aim-point. Depending on how certain the CO was of his own estimates, he could choose a concentrated or scattered fire mode. When to fire the first torpedo of a salvo and how large the salvo should be would be the subject of intense discussions as the first months of the war progressed and experience was gained. It would be 1943 and later before the Royal Navy was able to introduce major improvements and automation to the fruit machine.

The torpedoes to be used in the internal tubes were lowered nose first into the torpedo stowage compartment. From there, those going into the tubes were brought forward, through the watertight bulkhead into the tube space and loaded. The reloads were kept in the stowage compartment until such time as there was an empty tube available. The external torpedo tubes were loaded before departure from base and remained empty when fired. Torpedo Gunner's Mate Joe Brighton of *Porpoise* narrated:

The torpedo was fitted with side lugs which rested on runners inside the torpedo tube to prevent the torpedo from turning. On the top of the torpedo was a steel block, called a 'top block'. When the torpedo was loaded into the tube, the top block butted against an air-operated stop which was known as the 'top stop'. A spring-operated stop also entered the tube at the rear of the top block and the torpedo was prevented from moving in any direction until [the required speed, depth and gyro data had been set and] the firing gear was operated. Great care was essential when loading the torpedoes. Settings had to be checked and the propeller had to be lined up to ensure that the engine pistons were in the correct position for starting. The main body of the torpedo had to be fairly tight, as any small object could jam the torpedo in the tube. In wartime this would be disastrous and was a TGM's Nightmare. [. . .] The thought of a torpedo with engine running, jammed inside a tube while in contact with the enemy is too horrible to contemplate. It could, and probably did, happen. There would be no survivors to tell the tale. In my experience, in peacetime, it happened on at least two occasions with practice torpedoes. This could have been caused by faulty firing gear, by insufficient air impulse or by some small object jamming the torpedo in the tube.[29]

Firing a torpedo meant the sudden loss of a ton and a half of weight forward – to avoid bringing the boat to the surface, water was needed to replace the torpedo the minute it left the tube. This was achieved through an elaborate system of compensating systems, quickly bringing the correct amount of water into the tube while preventing the air used to fire the torpedo from escaping to the surface. Firing several torpedoes augmented the risk of surfacing and required well-exercised co-operation between several men. Brighton continued:

> The firing gear was a collection of devices designed to launch the torpedo from the tube by air pressure, but the air impulse could not be allowed to follow the torpedo from the tube, as this would cause large bubbles on the surface which could easily have been seen by the enemy. To avoid this, an automatic inboard venting system had been arranged. This came into operation as soon as the torpedo had been given its initial launch forward by the air impulse. An air-operated valve opened automatically, allowing the air impulse to be diverted to an open tank, called the AIV-tank, under the tubes. In addition to the air a quantity of water had to be taken into the boat to make up for the weight of the torpedoes which had been fired. [. . .] Perched on the seat at the rear end of the tubes was my position at the firing panel with the firing levers (six on *Porpoise*). The three fore-endsmen in the tube space attended to the alteration of torpedo settings and carried out any emergency instructions. [. . .] The captain, in the Control Room, would decide the time interval between the firing of each torpedo, and this would be passed by 'phone to an officer in the fore-ends. [. . .] At the order 'Fire!', the firing lever for the particular tube would be pulled back, held back for two or three seconds, then replaced. [. . .] The sequence was repeated when each tube was fired. It was quite noisy in the fore-ends, with air and water sounds, but in the remainder of the boat there was a bit of a shudder when each tube fired and a build-up of air pressure.[30]

The forward part of the torpedo contained the warhead and its detonator, the rest of the space was taken up by the propulsion system and the stabilising devices. Most early torpedoes usually had two contra-rotating propellers on a single shaft to keep them stable in the water. The depth-keeping mechanism of a torpedo usually consisted of an adjustable hydrostatic valve, set to the anticipated draught of the target and the type of detonator used. Servomotors connected to the horizontal rudders and vertical tailfins kept the torpedo running straight and level, acting on input from the depth-keeping mechanism or the gyroscope that was set spinning when it was fired. The gyros in the Mk VIII torpedoes sometimes failed, with the result that the torpedo turned in a large circle back towards the submarine from where it was fired. The asdic operators were well aware of this issue and listened carefully for any torpedo not running straight. If they reported one turning off course, the CO would take his boat down to get out of the way. Though usually no more than a nuisance, it meant at least one torpedo was lost and, during periods of attention from enemy escorts, added stress to a challenging situation.[31]

As the war wore on, some older torpedoes from the Great War were also issued to the submarines on patrol during the hectic summer of 1940. This inevitably led to a number of duds where the motors malfunctioned, the torpedoes falling lifeless to the seabed, or the steering failed, sending them off on a stray course, or they simply did not explode even when they hit. As on board the German U-boats, where the torpedo problem was crippling, the frustration when this happened was intense.[32]

Deck Guns

Deck guns on submarines may sound contradictory to their purpose of operating under water. It was, however, seen by many submariners as an essential weapon to sink defenceless ships when surprise was not necessary, saving the use of an expensive torpedo, or against targets on land. There was also an option for self-defence in case the boat was for some reason unable to dive. Most T-class boats had a 4-inch Mk XII 100-mm/50-calibre gun while most S- and U-class submarines had a specially designed Mk I 3-inch gun. Some of the earlier boats had to make do with an older alternative, though, and Lieutenant Commander Bryant of *Sealion* found his deck gun temperamental:

> I could find no way to make the breech reliable. As it was originally an army Ack Ack gun, I sought guidance from the gunners at Malta. [. . .] An elderly warrant officer, however, [. . .] could only suggest that we should throw it away as the army had done years before. Actually, apart from the fact that the breech jammed at the most inopportune moments, that the shell was too light for the job and that it was in no way designed to withstand the exposure to submarine life, it was a very good little gun. Most of its ailments could be cured by a strong man with a lead mallet . . .[33]

Pre-war exercises with the deck gun were frequent and the record at the China Station was ten rounds into a 10-foot-square target at 600 yards in a minute, the exercise beginning and ending with the boat submerged.[34] Positioning the gun was a compromise between quick accessibility, ease of ammunition handling and stability. Usually it was either sited in a casing in front of the conning tower or directly on the deck. Ready-use

A gunlayer on board *Ursula* checking his 3-inch gun at sea. (S Clewlow)

lockers held a few shells to speed up firing, while a chain of ratings passed additional shells up from the magazine below. To man the gun, four or five men were usually needed, including ammunition handlers. As the war progressed, use of the deck gun proved rather limited in North European waters. Adverse weather and high waves made hitting anything rather difficult, while the constant danger of aircraft made it risky to have too many men on deck when on the surface.

Periscopes

Periscopes allow a submarine commander to see above the surface from a submerged position. Operated by rams and wire pulleys working off the telemotor system, the periscopes retract into wells in the control room deck when not in use. A watertight gland where the periscope passed through the pressure hull allowed it to be rotated without excessive force around 360 degrees for ease of observation.

The experienced submarine commander used his periscopes sparingly in tactical conditions as, under most conditions, it would create a tell-tale wake, or 'feather', giving away the submarine's position. Seeing a target in the search-periscope, the CO or the officer of the watch would adjust the handle until the two images of the vessel were one above the other. On a word, the ERA standing behind him could then read off the range shown on the periscope stem and pass that to the other officers and men of the control room.

British WWII submarines had two periscopes: a long-distance, high-power search-periscope and a close-up, attack-periscope. Both periscopes were made of bronze so as not to affect the magnetic compass. This made them light but also less rigid, requiring the characteristic support standards rising up above the bridge.

The forward of the two, the search-periscope, was binocular and bifocal with two settings: 1.5x magnification with 40 degrees field-of-view for a swift all-round look, and 6x magnification with 10 degrees field-of-view for identification of objects and scanning detailed areas of the horizon. This periscope had the ability to look upwards at an angle, known as a 'skyscrape', to search for aircraft before surfacing.

The second periscope, the attack-periscope, had a smaller diameter than the search-periscope (7.5 inch versus 9.5 inch) and only one setting: 1.5x magnification, which gave the commander a monocular view suitable for the latter stages of an attack. The smaller diameter made it less conspicuous when raised, giving less wake. It had poor light-transmission though, and was used as little as possible.

Ideally, the periscopes should be as long as possible to allow them to be used from maximum depth below the surface while still being accommodated within the pressure hull. The compromise was about 34 feet (10.3 metres), which meant a periscope depth of 30 feet (9.1 metres) in the S- and T-class submarines. In the smaller U-class, the periscopes were shorter, giving a periscope depth of only 27 feet (8.3 metres) – too shallow in clear water, as the shadow of the boat could be seen from the air at times.

Tetrarch, one of the latter group one T-class boats was equipped with experimental 40-feet (12.1-metres) periscopes, with tops protruding above the standards even when down. This was partly successful, making depth-keeping at periscope depth easier. Allocating resources to a renewed periscope design was difficult, however, and the early wartime Royal Navy submarines would have to make do with the standard 34-foot type.[35]

Asdic and Communication

At the end of WWI, the British Navy had developed a prototype for active underwater sonar submarine-detection gear, the so-called 'asdic'.[36] This works by sending a narrow, ultrasonic sound wave, created by an oscillator, through the water. Striking anything, including the hull of another submarine, an echo bounces back and can be picked up by hydrophones, recorded as electrical impulses heard by an operator, and displayed on a screen or as marks by a stylus on a paper roll. The hydrophones of 1939 could determine the direction of the echo quite accurately. The distance to and the depth of the object producing the echo was not given, though.

By the outbreak of WWII, four different asdic sets for various types of surface vessels had been developed, as well as one for submarines: Type 129. *Oberon* was the first submarine to carry asdic and it was quickly found that the device could be put to good use under water. Above all, the hydrophones of the asdic sets were far superior to the regular sets and, as the asdic could be turned 360 degrees, the direction of the sound could be determined with almost pinpoint accuracy. Accurate range-finding needed active use of the sonar, though, which was normally avoided as it would reveal the presence of the submarine to anybody nearby. A skilled asdic operator might have a fair opinion as to the distance of the source of the sound he was picking up, but the CO would have to realise

The telegraphist onboard *Tribune* at his set. Conditions are rather basic. The bulbs tended to break during depth-charge attacks and were easily replaced. (IWM A10905)

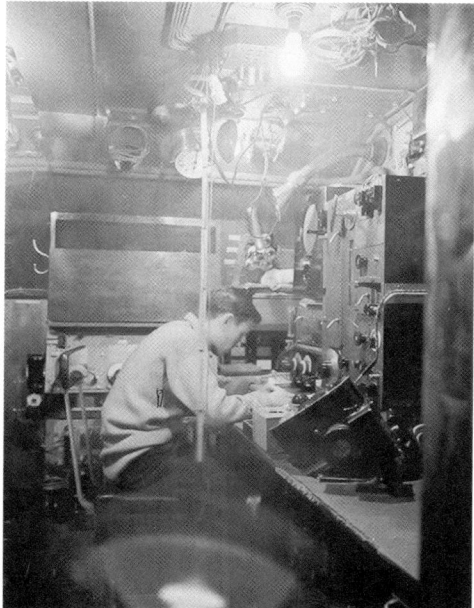

that this could easily be misleading. The asdic was sometimes used for navigation in tight waters, where rocks and shallows could be detected, and even mines. On the surface with diesel engines running, the asdic was useless, as the vibrations and sound made by the submarine's engines negated its use.[37]

Interestingly, the asdic was also used for very effective communication between submerged submarines. As the beam could be pointed directly towards the receiver, Morse signals in plain text were sent from one boat to the other when within range. The sound pulses were received clearly over a moderate distance, but not picked up further away, like radio signals. Radio signals to and from submarines during WWII were mostly sent via the Rugby radio station in Warwickshire.[38] From here, signals from Vice Admiral Submarines – VA(S) – or the respective flotillas were transferred to Very Low Frequency (VLF) signals and re-transmitted at about 16 kilocycles, which could be received by a submerged submarine on the loop aerial in home waters while still submerged, close to surface. For this to be possible, the boat turned roughly in the direction of Rugby as the aerial was strung out along the forward jumping wire, running from the bow to the periscope standards to prevent nets or other obstructions snagging on the superstructure. Obviously, this affected operations and was not always possible. High-frequency flotilla signals could only be received when at the surface with the mast aerial raised. Signals were usually transmitted every four hours and each submarine had its own call signal. Important signals could be sent at any time and the telegraphist had to listen in whenever he could.

Coming to periscope depth at set times was not always convenient. On 9 February Lieutenant Commander Rupert Lonsdale brought *Seal* near the surface at 18:00 to listen in to the routine afternoon broadcast. His telegraphist heard nothing until 18:13, when he received: 'Nothing to communicate'. Angered, Lonsdale wrote in his log:

> During this time, *Seal* had been in a dangerous position at thirty feet, when it was too dark to see and speed and water noises were handicapping the reception [. . .]. It is submitted that it is most important for Rugby to make this operating signal at once if they have no signal to make. [The signal must be on schedule] to reduce the time that a submarine has to remain in a possibly dangerous position while receiving messages of no importance.[39]

To send a signal, the submarine could in theory use an antenna attached to one of the periscopes, but this gave a weak signal that was not always received, not even from within the North Sea. The safest procedure was to surface and raise a telescopic or hinged mast. Hence the transmissions from the submarines were kept to a minimum. All the more so after early 1940, when it was realised that German land stations could intercept the signals and track the senders.

Propulsion and Batteries

On the surface submarines were powered by diesel engines, and when submerged by electric motors, the batteries of which were recharged by the diesels while on the surface. The U-class submarines had a diesel-electric system where the propellers were driven at

The motor room of *Tribune*, looking forward towards the diesels of the engine room. Note the engine room telegraphs behind the artificer. The electro motor is below the floorboards of the central passageway. (IWM A10896)

all times by the motors, while the diesels were used to generate electricity and charge the batteries when surfaced. Two shafts was the norm, each with one propeller.

When operating under water, the submarines of WWII relied entirely on batteries to drive the electrical engines. The batteries were large, heavy hardware, usually grouped in two or three cell-tanks underneath the decking inside the pressure hull in the forward part of the boat to balance their weight with the engines and motors aft. Depending on the type of boat, the total battery weight could exceed 150 tons. The cells were arranged so that if one fell out, one or two would still be in operation.

At full speed submerged, most of the battery capacity would be drained within an hour or two. At economical speed it would still last no more than thirty hours or so, even with the most careful use. Hence, the status of the batteries and how to recharge them would constantly be on the mind of the CO and his chief engineer. Running out of amps meant the submarine would be forced to surface, irrespective of what waited for it there. And the lower the battery was drained, the longer it took to recharge. In general, twelve hours or more submerged necessitated at least four to five hours charging at maximum rate. The reports from submarines operating in the northern part of the North Sea as spring progressed towards summer in 1940 all contain comments on the difficulties of charging the batteries fully during the shortening periods of darkness, thereby limiting the charge available to operate meaningfully under water during daylight. VA(S) Horton took steps to improve the quality of the batteries during 1940, but this took time to implement and could only be performed during maintenance periods in the yards.

When on the surface, the batteries were charged by one of the main engines. Charging would take most of the output from this engine and, in the meantime, there was only one engine available for propulsion. Charging too fast would heat up the batteries and damage or even destroy them. Consequently, a minimum period of six hours was normally required at the surface to ensure fully charged batteries. During charging, great care had to be taken to ensure the ventilator systems were working properly as the batteries were liable to give off explosive and toxic gas.

DSEA

The Davis Submerged Escape Apparatus, or DSEA, had been adopted by the Royal Navy in the late 1920s. It consisted of a rubber breathing bag carried across the chest by a strap over the neck and a belt around the back, much like a lifejacket. The bag contained a steel high-pressure cylinder holding oxygen and a canister of barium hydroxide to scrub the exhaled CO_2. Opening the cylinder's control valve admitted oxygen into the breathing bag, charging it to the pressure of the surroundings, whether water or the confines of a submarine. Wearing the DSEA, breathing took place through a mouthpiece connected to the canister of CO_2 absorbent with a flexible corrugated tube. The nose was closed by a clip and goggles were also supposed to be worn. During the ascent to surface, air from the breathing bag was allowed to escape, as water pressure decreased, through a non-return release valve. At the surface the valve could be closed and the breathing bag would change to a buoyancy aid.[40] To control the ascent, a very effective rubber apron could be unrolled and held out horizontally by the escaper after he left the submarine.

All men had to pass an escape test, wearing the DSEA apparatus, before they were posted on board submarines. This took place in a tank at Fort Blockhouse. Those who did not manage to climb down the 30-foot ladder, spend some time on the bottom and then ascend in a controlled manner to the surface would not serve on board one of the Royal Navy's submarines.

A submariner wearing the Davis Submerged Escape Apparatus, DSEA. (Author's Collection)

The 'Ursula Suit'

Suitable clothes for the harsh North Sea conditions were not at hand for the British submariners in the early days of WWII – unlike their German colleagues. The oilskins provided in the beginning were too thin and the wool underneath became damp when on the bridge. Multiple layers of clothes were used, supported by towels, gloves and heavy sea boots.

Lieutenant Commander George Phillips of *Ursula* found this extremely inconvenient. In 1938, when observing his navigating officer, Lieutenant Richard Lakin, wearing a one-piece over-suit when riding his motorcycle, he had an idea. Lakin's suit was made by Barbour of South Shields from coloured waxed cotton, and appeared very efficient, keeping him dry, even when doused with water from a fire hose.

Phillips decided that the overalls, with a few alterations, might be suitable for submarine lookouts and bridge personnel. He contacted the Barbour factory, convincing them to make the existing garment into a two-piece *'Ursula* suit' with a hooded jacket. This was done at Phillips's own cost until the Admiralty became involved and took over. Further improvements included elastics at the waist and ankles, chest pockets removed and the civilian tartan lining replaced with heavy dark-blue cotton. The suits proved to be extremely comfortable, warm and waterproof, and were eventually issued as standard to all RN submarines, most often worn with the traditional cream, roll-neck 'woolly pully' and suede sea boots.[41]

Bearded Lieutenant Commander Phillips of *Ursula* and one of his officers are wearing early versions of the '*Ursula* Suit'. The third officer is wearing a regular raincoat. (S Clewlow)

— 3 —

The Submariners

Training and Tactics

FIRING TORPEDOES WAS MUCH practised by British submariners between the wars, partly under competitive conditions. By 1937, practice torpedoes had a special collision head, so that it could be ascertained whether the torpedoes had actually hit their target or not. The depot ships of each flotilla or some other support ship usually acted as target for mock attacks. Exercises under realistic conditions against escorted warships or convoys were rare, though. In spite of arguments from the COs that night attacks on the surface would be an essential skill to master, practising such skills was not allowed for fear of collision. For security reasons, the submarines were instructed to dive some 2,000–3,000 metres (2,200–2,300 yards) away from the big ships, and fire their practice torpedoes from a distance of at least 1,000 metres (1,100 yards). Under no circumstance were the submarines to surface less than half a mile from any surface ship; they should only fire yellow signal rockets to reveal their presence and then go deep until safely away. The realism of such exercises against large fleets can easily be questioned. In addition, the officers of capital ships and cruisers in particular wanted little to do with submariners and their boats – partly because any collision might influence their careers, whether they were blamed or not, and partly because operating together with submarines was difficult and restricted their own movements. As a result, most Royal Navy officers in 1939 had very limited knowledge of the tactical use of submarines, their strengths and weaknesses, and how to fight them.[1] The fact that submarines operated in three dimensions was ignored.

Ben Bryant wrote:

> In vain did we protest on fleet exercise when, as usual, we were adjudged sunk, that no allowance had been made for depth. We were merely told that we had been sunk and not to argue. Only a few months later, frantic efforts were to be made to devise material techniques to deal with the deep submarine. Many ships were to be lost and the U-boats escape because our own submariners had not been listened to. In the Combined Fleet Exercises of the spring of 1939, Ruckers had at last got permission for his boats to operate at night without navigation lights. Bickford (*Salmon*) and I (*Sealion*) had spent a considerable period at night, unseen, in the midst of the 'enemy' fleet. Bickford had 'torpedoed' HMS *Courageous* with a salvo and she was adjudged to have had her speed reduced by 2 knots. [. . .] The CO of the cruiser which *Sealion* torpedoed would admit to no damage. When I asked him why at Gibraltar some days later, he replied that a submarine had no right to be on the surface, darkened amongst the fleet at night.[2]

Similarly, Hugh 'Rufus' Mackenzie, at the time serving briefly on board the capital ships of the Mediterranean Fleet as a submarine expert, wrote:

Submarines only occasionally played a significant role in these [fleet] exercises and even when they did, the scale of 'casualty' or 'damage' imposed on their targets as a result of a successful torpedo attack was totally out of keeping with reality. The lack of appreciation of the submarine threat may be explained by the withdrawal in 1931 of the ageing Great War L-class submarines from the Mediterranean Fleet, to be replaced a year later by the new R-class submarines. Another factor was the safety rules which required all submarines to be on the surface at night, burning navigation lights and taking no part in any of the exercises during dark hours.[3]

Later, having been sent back to Britain and serving as a first lieutenant on board *Osiris* in September 1939, he added:

Actually, I think, when war did come, we were confident, possibly over-confident. But we very quickly learned that our training really hadn't fitted us for fighting a 1939 war. When I look back now, although we were quite good at firing torpedoes and the technical side of how to conduct a patrol, the British submarine service was, right up to the outbreak of war, very poorly trained for wartime operations. As an example of this, in Fleet exercises, submarines were not allowed to dive at night. They had to surface at sunset, switch on their navigation lights and take no further part in the exercise or operation until daylight the next day. This gave us a completely false outlook on how one should conduct an operational patrol in wartime. The whole tempo of our existence really did not prepare us for the dangers one had to face going into enemy controlled waters on an operational patrol in wartime.[4]

Always somebody left behind. Newly commissioned *Sealion* (behind) and *Shark* (nearest) preparing to sail from HMS *Dolphin*, Gosport, to join the 1st Flotilla at Malta in March 1935. (Author's Collection)

Such was the confidence in the effectiveness of the asdic on board the destroyer escorts that hardly any tests or exercises were conducted under realistic conditions, finding out what happened as the submariners learned how the sonars worked and how the escorts used the information they obtained. This created flawed perceptions of risk from, and defence against, submarines among the officers of the surface ships as well as distorting the overall concept of risk among the submariners, focusing on an operational situation they would rarely, if ever, be in. Above all, it simplified and to some extent neglected the menace of extended counter-attacks, especially from the air.

In the exercises that were held, it was often found that the asdic failed, and even when it did work it had a number of weaknesses. British submarine commanders found, after a while, that it was relatively easy to escape asdic-equipped destroyers once they learned their tactics. Repeatedly, the submariners penetrated the screens in groups and 'laid mines' or surfaced firing flares, signifying they were within torpedo range without having been detected. The fact that they did exactly what German submariners were training to do, and did so successfully, was ignored and dismissed as reckless behaviour. On the other hand, if one of the destroyers passed close to a submarine, the submarine was immediately deemed sunk and out of the exercise.[5]

Except for pressure from people like Captain Philip Ruck-Keene, C-in-C of the 1st Flotilla in the Mediterranean at the time, to allow diving at night and operating without navigation lights during the Abyssinian crisis, there were few voices raised against the general policy of training the Submarine Service. It would be 1938 and the Munich crisis before it was felt by the Submarine Service that they were being taken at least halfway seriously. There was still a lot of room for improvement, though. Lieutenant Commander 'Shrimp' Simpson of *Porpoise*, for instance, discovered that the mouth of the River Ems, where he was to lay mines should the crisis escalate, had only 15 metres of water – at least 5 metres less than the minimum needed to cover the boat with room to manoeuvre. When made aware of this, the CO of 2nd Submarine Fleet, Captain Jock Bethel answered:

> Now, my orders to you are that you should lay these mines to the north and west of the positions given, provided visibility allows you to fix where you have laid them, provided there is adequate depth of water during the approach and provided . . . you return here safely. . . . The next lot of orders will be issued by Flag Officer Submarines, so we won't have any repetition of this suicidal stuff.[6]

Later, in mid-1939, Simpson was ordered to carry out some practical experiments from *Porpoise* to test the feasibility of 'stop-and-search' practices on merchantmen at sea, including placing prize crews, in accordance with the prevailing international naval treaties. *Porpoise* was to operate against a group of fleet auxiliaries off the Isle of Wight and she would first have to find one of them, get close enough to surface and stop her at gunpoint, before opening the casing, launching the collapsible boat and pulling across to board the quarry. All the time, they would be under time pressure from a Coastal Command aircraft known to be approaching from a nearby land base, alerted by radio the minute that the submarine was sighted from the auxiliary. Hence, the exercise set-up was very realistic. Simpson wrote:

We had two days of this farcical boating picnic and in conditions of flat calm with all in favour of the boat. On the first occasion the boat did get seaborne and a few yards on her journey. On all subsequent occasions the very slow aircraft was always overhead before the collapsible boat was on deck and erected for launching. When war was declared, the first action taken by submarines was to land all collapsible boats and clear the casings of all rope and other gear which might float as a result of depth-charging, or might foul the propellers.[7]

Still, even if the tests were clearly found to be futile, no changes to the overall instructions of adhering to the prize regulations were made. On the other hand, the swift and efficient reaction of Coastal Command to the distress signals might have given a somewhat deceitful sense of security for ships in the coastal areas as it was presumed that German submarines also adhered to the international regulations.

In spite of the obvious gaps and shortcomings, the Royal Navy's training of its submariners was nevertheless sound and thorough. Most of the young officers developed their boats and men in a manner they considered necessary. They talked freely among themselves, discussing experiences and practices, to the extent that most were physically and mentally prepared and adapted quickly to the realities of war, when it came.

Tightly Knit

On board a submarine, life or death depends on every man knowing and doing his job, all the time. Inevitably, the crews of most submarines were young; mostly in their early twenties, some even in their teens. Few if any of the officers were past 35. This meant that, unlike larger surface vessels, command was in the hands of young men with little previous experience of war. On the other hand, the small size of the crew and the cramped living conditions often created a deep feeling of unity and belonging as well as pride in their captain, on whom they depended for success as well as survival. There was also a strong feeling of being part of an elite: discipline being relaxed and rules judged by necessity – which the most skilled commanders would use to great effect, increasing the proficiency of their boats.

By 1939, around 270 officers and 2,500 petty officers and ratings served in the Submarine Service, some 5 per cent of the total number of men in the Royal Navy.[8] Far from all British submariners were volunteers. Conscription was necessary at intervals, and in the late 1920s half the training classes were conscripts and half volunteers. Nevertheless, most who came into the Submarine Service chose to stay on. Life on board a submarine gave certain advantages. Submariners were, with all allowances, paid almost double what most other men in the Royal Navy received. Pay increased proportionally with rank and was undoubtedly a reason quite a few accepted the risks of the trade in the first place – and once there, remained. When at port they were usually billeted ashore and the food was good, at least while in port and during the first part of a patrol. For many, it appears that avoiding the rigours and discipline of the big ships was at least as important as the money. In addition, most officer candidates faced the prospect of command, if not as CO, at least as first officer, and responsibility came early. On the other hand, the boats were dangerous even in peacetime and no fewer than fourteen British submarines were lost between 1919 and 1939, mostly from collisions or mishandling during diving or surfacing.[9]

Those that were deemed unsuited, through claustrophobia, incompetence or plain disinterest, were usually given a way back to surface roles in order not to endanger their boats. Most settled in though, taking the risks and discomforts along with the advantages. Conscripts had to stay for three years, volunteers for five. Most of the submariners that stayed on in the navy beyond the minimum term opted to stay in the Submarine Service and few actively sought transfer to another branch. In wartime there was no doubt that the dangers would increase sharply, but still young men of all ranks requested transfer to the Submarine Service.[10]

Officers of the Royal Naval Reserve (RNR) joining the Submarine Service were normally considered very useful as navigation officers, their skills in most cases superior

Tightly knit: officers, NCOs and ratings of *Thunderbolt* in 1940. In the middle is First Lieutenant John Stevens, a particularly competent and well-liked officer. Note the age differences of the men around him. (Author's Collection)

to those coming fresh from officer training. Men from the Royal Naval Volunteer Reserve (RNVR) were at first few and far between among the submarine officers, but from the winter of 1940/41 the first ones appeared, heralding a steady flow of volunteers, who in most cases were as qualified and competent as the professionals.

The crew of a submarine would usually stay together over a long period of time. It was recognised that it was vital that they worked as a team and knew each other well. Throughout the war, though, there was a constant flow of new boats coming into commission, absorbing the newcomers and, to ensure learning and transfer of experience, senior POs would often be transferred to the new boats as one of the first of their crew. Young officers were regularly rotated between boats as they were promoted, to gain multiple experiences from different boats and commanding officers.

The CO of a submarine at the beginning of WWII would unmistakably put his stamp on his boat. Most of them were in their late twenties or early thirties. 'Old enough to have experience, self-confidence and judgement, young enough not to think too much,' according to Ben Bryant who added, 'at 35 most men are getting too old, over cautious.'[11] This meant that as a small community, away from senior officers for weeks at a time, each boat would develop its own culture, largely predominated by the style of the CO. Some were buccaneers, some were arrogant and distant, maintaining command through a

Another day in the office. 'Torps' Sub-Lieutenant McKenzie of *Seraph* in front of the torpedo control panel. Beside him is Able Seaman Payne keeping the log. (Author's Collection)

cloak of indifference. Others, like Rupert Lonsdale of *Seal*, gained their respect through a quiet, low-key empathy that made the men do their utmost to comply. As in most things beyond the physical mechanics in a submarine, there were few guidebooks to refer to and individual management styles had to be improvised and tested out.

There was hardly any electronic equipment on board a submarine and, when submerged, the CO was the only one able to see what was going on above using his periscope. His orders had to be followed to the letter and there was normally limited time for advice or discussions. Decisions would have to be made in a split second and, if wrong, could have disastrous consequences, even in peacetime. Although young and of medium rank – normally lieutenants or lieutenant commanders – their responsibilities were huge. Still, the main attraction for most submarine captains appears to have been a blend of being given command of a vessel early in their career and the freedom of acting without too much supervision from the higher ranks. Some were not up to it and were unceremoniously transferred to other jobs.

The CO was not alone though. He might be in absolute command, but his success depended ultimately on the skills and efficiency of his crew. Every man counted and a successful attack was far more about teamwork than in other ships. One man making a small mistake or losing his concentration could mean the torpedoes missed or even endangered the whole boat. Hence, discipline was different on board a submarine. The separation between officers and men was unavoidable, but it was less of a gap at sea during a patrol. Each man was important and had to know his job to perfection. This made the chain of command very short and created a bond between the ranks rarely seen in surface ships. The rapport between the CO, his first officer and the senior ratings of the submarine would be vital. The successful commander had a crew who trusted him fully, knowing that he knew them as well as he knew their equipment. As the war progressed, it became obvious to all submariners that their lives depended on each other and only when the commanding officer knew that he could trust his entire crew to do their job, could he focus on the tactical and operational side of the patrol.

On land as well, the flotilla commanders had challenging tasks, especially as the losses mounted. Most of them were old submariners themselves. Many had been to war and had great concerns about sending boats on some of the missions. When submarines became overdue or were known to have been sunk their grief was genuine.

One of the most outstanding flotilla commanders at the time was Captain Philip Ruck-Keene, commonly known as 'Ruckers'. According to Ben Bryant, he was 'the most forward-looking submariner between the wars'[12] – he provided relevant training for his boats and crews and managed to break down some of the 'well-meant but grandmotherly' rules of submarine conduct during fleet exercises.[13] In particular, when at Malta in the late 1930s he and his four young S-class commanders, Bryant, Bickford, King and Buckley – of *Sealion*, *Salmon*, *Snapper* and *Shark*, respectively – made up an outstanding team full of competence, ideas and initiatives that were to be priceless when war commenced.[14]

'Ruckers' was a 'huge bull of a man with a ruddy countenance, bushy eyebrows and eyes so deep-set it was impossible to see their colour,' Lieutenant Commander William 'Bill' King wrote, continuing:

[He] was determined to prepare properly for war – if it came. [. . .] A legend for his outbursts of rage, his realistic concepts and his original ideas, Ruckers either loved you or hated you. He radiated *joi de vivre* and could not hide his fury at those who were not aware of life and danger to life. [. . .] Because he never bothered to hide his opinions, even to senior officers, he was not always popular [but] we accepted any dressing down from this man because his roars were heartfelt and we knew we deserved them. One didn't forget a reprimand from Ruckers – it was the experience of a lifetime.[15]

The Perishers

Officer candidates were thoroughly trained in most aspects of operating a submarine. And more than in most branches of the Royal Navy, the training was very much hands-on, first at a submarine training class at HMS *Dolphin*, the submarine headquarters base at Fort Blockhouse, Gosport then on board a training boat.[16] Ben Bryant wrote:

In the mornings we would have lectures and in the afternoons go and actually work the things we had heard about, in the boats alongside. On Fridays we would usually go to sea for the day in one of the training boats. By the end of our four months' course, we were able, after a fashion, to do every job in the submarine ourselves.[17]

Before continuing their career, most submarine officers did a year in general service, usually on board a surface ship. This was not welcomed by all submariners, but probably a wise provision in the long run. There is no record of a similar year being considered the other way, though, not even for those officers destined to command anti-submarine vessels.

Having qualified as a submarine officer, each man spent time at the different positions on board, first as navigator and later as torpedo officer, before being considered for command. Most sub-lieutenants or lieutenants would serve on various boats under captains who observed them closely and gave their recommendations. If still found potentially suitable, each officer would serve as first lieutenant, first on board one of the older boats, then one of the newer boats. Those considered qualified would finally be assigned to the submarine commanding officers' qualifying course, also known as the 'periscope school' or 'perisher course'. The candidates, five or six at a time, assigned to each five-week course were commonly known as 'perishers'. The first part of the course took place in the 'attack teacher', a rough simulator near Fort Blockhouse. Here, model ships were observed through a periscope mounted in a replica of a control room and the candidate had to show that he could manoeuvre his own vessel safely while still keeping a three-dimensional picture of multiple targets in his head with a minimum of aids. All the time, his classmates, assisted by the staff of the simulator, tried to outwit him, manoeuvring the ship-models that he was supposed to attack. The first RNVR officer accepted to train for submarines was Edward Young in May 1940.

The second part of the course took place at sea on board a real submarine, usually one of the old H-class boats. The candidates were given command of the submarine while its regular captain watched from the side and would only intervene in cases of acute danger.

Each attack was recorded and analysed in detail afterwards, providing effective learning. Not all candidates passed and those who failed returned quietly to general service; a failed CO candidate was not considered useful in a submarine. In 1937, at 27, Bill King considered that the perisher course marked a very great signpost in his life:

> Many excellent officers failed to pass this particular examination and went on to command bigger ships with great success. To attack with a submarine requires a certain eye and a certain flair which is difficult to reveal until you are actually undergoing the course. [. . .] How can I explain it? Perhaps one might compare a singer with sufficient voice but sort of a lack of ability to hit absolutely true. Of course I wanted to pass and do well.[18]

Bill King passed – but he was not too sure of himself:

> Having qualified to command a submarine, I spent a short time as Staff Officer Operations at the anti-submarine training flotilla at Portland. I had plenty to think over – perhaps too much. [. . .] To fire [the torpedoes] you had to point the submarine like a bow and arrow. It needed a virtuoso to do it well and in mock attacks, I had learnt how often I lacked brilliance, wallowing around like a stuck whale in the path of the oncoming target-ship. If war came – would I be any good?[19]

He would indeed.

Perfect Buoyancy

As in most Royal Navy vessels, the first officer of a submarine had the role of maintaining crew discipline, assigning duties to each man, and keeping the boat ship-shape. He would also be responsible for the welfare of the men as well as their training and competence to make the boat an efficient fighting machine. When at sea, the first officer was responsible for the care and maintenance of the batteries as well as the most important task of all: the diving and, once below, the trim of the boat. This required a perfect understanding of the maze of wheels, pipes, valves and switches inside the submarine in addition to the functions of each ballast tank and the consequence for the boat's behaviour of increasing or reducing the amount of water in them, individually or in series. If the CO wanted to look through his periscope, it would be the first officer's task to get him to periscope depth as soon as possible – and stay there. A bad trim could dip the lens of the periscope under at a critical moment, or worse, cause the boat to break surface.

When the commander of a WWII submarine wanted to submerge his boat, he did so by ordering the main ballast tanks to be flooded. On most submarines these were welded onto the sides and hence known as saddle tanks. Tanks inside the pressure hull usually had valves at their top and base that needed to be opened manually or hydraulically from the diving control panel when flooding was ordered. Outside tanks were open to the sea at their base and the water kept out by the pressure of the air trapped inside when the boat was on the surface. To dive, vents were opened, usually by hydraulics, on the top of the tanks, letting the air out and allowing the water to flow in from the bottom. Most boats at the time also had the number one (forward) tank or 'Q-tank' included as part of the central system for diving. This was used for quick-diving, as filling it would force the bow down and the boat under. As the submarine was nearing the desired depth, the Q-tank was blown empty with high-pressure air, which raised the bow – levelling off the boat, assisted by the hydroplanes – after which the first officer adjusted the trim until the boat was level and steady at the required speed. To surface, the water was forced down out of the tanks by blowing high-pressure air into them. To expedite surfacing in an emergency, the vents of the main tanks were always kept closed, so that high-pressure air could be released promptly, forcing the water out as quickly as possible.

A German U-boat with an experienced crew could dive in less than thirty seconds. British boats were in general slower, requiring up to a minute unless well trimmed down in advance. The more buoyancy a submarine had, the longer it took to dive, and buoyancy was required to keep the bridge reasonably dry when at the surface and allow the lookouts a useful range of observation. When running into heavy seas, the S-boats in particular tended to get waves underneath the bow, delaying diving. In such circumstances, the Q-

Depth-keeping onboard *Seraph*. Below the depth gauge, showing the boat to be at 30 feet, is a spirit-level showing if the boat is horizontal or at an incline, bow up or down. The wheel controls the hydroplanes. (Author's Collection)

tank would be partially flooded when at the surface to keep the bow down. This, however, could be dangerous in heavy seas as the boat became sluggish, manoeuvring poorly. As in most things related to submarines, there was a balance between the different risks as conditions changed.

The stability of the boat when underwater was controlled by rudder, hydroplanes and trim tanks – small tanks inside the pressure hull – which could be filled or emptied as needed. This sounds easy, but in the days when most of the operations were manual, keeping the boat safe and steady at the right depth was far from easy. To achieve neutral buoyancy or 'perfect trim' and avoid sinking or rising, the first officer had to constantly monitor the trim and adjust it by varying the water levels in this series of compensating tanks. The weight of torpedoes being moved around or fired, fuel being used, stores being moved or even crew moving about the boat would all affect the trim. Also the temperature and salinity of the water outside and the speed of the submarine would necessitate adjustments. A certain minimum speed was usually needed, depending on the type of boat. If completely stopped, the boat would inevitably rise or sink and so need constant trimming. The slower the speed, the more challenges for the first officer to keep the boat at a constant depth. However, frequent use of the pumps when submerged drained the batteries and could be detected by the enemy, so a virtuous first officer always worked towards stabilising the boat with minimal use of machinery. Captain(S) Henry Oram of 5th Submarine Flotilla in 1939 later wrote:

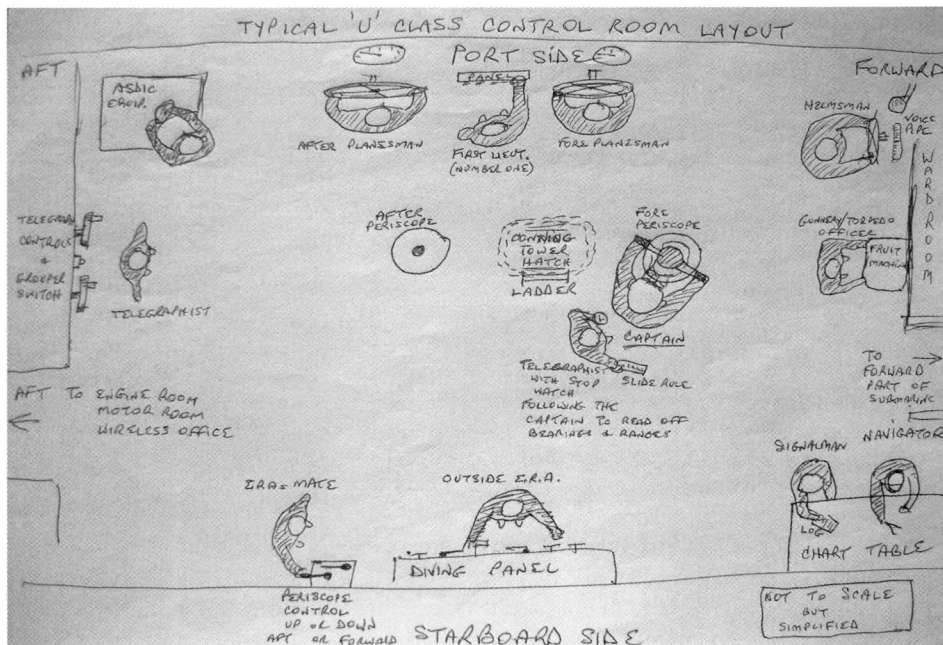

A free-hand sketch of the control room of *Ursula* made by Jimmy Green who served there. (with kind permission through S Clewlow)

Calculating the amount of water to be let into the tanks so that the submarine submerges and then maintains the correct depth with the proper buoyancy is called 'putting on the trim'. The outside ERA (so-called because he is the Engine Room Artificer responsible for all machinery 'outside' the Engine Room) and his mate, a stoker, are standing by in the control room near the valves which they operate when the order to dive the submarine is given. Each man has a specific job to do at diving stations. He must concentrate on that job, do it and report that he has done it. Submarines are designed to sink, but under controlled circumstances.[20]

All commanding officers had served as first officer before being accepted on the perisher course. This meant that they all had a thorough first-hand knowledge of operating a submarine, including the challenges and risks involved. Not all first officers moved on to become a CO though. Some were not suited for it or did not want the extra burden of being in overall command. Others were lost when their boats were sunk and would never have the chance to emerge from the shadow of their more famous COs.

The engineering officer, usually a lieutenant or warrant engineer, would be responsible for the smooth and trouble-free running of engines and motors – at times a very challenging task in a WWII submarine. The third hand would be the torpedo officer, responsible for storing and maintenance of the torpedoes when on board and firing them when the CO decided he had a proper target in sight. The fourth officer or navigation officer, usually a sub-lieutenant, would be responsible for the position of his own boat, as well as that of any friend or foe nearby. He would have few aids to help him and after extended periods submerged without any form of calibration from sightings of land, buoys or lights, the precise position of the submarine could become very difficult to confirm.

During a torpedo attack, the fourth officer would usually work the fruit machine.

On Patrol

For every submariner, the first patrol was special. No more so than for the CO taking his boat to war for the first time. Lieutenant Commander William 'Bill' King wrote:

> Can any man forget his first wartime patrol? I was 29. I had commanded *Snapper* for six months. I hoped to use her swiftly, ambitiously in her own specialized way, and to return with prizes. When at sea a submarine captain hardly sleeps. He lives between the chart table and the periscope. He never undresses. He never ceases to be on the alert. Unlike the captains of surface ships he is not in direct communication with his superiors. He carries sealed orders. Every decision is made by him alone. [. . .] Alone on the bridge in a murky night, setting out into a 15-day patrol in the North Sea, a terrible isolation had to enfold each one of us who were so entirely responsible for our men's lives and our ship's prowess.[21]

When on war patrol, the routine for British submarines would be to remain submerged during the day, keeping a periscope lookout, to avoid being detected, whether in transit or on patrol at an assigned billet. At nightfall, the boat would be taken to the surface and, running on main engines, the batteries would be charged while steering away from the central billet, before turning back to dive again well before first light. Stoker Hart of *Triad* wrote:

'Diving Stations!' The Cox'n sat in his little stool at the control of the fore-planes, with the Second Cox'n on the after-planes and the second senior Engine Room Artificer on the diving panel, from which almost everything of importance occurring in diving is motivated. We in the engine-room would shut off for diving. The Captain came down from the bridge, shutting the tower hatch behind him and ordered: 'Open main vents, fore-planes hard to dive, both motors full ahead,' to force the submarine down. The Second Cox'n would try and keep an elusive bubble in the exact centre of his gauge, which worked on the same principle as a spirit level, and therefore kept the vessel on an even keel [. . .] 50 feet . . . 70 feet . . . with a little pumping and flooding of the for'ard and after tanks she acquired a perfect trim.[22]

Normal, controlled diving routines meant taking the boat under in a couple of minutes. In an emergency however, it would take *Triad* no more than thirty-five seconds to go from cruising at the surface, diesel engines throbbing with a full watch on the bridge, until she was stable 100 feet below on electrical engines.

On patrol in any remotely dangerous area, the submarine would dive before dawn to pass the hours of daylight submerged, running at slow speed on the electric motors. Once below, things would settle down to a certain routine, usually going at two or three knots

No room for individuality. The seamen's mess in the torpedo storage room of *Seraph*. It is early in the patrol and the torpedoes are still in their cribs, making space restricted. Note the bread supply on the shelf above the men. (Author's Collection)

to save batteries while being manoeuvrable. At periscope depth, in the wintery North Sea, the surge of the seas above would still be felt, making life hard for those on watch. If caught by a large sea, the boat would break surface, which usually resulted in a hefty nose-dive with screaming motors as the officer of the watch fought to regain control. Surfacing at nightfall, to charge batteries and try to fix a position, conditions were even worse. Heavy seas were constantly smashing down on the lookouts and the wet clothes turned into ice-shields in the sub-zero conditions, of which there were plenty.

During the day, if nothing was sighted, the crew would be at watch-diving stations. This meant that a third of the crew would be controlling the boat, changing shift every three hours. The rest would be doing minor maintenance or repair jobs, sleeping, playing games or just idling. As little movement as possible was advised. Moving about would upset the trim of the boat, which meant using the pumps to adjust the balance, speeding up the motors or working the hydroplanes, using precious battery power. Also, less movement meant less breathing, conserving the available air. There was no artificial supply of air when the hatches were shut and after ten to twelve hours submerged breathlessness and gasping became rather common.

A WWII submarine used a large amount of compressed air, blowing tanks, firing torpedoes, etc. Thus a number of air-leaks into the boat were inevitable and the pressure in the boat built up, especially after a number of torpedoes had been fired, when the discharge pressure was vented inboard. On surfacing, the first man to open the conning-tower hatch, normally the CO, was in some danger of being blown out of the hatch by the built-up pressure inside the boat. Hence, it was quite normal for the second man up, usually the signalman, to hold on to the captain's ankles. If the build-up was very high, it was possible to run the air compressors for a while to bring the pressure down, but this required a lot of power and was avoided, unless it was known with certainty that the surface would be clear and remain so for the time needed to recharge the batteries.

Surfacing, usually after nightfall, was necessary to replenish the batteries as well as the air supply. Before surfacing, the boat would go deep, while the asdic operator listened carefully for ships on the surface, to avoid the enemy as well as accidental collision. Once above, the lookouts would scramble onto the bridge while the engineers started the engines and prepared to commence charging the batteries. One engine would be used for charging; while this took place, speed would be kept moderate. The small and slender submarines rolled badly, far more than most surface ships, and the bridge was taking heavy seas even in moderate weather, requiring a safety harness to be worn. If the weather was too poor, the captain could always choose to submerge, once the batteries were fully charged. Not that this always helped. On 5 March 1940, Lieutenant John Brown wrote in the diary of *Unity* after a day on patrol off south-western Norway:

> Proceeding at 80 feet owing to heavy swell. Submarine rolling 25° either side at periscope depth. An exceedingly heavy swell was running, in conjunction with a very rough sea and perfectly clear sky. Periscope depth was impossible for the majority of the day. [. . .] 09:50 – Hit bottom with 70 feet on the gauge, and a few minutes later hit bottom again with 80 feet on the gauge whilst withdrawing. As a result of this incident, the deviation of the Diving Compass, which had been swung after degaussing, changed completely.[23]

Artificer Blackwell of *Seraph* keeping an eye on his CO climbing the ladder to the conning tower as he blows the tanks to surface the submarine. On any signal of danger from the CO he would immediately reverse the process. (Author's Collection)

When on the surface, British routine was to have three men on the bridge, irrespective of the weather conditions. At the beginning of the war this was usually two lookouts and the officer of the watch, each being responsible for his own 120-degree sector. This was convenient, considering the crew on board and the space on the bridge of the older boats. It was insufficient in wartime, however, as the lookouts needed to give undistracted attention to their task, which the officer of the watch could not always do. Some COs therefore had three individual lookouts on the bridge, with the officer of the watch in overall charge.[24] The captain could of course spend as much time as he wanted on the bridge and most did so much of the time.

The front and sides of the tower were screened to give some protection against the elements and leather gear or oilskins, often both, were worn on top of sweaters and sea-boots. Nevertheless, the lookouts inevitably got soaked in anything but calm seas, enduring a miserable hour-long watch before being relieved. Some captains had one or more favourite lookouts who had proven their worth through good eyesight and particular vigilance; they were kept up top beyond regular watches, especially in tense situations.

Unless they had become soaked by seas breaking over the bridge, most submariners did not undress or change clothes for the duration of the patrol. Below, nothing ever dried anyway. Bulkheads were constantly damp and a revolting mix of water, oil, fat and seasickness was sloshing around underfoot. Life as a submariner was hard, both above and below the surface.

Normally, there were no restrictions on smoking when the boat was on the surface, except for a period when charging the batteries, and then only in certain places. Whilst diving, however, smoking was strictly forbidden. For many, the highlight of the day was when the boat surfaced after dark with an empty sea. Air was again dragged down the conning tower by the engines and it was permitted to smoke at will. Later, the rum store would be opened and the coxswain would serve out the rum issue of 1/8 of a pint per man. Joe Brighton of *Porpoise* remembered:

> This was more precious to us than the Crown Jewels. Several of the junior lads had no taste for the stuff, which was just as well . . . Bottling the stuff was against naval regulations, but more or less condoned in submarines as the lesser of two evils. The bottled rum was used as currency to get favours done later. On more than one occasion after a heavy depth charge attack, the Skipper would ask the cox'n 'what's the state of the rum-jars cox'n?' He would always reply: 'two jars are cracked, sir. We will have to break them off.' This of course meant an unofficial 'splicing the main brace'.[25]

Inevitably, though, the routine and boredom of patrolling in poor weather with many restrictions and few enemy targets set in. As Bill King recalls:

> I did not know that I was beginning a routine life which would go on week after week for six years; that my world would be bounded by the chart-table, the periscope and the bridge during almost all that time; that the smell of diesel oil, chlorine and unwashed bodies would be continuous and that our every day was to be passed below water in damp fug that would be cold in N. Europe, warm in the Mediterranean and an inferno in the Tropics.[26]

Habitability was not prioritised in British wartime submarines. Conditions were cramped and uncomfortable and in spite of excess motivation and close camaraderie, each patrol was a challenge for everybody on board. In November 1939, Lieutenant Gregory of *Sturgeon* wrote:

> After being on patrol for twelve days, the reduced efficiency on the part of the personnel was very marked and reactions to orders slowed up. It is difficult to keep an S-boat's crew keyed up for a much longer period of time and it is considered that no S-boat should carry out a patrol of a duration greater than fourteen days.[27]

The T-class boats were somewhat larger but Lieutenant Commander Robert Stirling-Hamilton of *Thistle* found that routine and discipline were still needed:

> During *Thistle*'s first patrols [in October, November and December 1939 in Skagerrak], when we were diving from roughly five in the morning until eight at night and it was

necessary to preserve the air in the boat by doing no cooking while under water, we evolved a routine of changing night and day. [. . .] The transition period was a bit difficult [. . .], but it served well once the scheme was under way. [. . .] Both the officers and the ratings were organized in three watches, the officers keeping two hour spells throughout and the men two hours while dived and four hours on the surface, although the lookouts on the bridge at night changed every hour. Only the watch on duty was used to dive the boat and we slipped under in fairly slow time, usually shortly after six a.m., while it was still dark, and retired to ninety feet until it was possible to see through the periscope. This was an hour to an hour and a half after diving, depending on the weather.[28]

During daytime, most of those off watch retired to their bunks to minimise the use of oxygen while watch was kept by listening and occasional use of the periscope. By the time darkness had returned, *Thistle* would prepare to surface, usually around 17:00 at this time of the year.

All hands were at their stations for surfacing as this was an anxious moment when the boat might have to crash-dive in a hurry. When all was ready below and the operators had had a good listen round to make certain no ships were near, tanks were blown and the submarine brought to the surface with all possible speed. I opened the hatch and went onto the bridge with the signalman as soon as the conning tower broke surface, and we had a quick look around to make sure that there was nothing near, followed by a more thorough search. Next, look-outs were placed, the tanks were blown some more to give the minimum buoyancy required by the weather conditions. The electric motors were stopped and a charge put on the batteries by one engine, while the other engine was clutched to drive the boat at about five to eight knots. [. . .] After all was settled for the night, hands off watch fell out and we had breakfast. Then everyone set to work.[29]

The time on the surface was spent cleaning up the boat, carrying out repairs, preparing hot meals – dinner at eight and tea at midnight. Stirling-Hamilton spent most of the night on the bridge, when not eating, planning courses or deciphering signals. Four-hour watches were normal on board Allied submarines, including the officers. There were many lessons to be learned as the war progressed and they turned out to be rather different from what had been expected in the peacetime Royal Navy. For instance, it had not been realised that night blindness – going from the lit interior of a boat to look-out duty on the bridge – lasts for up to thirty minutes. Later, deep-red lights only were used and the next watch wore dark glasses for half an hour before taking over. Another issue was binoculars. The few that had been issued – two per boat, increased to four in late October 1939 – were of mediocre quality and misted up internally from the wet conditions on the bridge. The COs 'begged, borrowed and stole binoculars' wherever they were to be found, according to Bill King, and both he and Ben Bryant wrote that they bought several pairs with their own money from trusted shops ashore.[30]

Sleep was a luxury for most commanding officers during patrol. Even if not part of the regular watch routine, and, in theory, they could rest any time they wished, few captains could really relax during a patrol near an enemy coastline. They all knew that their brains would not work properly without sleep, but they all also knew it would be difficult to escape the burden of command when on their own in alien waters. In the spring of 1940, when things hotted up and many submarines were deployed in the busy waters of the Skagerrak and the Kattegat, requiring constant vigilance from the COs, it was discussed at length if they should use Benzedrine or a similar drug to delay fatigue. Sooner or later, the CO's body would need rest, but the time of reckoning might come at an unpredictable moment, and Horton eventually decided against it, leaving the issue dead.[31]

The toilet, or 'head' as it was known, was a challenge. After each visit to the tiny room, a set of valves had to be opened in exactly the right order or water would blow into the submarine under pressure, together with the contents of the toilet.[32] This meant using the heads was avoided as long as possible and many men would rather 'hang on' for days. Betting on who could abstain the longest occurred in some boats. Emptying the heads was a noisy process and approval had to be obtained by the officer of the watch when on war patrol as the contents, together with a fair amount of air bubbles would rise to the surface. If in an area where enemy A/S patrols were known to operate, the alternative was to use sanitary buckets. This was even less popular and the request for sprinkler tins with disinfecting powder soon emerged.

Food was another issue on board the submarines. When leaving port, the refrigerators and larders were well stocked, including all kinds of fresh fruits and vegetables. However, this did not last long in the damp conditions. Whatever the arrangement, anything that was not tinned was usually stale with a pronounced taste of diesel within a short time. At first there were no dedicated cooks and each CO chose one or more ratings to make the grub as best he could – with mixed results, to say the least. On the surface hot meals were a particular challenge as the boats were tossed around in anything but the calmest seas. Some captains tried to help by having the hot meals served during early daytime when the boats were usually submerged anyway. As the war progressed, some men received training in preparing basic food and the amount and quality of the tinned food improved, making conditions somewhat better.[33]

In most cases after an attack had been carried out by a submarine, whether successful or not, came an almost inevitable hunt where the roles were reversed and the submarine was the target. In a bizarre manner, this was often a pitting of two minds against each other: that of the submarine CO versus that of the captain of the escort. Neither could see each other and both relied on the quality of their equipment as well as their men. Fear was inevitable during a hunt. When the escorts got close enough, they could be heard inside the boat by everybody and if the active sonar caught the boat in its beam, the resulting loud 'pings' usually meant that a depth-charge attack was imminent. To avoid any sound being picked up during a hunt, all noisy activity was halted, all machinery and pumps turned off and speed kept at a minimum to avoid motor noise as well as echoes from the wake. Once detected, it was a matter of increasing speed at the right time, after the charges had been dropped, changing course and hoping for the best. For most of this time the CO would be absorbed in receiving information about the enemy and the condition of his own boat, using this to think ahead and plan his escape. For the rest of the crew it was worse – much worse. Ben Bryant wrote:

> To aid you in your escape, you could make use of density gradients in the sea and variations in the temperature and salinity of the water, which deflects the beam. You could also make use of water noises such as the sea breaking [. . .] or best of all the

noise and disturbance caused by the last pattern of depth charges dropped on you. [. . .] The swish, swish of the propellers of the hunter passing overhead, the waiting for the explosion of the charges as they sank slowly down. Had they been dropped at the right moment? Were they set to the right depth? The knowledge that there is no escape, that you must just wait for it. Then the shattering roar, the lights going out, the controls going slack as the power is cut and the paint raining down. The silence and the faint sounds of running water where a gland has started a trickle.[34]

Lieutenant Commander Christopher Hutchinson of *Truant* held that it was a severe failure not to expose the submariners of the Royal Navy to anything even simulating depth charges.[35]

Left: Hugh Rufus Mackenzie; *right*: Arthur 'Baldy' Hezlet. Two key submarine officers who wrote openly about their experiences after the war. (Royal Navy Submarine Museum Collection)

— 4 —
'. . . the Violence of the Enemy'[1]

Vessels

THE ACTIVE ANTI-SUBMARINE TECHNOLOGY of the Kriegsmarine in the first part of
the war was focused around three main fundamentals: hydrophones, depth charges
and small A/S vessels. The task of taking on the British and Allied submarines after
September 1939 was given to minesweepers, trawlers and auxiliaries. Some were
specialists of the so-called *U-Bootsjagdflottillen*, submarine hunting groups, for others
it was part of the everyday work. The men of these vessels were largely reservists. They
had received limited pre-war training and literally had to learn the operational and
tactical game on the job, after the outbreak of the war. Destroyers and large torpedo
boats had A/S capacity but were not much used for this task on a regular basis. If
they did become involved, they lacked the necessary competence and skills and usually
obtained little.

In the 1920s and early 1930s, the priority in terms of small ships in the Kriegsmarine
was given to minesweepers and torpedo boats. These ships could also take on submarines
if necessary, it was believed. Only in the second half of the 1930s was the need for a
specialised anti-submarine vessel, or *U-Jäger*, acknowledged by the Oberkommando
der Marine (OKM), Germany's Naval High Command. The specification for such a
vessel was difficult to agree, however, and by September 1938, during the Munich crisis,
no orders for *U-Jäger* had yet been placed. Instead, several modern, large trawlers and
whale boats were requisitioned by the Kriegsmarine and deployed in two *U-Jagden*, or
anti-submarine flotillas, the 11th A/S Flotilla (11.U-Jagdflottille) under Fregattenkapitän
Günther von Selchow, based at Flensburg, and the 12th A/S Flotilla (12.U-Jagdflottille)
in Wilhelmshaven under Korvettenkapitän Hans Felix Korn. The boats were armed and
equipped for A/S work, including having S-Gerät sonars installed. The crisis subsided
and after about two months of training, the flotillas were decommissioned and the men,
virtually all from the reserve, returned to civilian life.

On 3 September 1939, after Britain and France declared war, the 11th and 12th flotillas
were re-mobilised. This time two more flotillas were added: the 17th A/S Flotilla and the
smaller 13th A/S Group in Kiel, both with requisitioned fishing boats. Within the flotillas,
the boats were organised in groups of two to six vessels, operating together tactically,
so-called *Jagd Gruppen* or 'hunting groups'. Many of the requisitioned trawlers intended
mainly for mine-sweeping received only passive listening gear. In addition they were
slow and, by mid-1940, many British submarine COs considered them easy to avoid by
staying shallow and observing them by short glimpses through the periscope, aided by
their own asdic listening devices.

Meanwhile, the concept of a specialised submarine-hunting vessel was researched. The
German naval designers, as usual, tried to add several alternative tasks to the *U-Jäger*,
though. This made them too complicated and resource demanding for war production

An A/S training flotilla, *Schulverband*, off Wilhelmshaven just after the outbreak of the war. (Author's Collection)

and the project was cancelled in 1940. Trawlers, minesweepers, R-boats and S-boats, it was decided, could adequately handle the A/S tasks.[2]

An example of a German A/S trawler was *UJ128 Franken*. The 435-ton, coal-fired vessel was built in 1938 for the 'Nordsee' Deutsche Hochseefischerei Bremen-Cuxhaven AG, a fisheries organisation on the German north-west coast and subsequently requisitioned at the outbreak of the war. Her fish holds were converted to accommodation for the enlarged crew, consisting of the original fishermen, unceremoniously enlisted into the Kriegsmarine, a handful of reservists and some younger trained personnel in specialist jobs, such as radio, sonar and gunnery. The officers were also a mix of older reservists and younger cadets or recently promoted juniors needing active service experience. In all, some thirty-five officers and men were on board.

An old 8.8-cm gun was mounted on the foredeck and an A/A gun aft while twenty-five depth charges were loaded onto the poop deck. There were no throwers and the depth charges were rolled over the stern.[3] To locate lurking British, French or Polish submarines, *UJ128* was equipped with a hydrophone listening device, but there was no asdic. *UJ128*'s captain in 1940 was Kapitänleutnant Otto Lang, a reserve officer recalled from his engineering land-based job to which he had retired after serving in the Great War. His first lieutenant was Heinz Nolte, a 22-year-old regular officer. These two men worked well together and *UJ128* became, like many of her compatriots, an efficient anti-submarine weapon after some months in operation. With few exceptions, the men of the *U-Bootsjagdflottillen* were all reservists from all levels of German society and geography. In many of the boats the ratings had a core of the original fishermen, good for running the boat, but perhaps not so good for discipline and naval 'polish'.

The German A/S forces were not given much priority early in the war. Only after the cruisers *Leipzig* and *Nürnberg* had been damaged by *Salmon* and *Ursula* in December 1939 did the German Naval Warfare Command (Seekriegsleitung or SKL), realise that an active A/S policy was necessary – see chapter 9.

Organisation of the Kriegsmarine at the outbreak of WWII

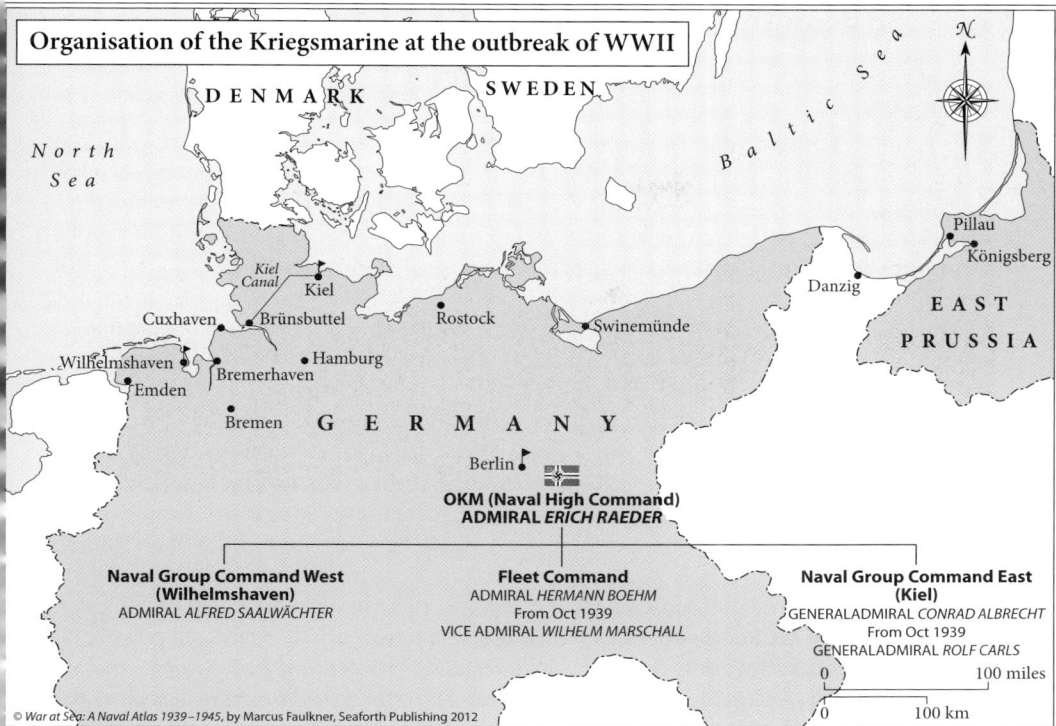

DENMARK

SWEDEN

Baltic Sea

North Sea

Kiel Canal

Kiel

Pillau

Königsberg

Cuxhaven

Brünsbuttel

Rostock

Danzig

EAST PRUSSIA

Wilhelmshaven

Bremerhaven

Swinemünde

Hamburg

Emden

Bremen

G E R M A N Y

Berlin

OKM (Naval High Command)
ADMIRAL *ERICH RAEDER*

Naval Group Command West (Wilhelmshaven)	**Fleet Command**	**Naval Group Command East (Kiel)**
ADMIRAL *ALFRED SAALWÄCHTER*	ADMIRAL *HERMANN BOEHM* From Oct 1939 VICE ADMIRAL *WILHELM MARSCHALL*	GENERALADMIRAL *CONRAD ALBRECHT* From Oct 1939 GENERALADMIRAL *ROLF CARLS*

0 ——— 100 miles

0 ——— 100 km

© *War at Sea: A Naval Atlas 1939–1945*, by Marcus Faulkner, Seaforth Publishing 2012

M1907 Heinrich Baumgarten. 467 tons, built in 1937 for the company Hochseefischerei Carl Kampf P/R in Wesermünde and taken over by the Kriegsmarine in September 1939. Boats like this, equipped with a gun, a couple of machine guns and some depth charges, bore the brunt of the German coastal defences, including minesweeping and A/S work. The bar in front of the bow is for the minesweeping bow-gear. When folded down, it would keep the sweep ahead of the boat and under water. (Author's Collection)

Sonar Equipment

Two types of equipment existed, the passive Horchgerät and the active S-Gerät. The problem of locating a submerged submarine had received considerable attention from German naval scientists, but, contrary to their British counterparts, they focused on passive reception of the sound and not active sonar. Nevertheless, visual observations were still paramount. Patience, a pair of keen eyes and some good binoculars were still key A/S tools well into 1940.

The Gruppenhorchgerät (GHG) was a passive listening apparatus with hydrophones, capable of picking up sounds at a significant distance when the receiving ship was at standstill. When moving, however, there were several limitations, bringing the practical range down to 500–700 metres and the receiving vessel could only move slowly, 5–8 knots at the most, depending on type of vessel, with all auxiliary engines turned off. In anything above moderate seas, the GHG became almost useless on board smaller ships like trawlers and minesweepers. Sometimes the hydrophones were also towed behind, although this made distinct noises which made them easy to avoid as they had limited directional capacity.

The GHG was fitted into most surface vessels and virtually all submarines. It consisted of sets of underwater microphones mounted on each side of the forward keel, picking up underwater noises. The number of microphones and their arrangement varied between ship types. By measuring the amount of time it took for the sound to arrive at each of the microphones, the device would give a rough indication of the direction from which the sound came, as would the strength of the sound as the microphones or the vessel was moved. The range was not given, but experienced operators could still give the captain an indication and, after some plotting, the direction and speed and what kind of vessel it was. The effectiveness of the GHG depended to a large degree on the operator, and a skilled man at the apparatus was an asset for any A/S vessel.

Early GHGs could not be rotated and the captain had to turn the ship slowly in a circle while the operator listened. The reception was best when the A/S vessel had its side to the target, but dwindled as the source moved to the front or rear of the ship. For best effect, the ship had to stop its engines while the hydrophone operator listened for a few minutes, which had the added effect that the A/S vessel became passive and difficult to detect by the submarine. GHG was installed in U-boats from 1935 onwards. Single vessels could be picked up 10 to 12 miles away and multiple ships at up to 50 miles. The detection range depended on the operator, of course, but also sea conditions or wind on the surface, temperature, saline layers, large schools of fish, depth charging by other vessels and so on. The British did not fully realise the Kriegsmarine's reliance on passive sonar and its quality until the summer of 1941 when *U570* was captured with its GHG set intact and its functionality could be assessed.

The Sondergerät für Aktive Schallortung, or S-Gerät, was an active echo-sounder, equivalent to asdic, though not as robust or functional.[4] German intelligence had very limited knowledge of the British asdic, and the S-Gerät was largely an independent development, installed in individual ships from 1938. Production was limited, though, and the sets were mostly earmarked for destroyers and large torpedo boats. Like the asdic, the S-Gerät transmitted sound pulses and timed the returning echo to detect underwater objects, up to 4,000 metres away. The range, however, depended on many factors such as water depth, temperature, salinity, etc. The apparatus was a complicated construction, and it had to be switched off for ten minutes every hour and up to half an hour every four hours to work satisfactorily. Usually, therefore, where several boats operated a general search-line with unknown enemy boats in the area, one boat would be in the middle, slightly ahead of the others, to have a free area of search, operating its S-Gerät. The other boats were line-abreast behind the lead boat, about 1,000 metres (1,100 yards) to each side, using their GHGs. Every three to four hours, the lead boat would change so that the S-Gerät could be turned off and another ship's set used instead. During depth-charge attacks, if many charges were dropped, explosions near the A/S vessels would mean the S-Gerät would shut down for up to fifteen or twenty minutes, making a continuous search rather challenging.

Tactics

During the first months of the war, most boats of the *U-Jagd* or A/S groups were equipped with both GHG and S-Gerät as well as echo-sounders and other equipment for navigation in shallow waters. In cases where an A/S group had a suspected contact, one vessel, with the active sonar operating, usually drifted or moved slowly, directing its companions as they attacked. The German war diaries contain many reports where A/S captains complain that their S-Gerät failed when they needed them the most and they had no specialist on board to fix it. Heavy manoeuvring in high seas and the detonation of depth charges nearby frequently made the apparatus unstable and prone to shut down. If it did, it would take up to half an hour before the operator reported that it was working again. There are also many examples of A/S vessels chasing echoes for quite some time, dropping several depth charges, before concluding that they had been wasting time on a wreck or simply a crag on the seabed. The wrecks of the submarines *Undine* and *Starfish*, sunk in the Heligoland Bight in January 1940, were marked with buoys, partly for them to be recognised as wrecks, partly for inexperienced GHG and S-Gerät operators to use them for practice so that they learned the signatures and sounds of British submarines lying on the seabed as well as wrecks in general.[5]

How to use the equipment at hand for submarine hunting had to be learned, technically and not least tactically. This would take time, all the more so as both the active and passive devices ceased functioning when the *U-Jäger* moved towards the echo at speed to attack. In the early part of the conflict, this resulted in a quantitative use of depth charges to carpet-bomb the area where the enemy submarine was believed to be, quickly expending the stock of charges without success. Once the German A/S crews gained experience, though, their success rates rose and the combination of aircraft and multiple escort vessels would start to take its toll on the Allied submarines. Aircraft searching a wide area ahead of and to the sides of an advancing convoy would drop bombs if a submarine was sighted, to ensure that it stayed deep, and would fire flares to mark the site where it had been seen and attract the A/S vessels.[6]

One tactic developed during the spring of 1940 was for a group of boats to search an area line-abreast about 1,000 metres (1,100 yards) apart. If one boat made a sighting or a

Minesweepers of 17.Minensuchflottille lining up for an anti-submarine sweep off Hela in the Baltic. *M1704 Alexander Becker* to the right and *M1708 Aldebaran* in centre. (Author's Collection)

contact, it would go straight in, dropping depth charges and one or more marker-buoys to keep the location. The nearest boat in the line would then turn towards the location and cross the track of the first boat at 90 degrees, dropping its charges on each side of the first salvo.[7] This was fine in theory, but as most A/S vessels were rather slow, there was usually plenty of time for the hunted submarine to move some distance away from where it was first detected by the time the second hunter appeared.

Surprisingly, there is literally no mention in German documents of co-operation or transfer of experience between the U-boat crews and the A/S vessels after the outbreak of war. During pre-war exercises, the U-boats were allowed to practise attacking formations of cruisers and destroyers and their experiences were then discussed and used to find the best defensive formations for the surface vessels. The exercises seem not to have been used the other way, though, to develop A/S tactics, and for some reason, the constructive communication appears to have stopped completely after the outbreak of the war. After the battleship *Gneisenau* barely survived the torpedoes of the submarine *Clyde* off Trondheim in late June 1940 (see chapter 22), Kapitän zur See Hellmuth Heye of the cruiser *Admiral Hipper* added some remarkable comments to his war diary:

> The submarine attack on *Gneisenau* has once again shown the lack of efficient A/S escorts. It has also however, highlighted the challenges facing ships operating far from their own bases against a numerically superior enemy, well equipped for a naval war. . . . I can at this stage only regret that the U-boat arm was taken away from the Fleet, making exercises and tactical training of the destroyers in A/S measures impossible. Perhaps it could be important to transfer at least some of the experiences our own submariners have gained from their contacts with British A/S measures to our destroyers and escorts.[8]

When no firm enemy contact had been made for a while, flotillas would normally split up in groups of two, three or four and sweep a larger area some miles apart. British submarine captains found the trawlers easy to keep at arm's length, provided they became aware of them early enough to steer clear. Time and again, the British submarine reports tell how a group of trawlers were sighted and almost casually avoided by a shift of course away from the A/S vessels' line of advance.

S-boats, R-boats and minesweepers were much faster than the trawlers and on paper better equipped. However, when running on anything but slow speed, they emitted loud engine noise which made them recognisable at a significant distance. Having been hunted on several occasions by what he termed *Schnellbooten*, meaning S-boats or MTBs, off Lindesnes and Lista, in April 1940, Lieutenant Commander Philip Roberts of *Porpoise* wrote:

> The tactics of these boats are not quite understood. Though they were obviously aware of *Porpoise*'s presence in the vicinity, they were extremely inefficient when in close proximity. On one occasion, when within 600 yards of *Porpoise*, they did not get in firm contact. They appear to release depth charges fairly indiscriminately, obviously in the hope of making one move actively. And, depth charges in the vicinity do not indicate, by any means, a firm contact. [On one occasion] these boats managed to get each side of *Porpoise* and dropped three charges, but were not very close.[9]

The chasers were never very persistent and would break off the search after an hour or two. In conclusion, Roberts wrote that he found it 'irritating and rather humiliating to be chivvied by such insignificant things as these *Schnellbooten*', and recommended an 'occasional sweep of the coast by destroyers' to discourage them from coming offshore.[10]

German destroyers, known as *Zerstörer*, were well equipped for submarine hunting, but had little training and were, with very few exceptions, only engaged in A/S activities when responding to attacks on ships they were escorting or if they actually stumbled serendipitously across a target.

On 10 April 1940, *Spearfish* ventured into a group of escorts that had been screening a convoy attacked by *Triton* shortly before. The commanding officer of *Spearfish*, Lieutenant Commander John Forbes, wrote on the tactics used by the German destroyers:

> Weather was flat calm and A/S conditions were well-nigh perfect. One destroyer kept on either bow, on a steady bearing. Third destroyer stopped, listening and directing. 'Speed-up' to come in was definite, but only to about 160 revs. Attack was by one, two and, at least once, all three – practically simultaneously. Conclusions drawn, as none of the charges were very close, was that listening device was excellent directionally, but they found difficulty in ranging through directing ship. It was remarkable how quickly destroyers got back in station and how steady their bearing then remained even after large alteration of course by the submarine. Their A/S transmission (heard over a period only) was a 'hollow-tin noise' just below 10 k/cs. They swept the whole time with single transmissions over a fair-sized sector, in short steps, on approximately the correct bearing. In spite of the fact that they were often dead-on, they never appeared to get contact and continued sweeping backwards and forwards over an arc.[11]

Weapons

At the beginning of the war, the main A/S weapon available to the Kriegsmarine was the depth charge. This was little more than a free-sinking cylindrical container filled with explosives, in principle little different from those of the Royal Navy. There were several models of depth charges available: WBD, WBF, WBG and WBH, with WB signifying *Wasserbombe*, or water bomb. Their difference mainly related to explosive charge and overall weight. The WBD had the largest explosive charge of 180 kg (396 lb), the others had 60 kg (132 lb) each.

The heaviest depth charge was WBH, which weighed 240 kg (529 lb), resulting in a sinking velocity of about 4.35 metres (14.3 feet) per second. This meant it took twenty-three seconds from the surface to 100 metres (330 feet). The depth charges were detonated by a firing pistol activated by hydrostatic pressure with six fixed settings at 15- to 25-metre (50- to 80-feet) intervals between 15 and 150 metres (50 and 500 feet). The smallest charge, the WBF, could not be set to explode deeper than 75 metres (250 feet).

At the beginning of the war, fifteen to twenty depth charges on board a vessel as it left port was considered adequate. It was quickly realised this was insufficient and the number was increased significantly, up to fifty on the larger boats. Initially, most trawlers and auxiliaries could only roll their charges off a ramp at the stern, but gradually more and more of them also had single-barrel throwers to send the depth charges over the side as well, 'framing' the submarine in a deadly grip once detected.

In theory, if a WBD charge exploded within 7–8 metres from the hull of a submarine, it would be destroyed. At more than twice that distance, damage could still be significant,

Depth charges ready on the afterdeck of the minesweeper *M9*. Those behind the operator are already in the throwers. The nearest are reloads. (Author's Collection)

often forcing the boat to surface. For the smaller charges, the destructive radius was considered to be 5–6 metres.

Knowing where the submarine actually was, even if detected by sonar, was far from easy though, and required quick three-dimensional thinking by the A/S captain as well as a skilled sonar operator capable of interpreting the confusing echoes into intelligible information for his officers – even more so as contact was lost when the escort increased speed, closing the distance to deliver the attack. In difficult sonar conditions, or when the water was disturbed by multiple depth-charge explosions, the chance of a submarine escaping a single A/S vessel was relatively good. Two or more vessels operating in unison significantly reduced the chances for the submarine. Being at the receiving end of a German depth-charge attack would have been harrowing at best. Stoker Hart of *Triad* wrote:

> It was possible to hear depth charges speeding down through the water towards us and even before they exploded, easy to realise they were coming annoyingly close. Then, for a fraction of a second, the whole undersea seemed to burst wide open. The whole of *Triad*'s interior became nothing but a blurred vision, for all the world like a cinema screen when the film being displayed runs off the rails and goes crazy. Paint tore off the bulkheads, lights tinkled down to the deck as if somebody had been using them as targets at an Aunt Sally stall. And before the crashing din of the first attack had died down, a second pattern of depth charges was speeding through the water towards us. All eyes turned up towards the deck-head. Whoomph! Tah-whoomph! Whoomph! There was the same fantastic blur inside our narrow ship; she bucked and plunged as if she were a bronco being spurred to madness. A voice grunted: 'By the b—y hell, those were close![12]

Torpedo Gunner's Mate Joe Brighton of *Porpoise* narrated:

> I have often been asked what it was like during a depth charge attack. It was bloody awful. . . . Inside the submarine, when the attacking vessel was in firm contact, a prolonged, repeated 'piiing-ging' like a mighty tuning-fork could be heard. This was no comfort to us at all. All we could do was wait and take what was coming to us. We could plainly hear the propellers of the attacking ship as it came in for the attack. We could hear the depth charges as they were thrown in the water and just had to wait for the crashing explosions that followed. . . . The structural strain (on the hull of the boat during the explosion of a depth charge nearby) transmits itself to the human body almost as an electric shock, causing the same kind of vibrations.[13]

British submarines were noisy and had a lot of equipment on board that made sounds detectable by German A/S vessels. In particular, the telemotor and the ballast pumps were noisy and most COs avoided changing depth by using the pumps when hunted. The asdic generator and Sperry gyro compass also made detectable sounds. Hence, if the A/S vessels came really close, these motors were stopped too. With the pumps shut down, it was usually possible for a submarine to sneak away from the passive German sonar. German U-boats dived deep when depth-charged but many of the British captains 'adopted shallow tactics', staying above 30 metres at slow speed, bursting away when they believed they were out of contact.[14]

Occasionally, while being hunted, British submariners reported hearing 'scraping noises' from the outside of the submarine, believed to be coming from wires being towed by the A/S vessels. Coming home, minor damage was at times found on the submarines, most likely from these wires.[15] This was actually a WWI concept called *U-Bootsdrachen* still used at the beginning of WWII. In its most primitive form, it was a sweeping wire with a grapnel at the end. In theory, when the grapnel hooked the submarine, it would pull an explosive charge down which would explode on contact with the outer hull. Alternatively, the crew on the deck of the A/S vessel could, on seeing the wire tighten as the grapnel hooked on, push the charge overboard. In practice, this was not so easy. Firstly, the submarine needed to be fairly accurately located before the grapnel could be used effectively. Secondly, there were not many places where the grapnel could fasten, making the submarine a difficult target. If the submarine lay on the bottom, which the British boats very often did in the shallow parts of the North Sea when hunted, it was only through extraordinary luck such a weapon might be expected to work. Later attempts at towing a charge behind the A/S vessel and detonating it by remote control if the submarine was believed to be near or by electrical short-circuit detonators should it hit something, were not very successful.[16] It has not been possible to find any documents describing the successful deployment of *U-Bootsdrachen* – far less sinking or even damaging an Allied submarine.

A habit of the German A/S forces was to drop a few depth charges at irregular intervals in areas where submarines had been reported or could be expected. These *Schreckbomben* or 'scary bombs' were intended to frighten the submarines away or at least keep them down, but in most cases did little else than tell the British submarine commanders where their adversaries were so they could steer outside the range of their echo-sounders.[17]

British submarine commanders noted that the A/S trawlers frequently stopped or proceeded very slowly, correctly gauging that this was necessary to optimise the use of their sonars. German anti-submarine tactics were not well known early in the war and this was one of the first real observations. At first, the British submarine commanders frequently used a tactic of sneaking in behind the German screen to attack the convoy on a broad track pushed in from abaft the screen. The German escorts learned rapidly though, and by having some ships staying astern of the convoys, undetected British attacks became more and more difficult. To British submariners, the German A/S tactics appeared 'curious'. 'They frequently pass one another, circle around and occasionally get stern-on to each other,' wrote Lieutenant Commander Slaughter of *Sunfish*, continuing that the Germans 'appear reluctant to trust their instruments to drop charges'. Lieutenant Commander Bryant of *Sealion* found the trawlers 'disciplined', operating in pairs, but still fairly easy to avoid.[18]

On the other hand, after having been chased for four and a half hours by the torpedo boats *Luchs* and *Greif* off southern Norway in April 1940, after torpedoing the cruiser *Karlsruhe*, Lieutenant Commander Christopher Hutchinson of *Truant* wrote:

> After each attack, [torpedo boats] stopped to listen, used echo-sounding, but appeared not to transmit on any super-sonic set. They appeared to drop some form of device which made a sound like gravel dropping on the hull of the submarine. A/S conditions were very good and enemy appeared to be uncomfortably efficient at hunting and most persistent. I hoped forlornly that they would retire after dark on more important business.[19]

It was not to be the case. In all, thirty-three depth charges were counted, most of them close – see page 182.

Mines

At the beginning of the war, there were two types of German anti-submarine mines: the standard UMA and the slightly heavier UMB, in use from the winter of 1940/41. Both were of the horntrigger- type laid by surface vessels.[20]

	Diameter	Charge weight	Total weight	Horn triggers
UMA	800 mm	30 kg	810 kg	5
UMB	840 mm	40 kg	c. 800 kg	5

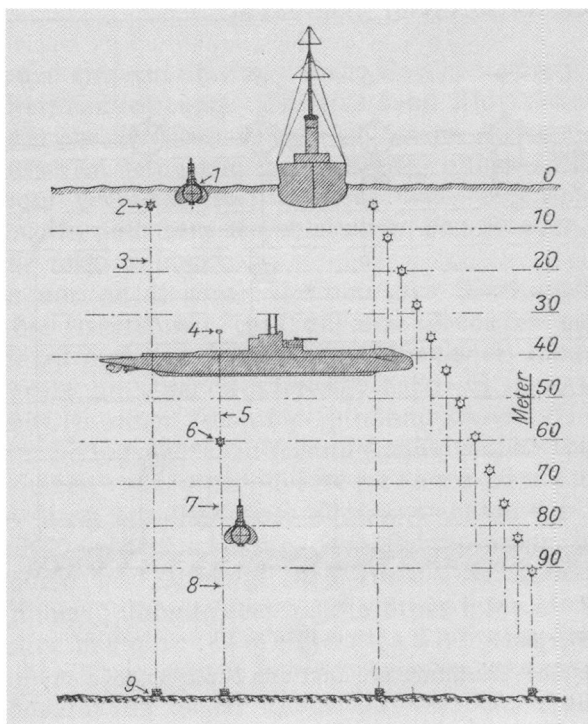

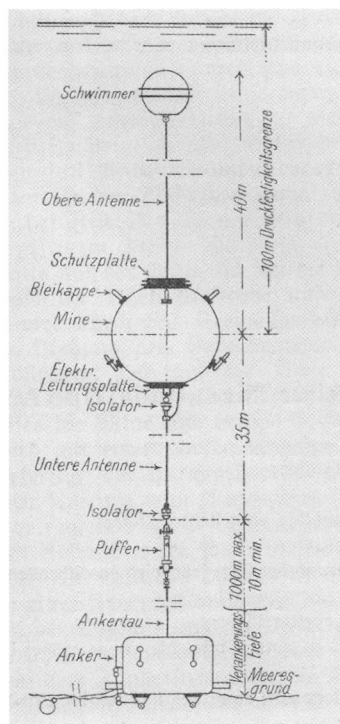

How the Germans envisaged an anti-submarine barrage to work. The mines are placed at various depths from the surface down to, in this case, 90 metres. Some mines (number 6 in the figure to the left) have contact horns as well as sensors (antennae) above and below the mine proper. These would ensure the mine exploded if the submarine hit the wire up to 25–30 metres above or below the mine proper. Other mines placed higher in the sea (number 2 in the figure to the left) have only contact horns on the lower half, to avoid it being triggered by surface ships. (From *Marine-Rundschau* 40/4 1935)

These mines would usually be laid in stripes across known or expected submarine tracks. Their anchor-lines were adjusted so that the mines, which were liberally covered by both chemical and switch horn triggers, ended up at a depth of between 10 and 15 metres. Regular mines could also be dangerous to a submarine at the surface, but in most cases the moderate draught of a submarine would take it safely over an anchored mine. Drifting mines should in theory have rendered themselves safe when released from the mooring tension, but this was often not the case. For all anchored mines, it was a great risk that, should its wire become snagged by the hydroplanes or some other part of a submarine, it might be pulled against the hull, irrespective of the depth it was anchored at. Magnetic mines were less of a threat to a submarine as it would normally seek to operate in waters of greater depth than these mines usually were laid in.

Mines were laid by both sides almost immediately after the outbreak of hostilities. In the North Sea, a huge area, known as the Westwall, was announced by the Kriegsmarine on 3 September. It covered a rectangular area from just west of the Ems estuary past Horns Reef towards the Great Fisher Bank, protecting the approaches to Hamburg, Emden, Wilhelmshaven, Bremerhaven and Cuxhaven. The first 650 mines inside this area, known by the Allies as the 'German Declared Area', were laid on 5 September and within three weeks a total of 4,000 mines, surface as well as anti-submarine, had been laid inside the Westwall. A narrow sea-lane existed between the southern end of the field and the Dutch West Frisian Islands; otherwise the entrance to the Bight was from the north, i.e. from the Skagerrak.

In reality, the Westwall was not one field, but a series of overlapping 'mine-stripes', fifteen in all, inside the declared area, making it impossible to sail in a straight line from east to west or north to south. Each stripe consisted of 200–300 mines, interspaced with numerous explosive *Sprengbojen* to prevent sweeping.[21] Below the regular mines, a network of anti-submarine mines made a three-dimensional death-trap. New stripes were added at intervals to maintain the effect of the declared area and catch Allied ships trying to sneak through. The Westwall being far offshore, exact positioning was sometimes difficult and the start and end point of a few of the stripes were several miles from the initially intended position. For those who knew where the stripes were, it would be possible to navigate through the Westwall. In particular, two diagonal routes were established, *Weg I* and *Weg II*, used by naval ships and U-boats to and from the southern North Sea. After a while, a chess-like game developed, with the British trying to close the routes without the Germans knowing it and the Germans trying to keep secret where the routes actually were. In an attempt to keep *Weg II* open, a fake stripe was laid across its western exit in such a way as to be observed, to try to confuse the Royal Navy.

In February, *Sealion* discovered a light buoy north-west of Heligoland, east of the Westwall, believed to be the starting point of a swept channel through the southern part of the mined area. This marker was used by *Sunfish* to sail through the minefield on the 19–20 February. Later, this marker was referred to as 'Sealion's buoy' or by some as the 'Sunfish buoy' and used by British submarines, at least up to the second half of April, when *Narwhal* reported it to be at least one mile off position. The Westwall was usually known as the 'cabbage patch' to the British submariners.[22]

Aircraft

Unlike the Royal Navy, the Kriegsmarine considered aircraft an important supplement to the surface ships' combat capabilities, performing long-range reconnaissance and mine-laying as well as bomb and torpedo attacks. Following the creation of the Luftwaffe, C-in-C of the Kriegsmarine, Admiral Raeder and Head of the Air Force Field Marshal Göring had originally agreed that naval aviation should be under the control of the navy, while the Luftwaffe supplied men and machines. In late 1938, however, Göring saw that the new aircraft carriers being planned would become prestigious projects and decided that the Luftwaffe should be fully responsible for all aspects of flying from them. For good measure, he also added all naval air operations, such as attacks on ships and submarines and reconnaissance, claiming, 'Anything that flies belongs to me!' This meant that the ambitious plan for a naval air force was all but abandoned in favour of fighters and army support aircraft. Even worse, as the total responsibility also included communication, it meant that any information from the aircraft was delayed for several hours while it was passed up the Luftwaffe system and then back down through the navy to the ships.

By the autumn of 1939, fifteen naval reconnaissance units were operational, organised in five groups totalling some 154 aircraft in the North Sea region and the Baltic. Most of these were equipped with Heinkel He115, He59 and He60 floatplanes or Dornier Do18

An Arado Ar196. Designed as a shipboard reconnaissance aircraft for the capital ships of the Kriegsmarine, these nimble, manoeuvrable aircraft also gave sterling service in the A/S role. It had a crew of two and a range of just over 1,000 kilometres (620 miles). Maximum speed was some 310 km/h (190 mph). This particular aircraft, 6W+AN from 5.BFGr196, was assigned to the cruiser *Admiral Hipper* at the time the photo was taken in early 1940. (Author's Collection)

Heinkel He115 B-1 of KüFlGr 106. A sturdy but rather slow multipurpose seaplane taken into service just prior to the outbreak of WWII. It had a range of well over 2,000 kilometres (1,240 miles) and could carry a fair load of bombs, mines or torpedoes. Cumbersome, with a maximum speed of 325 km/h (200 mph), it was not well suited for either air combat or attacking diving submarines. Nevertheless, due to its range, the He115 was extensively used for reconnaissance and convoy escort in the first part of WWII. (Author's Collection)

flying boats. In addition, there were two *Bordflieger* units which supplied Arado Ar196 aircraft on board battleships and cruisers and three *Träger* squadrons, training to operate from the planned carriers.

Slow, poorly armed and cumbersome, the German naval aircraft were still robust and the Do18 in particular had a considerable operational radius. The He115 could carry a fair load of bombs as well as mines and torpedoes but was feebly armed and rather helpless as a bomber. The He59s and He60s were quickly found to be unsuited for combat and relegated to secondary tasks as fast as they could be replaced. On the other hand, the Ar196 was, somewhat surprisingly, found to be well suited for convoy escort and submarine patrols. This proved invaluable during the winter and spring of 1939/40 when many of the heavy ships of the Kriegsmarine were either sunk or still in the yards and their aircraft were left with no meaningful tasks for the time being.[23]

Prior to the attack on Denmark and Norway, the naval aircraft in the west largely operated from bases on the North Sea islands Norderney, Borkum and Sylt as well as Wilhelmshaven. This meant they occasionally sighted one of the British submarines on patrol in the German Bight. The aircraft were largely on reconnaissance missions, though not specifically on anti-submarine patrols and encounters were few and far between. This changed dramatically on 16 April 1940, one week after the attack on Denmark and Norway, when a signal from the SKL was received by the General der Luftwaffe beim ObdM, the air force liaison officer at the naval headquarters. It stated that, with immediate effect, Air Force Command East was responsible for convoy escort and submarine hunting in the Kattegat and the Skagerrak and that the necessary aircraft would be made available. The increased mobilisation of naval aircraft for anti-submarine patrols had actually started a few days earlier in response to the augmented British and Allied submarine efforts. For a number of reasons (beyond the scope of this book) things would not be quite as organised as anticipated on the German side. Nonetheless, for the British and Allied submarines, this decision was to indicate a dramatic change in their ability to operate east of the Skagen–Lindesnes line (see chapter 15 to 21).[24]

In the areas most exposed to submarines, the Luftwaffe deployed just about anything that could fly to search for the Allied boats. In particular, the large number of Arado AR196 floatplanes of the units 1./196 and 5./196 that were not employed on board cruisers and battleships as intended made a significant impact during the summer and autumn of 1940. From bases in southern Norway, the Frisian Islands, France and the Bay of Biscay, these nimble aircraft were a constant threat to any Allied submarine in their sector.

The German aircraft flew low when on A/S patrol, usually lower than their British counterparts. This meant that they lost the ability to see as far on either side of their flight-path, but then the feather of a periscope was not easy to see from up high anyway. Above all, though, it meant that if they did see a submarine – on the surface or at periscope depth – they could attack almost immediately. More than once, a British submarine crew could ascribe their survival to plain luck, with the small bombs not causing any real damage unless there was a direct hit on something exposed, such as the rudders or diving planes. In some cases, the bombs did not explode at all, possibly as they were dropped from too low, or because they came in at too low an angle for the detonators to be triggered by hitting the water if they missed the hull.

— 5 —

'. . . the Dangers of the Sea'[1]

ON 3 SEPTEMBER, TWO signals were issued from Whitehall in London to all British naval units. The first was timed 11:17 and read 'Most Immediate: Total Germany', which in plain language translated as: 'Commence hostilities at once with Germany'.[2] The second signal a few hours later, read simply 'Winston is back'. The 65-year-old Winston Churchill had been re-appointed First Lord of the Admiralty by Prime Minister Chamberlain and offered a seat in the War Cabinet, both of which he immediately accepted.

As shown in the table below, the number of British and German submarines was equal at the outbreak of the war. The table is somewhat misleading, however. The German U-boats were new and of modern design, whereas a large number of the British submarines were obsolete, only fit for training purposes – or, at best, service in regions where the war had not yet erupted. In addition, the Kriegsmarine could focus their resources on the merchant lines around Britain, while the Royal Navy had multiple commitments in several far-flung places.

Table 3: Comparison of German and British submarine strengths

Royal Navy			Kriegsmarine		
	Sept 1939	May 1940		Sept 1939	May 1940
H-, L-class	12	12	Type I	2	2
O-, P-, R-, River-class	21	20 (-1)	Type II	30	27 (+4/-7)
Grampus-class	6	6	Type VII	18	14 (+7/-11)
S-class	12	9 (-3)	Type IX	7	4 (+3/- 6)
T-class	3	8 (+7/-2)			
U-class	3	1 (-2)			
Total	57	56		57	47

As the war approached, boats held in reserve began to be manned from the beginning of July 1939, and by 1 September the operational strength of the Royal Navy's submarine fleet was fifty-seven, twelve of which were single-hulled WWI design.[3] Geographically, they were deployed in four major theatres: home waters, Mediterranean, Indian Ocean and China Station, and when war was declared, several rotations were made, based on an overall priority at the time. The minelayers *Porpoise*, *Narwhal* and *Cachalot* and four S-class boats, *Shark*, *Sealion*, *Salmon* and *Snapper*, were called home from the Mediterranean, concentrating the modern submarines in home waters, while three O-class boats were kept in the Mediterranean. For several months, *Osiris*, *Otway* and *Oswald* had very little meaningful to do, except exercising with the trawlers of the 28th A/S Group and alternating between the bases at Malta and Alexandria. *Oxley*, on the other hand, up until now used for training at Gosport, was sent to the 2nd Flotilla at Dundee to become operational. A number of the old H- and L-class boats were mobilised from the reserve and made operational as 5th Flotilla at Portsmouth. *Oberon* was in the yards and when completed in mid-September also attached to the 5th Flotilla, to be used for training. Fifteen O-, P- and R-class boats were retained at the China Station, while *Severn* and *Clyde* were temporarily diverted from home waters to Freetown to search for raiders in the South Atlantic.[4]

One S-class and a dozen T-class submarines were under construction, eight of which would be commissioned before April 1940.[5] Many of the boats nearing commission in September 1939 were rushed through the final stages of completion and testing and taken into service a month or more earlier than planned.[6] In May, as France was reeling and the likelihood of Italy entering the war was high, all remaining O-, P- and R-class boats from the China Station and Indian Ocean were transferred to the Mediterranean Fleet. The last to sail from Singapore was *Rover*, which did not finish her refit until August.

It was by no means clear from the start how the British submarines were to be used during the war, either in a strategic, tactical or operational sense. In the Admiralty Fleet Order 1/38, Rear Admiral Submarines was given:

Starfish 19S and *Seahorse* 98S, May 1939, alongside destroyer *Mackay*. (P A Vicary)

general administrative charge over all matters affecting service in submarines in order to ensure co-ordination and uniformity in questions of personnel, training and in matters affecting seagoing efficiency. The direct responsibility for the efficiency of submarines and flotillas will rest with the Flag Officer and Senior Naval Officers under whose command they are placed.[7]

Thus, Rear Admiral Bertram Watson, appointed RA(S) in December 1938, had only administrative command of his boats before the war. Operational and tactical control of submarines operating in home waters, including the North Sea and much of the North Atlantic, rested with the Flag Officer Home Fleet as it did with the regional commanders in the Mediterranean, Far East and other overseas stations. As war commenced, Watson would assume operational control of the flotillas in the North Sea, but he would remain under the immediate orders of the C-in-C Home Fleet, Admiral Forbes. Command of the 5th Submarine Flotilla operating in the Channel and the Western Approaches would be held by Captain(S)5 reporting to the C-in-C Portsmouth. The role of the Admiralty regarding the submarines remained somewhat unclear.[8]

By mid-August, all reserve submarines were either in commission or working-up and from the 21st onwards, the Submarine Service was assuming an increased state of readiness. Several boats were moved from Portsmouth to Blyth and Dundee as soon as they were ready for sea. Others were sent to the yards for a final check before going to war. Finally, Watson moved his headquarters from Fort Blockhouse at Gosport to Corriemar House at Aberdour, near Rosyth, on 30 August, visiting 6th and 2nd flotillas at Blyth and Dundee on his way. The main reason for the move was to facilitate communication with the Home Fleet and Coastal Command. Most of the Submarine Staff remained at Fort Blockhouse. The move of the C-in-C with most of the fleet to Scapa Flow shortly after lessened the effects of Watson's transfer significantly and he requested that he should be allowed to move back to Gosport once the flotillas stationed in the north were operating satisfactorily. No action was taken until the arrival of Admiral Horton in early 1940.[9]

As with the German U-boats, British submarines were also sent on patrol prior to the actual outbreak of war. On 31 August 1939, five submarines were off southern Norway, while six were in the Heligoland Bight.[10] Highlighting the complex command structure, the entire 6th Flotilla was sent into the Heligoland Bight without consideration as to how they should be replaced when they headed back at more or less the same time. When the U-class boats *Undine*, *Unity* and *Ursula* returned from their first patrols, it was found that all three had extensive cracks in the main engine frames. Repairing this put them out of service for at least a month, further reducing the strength of the submarine grid. With somewhat more foresight, the 2nd Flotilla was instructed to have five boats off the coast of Norway in a rotational manner where they could be replaced when they had done their time without leaving gaps in the chain.

Neither Forbes nor his staffs comprehended that submarines needed to be operated differently from other ships, their most efficient use being a rolling deployment where about half the force was at sea and the other half in transit or in port for rest and recreation for the crew and maintenance of the boats. Above all, it appears to have taken some time to appreciate that submarines, at a risk, could operate unsupported for relatively long periods, even in areas where own forces did not exercise superiority on the surface.

Interestingly, it appears that the use of submarines was studied far more from a moral and legal aspect than from a tactical and operational one in Britain between the wars. Based on the treaties of the naval conferences in the 1920s and 1930s, the British government basically concluded that submarines could not be used against merchant vessels without breaking the laws of war. The only ships which could be attacked and sunk without warning were enemy warships and auxiliaries clearly recognised as such. According to the Prize Regulations of the 1930 London Naval Treaty, all other ships should be stopped and searched and, if found to be enemy operated or carrying contraband, only sunk if impossible to take to port as a prize and only after crew and passengers were safe. A submarine could not:

> sink or render incapable of navigation a merchant vessel without having first placed passengers, crew and ship's papers in a place of safety. For this purpose, the ship's boats are not regarded as a place of safety unless the safety of passengers and crew is assured in the existing sea and weather conditions by the proximity of land or the presence of another vessel which is in a position to take them on board.[11]

The Admiralty's *Naval Prize Manual*, issued to the submarines after the outbreak of the war, went one step further. Recognising that it would not be possible for a submarine to abide by these rules, it stated that enemy merchant ships should, as far as possible, be sent to a British-controlled port with a prize crew on board. In addition it concluded that 'H.M.Submarines should regard themselves as "precluded from sinking neutral vessels" under any circumstance and rather let them go if they could not be forced or persuaded to go to a British port.'[12] In consequence, initial general instructions from the Admiralty told RA(S) to prioritise reconnaissance over attack even if favourable opportunities to harass the observed vessels 'should not be neglected':

> The primary object of submarines in [the North Sea] patrol is to report movement of German war vessels, but no favourable opportunity of attacking them should be neglected, providing that this can be done without prejudice to the primary object. Other vessels acting suspiciously are also to be reported. Submarines should bear in mind that retaliatory action by light forces, should the submarine attack, may prevent the submarine passing vital information to C-in-C Home Fleet. [. . .] Commanding Officers must decide for themselves according to circumstances, whether the importance of the enemy to be reported, and the possibility of the submarine being detected by enemy surface ships or aircraft justifies surfacing to report. [. . .] It may be that detection must be accepted, if the importance of the enemy justifies it.[13]

These orders were unfamiliar to the submarine crews who pre-war usually had found themselves involved in fleet actions, supporting their own surface ships, or, if alone, intercepting and shadowing enemy surface forces. Waiting for an enemy fleet to appear had, up until now, meant staying submerged in order to avoid all risk of detection. Patrolling an area for an extended time turned out to be challenging – particularly if that area could be reached by enemy shore-based aircraft, which made proceeding on the surface during daylight hazardous and even using the periscope incurred some risk. It was found extremely difficult to maintain static position on a patrol line over time due to currents, poor weather and limited opportunities to check position. Hence, revised orders were issued from RA(S) to his boats on 20 September, making it clear that, while all German war vessels should be reported as soon as convenient, whether attacked or not, 'the object of all submarines is to attack enemy war vessels', adding that 'submarines, when in their patrol zones, have full freedom of action for the attainment of their respective objectives.' This was more in line with expectations and morale on board the boats rose. Merchant ships were still to be intercepted on the surface and preferably sent to Kirkwall with a prize crew, or, if she had to be sunk, the German crew was to be taken on board the submarine if not very close to land.[14]

During the first part of WWII, British and Allied submarines were to fight their war in home waters under conditions very different from those of the majority of the German U-boats. 'Home waters' for the submariners meant north to the Barents Sea, south to Gibraltar and the Azores, west to the Denmark Strait and east to the Skagerrak and the Kattegat and into the Baltic – if they could get there. In theory, British naval superiority was absolute in this area – in practice, not quite. Especially as German aircraft and airmen would prove themselves, at the very least, equal to anything the British could muster at the time. The central part of the home waters, the English Channel, the North Sea, the Skagerrak and the Kattegat were mostly shallow waters, strewn with minefields and rather close to enemy aircraft bases and A/S forces. Characteristically, until the German invasion of Norway and Denmark, and subsequently the Lowlands and France, changed the whole strategic situation, British submarine patrols were largely tedious affairs under harsh climatic conditions, interrupted by brief moments of fear when attacked by aircraft or entangled in an unknown minefield. On a few occasions, German cruisers or destroyers were sighted, but only rarely did the British submarines manage to get on to a firing course.

Germany's relatively inland position meant it was much less dependent than Britain on its overseas shipping lanes. The subsequent limited German merchant traffic in the North Sea and adherence to the Prize Regulations resulted in few British submarine attacks on German shipping in the first seven months of the war. The majority of merchant traffic, which was largely neutral anyway, hugged the coasts of the Nordic countries, staying inside territorial waters. Only at night did they venture outside if necessary and then at maximum speed. This was as much to avoid German U-boats as British submarines.

After the immediate cessation of the German ore shipments from Sweden at the outbreak of war, it subsequently recommenced during the autumn, first in the Baltic, then also through Narvik in Norway. German ore ships from Narvik followed the Norwegian Inner Leads southwards, which they were fully entitled to do. The Skagerrak was crossed at night from somewhere between Lista and Lindesnes towards Skagen where they entered Danish waters to the east or west, depending on the port of destination in Germany. The British Admiralty considered that the use of Scandinavian territorial waters by the German ore ships meant that any success in halting this traffic would require a political decision by the War Cabinet that such waters could be violated. Pending such a decision, neutral waters should be respected. Not one German ore ship was intercepted between October 1939, when the trade was resumed, and March 1940.

Eventually, a patrol line, nicknamed the 'Thin Grey Line', was set up across the North Sea as a precaution against German ships trying to approach the British east coast. The number of submarine attacks on U-boats in transit through the North Sea though, and in particular the successes of *Salmon* and *Ursula* in December, made the U-boats proceed underwater at fixed times along a few set routes, and under escort near land. This slowed down operations and diverted resources. Later, after the German occupation of Denmark and Norway on 9 April 1940, when these Prize Regulations were lifted, the supply lines to Norway became prime targets, forcing the Kriegsmarine to allocate significant resources for A/S protection of their own convoys.[15]

During the first months of the war, the suboptimal performance of the main aircraft of the Coastal Command, the Avro Anson, would influence the disposition of the Royal Navy's submarines. The Anson was a sturdy, reliable workhorse, but lack of speed, range and armament made it totally unsuitable for reconnaissance patrols into the North Sea.[16] With a range of no more than 510 miles the Ansons could not even make the return flight to the Norwegian coast from Montrose, having to turn back 60–80 miles short of the territorial boundary. Hence, the easternmost part of the patrol line had to be covered by submarines, stationed at 12-mile intervals off Obrestad Lighthouse, south of Stavanger. The first five boats on what was to become known as the Obrestad Line, *Seahorse*, *Starfish*, *Triumph*, *Spearfish* and *Sturgeon*, were in place from 26 August 1939 onwards.[17] They quickly experienced significant difficulty maintaining their positions owing to problems with radio fixing and reluctance by the commanders to surface during daylight because of the risk of being sighted by German aircraft. Later, towards the end of September, as sufficient Hudson aircraft became operational and Coastal Command was capable of covering the whole length of the reconnaissance line from Scotland to Norway, the submarines were given a freer hand off the south-west coast of Norway and into the Skagerrak, with each boat having a fairly large area within which it could work with significant freedom.

After the first mass deployment of the 6th Flotilla in the Heligoland Bight, a rolling patrol system was set up from Horns Reef to Terschelling, on either side of the 'German Declared Area'.[18] This close to Germany, however, the number of A/S patrols and aircraft made conditions challenging and there is little doubt that operating east of the Westwall for any extended period was somewhat disquieting for the British submariners.

Once outside their base, a submarine had no friends and every ship or aircraft was potentially dangerous, irrespective of whether they were friend or foe. Bill King of *Snapper* wrote:

> We realised war's reality when a British patrol boat in the Channel charged us out of the mist, mute but obviously determined to ram! I put *Snapper*'s stern to her and she missed by feet. [. . . Later] *Snapper* joined a convoy which trailed bleakly up the East Coast till one dark night a neighbouring merchant ship suddenly realised that some kind of submarine was in the vicinity. 'U-boat alarm! Turn to ram.' Our officer of the watch did his job well, for I arrived on the bridge just as a large freighter's propeller covered us with spray. Commendable as the British zeal in anti-submarine work might be, I did wish they would stop practising on *me*![19]

Seahorse. (Abrahams)

On 4 and 5 September, respectively, *Sturgeon* and *Seahorse* were attacked by RAF aircraft while returning to Dundee from their first patrols. The aircraft had been routed away from the submarine lanes, but in the case of *Seahorse*, the Anson from 233 Squadron was more than 35 kilometres off course. Pilot Officer George Yorke became quite enthusiastic when he saw a submarine at the end of a long patrol, and diving in, dropped his entire bomb load on the diving boat. Elated by the successful attack which he believed had seriously damaged the submarine, Yorke set course for Leuchars, only to find that shrapnel from the exploding bombs had damaged his wing tanks and, running out of fuel, he had to land his aircraft in the River Eden estuary. The crew got into the dinghy and were quickly rescued. The bombs exploded uncomfortably close to *Seahorse*, and though there was no internal damage, the after hydroplanes jammed. Hitting the seabed at about 80 metres (260 feet), the A/S dome was damaged, necessitating docking after arriving at Dundee.[20]

The two incidents led to an immediate revision of routines to keep aircraft and submarines even further separated. The necessity for the submarine to fire recognition signals and not just dive was emphasised, as was the preference for making the last portion of the return journey in darkness. In some areas, known as 'sanctuaries', near the main submarine bases, no submarines could be attacked, even if positively identified as German. In others, a challenge would have to be made before an attack could be instigated, and in others still, surface escort was provided. In all cases, the scheduled passage of submarines through the coastal areas was forwarded from RA(S) to Coastal Command and the regional RAF command centres. Nevertheless, adverse weather and challenging navigation resulted in rather frequent attacks on boats as they departed from or returned to base by eager airmen. Recognition signals had limited use as few captains stayed on the surface long enough to use them when sighting an aircraft.[21]

British Naval Structure 1939–40

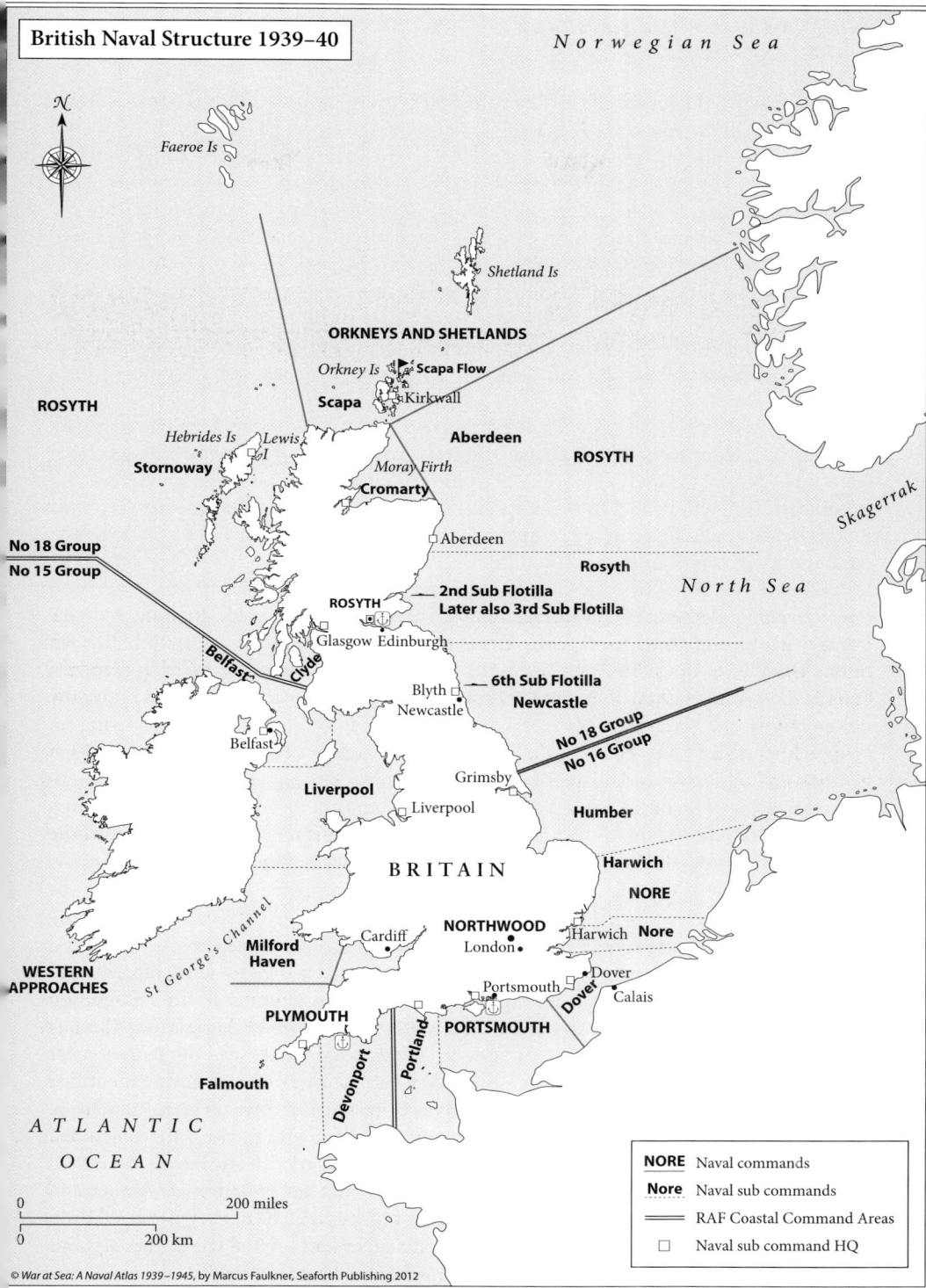

Norwegian Sea

Faeroe Is

N

Shetland Is

ORKNEYS AND SHETLANDS

Orkney Is **Scapa Flow**

ROSYTH

Scapa Kirkwall

Hebrides Is Lewis

Stornoway

Aberdeen

ROSYTH

Moray Firth

Cromarty

Skagerrak

No 18 Group

No 15 Group

Aberdeen

Rosyth

North Sea

2nd Sub Flotilla

Later also 3rd Sub Flotilla

ROSYTH

Glasgow Edinburgh

Belfast

Clyde

6th Sub Flotilla

Blyth

Newcastle

Newcastle

No 18 Group

No 16 Group

Belfast

Grimsby

Liverpool

Liverpool

B R I T A I N

Humber

Harwich

NORE

Northwood

Nore

Harwich

St George's Channel

Cardiff

London

Nore

Milford Haven

Portsmouth

Dover

Dover

WESTERN APPROACHES

Portsmouth

Calais

PLYMOUTH

Devonport

Portland

PORTSMOUTH

Falmouth

ATLANTIC OCEAN

NORE	Naval commands
Nore	Naval sub commands
═══	RAF Coastal Command Areas
□	Naval sub command HQ

0   200 miles

0   200 km

© War at Sea: A Naval Atlas 1939–1945, by Marcus Faulkner, Seaforth Publishing 2012

*   *   *

In mid-October, intelligence available to the Admiralty indicated that German surface ships might raid the east coast of Britain. In addition, the North Sea convoys from Methil to Bergen were becoming regular and provided a potential target. Hence, on 28 October, a patrol line was set up again in the North Sea. Nine submarines, *Thistle, Starfish, Sunfish, L26, Cachalot, Seal, Sealion, Shark* and *Salmon*, were formed in a line running from the Dutch coast off Ijmuiden northwards, along the western edge of the German Declared Area, to the southern entrance to the Skagerrak, 12 miles apart. The boats were instructed to attack 'enemy surface ships, including transports, except when conditions appeared to be unfavourable for air reconnaissance, in which case reconnaissance was the primary role'. Submarines were not to be attacked unless identified with certainty as a U-boat. Nothing came out of this set-up, however, and the patrol line was abandoned on 5 November.

Nevertheless, the disposition of the submarine forces had been highlighted again, resulting in a letter from RA(S) to the Admiralty on the 6th with extensive suggestions as to how the war should be run underwater. His suggestions, while emphasising that submarine dispositions required a large degree of flexibility, included the idea that most S-class boats should be gathered in the 2nd Flotilla at Dundee, including those returning from the Mediterranean. In addition, he suggested that two 'Atlantic flotillas' should be formed: one consisting of six T-class boats, supported by the depot ship *Maidstone*, and one consisting of the three River-class boats, supported by *Cyclops*. The four available minelayers, he suggested, were to be used in the North Sea, or, if not required to lay mines, attached to one of the Atlantic flotillas. The three U-class boats and the operational ones of the L-class were to remain at Blyth for North Sea duties. In the RA(S)'s mind, the

> flotillas in the North Sea are to act with the object of destroying enemy submarines and surface craft and reconnaissance duties generally. One Atlantic Flotilla, based on the west coast of Scotland, to patrol to the westward of the Outer Hebrides with the object of discovering the passage routes of U-boats and to destroy any encountered. The other Atlantic Flotilla to reinforce the Hebrides patrol, if its present employment at Freetown proves unfruitful.[22]

The Admiralty discussed the suggestions at length, and concluded that even if such dispositions might affect German U-boat operations, the expectations of actual results were rather limited and that, although worth a try, the main areas for submarine operations should be off the Norwegian Coast, Horns Reef, the Skagerrak, the Fair Isle Channel and north of Shetland. Anti-U-boat patrols west of Scotland by T-class boats were instigated at the end of October, but after two or three fruitless weeks in poor weather, this patrol was terminated. The Home Fleet flotillas, 2nd, 3rd, and 6th, were all gathered on the east coast for operations in the North Sea area, while the minelayers *Narwhal, Cachalot* and *Seal* were deployed as convoy escorts, operating partly out of Halifax, partly out of UK ports. At times, when in the UK, these boats were also used as escorts on the ON/HN convoys between Bergen, Norway and Methil.[23]

After further discussions, it was decided in early November that the Dundee-based 2nd Flotilla under Captain William Stephens should focus on the German iron-ore traffic in the northern North Sea and merchant ships that had eluded the Northern Patrol. It would be composed of the T-class boats *Triton, Triumph, Thistle, Triad, Trident* and the two Polish boats *Orzeł* and *Wilk*. The minelayers *Narwhal, Seal* and *Cachalot* were initially assigned to 2nd Flotilla but shortly after transferred to 5th Flotilla under operational control of Rear Admiral 3rd Battle Squadron for Atlantic duties on the Halifax convoy route. The depot ship *Forth* was also assigned to the 2nd Flotilla.

The 6th Flotilla operated from Blyth under Captain Jock Bethell with *Undine, Unity, Ursula, Sturgeon, Seahorse, Starfish, L23* and the depot ship *Titania*. In January 1940, *Severn* and *Clyde* were also transferred to the flotilla from Freetown, as their unproductive patrol area in the South Atlantic was taken over by French submarines based at Dakar.[24] The 3rd and 6th flotillas were to operate in the central and southern North Sea, targeting German naval vessels, including U-boats. German air raids on northern Britain commenced during October – not on any significant scale, but enough for the Admiralty to decide on 13 November that 2nd and 6th flotillas were to relocate to Rosyth, until adequate A/A defences had been set up at Dundee and Blyth, respectively.[25]

The new 3rd Flotilla instituted at Harwich in mid-November consisted entirely of S-class boats: *Seawolf, Sunfish, Shark, Sterlet, Swordfish, Spearfish, Sealion, Salmon* and *Snapper*. The flotilla was under the command of Captain Philip Ruck-Keene with 'Shrimp' Simpson as second-in-command and John Illingworth as its highly competent flotilla engineer. The main task of the flotilla was to patrol the northern English Channel and southern part of the North Sea, off the Dutch and Belgian coasts, in search of German warships and escort convoys. In addition, general reconnaissance would be important, especially in weather conditions that hampered aerial reconnaissance. The depot ship

Scraping the barrel: *L27*. Built at Vickers Ltd, Barrow-in-Furness, in 1918, she was obsolete at the start of WWII, but nevertheless called to war. (Cribbs)

Cyclops was assigned to the 3rd Flotilla and, while waiting for it to arrive from a refit, *Salmon* and *Snapper* were based at Sheerness south of the Thames estuary. This was an awkward arrangement and as soon as *Cyclops* arrived in November, the whole flotilla assembled at Harwich. To obtain the skilled labour needed in the docks and workshops to keep his flotilla operational, Ruck-Keene simply advertised in the newspapers, picked those he wanted and sent the rest of the list of applicants to the embarrassed director of dockyards at the Admiralty, who had told him there was no skilled labour to be found any more in Britain.[26]

At Gosport, Captain Cyril Coltart's 5th Flotilla, originally intended for training, covered the southern Channel and Western Approaches with *Oberon, H28, H31, H32, H33, H34, H43, H44, H49, H50, L26* and *L27*. Training and familiarisation of new submarines remained with the 5th Flotilla and *Tribune* and *Truant* were also temporarily assigned until deemed fit for war, as were most later new builds. While refitting, *Thames* and *Porpoise* were also nominally under control of 5th Submarine Flotilla. The old *Alecto* was assigned as depot ship, but was not used much as it operated out of Fort Blockhouse, the main submarine base.

Modifications to these assignments would be frequent as refits, repairs, damage and losses reduced the number of active boats in any one flotilla and which boat was assigned to which flotilla changed several times during the first months of the war (see Appendix III).[27]

— 6 —

A Slight Drizzle

SUBMARINES HUNTING SUBMARINES APPEARS intriguing, and this was seen as one of the primary tasks for British submarines by many Royal Navy officers. It was, however, quickly found to be a far from easy task. Several attempts to take out enemy boats occurred over the first months of the war but it became apparent that submarines were not ideal weapons to hunt enemy submarines. Firstly, finding and tracking another submarine was difficult, to say the least, with the tools available at the time – not to mention identifying it as friend or foe. Secondly, the torpedoes of the day were not suitable for an attack on a submerged adversary, limiting interception to cases where the target was on the surface. Thirdly, the submarines were small with shallow draught and the attempted attacks often failed as the torpedoes went underneath the target. Finally, there was the constant fear of misidentification, firing on one of your own boats. Nevertheless, the British Admiralty believed their own submarines could effectively intercept German U-boats.

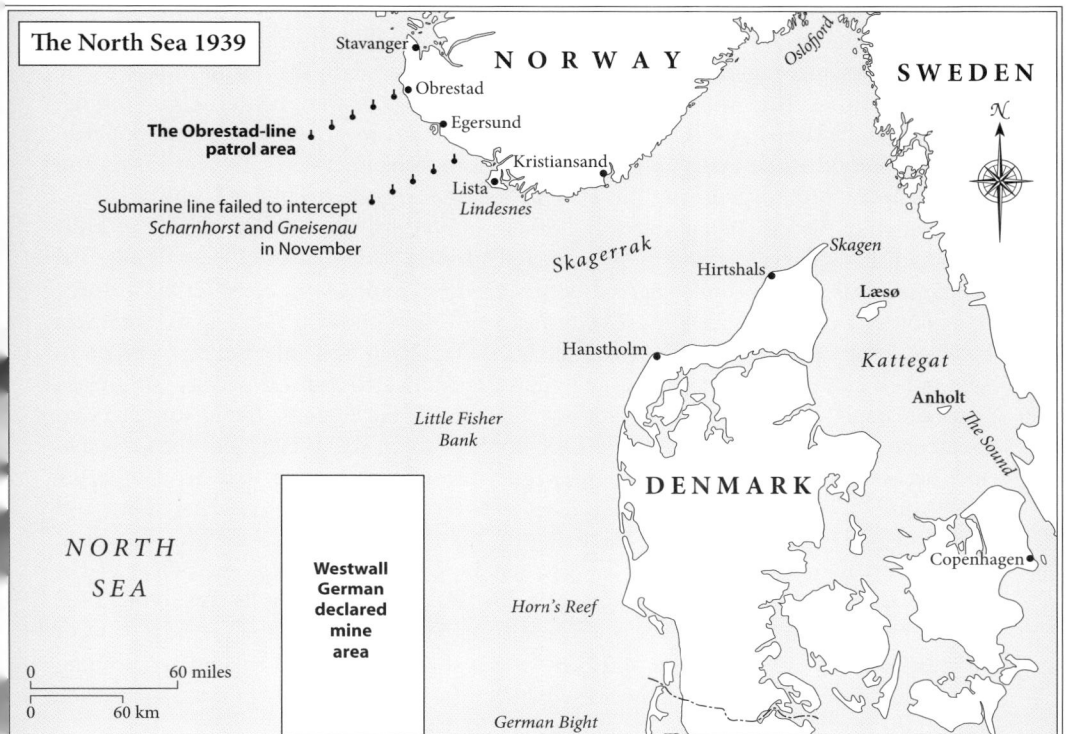

The North Sea 1939

Stavanger
NORWAY
Osloford
SWEDEN
N

Obrestad

Egersund

**The Obrestad-line
patrol area**

Kristiansand

Submarine line failed to intercept
Scharnhorst and *Gneisenau*
in November

Lista
Lindesnes

Skagerrak

Skagen

Hirtshals

Læsø

Hanstholm

Kattegat

Anholt

Little Fisher
Bank

The Sound

DENMARK

NORTH
SEA

**Westwall
German
declared
mine
area**

Copenhagen

Horn's Reef

0   60 miles

0   60 km

German Bight

On 3 September, *Spearfish* had just arrived on the Obrestad Line west of Egersund when the 'Total Germany' signal arrived. Literally minutes later, a torpedo track was observed ahead, missing the submarine by a few metres. It 'appeared to have been set for a shallow depth and was most noticeable when passing through waves', Lieutenant John Eaden, *Spearfish*'s commander, wrote. He ordered an emergency dive and turned in the direction that the torpedo had come from, asdic alerted. Strong hydrophone effects were picked up and a nerve-racking cat-and-mouse chase followed. At one stage, the two boats were probably no more than 20 metres (65 feet) apart, but there was no contact and about six hours after being fired at, Eaden surfaced. The U-boat, *U20*, was nowhere to be seen.[1]

A week later, on 9 September, Lieutenant Commander George 'Scraper' Phillips of *Ursula* fired four torpedoes at *U35* north-west of Borkum. The distance between the boats was some 900 metres (980 yards). The splash of the discharge was seen by the German lookouts in spite of the failing afternoon light, and the IIWO Leutnant Hans-Joachim Roters was able to turn the boat sharply to port, towards the stalker, combing the tracks.[2] Once through, he turned away at maximum speed. The CO of *U35*, Kapitänleutnant Werner Lott, who rushed up top when the boat geared and increased speed, realised they had escaped destruction by a hair's breadth and wrote in his diary: 'The torpedo passed only metres away, and everybody on the bridge looked a bit pale. Me included! A genuine baptism of fire for a U-boat.' The visible splash of the discharge was an issue with the U-class boats known from early trials, but it had not been properly rectified by the outbreak of war.[3]

U35 was one of five U-boats leaving Wilhelmshaven that morning, heading for the southernmost opening in the Westwall minefield, to operate in the northern part of the English Channel. The other boats, *U21*, *U23*, *U31* and *U36*, were behind *U35*. Through signalling with lamps and star-shells, they were warned to give the area a wide berth. Some ten minutes after firing on *U35*, though, another shadow was seen from *Ursula* and Phillips fired a fifth torpedo, but this also missed, the target being either *U21* or *U23*.[4]

Meanwhile, *Oxley*, *Triton* and three other submarines were on the Obrestad Line, some 12 miles apart according to orders from Admiral Forbes, C-in-C Home Fleet. The separation was a compromise agreed between Forbes and RA(S), considering the area to be covered and the number of submarines available, while also allowing for what was believed to be a safe margin. The two submarines had been in regular contact, and on 10 September, communication during the afternoon indicated that *Oxley* was fairly close – at one stage just over 2 miles – but not dangerously so. At 19:55 *Triton* surfaced and Lieutenant Commander Hugh 'Pat' Steel had his position fixed relative to the Obrestad and Kvassheim lighthouses on the Norwegian coast. Ascertaining that his submarine was inside its designated patrol area, Steel initiated a slow zigzag, steering south and switching one engine to charging the batteries. Assuring himself that the area was clear, except for a merchantman in the far distance, he gave the bridge to the officer of the watch, Lieutenant Harry Stacey, and went below, leaving orders that he was to be called if anything unusual appeared. Shortly before 21:00, Steel was called to the bridge: 'I went straight up. The night was dark and there was a slight drizzle and I could see nothing except the shore lights. The Officer of the Watch informed me that there was a submarine fine on the port bow, which for the moment I could not see.'[5]

Triton. (WSPL)

Shortly after, when Steel could make out the shape of an object in his binoculars, he took command of his boat. Orders were given to proceed on the main motors, ending the charge. Leading Signalman Eric Cavanaugh was sent for to ensure any signalling was executed correctly and the control room was instructed to ensure the external bow tubes, numbers seven and eight, were standing by, ready to fire. This automatically made First Lieutenant Guy Watkins, in charge below, order the men to diving stations. Getting accustomed to the dark, Steel realised that he was observing a submarine, steering in a north-westerly direction:

It occurred to me that it might be *Oxley* and I dismissed the thought almost as soon as it crossed my mind because earlier in the day I had been in communication with *Oxley* and given her my position accurately [. . .]. I then ordered the challenge to be made as soon as my sights were on and I knew the armament was ready, and the signalman made it slowly. No reply was received. After about 20 seconds I ordered the challenge to be made again. During this time I had been studying the submarine very closely indeed. She was trimmed down very low and I could see nothing of her bow or shape and the conning tower did not look like *Oxley's*, and I could not see any outstanding points of identification such as periscope standards, etc. Accordingly, I ordered the second challenge to be made. Receiving no reply to the second challenge, I made a third challenge again after a short interval. Receiving no reply to the third challenge I fired a rifle grenade which burst correctly. [. . .] By this time I was completely convinced that this was an enemy submarine. I counted fifteen slowly to myself [. . .] and gave the order to fire. No. 7 and No. 8 tubes were fired at three second intervals. About half a minute after firing, indeterminate flashing was seen from the submarine. This was unreadable and stopped in a few seconds. [. . .] Very shortly afterwards [. . .], one of my torpedoes hit.'[6]

At this time Lieutenant Stacey took a fix, using Obrestad and Egerø lighthouses, putting *Triton* well inside her own sector. The grenades referred to are rifle grenades carried for

Oxley in 1932. (W&L)

challenging other submarines at the surface. They were old, considered unreliable and were generally only kept in service at all for want of something better.

Remaining on the surface, Steel took his boat towards the area of the explosion to investigate; cries for help were soon heard – in English. The light from the Aldis lamp revealed three men swimming amid oil and debris. Lieutenant Commander Harold Bowerman, *Oxley*'s commanding officer, and Able Seaman Herbert Guckes, one of the lookouts, were rescued. The third person in the water, Lieutenant Manley, was not recovered. In all, fifty-three men were lost.

A board of inquiry found that *Oxley* was 'considerably to the eastward of her estimated position', probably due to an unexpected tidal current. The crew of *Triton* had acted correctly and was not to blame for the sinking. The lack of response from *Oxley* was explained by Bowerman as follows:

> On emerging from the upper conning tower [to the bridge], the Officer of the Watch told me that a submarine was just abaft the starboard beam and had fired a grenade. He told me that we had fired a grenade in answer but that it had failed to function. I asked him if he had made the private signal reply. He answered yes, but must have been hesitant or doubtful because I remember telling him to make it again to be certain. He had just commenced making it and I had by this time got out of the conning tower and was looking to the starboard [. . .] when I saw a flash immediately beneath me and heard a dull explosion and the ship shook. She seemed to list to port and break in two from the centre.[7]

Lieutenant Manley, *Oxley*'s officer of the watch, thus believed he had answered *Triton*'s challenges. No signals were observed on board *Triton*, though, other than the 'indeterminate flashing', not recognised as Morse, after the torpedoes had been fired.

The main burden for the tragedy was attributed to *Oxley*'s navigation and watch-keeping on the evening she was sunk. Lieutenant Commander Bowerman was not blamed directly, but there was no doubt it was his responsibility that *Oxley* was out of position. A reconstruction at the inquiry put *Oxley* close to the eastern limit of its patrol area in the afternoon, and found that the course Bowerman had steered subsequently did not allow for the currents in the area. The main blame for the disaster was nevertheless attributed to Lieutenant Manley, for not 'having kept or seen kept a proper lookout'. *Oxley* had only three men on watch, the officer of the watch being responsible for his own 120-degree sector. This was convenient, considering the crew on board and the space on the bridge, but inappropriate for wartime conditions. On board *Triton*, there were also three men on the bridge, but in this case the two lookouts had a 180-degree sector each, with the officer of the watch in general charge. In addition, there was a change of personnel on board *Oxley* at the critical moment as Able Seaman Guckes came onto the bridge a minute after nine, taking over as port lookout, well after *Oxley* had been observed from *Triton* and about the time when it was recognised on board *Oxley* that a submarine was near.[8]

For several reasons, the disaster was kept from the public, all the more so as Lieutenant Commander Bowerman was considered free from blame and not tried before a court martial. The disappearance of *Oxley* could not be concealed from the men of the Submarine Command though, and in spite of the exact circumstances remaining obscure, it was common knowledge that she had been sunk by one of their own boats. The boats still on the Obrestad Line were spaced another 4 miles apart and instructed to show extra vigilance.

Lieutenant Commander Steel was completely exonerated, but being 36, he was posted as an instructor on the perisher course at Gosport, before spending the rest of the war on board submarine depot ships and cruisers. The 35-year-old Lieutenant Commander Bowerman was declared free from blame by the Admiralty. Nevertheless, he was transferred to destroyers shortly after and served as commanding officer in several during the war.[9]

On 12 September, *Seahorse*, on her way to her billet off Norway, attacked a U-boat with torpedoes at long range while the German was busy attacking a merchant ship with gunfire. This had no effect, however, and the U-boat vanished, the lucky merchantman heading away at her best speed.

That same evening, intelligence was received by the Admiralty that there were five German cargo ships at Kopervik near Haugesund and *Triton*, still on the Obrestad Line, was ordered to investigate. Lieutenant Commander Steel took his boat into the Skudenes Fjord, inside Norwegian territory, but did not journey far enough north and so did not find the ships. Had they been found, the orders were to intercept them with gunfire and, with the German crew removed, sink the ships or if possible take them to Kirkwall.[10]

A few days later, on 14 September, three torpedoes from *Sturgeon* narrowly missed *Swordfish* east of the Firth of Forth. *Sturgeon* was outbound; *Swordfish* was on her way home – Lieutenant George Gregory of *Sturgeon* should have been informed that *Swordfish* was expected, even if not exactly where. He was later criticised for not actively seeking knowledge of other submarines when not properly informed, and above all for not challenging before firing torpedoes close to home. Measures had been taken to separate outward- and homeward-bound submarines, but these were obviously insufficient. When a submarine was encountered on a northerly course, after *Swordfish* had had to alter course to avoid a coastal convoy, Gregory acted on instinct when the submarine was observed to dive and virtually 'fired from the hip'. He stated later that, with the course it was steering, he was never in doubt that it was a German U-boat he fired upon. Consequently, no challenge was made.[11]

Swift reactions from First Lieutenant Leslie Bennington, on watch on board *Swordfish* – diving without waiting for his commander's orders when he sighted the other submarine – meant that at least one of the torpedoes actually went *over* the intended target, exploding in shallow waters. Stricter procedures for separation of outbound and inbound submarines, as well as disseminating information on the whereabouts of friendly boats, were introduced and on the last stretch towards base, surface escort was introduced.[12] On 21 October, RA(S) issued the following orders to all submarines: 'Submarines met during your passage to and from your patrol are not to be attacked unless they are recognised as German or give incorrect identification signal. Failure to make an identification signal after being challenged is not to be proof that the submarine is hostile.'[13]

But the concern was still there.

On a request from C-in-C Western Approaches Admiral Dunbar-Nasmith, RA(S) and the Admiralty agreed to detail one H-class boat, *H33*, from the 5th Flotilla for special operations. The submarine was to work in combination with an A/S trawler, which would act as an ordinary fishing vessel to lure U-boats off the west and south coasts of Ireland to attack it. It was believed that the submarine would then be able to track the U-boat and act offensively. There was also a notion in the Admiralty that U-boats might be using isolated bays on the Irish west coast to refuel from tankers, and places like Blacksod Bay were patrolled at times.[14]

The first trawler to operate with *H33* in October 1939 was *Tamura*; the trawlers *Comet* and *Manor* were also subsequently detailed for these operations, as well as the submarine *H43*. In the north, *H34* performed similar patrols from Scapa Flow with the trawler *Euryalus*. These patrols continued somewhat erratically until May 1940, without any results whatsoever. Quite the contrary, on several occasions the submarines were

H33. (Author's Collection)

identified as hostile and attacked by their own aircraft or trawlers. On 30 September, *H34*, on her way to Scapa Flow from such a patrol west of the Hebrides, fired two torpedoes at what appeared to be a German U-boat off Kinnaird Head. Both torpedoes missed what was probably not a genuine target at all: there were no U-boats in that area at the time.[15]

In spite of being small, the H-class boats did well in the rough offshore seas, both on the surface and at periscope depth, when operated by an experienced crew. Being pitched about on the surface was very tiring for the men, however, and increasingly uncomfortable as weather worsened into the winter. Furthermore, the concept of binding a submarine to a small surface vessel was not a good one. Communication was difficult, and should an enemy U-boat be encountered, it might take some considerable time before the submarine was in a position to attack it, during which the escort vessel would be at risk, although trawlers were not favourite targets for U-boats – in general they were looking for larger prey. Furthermore, the U-boat might well be detected by the submarine itself, questioning the need for the trawler in the first place. Later attempts to use the trawlers as scouts for the submarines, which were given freedom of choice as to their own movements, did not produce any improved results.[16]

During the autumn of 1939, the Admiralty was very much concerned about the risk of surface raiders breaking out into the Atlantic to attack the newly organised convoys. In addition, the convoys across the North Sea, to and from Norway, as well as the Northern Patrol – the picket line of armed merchant cruisers (AMCs) and older cruisers organised to intercept German blockade breakers attempting to return home – would be at risk, should the Kriegsmarine flex its muscles.

In a note from the Plans Division of the Admiralty dated 24 October 1939, it was argued that an effective reconnaissance of the northern North Sea would be of paramount importance in the months to come. It was to be expected, especially as the nights were about to grow longer and poor weather become more frequent into the winter, that German raiders would attempt to break out in order to escalate the war on commerce. In addition, raiders were already out and a number of German merchant ships were believed to be homeward bound, or would be so shortly. Air reconnaissance of the various exits and entries to the North Sea had been established, but this would be less than effective at night or in foggy weather, the note argued. Trawlers, destroyers and cruisers might fill the gap, but were in great demand elsewhere and the Plans Division concluded that 'the only suitable ships which we can draw on in strength, without prejudice to other vital requirements, are our submarines.'[17] The note continued with a curious lack of insight into submarine operational matters:

> At the moment, our submarine effort is widely dispersed in respect of function, locality and time, with the result that although of undoubted value in a subsidiary way, it does not contribute in any great measure towards our primary objective at the moment. This is particularly so in regard to reconnaissance because a number of vessels over an area provides a very much less effective reconnaissance than when on a concentrated line. Although operating at strategic points, any intelligence which they obtain is largely wasted because we cannot maintain other forces close to them with which to institute further search immediately. [. . .] Air reconnaissance being ineffective at night and in low day visibility, it is clear that the maximum reconnaissance effort will be obtained

from a limited number of submarines by concentrating them on a line at such a time and in such a position as to provide the best possible insurance against the failures of air reconnaissance. To provide the complement to air reconnaissance, clearly submarines are required to make their effort during darkness and low day visibility. Ability to detect ships at long range by using their asdics as hydrophones renders them particularly suitable for this purpose. It is understood that reliance can be placed on the detection of large ships passing at high speed at a distance of at least five miles, thus enabling them to be spaced ten miles apart. [. . .] Charging of batteries would then have to be undertaken in good day visibility and attacks on U-boats would of course, have to be prohibited.'[18]

Even more curious is the comment in the report made by Rear Admiral Tom Phillips, Deputy Chief of the Naval Staff, who wrote that he believed the raiders would keep close to the Norwegian coast and, keeping in mind the experiences from the Obrestad Line, the submarines would locate nothing at all. And if they did, he could not see 'how the submarine can tell whether it is a warship or a submarine'. It appears that these officers discussing the strategic and tactical use of the British submarine force had not spent much operational time on board an actual submarine. At the time of issuing the note, there were twenty-three submarines in home waters, including training boats and three minelayers. It was reckoned that sixteen of these would be available for the two weeks of each month when there was no moon and German raiders or blockade breakers were anticipated to attempt a breakout or return to port. 'Spaced ten miles apart, this number would provide a line 160 miles long which is sufficient to cover the whole North Sea entrance.' Surprisingly, the submarines were not expected to attack, just report their observations 'so as to enable other forces to investigate reports, shadow, cripple and finally destroy a ship proceeding through the line at high speed. Submarines cannot be relied on to carry out these functions without prejudice to their main role of reconnaissance.'[19]

Such rigid schemes for submarine deployment were never fully attempted. In late November 1939, *Trident* was one of several submarines ordered to take up billet along a line south-westward from Lista Lighthouse off the coast of Norway. Fifteen miles apart, they were attempting to intercept the German battleships *Scharnhorst* and *Gneisenau* returning home from having sunk the armed merchant cruiser *Rawalpindi* in the Norwegian Sea a few days earlier.[20] The battleships were not encountered, but on 5 December Lieutenant Commander Gould wrote in his war diary:

> 23:02, course 180. Sighted darkened ship, subsequently identified as a submarine, bearing 120° at approximate range 600 yards, steering about 250°. Turned towards and flooded up all bow tubes. As *Trident* was reaching a firing course, submarine made unreadable 3 letter group by lamp. In view of this and Rear Admiral(S) 18:43 of 4th December, it was decided that submarine was probably friendly. By this time, it was realised there was imminent danger of collision and the appropriate steps were taken, *Trident* eventually passing clear astern by about 50 feet. In the meantime an identification grenade was fired and the challenge made. This was answered by 'Pendants 80'. The challenge was made again and the correct reply was received, followed by 'Pendants 81' (*Sunfish*). [. . .] *Trident* then lost touch and although *Sunfish* was called by SS/T, no explanation was offered to account for his presence 30 miles from his position.[21]

U23, the first U-boat of Otto Kretschmer, who was to sink the largest tonnage of Allied ships during WWII. Between September 1939 and February 1940, Kretschmer made eight patrols with *U23*, sinking eight ships, including the destroyer *Daring*, totalling some 27,600 tons. (Author's Collection)

This account is chillingly similar to that of *Triton* and *Oxley* and another tragedy was only avoided by the vigilance of Lieutenant Commander Gould.

On 14 October, Lieutenant Gregory of *Sturgeon* brazenly attacked *U23* 20 miles west of Skagen, but again failed to hit with any of the three torpedoes fired. Two explosions were heard on board *U23*, but no torpedo tracks were seen and the boats quickly lost contact.[22] This was one of several unsuccessful attacks by a submarine on a U-boat within a short period of time and RA(S) issued instructions that, should conditions be favourable,

Lieutenant George Gregory of *Sturgeon*. He was a very experienced submarine officer, graduating from the 'perisher course' in 1938. After leaving *Sturgeon* in late 1940, at the age of 31, he served in various onshore and staff roles for the rest of the war. Vice Admiral Gregory retired from the Royal Navy in August 1966. He died in 1975. (IWM TR487)

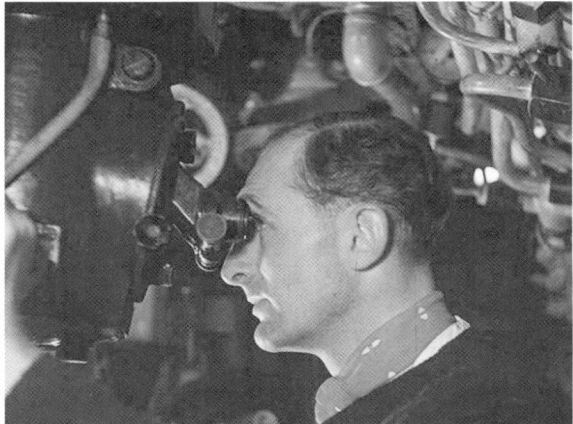

U-boats were targets worth a full salvo.[23] Still, on 6 November, *Sealion* missed *U21* with six torpedoes in foul weather near Dogger Bank. On this occasion, as there was full daylight and the distance was around 5,000 metres (5,500 yards), there was ample time for the German boat to turn away and avoid the torpedoes.[24]

On 20 November Lieutenant Gregory could finally claim his first success – which was also the first sinking of an enemy vessel by any British submarine during WWII. On this day, he fired four torpedoes at two German anti-submarine trawlers northwest of Heligoland. One of them, the 428-ton *V209 Gauleiter Telschow*, was hit and sank. Not everybody believed that such small vessels were appropriate targets for British torpedoes. Others believed that firing at them from time to time would keep them on their toes and lessen their eagerness to search for submerged submarines. A hefty discussion followed, but there was never a simple answer to this dilemma.

The Polish Predicament

WHEN THE POLISH STATE was created after WWI, its navy, the PMW, was tasked with creating a credible deterrence against Soviet and German aggression, focused around a number of fast submarines with mine-laying capability. French capital loans for naval development came with conditions for use in specific French yards, however, and Polish plans for nine submarines were changed to three submarines plus two destroyers, though the latter were initially not wanted. The submarines, *Wilk*, *Ryś* and *Żbik* were rather poor designs and plagued by operational problems from the start. Trying to restore the original plans for mine-laying submarines, orders for two large, sophisticated vessels were eventually placed in Dutch yards: *Orzeł* paid for by public subscription, and *Sęp* by normal naval directorate funds. *Orzeł* and *Sęp*, both commissioned in the spring of 1939, were fine ocean-going boats, each well-armed with a 105-mm gun and twelve torpedo tubes. Faster than most contemporary submarines, they were capable of 20 knots on the surface and 10 submerged. At 1,473 tons submerged, though, they were quite large for the shallow waters of the Baltic and smaller, coastal boats would arguably have been more suitable.[1]

When the hostilities escalated in 1939 and the war seemed inevitable, the five submarines, *Orzeł*, *Wilk*, *Sęp*, *Żbik* and *Ryś*, were supposed to create a defensive screen

Ryś under construction at Nantes in 1929. When launched, she would displace 980 tons on the surface and 1,250 tons submerged. (Author's Collection)

Submarine *Sęp* and destroyer *Błyskawica* just prior to the outbreak of WWII. (Author's Collection)

in and around the entrance to Danzig Bay, attacking German convoys to East Prussia and naval vessels shelling coastal positions. The plan, collectively known as Operation Worek, called for *Wilk* to operate in Danzig Bay, *Sęp*, *Żbik* and *Ryś* outside in the Baltic and *Orzeł* to stand by as flexible reserve in the Bay of Puck. The captains had strict orders not to lay their mines until specific orders arrived and to conserve their torpedoes for 'significant military targets'. This disposition was far less aggressive than expected by the Kriegsmarine which anticipated that the Polish boats would operate against their own warships and transports in the entire southern and western Baltic. In the shallow, coastal waters, the submarines would be vulnerable to A/S countermeasures and the Worek plan actually took the submarines away from where the enemy would be. In the event that the Polish naval bases were overrun, the submarines should remain as long as possible in the Baltic, inflicting maximum damage, and then leave for Britain. If this was not possible, refuge should be sought in a neutral port.

In the morning of 1 September, *Sęp*, *Żbik* and *Ryś* were at Hela, while *Orzeł* and *Wilk* were at Oksywie naval base outside Gdynia. The emergency call from Danzig, announcing the commencement of hostilities, sent all five submarines to sea. Air activity was intense, however, and, having to stay submerged, it would be evening before they were in place as planned. Only on 5 September were orders issued to *Żbik* and *Ryś* to lay their mines in the waters around Hela. There was a shortage of mines suitable for the submarines and they only carried some twenty each, half their capacity. It is unclear if the order to lay the mines was withheld by Allied demand or from a perception by the Poles that the Allies might not approve until after the effects of the declaration of war on Germany were seen.[2]

Lieutenant Commander Boguslaw Krawczyk of the submarine *Wilk* took on board ten torpedoes, twenty-two mines and 114 shells for the 10-cm deck gun before taking to sea.

Polish Submarines in the Baltic

0 ——————— 100 miles
0 ——————— 100 km

FINLAND

Turku

Helsinki

Gulf of Finland

SWEDEN

Stockholm

Tallinn
Orzel
Arrives 13.09
Departs 18.09

ESTONIA

—— *Rys*
—— *Sep*
—— *Zbik*
Interned in Sweden

Tartu

Gulf of Riga

Baltic Sea

Riga

LATVIA

Submarine *Wilk* also
succeeded in escaping
to Britain

LITHUANIA

Operation Peking
—— *Błyskawica*
—— *Burza*
—— *Grom*
Destroyers to Britain 29.08
Arrived 01.09

Operation *Worek*
**Attempted Polish
submarine blockade**

Gdynia

Königsberg

Danzig

GERMANY

**DANZIG
FREE STATE**

**EAST
PRUSSIA**

POLAND

Westerplatte

Danzig

Inset map (Danzig Bay / Puck Bay):

Sep

Seaplane
base

Puck

Orzel Jastarnia

Zbik

Rewa

Mechelinki

*Puck
Bay*

Hela

Rys

Oksywie

Gdynia

Wilk

0 ——— 5 miles
0 ——— 5 km

Danzig Bay
⚓ Major AA battery
◣ Major coastal battery
⊿ Submarine

© *War at Sea: A Naval Atlas 1939–1945*, by Marcus Faulkner, Seaforth Publishing 2012

During the morning of the 2nd, the German destroyer *Erich Steinbrinck* was sighted, bombarding the naval base on the Hela Peninsula. Krawczyk prepared to attack, but while getting into position, *Wilk* came under attack herself by a group of A/S vessels, forcing Krawczyk to dive deep and withdraw. Three days later, preparing to lay her mines off Hela, *Wilk* was again attacked by German A/S vessels. Again she escaped and Krawczyk decided to withdraw north towards the coast of Sweden.

On the way, *Wilk* was constantly harassed by German A/S vessels and it was obvious that she was leaving a trail of oil from leaking tanks. Krawczyk decided it was better to lose his boat fighting than fleeing and prepared to surface. By the time he broke surface though, the sea was empty. Undoubtedly relieved, he continued northwards, cleaning the leaking tanks to stop leaving a trail. In addition, the fore hydroplanes were damaged and unreliable while a leak through the engine exhaust necessitated continuous pumping when submerged.

Two days later, on the 11th, the cruiser *Hipper* was sighted and Krawczyk prepared for an attack. Before he could get into position, however, the German turned away. Later the same day, orders were received from the Polish Naval Command for all submarines to head for Britain. Krawczyk waited until a convoy appeared on a westerly course near the Swedish coast and surfaced, positioning his submarine close by. Approaching Öresund at dusk on the 14th, the German destroyer *Richard Beitzen* and the torpedo boat *T107* were sighted, but they, as Krawczyk had hoped, believed *Wilk* was a Swedish submarine escorting the convoy and did nothing. Krawczyk took his boat through the Kattegat and towards the North Sea; on the 20th, *Wilk* arrived off May Island, from where she was escorted to Scapa Flow, her crew exhausted.[3]

Orzeł was ordered to slip anchor and head for her pre-determined sector in the Bay of Puck on 1 September, immediately after the first air raids on Oksywie. German aircraft and A/S vessels kept the submarine submerged most of the time, though, except for a few hours every night. Hence, Komandor Podporucznik Henryk Kloczkowski, 'Klocz' to his men, did not receive the warning to look out for and attack the battleship *Schleswig-Holstein* should she leave Danzig.[4] Learning that most of the Polish surface ships had been sunk, Kloczkowski nevertheless decided to leave the Bay of Puck and head for the Baltic. During the evening of the 3rd, the German destroyers *Leberecht Maass* and *Max Schultz* were sighted from *Orzeł*, but as they were in the sector assigned to *Wilk*, Kloczkowski did not attack. Just hours earlier, *Orzeł* had been bombed by a German aircraft, and that might also have increased his reluctance to reveal the presence of his submarine, as there was total German air superiority over Danzig Bay. On the way towards the mouth of the bay, *Orzeł* met briefly with *Wilk* and the two captains discussed fleetingly what options they had.

The next day, the 4th, there were still aircraft overhead and Kloczkowski decided to place his submarine on the bottom, sitting things out. At 15:00 his patience ran out and, against the advice of his officers, he decided to surface and take a look. Poking the periscope out of the water, it was immediately sighted and several aircraft attacked. Reinforcements were also called and, before long, *Orzeł* was subjected to a particularly violent attack by the minesweepers *M4* and *M3*. One depth charge exploded just above the boat, sending it crashing into the seabed. All lights went out and water started leaking through the diesel exhaust valve. The attack lasted all day but eventually *Orzeł* managed to get away under cover of darkness. For the next week, Komandor Podporucznik Kloczkowski decided to patrol the waters off the Swedish island of Gotland. What he hoped to find there was unclear to his officers, and when he ignored orders from Hela to return to Polish waters a tense atmosphere developed. After a few more days Kloczkowski declared that he was sick, which prompted further instructions from Hela to return immediately or land the captain in a neutral port. Meanwhile, a leak in the hydraulic system had developed, which could not be repaired at sea, and Kloczkowski decided the best thing would be to enter Tallinn in neutral Estonia to seek assistance.

Arriving in the outer harbour of Tallinn in the early hours of the 14th, *Orzeł* was shortly taken into the inner basin, as far away from the entrance as possible, by two Estonian patrol vessels. The 37-year-old Kloczkowski and Petty Officer Barwinski, who had also fallen sick, left the submarine as soon as she had been tied up, to seek medical attention.[5] The 32-year-old First Officer Kapitan Marynarki Jan Grudzinski took over command of *Orzeł*.[6]

At first the Estonians honoured the Hague Convention and measures were taken to facilitate repairs. There was immediate pressure from Germany, however, and on the morning of the 15th, Grudzinski was called to the Estonian harbour master. There, he was informed that they would not be allowed to leave until at least six hours after a German merchant ship, which was scheduled to depart during the coming night. Nevertheless, in the afternoon, an armed detachment boarded *Orzeł*, declaring that the Estonian government had decided to intern the boat. Maps and navigation aids were immediately confiscated, as well as the Polish flag, which had been flying since their arrival. During the night, the breech mechanisms of the deck guns and their ammunition were removed, and unloading of the torpedoes commenced. By midday on the 16th, all forward torpedoes had been landed, but a Polish seaman managed to sabotage the torpedo hoist and the six torpedoes aft were left on board.

Angered by the Estonian hostility, Grudzinski and the new first officer, Porucznik Marynarki Andrzej Piasecki, worked out a plan for escape. Dismantling work on the engines was delayed under all kinds of pretexts and one of the petty officers, pretending to be fishing, sounded the water depth of the inner harbour. The radio and gyro compass were covertly set in working order. On the night of 17/18 September, the Estonian guards in the control room were overpowered, while one of the seamen cut the main electric cable supplying the inner docks, taking out all the lights. On a signal from Grudzinski once all were back on board, the mooring wires were cut and *Orzeł* got under way.[7]

The alarm was raised and some light guns of the harbour defences opened fire. Fortunately for the Poles, the larger guns held back, allegedly from fear of hitting their own ships moored around the port. In reality, most of the Estonian military probably cheered the Poles as they raced for the open sea. *Orzeł* touched a sand bank near the exit of the harbour, but Grudzinski managed to get her off by use of the trimming tanks and the submarine slipped into the Baltic.

There were no charts on board and, with the Polish Navy disintegrating fast – its ships being sunk or interned and the land bases overrun – there was no help to be found. Quite the opposite, as Russia also attacked Poland on the 17th, so Soviet ships were also hunting *Orzeł* in addition to the massive German force sent to find her. For the next couple of weeks *Orzeł* moved back and forth in the waters off the Swedish island Öland – sometimes north towards Gotland, other times west to Bornholm. Grudzinski needed maps and his intention was to board the first German merchant vessel encountered and take her charts and logbooks. No German civilian ships were encountered though, only warships and aircraft looking for them.[8]

After three weeks of fruitless searching for something on which to use her remaining six torpedoes, Grudzinski finally decided it was time to leave the Baltic, heading for Britain. Supplies of freshwater and food were running short and there was nowhere to go to for replenishment. Internment in Sweden was not an option. The Belts were closely guarded by German A/S ships, but *Orzeł* managed to crawl through with the help of a map drawn from memory by the navigating officer, Sub-Lieutenant Mariana Mokrskiego, and a list of Swedish lighthouses. Whenever they had to come to the surface, Grudzinski flew a Swedish flag, and this, combined with heavy rain and low visibility, brought them through. On 14 October, some fifty days after she sailed from Oksywie, *Orzeł* made landfall, off the east coast of Scotland. A signal was sent by radio in plain English and a British destroyer came out to escort her into Rosyth, much to the surprise of the Admiralty who had thought her long since sunk.[9]

Orzeł's sister boat *Sęp* had been rushed home from the Dutch yard a few months earlier and was not fully tested by her crew when she took to sea. On 2 September, *Sęp* fired a single torpedo at the German destroyer *Friedrich Ihn*. The speed of the destroyer was underestimated, though, and the torpedo missed, in spite of the submarine being only 400 metres (440 yards) away. *Ihn* counter-attacked with a vengeance and the submarine crawled away with severe oil leakages as well as other damage, water seeping into the boat. On the 3rd, *Sęp* was at the receiving end of a torpedo from *U14*, but the torpedo exploded prematurely and she escaped again. The crew of *U14* saw and heard the exploding torpedo and erroneously reported the submarine it had attacked to be sunk.

Polish submarine *Sęp* interned in Swedish waters in November 1939. (Wikipedia)

On 13 September, orders were received to sail to Britain if possible or, if not, to a neutral Swedish port for internment. By now conditions on board the boat were severe, owing to the extensive damage and leaks and when Hela confirmed it would not be possible to return there, her CO decided the best he could do would be to seek refuge inside Swedish territorial waters. On 17 September, *Sęp* appeared off Stockholm requesting permission to enter the harbour for repairs, knowing this would mean internment.

Ryś had also been damaged through repeated attacks from German A/S forces and aircraft and her captain decided to head for Sweden on the 18th. Both submarines were interned for the duration of the war and taken to Vaxholm, north-east of Stockholm. On the 25th, they were joined by *Żbik*, her captain also having concluded that his boat was not in a condition to break out for Britain.[10]

Except for *M85*, which foundered on a mine laid by *Żbik*, no German ships were sunk by the Polish submarines during the campaign. On the other hand, none of the submarines were sunk either, in spite of German claims to the contrary.[11]

— 8 —

A Most Appalling Crash

To THE MEN IN a submarine, the sea is full of noises, some easily recognisable, such as those from a pump or an engine, others more mysterious. In December, *Tribune* reported hearing 'parrot noises', resembling 'the chortling of a parrot accompanied by a whistling'. The sounds were heard close to an undersea telegraph cable, but it was never ascertained that this had anything to do with the phenomenon. Many boats also reported hearing the so-called 'North Sea grunt', gurgling sonic impulses of unknown origin. These were at first believed to originate from a novel, secret seabed detection system connected to onshore stations, adding to the unease of operating too close to the German coastline. After a while, it became known that similar noises had been heard during the previous war and the phenomenon was ascribed to natural causes, although never fully explained. It is very likely that in many cases these sounds actually came from whales, dolphins or porpoises roaming the North Sea.[1]

In the small hours of 25 September, an emergency radio signal was received at the Home Fleet from the submarine *Spearfish*. She had been badly damaged off Horns Reef during a lengthy chase by German A/S trawlers the day before, and was unable to dive. The previous night, *Spearfish* had been on the surface all night in a howling gale off Norway. At dawn on the 24th, Lieutenant John Eaden decided it was time to dive and, after doing so, headed south across the Skagerrak towards the Danish coast. A few hours later, when the crew was preparing for a late breakfast, a depth charge exploded without warning in the vicinity. Eaden decided to have a look and ordered periscope depth. Before the first

Spearfish in 1937. (W&L)

lieutenant could take the boat up, however, a second depth charge exploded even closer. They were obviously being attacked. Instead of continuing up, all machinery was stopped and they sank towards the shallow seabed, settling in for an extensive hunt, observing absolute silence. In the next hour,

> 6 single charges were exploded at various ranges. The ratings started a sweepstake as to when the next charge would land. Enemy A/S forces must have had strong contact with some object, possibly a wreck, luckily not us. 25 single charges of varying strengths were exploded between 14:30 and 16:10. These charges 'thumped' the boat but did no damage. At 17:20, some form of wire or grapnel was heard passing over the after jumping stay. Next, a bump on the after casing followed by a series of short bumps moving aft. The charge then exploded with a most appalling crash. The whole ship appeared to spring inwards and then open out again. Nearly all lights were smashed including glass shades. In the darkness, spurting of water and hissing of escaping air could be heard.[2]

Spearfish had obviously escaped destruction by the narrowest of margins. What may have been an explosive sweep had exploded outside the engine and motor rooms, severely twisting and denting parts of the pressure hull. After fitting a few new light-bulbs, with the least possible noise, Lieutenant Eaden decided it was time for a 'tot of rum to all officers and men'. While this was savoured, damage was checked and it was clear that the boat was in severe peril. There were several leaks aft and water was squirting into the bilges; one motor and both the engines were out of action and the high-pressure air system was leaking in half a dozen places. They would have to surface soon – if at all. The air quality inside the submarine was becoming so poor that a decision had to be made quickly. Darkness was approaching and Lieutenant Eaden decided to ascend and, if necessary, fight to the finish. A demolition charge would be placed under the warhead of one of the torpedoes and, if necessary, set off to avoid the submarine being captured once the crew had abandoned the boat. Somewhat to Eaden's surprise, an air of relief and eagerness spread through the submarine when he mustered the hands and informed them of his intentions. They stacked ammunition for the guns, checked the torpedoes and prepared the demolition charges. The Germans seemed not to have realised what had happened, however. Further depth charges exploded from time to time, but gradually they moved away and when, at 20:30, the battered submarine reached the surface, no other ships were in sight.

Leaks from the high-pressure air bottles meant that opening the conning-tower hatch would release the over-pressurised air inside the boat with some force. Hence, it was with a 90-kg signalman grasping his legs that Eaden stood on the ladder to the conning-tower hatch and knocked off the clips. As the hatch flew open he was pulled off his step and his binoculars flew off into the night.

Surveying the damage to *Spearfish*, things were even worse than anticipated and it was obvious that they could not dive again due to the extensive damage to the pressure hull. The engines were disabled and all they could do was to crawl away from the scene on one motor. After two hours' hard work, though, one of the engines could be started and things looked a little better. All the more so when wooden plugs had been fitted to the worst of the leaks and it was reported that the pumps could cope. Lieutenant Eaden endeavoured to get his boat home via Danish territorial waters; when a new antenna had been rigged up sometime after midnight, he transmitted a message, asking for an escort to take them back home across the North Sea.

Admiral Forbes ordered 2nd Cruiser Squadron's Vice Admiral Edward-Collins in *Southampton*, with *Glasgow* and destroyers *Jervis* and *Jupiter*, to sea with all dispatch, while Captain (D)6 Randolph Nicholson with *Somali*, *Mashona*, *Matabele* and *Eskimo*, already off the Norwegian coast south of Bergen, was ordered to set course for Denmark and meet up with 2nd Cruiser Squadron on the way. Meanwhile, the rest of the Home Fleet also took to sea. *Hood* and *Renown* with 18th Cruiser Squadron and destroyer support were positioned to cover the rescue operation from the north while Forbes positioned himself with *Nelson*, *Rodney*, *Ark Royal* and six destroyers in the Bergen–Shetland narrows.

Meeting up with *Spearfish* north of Ringkøbing at 00:55 on the 26th, *Somali* and *Eskimo* took station on the submarine while *Mashona* and *Matabele* remained with the 2nd Cruiser Squadron, reinforced by cruisers *Aurora* and *Sheffield*, screening from a distance. Later in the morning of the 26th, Do18 flying boats of 2./506 and 2./306 sighted the British covering forces, which the B-Dienst had reported to be at sea, north of Great Fisher Bank, resulting in heavy bombing attacks on them.[3] *Spearfish* was not interfered with though – except for one Do18 that got too close for comfort and was promptly shot down by Skuas from *Ark Royal* – and arrived in Rosyth without mishap next morning. From Rosyth, *Spearfish* was transferred to Newcastle upon Tyne for repairs and remained there until the middle of March 1940.[4] By that time, Lieutenant Commander John Forbes had taken command of the boat.

The ordeal of *Spearfish* was the first really serious depth-charge attack on a British submarine in the war, and it made a severe impression throughout the Submarine Service. Reports were widely distributed and it appears that Lieutenant Eaden spoke or lectured to most other submarine officers that he came across. One can also take it for granted that, while *Spearfish* was in the yards, her ratings and NCOs spoke freely of their experiences to other submariners in messes and pubs throughout the country. For months, just about every account of being hunted by German A/S units contained the phrase 'Bearing in mind the experience of *Spearfish* . . .' or something similar when the commanding officer explained how he had chosen to act and why.[5]

From 29 October to 6 November, a Dogger Bank patrol of ten submarines was maintained on instructions from the Admiralty in an attempt to intercept German U-boats passing through the North Sea. During this period, *Sealion* unsuccessfully attacked one U-boat. In addition, *Sunfish* sighted another submarine, though did not attack as its identity could not be established. The other boats on this patrol encountered little apart from atrocious weather, which made station-keeping virtually impossible – often ending up more than 20 miles off position – and the concept was abandoned.[6]

In late November, *Triad* under Lieutenant Commander Ronald Jonas was on patrol in heavy seas off south-western Norway when a particularly vicious sea jammed the aft hydroplanes in the maximum 'ascend' position, at an elevation of 70 degrees. The connection between the telemotor systems and the hydroplane axles had failed owing to split securing nuts and the planes were locked in the near-vertical position, from where the manual back-up systems could not retrieve them. After an initial emergency routine, closing all watertight doors, it was assessed that the boat was not in any immediate danger, but it was virtually impossible to make headway, the planes acting as huge breaks and *Triad* could not dive, except statically in an emergency. For all practical purposes, *Triad* could only proceed stern-first, into the weather, at about 2 knots. The destroyers *Inglefield* and *Maori* were detached from the Home Fleet to come to her assistance.[7] Captain Percy Todd of *Inglefield* narrated:

> At 14:00 [on 27 November], I located *Triad* and proceeded to take her in tow. This was completed by 16:15 and I proceeded for Rosyth at 5 knots. At 18:00 the tow parted and as I had not another suitable wire, I ordered *Maori* to take *Triad* in tow. From 18:00 to 09:00 on the 28th, *Maori* endeavoured to take *Triad* in tow, but the weather was deteriorating and conditions were quite unsuitable. I ordered the submarine to proceed stern first into the wind, which was her only method of progression. The destroyers proceeded to patrol round the submarine.[8]

Shortly after, three Coastal Command Blenheims arrived to assist in the escort. One of them was given the status by visual signalling and ordered by Captain Todd to move well clear of the ships before forwarding this message by radio signal to C-in-C Home Fleet. The weather deteriorated further and by nightfall a full gale was blowing, with heavy seas. During the night, communication with *Triad* was lost, but by 08:00 on the 29th the

Triad proceeding stern-first in heavy seas off southern Norway. The photo is taken from a Hudson of 224 Squadron flying out of Leuchars. (NA-AIR 28/470)

two destroyers had regained contact. By then, the weather had moderated somewhat. The sister-submarine *Triumph*, which had met up with the group during the previous afternoon, vanished during the night and was not to be seen. During the day *Triumph* was ordered by radio to resume patrol off Jæren as she could contribute nothing in the foul weather and was better off handling the storm on her own.[9]

A new aircraft, a Hudson this time, arrived and, following the same procedure as the day before, updated the C-in-C on the situation. Tugs had not been able to depart Rosyth; during the morning, Todd, who had considered taking the crew off the submarine and scuttling her, received:

> a signal from the Admiralty to return to Norwegian territorial waters with *Triad* to await the arrival of (the tug) *Bandit*. Almost simultaneously, a signal was received from the C-in-C Home Fleet, ordering me to continue the tow to the Westward. In view of another gale warning and the fact that *Triad*'s last towing pendant was in use, I decided to take *Triad* into territorial waters and endeavour to effect temporary repairs with the combined resource of destroyers and submarine to enable the latter to return to Rosyth under her own power.[10]

The three British ships dropped anchor in Mastrafjord north of Stavanger in the morning of 30 November. Under the prevailing conditions, and with *Triad* having sustained genuine weather damage, this was legitimate, provided the Norwegian authorities were notified of their presence. It is not clear if the Norwegian authorities were properly notified, but the chief pilot at Skudeneshavn, north of Stavanger, called the naval authorities in Stavanger at 08:20, reporting that 'an English Man-of-war towing submarine *T53* has been observed, heading for Stavanger'.[11]

Norwegian torpedo boat *Stegg* is dwarfed by *Inglefield*. (RA PA-1209Ui199-401)

Triad in Mastrafjord. Note how she is trimmed bow-down to lift the after hydroplanes as much as possible out of the water. The forward hydroplanes are folded up as usual on the surface. The aft hydroplanes are still out, almost vertical, seen below the two men on the after deck. (RA PA-1209Ui199-401)

A few hours later, a Norwegian MF.11 seaplane landed alongside *Inglefield*. The observer, Lieutenant Fredriksen, climbed on board, saluted smartly and enquired the reason for their presence. After Captain Todd had explained the situation, Fredriksen informed him that, according to the Norwegian neutrality regulations, the destroyers would have to leave within twenty-four hours, while the submarine could remain until repairs had been effected. Radio could not be used by any of the ships.

Not long after, another MF.11 landed, with a senior naval officer, Kaptein Eivald Røren, on board, while the torpedo boat *Stegg* arrived from Skudeneshavn. Kaptein Røren and Kaptein Johan Dahl of *Stegg* both came aboard *Inglefield* and Todd again explained the situation. It was obvious that it would not be possible to repair *Triad* on site and it was agreed that arrangements should be made for her to be towed to Rosenberg Yard in Stavanger by a Norwegian tug. The two Norwegian officers could see for themselves that the hydroplanes had jammed in a vertical position and could not be repaired at sea as the only access to the broken parts was from the outside, below the waterline. Once the tug had arrived and all arrangements were in order, the two destroyers left Norwegian territorial waters.[12]

Everything was arranged according to the neutrality regulations. In all the reports and accounts of these events from the Norwegian side, though, it is obvious that promptness and succour was added with pride, since the submarine was British. The Norwegians may have been neutral, and wished to remain so, but there is no doubt who the people of Stavanger, the nearest town to Britain across the North Sea, saw as their friends.

The next morning, Friday 1 December, armed guards were posted around Rosenberg Yard, including a handful of policemen, to ensure nothing untoward took place. Meanwhile, Kaptein Røren discussed with the management of the yard what needed to be done. To simplify matters and save time, it was decided to haul the submarine up onto a slipway, stern first, only as much as was needed and not take her into the dry dock. The repairs were straightforward once the boat was sufficiently out of the water and *Triad* was refloated in the afternoon of the next day, fully seaworthy.

Meanwhile, the C-in-C Norwegian West Coast, Admiral Carsten Tank-Nielsen, flew down from his office in Bergen to ensure that everything possible was done to effect the repairs. He was also able to inform Lieutenant Commander Jonas that no German ships were waiting outside Stavanger as he had reconnoitred the area on the way down. Thereafter *Triad* quickly left Norwegian waters, escorted to the territorial border by *Trygg*, another of the Norwegian torpedo boats. *Triad* was back at Rosyth on 4 December.

This episode has many interesting aspects, among them the inability of the destroyers to actually assist *Triad*, the Admiralty's direct interference in the operation and the prompt Norwegian support given to a British submarine. During the winter, all T-class boats were docked to inspect, and if necessary repair, their hydroplane tiller arm to prevent similar incidents.[13]

On some occasions, Norwegian territorial waters were entered by British submarines without approval of the Norwegian authorities. At Christmas in 1939, *L23* was on patrol in the Skagerrak off southern Norway. Lieutenant Leslie Hill, on his first patrol as commander, wrote in his report:

> At dawn on 26th, patrol was taken up off Kristiansand in accordance with Admiralty's 0155/26. As there appeared to be an unusual amount of smoke over Kristiansand, it was decided to dive into the entrance of the fjord to investigate. One Norwegian seaplane and two single engine landplanes were sighted flying over the harbour. One B-class submarine with white squares painted on the casing above the fore-planes and white patches on the conning tower was anchored in the naval anchorage. There appeared to be no unusual activity. Territorial waters were left at 09:30 and patrol resumed 6 miles off the entrance to the fjord.[14]

Captain Jock Bethell, CO of the 6th Flotilla, added that he considered this action to have been 'correct', although 'taken in full knowledge of the risk of attack from Norwegian forces'.[15]

The North Sea is treacherous at the best of times, the southern section all the more so for a submarine, needing room to operate underwater, preferably unrestricted by shallow sandbanks and strong currents. Off the coast of Holland during a particularly harsh period in the autumn of 1939, things went wrong for *Snapper*. Bill King wrote:

> After several days' continuous north-westerly gales, I had little idea where we were because the tidal stream forked in our area. [. . .] About half an hour before dawn [. . .], I was in my bunk when the officer of the watch sent me a message: 'Light ahead. Apparently the shore'. We must have taken the wrong tidal stream. *Snapper* was heading

fast into the Dutch coast. [. . .] I leapt up in a flash, for I slept in oilskins. I knew we must be driving ashore with a full gale behind us. 'Hard-a-port' I shouted to the helmsman in the control room and as I sprinted up the conning-tower ladder my heart turned to lead. A moment after I reached the bridge we struck bottom with a shuddering jar. If the helmsman had not reacted to the split second we would have been finished.[16]

Thanks to the swift reaction of the helmsman, *Snapper* was pointing out to sea when she struck bottom, instead of pointing inland with the waves coming from behind. Fortunately, the seabed was all sand; every crest in the waves lifted them off and every trough slammed them down again. Skilfully, King used the electric motors, ordering 'Full ahead' every time they were lifted and 'Stop both' as they dropped. Against the odds, a thoroughly relieved CO, after what seemed like an eternity, registered that the bumping was becoming less severe and then stopped altogether as they reached deeper waters.

Floating mines were a constant threat to all the submarines in the North Sea. Due to the large number of mines in the area and the prevailing currents, the area where the Skagerrak and the North Sea met was particularly dangerous. The mines should have been rendered harmless if they broke adrift, but often they remained 'live', irrespective of who had originally put the mine in place. Normally, a drifting mine would be swept aside in the bow wave from a submarine, but not always, and it was never worth taking the risk if the mine was seen in time.

On Boxing Day 1939, *Triumph* was on patrol north of the German Declared Area. Before going below after surfacing, Lieutenant Commander John McCoy had put his submarine on a southerly course at 6 knots, with port engine on the propeller, starboard on the charge. First Lieutenant Leslie Bennington was officer of the watch with three lookouts on the bridge. At 23:06, the moon came out from behind a cloud and he sighted a rogue mine floating sluggishly dead ahead, only a few metres away. There was no time to react other than to shout 'hard-a-starboard' down the voice-pipe and hope for the best. With starboard engine declutched from its propeller, the boat was slow to answer the helm, however, and

Triumph. (W&L)

the mine struck fine on the port side of the bow. It exploded with a large sheet of flame, temporarily blinding the men on the bridge. Below, a rather inconspicuous metallic crash brought most men rushing to their diving stations, closing watertight doors and wondering what had happened.[17] Extraordinarily, none of the torpedoes exploded, in spite of a large part of the bow being blown away and the torpedoes completely wrecked. The type-3F pistols had been fitted ready for service on the torpedoes loaded in the tubes. Their built-in safety mechanisms functioned as intended, though, preventing the warheads from detonating. From one tube, the whole torpedo was missing; in another, all that remained was the tail end while a third had severe damage to its warhead.

About 3 metres of the bow had been blown off, leaving only a part of the lower hull, below the lowermost torpedo tube. The structure of the entire bow had been forced to starboard, causing stretching on the port side and 'rippling' on the starboard.

There was damage to the pressure hull and cracks in the forward bulkhead, but the watertight partition leading to the torpedo space held. The main watertight doors had

The damage to the bow of *Triumph* was extensive. Note that the two external torpedo tubes above the pressure hull are also damaged. (NA-ADM 267/89)

been open at the time of the explosion, but the door between the torpedo space and the seamen's mess (no. 40 bulkhead) had been jarred shut, locked itself and was now totally jammed. Access to the wrecked torpedo space was gained through the escape chamber in the same bulkhead. The doors at the fore end of the torpedo space had been shut and remained so, probably preventing the force of the explosion penetrating fully into the submarine. When opening the port fore door cautiously, it was discovered that water was ingressing through several leaks and the water level was above the floor planks. The leaks were plugged as best as possible and the forward bulkhead was shored up. After this, the pumps were switched on and appeared to hold the water. Still, a pressure gauge was rigged up in case it would become necessary to shut the fore end doors and apply air pressure forward to hold the water out. McCoy hoped that this would not become necessary as he anticipated that if he had to close the watertight doors, sealing off the damaged areas, too much water would enter, which the pumps would not be able to cope with, and the boat would sink. It was a better alternative, he believed, to let some water in, keep all pumps operating at full capacity, plug as many leaks as possible and head for home.

The weather was poor, and an agonising 4.5 knots was all that could be made. German aircraft did emerge, but by the time the Luftwaffe had co-ordinated their forces for an attack, a battle flight of Hudson aircraft had arrived, driving the Dornier flying boats away. Eventually, *Triumph* limped into the Firth of Forth, to spend six months in dock.[18]

Luck and Good Fortune

DURING TEN DAYS IN an otherwise rather bleak winter, when most submarines were billeted in the North Sea, *Salmon* was to have an epic patrol, achieving results otherwise unheard of at this stage of the war.

Salmon's commanding officer, Lieutenant Commander Edward 'Bickie' Bickford, was universally seen as a man of great integrity with charm and intelligence well above most. According to Bill King,

> As a Lieutenant he was using his first-class brain to fight for the interests of submarines against those surface-ship senior officers who regarded us merely as clockwork mice designed for them to hunt. 'One day you will really need submarines,' Bickie pleaded. 'If you neglect their proper training you won't have them for long.'[1]

Salmon left Rosyth for patrol in the North Sea on 2 December. Little happened until 13:30 on the 4th, when, cruising submerged some 90 miles south of Egersund, First Lieutenant Maurice Wykeham-Martin, who had the watch, called Bickford to the control room. Wykeham-Martin had sighted in the periscope what he believed was a U-boat. Shortly after, the asdic station reported hydrophone effects on the same bearing. They had stumbled across *U36*, under the command of Korvettenkapitän Wilhelm Fröhlich, on her way into the North Sea. Bickford made an instant decision:

Commander George 'Scraper' Phillips (*left*) and Commander Edward 'Bickie' Bickford (*right*). Both just promoted, but not yet wearing their DSOs. At the time, Phillips was 35 and Bickford 30 years old. (S Clewlow)

On going to the periscope, I found the U-boat to be steering approximately 350 degrees, evidently on passage outward bound. I was a long way off track and closed her at full speed and eventually fired at 5,000 yard on 110 degrees track, the salvo being spread at seven-second intervals, torpedoes being set at eight feet. At least one torpedo broke surface and much disturbance was visible on the surface on firing. I lost trim temporarily but regained it in time to be at periscope depth before my shot could have taken effect. I saw her through the periscope blown to small fragments which rose at least 200 feet into the air. I surfaced to pick up survivors but found nothing but oil, wreckage, one dead body and a lifebelt. Bubbles continued to come up from the bottom for some time. Many volunteered to swim out through the oil to retrieve the lifebelt as a memento. I considered this unnecessary and, fearing aircraft and the possible presence of another U-boat, I dived once clear of the oil patch.[2]

Forty German sailors had found an immediate and violent death. This was the first U-boat sunk by a submarine after seven unsuccessful attempts and the expenditure of over twenty torpedoes.

Nine days later, at dawn on 12 December, still in the same general area, *Salmon* was forced to dive just before dawn by a German aircraft. Bickford found it curious that the aircraft should be so far from home so early in the day. The riddle was solved an hour and a half later when the asdic operator reported HEs (hydrophone effects) to the north-east. Coming to periscope depth, a huge liner was seen to cross the stern of *Salmon* at high speed. It was the 51,731-ton German *Bremen*, easily recognised, though painted in drab, grey colours.[3] Bickford turned onto an attack course and studied the liner through the periscope, to see if she carried any offensive armament, while he approached. He could see none, and under orders to sink warships only, Bickford took *Salmon* to the surface:

I decided to surface on a firing course and stop her with my gun with the intention of firing torpedoes if she opened fire on me, or gunning her only if she refused to stop but did not open fire. 09:40, surfaced and made international [signal X for 'stop'] by Aldis lamp five times over the space of a minute. There was no reply and I ordered a round to be fired ahead of her. Just as the gun layer was about to fire, a Dornier DO18 appeared and I was forced to dive.[4]

Bremen was travelling fast and with *Salmon* under water, the distance between them was nearing the limit of effective torpedo range. It would still have been possible to attempt a salvo at the huge target, but Bickford decided he would be 'unjustified in firing torpedoes at her' even if she was under escort by aircraft. *Bremen* had arrived in Murmansk on 6 September, escaping British pickets off Canada on the way home from New York. After a few months in Russia, she departed the Kola Inlet during a snowstorm on 10 December with a minimum crew and unarmed, carrying no war material or troops. Bickford had seen no sign of her being armed or under naval command and, as he had not had the time to fire any warning shots, proper protocol for firing torpedoes had not been met. 'I had no special instructions with reference to intercepting *Bremen*,' Bickford later wrote, 'and considered myself bound by international law, a rigid adherence to which had been specifically stressed to Submarine Commanding Officers at the beginning of the war.' To

Bremen steaming briskly past an escort from 12th A/S Flotilla shortly after having outrun *Salmon*. These escorts could not keep up with *Bremen* and were posted as pickets along the route, listening for submarines and looking out for drifting mines. (Author's Collection)

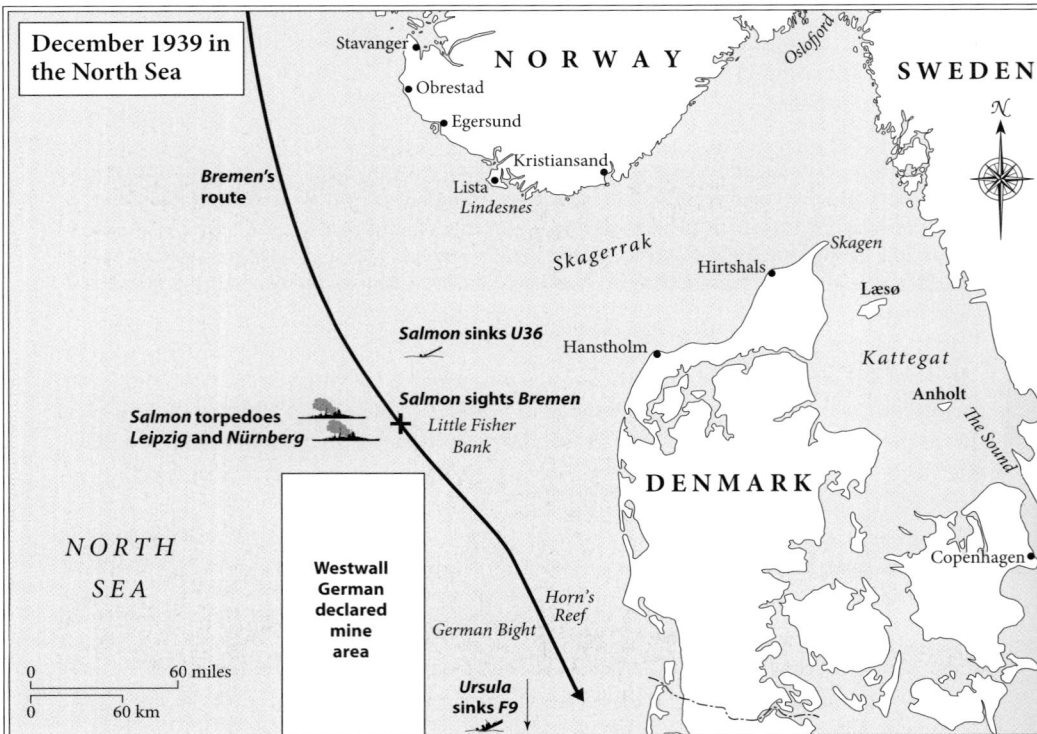

December 1939 in the North Sea

Stavanger
Obrestad
Egersund
Kristiansand
Lista
Lindesnes

NORWAY
Oslofjord
SWEDEN

Bremen's route

Skagerrak

Skagen
Hirtshals
Læsø

Salmon sinks *U36*

Hansholm

Kattegat
Anholt

Salmon sights *Bremen*
Little Fisher Bank

Salmon torpedoes *Leipzig* and *Nürnberg*

DENMARK

The Sound

NORTH SEA

Westwall German declared mine area

Horn's Reef

German Bight

Copenhagen

0   60 miles
0   60 km

Ursula sinks *F9*

his friend Bill King of *Snapper*, however, Bickford was somewhat less politically correct: 'I nearly died of temptation to fire at her,' he said. 'I guessed she must be carrying troops and I itched to torpedo her.'[5]

Instead, *Salmon* surfaced at 10:40, sending a signal to the Admiralty that *Bremen* had been sighted, before continuing the patrol. Shortly after, a signal from the Admiralty to *Ursula* was intercepted, stating that *Bremen* was not a target. Bickford 'felt much relieved'. *Salmon*'s patrol was far from over, but as he had been seen from both the liner and the aircraft, Bickford expected the area to become 'unhealthy' and steered west, towards Great Fisher Bank, where U-boats had lately been observed by British aircraft.[6]

The German light cruisers *Köln*, *Leipzig* and *Nürnberg*, under the command of Konteradmiral Günther Lütjens had left Wilhelmshaven in the morning of 13 December, to meet up with the destroyers *Hermann Künne*, *Friedrich Ihn*, *Erich Steinbrinck*, *Richard Beitzen* and *Bruno Heinemann*, north of the Westwall minefield. The destroyers were on their way back from a mine-laying sortie off Newcastle upon Tyne and the cruisers were to secure their return home, in case British surface forces were in pursuit. The estimated meeting time was around 11:30 German time (GeT). British submarines had been reported in the area, but there were no suitable A/S escorts available for the cruisers, which would

Above: *Leipzig*. *Below*: *Nürnberg*. Both cruisers were commissioned in 1931. They were 8,100 tons, armed with nine 15-cm (5.9-in) guns and capable of 32 knots. (Author's Collection)

have to rely on aircraft and their own speed for security until the destroyers arrived at the meeting point.[7] Lütjens had complained to his superiors at Naval Command West about this, but had been instructed to go ahead with the mission as planned. The report from *Bremen* of having been chased by a submarine the day before was disturbing, but Lütjens expected that it had moved away as its position had been compromised. A second submarine, registered further west from intercepted radio signals, was ignored. At first light, Lütjens grouped his cruisers with *Leipzig* and *Nürnberg* in line-abreast 1,200 metres (1,300 yards) apart, with *Köln* between them, half a mile behind. They were zigzagging with frequent course alterations, changing speed at intervals between 24 and 28 knots.[8]

At first light, two of the cruisers' own scout planes were sent up with orders to stay close to the ships, one on either side of the formation. It was intended to replace these aircraft with seaplanes from the island of List, but snowfall there caused delays and when the scout planes ran low on fuel and had to set course for land, the cruisers were without air escort from about 10:30 German time.

Shortly after the aircraft had left, the Danish steamer *Charkow* came into view. While a prize crew was prepared on board *Leipzig*, it was established that the Dane was on a list of ships approved for transit and Lütjens decided it was not necessary to inspect her after all. The three cruisers continued southwards at 24 knots. At 11:10, a British reconnaissance aircraft was observed, but this stayed outside gunnery range and when two He115s of 1./506 finally arrived from List shortly after, it disappeared. At 11:20, radio contact was established with the five returning destroyers, which at that time were some 40 miles to the west-south-west. Course was set towards them in order to ensure a swift encounter. Shortly after, just as the first destroyer came in sight – at 11:25 German time, according to the cruiser's war diary – a torpedo hit *Leipzig*, amidships on her port side.[9]

On board *Salmon*, First Lieutenant Wykeham-Martin had the watch and subsequently was the one who called Lieutenant Commander Bickford to the periscope. He could

Salmon. (W&L)

see what were undoubtedly German naval ships. The distance was significant, though: almost 11,000 metres (12,000 yards), and Bickford misidentified them as capital ships *Scharnhorst* and *Gneisenau* with cruisers. Most likely he counted the Danish *Charkow* into the group as well. At first, there was little hope of coming into an attack position, but when the German ships turned west-south-west to meet with the destroyers, the situation changed. With some eagerness, Bickford took his submarine closer for an attack:

> 10:36. Fired [six torpedo] salvo at *Leipzig* and *Hipper* [actually *Nürnberg*], the two rear ships, the salvo being spread at eleven second firing intervals. At this moment *Leipzig* was on a 90 degrees track, range 5,000 yards, and *Hipper* [*Nürnberg*] appeared slightly out of station on the starboard quarter of *Leipzig*. I gave their speed as twenty knots, but on further consideration I now think that was under-estimation. I fired a spread salvo with point of aim just ahead of *Leipzig*'s bow with the object of winging two ships rather than sinking one, hoping thus to provoke a fleet action. Went deep and altered course to 90 degrees from firing course at full speed. 10:40. Heard a loud explosion and said, 'that is the *Leipzig*'. 10:41. Heard two loud explosions which were either hits on the third ship or the commencement of depth charging. Until this moment I had been attempting to regain trim for a periscope observation, being very heavy forward after firing (I had flooded 'A' to keep her down). Now, however, I considered it unwise to return to periscope depth as I was still not under slow speed control. So I continued at full speed. 10:46, heard three explosions which were considered to be remainder of the salvo hitting the bottom. [. . .] 10:50. Took evasive action. [. . .] *Salmon* was subsequently depth charged until noon.[10]

The Heinkel aircraft saw the torpedo tracks and one of them dropped two 250-kg bombs where they appeared to come from. Neither of the bombs exploded and it appears they were not registered on board *Salmon*, possibly as they hit the water some distance away from the submarine. While Bickford and his men were struggling to regain control of their boat, the feather of the periscope breaking surface was sighted from the aircraft. Fire was opened during the brief moments it was seen, but this also appears not to have been registered on board *Salmon*. On board *Nürnberg*, what appeared to be the tower of a submarine was seen for about twenty to thirty seconds and fire was opened from the aftermost turret. The detonations of two of these shells were most likely the explosions heard by Salmon at 10:41. Immediately the torpedo hit *Leipzig*, the order 'Hard-a-port' was given and copied to the two other cruisers. Both reacted fast, but not fast enough. One torpedo was seen passing right in front of *Nürnberg*, one hit the cruiser in the bow and three torpedoes were seen passing aft. These three torpedoes were heard to explode in the shallows nearby, matching the observations noted in *Salmon*'s diary at 10:46.[11]

On board *Leipzig*, the torpedo hit amidships just below the waterline at the bulkhead between two of the three boiler rooms. The massive explosion damaged the keel, and part of the armoured deck was bent upwards. Some 1,700 tons of water entered the ship and both boiler rooms were flooded. Eventually, only the auxiliary diesels were functioning, speed being reduced to 12 knots. Most of the ship's electrical power failed, including the rudder engines, making manual steering necessary, severely limiting manoeuvrability. Central gunnery control was gone and all guns, including all A/A guns and main turrets,

The damage to *Leipzig* was extensive. Inside the huge hole in the port side, measuring c. 10 x 5 metres, several 'tweendecks and bulkheads were ripped apart. Also parts of the upper, armoured deck were buckled and cracked. Much of the machinery, boiler and pump systems were also destroyed. (NARA T1022-2794)

would have to operate under local control should she come under attack. *Nürnberg* was less damaged and reported that she was capable of 15–18 knots with good manoeuvrability. Flooding was minimal. The central A/A gunnery control was lost, but local control of the main turrets remained intact. *Köln* had not been hit.[12]

On board the destroyers, it had not been realised that the cruisers were as close as they actually were and when smoke was sighted around 11:30, it was at first believed to stem from a vessel being bombed by aircraft seen shortly before. Only when the emergency signals came from the cruisers with orders to hasten to their assistance did the events emerge. By then, two of the destroyers, *Friedrich Ihn* and *Erich Steinbrinck*, had been dismissed directly to base with engine problems and low fuel reserves respectively. Hence, only three destroyers, *Hermann Künne*, *Richard Beitzen* and *Bruno Heinemann*, closed the cruisers at 13:40. During the manoeuvring to avoid the torpedoes, *Nürnberg* and *Köln* had become separated from *Leipzig*. Lütjens decided they were better off this way and gave orders for *Leipzig* to head independently for home, temporarily assisted by *Charkow*, which was still nearby. The two other cruisers circled to the north, before steering east and then south-east. When the destroyers finally arrived, Lütjens let *Köln* join *Beitzen* and *Heinemann*, standing by *Leipzig*, while *Künne* covered *Nürnberg*. *Charkow* was dismissed. The two groups were in sight but far apart and, due to different speeds, they did not reunite. A couple of aircraft remained above as long as they could.[13]

Bickford believed that *Salmon* was being hunted by the escort and that depth charges were dropped. This was not the case, though, and there is no report from any of the destroyers to this effect. Most likely, besides the shells fired from *Nürnberg*, the explosions of bombs dropped from a few British aircraft attacking *Nürnberg* shortly after were mistaken for depth charges. After a while, things grew quiet and when *Salmon* was back at periscope depth shortly before 15:00, the sea was empty. Reports were duly submitted and, after dark, Bickford surfaced and set course back to the area where the torpedoes had been fired, to search for wreckage. Finding nothing but a large patch of oil, he gave the order to 'splice the mainbrace' and, with no torpedoes left, eventually set course for home.[14]

Early in the morning of the next day, the destroyers *Friedrich Ihn* and *Hermann Schoemann*, coming out from Wilhelmshaven, fell in with *Leipzig* and *Köln*. In addition, the smaller escorts *F7* and *F9* arrived as well as 2nd Minesweeper Flotilla and 1st R-boat Flotilla to assist the cruisers back to safety. Around 10:00, when the new escorts had found their places, Group West ordered *Köln* to proceed at maximum speed to Wilhelmshaven in the company of *Schoemann* and *Ihn*. *Nürnberg* was already far ahead doing 18–20 knots in the company of *Künne*. Trotting along at 12 knots, *Leipzig* was covered by the destroyers *Richard Beitzen* and *Bruno Heinemann*, the escort vessels *F9* and *F7* and the minesweepers *M9*, *M10*, *M12* and *M13*. The R-boats *R33*, *R35*, *R36*, *R37*, *R38* and *R39* were sweeping a wider area around the larger vessels.[15]

The crew of *Salmon*, proudly lining up on deck, coming home from one of the most successful submarine patrols in the early part of the war. Lieutenant Commander Bickford is in the middle. (Royal Navy Submarine Museum Collection)

* * *

A second British submarine, *Shark*, had on the night of 13 December been ordered to proceed through the Westwall to a billet off the Jade River. At 10:45 on the 14th she had passed through the minefield when 'one cruiser and four destroyers' were sighted some eight miles away, off Heligoland. This was undoubtedly *Leipzig*, but Lieutenant Commander Peter Buckley never got close enough to fire his torpedoes. Instead, he had to satisfy himself that some loud explosions heard less than an hour later signified that one of his fellow submarine COs had managed to achieve an attack position.

Indeed, Lieutenant Commander Phillips, already on patrol with *Ursula* south-east of Heligoland, was in luck on this day. In the early morning he had sighted one group of patrol vessels at great distance but decided to let them go, hoping for larger prey. He was to be handsomely rewarded:

> At 11:15 sighted *Köln*-class cruiser and six destroyers [steering south]. *Ursula* was ahead of the leading ship of the port column. It was not certain at first whether *Ursula* was immediately ahead of the enemy or astern, and course was altered towards the formation. [. . .] Getting dangerously close to the leading destroyer, went to 50 feet and turned in under her on to the firing course. At this stage of the attack, the asdic was invaluable as it indicated that the turn had to be made quicker than was anticipated [. . .] to get an accurately aimed shot instead of firing on the swing. At 11:31 fired 4 torpedoes at 6

Ursula. (Real Photographs)

seconds interval, range 1,200, estimated speed 16 knots. 1 minute 10 seconds after firing a tremendous explosion occurred, followed 6 seconds later by another even heavier. [. . .] This explosion broke electric lights in the submarine. Hydrophone effects from the target stopped immediately and was succeeded by various noises described by the operator as 'like nothing he had ever heard in his life'.[16]

Unknown to Phillips, the torpedoes had all missed the cruiser. The starboard bow escort, *F9*, had been hit though, possibly by two torpedoes, and was sinking fast. She capsized rapidly to port and the broken-off stern stood solemnly vertical for about twenty seconds before the escort had completely disappeared. At the time she was hit, *F9* was 600–800 metres (660–875 yards) ahead of *Leipzig* and at least one torpedo track was observed crossing the bow of the cruiser. In all likelihood, Phillips overestimated the speed of the German warships, which were doing no more than 12 knots due to *Leipzig*'s damage. After firing, Phillips dived to 20 metres (65 feet) and brazenly kept *Ursula* moving at slow speed towards the last position of the cruiser. This seems to have outsmarted the destroyers *Beitzen* and *Heinemann* that came searching for her as they never gained contact and no depth charges were dropped, reflecting the lack of A/S practice common to German destroyers at the start of the war. Eventually, only one depth charge was registered on board *Ursula*. According to the war diary of 2nd Minesweeping Flotilla, *M12* dropped a few depth charges on what was believed to be a contact. Only one of the depth charges exploded, though, and no success was observed. Lütjens later wrote in *Leipzig*'s war diary that in his opinion:

the fact that there could be a second submarine attack at all was largely due to the inadequate anti-submarine tactics of the escort. The individual vessels – in particular the destroyers – had repeatedly to be ordered to increase their speed, to steer a zigzag

F9. One of ten so-called *Flottenbegleiter* (fleet escorts) commissioned between 1935 and 1938. These were among the least successful German naval vessels. Poorly designed, with unreliable technical systems, they saw very little service and spent most of the early war taking up resources in the yards until taken out of service altogether. (Author's Collection)

course and to search their sectors more closely, without wandering too far off. Too often, the ships would move at low speed on parallel courses. It looked as if the escort felt *too* sure and did not really believe there could be another attack. In contrast to this, the R-boats – in spite of the, for them, uncomfortably rough seas – performed their tasks eagerly without having to be advised. After the attack the vessels on the starboard side of the screen, from where the torpedoes appeared to have come, scattered about, but failed to locate the submarine. Thus, the starboard side of *Leipzig* was at times left unprotected. After a period of futile search, the escort vessels had to be ordered by radio to start dropping depth charges to scare the submarine away. In spite of this order, however, only *one* depth charge explosion was registered. In short, it must be concluded that the escort vessels had not proved themselves equal to their task.[17]

A total of 120 men of *F9*'s crew went down with her; only fifteen men were pulled out of the water alive. The two R-boats *R36* and *R38* were left behind looking for survivors while the others hastened away towards the safety of the Elbe estuary. Group West wanted *Leipzig* to head directly for the yards in Wilhelmshaven, but Lütjens ignored this and steered for the nearest safe haven to the east, to avoid passing any more loitering submarines. The conditions on board *Leipzig* were becoming challenging and he did not want to push his luck any further.

Some forty-five minutes after firing his torpedoes, Phillips took *Ursula* to periscope depth. He could see the two R-boats, but nothing more and withdrew westwards, believing he had sunk a cruiser.

The SKL concluded from the episode that the Royal Navy had intensified their efforts in the German Bight inside the Westwall. Hence, larger warships should not operate in the southern and central North Sea any longer, as there was all the more reason to believe they would have even more submarines there. Furthermore, they agreed with Lütjens that the A/S capacity of the escorts in general was unsatisfactory, and, so far in the war, not a single British submarine was known to have been damaged, far less sunk, with certainty. From now on, anti-submarine efforts should be intensified; it was, as a minimum, expected that ships in the German Bight should be safe from British submarine attacks.[18] Captain Philip Ruck-Keene of the 3rd Flotilla wrote:

> It is impossible to speak too highly of the Captain Officers and crew of the *Salmon*. At first sight it may appear that luck and good fortune played a large part; undoubtedly the opportunities were there, but the way in which they were exploited and the whole conduct of the patrol is an example to submarine officers for all time. Small touches in the narrative, which might be unnoticed except by a submarine officer, reveal the hand of the artist. If he had not made the instant decision which he acted on at full speed, the attack on the U-boat would never have been possible, the exactly correct and imprudent action in the attempt to stop the *Bremen* shows resource and initiative at its best, only possible by someone who has thought deeply on all phases of submarine war. There can be no doubt that two cruisers were hit. [. . .] I consider that this officer should be immediately promoted to the rank of Commander. Recommendations for decorations [. . .] are attached.[19]

Big words, but in almost all contemporaneous accounts, these episodes are seen as a watershed when the British submariners started to feel they were able to hit back. Their

Lieutenant Commander Phillips of *Ursula*, wearing an early version of the *Ursula* suit, is informing Captain 'Jock' Bethel of the patrol. (S Clewlow)

The crew of *Ursula* being welcomed home by wives and girlfriends. (S Clewlow)

fellow captains were full of envy for the chances Bickford and Phillips had had, but also of the way they had handled the opportunities. Both were awarded the DSO and promoted to commanders, while *Salmon*'s First Lieutenant Wykeham-Martin was awarded the DSC. Several POs and ratings on board both submarines also received orders or a mention in dispatches.[20]

Churchill was most enthusiastic and announced in a radio broadcast on 18 December that a 6,000-ton German cruiser had been sunk. For *Salmon* and *Ursula*, he staged a heroes' welcome with families and girlfriends waiting quayside when the two submarines returned home – with press and photographers to record it all. In fact, both cruisers managed to limp home, but went straight for the yards, where they would stay for a long time. *Leipzig* would never become fully operational again and ended up as a training ship in the Baltic.

Bickford was invited to London for lunch with the First Lord to give his story first-hand. After the meeting, Churchill took Bickford aside and suggested he should spend some time ashore, both to let officers of the Admiralty benefit from his experiences and to give him and his crew a rest. He also suggested that *Salmon* should go to Devonport as an extra training submarine for a few months.[21] Nevertheless, when *Salmon* left for her next patrol, Bickford was on the bridge. *Salmon* was lost with all hands in July 1940 (see page 349).[22]

— 10 —

Something Less Than God

A FEW WEEKS INTO the war, questions arose as to the proper use of the British and Allied submarines. Little had been achieved, and compared to the aggressive use the Germans made of their boats, British tactics looked tame. During October, discussions were initiated in the Admiralty and there were numerous suggestions. Admiral Dunbar-Nasmith, C-in-C Plymouth and Western Approaches Command, argued for a flotilla of submarines to be stationed in the south-west to hunt U-boats in the Atlantic off Ireland. Others wanted submarines as convoy escorts or blockading neutral ports in Spain and the West Indies where German merchant ships had sought refuge.

First Lord Winston Churchill wished to take the initiative and be aggressive. The challenge at this stage of the war was the small number of German ships at sea, outside the Baltic, the Skagerrak and the Kattegat. Hence, Churchill instructed the Admiralty to consider sending a naval force, including three old battleships, an aircraft carrier and five cruisers supported by destroyers, submarines and auxiliaries, into the Baltic – Operation Catherine. The strategic gain of such a show of force, besides cutting off German iron-ore supplies, would, in Churchill's opinion, be to have the Scandinavian countries join the war against Germany. The logistics of Operation Catherine would be awesome, however, not to mention the risk that probably none of the ships involved would come back out again as long as the war lasted – if ever. First Sea Lord Admiral Dudley Pound was very much against the plan as the ships and resources, in his opinion, were needed elsewhere and the loss of such a large force of ships would cripple the Royal Navy. Rear Admiral Watson also opposed the plan, believing his submariners needed far more experience and adaptation to war before being sent into such alien waters. Churchill pushed hard for Catherine through the autumn, but the opposition remained strong and, in January 1940, the operation was shelved.

Rear Admiral Watson never had a good rapport with Churchill, and his reluctance to support Operation Catherine widened the gap. After the complete failure of British submarines to intercept *Scharnhorst* and *Gneisenau* in late November, after the battleships had sunk the Armed Merchant Cruiser *Rawalpindi*, Watson's time was up. Churchill contacted Vice Admiral Max Kennedy Horton, at the time C-in-C Northern Patrol, offering him the job as head of submarines. Horton, himself an old submariner, was delighted to accept and on 9 January 1940 he was appointed Vice Admiral Submarines, VA(S).

The post of Flag Officer Submarines was normally held by a rear admiral, but a new Admiralty regulation that the post should be held by an officer who had served in submarines at war limited the choice substantially. Persistent rumours had it that the desire of some within the Admiralty to have Horton revitalise the Submarine Service was so great that the regulation was introduced in order to ensure Horton was the only real contender for the post. Horton was only too happy to be back with submarines, provided he would be given the 'free hand' promised him by Admiral Pound.[1]

Admirals Max Horton (*left*) and John Tovey (*right*). The photo is taken on 28 September 1942. At the time, Tovey was C-in-C Home Fleet while Horton was A(S), Admiral (Submarines), having been promoted to full admiral in January 1941. Less than two months after the photo was taken, Horton was appointed C-in-C Western Approaches Command. (IWM A12102)

* * *

With this appointment, one of the Royal Navy's most experienced submariners had been put in exactly the right place. When WWI had broken out in 1914, Horton was commander of *E9*, an 800-ton submarine operating in the Heligoland Bight. On patrol, his crew knew him as cold-blooded, composed and imperturbable. On 13 September, only a few weeks into the war, Horton had *E9* approach the entry to Heligoland harbour in thick fog. As the fog lifted, he submerged and, shortly after, the light cruiser *Hela* appeared in his periscope. Horton fired two torpedoes and dived deep. When the torpedoes were heard to explode he came up again to have a look and saw the cruiser sink. The periscope of *E9* was sighted, though, and it took almost twenty-four hours to get away from the German escorts that hunted him with guns and depth charges.

This was the first time ever that a British submarine had sunk an enemy ship: elated, Horton was flying a small home-made 'Jolly Roger' when he returned to Harwich, initiating a new tradition. Indeed, it was a game-changing event in naval strategy, but one that was missed by most – even the Lords of the Admiralty. Big guns would still reign supreme, in spite of their extreme vulnerability to the torpedoes of a small but determined submarine.[2]

In September 1915, it was decided to send a British submarine flotilla to the Baltic to assist the Russian Fleet there preventing the German iron-ore imports from Sweden. Eleven boats were sent: seven E-class and four C-class. One was lost during transit and one was damaged and had to return, but the other nine operated with quite some success against the German traffic from Sweden.[3] It also kept a significant German naval presence in the Baltic, to protect their trade routes and training grounds. Horton took *E9* safely through the Belts and, along with several other submariners, made a name for himself sinking several merchant ships as well as the torpedo boat *S148* and damaging the German cruiser *Prinz Adalbert*. In December 1914, aged 31, Horton was promoted to commander.

Returning from Russia in 1915, Horton was appointed to command the new 1,200-ton *J6*, with which he made a number of demanding but uneventful patrols in the North Sea. Later, Horton was selected to command and supervise the building of the experimental submarine *M1*, which was armed with a 12-inch gun in a turret. By the time she was operational, the war was almost over and Horton never tested his new command at war. Instead, he was appointed to the *Maidstone* and sent back to the Baltic with a submarine flotilla to assist the smaller states there against Russian aggression. In the spring of 1920, the situation in the Baltic had settled and the British naval forces were called home – Horton with a second bar to his DSO.

In 1922, Horton was appointed to the cruiser *Conquest* and given command of a flotilla of K-class submarines in the Atlantic. There ensued some years of shore service at the Admiralty and as Chief of Staff to Admiral Keyes at Portsmouth before he was given command of the battleship *Resolution* and sent to the Mediterranean. On 17 October 1932, Horton was promoted to rear admiral and given command of the 2nd Battle Squadron with his flag on board *Malaya*. In this function, he was also second-in-command of the Home Fleet. Three years later, he shifted to 1st Cruiser Squadron and moved his flag to the cruiser *London*. This took him again to the Mediterranean and the Spanish Civil War. Promoted to vice admiral in 1936, he left active service for some time before taking up command of the Reserve Fleet in 1937.

With the onset of WWII, the 140 vessels of the Reserve Fleet were to be integrated into the Royal Navy, a process made very much easier by Horton's energy and inspiration. His task completed, Horton was given command of the re-established Northern Patrol, enforcing British control of the sea lanes between Greenland, Iceland and the Faeroes.[4]

Horton had proven his worth as a submarine commander and his unquestionable courage and competence created confidence in most of those that served under him. In October 1907, while Horton was a lieutenant and commander of *A1*, his commanding officer wrote: 'Good at his boat and bad socially. Made very good attacks in *A.1*. Always supposed to be very good at engines. Troublesome in the mess – insubordinate to First Lieutenant. Bad language – but extremely intelligent.'[5]

Horton was a complex man: a lone wolf, ruthless and blunt to the point of rudeness; yet he cared for his men in an extraordinary way. One minute, he could strip a submarine captain of his command and send him to an escort vessel in the Atlantic, the next he could send signals like the one he sent to Captain George Voelcker, C-in-C 6th Flotilla, on 5 June 1940:

> My warmest congratulations are to be conveyed to the Commanding Officer HMS *Narwhal* [Lieutenant Commander Ronald Burch] on his conduct of a patrol which not only included minelaying under difficult conditions but also the undoubted infliction of considerable damage on an enemy convoy. The officers and ships company are also to be commended for their admirable conduct under trying circumstances during the depth charge attack on the 1st May.[6]

Honest mistakes were tolerated if confessed to immediately, but woe betide any subordinate who was caught in neglect or trying to bluff a higher competence than acquired. Commander Denys Rayner of the corvette *Verbena* wrote:

Horton's own staff regarded him as something less than God but more than Man. If they had not done so they would have found themselves relieved. He had more personal charm than any man I ever met, but he could be unbelievably cruel to those who fell by the wayside.[7]

Horton made up his mind regarding a subordinate in minutes, and unless favourable, he ruthlessly replaced those he considered unskilled for the job at hand. Frequently accused of being intolerant and inflexible, his callousness and rough manners annoyed many fellow officers who often held that similar results to those he undoubtedly obtained could have been achieved with less rigorous methods. There is absolutely no doubt though that, as an ex-submariner, he had the well-being of his men at the top of his list. A submarine commander wrote:

> I know he spent many miserable hours thinking about us, and he was terribly cut up when a submarine was lost. He would not show it, but would concentrate on the job even more fiercely than usual. He wished to make certain that training and good material would minimise future losses.[8]

As Vice Admiral Submarines, Horton was responsible to the Admiralty for the general administration of the Submarine Service. Operationally, however, he was only responsible for those submarines allocated to the Home Fleet, operating in the North Sea and the Atlantic, as the submarines in the Mediterranean and Far East were subordinated to the local C-in-Cs in those areas. Thus, in operational matters Horton reported to C-in-C Home Fleet, Admiral Forbes.

Nevertheless, Horton felt that Aberdour was too far from the Admiralty because an efficient use of his submarines required close co-operation with the Naval Staff and above all the aircraft of the Coastal Command, more than the surface ships of the Home Fleet. Hence, at the end of March 1940, Horton moved his headquarters from Aberdour to Northways, a converted set of flats near Swiss Cottage in north London, far enough from the Admiralty to give him a free hand, and close enough for day-to-day contact with the Naval Staff and the Coastal Command. Still he was in regular contact with the Home Fleet and now for all practical purposes no further away than he had been at Aberdour. The submarine staffs were moved up from Gosport, initiating a very efficient headquarters for the service.[9] A staff officer wrote:

> Max frequently visited the flotillas and his presence and bearing inspired them. He was a tiger to his staff, and we realised it within a few hours of his joining. But a tiger in whom we all had supreme confidence, and though he could and did bite hard when bites were needed, and though his growl was exceedingly fierce, to the trained ear that growl had a distinct note of friendliness on many occasions. His staff had to know their job or had to quickly learn it. If a mistake were made and frankly confessed with full reasons for making it, Max would be as tolerant as anyone, provided the mistake was not made through slackness. He worked hard himself, very hard, but he rightly saw to it that his staff worked harder. Yet he did not *make* work and was very critical of any actions by his staff that might lead to making unnecessary work. He had always kept in close touch with the Submarine Service and had a tremendous store of submarine knowledge and experience. Within a few days, he was able to pick up the threads of all submarine matters and quickly spanned the interval that had

elapsed since he was last an active submariner [as flotilla captain in 1925]. He would personally delve into the minutest problem connected with submarines, and woes betide any officer who tried to bluff that he had more knowledge of a subject than he in fact had. When any signal was received requiring action, no matter how trivial or without urgency, it was a cardinal maxim that the action required should be initiated at once.[10]

Above all, the move and reorganisation created a vital co-operation with the Coastal Command. Horton and the C-in-C Frederick Bowhill met regularly, creating an excellent rapport, and naval liaison officers were placed at the staff of Coastal Command.

Within a few weeks of his arrival, Horton initiated a major shake-up of the senior personnel of the Submarine Service, later to be known as 'Horton's Purge'. Captain Stephens of the 2nd Flotilla was unceremoniously replaced by Captain George 'Colonel' Menzies at the end of January, while some twenty commanders considered unsuited or too old were moved from their boats to other jobs. The vacant spaces were filled with younger men who had been waiting in the wings as there had been no boats available for them after they had completed their perisher course. Many of those purged by Horton later delivered sterling service in staff positions or commanding smaller surface vessels.[11]

Rear Admiral Reginald Darke, C-in-C of the Submarine Depot at Fort Blockhouse, Gosport wrote: 'As Flag Officer Submarines, Max was superb in his operational and

Admiral Horton talking to Polish Naval officers Kapitan Marynarki Borys Karnicki (DSO) and Kapitan Marynarki Jerzy Koziolkowski (DSC) on 28 July 1942 at the Admiralty in London. Both have just received their awards. (IWM A11109)

administrative actions. He had an intuition of what the Hun would do, which was quite uncanny. As an instance, I take the German invasion of Norway.'[12] The intuition was undoubtedly backed up by a large amount of information and logical analysis.

Having declined the offer to take command of the Home Fleet in October 1940, Horton was nevertheless promoted to full admiral on 9 January 1941. On 17 November 1942 he was appointed Commander-in-Chief, Western Approaches to fight the German U-boat menace.[13]

Negative Flag

HORTON'S ARRIVAL AT ABERDOUR coincided with one of the worst disasters of the British submarine command in the first part of the war and a major success for the German anti-submarine forces. The submarines *Unity*, *Undine*, *Seahorse* and *Starfish* had all sailed at the end of December or beginning of January to patrol in the Horns Reef–Heligoland Bight area, east of the German Declared Area. All four submarines had similar basic instructions: to pass north of the Declared Area into Zone E between the northern part of the minefield and the coast of Denmark and operate north-west of Horns Reef. After two days there, they should proceed southwards into Zone B, off Heligoland, operate there for four to five days, and then return to Zone E, again along a different route. After a further two to three days in Zone E, course was to be set for home. Each submarine would be followed by another, with a few days between them, in a rotational system. The area between Heligoland and the mouths of the rivers Jade, Weser and Elbe was not suitable for sustained submarine patrols, owing to the high number of German vessels in the area making surfacing to charge the batteries virtually impossible. Hence, this area and the shallow waters off Esbjerg were to be avoided.

Unity returned to Blyth as planned on 5 January. *Seahorse* should have been back on 10 January. She was not, and as no signal of delay was received, anxiety rose. The other submarines on the route, *Undine*, *Ursula* and *Starfish*, were ordered to leave the area east of the Declared Area as soon as they could and not enter if they had not yet done so. *Ursula* remained to the north, did not enter Zone E and returned as expected on 24 January. Nothing was heard from *Ursula* and *Starfish*. On Tuesday 16 January the Admiralty declared that *Seahorse*, *Undine* and *Starfish* had been lost.

Undine. (W&L)

Seahorse in October 1933. (W&L)

At first it was believed that the losses might be connected to extensive new German minefields, possibly linked to hydrophones or controlled from land or guard vessels, or to some new kind of weapon. As we know today, however, it was just plain bad luck, along with some unfortunate decisions and a pinch of misjudgement.[1]

Lieutenant Commander Alan Jackson took his submarine *Undine* from Blyth on her fourth war patrol on 31 December 1939. Shortly after departing, it was found that her asdic was not functioning properly: the dome in which it was housed had flooded. The asdic had just been overhauled and the leak most likely stemmed from a faulty rubber seal, not properly fitted when assembling the dome again. Jackson decided that he could carry out the patrol satisfactorily without the asdic and continued towards the northern end of Zone E, off Horns Reef. Nothing happened there and, following orders, he continued into Zone B after a few days. At 09:50 on 7 January, some 10 miles west-south-west of Heligoland, two German mine-sweeping trawlers were sighted, about a mile away. Jackson immediately prepared for an attack. There had been significant disagreement among the submarine commanders regarding the merit of attacking trawlers and other small auxiliary vessels. In spite of repeated requests for an official view on the issue, instructions from RA(S) Watson were ambiguous. Nonetheless, Jackson moved *Undine* into position and fired one torpedo at the leading trawler on a 90-degree track. It missed astern by a few metres, the trawler's speed having been underestimated. Without showing the periscope again, Jackson turned *Undine* westwards, attempting to sneak away with all machinery stopped.[2]

In fact *Undine* had run into the minesweepers *M1204 Anna Busse* and *M1203 Bürgermeister Schmidt* of the 12th Minesweeper Flotilla and the torpedo had been aimed at *M1204*.[3] Retaliation was swift, and minutes later there were several explosions as the minesweepers threw their first depth charges. *Undine* was in less than 30 metres of water, trying to creep away some 20 metres below the surface, almost blind due to the loss of the asdic and the poor quality of the hydrophones. After a while, the attacks stopped and Jackson started to hope he might have escaped:

> A period of complete quiet followed for about five minutes. Thinking there might be a possibility of attacking again or that the enemy had broken off the hunt, I returned to periscope depth and raised the Low Power Periscope, to look directly at a trawler on the starboard beam, so close that I could see only her port side from the bridge to the aft end of the engine room casing. I immediately ordered 'Down periscope, 60 feet', but before the submarine had really started to go down there were three violent explosions, one aft, one forward and another. (I was informed recently by Leading Telegraph Monserrat that he heard a noise on the port side of the Control Room which sounded like a depth charge scraping the pressure hull, but I have no personal recollection of this.) The submarine was blown upwards, some lights and glass broken, there was a steady leak in the engine room from near the hatch, a leak in the galley and I was later informed that the Fore End had flooded and had to be abandoned. Both sets of hydroplanes were reported out of action, (the fore hydroplanes hard-a-rise) but the after hydroplanes appeared to be working. I ordered 'Take her down, flood o' but the submarine continued to rise until the periscope standards broke surface, giving many of the crew the impression that the drop keel had fallen off. I therefore raised the Low Power Periscope and saw a trawler bows-on on the starboard beam at a range of approximately half a mile. Considering that it was impossible to get the submarine down again to a safe depth before being rammed, I ordered 'Surface, burn the [Confidential Books], prepare the charge' and went to the bridge, followed by the Leading Signalman who acting on my orders, waved the Negative Flag, which was the best substitute for a white flag available.[4]

Undine was not fitted with a gun and could not fight back. First Lieutenant Mike Harvey opened the main vents before he abandoned ship, as the scuttling charges were not accessible due to the flooding. Lieutenant Commander Jackson ordered 'abandon ship', and the men started to muster on the fore-casing before going into the water. Even though the German gunners continued to fire enthusiastically a short time after the flag of surrender had been shown, all the crew were able to leave the boat and were rescued from the freezing cold waters.

Meanwhile, a third minesweeper, *M1201 Harvestehude*, with the flotilla commander Kapitänleutnant Fritz Petzel on board, arrived at the scene, taking command. *Undine* was still afloat and some men, led by Petzel, went on board to retrieve as much confidential material as possible, stop the engines and close vents and hatches in an attempt to save the boat from sinking.

While they were below, *M1201* managed to get a towing hawser attached, but it was too late. Petzel and his men were forced back up due to chlorine gas leaking from the flooded batteries, without achieving much; all the more so as confidential papers had been burnt. Some of the minesweeper crew boarded *Undine* a second time with gas-masks and flashlights, but as soon as the engines were stopped, the submarine sank.[5]

As *Undine* went down, it could be seen that at least one of the fore hydroplanes had been locked in hard-a-rise position by one of the exploding depth charges, explaining why she had been forced to the surface. Jackson and his crew spent the rest of the war in German POW camps.[6]

The sinking of *Undine* was the first documented success of the Kriegsmarine against the British submarines and it was noted in the war diary of the SKL that it was about time, as they had started doubting the efficiency of their own A/S flotillas.[7]

At 13:18 on 7 January 1940, ships of the German 1st Minesweeper Flotilla sighted a submarine on the surface some 20 miles west of Heligoland. By the time they arrived at the location, the submarine had dived, but some eight or ten depth charges were dropped. No effects were seen on the surface, but noises were heard through the hydrophones and a buoy was dropped to mark the search area. A dozen more depth charges were dropped, after which no further contacts were obtained. During the afternoon, a heavy fog set in and the ships returned to Wilhelmshaven, leaving one minesweeper behind at anchor during the night. Several sources hold that this submarine was *Seahorse* and that it is likely that she was sunk by the minesweepers. A detailed analysis of the known facts made by Robert Coppock of the Naval Historical Branch in 1985 gave another, much more likely story.

Lieutenant Dennis Massy-Dawson took *Seahorse* to sea from Blyth in the afternoon of 26 December. Following the routine, he was to head for Zone E north-west of Horns Reef,

Submariners from *Seahorse* in 1938. (Author's Collection)

passing well north of the German Westwall minefield or Declared Area. After midnight on 29/30 December, he was to continue south, into Zone B west of Heligoland keeping east of the longitude 7°E. After midnight on 4 January, *Seahorse* was to return to Zone E, keeping to the west of 7°E, and from there to Blyth where she was due back on 10 January. *Seahorse* did not return as planned though, and nothing was ever heard from her.[8]

In parallel with establishing the Westwall, half a dozen anti-submarine minefields were laid inside the Bight, west and north of Heligoland. The mines of these fields were laid in dense stripes and moored quite deep so that surface ships could pass safely over them, while submarines would be at severe risk if they passed through. If a mine was not hit directly, there was a good chance one of the retaining wires would be snagged by the submarine; the mine's anchor would hold firm and the mine would be pulled towards the boat. By 15 September 1939 more than 2,700 anti-submarine mines had been laid inside what was known to the British submariners as Zone B. It has not been possible to find firm evidence of how well the Admiralty and RA(S) were aware of these minefields and their locations. Coppock in his analysis states that 'Admiralty intelligence in the above-mentioned minefields was lacking.' He added that:

> *Ursula* had earlier reported a probable searched channel between Heligoland and the chartered position of the Vyl Lightship. Whereas this information was passed to the *Seahorse* without any instructions on how to approach Heligoland should she decide to do so, the *Undine* and *Starfish* were directed that should they operate near Heligoland they were to approach and leave along a line between Heligoland and Vyl Lightship [off Esbjerg]. This line, as it happened, ran to the eastward of the minefields, which meant that both *Undine* and *Starfish* kept clear of them when moving from zone E to Zone B. [. . .] *Unity*'s captain, who similarly was informed of the probable existence of the searched channel but also given no directive, chose to approach the latitude of Heligoland much further to the westward . . . contrary to her patrol orders.[9]

On 13 September, 960 UMA mines were laid by the minelayers *Cobra*, *Kaiser*, *Roland* and *Hansestadt Danzig* in a field known as 'Sperre b Martha Eins' – 'Stripe b Martha One'. This was due west of Esbjerg and Horns Reef, just north of the boundary between the British Zones E and B. Water depth at this location is around 30 metres (100 feet) and stripe b would have made a 20-nautical-mile broad wall, two to four rows deep, almost impenetrable for a submerged submarine. Some 70 miles further south, stripe f – with over 600 mines – made a similar barrier; further south yet was stripe d.[10]

In all likelihood Lieutenant Massy-Dawson, according to orders, set course from the billet north-west of Horns Reef towards Zone B during 29 December, some miles to the east of 7°E. If so, *Seahorse* would be on a course straight into several anti-submarine minefields. Following the instruction to pass into Zone B just after midnight on the 29th, *Seahorse* would likely have passed the area of stripe b at dusk (and hence still submerged), planning to come to the surface at nightfall. If stripe b was crossed on the surface at night, stripes f and d would have been approached submerged during daylight the following day. Hence, the likelihood of *Seahorse* encountering one of the mines in stripe b, stripe f or stripe d is considerable – either directly or pulling one towards her by snagging the mooring line.

Starfish in July 1937. Note the camouflage paint, which she did not carry by January 1940. Also note the man in the dinghy and the collapsible crane used to lower the float into the water after it has been inflated and retrieved when the job was done. (R Perkins)

To date, the wreck of *Seahorse* has not been located. It is, however, very likely that she is to be found somewhere north of Heligoland, to the east of 7°E. Five officers and thirty-four ratings remain on board *Seahorse*.[11]

*   *   *

The third submarine lost in this dramatic period was *Starfish*. Lieutenant Thomas Turner took her to sea from Blyth on 5 January on his sixth war patrol. At 09:30 British time (BrT) on 9 January, in Zone B, west of Heligoland, he sighted and attacked what he believed to be a German destroyer. The attack failed due to faulty drill and the torpedoes remained in the tubes when Turner gave the order to fire. Going back up to periscope depth to prepare for a second attack, Turner found the target, the minesweeper *M7*, lying stopped less than 100 metres (110 yards) away.

The crew of *M7* had located *Starfish* on their S-Gerät only minutes after Turner had seen them through his periscope. The periscope of *Starfish* was seen 10:53 GeT (09:53 BrT) only 70 metres (75 yards) ahead and Oberleutnant Heinrich Timm did not hesitate:

> Full speed ahead was ordered and rudder given to run over the position where the periscope had been sighted. Two depth charges were dropped over the stern, but due to a miscommunication the throwers were not fired. The S-Gerät operator reported that he still had the echo and three buoys were dropped to mark the site. At 11:40 [GeT] six depth charges were dropped in a second attack. No result observed. At 12:56, two more charges were dropped inside the marked area. After this, the increasing state of the sea limited the use of the S-Gerät.[12]

The explosions from the two first depth charges, which occurred as *Starfish* was levelling off at 20 metres (65 feet), cut the power to both of *Starfish*'s hydroplanes. They froze in a 15-degree rise position. Turner stopped the motors and let water into the A, Q and Z ballast tanks, taking his boat to the bottom to see if they could be reactivated. The water depth was about 30 metres (100 feet). *Starfish* settled on a level keel and orders were given for complete silence while repairs were attempted to the hydroplanes.

Turner, as most submarine commanders, had been thoroughly informed of the experiences of sister-ship *Spearfish* some months earlier and considered the best tactic would be to get under way in order to evade further attacks. Hence, when the electrician asked for permission to restart one of the Sperry motors to prevent the gyro from wandering while they were lying still, permission was granted. Shortly after, four depth charges exploded fairly close, causing widespread damage. Turner assumed the noise from the Sperry motor had been giving *Starfish*'s position away and decided to turn it off again and remain on the bottom in silence until dark. There was no way of course he could have known that, by doing so, he remained inside the area *M7* had marked with buoys on the surface.

Oberleutnant Timm waited patiently above, knowing that for the time being he had the upper hand. Very well aware that the British submarine still had sharp fangs, he changed course and speed constantly and the gun crews were kept at high alert, should the enemy attempt to surface or fire torpedoes from periscope depth. A few depth charges were dropped at times when the S-Gerät operator reported a reasonably confident position of the submarine. It is notable that not once during this period was any oil seen on the surface. The hull of *Starfish* remained intact and the fuel tanks were well protected on the inside.

Around 15:00, sea conditions had improved and some twenty depth charges were dropped in two attacks. Some of the charges exploded fairly close to the submarine and this time, the damage was very serious. Rivets in the pressure hull were sheared and seams cracked in several places. Heavy leaks were caused in the fore end and air bubbles could be seen on the surface, pinpointing the location of *Starfish* to those above. Several new buoys were dropped, some with lights attached, as daylight was fading. The leaks could not be stopped, and by 18:00, the situation inside *Starfish* had become critical. Both torpedo trenches and bilges were nearly full, while water was lapping the starboard main motor casing. The German adversary was not likely to leave and the chances of *Starfish* escaping were dwindling by the minute. At 18:20 (BrT), Turner gave the order to surface.

Above, *M5* had come to the assistance of *M7* and the two minesweepers pinned *Starfish* down with their searchlights as soon as she surfaced. A few machine-gun bursts were fired to let the submariners realise they were trapped, but they were wide of the bridge and no one was hurt. Turner realised his plan of sneaking away on the surface had failed and he saw no other option but to scuttle his boat. Orders were given to flood the main ballast tanks one side and throw all confidential papers overboard while a white flag was raised. Once this happened, no further machine guns were fired. A dozen men who jumped into the water were picked up by a buoy-boat, while *M7* came alongside, taking the rest directly on board in spite of the submarine listing heavily as the ballast tanks filled. *Starfish* sank before it was possible for any of the Germans to get on board.[13]

*   *   *

German minesweeper *M7* of the M35 class. At 682 tons, these boats were versatile and fast, capable of over 18 knots. They were also well armed and carried a large number of depth charges, making them a feared opponent for the Allied submarines. Fortunately for them, there were few of them around and they were constantly in demand for escort, mine-sweeping and mine-laying missions. (Author's Collection)

The loss of the three boats within a week naturally caused deep concern in Submarine Command. For a while, there was fear that some kind of new enemy weapon system had been adopted or a kind of trap had been instigated. In fact, though, both *Undine* and *Starfish* were lost from a combination of inexperience and foolhardy attacks on manoeuvrable A/S vessels in shallow waters. The only new element was the German A/S tactic of stopping and listening, confusing the submarine captains, who were used to different tactics when exercising with British vessels. The German hydrophones and echo detection sets worked best when the ships were stopped or moving at very slow speed. Early in the war, only a limited number of vessels in each flotilla had been equipped with hydrophones, giving instructions to the others. The German echo-sounding system was more primitive than the British asdic, but technically complicated and sensitive to water conditions. It was generally used for direction and ranging purposes after contact had been obtained through hydrophones. In addition, it needed to be shut off at intervals to reset.

As a consequence of the losses in January the patrols in the western Skagerrak, off the Dutch coast and to the west of the Westwall were strengthened, while those to the east of the German Declared Area were suspended for the time being. VA(S) informed the Admiralty and the C-in-C Home Fleet that he did not intend to send further submarines east of the German Declared Area, into Zone B and Zone E – except in an emergency to intercept verified German ships – until more information on the conditions in this area had been obtained. Furthermore, he added, no submarine would be sent into any zone previously occupied by another submarine until the latter

British Submarines lost in January 1940

DENMARK

Seahorse sunk

Zone E
Zone B

*North
Sea*

Westwall
German
declared
mine
area

Starfish sunk

Heligoland

7° E

Undine sunk

Cuxhaven

Hamburg

Wilhelmshaven •   • Bremerhaven

• Bremen

NETHERLANDS   G E R M A N Y

0   40 miles
0   40 km

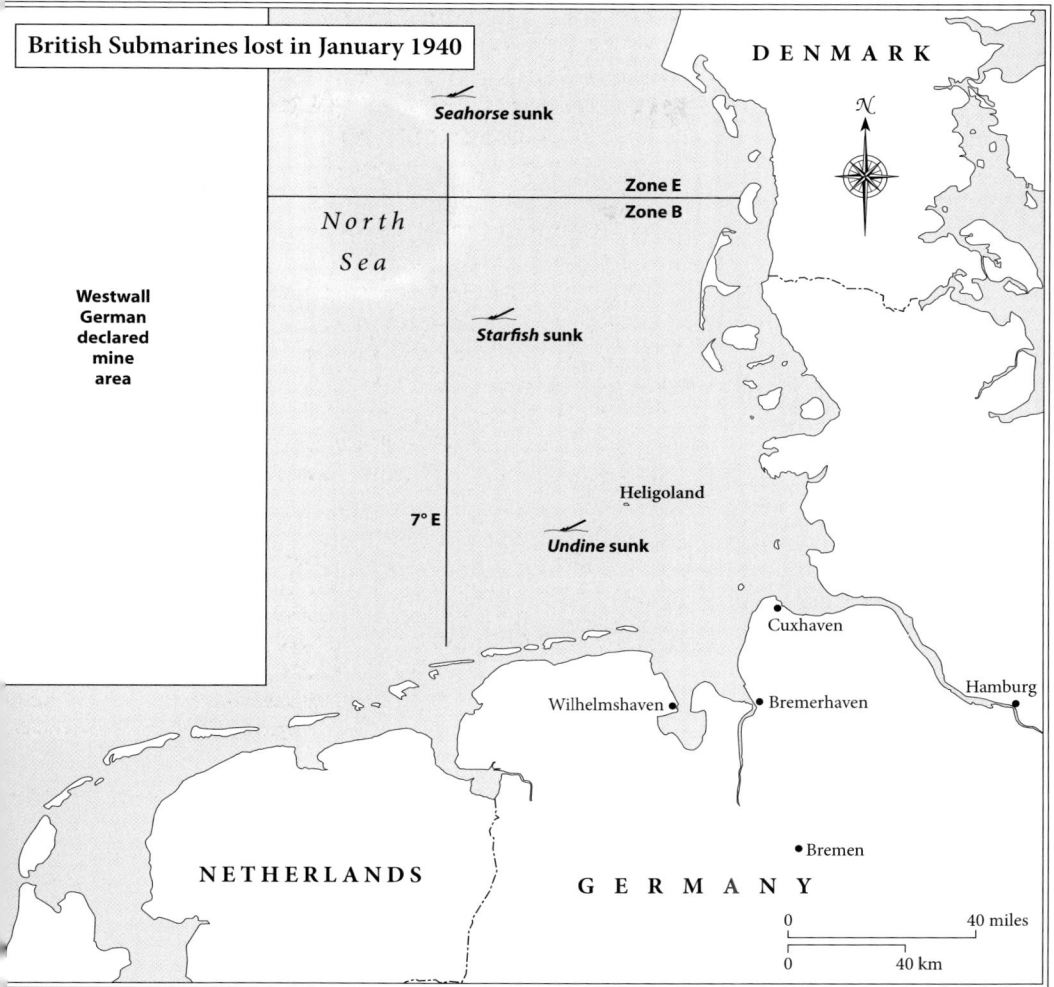

had acknowledged its safe departure from that area. Both the Admiralty and the C-in-C Home Fleet concurred with this policy.[14]

The Kriegsmarine made several attempts to raise the wrecks of *Starfish* and *Undine*, but did not succeed. Some parts were retrieved by divers or by dredging, although little of real importance.

First Blood

THE WINTER OF 1939/40 was unusually hard. Movement of smaller vessels, including submarines, became difficult from late January to early February, largely as the extreme ice conditions along the North Sea coasts kept most vessels in harbour for several weeks. Those submarines that did go on patrol had few encounters with German ships in general, and none with warships that would make good targets. Strict adherence to international prize law made the merchant ships virtually immune as the number of German aircraft and A/S escorts for all practical purposes prevented any 'stop-and-search' procedures from being followed.

On a request from the Admiralty, *Trident* sailed from Rosyth on 27 December 1939 for a patrol to the north of the Russian Kola Inlet. The intention was to determine if it would be possible for a submarine to operate in the north during wintertime and, more specifically, be capable of detecting the sailing of an expedition from Murmansk towards Norwegian ports during the long winter nights. Before sailing, fifty flying suits were taken on board to use against the expected severe cold in the Arctic. *Trident* was otherwise provided for

Ice conditions were at times quite severe during the winter of 1939/40. Here, *Sealion* at Harwich. (Royal Navy Submarine Museum Collection)

a thirty-day patrol, so conditions inside were cramped as Commander James Gould took his boat to sea.

Trident returned to Rosyth on 12 January and Gould reported that it would be quite possible to operate in the Arctic, in spite of periods of severe fog hampering visual observation. During times of fair visibility, operating in the area would not be very different from operating off northern Norway. He had only been off the Kola Inlet for five days, though – until a signal from VA(S) instructed him to return to Britain – due to the prevailing fog providing minimal visibility. The cold was not as intense as expected and the flying suits were not needed except by those on the bridge. Weather was fairly calm during *Trident*'s stay off Kola and as she did not stay long enough to experience the full force of the weather conditions, Gould's report probably gave the Admiralty a somewhat false impression of the hardships of operating in the Arctic during wintertime.[1]

After a patrol off the Danish coast, Lieutenant Commander Stirling-Hamilton reported that *Thistle* had had several encounters with the bottom while diving from German aircraft, giving the hull of the boat a hard time as well as the nerves of the crew. He also found it difficult to hold position in the shallow waters owing to the constant surging up and down draining the batteries to control the boat. On 2 February 1940, *Thistle* docked at Rosyth having completed five patrols in the Skagerrak and the northern Kattegat. Seventy-four days had been spent at sea, thirty-four of them underwater. Eleven thousand miles had been steamed, 2,000 of them under water. No breakdowns had been experienced – but no successes either.[2]

War or not, fishing vessels, particularly from neutral Denmark, were active in the northern North Sea, causing challenges for the submariners. They regularly used nets for fishing and vigilance was needed when nearby. Lieutenant Commander George Davies of *Tribune* wrote in December 1939:

> A large number of fishing vessels were sighted [off the Skaw]. The fishing ground is approximately the area inside the 40 fathom line to the east of longitude 10E and vessels operate from Skagen. Vessels appear to be employed on seine net fishing and their nets cover a very wide area. They carry the appropriate lights at night, but one vessel of the fleet carries two additional vertical red lights and appears to act as patrolling craft. These vessels proceed to and from the fishing grounds at about 10 knots (175 revs) and use their engines intermittently while fishing. The sound of their [high speed] engines is easily heard on H.E. and closely resembles that sound of destroyer engines.[3]

The large number of fishing vessels was somewhat suspicious, and the submarines were instructed to intercept fishing vessels acting suspiciously, even if neutral, and, if considered necessary, bring them to Britain with a prize crew. This necessitated the use of guns from submarines on the surface and all commanders were ordered to carry out firing practice when convenient. The U-class boats were as yet unarmed, but in a meeting on 5 February 1940 between Admiralty and submarine officers, it was decided to fit 12-pounder HA9 guns to all U-class and 3-inch low-angle guns with increased elevation to all S-class submarines.[4]

On some occasions it appeared that the sea was full of ghosts. In the patrol report of *Tribune* Lieutenant Commander Davies wrote on 13 January 1940 that, at 19:00, his

A Danish fishing vessel, of which there were many in the north-eastern North Sea. (Author's Collection)

submarine crossed 'two torpedo tracks' in the Skagerrak, between Skagen and Arendal. He immediately sounded the alarm and took *Tribune* down, but nothing further was heard or seen. No German U-boat is known to have been in the area and the 'attack' was most likely imagined.

Four days later, on 17 January, while about 15 miles east-north-east of Skagen in good visibility, Davies wrote in his report:

02:43 Sighted a darkened object on the port bow. Sounded Night Alarm and altered course towards. Proceeded slow grouped down on one motor.

02:46 All internal tubes ready, Object identified as a submarine on the surface [. . .] at a range of 2000 to 2500 yards.

02:48 Target appeared to be stationary [. . .] A/S operator reported hydrophone effect right ahead.

02:50–02:51 Fired torpedoes from internal bow tubes 1–6. Waited results of these shots. Torpedo tracks were seen approaching target and A/S operator reported all torpedoes running.

02:53 Decided to fire external tubes, firing Nos 7 & 8 from the surface and then diving to fire Nos 9 & 10 by A/S from submerged.

02:54 Dived. The submarine gave a heavy shudder while I was in the conning tower, sufficient to cause me to lose my balance. I was surprised to find that this had not been noticed in the control room, but at this time everyone was fully occupied with diving the boat and there were considerable noises from blowing 'Q'. On subsequent investigation it was found that ratings in all compartments except the control room had felt this shudder. One remarked, 'that was a hit all right'.[5]

Unfortunately not. No German U-boat was in this area at the time and certainly none was lost. It has never been ascertained what *Tribune* actually fired ten torpedoes at. No definite explosions were heard, although the asdic operator maintained that he had clearly heard hydrophone effects from what he considered to be a U-boat and the torpedoes running towards it. Later in the day, Lieutenant Commander Davies put himself on the sick list with a fever and First Lieutenant Archibald Cheyne took command, taking the boat home to Rosyth.[6]

To protect their own and chartered ships from Scandinavia to Britain, the Admiralty introduced a convoy system across the North Sea a few weeks into the war. Following neutral sea lanes to collection points in south-western Norway, ships loaded with fish, butter, meat, timber, pulp, aluminium, ferro-alloys, minerals and other commodities were eventually assembled in convoys and escorted across the North Sea to Methil, from where they dispersed, according to destination. In the other direction, the convoys assembled at Methil from where they were taken to various entry points to the Inner Leads off Bergen. The North Sea convoys caught the attention of the SKL, which declared that ships joining the convoys did so at their peril. Still, no German surface ship was ever sent to attack the convoys and, even more surprisingly, no submarines either. A few attacks occurred accidentally when U-boats happened to run into a convoy.[7]

Anticipating German surface attacks on these convoys, Allied submarines were often added to the convoy escort, when available. The concept was that they could attack heavy surface ships that were attempting to harass the convoy, thereby acting as a deterrent and reducing the need to deploy capital ships. This was something the submarine commanders were not well prepared for and the service, inevitably boring and uninspiring, was dreaded. All the more so as there was a constant risk of being run over by a merchantman heading off course or being mistaken for a U-boat by one of the other escorts.

In the early morning of 18 February, while on the surface some 40 miles east of Pentland Firth, Kapitänleutnant Otto Kretschmer in *U23* ran into convoy HN-12, about thirty ships, from Bergen to Methil.[8] At the time, the local escort consisted of the destroyers *Daring* and *Ilex* on the port and starboard quarters, respectively, while *Delight* and *Inglefield* were on the port and starboard bow. The A/A cruiser *Calcutta* and the submarine *Thistle* were also in company, while the cruisers *Edinburgh* and *Arethusa* with destroyers covered at a distance. Kretschmer decided the situation was too good to miss and resolved to attack. None of the destroyers had sighted *U23* and, being on the surface, she had not been picked up by their asdics. Brief flashes of light were seen on board one of the destroyers when the black-out curtains were opened as men moved through them, so positioning the boat for an attack on what turned out to be *Daring* was easy. One torpedo was fired, after which *U23* turned quickly around, heading away, though still on the surface. On the way a second torpedo was fired at *Thistle*, but this missed and appears not to have been registered on board the submarine.

The torpedo from *U23* hit *Daring* on the port side aft. Shortly after detonating, it was followed by a secondary explosion, most likely as her after magazine went up, breaking the destroyer clean in two. The stern section towered up and sank rapidly until only a small part remained visible. The fore part capsized in less than thirty seconds and remained floating for about half an hour.[9]

Thistle in 1939: one of the most poignant photos of any British submarine. (P A Vicary)

On board *Thistle*, Lieutenant Commander Robert Stirling-Hamilton had just gone below, as all seemed peaceful, when two loud explosions rang through the boat. Believing it was depth charges from one of the escorts, he went above to investigate, but without calling the alarm. The officer of the watch told him that just after the explosions a column of black smoke had risen from the direction in which *Daring* had last been observed, but as the moon was about to set, it was difficult to see much. Closing, strange shapes could be seen in the water, but as none of the convoy or the other escorts seemed to react, it took some time before the men on the bridge of *Thistle* realised that it was *Daring* – which was nowhere to be seen – that had been sunk. A mine was unlikely due to the water depth and Stirling-Hamilton realised with a chill that a U-boat was around. That a torpedo had already been fired at them and missed seems not to have been registered at all:

> We circled near the wreck, keeping an eye open for survivors, looking and listening for the U-boat. With no signs of either, I could not close and stop without the risk of the submarine sinking us as well, for he would still be in the dark sector. At the same time I was every moment expecting the destroyer which had been ahead of *Daring* to drop back, but they evidently had heard nothing and it was only after a long pause that we were able to attract the attention of a destroyer to starboard of the convoy [*Ilex*]. She closed *Thistle* and when I had informed her captain of the situation he steamed off to the west saying that he would look for the U-boat while we were to pick up survivors. Unfortunately he lowered no boats and was out of sight before I could ask for them.[10]

Only three men were to be found. One disappeared before he could be picked up, one was relatively safe on board the still-floating bow of the destroyer, while the third clung to a small raft. The latter called that his arm was broken so he could not swim and Stirling-Hamilton brought the stern of his submarine as near to the raft as he dared.

Thistle's RNR Lieutenant [Roland Ennor] swam to him with a line. Instead of waiting to be towed alongside, raft and all, which was intended, the man let go and clung to the officer, taking both under water. When the latter had freed himself and grasped the man again, he could not hold him because everything was covered with oil and this unfortunate rating sank and did not reappear. The sea was not rough but the moderate swell made a big motion relative to the submarine's stern and the officer ran a considerable risk of being severely injured on a propeller or other projection and he was bruised, exhausted, bitterly cold and disappointed of having lost the man after his gallant effort.[11]

Ilex then returned briefly, lowering two whalers before taking off again in search of the U-boat. The officer of the watch on board *Ilex* believed the explosions were from depth charges and informed Lieutenant Commander Saumarez accordingly. As nothing else happened, he saw 'no reason for concern' until the signal from *Thistle* was finally seen fifteen minutes later. Saumarez was later criticised by C-in-C Home Fleet and C-in-C Rosyth for not lowering his boats earlier.

The boats from *Ilex* greatly facilitated the rescue work and the man from the stern, Able Seaman William McBride, was taken care of, though getting him on board the submarine was no easy task in the swell. At dawn it became obvious that there were no further survivors to be found and *Thistle* and the other escorts out searching were ordered to rejoin the convoy. Picking up speed in the growing light, a raft with a group of men was sighted and brought to the attention of a nearby destroyer to pick them up. The six men on the raft had fought the cold and the heavy swell throughout the night, clinging to it as best they could. To keep spirits up they sang songs and cheered themselves with the thought that they would be entitled to fourteen days' leave. When daylight came there had been no sign of the wreck or any other survivors, but after some time, to their immense relief, the destroyer *Inglefield* came into view, heading straight for them. By the time they were taken on board; the six men were close to exhaustion and would not have lasted much longer. They were to be the only survivors from *Daring* in addition to McBride on board *Thistle*.[12] Kretschmer continued to stalk the convoy from a distance during the day, but ran into several A/S groups and another heavily escorted convoy, protected by aircraft, that could not be attacked during daylight. After that, HN-12 was no longer to be found.[13]

A week later, the commander of *U63*, Oberleutnant Günther Lorentz, received a signal from the German U-boat Command that he was in a favourable position to intercept convoy HN-14, which had left Bergen for Methil on 24 February. The convoy, fifteen to eighteen merchant ships, was heavily escorted by cruisers *Edinburgh*, *Arethusa* and *Cairo*, the destroyers *Escapade*, *Eclipse*, *Escort*, *Electra* and the minelayer submarine *Narwhal*.[14] In the early morning of the 25th, *Electra* and *Eclipse* were detached to go north of the Orkneys with some ships destined for the British west coast while *Inglefield* and *Imogen* fell in, coming from Scapa Flow. At this time *Escapade* was on the port bow of the convoy, with *Escort* on the starboard bow and *Narwhal* abreast the leading ship of the port column. At 07:55, east-south-east of the Orkneys, *Narwhal* reported: 'Suspicious object 025 degrees'. Lieutenant Commander Eric Oddie had immediately turned his submarine towards the sighting, working up speed, and Commander Harry Graham in *Escapade* followed suit, receiving the same signal. At that time, the weather was calm with a swell

Narwhal in July 1937. (R Perkins)

from the north: shortly after, *U63* became visible on the crest of a swell. Graham held his fire, hoping to get closer, but Lorentz dived rapidly.

Narwhal was ordered back to take care of the convoy, to avoid confusion, while *Escapade* – joined by *Inglefield*, *Escort* and *Imogen* – commenced the attack. Damaged by depth charges, Lorentz was compelled to take his boat to the surface, where he was met by heavy gunfire from the destroyers. *U63* sank within minutes, but twenty-four men including Lorentz were rescued. One man perished. In spite of having been sent away from the attack, *Narwhal* was credited for having sighted the U-boat and promptly leading the destroyers to her destruction.[15]

On 18 February 1940, *Scharnhorst*, *Gneisenau* and the newly commissioned cruiser *Admiral Hipper* headed into the North Sea with the destroyers *Heidkamp* and *Galster*. The destroyers *Jacobi*, *Riedel*, *Schoemann* and *Maass* departed Wilhelmshaven at the same time, but early next morning, off Skagen, they turned east into the Skagerrak to look for merchant ships carrying contraband. The operation was codenamed Nordmark and had two objectives. The surface ships were looking for reported convoys from Norway and, as their presence was expected to draw British forces into the North Sea, nine U-boats were placed between Kinnaird Head and the Shetlands to intercept the Home Fleet should it take to sea in response. Distracted by the *Altmark* incident erupting the day before, Operation Nordmark got off to a bad start as fog and ice kept the normally efficient German reconnaissance aircraft at base. Hence, Admiral Wilhelm Marschall, leading the operation from on board *Gneisenau*, operated solely on radio intercepts and signals intelligence. He did not appreciate this and, finding nothing but neutral Norwegian fishing vessels, turned back during the night of the 19th/20th.

Unknown to Marschall, his sortie had been sighted by British aircraft off Heligoland in the early morning of the 18th. The westbound convoy HN-12 was already nearing Scotland, while the next eastbound convoy heading for Norway was held back at Kirkwall to be out of harm's way. Parts of the Home Fleet had already taken to sea to screen the operations against the *Altmark* and were directed towards the North Sea. Admiral Horton saw a chance for his submarines and ordered *Salmon* and *Sunfish* towards Heligoland, near the eastern end of the probable channel through the declared area. *Orzeł* was ordered towards Horns Reef, while *L23* and *Seal* were positioned north of the declared area. *Triton* and *Triad* were kept off Norway, covering the entrance to the Skagerrak, while *Truant* was sent with dispatch from Rosyth to cover the gap between *Seal* and *Triton*. The purpose of the German sortie was not known, and the dispositions were meant to cover a possible attack on the North Sea convoys as well as an attempt to relieve *Altmark*, still in Jøssingfjord. It was also known that half a dozen German merchant ships had left Vigo in Spain a week earlier and were, as far as was known, attempting to return to Germany. The sortie might therefore also be an attempt to team up with these as they came south from the area off Iceland, escorting them home.[16]

Further air reconnaissance was hampered by the poor weather and when the *Salmon* reported '*Scharnhorst, Gneisenau, Hipper* and *Königsberg* steering south at high speed' during the morning of the 20th and *L23* reported 'one cruiser and two destroyers steering south-east' a little later, confusion reigned. Both submarines had to go deep to avoid the escorts and could not pursue; off Heligoland, *Sunfish* was kept down by destroyers while *Salmon* sighted nothing but a few trawlers. Eventually, during the 19th the British submarine lost the trail altogether and as the Home Fleet turned back before running into the German U-boat lines, the almost bizarre situation developed where two fleets and fifteen to twenty submarines moved around in the North Sea without intercepting

German supply ship *Altmark* heading for shelter in Jøssingfjord, south of Stavanger, hotly pursued by British destroyers *Intrepid* and *Ivanhoe*. Photo taken from *Ivanhoe*. (Briggs Collection)

each other. Late in the morning of the 20th, *Salmon* finally sighted the German ships escorted by three destroyers steering south, off Heligoland. They were far outside torpedo range, though, and during the evening of the 20th, all German ships returned to port.[17]

In the early hours of 20 February *L23* was heavily depth charged north of the Westwall by *M1*, *M5* and *M7* and limped home with severe damage. The minesweepers, which were part of the screen for Operation Nordmark, observed a lot of oil on the surface as well as a series of air bubbles and reckoned that they had sunk another submarine. This was not the case though. The oil came from the ruptured number six external tank and it was also seen and smelt by the men of *L23* when they were back on the surface later in the morning.[18]

The main reason for generating all this commotion was the incident of the German supply ship *Altmark* which had sought refuge from British destroyers inside Jøssingfjord in Norwegian waters south of Stavanger. On the night of 16/17 February, the destroyer *Cossack* entered the fjord, released the British sailors held prisoner on board her and left the *Altmark* grounded, though otherwise relatively undamaged.[19] Learning that *Altmark* had not been sunk, the Admiralty instructed Horton to make a cordon of submarines outside Jøssingfjord in case she should try to leave. *Seal*, *Orzeł* and *Triad* were to patrol outside the fjord with *Triton* further out, in case other German ships should attempt to enter the fjord in assistance. After some days, it became clear that *Altmark* would stay in the fjord for a while and the four submarines were instructed to resume their patrols or return to base. Meanwhile, Lieutenant Commander Christopher 'Jockey' Hutchinson received a signal to steer *Truant* towards Norwegian waters, report if *Altmark* left the fjord but remain inside Norwegian waters and attack if she ventured outside. On 23 February, he was off the entrance to Jøssingfjord, inside Norwegian territory. Underwater conditions were challenging in the area, including many fishing nets and lobster pots. The German tanker was not to be seen. Hutchinson's entries in his war diary of 23 February are revealing:

17:56. Surfaced, Proceeded to vicinity of Jøssingfjord in accordance with [signal from 2nd Flotilla].

19:08. Received Admiralty 1735/23, (*Altmark* probably sailing tonight), increased speed.

20:56. Flooded up all internal bow tubes. Commenced patrol south of Siragrunnen. [. . .] Visibility landwards less than 2 miles. In these conditions, egress from Jøssingfjord could not be seen. Proceeded to close Jøssing entrance from north-westward.

23:07. British Lockheed aircraft patrolling overhead.

23:20. Stopped 2 cables from the cliffs by Rekefjord to watch what was considered the only exit from Jøssing for a ship of any appreciable size. Pancake ice. No navigational lights in vicinity. Visibility 1½ miles.[20]

It is not specifically mentioned in the logbook, but Hutchinson later said that he went so far into the fjord, on the surface using the electric motors, that he could actually see *Altmark* and some of the Norwegian torpedo boats. For a while he was tempted to send a torpedo into the German tanker, but decided against it and pulled out. He did not mention seeing *Wiegand*, a German ore-ship which had stopped by on 21 February en route from Narvik to pull *Altmark* off the bank on which she was grounded. Ascertaining that *Altmark* was able to make herself seaworthy with the men and equipment on board, *Wiegand* prepared to leave.[21] As *Truant* emerged from Jøssingfjord, Hutchinson positioned his boat at the Siragrunnen shallows. This position commanded both exit routes from the fjord should *Altmark* depart, but it also contained a myriad of fishermen's buoys which looked like floating mines, creating some unease until it was realised they were harmless. *Truant* stayed off Jøssingfjord for several days.

24th February
04:00. Received Admiralty signal that SS *Wiegand* sailed from Jøssingfjord at 22:30. H.E. from this would not be heard through own engine noises. Closed the west entrance.
05:50. Dived. Patrolled S.E. of Siragrunnen. Depth keeping in the swell was extremely difficult, consistent with a good periscope watch. Definite ships giving H.E. could hardly be seen against the high land. *Altmark* might well have sailed unobserved if she kept close to the land.
17:51. Surfaced. Strong moonlight. Patrolled in eastern end of Siragrunnen.
21:30. Small aircraft active in entrance to Jøssingfjord.

25th February
Noon–15:00. One aircraft seen on numerous occasions near entrance to Jøssingfjord.
18:55. Surfaced. Patrolled on east end of Siragrunnen.
20:15–21:15. Shadowed large suspicious merchant vessel navigating with extreme caution within half a mile of the land from Siragrunnen to Lista. Her identity could have been established by disclosing our presence, but this was considered undesirable with *Altmark* still in harbour.

26th February
04:00–05:00. Seen twice by fishermen in small boats.
05:45. Dived – patrolled close to S.E. of Siragrunnen. Wind and sea increasing.
09:00–10:00. Broke surface three times trying to see over the waves at periscope depth. At 29 feet could just see over waves. At 28 feet came right up and broke surface.
13:00. Periscope depth became valueless. Dived to 60 feet – coming up to periscope depth every 20 minutes, or to investigate any H.E.
13:30. Became mixed up with large fishing fleet in small motor boats.
18:32. Surfaced. Patrolled off S.E. Corner of Siragrunnen. Sea moderate during night.

27th February
00:30. Visibility closing down. Moved to patrol off S.E. corner of Siragrunnen. Ran into thickly sown patch of large fishermen's floats 1 mile south of Siragrunnen patch. Fouled port propeller. Used high speed on port engine to clear foul. By 06:00, all floats were adrift except one.

07:00. In thick fog and sea 2–5, trimmed up aft and cut remaining float adrift. Remained on surface patrol S.E. of Siragrunnen in fog, visibility 1–5 cables. Set A/S watch.[22]

Truant remained off Jøssingfjord for another uneventful four days before setting course for Rosyth. At the end of his report, Hutchinson added that he was greatly relieved when he, upon returning to base, learned that *Altmark* was still in Jøssingfjord and had not managed to sneak out undetected while he was waiting for her outside. Interestingly, he concludes that, had he had a collapsible dinghy on board, he would have sent an observer ashore 'to signal the sailing of *Altmark*'. Sending a man in swimming was precluded by the low sea and air temperatures.

In the morning of 6 March, *Altmark* finally left Jøssingfjord, escorted by Norwegian destroyers. The British had meanwhile abandoned the demand for the tanker to be interned and made no comment. Nevertheless, the Admiralty was duly informed by Norwegian contacts that *Altmark* was preparing to depart and *Unity*, on her way to a routine patrol west of Skagen, was diverted northwards with utmost dispatch by a priority signal from VA(S) in the early hours of 3 March. By the 5th, she was in place outside Jøssingfjord with orders to attack if *Altmark* ventured outside Norwegian territorial waters. She never did, though, and with the Norwegian destroyers keeping close guard, Lieutenant Brown could only observe and report her movements. After the *Altmark* had passed Lista Lighthouse, *Unity* withdrew westwards to transmit an enemy report.

Three weeks later, *Altmark* slipped quietly southwards through Swedish and Danish waters and, assisted by a tug, reached Kiel, in the evening of 27 March.[23]

On 28 February, the 7,848-ton German blockade-breaker *Wangoni* was identified by *Triton* off Lindesnes, though well inside Norwegian territorial waters. Lieutenant Commander Pizey stalked the merchantman from outside the territorial waters until nightfall when she attempted to cross the Skagerrak, steering for Hanstholm on the

Triton in June 1939. (W&L)

Danish west coast. When she did appear, Pizey held back for some time until he was certain she could not double back when intercepted. Unfortunately, he waited too long and when *Wangoni* did not stop when challenged, *Triton*'s speed was insufficient to overtake her and eventually the chase had to be abandoned.[24]

Unknown to the submariners, political events were to change their war completely. After six relatively uneventful months, the British and Allied submarines deployed in the North Sea would move to the forefront of events and become involved in a totally different kind of warfare compared to what they had experienced so far. The preparations for the Baltic sortie had nevertheless resulted in many submarines not being sent out on patrol. Similarly, many other boats had been 'degaussed' as a result of the increased German use of magnetic mines.[25]

On 19 February, the Admiralty and the Cabinet were informed by the embassy in Stockholm that, due to the severe ice conditions in the Belts and the Baltic, German ore ships from Narvik were now crossing the Skagerrak from Norwegian waters towards the German North Sea ports. Halifax brought this up with Churchill, commenting that while the navy was 'always pressing for leave to intercept in territorial waters, here was all the ore trade passing through non-territorial waters'. This was not what Churchill was after, though, and apparently caught off guard, he asked Admiral Pound 'what answer to give him, apart from the proximity of German shore-based aircraft'. Admitting that Lord Halifax had a good point, Pound nevertheless realised that his First Lord did not want to pursue this angle and eventually all that happened was that VA(S) Horton was instructed to intensify the efforts of his submarines in Skagerrak.

What Churchill wanted were more aggressive naval measures. The *Altmark* incident, in his opinion, had given all the reasons necessary to bring forward plans rejected by the War Cabinet some months earlier to lay mines inside Norwegian territory, disturbing the German ore traffic out of Narvik. Such operations, Churchill held, could be justified by pointing to Norwegian lassitude in Jøssingfjord. This would undoubtedly provoke a German reaction and lead to a kind of war where the Royal Navy would have the upper hand. Encouraged by support from various military and Cabinet members, Churchill ordered the Admiralty to initiate urgent preparations for a mine-laying operation, which, 'being minor and innocent, may be called Wilfred'. Landing in Norway without Norwegian agreement would be a mistake, Churchill held, but he was fairly certain that mining of selected places in the Leads could be carried out without confronting the Norwegian Navy. Prime Minister Chamberlain and Foreign Minister Halifax were against such measures at first, as well as supplying help to Finland, but after considerable pressure from France, the British War Cabinet gave in on 11 March and agreed to land troops in Narvik, even without Norwegian consent. This would immediately halt the German ore traffic and create a basis for troops to be sent to Finland.

In the early morning of 13 March, the embarkation of the Allied expeditionary force for Narvik began. The day before, all of Horton's available submarines had been ordered to gather in the North Sea to screen the surface ships that would bring the troops across. A few hours later, however, the news of the ceasefire in Finland broke, the expedition was cancelled and the soldiers were ordered by a relieved War Cabinet to disembark and stand down. Churchill argued that the primary goal of the expedition remained and urged that the Narvik landings at least should still go ahead – but to no avail. There would be no Scandinavian mission for now. German intelligence was aware of the positions of thirteen of the submarines – twelve of them named – and concluded that the Heligoland Bight had been 'sealed off' to protect an Allied attack on Norway.[26]

In parallel with the plans for Narvik, Ruck-Keene and 'Shrimp' Simpson had, towards the end of February, received orders to start preparations for their six operational S-class submarines and six new T-class boats to enter the Baltic as part of the planned operations to assist Finland. Once the ice allowed, they were to operate out of Åbo in Finland and, while Ruck-Keene and his staff would fly over, Simpson was to sail from Cardiff to Trondheim with 500 tons of stores and spares and take them from there to Stockholm by train. Norwegian and Swedish neutrality does not seem to have been considered a hindrance. By 12 March everything was crated and ready to go, when the operation was abruptly cancelled by the news of Finland and Russia having signed a ceasefire that same morning.[27]

As the ice conditions gradually slackened during early March, Vice Admiral Horton focused the majority of his British submarines in the North Sea, Skagerrak and Kattegat, while the French 10th Submarine Flotilla covered the Dutch and Belgian coasts, operating out of Harwich. Irrespective of plans for an expedition to Norway, this meant a significant increase in the number of submarines operating north of Germany, which created profound concern in the Kriegsmarine. In Germany, the war also accelerated after the *Altmark* incident. Catalysed by the events in Jøssingfjord, German plans for Operation Weserübung, the invasion of Norway and Denmark, were focused and advanced in the German High Command.[28] On 5 March, 'Operations Order No. 1 for the Occupation of Norway' was issued and the wheels started to roll. The persistent severe ice conditions in the Baltic, however, delayed the departure of warships and transports from their eastern ports and there was growing concern that Allied interventions in Scandinavia might happen first. In a status meeting with Hitler on 9 March, C-in-C of the Kriegsmarine, Admiral Raeder, held that in his opinion the current development of the situation in Finland made Operation Weserübung 'urgently necessary'. If the Allies were to use the pretext of helping Finland, as intelligence indicated, they would certainly occupy Norway and Sweden en route, completely severing the supply of iron ore and establishing offensive bases.

On 10 March, it was noted in the SKL war diary that 'the totality of the reports point in a compelling manner towards the possibility of immediate action by the Allies in Norway.' Radio intercepts during the 13th tracked no less than thirteen British submarines deployed in the North Sea and at the entrance to the Skagerrak, with two more underway from Rosyth. This was more than twice the usual number and a clear signal that something was going on. Most likely, in the opinion of the Kriegsmarine, the British submarines were covering the flank of an Allied landing operation in Norway that other intelligence indicated was developing. Nothing was ready on the German side and as news was coming in from Moscow that Finland had capitulated, it was decided to do nothing, other than alerting U-boats in the area to be extra vigilant.[29] On the 15th, further intercepted signals ordering the submarines to disperse revealed that the Soviet–Finnish ceasefire had indeed upset the Allied plans. Interpretation of the signals indicated that the operation was not cancelled, just put on hold with forty-eight to ninety-six hours' notice. The SKL noted:

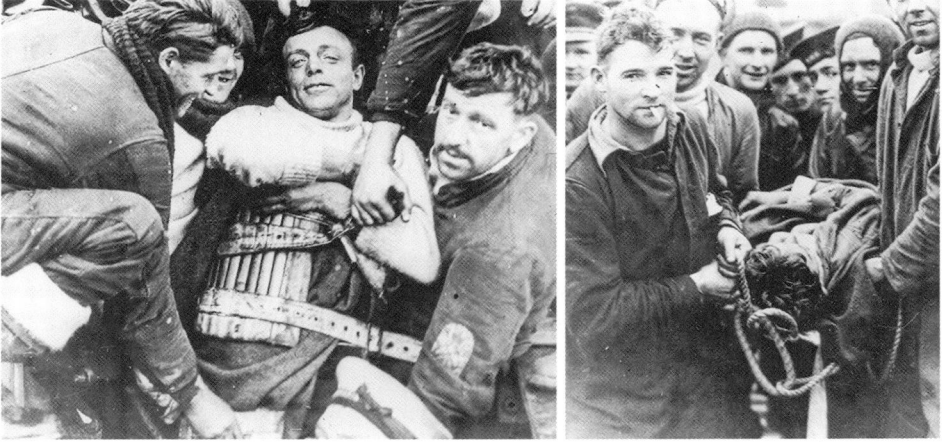

Survivors from *Protinus* being taken off from *Unity* to be landed in Rosyth. (Author's Collection)

The consequence of the Finno-Russian ceasefire for Germany's warfare is as yet unclear. The Allied plans for an immediate landing in Norway . . . seem to have been deferred for the moment. The SKL believes England's strategic goals in the north have not changed and the planned action will be initiated when another favourable occasion has been found.[30]

The war had stalled for a moment but things remained in high tension. In mid-March, Heinkel He111 aircraft from KG26 were hunting for what was believed to be armed British trawlers in the North Sea. One of those encountered on the 20th was the 202-ton Dutch trawler *Protinus* from Ijmuiden, fishing on the Middle Rough Bank, east of Newcastle. The Heinkel dropped a series of small bombs, one of which hit the *Protinus*, in spite of a large Dutch flag being waved. The bridge and the engine room were destroyed and the captain and a deckhand killed. The remainder of the crew took to the lifeboat as the *Protinus* started to sink. Some reports include the fact that the aircraft also strafed the crew as they made for the boat, but this is not confirmed with certainty and nobody was hit. There was no compass on board the lifeboat, no food and very little water. The ten Dutch fishermen started to row in the direction in which they believed they would find Denmark.

On 25 March, *Unity* sighted the small boat at 16:00 and, after establishing it was not a trap, Lieutenant John Brown approached to investigate. The Dutch sailors were by now in poor condition, having spent five miserable days in an open lifeboat. Two of the original survivors had perished, their bodies having been put overboard, and the remaining eight were suffering badly from exposure and hunger. Three of them had to be helped on board the submarine, where hot drinks and warm, dry clothes soon improved the situation. Keeping the men on board the small submarine was inconvenient and Brown took *Unity* towards Rosyth to land them. Off May Island, the survivors were transferred to the trawler *Agate* in the morning of the 28th, before *Unity*'s patrol was resumed.[31]

* * *

Lieutenant Commander George 'Scraper' Phillips took *Ursula* to sea from Blyth on 12 March, heading for a patrol area between Skagen and Gothenburg. It was to be a testing patrol in many ways. First of all, there were still ice floes floating in eastern Skagerrak, coming out from the Belts. Being difficult to register, *Ursula* surfaced twice in the midst of them, damaging the torpedo bow shutters and the attack periscope, which became bent and stuck in the fully raised position – as a result, it showed above the surface when at periscope depth.

The first week of the patrol was rather uneventful except for the encounters with the ice. Several merchant ships were sighted, but all inside Swedish or Danish territorial waters. At 21:46 on 21 March, however, the dim navigation lights of an otherwise darkened ship were sighted north-east of Skagen, some 8 miles off the point. Unknown to Lieutenant Commander Phillips at the time, he had just intercepted the 4,947-ton German ore ship *Heddernheim*, which was bringing a load of 7,000 tons of pyrite and copper ore from Thamshavn in Norway to Germany.

Signalling for the freighter to stop produced no result – quite the contrary, she increased speed, with dense smoke appearing from her funnel. Only after a warning shot had been fired did the vessel heave to. When asked to identify itself, the freighter signalled 'Estonian'. This was dismissed as 'nonsense' by Lieutenant Aston Piper, *Ursula*'s navigating officer who was RNR and had sailed on merchant ships in the Baltic before the war. There were no Estonian ships that large in his opinion. Meanwhile, *Ursula* crossed close astern of the darkened ship and, in the light of the Aldis lamp, the name '*Heddernheim* – Bremen' could be read, removing all doubt. A German ship had finally been caught in international waters.

The crew was ordered to send a boat across with papers, but the operation of lowering the boat went suspiciously slowly, with frequent requests for repeated information. When *Ursula*'s radio operator reported that *Heddernheim* was signalling that she had been intercepted by a submarine, instructions were given to abandon ship altogether.

Heddernheim. The 4,947-ton freighter was laden with 2,000 tons of copper ore when sunk off Skagen. (Author's Collection)

This speeded things up, but only a bit. Eventually, a lifeboat approached *Ursula*, the crew asking what the matter was. By now Phillips's patience had run out and, after a quick interrogation, confirming that the ship was indeed German, the boat was sent back to tell the rest of the crew that their ship would be sunk in fifteen minutes. The message was signalled back to the ship by hand light, but still things went very slowly. It was obvious that they were playing for time and a second warning shot was fired. This finally produced an flurry of activity and eventually both lifeboats pulled away.

As this was the first German ship sunk, Phillips wanted a prisoner and Aston Piper, who spoke some German, asked for the ship's captain to come aboard the submarine from the lifeboats. He was told that the master, Kapitän Teichmann, had shot himself. This did not seem very likely, but when Chief Engineer Sinn agreed to come in his place, this was nevertheless accepted.

To Phillips's frustration, it took three torpedoes to sink the stationary *Heddernheim*. While *Ursula* was manoeuvred into a firing position, number one tube was fired prematurely through a mistake in the drill, missing the freighter altogether. Shortly after, it was reported from the torpedo room that only number two and number five tubes were ready, numbers three, four and six having been damaged by ice. Number two torpedo was fired first, but failed to run, probably as ice had also damaged its port. Annoyed, Phillips ordered number five tube to be fired. This ran true and struck the *Heddernheim* amidships on the starboard side, after which it sank rapidly. At this time, a searchlight appeared from an approaching craft and Phillips decided it would be best to head off. The shore was close enough and the sea was calm, so with another ship approaching, the safety of the thirty-five men in the lifeboats seemed assured.[32]

It is noteworthy that the German SKL comments in its war diary that 'finally, the British have realised that it is necessary for them to attack the German iron-ore traffic in the Skagerrak and that there has been an option to do so, now the Baltic is closed by ice, that they, somewhat surprisingly, had hitherto failed to utilise.' Two days later, on 23 March, the 1,489-ton Danish merchantman *Sejrö* was also stopped by *Ursula*. Her papers were in perfect order, though, and she was allowed to sail on unharmed, while Phillips set course for Blyth.[33]

Still, this day would see the second British sinking of a merchantman as Lieutenant Commander 'Jockey' Hutchinson in *Truant* sank the 2,189-ton German freighter *Edmund Hugo Stinnes IV* off Bovbjerg Lighthouse – inside Danish territorial limits.

Truant had left Scotland during the evening of 12 March, and crossed the North Sea in very poor weather. Two days later, off the Danish west coast north of Ringkøbing, the 1,400-ton Danish vessel *Skodsborg* was intercepted and stopped. The sea conditions were too poor for Hutchinson to insist on the Danes sending a boat over with the papers and after ascertaining she was truly the *Skodsborg*, she was released and *Truant* dived, continuing around the south, patrolling between the east side of the German Declared Area and Horns Reef. Few ships were seen for several days. On the 22nd a few German A/S trawlers picked up the scent of the British submarine and got fairly close one time before Hutchinson managed to sneak away on the surface at nightfall.

Edmund Hugo Stinnes was on her way from Wesermünde to Copenhagen with a cargo of coke when she was intercepted. *Truant* had sighted her at 22:00 and stalked her for a while on the surface from outside the territorial limit, when, according to Hutchinson:

At 23:00, the ship altered course to 190° and thereby came outside territorial waters. No attempt to close was yet made owing to the proximity to Bovbjerg. It was desired to stop her in a position where coastguards would not be watching and reporting the proceedings. At 23:30, after a careful fix had been taken, the ship was found to be ½ mile outside territorial waters. She was closed at speed [and] a 6-inch Aldis lamp was switched onto her stern. Ship's name and Hamburg port of Registry read, Nazi ensign sighted. Signal was made in English: 'Stop, do not radio'. Ship proceeded and did not answer. One blank round was fired, followed by a repetition of the above signal and 'Send boat'. The German then altered course towards land [. . .] increasing speed.[34]

When the radio room reported SOS signals in German, Hutchinson ordered two live high-explosive (HE) rounds to be fired into *Stinnes*'s bridge structure. The signalling did not stop, and three more rounds were fired, all finding their mark, after which the signalling stopped altogether. With the freighter eventually coming to a complete halt, the crew then took to the boats. A short while later, *Stinnes* was seen to list and settle. Both lifeboats were pulling hard towards land and *Truant* gave chase. Catching them, the master, Kapitän Albert Weiss, was taken prisoner on board *Truant*. The rest of the crew was safe in the lifeboats, close to land, only one man being lightly wounded. According to Chief Engineer Room Artificer William Pook, Kapitän Weiss:

> was a very pleasant chap. He'd been a prisoner of war in the First War and we got on very well with him – He was quite happy to be a prisoner of war. We spoke to him and he could speak English. He joined with us and talked to us, so it was no problem with him at all.[35]

Stinnes was taking rather a long time to go down, though, and Hutchinson was getting impatient. He had been at the site for quite a while and, as dawn was approaching, German aircraft could appear at any time. To expedite the sinking, two torpedoes were fired into the freighter, after which *Truant* withdrew to the west.

By this time, she was undoubtedly inside Danish territorial waters. According to Hutchinson, *Stinnes* was outside territorial waters when first challenged by *Truant* and scuttled herself only after escaping inside. That might be, but Hutchinson admits that by the time the last shots were fired, she was inside Danish territorial waters – as she undoubtedly also was when he fired the torpedoes.

A Danish protest was delivered during the first days of April, requesting that the prisoner from *Edmund Hugo Stinnes IV* should be repatriated and compensation paid. Before much consideration could be given to this, the event was overshadowed by the German invasion of Denmark and Norway. Horton was delighted and commended both captains for their actions. Nevertheless, something bigger was apparently going on: in a signal dated 4 April, he informed submarines operating in the Skagerrak and the Kattegat that the boats should conceal their presence as much as possible and leave regular merchant ships alone. If, on the other hand, transports were encountered in the company of warships, and thus were legal targets, they should be prioritised in the attack.[36]

At the Führer Conference in Berlin on 26 March, intelligence was presented showing how close an Allied intervention in Norway had been when the Finnish–Russian ceasefire was announced. Admiral Raeder added that even if the imminent danger of such an operation

Danish and Norwegian Waters
March – April 1940

S W E D E N

N O R W A Y

• Larvik

Moonsund **sunk by** *Snapper*

Stedingen sunk by *Trident*

Brummer sunk by *Sterlet*

Ionia **sunk by** *Triad*

Amasis sunk by *Sunfish*

UJB sunk by *Tetrarch*

Antares sunk by *Sunfish*

Lysekil •

Florida **sunk by** *Snapper*

Schiff 40 Schürbek damaged by *Sunfish*

M1701 **and** *M1702* **sunk by** *Snapper*

• Lillesand
Kristiansand •

Rio de Janeiro sunk by *Orzel*

Karlsruhe **sunk by** *Truant*

Lützow damaged by *Spearfish*

Hamm sunk by *Seawolf*

Skagen •

Schiff 35 Oldenburg **sunk by** *Sunfish*

• Gothenburg

S k a g e r r a k

• Hirtshals

Heddernheim sunk by *Ursula*

Friedenau, Wigbert **and** *V1507 Rau VI* **sunk by** *Triton*

Læsø

M1302 **sunk by** *Snapper*

• Hanstholm

• Aalborg

K a t t e g a t

Anholt

August Leonhardt sunk by *Sealion*

Edmund Hugo Stinnes IV **sunk by** *Truant*

D E N M A R K

• Bovbjerg

• Helsingborg

• Esbjerg

Copenhagen •

• Malmö

0 _____ 40 miles

0 _____ 40 km

had been reduced, the ultimate objective of the Allies to sever the iron-ore supplies to Germany remained and an intensified effort against German merchant traffic in neutral waters was to be expected. Sooner or later, Allied plans for an intervention in Norway would re-emerge and Germany would have to carry out Weserübung. The operation had originated from the premise that Germany could not accept British control of Norwegian territory and that only a pre-emptive occupation could avert that. Therefore, Raeder suggested, Weserübung should be initiated in the next new-moon cycle and no later than 15 April. Everything was ready and the dark nights needed to cover the transit would soon become too short, increasing the overall risk to the operation. Virtually all operational U-boats had been deployed along the Norwegian coast or in the North Sea during March and would start running low on fuel and provisions by mid-April, thus closing the current window of opportunity. Sooner or later it would also be noted in London that other naval operations had been suspended. Hitler concluded that it was not to be expected that the Allies had abandoned their strategy in the north; threats of a German attack in France could trigger an Allied intervention in Norway to threaten Germany's weakly defended northen shores. Hence, a preliminary date for Weserübung was set between 8 and 10 April. The SKL, on Raeder's instruction, issued orders that all ships should remain on stand-by and arrangements for embarkation of troops and equipment continued until further notice – as should all security measures.[37]

In London on 28 March, at the first meeting of the Supreme War Council with Paul Reynaud as French prime minister, various types of actions against Germany were discussed. After some discussions, the laying of floating mines in the Rhine synchronised with mining of the Norwegian Leads – Churchill's Operation Wilfred – were agreed. Landings in Norway had not been mentioned in the meeting at all, but Churchill and the Chiefs of Staff saw an opportunity and the next day, the British War Cabinet almost casually added 'a British brigade and a French contingent' to be 'sent to Narvik to clear the port and advance to the Swedish frontier in case of German countermeasures to the mining' – Plan R4. At first, the mine-laying was planned for 5 April, but later moved to the 8th, with Plan R4 following shortly after, when it was clear that Germany had taken the bait and 'set foot on Norwegian soil, or there is clear evidence that they intend to do so'.[38]

— 13 —

Action Taken

VA(S) HORTON WAS CONVINCED that an Allied intervention in Norway would bring immediate German countermeasures and, having been informed of Operation Wilfred, he summoned the commanders of 2nd, 3rd and 6th flotillas to a meeting at his new headquarters in London on 1 April. There they were told that, in Horton's opinion, the British mine-laying would inevitably generate a German reaction, possibly even an invasion of Norway. Orders were given for all available submarines to be at sea by dawn on the 5th, covering the exits from the Bight, Kattegat and Skagerrak as well as likely German landing points in southern Norway.

At the time of the conference, *Triton* and *Swordfish* were off Skagen and *Trident* off Arendal. During the next few days, *Sealion*, *Sunfish*, *Unity*, *Thistle*, *Truant*, *Triad*, *Ursula*, *Clyde*, *Seal* and the Polish *Orzeł* took to sea to join them. *Tarpon* and *Severn* were to the north-east of the Westwall, while *Shark* and *Seawolf* were in the Heligoland Bight. *Narwhal* also sailed on the 2nd to lay mines north-west of Heligoland, where an opening in the German minefield had been discovered. *Seal* was sent to patrol off Stavanger. In the evening of the 4th, after Operation Wilfred had been postponed to the 8th, Horton moved some of the boats deeper into the sea lanes: *Orzeł* east of Lindesnes, *Trident* off

Sealion coming alongside at Harwich in April 1940. (Royal Navy Submarine Museum Collection)

Larvik, *Sunfish*, *Triton* and *Sealion* into the Kattegat. The latter was placed very far south in an attempt to cover the exits from the Danish Belts. It was, as Lieutenant Commander Bryant remarked, 'a position of honour, although not likely to inspire one's insurance company with enthusiasm'.[1]

The boats received orders not to compromise their position by intercepting merchant vessels, but focus on warships. Not an easy order to comply with. On the 7th, Bryant wrote in his war diary:

> Some 25 merchant vessels were sighted during the day, mostly northbound. Some were suspicious, but none that I could say definitely were German transports [. . .] One small ship marked Estonia had a funnel corresponding to that of Saaberk Co of Hamburg. Five ships had no flags or markings, three being greyish. It was not possible to surface and investigate them so no action was taken. [. . .] I was much concerned that I might be letting enemy ships by owing to taking no action. On the other hand, orders received conveyed the impression that it <u>was</u> essential not to compromise my position. The definition of a 'transport' was not clear in my mind, these suspected ships were certainly not 'Troop Carriers', were in territorial waters and the fact that they flew no flag was not absolute proof they were enemy.[2]

In his memoirs he added:

> As we crept south, another trouble beset us. The melting snow had freshened the water of the Baltic and Kattegat. We pumped out more and more ballast water and still we got 'heavier'. We were ballasted for salt ocean water; our destination had been too secret to enable us to have some of the lead ballast removed from the boxes in our keel before starting. Presently we had only just sufficient ballast water in our auxiliary tanks to give control. We had to pump out our fresh water, leaving only just enough to drink. The order went round: 'No washing, not even the hands.'[3]

Due to improved signal discipline, German B-Dienst had problems tracking the Allied submarines compared to a few weeks earlier and was largely unaware of their number and whereabouts. Except for *Trident*, which had already stopped and examined several neutral merchant ships off Lista on the 4th and 5th, and *Unity*, which had made an unsuccessful attack on the German U-boat *U2* in the Heligoland Bight on the 5th, there had been few indications of where the submarines were hiding.[4]

Based on the amount of land-based radio traffic, however, the B-Dienst estimated that some fifteen to twenty submarines were at sea. This number worried the SKL, as it might indicate that the Admiralty was aware of Operation Weserübung and was preparing a trap. On the other hand, it might be that the large number of submarines was a defensive measure for their own operation against Norway, as in March. Either way, the submarine alert was heightened and preparation for increased air and sea protection of the transfer convoys was ordered.[5]

By midday on 7 April, receiving information that a German fleet was at sea, Horton had no doubts that a German intervention was developing. He ordered all remaining boats – *Ursula*, *Shark*, *Severn*, *Sterlet*, *Spearfish*, *Snapper*, *Clyde*, *Triad*, *Truant*, *Thistle* and *Tarpon* – to sea with utmost dispatch, irrespective of status, bringing the number of submarines at sea up to over twenty, including two French boats.

Departing the Baltic on 8 April for Oslo. Most of the ships from 1st and 2nd Transport Group bringing men, weapons and equipment to the Norwegian capital were gathered in one large convoy. By the time they were to arrive, Norway was expected to be under German control. Photo is taken from the 2,643-ton *Scharhörn*. The four ships in the back are, from left to right, *Hamm*, *Antares*, *Espana* and *Muansa*. Reaching the Danish Belts, the men were ushered below deck and the ships spread out somewhat, re-gathering in the Kattegat. (Author's Collection)

Seawolf and *Shark* took to sea from Harwich in the evening of the 7th. During the 8th, they passed through the Westwall minefield on the surface by 'route 2' along latitude 55°46'N, 5 miles apart with *Shark* in the lead, ending up north of Heligoland. On the way, they passed a large number of floating mines, but otherwise made little ado of passing through one of the major German naval defence barriers.[6]

In the morning of 8 April, *Seal* arrived off Norway, south-west of Stavanger. During the day, periscope visibility was poor due to fog, getting even worse into the afternoon. Ships were heard through the hydrophones, some at high speed. Surfacing at nightfall, Lieutenant Commander Rupert Lonsdale ensured all torpedo tubes were ready and settled down with the officer of the watch and the lookouts on the bridge, engines at dead slow, straining eyes and ears for lights or sounds. At a quarter to midnight, starboard lookout suddenly yelled: 'Light dead ahead'. A large ship was coming right at them. Lonsdale instinctively rang down the telegraph with 'full ahead' and yelled 'hard-a-starboard' into the voice-pipe. It was the Estonian freighter *Otto*, which side-scraped down the submarine, ending with a violent crash as the bow of the freighter struck the hydroplane guard aft. It had been the closest of escapes. Some rivets were leaking and *Seal* was taking a small amount of water, but there was no question of returning to base.[7]

*   *   *

Further south-east from *Seal*, the Polish submarine *Orzeł* was cruising at periscope depth in the Skagerrak during the morning of the 8th. She was on her fifth war patrol after escaping the Baltic for Britain in September 1939. The first patrols had been rather uneventful, but this time it was clear that something was different. After a meeting with Flotilla Command just before departure, Lieutenant Commander Jan Grudzinski had arrived back at the boat visibly excited and ordered everything to be made ready for sea – on the double. At nightfall on 3 April, *Orzeł* had left Rosyth, arriving off southern Norway two days later, having been delayed by a minor defect in one of the fuel pumps. The first days of the patrol were quiet, except for a few distant explosions on the 7th. Nothing was seen when surfacing shortly afterwards, but the tension remained and the lookouts were very alert throughout the night. The next morning, at 09:45, submerged off Lillesand, the officer of the watch sighted the smoke of an approaching merchantman. So far in the war, they had encountered no German ships at all, and it was routinely assumed this was just another neutral ship. Hence, Grudzinski took his time before arriving in the control room. The merchantman carried no flag and no markings but her course was suspicious, coming from due south, apparently heading for Norwegian waters. Grudzinski approached slowly with the periscope at maximum magnification. Eventually he was able to read the name *Rio de Janeiro* on her bows. Aft, the home port had been painted over, but rather sloppily, and to his joy he could read 'Hamburg' when close enough. Finally – a legal German prey they could attack.

The 5,261-ton *Rio de Janeiro* was originally built for the Hamburg Süd Line in 1914, operating on the route to South America after WWI. Being once again confined by war, she was requisitioned by the Kriegsmarine in March 1940 for troop transport. (E Skjold Collection)

Unknown to the Polish submariners, *Rio de Janeiro* was one of the transports assigned to the transport group heading for Bergen. Originally a 5,261-ton liner carrying cargo and passengers between Europe and Latin America, she was now loaded with large amounts of military equipment, including four 10.5-cm guns, six 20-mm A/A guns, seventy-three horses, seventy-one vehicles and 292 tons of provisions in her spacious hull. In addition there were 313 passengers and crew, most of them wearing uniform.[8]

Grudzinski brought *Orzeł* to the surface and hoisted a series of flags signalling: 'Stop engines. The Master with ship's papers is to report on board immediately.' The freighter appeared to slow down in submission, but turned shoreward and did not stop. *Orzeł* could do 20 knots on the surface and closed rapidly. No activity was observed on board, but a few bursts from *Orzeł*'s machine gun across the freighter's bow resulted in the signal 'Message read and understood' being hoisted and *Rio de Janeiro* started to slow down in earnest. *Orzeł* followed suit, pointing the torpedo tubes in her direction as well as the breech-block-less deck gun, hoping that the Germans would not notice its deficiency. When fully stopped, a boat was lowered from *Rio de Janeiro*. It stayed close to the ship, however, in spite of a few sailors pretending to be rowing. After a while, Grudzinski and First Lieutenant Piasecki agreed that they were just putting on a show and had no intention of coming over. Something was really strange about the vessel as well – all the more so as *Orzeł*'s radio operator reported intercepting a coded radio signal from it. At 11:20, Grudzinski hoisted a signal to abandon ship as he was going to fire a torpedo in fifteen minutes. Still, there was no reaction other than another 'understood' flag being hoisted. No lifeboats were made ready or even swung out, not even when a repeat signal notified them that only five minutes remained until the torpedo would be fired.

Meanwhile, the Norwegian coaster *Lindebø* and the fishing vessel *Jenny* chanced to pass nearby. They were not in harm's way, though, and at 11:45 Grudzinski gave the order for one torpedo to be fired. At the time, *Orzeł*'s navigation officer estimated the German freighter to be 1.8 miles outside neutral Norwegian territory, although this may be an exaggeration according to Norwegian sources.[9] The range was point-blank and the torpedo struck amidships. Steam and dense smoke poured from *Rio de Janeiro* and suddenly her deck came alive with men in field-grey uniforms, falling or jumping into the sea. Lifebelts and pieces of wood were thrown over the side as more men followed into the water. Only after a while did someone start lowering some of the lifeboats. 'Where on earth did all these men come from?' asked Grudzinski, while observing the frenzy of activity in his binoculars. Before anybody could provide an answer, an aircraft was reported approaching from landwards and orders to dive were given.

At 11:15, the Norwegian sea defence sector in Kristiansand (SDS 2) had received a signal from Justøya Coastguard Station that they could see the tower of a submarine on a westerly course just outside the territorial limit and a merchant ship, which appeared to be idling next to it. The nationalities of both vessels were unknown. An MF.11 reconnaissance aircraft was ordered up from the naval air base at Marvika and took off shortly after. It arrived just as the torpedo struck and Løytnant Ragnar Hansen could see chaotic conditions on board the listing ship. People were running through flames and smoke, tumbling into the sea and trying to reach a few nearby floats. Several dead men were floating face down and horses were also in the water, adding to the horror. The submarine, which dived as the aircraft arrived, had vanished. A brief signal was sent to

Marvika at 12:07 as Hansen headed back towards Kristiansand to report. *Lindebø* and *Jenny* moved in to assist.

Rio de Janeiro listed to starboard, but did not appear to be sinking. Grudzinski, who had taken *Orzeł* around to the other side under water, fired a second torpedo from periscope depth. It struck at 12:15 and the bow of the transport broke off, vanishing quickly. Splinters from the explosion flew over *Lindebø*'s deck and several of the rescued sailors were killed or wounded. The hull of *Rio de Janeiro* rolled over and sank minutes later, leaving hundreds of men to fight for their lives in the freezing water. Soon the surface was littered with lifeless bodies. The Norwegian destroyer *Odin*, which also had been sent to investigate, arrived at 12:45, and eventually some 150 men were rescued by the various Norwegian vessels. Around 180 men perished, nineteen crew and some 160 soldiers, plus all the horses.[10] An accurate cross-plot of the position made from Justøy and Høvåg coastguard stations concluded that *Rio de Janeiro* had been just outside the Norwegian 3-mile territorial limit when torpedoed. Lieutenant Commander Grudzinski took *Orzeł* away from the carnage and eventually surfaced to send a report.[11]

Odin headed for Kristiansand with seventeen wounded and eighteen dead under a tarpaulin on the deck, flying her flag at half-mast. Most of the others ended up in Lillesand. The dead were taken to the chapel at the local cemetery. The lesser wounded were treated by three local doctors in the harbour area while the seriously wounded were sent to the hospital in Arendal. The Germans were wet and miserable and obviously shaken by their ordeal. The Norwegian police officer in charge of the operation in Lillesand, Nils Onsrud, became very concerned when he discovered that virtually all of the survivors were wearing uniforms and that some even had guns. Someone who was obviously an officer was trying to maintain some order, shouting: 'Wehrmacht hier! Marine hier!'[12] These men were no ordinary sailors! Questioning them, Onsrud was told that they were soldiers heading for Bergen to assist the Norwegian Army against an Allied invasion – at the Norwegian government's request. The officer, presenting himself with a salute as Lieutenant Voss, on the other hand maintained that *Rio de Janeiro* had been nothing but a merchantman loaded with general provisions. Onsrud was certain the man was lying and that he had stumbled onto something of great importance. He cordoned off the harbour area as best he could and organised dry clothes, food and cigarettes to keep the Germans busy, while he went looking for a telephone. Unknown to himself, and anybody else in Norway, the German plan for Operation Weserübung Nord, the invasion of Norway, had been unmasked.

Onsrud's call to Naval Command in Kristiansand came through at 14:30, but to his astonishment, the officer he spoke to doubted his findings and saw no need to initiate any actions other than the on-going rescue operation. To take care of the survivors and guard them, Onsrud was advised to contact the army 'as the men were already on land'. This he did, but the army saw no reason to interfere either. After nearly two hours of fruitless telephoning and discussions, Onsrud was tired of being pushed around and called Undersecretary of State Rognlien at the Lord Chancellor's Office in Oslo. Rognlien believed Onsrud and called both the General Staff and the Admiral Staff to inform them. He was greatly surprised to learn that the Admiral Staff already knew about the Germans in uniform claiming they were heading for Bergen, having received the same information upon *Odin*'s return to Kristiansand, but they did not consider the matter much to worry about compared to the British mines. The defence minister had been informed, but initiated no actions. Rognlien could only call Onsrud back and ask him to do his best.[13]

The reports from Lillesand and Kristiansand were forwarded to the Ministry of Defence and the Foreign Office around 18:30 and referred by Defence Minister Ljungberg to the Storting (the Norwegian Parliament) shortly after 20:00. Nobody reacted and no precautions were taken. In London, Grudzinski's report never reached the Admiralty. They only heard of the sinking of *Rio de Janeiro* through Reuters and apparently thought little of it.[14] Quite the opposite: VA(S), to his surprise, received instructions from the Admiralty to withdraw the boats off Norway and re-deploy them to a line across the North Sea, south of Stavanger, intercepting German naval forces heading home to bases in the Heligoland Bight. Before these instructions could be put into force, however, reports were received from Oslo that the *Rio de Janeiro* had been sunk and that German soldiers were being rescued. Horton took this to mean he had been right all along and made only minor adjustments to his dispositions, instead of the major realignment instructed by the Admiralty.

Having to spend two torpedoes on a stationary target at point-blank range as he had no operable gun was such a waste in Grudzinski's opinion, and he wrote in his war diary that he was not satisfied with the way *Rio de Janeiro* had been intercepted and sunk. Still, it was the first success of the Polish Navy since the capitulation six months earlier and it is easy to assume he was not entirely unsatisfied either. Later, in the afternoon of the 8th, *Orzeł* received orders to proceed further into the Skagerrak, east of Arendal and beyond.[15]

Already further east, off Svenner Lighthouse south of Larvik, *Trident* intercepted the 8,036-ton tanker *Stedingen* heading for Stavanger-Sola airfield with aviation fuel at midday on the 8th. She had travelled north inside Swedish territorial waters, but risked a dash across the open waters of the outer Oslofjord to save some time heading west. *Stedingen* was a civilian tanker, requisitioned by the Luftwaffe shortly after completion. She carried the name *Posidonia* for a while before being enrolled. When stopped by *Trident*, she had the name *Posidonia* painted over on the hull, and used *Stedingen* in her SOS. Lieutenant Commander Alan Seale wrote:

A large tanker, laden, with no national marks or name on her side was sighted steaming west outside territorial waters. This vessel appeared most suspicious and was thought to be a German Auxiliary. I decided to investigate and at 12:15 surfaced on her port quarter and fired a blank shot. She turned to starboard for territorial waters and increased speed. I then fired two rounds of SAP which fell just short in line with bridge. This caused her to stop engines. I closed on her quarter with 'Do not transmit' flying and made by lamp 'Abandon ship, I shall torpedo you in five minutes'.[16]

Stedingen was hastily abandoned by her crew when *Trident* opened fire. While the lifeboats were lowered by some, others opened the valve covers in the pump rooms and the telegraphist sent a brief SOS from the radio room. The lifeboats pulled clear and made for shore. *Trident* intercepted them and the German master, Kapitän Schäfer, and a sailor were taken on board the British submarine. *Stedingen* sank slowly and Seale finished her off with a torpedo before heading away.[17] The rest of the crew, some fifty men, continued

Shooting *Blücher* from *Emden* in the Danish Belts. There were journalists with cameramen and photographers on board many of the ships going to Norway, resulting in some of the most spectacular films and photos of WWII at sea. (J Asmussen Collection)

towards land and the lifeboats were eventually towed into Stavern by a pilot vessel. *Kreta*, one of the supply ships for Kristiansand, was also fired at by *Trident*, but she escaped into Norwegian waters.

Weather remained good in the Kattegat on the 8th with only a light breeze and a cloudless sky. As dawn broke, a group of warships headed out from Kiel Bay, steaming north towards the Danish Belts at 18 knots. The cruiser *Blücher* was in the lead, followed by cruisers *Lützow* and *Emden* and torpedo boats *Möwe*, *Albatros* and *Kondor*. This was Group V, bringing troops and administrative personnel to capture the Norwegian capital Oslo. The route took them between the Danish islands Fyn and Sjelland; when passing the Halskov Rev lightship at 08:00, entering open waters, the torpedo boats fanned out, flanking the cruisers, which took up a zigzag pattern. Overhead, aircraft arrived for escort. Nothing much happened during the day, except for a few false submarine alarms and, just after 13:00, a fishing buoy was riddled with machine-gun fire from *Blücher*, mistaking it for a periscope. The signal from the transport *Kreta*, around 14:00, that she had been fired at by an enemy submarine near the western entry to the Oslofjord raised tension, as did a Danish radio news-broadcast from Kalundborg reporting that heavy German naval units had been observed in the Great Belt, heading north. Towards evening, the ships were north of Hirsholmene, near the Skagen lightship and the deep swell from the open

Operation Weserübung North April 1940

0 ——— 200 miles
0 ——— 300 km

N

British routes
German routes
Airborne troops

British minefields
Laid 8th April
Alleged

Gneisenau
Scharnhorst

Renown

Gr I

Norwegian Sea

Narvik

Kiruna

Malmberget

Tromsø

Alta

Luleå

Mo

Mosjoen

Repulse

Gr II

Namsos

SWEDEN

Glowworm sunk

Kristiansund

Trondheim

Ålesund

Tynset

18th CS

Dombås

Lillehammer

Hamar

Home Fleet

Bergen

NORWAY

Fornebu

Oslo

Drøbak

Stockholm

Shetlands

1st CS

Stavanger

Egersund

Arendal

Kristiansand

Gr III

Gr IV

Mjölby

Gotland

Alvseta

Öland

2nd CS

Groups I, II

Gr VI

Aalborg

Gr V

DENMARK

North Sea

Esbjerg

Sylt

Copenhagen

Malmö

Bornholm

Kiel

Lübeck

Wilhelmshaven

Cuxhaven

Wesermünde

Hamburg

GERMANY

GREAT BRITAIN

Skagerrak could be felt. Darkness was not far away, but the sky remained clear. Suddenly, shortly after 19:00, *Albatros* on the starboard side of the cruisers hoisted a signal and flashed a warning. Submarine contact! This time it was real. Torpedo tracks were sighted, apparently aiming for *Lützow*, but she was already in a starboard gear as part of a routine zigzag manoeuvre and they all passed harmlessly ahead. *Albatros* stayed with the contact, dropping depth charges while the group resumed a north-north-easterly course into the Skagerrak.

Triton was on patrol between Skagen and Læsø Island when Lieutenant Commander Edward Pizey at 16:50 discovered that several heavy ships were overtaking him. He identified the first ship as *Gneisenau*-class (actually *Blücher*), the second as *Nürnberg* or *Leipzig* (actually *Lützow*) and the third correctly as *Emden*. The flotilla was travelling fast and he had little time to position his submarine. Also, he had to stay away from four suspected A/S trawlers that had been operating off Skagen since early morning. In order not to miss the chance, Pizey aimed all of his ten torpedoes at *Lützow*, the second ship in the line. Just as he was about to fire, though, *Blücher* zigzagged to port, coming into a more favourable position. Believing the cruiser was a battleship, Pizey saw her as the more important target and decided to switch marks, risking an 85-degree-angle shot of ten torpedoes from about 7,000 metres (7,650 yards). Just as the torpedoes were away though, the asdic operator reported that the target had increased speed from 14 to 20 knots. Pizey had allowed for 15 knots and all ten torpedoes missed astern of *Blücher*, actually coming close to *Lützow*.

Albatros came down the tracks but never found *Triton* and after a short search followed the rest of the fleet northwards. Pizey surfaced, sending a brief sighting signal at 18:25, using the mast aerial before an aircraft appeared and made him dive deep; the signal was not received in Britain. At 19:45 he was able to surface again and transmitted '1 German battleship *Gneisenau*-class with one heavy cruiser escorted by *Emden* and destroyers having passed Skaw westward 18:00. Speed 20 knots' using the main aerial.[18]

At 20:31, *Sunfish* reported observing '1 *Blücher*-class, 2 cruisers, 1 destroyer' 20 miles north of Skagen at 18:12, steering north and zigzagging away before coming close enough to attack. Admiral Horton was thrilled and ordered *Trident* and *Orzeł* to proceed with utmost dispatch to a position off Larvik, where he personally believed the flotilla was heading rather than risk entering the well-defended Oslofjord. This turned out to be a wrong decision and Group V slipped into the fjord unchallenged by further submarines.[19]

The German invasion of Norway and Denmark was about to commence.

A Most Unpleasant Day

AT 04:24 ON 9 April, the British Admiralty issued a signal indicating that German naval forces were invading ports in south and west Norway. Until this time, the submarines had only been allowed to attack 'enemy warships and transports'. Identifying which of the large numbers of merchant ships in the Kattegat and Skagerrak were German or indeed transports was no easy task, especially as escorts and air patrols precluded any attempt at surface interception. In the late morning of the 9th, the War Cabinet, after strong pressure from VA(S) and the Admiralty, approved that all German merchant vessels in the Skagerrak east of 8°E, or east of the German Declared Area, could be treated as warships and sunk without warning. This order was forwarded to all boats at 13:24.[1]

While the signal was decoded on board *Sunfish*, Lieutenant Commander Jack Slaughter was turning his periscope onto the 7,129-ton *Amasis*, just outside Swedish territorial waters off Lysekil. 'Just as the sights came on', he later wrote in his report, 'the last part of VA(S)'s 1324/9 was read out to me, so I fired.' One torpedo hit, and the ship sank, opening a series of successful actions by the Allied submarines. *Amasis* was not part of the invasion force though. On the contrary, she was on a commercial voyage from Stettin to Oslo with 7,300 tons of coal.[2]

During the 9th, there were several heavy air attacks on the surface ships of the Home Fleet off southern Norway, and C-in-C Admiral Forbes became convinced that, in the absence of fighter protection, his fleet could not operate safely in the North Sea. Instead, he recommended to the Admiralty that the Royal Navy should make a stand against the

Lieutenant Commander Slaughter on the bridge of his submarine *Sunfish*. (Royal Navy Submarine Museum Collection)

Germans further north, with the 'southern part being left mostly to our submarines as surface forces will find difficulty patrolling, etc. due to German [air] superiority'.

The Admiralty agreed that 'interference with communications in southern areas must be left mainly to submarines, air and mining, aided by intermittent sweeps when forces allow.' Landings were eventually made in central Norway and the Narvik area, while the seas to the south, across which much of the supplies and reinforcements had to be transported, were left to Horton and his boats.[3] Horton knew from his own experiences the navigational hazards of the eastern Skagerrak, Kattegat and the Belts. The shallow waters and narrow straits greatly favoured the A/S patrols and at times the water is so still that the shadow of the submerged submarine can be seen from the air. The slightest oil slick or feather of a periscope or antenna may give the boat away over long distances. Tides are also challenging in the area, as are the irregular variations in salinity from various freshwater sources which cause rapid changes in the density of the water. Boats in perfect trim may suddenly find themselves breaking surface when entering an area of increased salinity or, conversely, dipping periscope and heading for the bottom if entering a pocket of freshwater. Lieutenant Commander Bryant of *Sealion* wrote in his war diary on 9 April:

> A most unpleasant day. Glassy calm, surrounded by fishing boats, and enemy aircraft being sighted continually flying low and close. It was not possible to go deep (owing to density) and continual action to avoid being trawled up was required. Boat was driven slow, shafts in series, at 34 feet [. . .]. The boat could not be driven below 37 feet without flooding or speeding up. [. . .] Yet it is a wonder that we were not seen by the numerous seaplanes and other aircraft and this can only be explained by inefficient German patrols. Our periscope was used most judicially.[4]

In the afternoon of the 9th, *Unity* surfaced at 16:00 off Ringkøbing, inside the German Declared Area. Immediately, a vessel was sighted, hull down to the north, and Lieutenant Brown dived again and gave orders for an interception course. Approaching carefully, the ship was identified as the 3,000-ton *Casablanca*. Brown had at this stage not yet received VA(S)'s signal that German merchant vessels in the Skagerrak or east of the German Declared Area could be treated as warships and sunk without warning. Hence, he decided she was not a legitimate target without searching, which he did not wish to do as *Unity* carried no gun and would in all likelihood just compromise her position for no gain. Brown turned *Unity* slowly away from the merchantman, but decided to keep her under observation. When at 16:50 the vessel was dead astern, at about 900 metres, the asdic operator suddenly reported that she had stopped her engines. Brown found this strange and immediately raised his periscope to see what was going on. Before he had time to see much, two loud explosions shook the submarine but inflicted no serious damage. Brown lowered the periscope and turned *Unity* onto a course that would allow him to fire torpedoes as he was convinced what he had encountered was a German Q-ship, a trap to attract submarines by posing as an unarmed merchantman. Obtaining a firing position was not easy, though, as the German boat, who had started her engines again, kept bow-on to *Unity*. There was a heavy swell in spite of an otherwise glassy sea and any attempt at using the periscope made it dip one moment and rise high out of the water the next, making it easy for them to see where she was. Tiring of achieving nothing, Brown decided to quit before he ended up in a dangerous situation and turned *Unity* onto a westerly course at slow speed. After a while speed was increased as it was believed the submarine was at a safe distance. This was immediately followed by four explosions, however – the German ship was coming straight at them, obviously guided by some sort of listening device in addition to the observations of *Unity*'s periscope. Brown went deep and altered course away from the oncoming German. During the next hour, more than a dozen depth charges were dropped, while the surface vessel was heard to steam back and forth, stopping frequently, listening for where *Unity* might be. Brown kept his boat quiet, however, and slowly managed to increase the distance until, at 18:21, he was comfortable he had got away and could return to slow-ahead on both engines.[5]

This episode is rather strange. *Casablanca* was nowhere near the area, but her sister ship *Oldenburg*, which had left Wilhelmshaven on the 4th for an A/S patrol in the Bight, reported attacking a submarine assisted by the vessels *VP403* and *VP408* of the 4th Vorpost Flotilla on 8 April in this area. Except for the twenty-four-hour discrepancy, her account is similar to that of *Unity*'s and probably describes the same event.[6] Why the dates are different is not obvious, but as several German ships were involved on the surface it is easy to believe they had got the calendar right. Nevertheless, the way the attack is described by Brown, it appears that the German ships never had a firm contact and did not have professional drills and well-trained A/S crew. This matches the German report as the 2,312-ton *Oldenburg*, or *Schiff35*, was a converted passenger steamer requisitioned by the Kriegsmarine at the start of the war and converted to a submarine-trap; it was on her first patrol. She could do no more than 12.5 knots and was dependent on other ships assisting her in actually chasing the submarines that she might lure to attack her – the concept never became a success.

During the early morning of 9 April, German ships entered key Norwegian harbours, landing soldiers. In some places the operation went as planned, in other places there were challenges. By early afternoon Oslo, Horten, Kristiansand, Stavanger, Bergen, Trondheim and Narvik were all in German hands. To avoid becoming trapped in the fjords, the warships of the Kriegsmarine had orders to depart as soon as the soldiers and equipment that they carried had been unloaded. As predicted by the SKL, this was to become the most risky part of the operation and only in a few cases did the return leg go as smoothly as planned.[7]

At Kristiansand, the southernmost port of Norway, Kapitän zur See Friedrich Rieve, the captain of the cruiser *Karlsruhe*, was in command. Besides the cruiser, his small force consisted of the three torpedo boats *Greif*, *Luchs* and *Seeadler*, the depot ship *Tsingtao* and seven S-boats. *Greif* had been detached to land a small unit of soldiers at Arendal further east, but was back with the others during the afternoon. Thick fog and determined resistance from the Norwegian coastal fort covering the entry to Kristiansand had resulted in severe delays, threatening the success of the whole landing. Things had eventually worked out for the Germans, however, partly due to a misunderstanding among the Norwegian defenders who became confused by some signal flags in the dense fog and, believing some of the ships were French, held their fire. Around 16:00 the town and forts were firmly in German hands.[8]

Karlsruhe in Kristiansand harbour around midday on 9 April. (Author's Collection)

Rieve's orders after seizure of the port and town were rather loose, except that he should return to Kiel as soon as possible. Kristiansand was well within reach of British bombers and the longer he stayed the more likely an attack would be. By 18:00, the disembarkation of the troops and equipment from the larger warships had been completed and Rieve decided there was no reason to linger. *Karlsruhe* weighed anchor and left with *Greif*, *Luchs* and *Seeadler* in company. *Tsingtao* and the S-boats stayed behind. Offshore, the torpedo boats took up screening positions around the cruiser, which was zigzagging at 21 knots.[9]

Truant, under the command of 34-year-old Lieutenant Commander 'Jockey' Hutchinson, was loitering off southern Norway in the morning of the 9th, having left Rosyth three days earlier. Thick fog in the Skagerrak had made things difficult in the preceding days and although several ships had been heard, none had been identified with sufficient certainty to justify an attack. During the morning of the 9th, the fog started to clear and Hutchinson settled his boat at periscope depth. Explosions were heard at times and Dornier aircraft were sighted above on several occasions during the day. Something seemed to be going on, but it was not clear what.

At 17:23 three torpedo boats were sighted coming from the north-west, steering south at an estimated 22 knots. An attack was commenced, but discontinued when the ships were identified as 'Norwegian *Sleipner*-class destroyers'. This is definitely wrong as the only two such ships in the area, *Gyller* and *Odin*, were in Kristiansand harbour at this time, under German control. The vessels were most certainly the three minesweepers *M2*, *M9* and *M13* heading for home from Kristiansand – Hutchinson lost a good target. Together with *M1*, they had landed soldiers at Egersund further west; leaving that port, they then received orders to head for Kristiansand to assist the ships there. Upon arrival, their assistance was not required and three of the minesweepers left within a few hours, leaving *M1* behind with an engine problem.[10]

Truant. (Author's Collection)

On the positive side, the misidentification kept *Truant* concealed for larger prey and avoided counter-attacks from the minesweepers. Eventually, faint propeller noises were heard from the north and at 18:33 a German cruiser was sighted low on the northern horizon, steering south-south-east and screened by '3 *Maass* destroyers'. The escort vessels were not destroyers, but *Greif, Luchs* and *Seeadler*: capable of just over 30 knots and carrying some thirty depth charges each.

The range to *Karlsruhe* was 4,500 metres (4,900 yards) and decreasing. *Truant* would soon be in an excellent attack position and Hutchinson used his periscope as little as possible in order not to be sighted, particularly as he expected there would be escorting aircraft in the vicinity as well. Instead, he took *Truant* down to 20 metres (65 feet) and made a quick burst of speed to get inside the screen and ahead of the oncoming cruiser. A sudden easterly course alteration increased the relative speed of the cruiser, however, putting *Truant* in a most unfavourable position. All four ships were still within range, though, in an almost unbroken line and to Hutchinson it was 'now or never'. At 18:56 Hutchinson fired a full bow salvo of ten torpedoes, at a distance that was now estimated to be some 2,100 metres (2,300 yards). The two first torpedoes were set to run at 10 feet (3.1 metres). The next six, fired at six-second intervals, were set at 12 feet (3.6 metres) and the last two at 8 feet (2.5 metres). The shallower settings were intended to try to catch the escorts forward and aft of the cruiser, respectively.

In order to avoid breaking surface from the loss of the weight of such a large salvo, *Truant* was taken down as soon as firing commenced. About three minutes later, a loud explosion was heard, followed by another and then a third, accompanied by the sound of 'rending metal'. Hutchinson took *Truant* to periscope depth and sighted *Luchs* right on top of them. The hunt was on.[11]

On board *Karlsruhe*, four torpedo tracks were observed to starboard at 18:58. Kapitän Rieve immediately ordered 'both engines full ahead' and 'hard-a-port', but to no avail. In spite of three explosions being recorded by *Truant*, it appears that only one torpedo impacted on the starboard side of the cruiser, near the bulkhead between the auxiliary machine room and the cruising turbine room, compartments V/VI. Both engines and steering fell out and the cruiser stopped, listing 12 degrees. The situation was serious and

Torpedo boats *Greif, Albatros* and *Möwe* in 1940. (Author's Collection)

more so when the first officer, Korvettenkapitän Düwel, reported several compartments filling fast and all pumps out of action. Water and oil were soon up to the floor plates of the main rudder engine room and no. 1 generator room, coming through cracks in the bulkheads. 'The situation is serious,' Rieve noted in *Karlsruhe's* war diary.[12]

Luchs had narrowly escaped the torpedoes through emergency manoeuvring and was now combing down the tracks for retribution. On board *Truant*, which Hutchinson had taken to 20 metres (65 feet) again, turning away from the torpedo boat, the fore hatch sprang open and shut, water pouring into the boat when two depth charges exploded 'dead close'. The trim of the submarine was affected, but the closing mechanism of the hatch was not damaged and it was possible to tighten it again before any serious danger developed. The torpedo boats were not easily shaken off. *Truant* was chased for four and a half hours, with a further thirty-one depth charges being registered. 'Nearly all of them unpleasantly close,' according to Hutchinson, though not as close as the first two. The two torpedo boats were very persistent. After each attack, they stopped and listened, using echo-sounders. To get away from the hunters, Hutchinson took *Truant* below 350 feet (105 metres) at times. Later, he wrote:

After the first attack, which was unpleasantly close, submarine was taken to 320 feet in a depth of 250 fathoms. Speed of 3½ knots was maintained and not altered for fear of any alterations being heard. All other machinery, including the Sperry [gyro compass] was stopped, main motor coolers and bow caps shut and nearly all lights switched out.

Course was altered in an attempt to keep stern on, but the enemy continued to hold contact by hydrophone. Water was too deep for bottoming, so that that method of shaking off the enemy could not be tried. The submarine was making water too fast to attempt to hold a stopped trim. [. . .] Both hydroplanes went out of action but finished up capable of being operated, aft in local control and forward only on ship's telemotor system. This necessitated working the noisy telemotor pump when a destroyer was coming in to attack and not listening.[13]

One of the first explosions rendered the magnetic compass unserviceable and with the gyro compass stopped, *Truant* was moving around blindly for a while. Later explosions burst the aft trim-tank, increasing the leaks. Numerous short-circuits affected the electrical system and sparks flew from the main motor switch gear. The high-pressure air system developed leaks as well, increasing the pressure inside the hull and making breathing in the foul air very uncomfortable. One set of exploding depth charges cracked the Z-tank, starting several minor leaks, another jarred open the main engine cooling-water inlet valves, which resulted in flooding aft and sent the bows up 15 degrees. *Truant* was still under control, though, and level trim was not attempted, as using the pump would be noisy and there was a risk that oily water might reach the surface, revealing her location. Chief ERA William Pook later recounted:

I saw the water coming in through the tanks. The after tank was full up, the bulkheads started to leak and we were very heavy aft, so we were at an angle. Eventually, we were down to 420 feet which was way over our diving depth. We were like that for some hours. Every time we tried to come up, we were depth charged again. It went on until very nearly morning. [. . .] Stern glands were leaking and I had to tighten those up. We had to hammer up the bulkhead of the trim tank which had been damaged. We were jamming off valves which had blown open with the charges. Apart from that if there was nothing to do, we laid in bunks and waited. It was terrifying, there's no doubt about it. [. . .] It's not the charges that are frightening, it is waiting for them . . . when you hear the destroyers coming towards you. [. . .] You don't show it. You're probably churning over inside, but you don't show it.[14]

On board *Karlsruhe* it became clear that the cruiser was sinking and the survivors from below deck were ordered up. *Luchs* and *Seeadler* were instructed to break off the hunt for the submarine and come alongside the cruiser to take the crew off. Having done this, they set course for Kiel. Kapitän Rieve left his ship as the last man at 20:10, embarking *Greif*, which was ordered to remain. After a while, it was decided to sink the cruiser and a torpedo was fired from *Greif*. *Karlsruhe*'s forecastle was blown off but she remained afloat and it took yet another torpedo before she finally slid below, bow first, at 21:42.[15]

At that time things had been quiet for some time and Hutchinson decided to risk going up for a look. On the way up, more explosions were heard, although not as close as before and *Truant* was taken down to below 300 feet (91.5 metres) again. In all likelihood, these explosions were those of *Greif*'s torpedoes sinking the crippled cruiser. Things remained quiet after this and about an hour later, when the batteries were running low and the air was too foul to stand any longer, Hutchison ordered his submarine to rise again, very slowly and quietly.

Truant finally surfaced at 23:25, having been submerged for nineteen hours. Everything was quiet and nothing was seen of the enemy. All hatches were opened and the engines started to charge the batteries. None of the compasses worked, and the sky was overcast so it was difficult to know which way to go to clear the area. Assuming the direction of the wind had not changed much since the previous night, Hutchinson steered downwind, hoping this would be towards open waters. Eventually, the sky cleared sufficiently for the navigating officer to identify enough stars for a south-westerly course to be set for home. The crew was exhausted, and the boat damaged, so Hutchinson informed Submarine Command of the attack and that he was returning to Rosyth, in a signal at 01:12 on the 10th.

Most of the damage was made good during the day and in an update message, Hutchinson informed VA(S) that he still had six torpedoes remaining and asked if he should remain on patrol. The answer from Admiral Horton was swift and clear: 'All in good time. I want to see you first.'

The loss of a valuable cruiser to a single torpedo close to land was disconcerting to the SKL and Rieve was criticised for not attempting to take her in tow by the torpedo boats or call assistance from Kristiansand. Other senior officers pointed to the fact that, in spite of being in submarine-infested waters, the ship had neither been fully closed-up nor at 'action stations'. The condition of the ship had been serious after the torpedo hit, but it should not have been hopeless under the existing weather conditions. Based on the reports from Korvettenkapitän Düwel, Rieve maintained that the ship had been sinking and he did all that could have been done, considering the low level of training of the ship's young company. Still, it took two more torpedoes before *Karlsruhe* went down and perhaps more energetic damage control might have saved her. Rieve was temporarily made commander of the sea defences of the Oslofjord before he was promoted in August to Konteradmiral and appointed Chief of Staff at the North Sea Naval Command in Wilhelmshaven.[16]

The damage to *Truant* was slight and after a week in the yard, she was ready for her next war patrol, her seventh. Hutchinson received the DSO on 9 May 1940 for the sinking of *Karlsruhe*. The depth charging had taken its toll, however, and after another eventful patrol he was granted sick leave (see page 249). Lieutenant Commander Hugh Haggard was appointed CO of *Truant*.[17]

In the run-up to the invasion, *Thistle*, *Clyde* and *Seal* were stationed off Stavanger. During the 8th, they were moved westwards, away from the coast, 'to place them in the possible path of German heavy forces should they proceed up the west coast of Norway'.[18] This did not happen and the four German transports intended for Stavanger managed to slip into sheltered waters without being intercepted.[19] Based on air reconnaissance on the 9th, the Admiralty also believed (falsely) that a German destroyer was in Stavanger and instructed Horton to send a submarine into the fjord to investigate and attack if possible. Horton obligingly sent a signal to *Thistle* with instructions to enter Stavanger and 'attack enemy warships and transports' there, while *Clyde* and *Seal* were to close the coast further north.[20]

Lieutenant Commander Wilfrid Haselfoot, who had taken over command of *Thistle* two months earlier and was now on his second patrol, reported back that he was steering for the fjord, expecting to go in at nightfall. At 21:30, however, a second signal arrived at Northways: 'Expended six torpedoes on inward bound U-boat at entrance to Skudenes Fjord at 16:04. Result unconfirmed due to enemy air activity. Intend to carry out VAS 1249/9 tomorrow Wednesday with remaining two warheads, air activity permitting.'[21]

Meanwhile, the Admiralty had received information that there were no viable targets in Stavanger harbour and in a signal from VA(S), transmitted at 04:26 on the 10th, *Thistle* was instructed to cancel the entry into Stavanger harbour and rather take a billet off Skudeneshavn, keeping an eye on the entrance to Karmsundet. Nothing more was ever heard from *Thistle*, though – except for a brief statement on German radio that a submarine had been sunk, her fate remained a mystery until after the war.[22] The U-boat fired at was *U4*, which had returned to active service from a training unit in March to meet the need for extra boats during Operation Weserübung. At 17:05 (GeT), torpedo tracks were seen off the port quarter. Swift evasive action, turning away from the tracks, saved *U4*, with the nearest of *Thistle*'s torpedoes passing less than 10 metres (33 feet) away. At least three more torpedoes were heard by the sonar operator further ahead, indicating that Haselfoot had overestimated the speed of the U-boat. After some minutes, five loud explosions were heard on board *U4* when the British torpedoes exploded as they hit the coast.[23]

Oberleutnant Hans-Peter Hinsch did not appreciate being attacked at all and, taking *U4* down, he searched around for the perpetrator. Tension ran high in the U-boat as 'electric engine noises', heard at times, indicated that the enemy was still around. The batteries were low and Hinsch resurfaced at 22:17 to charge them while he kept searching, pulling further out to sea to get away from the dark background of the coast. At 01:57 the shadow of a submarine was sighted ahead and to starboard. It was too close to fire immediately and Hinsch gave orders to turn away from the British boat and shouted 'action stations – ready for surface attack' down the voice-pipe.

> We turn to starboard with both engines at 4/5 speed to get the enemy straight aft. Tubes I and III are made ready. After some 600 metres, I turn back to a reciprocal course. Enemy seems to have stopped. First torpedo (G7a) is fired as a straight shot. Observing the wake of bubbles, I see that the enemy's bows are shifting to starboard and that she is actually still slightly under way. The first torpedo misses. Immediately fire second torpedo (G7e) from around 400 metres, allowing for speed of 5 knots, direction 70. Hit amidships. Huge patch of oil and heavy smell. In the darkness we find nothing to retrieve.[24]

For some reason, the crew of *Thistle* had been caught off guard and earned the dubious distinction of becoming the first Allied submarine to be sunk by a U-boat. Haselfoot must have believed that the U-boat he had tried to sink earlier was long gone from the area as he surfaced to charge his batteries at nightfall.[25]

— 15 —

Freedom of Action

THE GERMAN INVASION OF Denmark and Norway completely changed the modus operandi of the British Submarine Service. Firstly, the submarine commanders were almost instantly given freedom of action and, secondly, there were targets to hunt almost everywhere. The following three weeks were to be among the most hectic and successful during the war, but also the most dangerous.

10 April

The bulk of the troops and supplies to secure the immediate sustainability of Operation Weserübung were to come through Oslo in a series of transport convoys following the initial landings. There had already been significant attrition of the first transport group, heading for the invasion ports outside Oslo. The following groups, bringing in more than 100,000 troops and their equipment, would go to Oslo only – partly as the sea lanes further west were under total British dominance, and partly as the main breakout towards the other bridgeheads was planned to come from the Oslo region.

This operation turned out to be not quite as easy as expected, mainly due to the one factor the Kriegsmarine had not fully prepared for: Allied submarines. Though not crippling, the attrition was high enough for the plan to be modified so that as many as possible were transported by air, while supplies and the rest of the troops were shuttled between northern Denmark and southern Oslofjord. On 10 April, the Admiralty informed C-in-C and VA(S) that they had decided 'interference with communications in southern areas must be left mainly to submarines, air and mining, aided by intermittent sweeps when forces allow.'[1] This was a formidable upgrade of the strategic significance of the Submarine Service – probably not fully recognised at the time – creating an undreamt of opportunity for VA(S) and his submarines.

Having continued east after sinking *Rio de Janeiro*, *Orzeł* had a rather quiet day on the 9th, largely hampered by fog. Three German mine-sweeping trawlers were sighted near their new patrol area off Larvik, but Grudzinski decided to leave them alone. The next day, the trawlers were sighted again and eventually he decided they were a convenient target for a few torpedoes. Two torpedoes were fired from close range. Both were heard to explode, but not due to hitting any German vessel. There was no hunt for the submarine afterwards, and the trawlers probably never even realised they had been fired at.

On the 12th, *Orzeł* detected a small convoy of at least two vessels under escort. The submarine was probably sighted before she could come into an attack position and was forced deep by aircraft while the merchant ships turned away. Subsequently, the escort hunted the Polish submarine for several hours, dropping at least twenty-one depth charges, before Grudzinski managed to steal away, having been down to over 70 metres (230 feet) and eventually bottoming with all engines turned off. During the next three days, *Orzeł* was attacked time and again by aircraft and A/S patrols and up to twenty hours per day were spent submerged. During one of the attacks, she was forced down to almost 100 metres (well over 300 feet), deeper than she had ever been before. On the 16th, course was set for Rosyth.[2]

During this patrol, over 100 depth charges and bombs were recorded by *Orzeł* as exploding in her vicinity, dropped from German warships and aircraft. Captain Menzies of 2nd Flotilla, however, believed most of these had not been specifically dangerous to the submarine and rather were the result of the German tactic of dropping charges at intervals to scare boats away. In the case of *Orzeł*, he believed that the crew's previous lack of exposure to A/S forces and their sensitive hydrophones gave them the impression that the hunting vessels were nearer than in fact than they were. Still, Grudzinski was praised for his aggressiveness and will to achieve.

At 16:35 on the 10th, *Triton* was still in northernmost Kattegat, when a large convoy of some fifteen ships steering north was sighted off Gothenburg, outside but close to Swedish territory. *Triton* was just inside Swedish territorial waters, in relative safety from German aircraft, but ready to move back into international waters if Swedish naval vessels should emerge. The convoy consisted of the majority of the transport vessels, heading for Oslo: *Scharhörn, Tucuman, Itauri, Espana, Friedenau, Hamm, Muansa* and *Wigbert*, escorted by *V1501, V1505, V1506, V1507, V1508, V1509* and some T-boats. The sea was very calm and the periscope had to be used sparingly to avoid detection by the escort, which included aircraft. At 17:26 the submarine was in position and Lieutenant Commander Pizey fired a 90-degree-angle shot of six torpedoes from about 2,000 metres (2,200 yards). Immediately the torpedoes were away, he turned *Triton* around, heading towards Swedish territorial waters, though staying just outside as the Swedish destroyer *Wrangel* was seen patrolling the inside, close by.

Friedenau sinking. (Author's Collection)

Six friends from Infantry Regiment IR 340 travelling to Norway on board *Friedenau*. The text on the back of the photo reads: 'Left to Right, Kunoth (missing), Krause, Miche (missing), Lehmann, Walcher (wounded) Schadeck (missing).' (Author's Collection)

No less than three ships were hit: the 5,219-ton *Friedenau*, the 3,648-ton *Wigbert* and the escort *V1507* (*Rau VI*). Total chaos broke out in the convoy. There had been no precautionary instructions and for a while it was every ship for itself. Some stopped to pick up survivors whereas others continued. Eventually, the transports were ushered on, while a few of the escorts stayed behind to pick up the remaining survivors. *Wigbert* sank on an even keel within fifteen to twenty minutes, while *Friedenau* remained for a while longer, floating on her forecastle. *V1507* vanished in seconds, taking nineteen men down with her.[3]

For the Germans, this was a disaster. Around 1,160 men were lost, the majority from *Friedenau*. The two infantry regiments IR 340 and IR 345 were decimated and few survived from the crews of the transports. There were a large number of horses on board *Wigbert* and some of these managed to break loose, swimming terrified around in the water. Soldiers from the surviving ships saw no other solution than to load their guns and start shooting them. While the main part of the convoy continued, the torpedo boat *T155* stopped, together with *V1501*. The transports *Espana* and *Hamm* halted for a while but were soon ordered to move on, lest also they should be torpedoed. Some 800 men were rescued, many by *Wrangel* that emerged from Swedish territorial waters to assist.

The counter-attack on *Triton* was heavy: seventy-eight depth charges were counted in all. Only once were four or five near enough to shake the boat, though, and Lieutenant Commander Pizey was able to get his submarine safely away within an hour. By 21:15, *Triton* was on the surface heading out of the Kattegat with no more torpedoes left.[4]

Later in the evening, the 2,500-ton *Antares* was stalked by *Sunfish* and sunk off Lysekil. She had lost the convoy and travelled alone, despite having 1,000 Austrian mountain troops on board as well as horses, guns and ammunition. *Antares* was hit by two torpedoes, causing what appears to have been an explosion in the ammunition stores. Panic ensued among the Austrians, most of who had never been to sea before, and several of the lifeboats and floats capsized, increasing the number of casualties.

Two photos of the rescue work on 10 April. To the left is *V1501* with *Espana* in the background. On the lower photo *T155* has also moved in. Notice the two men in the lower right-hand corner of the lower photo. They are apparently considered safe on the float and not given priority at the moment in spite of at least one of them being wounded. (Author's Collection)

Two trawlers of the 11th A/S Flotilla happened to be nearby on their way to the Oslofjord. Seeing the explosion of the torpedoes they rushed to the scene, but, by the time they arrived, *Antares* was sinking and all they could do was to pick up the survivors. This caused 'considerable activity overhead' according to Lieutenant Commander Slaughter, but no counter-attack developed and *Sunfish* slipped away to charge her batteries.[5]

Later in the evening, *Trident* and *Orzeł* both missed in their further attempts at the remaining ships of the convoy. The surviving transports reached Oslo during the 12th, followed by a more or less continuous stream of ships during the coming weeks.

After this catastrophic day, most of the larger ships were sent to Norway in small, heavily escorted convoys. Troops who could not be accommodated by aircraft or through the clandestine route through Sweden were taken by train to Denmark and shipped across from Frederikshavn or Aalborg to Larvik at the mouth of the Oslofjord. Some of the most important goods and units were taken up the fjord, directly to Oslo. Between 1,000 and 3,000 men were sent across each day, depending on the ships available. Some of the escorts also carried troops to speed up the transfer. The challenges for the escorts were many. Each convoy, whether it consisted of two transports or ten required a substantial screen. By the end of April, more than ten auxiliary or mine-sweeping flotillas, each with six to ten vessels, were active in the eastern Skagerrak, in addition to a dozen larger torpedo boats and escorts. This was somewhat unexpectedly pulling resources away from the naval support to the forthcoming assault in the west.[6]

The heavy cruiser *Lützow* was one of the ships which had taken troops to the Norwegian capital Oslo. The group had been severely delayed by resistance from the Norwegians and the lead ship, the cruiser *Blücher*, had been sunk by gunfire and torpedoes from the

The rest of the convoy steaming up the Oslofjord on 11 April. (Author's Collection)

forts at the Drøbak Narrows. *Lützow* had also sustained damage in the encounter and needed to return to Germany to be patched up before her next Atlantic sortie. Finally reaching Oslo at 08:45 in the morning of the 10th, Kapitän zur See August 'Curry' Thiele was in a hurry to leave as soon as possible.[7] Merchant warfare in the Atlantic was the *raison d'être* for the 'pocket battleship' and every passing week shortened the length of the nights in the northern waters and thus made the breakout into the Atlantic more difficult.[8]

The light cruiser *Emden* was left behind in Oslo while *Lützow* and the torpedo boat *Möwe* headed back down the Oslofjord around 15:00. *Albatros* and *Kondor* were already in the outer reaches of the fjord and would join them later. *Albatros* ran aground, however, and Thiele detached *Möwe* to stay with *Kondor* looking after *Albatros*. Hence, *Lützow* continued alone, in spite of several submarine alerts in the Kattegat. Thiele was not overly worried at losing his escort. The risk of interference by the Royal Navy in the Oslofjord or the Skagerrak was believed to be low and though British aircraft could appear at any time, the night would be sufficiently long for a high-speed crossing, he reckoned.

Leaving Oslofjord behind, the night was clear and starry with good visibility, moderate seas and a Force 4 north-easterly wind. Signals intercepted during the previous days put most of the British submarine contacts near the Swedish coast, and Thiele steered a westerly track in large zigzags at 24 knots. The general course was 138 degrees, heading towards the gap between Skagen and the Paternoster Skerries. An hour after midnight, German time, the ship's DeTe-Gerät radar picked up a contact ahead, fine on the starboard bow, at a range of 15,000 metres (16,400 yards). The echo was small and taken to be a fishing vessel, but Thiele gave port rudder to give it a wide berth. The distance increased, and when the radar reported the echo lost, starboard rudder was ordered to get back onto the main course.[9]

Spearfish, fresh out of the yards after her ordeal in September and with a new commander, Lieutenant Commander John Forbes, in charge, left Rosyth for her patrol area in the Kattegat on the morning of 5 April. Reaching her billet north of the German minefield in the morning of the 7th, extensive activity was encountered, both in the air and at sea. When surfacing to try to intercept a cruiser with escort that had been reported further west, they had to dive because of aircraft several times, making slow progress. On one occasion, at midday, only a panic-stricken emergency dive saved them from being hit by bombs from an aircraft coming out of the sun. One bomb exploded on the surface as *Spearfish* passed 6 metres (20 feet), shutting down the steering motor to the after hydroplanes. Forbes flooded the main tanks and the boat bottomed heavily at 30 metres (100 feet) with the bow 30 degrees down. It took an hour and a half until matters were under control again. In the evening of the 8th, *Spearfish* was ordered to reposition to inside the Skagerrak, north-east of Skagen. This position was reached in the early morning of the 10th. Several trawlers and minesweepers were sighted, but Forbes decided they were not significant enough as targets to reveal his position.[10]

Instead, when manoeuvring to approach what appeared to be a destroyer coming north out of the Kattegat shortly after 17:00, *Spearfish* suddenly received the attention of a group of escorts and A/S trawlers. It appears that *Spearfish* had been approaching the same convoy that *Triton* had attacked shortly before, having stirred up the escorts. During the chase for Lieutenant Commander Pizey and his boat, the Germans stumbled across *Spearfish* as well, shifting their attention to her. *Spearfish* was chased for most of the afternoon and seventy-nine depth charges were counted, causing high-pressure leaks and damage to hydrophones and periscope. Forbes wrote:

> Bowcaps were shut, main motor coolers shut off and fans stopped at the beginning of the attack. As 'U' boats are reputed to dive deep when charged, shallow tactics were adopted. The first part of the hunt was carried out at 45 feet, and the latter part at 55 feet. Slow speed was maintained throughout . . . The majority of the depth charges appeared to be set deep. When A/S transmissions were heard, an attempt was made to confuse the enemy with 'non-sub' echoes, by leading them into rocky Hierto Fjord (must be inside Swedish waters east of Väderöarna, where there is a small island called Hjärterön). When they ceased A/S transmissions the submarine turned round again towards the open sea. Bottoming was considered, but rejected as I felt that the enemy would sit down over us until dawn. . . . The actual depth charges were not as worrying as the danger that the submarine was being hunted to exhaustion.[11]

This must have become a real worry, as various leaks increased the pressure inside the submarine and, together with the foul air, made the crew exhausted and dizzy. To escape, Forbes used the disturbed waters after the explosions of depth charges to alter course but the A/S vessels always regained contact within minutes. Eventually, though, at 23:30 the hunters had finally been shaken off and Forbes could bring *Spearfish* to the surface after being submerged for more than twenty hours. Due to the pressure build-up inside the boat, Forbes was roped down when opening the hatch in order not to be sucked out and injured – a very necessary precaution, as the hatch flew open with a tremendous force as the air escaped.[12]

About an hour later, at 00:29 on the 11th, First Lieutenant Don Pirie sighted the bow wave of a large ship on the starboard quarter at about 3,000 metres (3,300 yards). Forbes, who was also on the bridge, believed it might be one of the escorts again and altered course to port to put the boat stern-on to avoid detection. Some minutes later, the vessel was seen to be very large and, later still, it was wrongly identified as *Admiral Scheer*.[13] The torpedoes were set to run at between 4 and 6 metres (13 and 20 feet). With both engines stopped, Forbes fired six torpedoes on *Lützow* from the conning tower by eye while swinging slowly to port. In spite of a very dark night, conditions were otherwise good and he risked a long-distance shot at over 2,000 metres (2,200 yards). Immediately after firing, orders were given for 12 knots and *Spearfish* was turned onto a westerly course. While still on the surface, a sighting report was sent to VA(S). After a couple of minutes, a large explosion was heard from the direction of the target.[14]

At the time when Thiele gave orders to bring *Lützow* back on her main course, Forbes's torpedoes were already underway. *Lützow* was still turning on starboard rudder when, at 01:29 GeT, a tremendous impact shook the cruiser aft. Nothing was seen prior to the hit. Just after, two or three torpedo tracks were reported at an acute angle off the port side. The rudder was jammed at 20 degrees to starboard and the cruiser kept turning while speed was reduced. Nobody in compartment II answered the telephone or the rudder indicator and it was obvious that there was significant damage. Several of the compartments aft started to flood and *Lützow* settled by the stern with a list to port. Thiele gave orders for emergency steering to be rigged, but

Lützow severely damaged off Skagen, surrounded by minesweepers and A/S vessels. Note that the central barrel of the forward turret is hanging down, damaged by a hit from the Norwegian guns at Oscarsborg when trying to penetrate the defences of Oslofjord. (Bundesarchiv, Bild 101II-MN-1025-13)

the rudder room could not be accessed and attempts to steer by the propellers had no effect: both propellers had been lost.[15]

At 01:55 an urgent signal was despatched to Group East giving the estimated position adding: 'Need immediate assistance from tugs', followed some ten minutes later by 'Probable torpedo hit aft. Engines are OK. Rudder not operational. Submarine protection is required.' And later still: 'My position is 10 miles off Skagen. Ship is un-manoeuvrable. Holding water. Both propellers lost.'

Eventually, the flooding was stemmed in compartment IV, but it was clear that the three after compartments were gone, including the aft magazines. With no propulsion or steering, *Lützow* drifted at about 2 knots south-westwards towards Skagen, broadside to the sea. Further submarine attacks were to be expected and in the good visibility the immobilised ship would be a dead duck. A sharp anti-submarine watch was set and all secondary guns manned. Thiele also ordered all crewmembers to don lifebelts and the lower decks to be evacuated, except by those assigned to the damage-control parties. Boats were swung out and made ready for launching. The aft turret was ordered to jettison all ammunition to help lighten the stern. By 03:00 the ship's trim had been improved by pumping oil and the main part of the hull was almost upright, even if the after deck was at an angle, partly underwater.[16]

At 03:08 Oberleutnant Vogler was sent off in a motor cutter towards Skagen to summon assistance from tugs and escort vessels. At about the same time, 17th A/S Flotilla, 19th Minesweeping Flotilla and 2nd S-Boat Flotilla were ordered by Group East to gather on the cruiser. The torpedo boats *Jaguar* and *Falke* were under way from Kristiansand, *Greif*, *Luchs* and *Seeadler* from Kiel and *Möwe* and *Kondor* from the Oslofjord.[17] Meanwhile, *Lützow*'s launch was set on the water with a crate of demolition charges and orders to circle the cruiser, throwing one or two in the water every now and then, passing off as depth charges, to scare further submarines away.

Between 04:30 and 05:00 the trawlers and minesweepers arrived and as many as possible of the ship's company were transferred to these, which thereafter took up screening positions. A temporary tow was rigged from three of the minesweepers (*M1903*, *M1907* and *M1908*) to provide a minimum of steering and keep the bow to the wind. *Möwe*, which arrived around 08:20, took charge ahead of the tow. Not long after, Oberleutnant Vogler returned from Skagen. He had not found any tugs but brought numerous fishing vessels and the Skagen lifeboat should an evacuation become necessary. At dawn, a standing patrol of He115 aircraft was established, reducing the danger of further submarine attacks significantly. The RAF mercifully stayed away.

The minesweepers found handling of the cruiser difficult as the wind and sea were building up, but in the afternoon the heavy tugs *Wotan* and *Seeteufel* arrived from Kiel to take over the job. When the rest of the torpedo boats arrived, taking up a proper anti-submarine station, it seemed as if it might be possible to save *Lützow* after all. Nevertheless, Kapitän Thiele ordered all unnecessary men off, including most of the gun crews, now that a proper escort was in place. Some 500 men were landed at Frederikshavn

Officers and men of *Spearfish* posing for the photographers after coming home in April 1940. First Lieutenant Don Pirie is second from left, standing; Lieutenant Commander Forbes is third from left. They believed wrongly that they had actually sunk *Admiral Scheer*. (Author's Collection)

The crew of *Spearfish* coming ashore for well-earned refreshments, having ended a busy patrol. (Author's Collection)

in Denmark, from where they were ingloriously sent home by railway. Several of the men had sailed with *Lützow* for years and pleaded to be allowed to stay on board during her time of plight, but Thiele had no time for sentiment. He was trying to save his ship, so off they went.

It was feared for a while that the increasing sea might break off the stern altogether as it appeared to be attached to the rest of the ship only by the two drive shafts, but the sea calmed somewhat and the structure held. In the end, *Lützow* had 1,300 tons of seawater below decks when the flooding was checked. This and her angled stern gave her a 12-metre (39-foot) draught astern, which became a huge problem as the shallow Danish inland waterways in some places were not very deep. On the other hand, Thiele preferred to risk grounding on a sandbank rather than having his ship sink in deeper water. Progress down Kattegat was slow: *Lützow* grounded on several occasions, but careful manoeuvring by the tugs and flooding of the bow to lift the stern freed her on each occasion. Eventually at 20:22 on 14 April, *Lützow* made it safely to the Deutsche Werke yard at Kiel.

Fifteen men died when the torpedo struck and their remains were buried in Kiel with full military honours. The SKL commented bitterly in their war diary that having used the heavy cruiser in the attack on Norway was a 'strategic blunder' which meant they had no Atlantic raiders available at the time when they were needed most. The repairs of *Lützow* would last well into 1941. Kapitän 'Curry' Thiele left the ship and within a few weeks was posted to Norway as Naval Commander, Trondheim.[18]

Also on the 10th, *Tarpon* attacked what turned out to be the Q-ship *Schürbeck* (*Schiff40*), west of Jutland. The torpedoes missed and in return *Schürbeck*, assisted by the minesweeper *M6*, chased the submarine, dropping depth charges for about four hours. *Tarpon* was never heard from again and was presumably lost with all hands in the counter-attack. Her wreck has not been located, though, and it is possible that she survived the attack only to hit a stray mine a day or two later.

Seawolf and *Shark* encountered little but A/S trawlers north of Heligoland and during the evening of the 10th they were ordered northwards, to the vicinity of Horns Reef: *Seawolf* to a billet north-west of Ringkøbing, *Shark* off Esbjerg. If anything, this area was even more infested with A/S trawlers and the submariners were kept busy as two or three groups of trawlers were in sight or heard on the asdic at any one time throughout the day.[19]

11 April

Meanwhile, the War Cabinet agreed a further extension of the freedom of action for the submarines and at 19:56 on the 11th, VA(S) submitted a signal to his captains that any ships, merchant or otherwise, under way within 10 miles of the Norwegian coast, south of 61°N, and anywhere east of 6°E, could be attacked on sight. By now, however, air and surface activity in the Kattegat and Skagerrak had increased considerably and it was becoming difficult to find safe areas in which to charge batteries during the shortening periods of darkness. Usually a full five hours were needed, but in April, the hours of proper darkness did not last that long off southern Norway, and it was important to find a quiet area with no interruptions. Some of the commanders forced the charging by increasing the charging voltage – not good for the battery, but it meant it could be fully charged in four hours.[20]

Sealion was deep into the Kattegat, some 15 miles south of Anholt Island. Lieutenant Commander Bryant wrote:

> In the afternoon, we sighted the bridge of a ship over the horizon and 'grouped up' to run in to attack. Very shortly we had to slow again for an [aircraft] and could not get in close. [. . .] It was a longish shot, nearly 3000 yards and we fired two torpedoes. The A/S vessels which had been troubling us earlier had gone off on a wild-goose chase over the horizon; and the air patrol had disappeared to the northward. It was one of these occasions, rare for a submarine, when one could wait [at periscope depth] and watch the shot.[21]

One of the torpedoes hit just aft of the funnel, a great column of water rising above the masts. The ship, which was the German freighter *August Leonhardt*, sank quickly in very shallow water, leaving her bridge and masts above water. *Leonhardt* had been part of the supply force for Kristiansand where she had docked during the afternoon of 9 April. After unloading, she had departed swiftly as there had been British air attacks on

The transport *August Leonhardt* approaching Kristiansand harbour in the afternoon of 9 April. The cruiser *Karlsruhe* to the left. Within some forty-eight hours they were both sunk by British submarines. Photo is taken from the torpedo boat *Greif*. (Author's Collection)

German ships in the harbour. Hence, she was on her way back to Germany to pick up more supplies for Norway when she was sunk off Anholt.

No attempt was made by *Sealion* to assist the survivors from *August Leonhardt* as there were many trawlers nearby, which Bryant assumed would come to the rescue. Instead he resumed patrol north of the Great Belt, hoping to intercept *Lützow*, or *Scheer* as he falsely believed, having received *Spearfish*'s sighting signal the night before.[22] Surfacing after seventeen and a half hours submerged, the fresh air rushing through the boat was most welcome.

To Bryant's relief, the nine o'clock signal from Rugby contained orders from VA(S) for *Spearfish* to move further north as the inner Skagerrak by now was considered too dangerous, flat calm seas with a bright moon at night making uninterrupted charging on the surface difficult. Bryant wrote:

> South Kattegat was becoming very strenuous with the moon, apart from the mill pond calms and the presence of patrols – luckily insufficient – no hour of the day or night passed without some avoiding action for fishing vessels being required. A move to the comparative peace of the North Kattegat was welcome.[23]

Bryant withdrew his boat to a new billet north-east of Anholt, close to the Swedish coast. Few ships were sighted outside Swedish territorial waters and the next day was used for engine repairs.[24]

Triad, where Lieutenant Commander Eric Oddie had replaced Jonas, moved into the Oslofjord on 11 April. She had left Rosyth three days earlier and had passed unnoticed through the North Sea and the Skagerrak. Entering the narrow Oslofjord, however, Oddie found it too risky to go too far up the fjord as the nights were short and moonlit and there were many A/S patrols around. Charging the batteries inside the fjord would be out of the question. Instead he lurked around the mouth of the fjord and sank the German transport *Ionia* after nightfall on the 11th. Afterwards, three A/S trawlers searched for *Triad* for several hours without gaining firm contact; 135 explosions were counted by her crew, going off at varying distances during the night, but none near enough to be dangerous. A large number of the explosions were probably small bombs dropped as deterrents from over a dozen aircraft patrolling the outer part of the fjord. The rest were 'scary bombs' dropped at irregular intervals from the trawlers.[25]

12 April

The next day, 12 April, following reports of German capital ships west of Lindesnes, Horton positioned *Severn*, *Clyde*, *Trident*, *Spearfish*, *Sunfish* and *Snapper* to cover the entrance to the Kattegat, between Lindesnes, Skagen and the Swedish coast north of Gothenburg. No naval ships were intercepted, but at the mouth of the Oslofjord, south of Hvaler Island, *Snapper* came across the small 321-ton tanker *Moonsund*. Lieutenant King wrote in his report:

> At 03:40, as dawn was breaking, a small steamer was sighted to the northeastwards, making for the northward. As it was getting light and aircraft were expected, it was desired to sink her quickly and two torpedoes were fired on a broad track. These missed astern. It was then seen that the steamer was smaller and nearer than at first estimated and that torpedoes were wasted on such a target as she could be chased and brought to. *Snapper* proceeded to chase and overhaul the steamer, which zigzagged and took no notice of the signal to heave to. [. . .] After a chase of seven miles, she was brought to with a shot across the bows. She then broke the German Merchant Flag. The order was shouted to abandon ship and the reply was heard, 'as you wish'. No efforts appeared to be made to get the boats out. The Lewis gun was then fired over the masts but produced no results. One round of HE was then fired into the forepeak and the cargo of aviation spirit burst into flames and the crew jumped over the side. Six out of the seven were picked up; the seventh could not be seen. Two of these subsequently died of shock and exposure in spite of strenuous efforts to save them. The remaining four, including the Captain kept in good heart for the rest of the patrol.[26]

In his biography he added:

> We nosed gently from one survivor to another, with two men hauling them in over the saddle-tanks and lowering the exhausted, wet bodies down the forehatch, which is about 20 ft. lower than the conning-tower and a dangerous place for the crew to be when there is a likelihood of an emergency dive. The last swimmer was dragged into our casing just as the first aircraft appeared. Deciding to abandon this one man and get the vital forehatch closed I ordered: 'Clear the foredeck and dive.' But Geoffrey Carew-Hunt, my third officer, begged, 'Let me get him down, sir'. Weakly I snapped: 'Do it quick.' Looking back I think I should have been heartless. The risk to my ship was unjustifiable. While perhaps fifteen seconds ticked by, Carew-Hunt bravely dragged the wet German down the steep cluttered forehatch and shut it.[27]

The tanker *Moonsund*. (H-J Heise Collection via E Skjold)

Two of the survivors were the 58-year-old master, Kapitän Johann Albers, and First Officer Hans Soltau. With everybody on board, King took *Snapper* down as quickly as he could, happy to get away from the smoking wreck that could be seen from miles away. Two trawlers and an auxiliary closed the burning tanker and, finding no survivors, initiated a search for the perpetrator. They did not find *Snapper* though, as she slipped quietly away southwards, towards Skagen. It is now known that *Moonsund* was part of the support fleet for the German invasion forces, under way to Trondheim with aviation fuel. Kapitän Albers maintained that they were heading for Oslo to receive orders and had no knowledge of what was happening in Norway. King had limited knowledge of what was happening himself, and could do nothing either way but continue his patrol.

Having spent the day dodging aircraft and A/S vessels, things became quiet by nightfall and *Snapper* surfaced to get fresh air and charge her batteries. The two dead Germans were buried at sea after a short ceremony and course was continued south towards the inner parts of Skagerrak. A/S vessels were everywhere and avoiding them was tedious work.

In Skagerrak, *Triad* experienced intense air activity. For a while, three A/S trawlers chased her, but Lieutenant Commander Oddie managed to break off contact by going in between some small islands inside Swedish territorial waters. He spent the rest of the day hovering off Koster Island with his back towards the Swedish border. Except for numerous aircraft overhead making periscope observations difficult in the glassy calm sea, all he sighted was 'three *Maass*-class destroyers' heading south, out of the Oslofjord, at 24 knots – gone before he could get within range.[28]

During the 12th, *Triton* and *Trident* started back for Rosyth while *Orzeł* moved east; *Shark* and *Seawolf* were ordered further northwards, closer to Hanstholm to try to catch *Hipper*, *Gneisenau* and *Scharnhorst*, which were reported returning to German ports. They were not encountered, though, and slipped behind the declared area in spite of more than a dozen boats looking for them. Most likely, intense tracking by the B-Dienst located some of the submarines so that they could be avoided or chased deep, while serendipity and the variable weather did the rest.

As the British and Allied submarines were unleashed when the invasion was confirmed, it instantly created a crisis in the OKW and the plans for moving troops and supplies to southern and western Norway had to be completely revised, diverting significant resources from other tasks to anti-submarine patrols. On 12 April, it was noted in the war diary of the SKL that: 'The severe threat from submarines in the Kattegat, the Skagerrak and the Oslofjord continues, necessitating deployment of all available resources as a countermeasure. There have been no results reported, in spite of a large number of depth charges having been used.'[29]

13 April

In the morning of 9th April, *Seal* had been instructed to close the Norwegian coast and sink any German ship sighted. Lieutenant Commander Lonsdale at first took his boat to a position off Skudeneshavn north of Stavanger in what he believed to be a good position to comply. Any ship passing between Bergen and Stavanger would have to close this area, whether going through the Leads or in open water. No German ships were sighted, though, and as heavy air activity forced *Seal* to stay submerged during

A view northwards from Stavanger harbour. The nearest ship is *Brita*. Behind her, between the mainland and the small island Tjuvholmen, is *Selje*, anchored so as to block the view into the harbour. *Seal* would have been in the waters behind *Selje*, unable to see which ships lay inside the harbour. *Selje* was painted with Norwegian neutrality markings, which is what Lonsdale saw through his periscope. (E Etrup Collection)

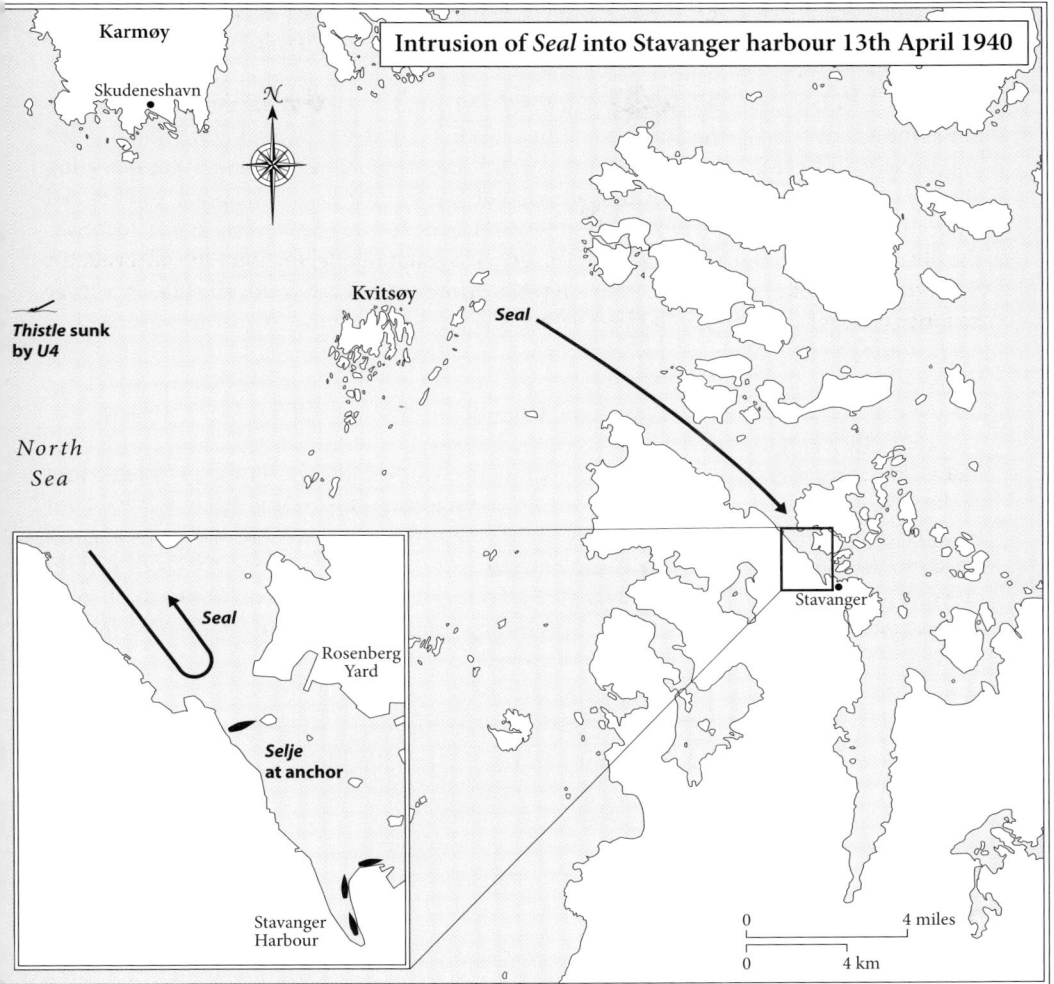

Intrusion of *Seal* into Stavanger harbour 13th April 1940

daylight hours, Lonsdale eventually decided to see which opportunities there were in terms of targets closer to Stavanger harbour. It was several days since Lieutenant Commander Haselfoot of *Thistle* had signalled his intention to enter that harbour looking for German warships and nothing more had been heard from him. It was of course unknown to Lonsdale, and VA(S), that *Thistle* at that time was a crushed wreck outside the entrance to Stavanger.

Lonsdale took the large, unwieldy *Seal* inside the mouth of Stavanger Fjord in the morning of the 13th, using the asdic to ensure he remained in deep waters mid-fjord, with short peeks through the periscope to ensure the course was right. It was a remarkable feat that took four hours of high tension up the narrow fjord. From 2.5 miles outside

Stavanger harbour proper, however, only merchant ships marked in Norwegian colours could be sighted and with the entire crew utterly disappointed, Lonsdale was compelled to turn back.

What Lonsdale did not know, was that, had he gone just a little bit further, he would have found the three German transport ships that had arrived in Stavanger harbour as part of the invasion force during the afternoon of the 9th: *Mendoza*, *Tijuca* and *Tübingen*. They were loaded with ammunition, fuel, equipment, A/A guns, heavy weapons, horses and vehicles as well as support and admin personnel, and were taking several days to unload. On the 13th all three were still in Stavanger, tied up at the inner quays of the harbour. To free quayside space and protect the valuable transports, several Norwegian ships that had been in the harbour on the day of the invasion were ordered to anchor outside. The 6,698-ton *Selje* had deliberately been placed as a *Hafensperre*, or blockship, in the gap between the small island of Tjuvholmen and the western side of the fjord – blocking the view into the harbour from outside, where Lonsdale looked through his periscope. *Selje* and other ships scattered around carried Norwegian neutrality markings with red-blue-white stripes fore and aft and a flag with her name amidships. Hence, Lonsdale was tricked by a simple deception and missed a very prestigious target. Whether it would have been possible to take the large *Seal* undetected on the eastern side of Tjuvholmen to get into a firing position without being detected is doubtful though. And, even if he had managed, damage to the city of Stavanger, including civilian casualties, would likely have been severe from a salvo of torpedoes exploding against ships and quaysides, so for the citizens of Stavanger it was probably just as well.

Coming back outside, in Haasteinsfjorden, what was identified as a 'German Torpedo Boat, T-class' was sighted from *Seal*. Lonsdale decided not to attack as a T-class torpedo boat would have a draught of no more than 6 feet (2 metres). *Seal*'s torpedoes had been set to run at 8 feet (2.5 metres) and would have to be pulled out of the tubes to be reset. Unmolested, the German vessel headed for Stavanger while *Seal* took station offshore. The 'Torpedo Boat, T-class' was probably the minesweeper *M1*, which had come up from Kristiansand to begin shuttling troops and supplies from Stavanger to Bergen. She had a draught of 2.65 metres (8.7 feet) and would have been worthy of a few torpedoes.[30]

In eastern Skagerrak, *Triad* was still hampered by glassy seas, enabling aircraft to see her when at periscope depth. At dawn, while approaching Færder Lighthouse submerged to look into the Oslofjord, the submarine was sighted and bombed by an aircraft. Twelve bombs were dropped, some fairly close, but they were small and caused no damage. At midday *Triad* was bombed again, this time while at 16 metres (50 feet). The German aircraft did not carry depth charges at this time and the bombs they used exploded when they hit the surface of the water. The chance of damage while 10–15 metres (33–49 feet) below was therefore small, but it kept the crew constantly on the alert and made going to periscope depth very hazardous.[31]

Further south-east, *Sunfish* was hugging the Swedish coast north of Gothenburg on the 13th. The batteries were not fully charged and so, to move about as little as possible, Lieutenant Commander Slaughter decided to stay on the bottom inside Swedish territory off Käringön where he would be relatively safe from German A/S trawlers, but could still observe the traffic outside by sonar and periscope when necessary.

At 12:00, *Sunfish* came to the surface for a routine periscope check. What appeared to be a merchantman was sighted on a southbound course. Slaughter estimated her to be about 3,000 tons, but she was high in the water and carried limited cargo – if any. The vessel carried no markings and no ensign, but the asdic operator reported with certainty that she was emitting active A/S pulses. Unknown to Slaughter at the time, this was the German Q-ship *Schürbeck* (*Schiff 40*) which had been unsuccessfully attacked by *Tarpon* three days earlier.

Slaughter emerged from Swedish territory and moved to attack. Two torpedoes were fired at 12:22, one of which hit forward. *Schürbeck* did not sink but as she drifted into Swedish waters towards Grönskären just north of Marstrand, the crew took to the boats. Unknowingly, the men of *Sunfish* had avenged *Tarpon*.[32]

Sunfish returned to Swedish waters and bottomed again at 35 metres (115 feet) depth, inside Måseskjär Island. At 18:45 Slaughter took his boat to periscope depth again to have a look outside. Four A/S trawlers were sighted close by, obviously searching for the submarine that had torpedoed *Schürbeck*. Again, Slaughter sought sanctuary inside neutral Swedish territory amongst the rocks and skerries and eventually the trawlers took their search northwards.

Sunfish returning from Norway on 23 April. (Author's Collection)

Further south, in the middle of the Kattegat, *Sealion* received orders on the midnight routine on the 13th to move further north to a billet in the Skagerrak. There were numerous A/S patrols around and Bryant decided to move north close to the Danish island of Læsø rather than straight up the main channel. This was fortunate as:

> the main channel on the east was illuminated by searchlights suddenly from time to time during the night and we would have been caught in the illumination. The Sperry had been stopped for counter A/S measures, the diving compass had been entirely unreliable since degaussing, the use of the [active sonar] was limited by presence of the A/S vessels and all the Swedish lights had been extinguished so that navigation was more interesting than accurate. Dived six miles short of Laeso Light Vessel, which was still burning. Battery was very low. [. . . At 05:45] sighted 8 light grey trawlers, steaming in pairs, course 130 degrees. Although I could see no gun, I took these to be enemy A/S trawler or M/S trawlers. They were not fishing. Avoided them.[33]

During the morning however, the trawlers got the scent of *Sealion* and came closer. The density of the waters around Læsø made an adjustment of trim necessary and Bryant had to allow the use of the pumps for a few minutes. This was picked up by one of the trawlers, which was seen through the periscope to steer straight for them. *Sealion* was taken as deep as the waters allowed while the pumps and all other machinery were shut down. The men settled down in silence. The trawler was heard to pass directly above the submarine, stop, restart, move around for some time and then make off, back to its companions. Bryant returned to periscope depth and proceeded north. The channel was infested with German A/S patrols, however, operating in pairs or in line-abreast formations. In all, some twenty grey-painted trawlers were sighted during the day, all of them skilfully avoided. At 20:45, north of Skagen and safely out of the Kattegat, *Sealion* finally surfaced with batteries almost completely drained. The nine o'clock routine contained a signal from VA(S) to *Sealion* with orders to return to Harwich. In his war diary Bryant concluded that although it had been a 'most enjoyable patrol' in general in spite of long hours, 'in a way, this patrol was deeply disappointing as having got what looked like a perfect billet, we in fact never saw a warship, except A/S craft.'[34]

14 April

On the next day, 14 April, after a night on the surface charging the batteries, *Sunfish* on the other hand rounded off a most successful patrol. Just as twilight settled in, the German Q-ship *Oldenburg* (*Schiff35*) was attacked west of Kungälv. After the encounter with *Unity* west of Ringkøbing a few days earlier she had now moved into the Kattegat looking for more British submarines. Slaughter fired two of the three torpedoes he had left when in position. Both hit and *Oldenburg* went down very rapidly, taking forty-five men of the 110-man crew with her. Korvettenkapitän Selchow's trawlers of the 11th A/S Flotilla, *UJ112*, *UJ114*, *UJ116* and *UJ176*, chased *Sunfish* for about an hour before returning to the site of the sinking to pick up the survivors. No firm contact was ever made on the submarine and no serious attacks developed. By 21:45 all was quiet and Slaughter

Lieutenant Commander Bill King on the bridge of *Snapper* in April 1940. (Royal Navy Submarine Museum Collection)

surfaced, setting course for home. Eleven torpedoes had been fired. Two of them misran while five hit, sinking three ships and damaging one beyond repair, totalling 14,500 tons – a very respectable performance.[35]

Snapper was also in luck on 14 April. In the early hours of the day, a vessel was sighted and attacked without result with one torpedo. The vessel was sighted at about 1.5 miles, but it was so fast that it was actually gaining on *Snapper*, in spite of the submarine going at full speed on the surface. The torpedo was fired in frustration on a very broad track without much hope of success.[36] A few minutes later, after turning north and giving up on the speeding vessel, *Snapper* was confronted by two escorts on a reciprocal course doing 20 knots, one on either bow, less than 200 metres (220 yards) away. An emergency dive literally between the two vessels took the submarine down before the Germans could open fire. King wrote:

One [escort] appeared to be fitted with a directional asdic of about 9kc/s. This vessel remained stopped or moving slowly as though directing the other vessel which had streamed a sweep. The second vessel was heard veering the sweep by a winch. [. . .] This attack was simple to evade, and in half an hour the vessels lost contact. As a noise was heard in the casing, *Snapper* surfaced to investigate possible obstruction or indicators. The vessels were still in the vicinity and renewed the attack without success, finally firing one charge and making off [after] three and a half hours.[37]

Meanwhile, dawn had arrived and *Snapper* continued southwards submerged during the morning and early afternoon. Trawlers were seen and heard all the time, but as the visibility was reduced due to fog, it was difficult to ascertain if they were fishing or submarine hunting.

At 14:00, midway between Skagen and Lysekil, near to where *Friedenau* and *Wigbert* had been sunk a few days earlier, two escorted freighters were sighted through the periscope, on a northerly course. The distance was about 2,500 metres (2,750 yards). By this time, defects had developed in the forward Automatic Inboard Vent (AIV) system as well as the telemotor system, requiring the bow caps to be kept shut as much as possible when submerged. Hence, King decided to fire a full salvo while backing away from the targets in an attempt to reduce the strain on the torpedoes. One tube misfired, but the other five torpedoes ran true.

A single explosion was heard after about ninety seconds, but King could not ascertain any hits as *Snapper* was taken deep as soon as the torpedoes had been fired to avoid breaking the surface. In fact, nobody on board the submarine had actually experienced a hit by one of their own torpedoes. An explosion was heard, appearing to come from where the target should have been, but success was not confirmed at the time.

Above: *Florida* mortally hit and (*left*) taking the final plunge. (E Skjold Collection)

The small convoy was part of the 3.Seetransportstaffel, third transport unit, and actually consisted of three vessels heading for Oslo with troops and provisions: *Moltkefels*, *Porto Alegre* and *Florida*. The escort consisted of *M3*, *M4*, *M6*, *M7*, *M8*, *M11*, *M12*, *M14*, *M20* and the torpedo boat *T190 Claus von Bevern*. The torpedo that the men onboard *Snapper* heard explode hit the 6,148-ton *Florida*. She did not sink immediately, but it was not possible to save her and she eventually went down.

Retribution from the escort was persistent, aided by a group of R-boats closing in support, though not very accurate. Except, that is, when the pump was started to get rid of excess water. Then the German listening devices came into their own and a 'shower of depth charges came uncomfortably close'. After about forty minutes, however, the escort moved on, presumably to screen the remaining transports, leaving only the R-boats. These boats had no or very poor active sonar and just relied upon listening systems. Hence, once the pump could be shut down *Snapper* was able to sneak away at slow speed, shaking the pursuers off at nightfall.[38]

15 April

On 14 April, the gunnery training ship *Brummer* embarked 409 soldiers for Oslo in the Danish port Frederikshavn. The embarkation was swift and *Brummer* headed to sea in the evening accompanied by *Jaguar*, *Falke* and *F5*.[39] Reaching Oslo next morning, the soldiers and their equipment were disembarked and the ships cast off again at 16:30, heading back to Frederikshavn for another batch of soldiers. At 23:00 on the 15th, off Jomfruland, the convoy passed through an area of fog and snow and Korvettenkapitän Max Gebauer ordered the escort into line-astern in order for them not to lose contact. *Brummer* was in the van and there was no A/S screen. At 23:07, two torpedoes passed in front of *Brummer* and the alarm was sounded. Before anybody could react, however, a third torpedo impacted below no. 1 gun, detonating the forward magazine. The forecastle was cut clean off, with gun no. 2 pointing towards the water at a wild angle.

At first it was unclear to the other ships from which side the attack had come and *Falke* and *F5* circled the scene, throwing depth charges and looking for a contact. Nothing was found, and *F5* was ordered to approach the wreck to take off the wounded while *Jaguar* joined *Falke* searching. When *F5* had evacuated as many as she could, she set course for Frederikshavn and Korvettenkapitän Gebauer, himself wounded from being thrown off the bridge by the explosion, ordered *Jaguar* alongside to take off the remaining crew. The wreck appeared stable but the damage was significant and she could sink at any moment in the choppy sea. A submarine contact was briefly obtained and the two torpedo boats gave chase, but the contact was lost and nothing achieved. A towing attempt was planned for dawn, but before it could be initiated, *Brummer* sank at 06:50, a mile off Tvesteinen Lighthouse, outside Arendal. There were fifty-one casualties, of which twenty-five were fatal. Virtually all of the killed and wounded had been in the forecastle.[40]

The assailant was undoubtedly *Sterlet*. After attacking *Brummer*, however, her fate remains uncertain. No further signals were ever received and she was eventually reported overdue and lost. From the reports of *Jaguar* and *Falke*, it seems likely that Lieutenant

Two photos of Oslo harbour in the afternoon of 15 April. *Above*: with one of the torpedo boats (*Jaguar* or *Falke*) inside. *Below*: *Brummer* – the torpedo from *Sterlet* impacted right underneath the double-barrelled 10.5-cm A/A gun on the foredeck, tearing off everything forward of the superstructure. (Author's Collection)

Commander Gerard Haward managed to bring *Sterlet* safely away, unless the boat had been damaged by one of the two dozen depth charges dropped, sinking to her destruction unnoticed. This, however, is not likely.

On 16 April, at 15:10, *M3*, *M7* and *M8* attacked a sonar-echo just east of Horten, well into the Oslofjord. The assumed submarine remained stationary throughout the evening and next day, air bubbles coming to the surface. This could have been *Sterlet*, but if so, Haward took a tremendous risk by going that far into the fjord. There would have been a good chance of finding prey, but the area was infested with A/S forces. No wreck has been found in the area and it is rather unlikely that this was the end of *Sterlet*.

In the evening of the next day, 17 April, a submarine fired two torpedoes unsuccessfully at a convoy off the Swedish island Måseskär, north of Gothenburg. During the attack, parts of the boat broke surface and it was subsequently heavily attacked by *UJ125* and *UJ126* of 12th A/S Flotilla. After about an hour, during which some forty depth charges were dropped, the contact was lost. It was assumed that the submarine had ventured into Swedish territorial waters towards the narrow waters around Käringön further inside to get away and no evidence of a kill was registered by the trawlers. There are no reports to be found from any Allied boat that matches these events as described in the war diary of 12th A/S Flotilla. Hence, it is very likely that this submarine was *Sterlet* and she could well have been damaged in the heavy counter-attack.

During the night *UJ128* joined her two companions and a search was set up just outside the territorial limit in case the submarine should try to set course for home. Just before dawn the next day, a heavy oil slick was seen, appearing to move southwards from a point just outside the Swedish islands where the submarine had vanished the night before. The slick was followed and several depth-charge attacks made on what appeared to be the source. At one stage, German oil barrels came to the surface, probably from one of the many wrecks in this area, but this does not exclude the fact that the A/S trawlers might have been following a real submarine. All the more so as firm echoes and submarine

Sterlet in April 1938. (W&L)

noises were reported by the operators of all three ships at various times. The assumed submarine contact moved towards the south-east in a zigzag course and was attacked repeatedly. Eventually, towards nightfall, the contact once again escaped into Swedish waters and vanished in between some islands, where the trawlers decided not to follow. No further contact was gained in spite of an active search by the German boats.[41]

It is likely that the submarine chased these two days off the Swedish coast was *Sterlet*. She would have sustained severe counter-attacks for several days, and, being damaged, perhaps even severely so, it is to be expected that Lieutenant Commander Haward would have taken his boat into Swedish territory to escape further beatings. The use of neutral Swedish territory around Måseskär/Käringön is reported by several other boats operating in this area at the time. Haward most likely spent the night of the 18th/19th off Käringön and then made an attempt to escape on the 19th. This was unsuccessful, and he may well have decided to go back inside neutral territory again further south. Whether *Sterlet* succumbed there to leaks or other damage, or later in the Skagerrak or the North Sea trying to return home, still remains speculation at this time. It is also possible that Haward and his men managed to patch *Sterlet* up for a safe return home and that she ventured into a minefield on the way.

For *Triad*, 14 April had been very busy, with several phases of hunting or being hunted, spending twenty-one hours submerged in total. On the 15th, Lieutenant Commander Oddie decided to see what conditions were like on the western side of the mouth of the Oslofjord, off the island of Jomfruland. Here, conditions were rather quiet and they 'saw nothing except aircraft but were not bombed'. Oddie was honest enough to add in his report that: 'This day gave the personnel a much needed rest, though not sought as such. We have all begun to feel the strain of the hunting and bombing although the morale keeps overall excellent.' Still, when charging on the surface after nightfall, two blue flares suddenly shot out of the sea mist no more than a mile away. *Triad* went down in record time, followed by eight depth charges, some rather close. Whatever had sighted them was not in the mood for a long chase though and headed off after the one attack.[42]

Luck continued to hold for *Snapper*, which was still north-east of Skagen on the 15th. King wrote:

> The German morning air patrols had recently been sent out late, so we remained on the surface to finish charging our batteries until 4 a.m. I was standing on the bridge with the officer of the watch Geoffrey Carew-Hunt and our three lookouts, peering into the misty half-light that heralded the approach of dawn when a dim shape showed in the gloom. 'Diving Stations! Night Alarm! Stand by all torpedo tubes!' [. . .] The tubes' bow caps were now always kept open when on the surface, with a man on watch, ready to fire them at immediate notice. Within sixty seconds of sighting the first ship, *Snapper* was ready to strike.[43]

At first, the darkened silhouette of a merchant vessel emerged in the mist, but it was shortly after followed by several more. King had run into another of the supply columns to Norway. This one from 3.Seetransportstaffel, third transport unit, consisting of the transports *Hohenhörn* and *Euroland*, escorted by *M1701*, *M1702*, *M1704* and *M1705*. To

M1701 H.M. Behrens and *M1705 Nürnberg* of the 17th Minesweeping Flotilla at Hela in the Baltic in December 1939. (Author's Collection)

King, there appeared to be ships all around, both transports and escorts, and he decided to stay on the surface and fire quickly. As they were in the mist, he assumed the convoy was running slow and applied a small deviation to his sights before giving orders to fire the last four torpedoes on a 90-degree track at 1,200 metres (1,300 yards), one every seven seconds. With all torpedoes gone, orders to dive were given. As they were descending, two torpedoes were heard to explode and one hit was observed through the periscope. A further two explosions were heard some minutes later and, optimistically, King believed that he had made four hits, the last two on ships on the other side of the convoy, not visible in the misty darkness. In fact, the ships hit and sunk were the two mine-sweeping trawlers *M1701 H.M.Behrens* (525 tons) and *M1702 Carsten Janssen* (472 tons). Both ships went down fast with a large loss of life, including the CO of 17th Minesweeping Flotilla, Korvettenkapitän Hermann Rehder.

The counter-attack was once again neither efficient nor persistent and *Snapper* was able to sneak away. One escort was heard to operate around the target area, stopping and starting at short intervals as if picking up survivors. Believing he was out of harm's way, King rose to periscope depth and sent a radio report about the convoy for other submarines with torpedoes left to act on. This was a mistake, though, as German direction-finding stations also picked up the signal and sent one of the A/S flotillas to the scene. The result was the severest round of pursuit that *Snapper* had experienced so far and it would take all day before King managed to extricate his boat. The pursuers used both listening devices and active sonar and could only be shaken off by curbing all noise-making activities inside the boat and running extremely slowly on one motor only. Towards the end of the hunt, when *Snapper* was sneaking away, the trawlers continued

The crew of *Snapper* giving the 'thumbs up' after returning home in April 1940. (Author's Collection)

to criss-cross the area of the last contact, dropping single charges now and again. Out of torpedoes, King set *Snapper* on a course for home.[44]

Seawolf and *Shark* had split up on the 14th, the former heading east past Skagen, towards the Swedish coast, the latter to a position off Kristiansand. On the 15th, *Shark* fired five torpedoes at the depot ship *Saar* (mistakenly identified as *Brummer*), which was escorting two transports. The torpedo tracks were sighted, though, and the German ships turned safely away. *Shark* was hunted by two trawlers for a while, but they never found her and no depth charges were dropped.[45]

16 April

On the 16th, the weather was poor in the Skagerrak with heavy seas from the south-west, unfavourable for the A/S trawlers and aircraft. On the other hand, it also made periscope observation difficult for the submarines, so there were few encounters reported. Nevertheless, on this day, *Porpoise* and *U3* were to have an unusual duel off Egersund.

The type IIA boat *U3* had left Wilhelmshaven three days earlier and was on a rather rare patrol for a German U-boat off southern Norway. This was an area where the Luftwaffe generally had permission to attack any submarine sighted, but most likely German intelligence had intercepted radio signals indicating there was a British submarine in the area as *U3* was directed into this area by a radio signal on the 15th.

Lieutenant Commander Phillip Roberts had taken *Porpoise* to sea from Rosyth on 13 April, heading for his billet off Egersund, south-east of Stavanger. He was in position in the early morning of the 15th. Little happened on that day or the next, until just after surfacing at dusk, to commence charging the batteries. At 21:30, while on a north-westerly course, parallel to the coast, a U-boat, also on the surface, was sighted on the starboard bow. Roberts immediately stopped the charge, engaging both engines at half speed ahead. The night was clear and the U-boat was visible just outside the track of the moon. It appeared to the men on the bridge of *Porpoise* that the other boat was stopped or moving at very slow speed almost broadside on to them. The course was altered to get the U-boat straight ahead. At this point, however, the enemy submarine got under way, her engines apparently making 'some smoke' as they started up. The U-boat turned to starboard, away from *Porpoise*, and vanished in her own smoke as she reached a course nearly stern-on to the line of sight from the bridge of *Porpoise*. The U-boat continued to turn, however, and emerged from the smoke almost broadside on again. Roberts gave a little starboard rudder to keep *Porpoise*'s bow pointing ahead of the U-boat and fired all six forward torpedoes, while swinging slowly back to port. The U-boat continued to turn as the torpedoes approached, combing the tracks, and was last seen bows-on to *Porpoise* signalling with a very dim light something that appeared to be the letter 'Q'. The entire behaviour of the U-boat was confusing and appeared 'rather unintelligent' to Roberts who gave the order to dive. The U-boat was heard briefly on the asdic after diving, but lost almost immediately. There were no indications that any of the torpedoes had hit, although fifteen minutes after firing there was a very loud single explosion.[46]

Robert's opponent was Kapitänleutnant Gerd Schreiber, a 28-year-old of the class of 1931 at the naval academy, the same class as Günther Prien and Fritz-Julius Lemp. He was a determined man, small of stature, but well spoken, who had served on board submarines since 1936, including in Spanish waters during the civil war. After a spell as torpedo officer on board the cruiser *Königsberg* in 1938–39, he was posted back to the U-bootwaffe and had his first war patrol in the North Sea under Kapitänleutnant Harald Jürst in *U59* in late 1939–early 1940, before being given command of the training-boat *U3*

Porpoise in April 1935. (W&L)

in January 1940. *U3* and Schreiber were transferred to active service in March 1940 and this was their second war patrol. No ships had been sunk so far.[47]

After nightfall on 16 April, Schreiber took his nimble boat to the surface after nightfall. Almost immediately, the shadow of another submarine was sighted. *U3* was in an awkward position in relatation to the moon, which was about half full towards the west; Schreiber ordered emergency speed ahead turning away from the opponent, intending to get himself out of the moonlight and draw the other boat into it. The unknown submarine – not yet identified and hence possibly also German – followed. The diesel engines of *U3* were not quite ready for the exertion of emergency speed (*äußerste Kraft*) so soon after being started and produced a large amount of smoke, and Schreiber lost sight of the other boat. Coming back through the smokescreen at maximum speed, the other submarine was now better positioned in the moonlight and could be recognised as a British minelayer of the *Grampus*-class. Closing at high speed to 1,000 metres (1,100 yards), Schreiber prepared to fire. Just then, the British boat appeared to start diving and he shouted down to the torpedo room to set the torpedo to run at 8 metres (26 feet). This took only a few seconds and thereafter one torpedo was fired. Why Schreiber only fired one torpedo when he must have had four ready in the forward tubes is not commented upon. Perhaps it was all he believed could be made ready as the enemy was diving. Whatever the reason, the one torpedo was aimed well, and actually seen from *U3* to pass over the foredeck of the diving *Porpoise*, between the deck and the jumping wire.

By this time, there was nobody on the bridge to see how close they had been to destruction as *Porpoise* was going down. Strangely, there is no mention in *U3*'s war diary of any torpedoes being fired at them and it appears nobody on board realised that they had just combed a salvo aimed at themselves. The detonation of *U3*'s G7a torpedo at the end of its run was heard by both submarines, but apparently nobody on board *Porpoise* realised what it really was. Having fired his one torpedo, Schreiber turned southwards again and vanished hastily from the scene, steering a zigzag course, just in case.[48]

It was believed for many years that *Porpoise* had sunk *U1* that day, but that is not the case. The duel was undoubtedly with *U3*, which was not sunk, while *U1* vanished around 6 April with all hands, north of the Frisian Islands.[49]

17 April

For *Seal*, nothing much happened in the days after she had entered Stavanger harbour. On the 16th, though, she received orders to take up a very precise station off Sola airfield, flashing recognition signals out to sea at a certain time and bearing. The position was found by asdic range and gyro bearing on Jarsteinen Lighthouse and at 04:20 in the morning of 17 April, the cruiser *Suffolk* and four destroyers passed 4 miles south of *Seal*, using the submarine as a beacon on their way towards bombarding Sola airfield. Having completed his part of Operation Duck, Lonsdale withdrew to the north to be out of harm's way.[50] Next evening, course was set for Rosyth. It had been an exciting patrol, though *Seal* and her crew still had all torpedoes intact.[51]

Meanwhile, *Triad* was bombed by aircraft on several occasions and it was clear that they could be seen through the calm water even when as deep as 15–20 metres. Occasionally, what was believed to be 'destroyers' were seen, but only on very few occasions did they manage to get into a favourable position for an attack. These 'destroyers' were most likely large torpedo boats, minesweepers or escorts and it is possible that, due to exercises with their own destroyers, the British submarine officers held them to be more dangerous than they actually were as German destroyers and large torpedo boats in general had limited A/S experience. Several attacks on convoys and smaller warships were performed, but there were no hits. On at least two occasions, the lack of results was considered to be due to faulty drill. Lieutenant Commander Oddie had joined *Triad* with some haste and there had been no time to test-fire torpedoes with the new crew before this patrol. In addition, the glassy calm sea and the constant presence of aircraft made periscope observations very difficult.

Numerous false reports were received at the Admiralty during the first weeks of the campaign in Norway, some of them creating confusing and at times dangerous situations. Acting on one such report on 13 April, of a German battleship off Molde, *Taku*, on passage to Norway, was directed to that part of the coast. The report was quickly found to be a misunderstanding and in the morning of the 14th, *Taku* was given revised orders to patrol off Trondheim, an area where British submarines so far had not operated. On the 16th, *Taku* received new orders to withdraw to the south to keep clear of a cruiser force sweeping along the Norwegian coast. Lieutenant Commander Voltelin van der Byl was not warned of the presence of other British ships in the area, however. Instead, a signal was received that warned (falsely) of German destroyers off Stavanger, heading north.[52]

During the day, *Glasgow* and *Sheffield* were sighted and correctly identified. When another warship was sighted in the early hours of the 17th, though, van der Byl took it to be German and fired four torpedoes from 2,750 metres (3,000 yards). Fortunately, the attack and the ensuing counter-attack both failed, as the target was in fact the British destroyer *Ashanti*. It must have been a sobering moment for the young commanding officer when the ship he had just fired torpedoes at turned towards him to attack in the growing dawn twilight and he recognised it as an unmistakable *Tribal*-class destroyer. Some minor damage was sustained from a pattern of depth charges that exploded around 35 metres (115 feet) away before *Taku* was able to surface and identify herself as friendly, but nothing that prevented her from continuing the patrol. After the incident became known, Admiral Horton ordered all his boats to remain south of Bergen for the rest of the campaign in Norway – until early June as things turned out.[53]

Following the return of the Weserübung naval forces from Norway, the Kriegsmarine's surface forces were in a severe predicament. Most of the larger ships were sunk or damaged but the successes of the Allied submarines called for unforeseen active German countermeasures, draining resources needed elsewhere. The SKL was deeply concerned and instigated increased A/S efforts with all available means, including aircraft and anti-submarine minefields. This had not been planned for and required a large degree of improvisation. Aircraft and crews for A/S patrols and convoy escort were taken from reserve units, flying schools and wherever they could be found. These measures employed were huge and in addition to the rapidly decreasing hours of darkness, made conditions for the Allied submarines in Kattegat and the eastern Skagerrak increasingly challenging. There was a lot of German traffic, though, and there were plenty of targets for those willing to take some risks.

The distance from Frederikshavn in Denmark – which could be reached by overland transport or by a short hop from Aarhus airfield – to Larvik in Norway, from which there was a fairly good rail and road connection to Oslo, as well as sheltered waterways, is 100 nautical miles. That meant ten hours at 10 knots or six and a half at 15 knots, most of which would be in exposed waters, with a constant threat from Allied submarines. South of Frederikshavn, the Luftwaffe had absolute air superiority, allowing for effective airborne A/S patrols and, after *Sunfish* and *Sealion* had been moved north, the shallow waters of Kattegat were considered relatively safe. Likewise, to the north of Larvik, the narrow Oslofjord was also fairly safe for vessels continuing directly towards the capital.

18 April

On the 18th, *Seawolf*, operating between Skagen and the Swedish coast, sank the transport *Hamm* south-west of Lysekil during a night attack. The 5,874-ton *Hamm* was part of a homebound convoy of three ships, escorted by four trawlers of the 2nd Minesweeping Flotilla. Lieutenant Commander John Studholme fired six torpedoes from 3,650 metres (4,000 yards) on the surface and observed *Hamm* first taking hits, and then catching fire. His asdic operator believed that he also heard another vessel taking a torpedo, but this was not correct. At one point, one of the escorts was only 1,000 metres (1,100 yards) away, but did not see the submarine as the moon had conveniently become obscured. Having fired the torpedoes, Studholme turned away, still on the surface, heading north-west at maximum speed. *Seawolf* was not chased and after a while speed could be reduced, allowing time to charge batteries and reload torpedoes. Later in the morning, a pair of torpedo boats and what was recognised as a destroyer escorting a large motor yacht were sighted in the haze, but there was no opportunity to fire torpedoes before they vanished into the murk.[54]

19 April

On the 19th, off Arendal, *Triad* carried out an attack on what was probably the depot ship *Tsingtao*, escorted by a group of trawlers. Four torpedoes were fired, though all missed as the German made a course change just at the time of firing.[55]

The 12th A/S Flotilla, which had its regular base at Wilhelmshaven, was to play a central role in the anti-submarine efforts in the Skagerrak in the coming months. C-in-C of the unit was Korvettenkapitän Hans Korn.[56] The whaleboats of the 12th A/S Flotilla were temporarily transferred from Wilhelmshaven to Kiel on the 17th in order to operate under BSO (Befehlshaber der Seestreitkräfte der Ostsee, or Naval Commander East), escorting convoys to and from Norway. For convenience the operational vessels of the two A/S groups, U-Jagd Gruppe 4 and 5, were combined in 5.U-Jagd Gruppe under the command of Korvettenkapitän Günther Brandt, who was also the captain of *UJA*. In addition to his own boat, *UJB*, *UJC*, *UJF* and *UJE* followed east. They were immediately put to use, and during the morning of the 18th, the four boats took to sea, escorting the tender *Brommy* and the 5,248-ton transport *Entrerios* in the direction of Frederikshavn.[57]

The Danish port was reached at midday on the 19th without mishap. There, *Brommy* was dismissed as she was going no further, while the steamer *Scharhörn*, loaded with ammunition for the troops in Norway, took her place.

The convoy left Frederikshavn at dawn on the 20th with two other convoys also heading for Norway. The other convoys were faster though and the ships under Brandt's command were soon left behind on their own. It was considered necessary to reach the mouth of the Oslofjord before nightfall so Brandt decided to risk a straight course and avoid zigzagging in spite of the valuable ships he was escorting.[58] Well over halfway to Larvik, at 14:20 GeT, three torpedo tracks were seen by the lookouts of *UJB* coming from the west. The sea was very calm and the tracks were seen from a considerable distance, allowing the whole convoy to turn against them and manoeuvre so that they could steer between the oncoming torpedoes. This they managed – just. The nearest torpedoes were only metres away from the ships. While the convoy turned back on course, covered by the *U-Jäger*, Korvettenkapitän Brandt took *UJA* and *UJB* at maximum speed towards where the torpedoes appeared to have come from. They had been fired from a considerable distance away though, and by the time the two whaleboats were nearing the area, the submarine was long gone and they found nothing. Satisfied he had successfully deterred the troublemaker, however, Brandt dropped a few depth charges for good measure and turned to rejoin the convoy. By nightfall, they reached the Oslofjord where *Entrerios* anchored for the night while *Scharhörn* was taken to Oslo during the night as her load of ammunition was urgently needed. Entering the fjord, they met another part of 12th A/S flotilla coming south with another batch of ships returning for more men and supplies for Norway. There was no lack of traffic in the eastern Skagerrak during these days.[59]

20 April

Swordfish, operating off Larvik that day, was chased from first light by aircraft. Eventually at 10:20 she was bombed by one while at periscope depth and Lieutenant Pat Cowell took *Swordfish* deep to get away. A few minutes later, engines were heard and Cowell took his boat up again to investigate. Bringing up the periscope to have look, he found *Swordfish* surrounded by no less than five F-class escorts and one larger vessel. Down they went again. This time, though, they were duly tracked and *Swordfish* was intensely chased for two hours. The depth charges, some of which came uncomfortably close, caused leaks in the outer tanks and the boat took water aft. To get away, all engines were stopped, including the Sperry gyro compass.

Undaunted, Lieutenant Cowell continued searching and within half an hour found a convoy of three merchant ships and four escorts. Six torpedoes were fired. The Sperry compass was still turned off, however, and course-keeping by magnetic compass turned out to be a challenge. Cowell wrote:

> After firing, *Swordfish* had 15° of port helm on, and helmsman stated that the ship had tried to swing rapidly to starboard, and that he had corrected this with Port Wheel. It is thought that as *Swordfish* took on an angle bow down to fire, the magnetic compass swung off, due to heeling error, and the helmsman chased it. Subsequent trials proved that with an angle on the ship, compass was liable to wander as much as five degrees.[60]

There were no hits, and *Swordfish* turned about, ran fast as long as she could, and when the escort came too close shut down as much as possible to creep away on one engine. But to no avail. Cowell and his men were chased for another six hours by the escort and the morning's hunting group which had been called to join the hunt. When finally able to surface at 20:44, the pressure inside the boat had built up so much that, when opening the hatch, it flew open so hard it knocked Lieutenant Cowell and a signalman unconscious. Cowell was unconscious for quite some time after this and First Lieutenant Harry Stacey had to take command for the next day and following night before command was restored.[61] The convoy they had attacked consisted of the freighters *Belgrano*, *Dessau* and *Curityba* and was escorted by Korvettenkapitän Selchow's 11.U-Jagdflottille. They had left Oslo the day before, heading for Kiel for another load of equipment and troops.

A few hours after having chased *Swordfish* away, a new submarine contact was reported and some twenty-five depth charges thrown. Contact was lost, however, and the convoy resumed course southwards. *Swordfish* remained off southern Norway for another week. Several convoys were seen or heard, but as she was constantly harassed by A/S patrols and aircraft, no opportunity to fire *Swordfish*'s remaining torpedoes emerged. Course was set for home on the 27th.[62]

Further west, still off Arendal, *Triad* made two unsuccessful attacks on the 20th. First, on a single transport with four escorts where the attack had to be abandoned as she lost trim just before firing. Shortly after, another convoy was sighted: this time three ships with four large escorts. Eight torpedoes were fired from 2,500 metres (2,750 yards) and one or two hits were registered on board *Triad*. There are no relevant German losses on this day, however. The counter-attack was swift, but mercifully short. Seven charges were dropped, some close, but Lieutenant Commander Oddie managed to extract his boat at slow speed and they got safely away. With no more torpedoes left, *Triad* set course for Britain at nightfall.[63]

Torpedo Tracks

Lieutenant Commander Ronald 'Ronnie' Mills took the Royal Navy's newest submarine *Tetrarch* to sea from Portsmouth on 13 April, having completed the work-up. *Tetrarch* had been assigned to 2nd Submarine Flotilla at Rosyth, but would make her first war patrol off southern Norway en route. The first days of the patrol were used to settle the crew into the routines of a war patrol, and tensions ran high through the boat when, at 18:37 on 23 April, deep inside the Skagerrak, between Larvik and Skagen, a southbound transport was sighted with heavy escort. This was the 2,988-ton *Ahrensburg*, escorted by the torpedo boats *T153* and *T155*, the escorts *F5* and *F8* and minesweepers *R33*, *R37* and *R40*, on passage to Frederikshavn. There was little time to think, and Mills decided to fire from the hip. Less than four minutes after the sighting, two torpedoes were fired from about 5 miles distance. Mills wrote in his report that 'Full salvo was not fired as it was thought to be a waste of ammunition at the long range. Also transport was southbound and therefore probably empty.' Why he fired at all is not explained. *Tetrarch* went deep and retired at high speed. No explosions were heard, however, and

Mills returned to periscope depth at 18:42, only to be met by a surprise when looking through his periscope:

> Saw three destroyers approaching down the torpedo track at high speed . . . in line abreast. *Tetrarch* fine on starboard bow of starboard wing destroyer. . . . Went to 300 feet at full speed under full helm, enemy being only about 1,500 yards away. First charges fired. Apparently well short. But why did the whole escort attack me and leave the transport unscreened?[64]

This was not Mills's best day on the job. The attackers were torpedo boats not destroyers, and the reason they left the transport was that there were several others staying behind that he had not seen. Over the next three hours, thirty depth charges were recorded in several attacks. Mills took *Tetrarch* down to well below 100 metres (300 feet), confident that his brand-new submarine could take it. She did, and with some relief the asdic operator announced around 20:30 that he could hear the hunt had been taken over by A/S trawlers, while the escorts appeared to have left, presumably to catch up with *Ahrensburg*, which had continued south. The new hunters were Brandt's 5.U-Jagd Gruppe and four trawlers from 12.U-Jagdflotille. Both groups had been deployed along the convoy route between Larvik and Frederikshavn as independent submarine-hunting forces. They were to take over whenever there was an alarm, allowing an escort to stay with their convoys. Now they both rushed to the area where *Tetrarch* was being hunted, called by an emergency signal from *T155*. The four regular trawlers of 12.U-Jagdflotille came first, while Brandt's five boats closed from the north, spread out in line-abreast, 800 metres (875 yards) apart, as dusk started to fall.[65]

Matters appeared to become a little less hectic for *Tetrarch*, as the hunters changed. The air was getting very foul inside the boat though, and pressure was high. Mills, who believed the worst was over, decided to surface and, if necessary, fight it out with the small number of trawlers that might remain above. At 22:20 BrT (23:20 GeT) he took *Tetrarch* up. As soon as the atmosphere had cleared somewhat the engines were started with all the fans turned on, while the torpedo tubes were made ready with the gun crew standing by. A pair of trawlers were soon sighted at about 1,000 metres (1,100 yards), closing. These were *UJB* with *UJE* right behind and *UJA*, *UJC* and *UJF* a little further away, though apparently not visible from the submarine in the growing darkness. Mills had brought his boat up right in the path of 5.U-Jagd Gruppe. Two torpedoes were fired 'to discourage their approach'. They both broke surface, but continued in the right direction. Mills ordered *Tetrarch* to dive again.[66] Brandt wrote:

> At 23:25 *UJE* on the left flank sighted a darkened vessel about 800 metres away in direction 260 degrees. She turned immediately towards it and gave full ahead. At 500 metres distance, the vessel was recognised with certainty as a submarine on the surface. At that moment, it started to go down. *UJE* immediately sounded the alarm by siren and fired white star-shells before dropping twelve depth charges on the site where the boat had dived, without any evident result. [. . .] Also *UJA* had detected the noise of engines and when the submarine alarm was given, 'hard-a-port' was ordered as well as 'full ahead'. Not long after, the echo-sound operator heard what he recognised as torpedo sounds. Before he could forward this information to the bridge, *UJB*, slightly ahead of 'E' and 'A', was hit by the torpedo and blew up.[67]

The torpedoes were also sighted on board *UJB* and Kapitänleutnant Neugebauer made the fatal decision to try to turn away. This put his boat right into harm's way, and the 330-ton vessel was literally blown to bits when the torpedo hit amidships. *UJA* and *UJC* hastened to the wreck site while *UJE* and *UJF* went for the submarine. There was little left of *UJB*, except some pieces of wood and empty lifebelts floating around in a heavy layer of oil. Four men were pulled out of the water, of whom only three survived.[68]

The result of the torpedoes appears not to have been observed on board *Tetrarch*. Some fresh air had been sucked into the boat by the diesel engines running on full speed for a couple of minutes before Mills decided to dive again. Once more, *Tetrarch* was exposed to depth charges. 'A tense period,' was the comment in Mills's report, 'charges exploded with great frequency.' The German tactic was to split their forces into several groups, plastering the whole area with depth charges rather than holding on until the submarine was found and go for a concentrated attack. One depth charge exploded close enough to cause the engine room hatch to lift and water to pour into the engine room.

Worse, when diving, Mills had ordered A, Q and Z tanks to be flooded, but for some reason the responsible operator emptied the Z tank instead. This resulted in a very unstable submarine, porpoising with limited control between surface and 400 feet (122 metres), deeper than any other T-class submarines ever recorded. To avoid catastrophe, Mills ordered nos 1 and 2 main ballast tanks blown and *Tetrarch* went straight up like an elevator, exposing herself on the surface for at least half a minute before going down again. Eventually, some buoyancy control was regained at about 300 feet (91.5 metres) and all machinery was stopped, except the forward hydroplane motor to allow emergency control of the boat. This was enough sound for the *U-Jäger* expert sonar operators to pick up, but not to locate with accuracy. Brandt kept his trawlers in the area and the depth charging continued for another hour and a half, although not dangerously close at any stage. Later Mills wrote:

> The experience of depth charging is like standing between the guns in a 15" turret. Charges are not close enough to upset one's balance, but depth gauges fluctuate violently. The enemy set their charges far too shallow, a criticism that it is felt should be kept Most Secret. The experience generally gave most people great confidence in the ability of modern submarines to stand the strain, but the effect of 'waiting' affected some men's nerves. Depth is all-important.[69]

Only when Mills decided to stop the hydroplane motor – as it became obvious the Germans could hear it – did he manage to sneak *Tetrarch* away from the pursuers. At this stage, at least one crewman was breathing through his DSEA apparatus. One reason for Mills's successful escape was probably also the news of French destroyers operating in the Skagerrak that night, as this distracted Brandt, making him very careful and alert, lest he should run into some of them.

Tetrarch eventually surfaced off Kragerø at 21:30 on 24 April, having been submerged for forty-three hours, except for the few minutes the night before. Several of the crew became sick from cramps, nausea and dizziness on surfacing and as this did not seem to disappear quickly, Mills set course for home. The men were no longer able to continue the patrol. *Tetrarch* was back at Rosyth on the 27th.[70]

*　*　*

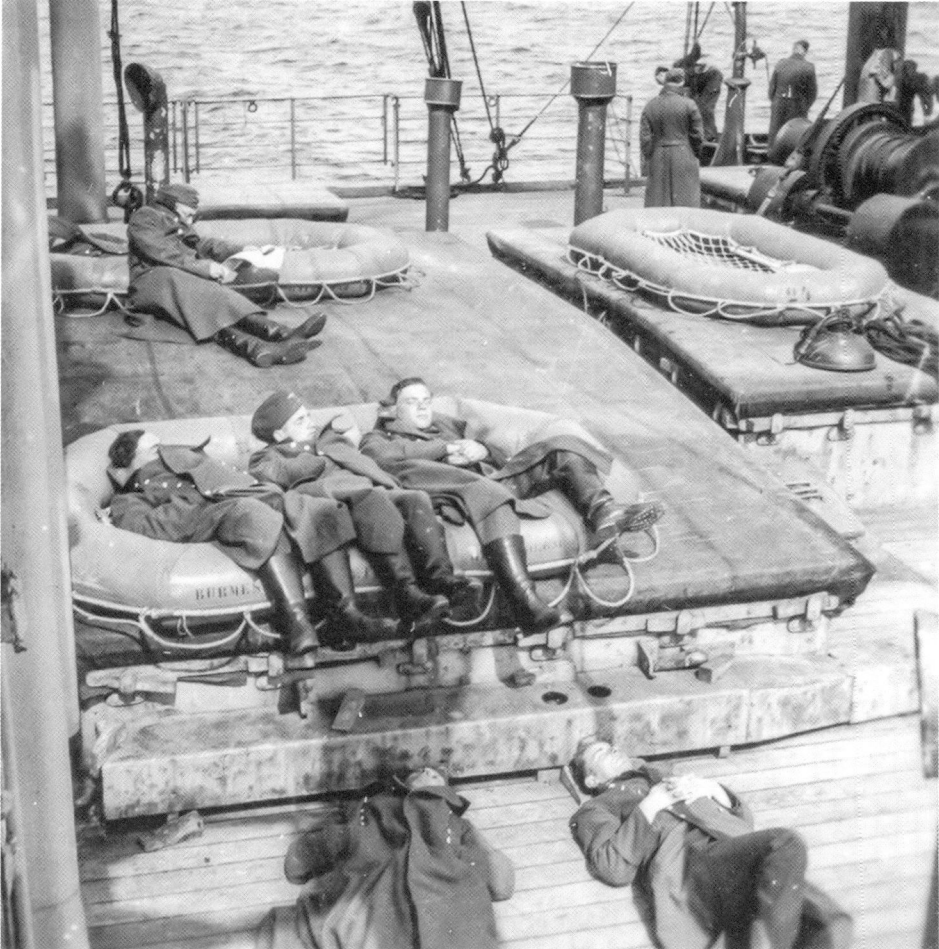

In the Skagerrak, late April 1940. Cold, but staying on deck. Floats are ready, but the life vests are used as headrests. The worst of the scare is over. (Author's Collection)

On 24 April, the SKL noted in their diary that due to 'energetic' anti-submarine measures, a reduction in the threat to the convoys had become noticeable. The countermeasures included heavy direct convoy escort, independent A/S patrols at sea and in the air, timing of convoys to cross the most dangerous areas during the nights, when the submarines had to withdraw to charge their batteries, and the laying of several anti-submarine minefields. Zigzagging was advised for the convoys and troops were kept on deck, life vests donned, with boats and floats ready. It was also strongly emphasised that if a ship was torpedoed, the rest of the convoy should continue, leaving the rescue efforts to the escorts and the nearest A/S units.

Korvettenkapitän Brandt and his 5.U-Jagd Gruppe, for example, after having buried the handful of recovered bodies from *UJB* at Horten in Norway and replenished their stock of depth charges, were sent back into north-eastern Skagerrak as an independent A/S group. They were not attached to any specific convoy, but screened them from a distance together with other similar groups along the route. For several days in late April they operated off the Swedish islands of Väderöerna, dropping 'scary bombs' from time to time and attacking contacts on several occasions. On 29 April, Brandt claimed a 'most likely sunk submarine' after a several-hour-long pursuit involving *UJA*, *C* and *F*, although there is no matching Allied submarine loss.[71]

The concentration of forces in the Kattegat and eastern Skagerrak left serious deficiencies in the North Sea and the Channel area, however, leading SKL to worry over the forthcoming events in the west. It also resulted in a heated discussion between Group East and GroupWest as to the deployment of the available naval vessels, including destroyers, torpedo boats, minesweepers and A/S flotillas.[72] There is little doubt that the intense efforts of the German A/S flotillas and aircraft eventually paid off, though. The inability of the Royal Navy and the RAF to seriously threaten – far less halt – the German supply-line to Norway greatly influenced the outcome of the ensuing campaign. By being able to bring in troops and equipment, including tanks and artillery, in far greater volumes than the Allies could, the outcome of the land war in Norway tipped in Germany's favour. Still, the Allied submarines sank over twenty German transports and naval ships, from cruisers to 200-ton trawlers, between 8 and the end of May. In addition, a large number of ships were damaged (see Appendix IV).

Throughout April, the submarines found the conditions increasingly difficult in the Skagerrak. The numbers of A/S patrols increased markedly and low-flying patrol aircraft were everywhere, forcing them to go deep continuously. Several of the boats were bombed without warning, even when submerged. By the second half of April, several of the submarines had been on patrol for nearly two weeks, some almost three, and they started running low on torpedoes. In addition, the rapidly shortening hours of darkness and the need for re-deployment pending the expected attack in the west, forced VA(S) to suspend patrols in the Kattegat and the eastern Skagerrak. In early May, after the attack on France, the submarines were forced to give Norway and Skagerrak 'a bit of a rest' altogether. Operations east of the Lindesnes–Skagen line were terminated for all practical purposes, leaving the supply convoys alone. One by one, the boats headed home.

One of the last attacks of this period was on 28 April when *Triad* took on a small convoy escorted by four 'destroyers'. Stoker Hart wrote:

> During those tense days, the 'brump' of the depth charges was continuous. Other submarines were having a bad time in the Skagerrak, but *Triad* had been reasonably lucky until we carried out our third attack of that particular patrol. We closed in towards the convoy at periscope depth. That convoy consisted of two or three supply ships and several motor torpedo boats – vicious, waspish crafts. The order was: 'Diving Stations!' Next came: 'Stand by Five, Six Seven and Eight!' There in the engine room, we had little or nothing to do beyond sitting and listening. [. . .] Four shudders shook *Triad*, which meant torpedoes had been fired. A yell from the control room followed: 'Shut off shallow water depth gauges!', so we were going deep. That meant the enemy escorts had spotted us. Less than a minute after firing, we were at 150 feet.[73]

After a few more rounds, the escorts suddenly gave up and left *Triad* to sneak away. With things settling down, the asdic operator could report that just before the depth-charge attack started, he had heard two of the torpedoes hit, but there is no German record of losses on this day. With no more torpedoes left, *Triad* headed for Rosyth and the comforts of home once more. There, however, totally overshadowing the one certain and two probable successes of her own patrol, was the news that sister ships *Thistle* and *Tarpon* had been lost, as well as *Sterlet*. A heavy price to pay for the Submarine Service.[74]

— 16 —

Out of the Fog

AT 17:30 ON 29 April, Lieutenant Francis Brooks took *Unity* to sea from Blyth for a patrol off Heligoland. Brooks was CO of *L23* and hastily transferred to *Unity* when Brown had been taken ill that same morning. Thick fog was rolling in and visibility was down to less than 75 metres (250 feet) as *Unity* turned northwards, down the swept channel towards St Abb's Head from where she would turn east further into the North Sea.

Brooks found the situation worrying and, in addition to the two lookouts and the officer of the watch, Navigation Officer Lieutenant James Trickey, he was on the bridge himself. Lieutenant George Hunt had just come onto the bridge to relieve Trickey, but had not yet done so. First Officer Lieutenant John Low was below in the control room. *Unity* had been given no escort and, without radar, the navigation depended entirely on eyesight and, in the dense fog, earshot.

Unknown to the submariners, a southbound convoy was also about to enter the swept channel off Blyth. They should have known, but the signal from C-in-C Rosyth with information about the presence of the convoy did not reach Brooks and his watch officers in time, apparently as it was for some reason not delivered to Brooks or any of his officers by the signalman. Neither had this information been given to Brooks during his last visit to the staff office before sailing. Hence, Brooks believed the channel was clear of traffic and *Unity* was doing 8 knots, as her sailing orders stated she was to proceed 'with dispatch'. No fog-siren was sounded.[1]

The first indication of other ships in the channel was a foghorn being heard from ahead, shortly after 19:05, to which Lieutenant Trickey answered with a similar blast.[2]

Unity in 1938. (A Wilmar Collection)

Immediately, Lieutenant Brooks took command, gave instructions for the engines to be stopped and the watertight doors to be shut, after which he ordered starboard rudder to avoid whatever was coming towards them. Suddenly, a different siren was heard very close, fine on starboard bow. The wheel was put amidships and Brooks gave orders for 'Full astern both'. Seconds later, the bow of a freighter loomed out of the murk – only 30–40 metres (100–130 feet) away and coming straight at them.

It was the 1,173-ton Norwegian freighter *Atle Jarl*. She had been en route from the UK to Norway in early April 1940 when Master Baltzer Thowsen heard of the German invasion of that country and turned back towards Methil. *Atle Jarl* had left Methil Roads that same day heading for Tynemouth in an MT convoy, eventually on her way to France. Neither vessel was aware of the other until the submarine spotted the freighter at about 50 metres (165 feet) on a collision course. Brooks ordered Lieutenant Trickey to sound three short blasts with the siren, shouted 'Collision stations – prepare to abandon ship!' down the conning tower and braced himself for the impact. He was aware that a collision was inevitable and that the small, single-hulled submarine would not stand much of a chance against the oncoming freighter. Brooks's quick and decisive action at this point probably saved the lives of many on board *Unity*, who would otherwise have been caught unawares.

Leading Seaman William Hill was on watch in the motor room when:

> I received the order 'Full speed astern both', and it was carried out at once. We were going astern for some time when I observed that Able Seaman Hare was attempting to shut the engine room bulkhead door. By motions to him and the engine room staff this was prevented till both engines were stopped, it was then carried out. We were still going astern when the First Lieutenant opened the door and gave the order 'Abandon Ship'. Both of us, myself and Miller, made to move forward to obey that order. Miller had preceded me slightly when I received the order to 'Stop starboard' I went back and stopped starboard. Then I picked up two life-belts and left the boat, throwing one to Miller.[3]

It is remarkable that Hill does not once mention noticing the collision or realising what was happening until being told to 'Abandon ship'. *Unity* was struck at the port forward hydroplane, just aft of the torpedo tube space. The impact was relatively gentle, but the bow of the freighter sliced through the pressure hull and water poured into the fore end of the submarine. Nobody was hurt by the collision and all men moved urgently but in an orderly fashion towards the control room to get out of the boat through the conning tower. Lieutenant Low organised the evacuation, ensuring all watertight doors were shut and calming down those who needed it on the way up the ladder. It appears he also searched through the boat as best he could to ensure nobody had been left behind. For some reason, the port motor remained going astern. Able Seaman Henry Miller volunteered to go back to stop it and Low followed him. They were seen going through the engine-room bulkhead door, shutting it behind them and then were never seen again. Low and Miller were both posthumously awarded the George Cross for their gallantry. *Unity* sank less than five minutes after the collision.[4]

Up top, Lieutenant Hunt met the men as they came up. He checked that they were OK and were carrying their lifebelts before sending them to gather on the after casing. He later narrated:

In those days we had no lifebelts worthy of the name, except we were issued with an inflatable rubber tube and of all the colours to choose from, it was covered in a blue sort of denim stuff! It also had a tube so that it could be inflated by mouth. Now, if you blew it up before you got out of the submarine, it made you so big it was difficult to get through the conning tower hatch. So the theory was you tied it round your body while deflated, came up to the bridge, and then got into the water and blew up your life ring – unless you had been able to do it on the bridge. It was ridiculous really, but then it was the beginning of the war and we were learning.[5]

Brooks, Trickey and Hunt stayed on the bridge. Hunt was ordered by Brooks to close the conning tower hatch when the last man was up and stand on it until *Unity* sank and the water pressure would take over, in an attempt to preserve some air for the two men still left down below. Hunt continued:

[All those close to the submarine when it sank] got sucked down quite a long way. As soon as we got back to the surface we tried to rally the chaps and we all tried to keep together as much as possible. They started a singsong in the water, so as they went around I advised them to 'keep your breath for staying afloat'. But they all more or less stayed together. A couple drifted apart and were drowned. There was a fair tide sluicing along, of course.[6]

Later, Lieutenant Brooks, who was rather shaky from having banged his head against something when *Unity* sank, commended Lieutenant Trickey for 'his assistance and

Atle Jarl photographed in the North Sea on 10 March while on her way towards the UK. The photo was taken from an Anson of 269 Squadron at Wick. (NA-AIR 28/941)

encouragement of ratings in difficulties in the sea', in spite of being a poor swimmer. It was early in the evening, the fog persisted and, unless the freighter was able to report the accident, nobody back at Blyth would know what had happened. Eventually, however, to everybody's relief, *Atle Jarl* loomed back out of the fog. Master Thowsen, who like Brooks was on the bridge of his ship owing to the fog, had glimpsed the White Ensign just before the accident and realised his ship had rammed an Allied submarine. Turning back was challenging in the fog with the other ships of the convoy nearby, but *Atle Jarl* was back to start the search for the men in the water within ten to fifteen minutes. Skilfully estimating the drift of any survivors due to the tidal currents, it was not long before the first bobbing heads were seen in the beams of the searchlights. Two lifeboats were lowered and within twenty-five minutes all men that could be found in the murk had been rescued. Two men drifted away with the tide before they could be rescued, making the total number of casualties four.

On board *Atle Jarl*, the survivors were given dry clothes, something warm to drink and a bed if they wanted. The Norwegian freighter had no radio on board though, and with the convoy gone, it was not until a destroyer was sighted next morning that the accident could be reported to Blyth. Thereafter, *Atle Jarl* took the survivors to the Tyne. Damage to *Atle Jarl* was relatively slight and in spite of taking on water forward, she was able to continue to her destination Rouen after some temporary repairs.

Lieutenant Hunt later reported that Master Thowsen had told him they believed that the lone, unescorted submarine would certainly be German and deliberately tried to ram her. The White Ensign was only seen at the last minute, too late to avoid the collision. It has not been possible to confirm this. At the board of inquiry, Lieutenant Brooks said Thowsen had told him he 'thought and hoped *Unity* was a German submarine'. Brooks had no doubt the collision was unavoidable, considering the course *Atle Jarl* held when his submarine became visible through the fog, less than 50 metres (165 feet) away – a distance covered in about thirty seconds.

Following the board of inquiry, Brooks was cleared of all liabilities and went on to command submarines *Upright* and *Utmost*, until, after a spell at Gosport, he was posted to the Operations Division at the Admiralty in July 1942.

After the inquiry, several routines and procedures were improved, particularly regarding communication and dissemination of important information; not least, all submarines were to be escorted in British waters. Otherwise, there was insufficient evidence to attach blame to any one person or vessel and the case was closed as an unfortunate accident. The officers and crew of *Atle Jarl* were officially commended by Their Lordships of the Admiralty for their 'efficiency and energy in rendering assistance to the ship's company of His Majesty's vessel and of the kindness and generosity shown during the night'.[7]

— 17 —

Le Grande Patrouille

THE FRENCH NAVY OR 'Marine Nationale' of the late 1930s was steeped in tradition, conservative in utilisation of new technologies and limited in individual opportunities. Still, at the outbreak of WWII, the Marine Nationale was the fourth largest navy of the world and in Europe second only to the Royal Navy. It could muster about 160,000 men and was far better prepared for war than either the French Army or Air Force with more than 200 relatively moden ships commissioned between 1920 and 1935.[1]

In June 1939, Vice Amiral François Darlan, was made Amiral de la Flotte and given command of the entire French Navy, including direct control of all operations in all theatres. As he was answerable directly to the government, it made him independent of general political support and to a large extent free from political control.

Darlan was not much in favour of co-operating with the Royal Navy and there was virtually no exchange of plans or points of view between the Admiralty and the French Naval Staff prior to the outbreak of war, largely due to common mistrust and no advisers advocating the need for a common strategy. Joint Anglo-French naval staff conferences were held in London on 31 March, 27 April and 3 May 1939, but these had little consequence for the practicalities in either navy. Vice Admiral Jean Odend'hal was appointed head of the French Naval Mission to the British Admiralty in London in 1939. He undoubtedly did his best to facilitate some sort of co-operation between the two navies, but against the dour unwillingness of Darlan he was not overly successful.[2]

Sous-marins

At the end of WWI, the French Navy possessed forty-seven submarines, eleven of which were captured German ones. The boats were mainly old, though, of many types and needed to be standardised. Hence, plans were made for an upgraded and modernised fleet. The proposals for banning submarines at the Washington Naval Conference and other meetings were actively opposed by France (and Italy). The restrictions in size of the various types of boats eventually imposed were largely respected though – at first.[3]

France constructed three types of submarines in the period between the wars: large ocean-going, long-range vessels for colonial service and for operation with the fleet (Sous-marins de Grande Patrouille), smaller boats for offensive patrols in European waters (Défense Côtière), and minelayers.

The first post-war French submarines, nine large, double-hulled boats of the *Requin*-class of the 1922 and 1923 programmes, were based on German U-boats that had been taken as reparations. They had a standard surface displacement of 1,441 tons submerged and were armed with ten 21.7-inch torpedo tubes, one 10-cm deck gun, and two machine guns. Commissioned between 1926 and 1928, they were found to be less than successful, in spite of extensive modifications in the mid-1930s.

The subsequent *Redoutable*-class, of which the first was commissioned in mid-1931, was far better, however, and, in all, thirty-one boats were built in three series between 1928 and 1937. They displaced 2,082 tons submerged; their maximum range was 10,000 miles at 10 knots on the surface, and their submerged endurance was sixty hours at 2 knots. They had a battery of eleven torpedo tubes (seven of them in two remotely controlled trainable external mounts) with a total of thirteen torpedoes, a 10-cm gun and a double 13.2-mm machine gun.

In 1923 the French Navy placed orders for coastal submarines with three different design bureaux. This led to three rather different designs, the *Sirène*-, *Ariane*- and *Circé*-classes, collectively known as the 600 series, to the same specification. These were followed a few years later by the slightly larger 630 series known as the *Argonaute*-, *Orion*- and *Diane*-classes, respectively. In all, ten 600 series and sixteen 630 series submarines were built. The French also constructed several smaller sea-going patrol-type submarines. The building programme also included the *Sirène*-class, nine of which were eventually built. Several other 600- and 900-ton patrol-type submarine classes were authorised in the years before the war, but not all were complete when France fell in June 1940. This way of building quickly resulted in logistical and operational challenges and in 1934 the navy opted for a standardised design, the *Minerve*-class of six boats were built, and in 1939 by the improved *Aurore*-class, the last series of French submarines constructed before the war. The boats of the *Aurore*-class displaced 893 tons and were armed with nine 21.7-inch torpedo tubes, three in an external, remotely controlled trainable mount, plus a single 3.9-inch deck gun and two 13-mm machine guns.[4]

Mine-laying submarines were limited to the six *Saphir*-class boats commissioned between 1930 and 1937.[5] These displaced 762 tons on the surface and could cruise for 7,000 miles at 10 knots on the surface. They had a submerged endurance of forty-eight hours at 2 knots and could operate safely down to a depth of 80–85 metres (265–280 feet). Five torpedo tubes were carried, two internal in the bow and three in a trainable external mount, with seven torpedoes in addition to a single 75-mm deck gun. The mines were carried outside the pressure hull in four groups of vertical wells, each with two mines, one above the other. Hence, there were thirty-two mines. These were released from the inside of the submarine by an air-pressure mechanism. The mooring depth of the mine could be adjusted by the operator shortly before laying, through a rather complicated process requiring the submarine to come to the desired depth for the mines to activate the hydrostatic device that placed the mine at the correct distance below the surface. The Sauter Harlé mines used weighed 1,090 kg on the surface (375 kg submerged) of which 220 kg was the explosive charge.[6]

The experimental submarine cruiser *Surcouf*, commissioned in 1934, was for many years the largest submarine of any navy. Designed for long-range commerce warfare, it displaced 4,373 tons submerged and had a range of 10,000 miles at 10 knots on the surface. It had a range of sixty hours at 2 knots submerged and could operate safely at a depth of 85 metres (280 feet). The giant's armament included no fewer than twelve tubes (eight in external mounts) with twenty-two torpedoes,[7] two 203-mm (8-inch) guns in a special turret mounting and a seaplane stowed in a hangar and launched with a catapult. The *Surcouf* was equipped with a special compartment to accommodate prisoners taken from intercepted vessels and a small motor launch to transport boarding parties. The submarine was useful in peacetime colonial policing but, marginal to wartime French naval strategies, it never really found a useful role to play after September 1939. Being costly to build and requiring a large crew of over 100 men, no further boats of this type were built.

French submarines were generally double-hulled, with an emphasis on good surface handling, even if this made them less efficient under water. Emphasis was also given to making the boats comfortable during long voyages and operations in southern latitudes where most of France's colonial empire was. A rather unique feature was the trainable, external torpedo mounts, built into the outer casing. These could be fired at various angles off amidships, but could not be reloaded at sea. French submarines carried torpedoes of two different calibres: 400-mm (15.75-inch) for use against shallow-draught targets such as escorts or transports, and 550-mm (21.7-inch) for use against larger warships. Some of the older boats carried a third variety of 450-mm (17.7-inch) only.

In 1939 France had a fleet of seventy-seven submarines in commission, one of the largest forces in the world at the time. Forty-one of these were modern, first-rate boats. About three-quarters of the submarines were based in the Mediterranean (mainly at Toulon, Bizerte or Oran); the rest were at Brest or Cherbourg, or in the colonies. There was no central submarine command. French submarines operated under the command of the fleet to which they were assigned. Like the Royal Navy, the French Marine Nationale in the late 1930s saw its submarine force working mainly in co-operation with the surface fleet, particularly in the Mediterranean. Long-range individual operations were largely seen as part of the protection of France's overseas territories and colonial empire.

The Best of Intentions

To ensure a more flexible use of the French ships, Churchill and Pound visited Maintenon in September 1939 to meet with Admiral Darlan. It was agreed that in addition to help protect the steady stream of British troops transported across the Channel, the Marine Nationale would participate in the escort of certain Atlantic and Gibraltar convoys as agreed on a case-by-case basis.[8] In return, asdic-equipped trawlers would be provided as well as general A/S and minesweeping competence. The mistrust between the two allies ran deep, though, and, in spite of the best of intentions, it would take time before any direct co-operation between the navies started to develop.

There were few targets for the French submarines deployed in the Atlantic and, after a while, the French Admiralty (l'Amirauté) decided to offer some of their long-range submarines as convoy escort, partly to free surface ships for other tasks, partly as it was believed the convoys would attract those German raiders and U-boats that might be at sea. From November 1939 to April 1940, the 1,500-ton submarines *Casabianca*, *Sfax*, *Achille* and *Pasteur* escorted at least eight Allied Halifax convoys as well as several convoys to Freetown or South Africa. *Surcouf* was also used for this purpose at times and the boats were occasionally diverted to purely French convoys to their own colonies.[9]

In early 1940, after the loss of *Seahorse*, *Starfish* and *Undine*, it was agreed that French submarines should augment British submarines in the North Sea, working from British ports. Hence, the 13th and 16th submarine divisions were transferred from Brest to

Jules Verne. Known as a *ravitailleur de sous-marins*, literally, a 'refuelling ship for submarines', the 4,350-ton vessel was an integral part of the French submarine forces operating from Britain in 1940. (Author's Collection)

Harwich. The first three, the 600-ton boats *Antiope*, *La Sibylle* and *Amazone*, supported by the depot ship *Jules Verne* and minelayer *Pollux*, arrived at Harwich in the evening of 22 March 1940 to make the core of what was to become known as the 10th Submarine Flotilla by the British and Groupe Jules-Verne by the French. Capitaine de Vaisseau Felix Raymond de Belot was in overall command of the forces.

The French submarines were to operate under British control, but as Horton was uncertain of their operational efficiency he deployed them in the less-exposed areas until they had gained more experience and proven their operational capabilities. By giving them billets in the approaches to the Heligoland Bight, west of the Westwall and in the northern approaches to the Strait of Dover, Ruck-Keene's 3rd Flotilla could be moved further north, off the Norwegian coast and into the Skagerrak. In mid-April, five more submarines, *Orphée*, *Doris*, *Thétis*, *Circé* and *Calypso* also arrived, as did the 1,500-ton boats *Casabianca*, *Sfax*, *Pasteur* and *Achille*. The latter four were transferred to the 9th Flotilla at Dundee at the end of their first patrols.[10] The final French submarine to operate from British ports in this period, the minelayer *Rubis*, docked in Harwich on 1 May, making the total number of French submarines in Britain thirteen.

The first of the French submarines to go on patrol from Harwich was *La Sibylle* on 31 March. The billet was off Terschelling and the patrol, which was quite uneventful, lasted for six days. After the patrol, the British liaison officer, Lieutenant Thomas Catlow, made a confidential report to Ruck-Keene and Horton of his observations, which makes for interesting reading:

The Commanding Officer [Lieutenant de Vaisseau Alphonse Raybaud] is an extremely competent and keen officer with a firm hold over officers and men. For a southern

Circé in 1932. 615 tons on the surface, 776 tons submerged, she could do 7.5 knots under water, but a mere 14 knots on the surface. She was commissioned in 1927 and ageing by the time she went to war. *Calypso*, *Thétis* and *Doris* were sister ships. The antennas had to be taken down before submerging. This was a cumbersome process, and the masts were not used when the boats operated from Britain in 1940. (Y Grangeon Collection)

Frenchman he has equable temperament and I never saw him panic. [. . .] I had no opportunity to see him under true action conditions due to an uneventful patrol. His only weakness to date is his inability to take his boat alongside well, one, I consider, to his considerations for his 'drowned' fore-'planes. Takes every precaution for the safety of his submarine, but [. . .] full of dash.

   [. . .]

   In the French navy, there is a special rating, a Petty Officer, who does a 3-year course in *Pilotage*. He looks after the charts and pilots the submarine under the supervision of the Captain and officers.

   [. . .]

   The coxswain of the submarine, the *Patron* [. . .], has complete hold on the crew and never at any time did I hear bickering or complaints. The crew of the submarine were keen and hardworking and of a pleasant disposition generally. Their discipline is very good and they show very marked respect towards their officers and Petty Officers [but] if a rating has an idea of his own, he immediately said so to the officer or Petty Officer, the matter was discussed and the best idea carried out.[11]

Overall, Lieutenant Catlow compared *La Sibylle* with a British S-class submarine. She had some external fuel tanks, though, requiring pumps to access. These pumps had limited volumes and, frequently breaking down, could make fuel a concern, even on shorter patrols. Also, she had above-water exhaust outlets and could not be trimmed down when on the surface. To obtain fully charged batteries, *La Sibylle* needed five to six hours on the surface.

   Submerged, depth-keeping was immaculate. Diving time was well over a minute, though Catlow believed they could do it significantly faster, once they had experienced

La Sibylle in 1933, just after commissioning. A slightly larger '600-ton' submarine, built some years after the *Circé*-class, she was 651 tons on the surface and 807 tons submerged. *La Sibylle* and her eight sister ships, including *Orphée*, *Amazone* and *Antiope*, could do a fair 9.5 knots submerged, but no more than 14 knots on the surface. (Y Grangeon Collection)

a real emergency. Should the boat take up an angle during the dive, however, Lieutenant Catlow feared stability might become a challenge as she has a large and wide casing outside the pressure hull. For some reason, the French submariners coped poorly with the deterioration of air quality inside the boat after being submerged for some time. In spite of purifiers and oxygen being fed into the submarine's atmosphere, they were troubled by the lack of fresh air, while Catlow was barely affected.[12]

The patrols that Lieutenant de Vaisseau Raybaud and his men made while stationed at Harwich during April and May 1940 were largely uneventful. Disaster was near, though, when Lieutenant Marcel Balastre of *Antiope* mistook *La Sybille* for a U-boat and fired three torpedoes at her, west of Terschelling on 20 May. Fortunately the torpedoes missed. On her last patrol before returning to France, numerous technical problems started to appear and a spell in the yards was obviously becoming necessary.[13]

Orphée under Lieutenant de Vaisseau Robert Meynier made only one short patrol out of Harwich, but this was quite eventful. In the afternoon of 21 April, two days into the patrol, while about midway between Ringkøbing and Dundee, two torpedoes were fired on what turned out to be *U51* under Kapitänleutnant Dietrich Knorr. Two U-boats had been sighted about fifteen minutes earlier and Meynier chased one of them at full speed to ascertain whether it was alien. When close enough, he and the British liaison officer, Sub-Lieutenant Peter Banister, agreed it was 'definitely not British' and decided to attack. On a parallel course to the German, on her starboard bow, the centre and stern torpedo turrets of *Orphée* were turned at a firing angle of 50 degrees. Time was of the essence, lest the U-boat should dive, and there was no time to set any gyro angles, just fire as soon as the tubes had been trained in the right direction. Only two torpedoes were fired, but Meynier ascertained they were running correctly through the periscope. Just before he went down, he could also see that the German started his diesels and made a small change of course, but believed this to be just routine. In fact, *U51* had problems with her port diesel engine and made several attempts to restart it at the time of the attack. *Orphée* was not sighted at all, just the torpedo tracks. Once these were reported, Knorr sounded the alarm and made an emergency dive while turning to port, away from the tracks. For some reason, both torpedoes exploded close to the U-boat, making it 'jump' several metres. There was no damage, though, and as nothing further was heard from the enemy submarine, *U51* fell back on her general course and continued homewards. Twenty-four hours later, she was safely moored in Kiel at the Tirpitzmole, having passed through the Kaiser Wilhelm Kanal during the afternoon of 22 April.[14]

On board *Orphée*, two explosions were heard at about the expected time at short intervals, and it was believed erroneously that the torpedoes had hit. Concern about the second U-boat that had been sighted and a low battery made Meynier take *Orphée* away from the area after a brief look for wreckage through the periscope. Two days later, *Orphée* was back in Harwich. At the time, it was believed that a U-boat had really been sunk and Lieutenant Meynier and his crew received some attention, including in the French press, as the boat was awarded a *Croix de Guerre* for the assumed achievement. *Orphée* returned to Cherbourg on 3 June.[15]

Another of the French boats operating out of Harwich in the spring of 1940 was *Doris*, a 600-ton, *Circé*-class coastal submarine. She had been commissioned in January 1930 after a lengthy building and work-up process and appears to have been continuously plagued by technical problems originating from being fitted with German Schneider diesels, which were unreliable and had a chronic lack of spares. Nevertheless, she was considered suitable for operating from bases in Britain as part of the 10th Flotilla.

A few days into her first patrol out of Harwich in late April, the port engine compressor broke down. This was serious as it meant the engine could not be used and *Doris* would only have the starboard engine available for running as well as charging. The patrol was terminated and *Doris* returned to Harwich on 25 April. There were no spare parts

Doris in 1938. (Author's Collection)

available on board *Jules Verne* and they had to be ordered from Toulon. This took time – all the more so, as the first crates with spares to arrive did not contain the actual parts needed.[16]

Even so, Capitaine de Corvette Jean Favreul was asked to prepare for a sortie in early May to a billet north of the Frisian Islands, off the Dutch coast. Something was brewing and, fearing that a German invasion of the Low Countries was being prepared, VA(S) considered it necessary to have as many boats as possible guarding the area south of the Westwall.

Discussing with his flotilla commander, Favreul agreed that it would be possible to take air from the working starboard compressor and run the port engine at half power. With only one and a half engines, the submarine would be a sitting duck should they actually run into the Germans they were looking for, but the men of *Doris* were willing to take the risk. A series of letters left behind by the crew for their families show that they recognised their vulnerability and left Harwich with few illusions.

In the evening of the 7th and early morning of 8 May, around a dozen Allied submarines, including *Doris*, departed for the coast off Holland. To avoid errors with so many different Allied submarines in the area, each commanding officer was given orders not to attack any other submarine, unless it could be identified with absolute certainty as being German. Intelligence received at the Admiralty indicated that the Germans could read the British cypher-codes and thus had knowledge of the disposition of the Allied boats. This has been difficult to verify with certainty in this specific case, and there are no indications in the war diary of *U9* that she was on anything but a normal patrol. It is true, though, that German intelligence to a large degree could read British naval signals at the time and could plot the position of vessels using their radios. In any case, new re-cyphering tables had been issued to most boats and the two that had not received new tables, *Antiope* and *Thétis*, were held back, patrolling the entries to Harwich.

U9. A type IIB boat, commissioned in August 1935. She would alternate between active service and training boat, until sunk in the Black Sea in August 1944 by Russian aircraft. (Author's Collection)

Doris reached her billet off the Dutch coast between Ijmuiden and Den Helder by nightfall. She was not alone.[17]

The 26-year-old Oberleutnant Wolfgang Lüth had taken his nimble type II U-boat through the Westwall, following the safe route *Weg I* the night before, towards a billet off the Dutch coast. By chance, this area overlapped partly with the southern part of the billet asigned to *Doris*. Due to numerous fishing boats, *U9* had stayed submerged all day and only surfaced after dark at 22:27. It was starlit, with a new moon and moderate to good visibility. The fishing boats had largely returned to port, but the lights from ten or twenty of them could still be seen to the east, towards land, as *U9* moved slowly southwards. About an hour and a half later the port lookout reported that what appeared to be the silhouette of a blacked-out submarine moved in front of some of the lights from the fishing boats, steering a northerly course, 3,000–4,000 metres (3,300–4,400 yards) away. Lüth turned towards the submarine (which was *Doris*), very carefully as he had the brighter western horizon behind him. *Doris* was apparently not zigzagging, but from *U9* it looked as if she turned from a north-westerly course almost 180 degrees towards the south and then, a few minutes later, back again towards the north-west. Still, it does not appear Capitaine Favreul or anybody else on board ever realised that they were being stalked.

Finally, at about a quarter past midnight on the 9th, German time, Lüth had *U9* in the position he wanted relative to his target and, turning towards it, fired two

Oberleutnant Wolfgang Lüth had many faces and was a rather controversial person. On one side, he was a determined submariner, charismatic and fatherly. On the other, he was a convinced Nazi who carried his Knight's Cross with pride. There is no doubt, though, that he was an exceptional U-boat captain. With *U9* he would sink seven ships in addition to *Doris*, totalling some 16,500 tons. In all, he would sink forty-seven ships, totalling 225,756 tons, becoming the second-highest scoring submarine commander of the war; he was awarded the Knight's Cross with Oak Leaf, Swords and Diamonds. Shortly after the armistice in 1945, he failed to answer a night sentry at the naval academy at Mürwick when challenged and was shot dead. (Author's Collection)

U9 after her patrol. *Left*: 29 May, in Brunsbüttel along *Usambara*. *Right*: in Kiel the next day, having passed through the Kaiser Wilhelm Canal. (Author's Collection)

torpedoes: one electrical G7e running at 2 metres (6.5 feet) depth and one conventional G7a running at 3 metres (9.8 feet). The range was only about 750 metres (820 yards) and after less than a minute, there was a huge fireball. According to *U9*'s war diary, the G7e torpedo passed in front of its target while the G7a torpedo hit *Doris* just aft of the conning tower. This apparently set off a secondary explosion of one or more of the warheads in the French boat's own dual mid-ship torpedo turret. Taking *U9* over to the site of the explosion, there was nothing to be found of the other submarine except a large patch of oil.

Doris went to the bottom with forty-five men on board. There were no survivors and it is not known if anybody on board *Doris* saw the torpedoes approaching. The British liaison officer Lieutenant Richard Westmacot, Yeoman of Signals Harry Wilson and Telegraphist Charles Sales were lost with *Doris*.[18]

On Patrol

The four 1,500-ton boats *Casabianca*, *Sfax*, *Pasteur* and *Achille* were ordered to depart Harwich in company on 18 April, heading for south-western Norway. It was a little over a week since the German invasion of that country and most of the British submarines were either still operating in the Skagerrak or the Kattegat, or on their way home to rest and replenish. Norwegian forces were still maintaining pockets of resistance north of Bergen and Allied forces had landed in central and northern Norway. It would be important to prevent any German reinforcements coming up along the western coast and the four French boats were deployed accordingly. While casting off, the after planes of *Achille* and *Pasteur* became entangled. *Achille*'s starboard propeller was slightly damaged, but she was still able to set off. *Pasteur* on the other hand was unable to submerge and had to abort her departure. The other French boats headed for Norway:

Sfax off Egersund–Flekkefjord, *Achille* off Stavanger and *Casabianca* covering an area south of Bergen.

Lieutenant de Vaisseau Marcel Groix of *Sfax* found the waters off Stavanger rather crowded. There were hydrophone contacts just about every day, though the ships sighted were generally small, and with low visibility it was difficult to get into a position from which to fire torpedoes. When visibility was fair, the escorts were numerous and the freighters travelled at high speed. On 22 April, several merchant vessels were sighted, however, of which one ventured near enough for a salvo of two torpedoes. The distance was still over 5,000 metres (5,500 yards); as the ship was travelling at over 20 knots, both missed.[19]

Further north, *Achille* made landfall off the island of Utsira in the early hours of Sunday 21 April and proceeded inshore to search the entrance to Karmsundet, the southern entry to the Inner Leads between Stavanger and Bergen. No ships were sighted, but numerous aircraft made Lieutenant de Vaisseau Ernest Michaud keep his boat submerged. On the 22nd, a large ship, identified as the 3,866-ton submarine fleet tender *Erwin Wassner*, was sighted, but was too far away to be able to get into an attack position, as the many aircraft overhead made surfacing impossible. Over the next couple of days, *Achille* stalked the entrance to the sound and many of the bays and inlets near it without encountering much other than fishing vessels and what was probably *Sfax*, well off station. On the one occasion when another large vessel was sighted, it was escorted by aircraft and Michaud decided to leave it alone. *Achille* was back in Dundee by 28 April. Upon reading the report from the patrol, the commander of the 9th Flotilla, Captain James Roper, called Lieutenant Michaud to his office to let him know that, in his opinion, it had been a mistake not to attack the vessel sighted, in spite of the aerial escort.[20]

Casabianca, a 1,500-ton submarine of the *Redoutable* class. She could do 20 knots on the surface and 7 knots submerged. (Author's Collection)

Further north still, *Casabianca* settled down off Selbjørnfjorden, one of the entrances to the Leads south of Bergen, occasionally moving to off Korsfjorden, further north. Why she was there and not further south at Sletta – the open stretch where ships following the Leads would have to come out behind the islands – is not clear. Predictably, there was little activity where *Casabianca* was, except on the 21st when a small MTB-type boat was sighted. Aircraft were regularly overhead, but none of them seem to have observed *Casabianca*, even when she was at periscope depth. On 25 April Capitaine de Corvette René Sacaze decided to take his boat into the fjord to see if there was anything worth his torpedoes there. Unfortunately there was not: only small freighters or fishing boats and a large number of aircraft patrolling the Leads, which made surfacing to inspect these more closely impossible. Nonetheless, he went back inside the Leads the following two days, again without encountering anything worth a torpedo. Shortly before midnight on the 28th, *Casabianca* set course back towards Dundee. Capitaine Sacaze later wrote that he found the 1,500-ton boat unsuitable for such inshore patrols as she was too large to manoeuvre easily in confined waters. In addition, he believed *Casabianca* would be easily detected if on the surface at night as the exhausts were very noisy and gave off streams of sparks visible several miles off.[21]

On their next patrols, the 1,500-ton submarines were deployed at the entrance of the Skagerrak on the same longitude as Lindesnes. This time they departed individually, between 7 and 10 May. For *Achille* the first days of the patrol, west of Lindesnes, were rather uneventful. Then on 14 May, while pursuing two merchant ships, she was bombed repeatedly and had to break off the chase. Now that the Germans knew they were there, *Achille* was attacked frequently, making it very hard to stay on the surface long enough to get a good charge in the batteries. To his relief, in the afternoon of 17 May, Lieutenant Michaud received orders for a new billet further to the south-west, away from the Norwegian coast. Moving there, another submarine was picked up on the hydrophones and chased for a while until lost again. A little later, during the night of the 17/18 May, a submarine was sighted on the surface about 1,000 metres (1,100 yards) away, most likely the same one that had been heard earlier. Two torpedoes were made ready hurriedly, but, uncertain of her identity, Michaud decide to fire a recognition signal. This made the other submarine dive swiftly without firing any signals back. The other submarine was chased for more than six hours by hydrophone, before finally being lost for good. The submarine chased was *Tetrarch*. Lieutenant Commander Mills recognised the other boat as French, but attempts at communication failed and he eventually sped away on the surface keeping the hydrophone effects of *Achille* well aft until they finally faded away.[22]

Finally called home on the 19th, *Achille* was on the surface west of Dundee in the morning of the 20th, well inside the security zone where Allied aircraft had standing orders not to attack any submarines, when an aircraft emerged from the clouds some 500 metres (550 yards) aft of the submarine. The recognition grenade failed to ignite and an emergency dive was initiated. While at about 25 metres (82 feet), several bombs exploded near the boat, causing havoc on board. Lamps burst, everything loose was thrown about, the compass and several battery terminals came loose, outside fuel tanks started to leak and both hydrophones and sonar ceased to work. *Achille* limped into Dundee at nightfall; the crew were alive, but furious at British airmen in general, and the men who could not recognise a French submarine from a German one on the surface in full daylight in particular. The pilot of the aircraft, a Hudson from No. 233 Squadron, later explained that he and his crew were unable to make any accurate observations owing to the intense glare of the morning sun on the smooth surface of the sea. The boat was seen to dive without sending any recognition signals and, as the navigator confirmed (falsely) that they were outside the 'no-bombing' zone, three anti-submarine bombs were dropped onto a clearly seen oil-track leading away from where the submarine had dived.[23]

The incident – for which no fault was ascribed to either side – highlighted several important issues. Firstly, the difficulty of determining the position of an aircraft at the end of a long patrol over open sea without regular radio bearings and fixes from ground stations; secondly, that the large French submarines were indeed prone to leave oil traces on the surface in calm weather; and thirdly, that a reliable system of recognition between aircraft and submarines was desperately needed.[24] Inspection of the damage to *Achille* in Dundee determined that she needed to go to France for repairs, all the more so as she was due for a refit in June anyway. Hence, *Achille* would not sail under British command any more.[25] On 18 June, when the Germans entered Brest, *Achille* was in dry dock and, unable to move under her own power. She was pulled out of the dock and scuttled in deep water to prevent capture.

Casabianca's second patrol off Lindesnes on the southern coast of Norway was uneventful for the first couple of days. There were many aircraft overhead, though, and one of them probably sighted and reported the French submarine. Just after diving in the early hours of 14 May, having charged the batteries during the limited hours of darkness, hydrophone effects of a fast vessel were picked up quite close. It turned out to be a small vessel of the MTB-type, probably a German R-boat or S-boat. Capitaine de Corvette Sacaze took his boat deep, shut down all noisy activities, and tried to sneak away. This turned out to be not so easy, as the 'MTB' was joined by a group of trawlers and depth charges were dropped: close by, but not particularly dangerous. Eventually though, around 06:00, the chase was abandoned and the A/S trawlers disappeared. Some hours later, the reason for all the commotion became evident: a convoy of eleven eastbound merchant ships with heavy escort, including aircraft, was sighted in the far distance, close to shore. *Casabianca* was too far away for any hope of getting into a suitable position to attack, as surfacing would be impossible with the escort around. The best Sacaze could do was to go to periscope depth and send an enemy report on the periscope aerial. Just as this was completed, a heavy explosion rocked the boat – they had been sighted by an aircraft, which had dropped a couple of bombs nearby. Sacaze took *Casabianca* deep and headed out of the area.

The next day, towards nightfall, *Casabianca* was back off Lindesnes. So were the 'MTB' and at least one of the trawlers. Depth charges were dropped, and they were chased for a couple of hours before being able to sneak away once again. After a few more uneventful days west of Lindesnes, *Casabianca* returned to Dundee on 21 May with some minor leaks and damage from the depth-charge explosions. Sacaze wrote in his report:

> This patrol has been particularly tiring. An average of 21 hours diving every day for 11 consecutive days. The air on board lacked oxygen at the end of each dive. The very short nights were exceedingly light because of the moon and thus gave no security to the submarine when charging. An unexpected and unpleasant impression was caused on

hearing the enemy patrol boat transmit absolutely identical supersonic transmissions to those of the Allies, the same method of search and attack. [. . .] I think that the patrol of a narrow sector in an area controlled by the enemy is not the best mission for this large [. . .] submarine. Its speed and radius of action [. . .] should make this submarine a good vessel for working in a wider field of action in which it could produce better results and in which it could regulate its movements according to information received. *Casabianca* should, in principle, commence refit on 1st June. Certain parts of the vessel begin to show signs of wear [. . .]. The submarine is nevertheless fit to make one more patrol and almost certainly yet another.[26]

Things were about to change, however, and no more patrols would be made during this phase. Following the German attack on the western front on 10 May, the 10th Flotilla, including the depot ships *Jules Verne* and *Cyclops*, was transferred from Harwich to Rosyth on 15 May, from fear of air attacks, with the submarines following over the period of a week as they returned from patrol. Two weeks later, on 4 June, *Jules Verne* and the French submarines remaining in Britain were called back to France. Apart from *Rubis*, which obtained quite significant results from the minefields she had laid, the other French submarines did not sink any German vessels while under British auspices.

In France, things went from bad to worse. Brest was occupied on 18 June and Cherbourg shortly after. *Jules Verne* and fourteen submarines escaped from Brest in spite of active Luftwaffe attempts to prevent them. The 1,500-ton boats *Achille*, *Agosta*, *Ouessant* and *Pasteur* were in the docks and scuttled more or less as the Germans arrived to prevent them from being captured. *Surcouf*, on the other hand, managed to get out in time, in spite of being in the process of refitting and out of commission. Admiral Darlan had given instructions to steer for a French port and the original idea was to go to Casablanca. With only electric motors for power and a jammed hydroplane preventing her from diving, however, *Surcouf* limped across the Channel at 4 knots, arriving in Plymouth during the night of the 19/20 June. From Cherbourg *Orion*, *Ondine*, *Junon* and *Minerve* evacuated in a hurry on the 19th, heading for Britain, while four submarines still under construction were destroyed.

At 18:00 on 22 June, the French government signed the ceasefire documents and the north and west of France fell under German occupation.[27] The unoccupied eastern part and the overseas colonies were under the control of the new French administration in Vichy. Most of the submarines escaped to Toulon or naval bases in North Africa under Vichy control.[28]

In Britain Les Forces Navales Françaises Libres (FNFL – the Free French Naval Force) was established on 30 June 1940. *Orion*, *Ondine*, *Junon* and *Minerve* joined *Rubis* as the core of the FNFL, operating under British control. Eventually, *Orion* and *Ondine* were cannibalised for spare parts for their two sisters and so were not used operationally. FNFL, commanded by Vice Admiral Emile Muselier, was the naval arm of Charles de Gaulle's Free French Forces (Forces Françaises Libres, or FFL). Admiral Muselier was the only flag officer of the French Navy to answer the call of de Gaulle and he was brought to Britain from Gibraltar by flyingboat.

The British government was concerned that the French fleet might be taken over by the German Kriegsmarine at the French armistice. Winston Churchill, in particular, wished

General de Gaulle and Vice Admiral Muselier visit the FNFL submarine *Minerve* in British port in late 1940. Muselier is to the left of the saluting Lieutenant de Vaisseau Pierre Sonneville. *Junon* is moored on the outside, but does not appear to be manned. (IWM A2173)

that the Marine Nationale should either actively join forces with the Royal Navy or be neutralised in some way to prevent the ships from falling into German or Italian hands. On 24 June, Admiral Darlan, on behalf of Vichy France, gave assurances to Churchill against such a possibility, but this was insufficient for the prime minister. He desired proof of allegiance and initiated Operation Catapult.[29]

The first stage of Operation Catapult concerned the French ships already in British ports. These were boarded by armed parties before dawn on 3 July and ordered to make it clear where their loyalties lay. At Plymouth and Portsmouth, most French sailors, including those on board the submarines *Orion*, *Ondine*, *Junon* and *Minerve*, reconciled and extended arms. On board *Surcouf*, however, several officers and men resisted the British operation. The acting liaison officer, Lieutenant Patrick Griffiths, proceeded to the wardroom accompanied by two ratings to explain what was happening to the French captain while Commander Sprague supervised the occupation of the rest of the giant submarine. Griffiths found the wardroom occupied by half a dozen French officers and about ten ratings, many of them armed. He managed to keep them talking for about fifteen minutes, but when Sprague arrived, announcing that the submarine was under British control, the French officers and men in the wardroom decided to scuttle their boat. Shots were fired and Sprague and Griffiths were gunned down, together with a British seaman and a French warrant officer. All four died.[30] At Dundee, *Rubis* remained under British operational control (see chapter 20).

The second stage of Catapult took place in North Africa. A Royal Navy task force, Force H under Admiral James Somerville, showed up outside the principal French anchorage at Mers-el-Kébir, delivering an ultimatum: either rejoin the fight against Germany, sail with reduced crews out of German reach or scuttle the ships. The French Admiral Marcel-Bruno Gensoul refused all options and the British opened fire. The battleship *Bretagne* was sunk and several other ships disabled or heavily damaged, while *Strasbourg* and a handful of destroyers escaped to Toulon. Almost 1,300 French sailors were killed. French submarines sortied from Oran, a few miles to the east, but were effectively constrained by British aircraft from *Ark Royal* and never got within torpedo range of Force H. On 8 July, a similar attack was made on Dakar, but the battleship *Richelieu* escaped almost unharmed.[31] These operations created a deep bitterness in the Marine Nationale and – except for men and officers loyal to de Gaulle, like those on board *Rubis* – shattered any prospect of future naval co-operation.

Churchill was not satisfied, however, and in September a new task force approached Dakar: Operation Menace. This time it included FFL forces, as de Gaulle had received intelligence that the colony was ready to swap sides and renounce its allegiance to Vichy. This was not the case, however, and hostilities ensued. On 23 September, the British destroyers *Foresight* and *Inglefield* sank the French submarine *Persée* and the day after *Fortune* sank *Ajax*, which was about to attack the task force. In return, the battleship *Resolution* took a torpedo from *Bévéziers* on 25 September while bombarding shore positions.[32]

By August 1940, *Surcouf* had completed her refit in Britain and was turned over to the FNFL. The only officer that had opted to stay on board after the take-over, Capitaine de Frégate Georges Blaison, was confirmed by the FNFL as her new commanding officer. There was bad blood, though, and it was decided to send *Surcouf* to Halifax, from where she would be used for trans-Atlantic convoy escort.[33]

— 18 —

Fear of Invasion

THERE IS NO DOUBT that the Allied efforts against the German supply convoys in the Skagerrak and Kattegat in the weeks after the invasion of Norway and Denmark were successful. Equally, there is no doubt that with a tactically co-ordinated effort, involving surface forces and aircraft as well, it could have been even more so. Instead, the Allied submarines found conditions increasingly difficult with rapidly shortening hours of darkness and increased numbers of German A/S patrols and aircraft. As April turned into May, Horton was obliged to suspend patrols in the Kattegat and the eastern Skagerrak east of the Lindesnes–Skagen line, largely leaving the supply convoys alone.

Only the veteran boats *Sunfish*, under Lieutenant Commander Slaughter, and *Sealion*, under Lieutenant Commander Bryant, were sent past Lindesnes during early May to keep the German A/S forces alert and see what could be achieved. Both found conditions extremely challenging. Still, *Sealion* succeeded in coming into position for an attack on a small convoy on 6 May off the Swedish Väderöarna. Bryant fired six torpedoes from over 5,000 metres (5,500 yards), but the tracks were seen and through some hard manoeuvring the 7,863-ton *Moltkefels* got away undamaged.[1]

Both submarines eventually withdrew with exhausted crews. Admiral Horton concluded that the risks run by submarines operating in Skagerrak, under the current conditions of calm seas, short nights and heavy German A/S efforts, were not worth the results they might obtain. Pending the return of more favourable conditions at the end of the summer, he moved his submarines westwards. The 2nd and 9th flotillas, at Rosyth and Dundee respectively, would focus on being in a position to intercept potential seaborne attacks on Britain across the North Sea. In addition, they would stage offensive operations on German communications to and from Norway in the areas between Karmøy and Lindesnes and a line from off Stavanger to the Westwall minefield. The boats of the 3rd Flotilla and the French 10th Flotilla were positioned south of a line across the North Sea from Newcastle to Esbjerg, outside the Westwall and south of the Frisian Islands and the Dutch coast.[2] Somewhat triumphantly, SKL noted repeatedly in their war diary during late May and June that the traffic towards Larvik and Oslo in Norway from Aalborg and Frederikshavn in Denmark was running 'without disturbances'. On the other hand, it was noted that German ships should not go west of Skagen–Arendal, unless it was unavoidable.[3]

Increased tension in France made Horton anticipate an attack on the western front. Hence, he reinstated half a dozen of the old H- and L-class boats to operational duties and had them transferred from Gosport to the 3rd Flotilla at Harwich to reinforce the North Sea Line. By 9 May, *Sturgeon*, *Triad*, *Snapper*, *Seawolf* and *Shark* were on patrol off the Dutch coast, as were the French *Doris*, *Calypso* and *Amazone*. Next day, French boats *La Sibylle*, *Antiope*, *Circé* and *Thétis* also joined the barrier. On 10 May, when the Germans finally attacked in the west, orders were issued that all ships north of Texel coming from Germany should be attacked without warning. However, it was emphasised that, due to the high density of Allied submarines in the area, care should be taken to ensure proper identification before attacking another submarine. In general, these patrols were uneventful, except for the sinking of *Doris* by *U9*.[4] As the situation in the Low Countries and France deteriorated, it was decided in a meeting in the Admiralty on 16 May, where VA(S) was present with several other branch commanders, that the H- and L-class boats of 3rd Flotilla should pull back from Harwich to Portland and Portsmouth – partly to reduce the number of submarines in the southern North Sea, partly to create an anti-invasion screen in the Channel. The south was not considered the most likely area of German aggression and the older boats would be adequate there.[5]

Three weeks later, the remains of the British Expeditionary Force had been evacuated from Dunkirk and the French government was considering capitulation. Fear that the Germans would not stop at the Channel coast spread in Britain. At the time, south-western France had not yet emerged as a base for the Kriegsmarine and only areas north of Dover were considered likely targets for a German invasion.

Caged Sealion

An in-depth analysis of the issue of a German invasion of Britain is beyond this book, but the fear of an invasion was to affect the dispositions of the Allied submarines to a large degree, causing instances of panic and unnecessary losses. In reality, there were no German invasion plans for Britain until Admiral Raeder brought it up in a meeting with Hitler on 21 May 1940, just prior to Dunkirk. Raeder and Hitler discussed the question of a possible landing in Britain again on 20 June, but then only as a concept and under which circumstances it might become necessary to consider. At this stage, Hitler showed no interest for such a venture and it would be 2 July, after further suggestions from his staffs, before he initiated an intelligence analysis to be prepared and gave orders to compile the first drafts of what was to become the plan for Operation Seelöwe (Sealion).

Later in July, orders were given that the preparations for the operation should be completed by mid-August. This meant that there would be no time to move forces for anything other than a potential diversion to Norway and that landings would have to be in southern England, close to French and Belgian ports. In general, the Germans were as surprised as the Allied commanders by the scale of their success in France and were not ready to take advantage of the position that it put them in. Neither Hitler nor his staffs had any long-term strategic plan for war against Britain. Everything was completely improvised and virtually nothing prepared or pre-planned.

What was being elaborated on in the German High Command was a plan of deception to divert significant British naval and air forces northwards. The plan, outlined by the C-in-C East Generaladmiral Rolf Carls, was known as Operation Herbstreise (Operation Autumn Journey) and included several fake convoys leaving Norway and the Baltic, covered by cruisers, seemingly heading for northern Britain. Combined with attacks on the Northern Patrol, this was meant to draw the main force of the Home Fleet away from the real invasion forces to be set up in the south. Carls's plan did not emerge before August 1940, though, and there are no documents to support any real German concept of an invasion of the British Isles before this. The

German SKL registered the invasion scare with some amusement and was not unhappy with the fact that this tied British submarines to defensive positions off their own east coast.[6] During August, the invasion was delayed to September and subsequently, on 12 October, Operation Seelöwe was put off until the following spring. In reality it was shelved for good, as the Luftwaffe had failed to gain air superiority during the Battle of Britain and German naval strength had been disastrously weakened by the losses during the campaign in Norway.[7]

Intelligence from the newly occupied countries, Norway, Denmark, Holland, Belgium and France, was meagre at this stage, as was information from Germany itself. Hence, British military leaders were to a large extent left with only analysis and assumptions as a basis for their forward planning. With no knowledge of the realities mentioned above, many analysts in Britain held that a German invasion was likely in 1940. Some believed that the Germans had a long-term plan and, after the French capitulation, a German invasion fleet could appear from anywhere between western Norway and the Bay of Biscay. Others considered that the amount of shipping available to the Germans in Norway and the Baltic, contrary to the recently occupied French west coast, made it likely that, should an invasion come, it would come from the north and be directed towards north-east Britain. If German ships, supplies and troops were made ready in southern France, they would inevitably be discovered and an invasion fleet would not be able to sail undetected. From Norway, however, the weather conditions and vastness of the northern North Sea made it conceivable that a fleet could be brought covertly to a position close enough to Britain to make the final leg of the journey under cover of darkness, as summer passed into autumn.

To give forewarning of any seaborne forces approaching, the submarines were stationed in defensive billets with reconnaissance as their main task. In particular, boats were stationed off the exits of the main Norwegian ports believed to be suitable embarkation points – Trondheim, Bergen and Stavanger. In addition, there were offensive sorties in the sea lanes between Stavanger and Kristiansand, in places where enemy traffic had to travel in open waters. In addition, a second patrol line was set up in the central and northern North Sea to intercept German submarines on their way to and from the Atlantic. After the fall of France, however, this traffic dwindled quickly as new bases were opened in the Bay of Biscay.[8]

The expectation of a German invasion of Britain was so serious that some submarine captains, unknown to their crews, had stowed away a large box of cash so that, in the event of a successful invasion of Britain they could pay for fuel at a Swedish port before crossing the Atlantic to continue the fight from Canada.[9]

General Edmund Ironside, Chief of the Imperial General Staff (CIGS), was one of those convinced that the German forces would not rest long when they had conquered France. In early June 1940, just after the conclusion of the evacuation from Dunkirk, he wrote in his diary that he expected a German invasion of the British Isles by air and sea after a brief but intense bombing campaign. Exactly what concrete evidence this assumption was based on is not clear, but in his analysis of the situation in mid-June, he wrote that the Germans 'will be very stupid if they delay much longer'.[10] No invasion materialised – only the bombers of the Luftwaffe – but General Ironside's constant predictions of a

German invasion made their mark on the British defence dispositions, even after he was replaced as C-in-C Home Forces on 19 July and, for all practical purposes, retired.

Within the Royal Navy, Admiral Drax, C-in-C the Nore, was one who feared a German invasion might become a reality. In a paper to the Chief of Staffs' committee on 25 July, he suggested that a massive German attack on northern Scotland might be feasible, capturing Scapa Flow and securing a foothold in the north.[11]

In a meeting at the Admiralty, chaired by the Vice-Chief of the Navy Staff (VCNS) on 16 May, Horton was advised that, from then on, the disposition of his submarines 'should be considered with a view to giving warning, and as far as possible prevention, of an invasion'. Three possible areas in Britain for such landings were given: the Shetlands, the coast between Sunderland and Flamborough Head, and the Norfolk–Suffolk coast. Horton accepted this and stated that in the last week he had disposed three submarines in defensive positions off the known entrances to the German minefield to meet just this threat. VCNS repeated his, and presumably the Admiralty's, view that the most important task for the submarines was that of distant reconnaissance, with offensive operations against the invasion forces clearly being a secondary objective. The submarines should not reveal their presence by attacking shore-hugging convoys, but rather lie low and observe.

Should an invasion fleet be discovered, the Submarine Service was seen as the first line of defence. Hence, a patrol line from Stavanger south to the Westwall was maintained by five boats, and the line west of the minefield by a further three to four boats, concentrating off the expected German exits. Finally, three boats were stationed in the gap between the southern edge of the Westwall and the Dutch coast.[12]

These dispositions created tension between VA(S) and C-in-C Home Fleet, Admiral Forbes. The latter, who had not been present at the meeting in the Admiralty on the 16th, pressed for continued submarine operations in the inner Skagerrak. Horton, on the other hand, particularly based on the reports of Slaughter and Bryant, found this too risky and vetoed the idea until conditions had improved. After further discussions, Horton and Forbes agreed that, with the addition of mine-laying off the coast of Norway, patrols off the major western ports of that country, Stavanger, Bergen and Trondheim, should continue. Otherwise, submarine operations in Home Waters during the summer of 1940 were mainly focused on anti-invasion measures and U-boat hunting. Admiral Forbes eventually agreed that a seaborne German expedition against Britain could well come from Norway.[13]

In spite of the successes of the Allied submarines during April and May 1940, the fear of a German invasion and the perceived need to use the submarines for reconnaissance therefore reintroduced most of the restrictions that the submarine commanders thought they had finally got rid of. Even more seriously, it put the boats in danger. Horton was warned by the Admiralty that a German invasion might be expected in the north around 6–7 July. He did not think so himself, but could not afford not to have his boats at sea.[14] By this time, the submarine patrols off the Dutch coast had been largely discontinued, partly as it was considered highly perilous keeping them there. Instead, the number of submarines off Norway, from north of Bergen to Kristiansand, were increased as much as resources allowed. Once again the British submarines were caught in a quandary of offensive actions and reconnaissance.

— 19 —

'We've 'it a Bleedin' Mine'

THE LANDING OF AGENTS and commando units on enemy shores and other special operations would become almost routine for Allied submarines as the war progressed. In 1940, however, this was a new and totally unfamiliar type of mission, the first of which took place in late April: to prevent the German occupiers in Norway from 'settling down'.

In the afternoon of 24 April, Lieutenant Commander Hutchinson took *Truant* to sea from Rosyth with a handful of MIR officers under the command of Lieutenant Colonel Brian Mayfield of the Scots Guards on board.[1] The officers were to be landed in the Hardangerfjord area near Bergen to assist Norwegian resistance in operating against German railway communications in southern Norway (Operation Knife).[2] Captain Peter Kemp, one of the MIR officers, later wrote:

> In the early part of the afternoon, we went aboard *Truant*, where our stores were already stowed. It proved difficult to find space to stow ourselves. Carrying her full complement of officers and crew, *Truant* had little enough space to accommodate even one or two passengers. Hutchinson and his First Lieutenant had to spend a long time finding odd corners where we could lay our heads among the machinery.[3]

Eventually, Kemp and the others were provided with mattresses and cushions and could lie down for the night while the submarine headed across the North Sea.

While on the surface, at 03:40 on the 25th, south of Aberdeen, *Truant* was damaged by an explosion, in all likelihood from a magnetic mine. A second explosion occurred shortly after. Kemp continued:

> The two explosions, coming hard on top of each other, penetrated my dreamless unconsciousness. Through my slumber I was vaguely aware that the first was somewhere near me, the second away for'ard. Suddenly I was fully alert as I heard the order 'Diving Stations!' relayed on the loud-speakers through the boat. I realised that the diesels had stopped. [. . .] Close by, a muffled voice broke the silence – Gawd! We've 'it a bleedin' mine.[4]

Nobody was seriously hurt and as the forward watertight bulkhead was holding behind the flooded torpedo room, Hutchinson at first wanted to continue. The steering gear had been damaged, though, and the boat zigzagged up to 20 degrees to either side when the diesels were restarted. In addition, there were many leaks and the main battery had been damaged so that chlorine gas began to seep through the boat and he had to give in and turn back. According to Kemp,

> [Hutchinson] said there was some flooding aft and several rivets were started amidships. 'If this had been any boat but one of these new T-class, we shouldn't have remained afloat.' [. . .] Much later he told us that he had concluded his signal to *Forth*,

reporting the incident, with the words 'will require at least three weeks' refit and a new Commanding Officer. [. . .] We met with no further incident on the way home, but the strained faces of Hutchinson and his officers told us that they looked forward to the end of the trip. [. . . On board *Forth*] we were filled with gin and plied with questions by incredulous submariners, who seemed astonished that *Truant* had managed to get home in such a condition.[5]

The operation was transferred to *Clyde* for a second attempt, but cancelled before she was ready to sail, as the situation for the Allies in Norway had deteriorated.[6] For Hutchinson, this was the last straw. He had not slept well for some time and had started using sedatives to rest. He had to admit that his nerve was gone and that he was a liability to his men and his boat and asked to be relieved. This was granted and after three months' sick leave, he was appointed Staff Officer Operations at Horton's headquarters. Later, he served at the Admiralty, then at Malta, before he ended the war on board the battleship *King George V* in the Pacific.[7]

Special Missions

As the campaign in Norway drew to a close, it became paramount to establish channels of communication that could provide the Allied authorities in Britain with information about what was going on. At first these attempts to establish such channels of information were rather improvised, not least for the Allied submariners, none of whom at this stage had the slightest experience of this kind of warfare, which later in the war was to become an integral part of the use of submarines.

On 2 July *Seawolf* took to sea from Rosyth with two Norwegian officers onboard: Kommandørkaptein Edvard Danielsen and Løytnant Harald Voltersvik; the latter was to act as the local pilot. After nightfall the next day, the two officers were landed at Ullerøy

Seawolf in May 1937. (Abrahams)

Island just west of Lindesnes by rubber dinghy (Berthon Boat) brought along especially for this purpose. This mission, known as Operation Thwart, was the first of many to land agents by submarine on the Norwegian coast during the war.

Danielsen had been a member of the Norwegian Admiral Staff at the time of the German invasion in April 1940. At the end of the campaign, he went to Britain in a small fishing dory. There he came into contact with the Scandinavian section of the Secret Intelligence Service (SIS). Operation Thwart came about in order to establish a radio transmitter in Oslo, providing information on the German forces in the capital.

From Ullerøy, Danielsen and Voltersvik were taken to the mainland by friendly countrymen and continued on to Oslo by train; the radio equipment was carried in a suitcase. In Oslo, the radio was rigged up in the basement of a fellow naval officer and became one of the first stations in any occupied country transmitting regular messages to Britain.[8]

Seawolf patrolled nearby, though well clear of the landing zone. Several ships, including trawlers and minesweepers, were seen at a distance, but none came near enough to attack. Smaller coastal vessels, observed near land, were not attacked from fear of jeopardising the chances of picking up the Norwegian officers again. During the night of 9/10 July, Danielsen and Voltersvik were picked up again from the location where they had been landed, this time in the company of Løytnant Johan Brinch of the the Norwegian Naval Air Service. As Operation Thwart was now considered over, three torpedoes were later fired at a large, armed trawler believed to be an A/S vessel, but all torpedoes missed. By 12 July *Seawolf* was back at Rosyth, successfully landing the three agents.[9]

In occupied France, there was also the need for information as the new reality of an occupied Europe emerged. On the night of 7/8 July, *H43* landed an officer of the Guernsey militia near Icart Bay in Guernsey (Operation Anger). Three nights later, Lieutenant George Colvin took his boat back into the treacherous waters, picking up the officer and bringing him safely back to Plymouth.[10]

A month later, on 2 August, *Talisman* landed two French agents near the Hourtin Lighthouse, south of the Gironde estuary, in a collapsible canoe. The submarine was brought slowly towards the beach until it touched bottom some 250 metres (275 yards) from land. There the agents climbed into the canoe and paddled ashore; the canoe was recovered by winching it back using a heavy cod-line following a signal from the men that they were safely ashore. Apart from the fact that the canoe was swamped and had to be punctured before it was possible to be hauled back on board, the operation was a success.[11]

A surprise for Allied submariners was the sudden appearance of small vessels carrying a handful of people onboard, heading westwards towards Britain from the occupied European countries. As the Germans tightened their grip on each country, officers, politicians, sailors, seamen – or just anybody who wanted to join the fight against Nazism – started gathering in groups looking for a way to come across the North Sea or the English Channel to join their free forces in Britain. The Germans were angered by the fact that these people did not accept the situation and wanted to continue the fight against them from abroad, and within a short time the penalty for being caught escaping occupied Europe was death, or at best a long-term sentence in a labour camp.

In the evening of 16 July, *Clyde* was on an otherwise largely uneventful patrol off Stadlandet, north of Måløy, when what was believed to be a motor fishing boat was sighted. Lieutenant Commander Ingram surfaced and approached the small vessel, which had the letters 'SF-52-SV' painted on her side. It turned out to be the 15-ton Norwegian cutter *Fredheim* with four men onboard, Hans Oppedal, Ananias Oppedal, Adolf Oppedal and Abraham Færestrand, all locals from the island of Vågsøy.

None of the four men spoke any English. As they were not fishing, in spite of having equipment onboard to do so, and could neither produce any relevant papers nor explain what they were doing so far offshore, Ingram decided to take them onboard and sink *Fredheim*, lest they would go back and inform German authorities of the whereabouts of the submarine. He was quite certain they were not Germans, but the lack of communication made the situation complicated and he decided to take no chances. The small wooden boat was rammed and vanished quickly. After another two weeks on patrol, the four men were subsequently landed in Newcastle.[12]

A similar episode occurred at about the same time. *Swordfish* intercepted the Norwegian sailing yacht *Marski* on 28 July. The four men on board, Theodor Jensen, Jens Ugland, Reidar Ytterlid and Olav Andersen, all officers of the Norwegian Merchant Navy, had left Arendal almost two weeks earlier. They had been given permission by the German harbour master to sail west along the coast for a small fishing vacation. This they did at first, but once they considered the situation opportune, they continued westwards into the North Sea, as had been their intention all the time. They encountered atrocious weather, however, and the small vessel ended up drifting around in the North Sea with ripped sails and a broken mast until *Swordfish* intercepted them. As the submarine was outbound to a billet off Norway, the four men were taken almost all the way back home before finally being landed in Blyth on 8 August.[13]

Intercepts

Throughout the campaign in Norway, from 9 April to mid-June, there was a substantial traffic of German ships of all kinds in the Norwegian Leads and fjords. One of them was the 5,295-ton German freighter *Cläre Hugo Stinnes I*. She had come from the USA with 8,000 tons of grain several weeks earlier, intending to pass through the Norwegian Leads on the final leg of her way to Germany. She ran aground, however, and as compensation for extensive repairs, her cargo had been confiscated. She left the dockyard near Trondheim on 6 April and continued homewards in ballast. *Stinnes I* passed through Bergen on 9 April, unaware of the German invasion. Acting on reports of an 'armed German vessel', a Norwegian torpedo boat intercepted her in the outer Hardangerfjord during the afternoon of the 12th. At the time, *Stinnes I* was flying a Danish flag, but her true identity was quickly established and she was taken to Eidfjord to serve as an accommodation ship for the Norwegian naval air group there. The crew was interned. On 26 April, *Cläre Hugo Stinnes I* was recaptured by the German minesweeper *M1*.[14]

Trident, now under the command of Lieutenant Commander Geoffrey Sladen, left Rosyth on 22 April. After a few days of patrolling south of Stavanger, including a failed attempt to torpedo the southbound supply ships *Palime* and *Pelikan* off Lindesnes on the

25th, Sladen set course for Korsfjorden and the entrance to the Bergen Leads. After two days prowling outside with no result, he decided to go into Bjørnefjorden, well inside the German-controlled area. At 09:30 on 2 May, a large ship, taken to be a German transport, was sighted on a northbound course. The ship was *Cläre Hugo Stinnes I*, once again on her way to Germany under the command of her original master, Oberleutnant Kleinen. Torpedoes were fired, but as the freighter was in ballast and high in the water, they ran under the ship. Sladen took *Trident* to the surface and ordered the 4-inch gun to be manned. After a 10-mile chase in broad daylight, where some seventy rounds were fired and over a dozen hit, the captain of *Stinnes* had had enough and put his ship aground on Skorpa, a small island located where the two fjords Bjørnefjorden and Korsfjorden meet. The Germans lowered the boats on the leeward side and rowed away. Sladen realised he had pushed his luck far enough and, after firing a last torpedo, which exploded on the rocks near her fore hold, he beat a hasty retreat. Off Marsteinen Lighthouse at the mouth of Korsfjorden, he was forced to dive by an approaching aircraft. S-boats sent out from Bergen conducted a persistent but ineffective search until late in the afternoon.

Nineteen depth charges were counted. None was really close, though a few were near enough to shake the boat thoroughly, including one near enough to lift *Trident's* bow, sending excess bilge water aft, threatening to flood the main motors. Not willing to pump out the water, as it contained oil that would be seen on the surface, Sladen had his crew man-handle buckets of water forward to regain trim. He later noted in his report that this 'proved a valuable occupation for all hands during the first attacks', adding that 'the greatest depth reached was 400' – needle of the depth-gauge just clear of the stop – angle 10° bow up.' *Trident* arrived safely at Rosyth on 4 May.[15]

Cläre Hugo Stinnes I aground on Skorpa near Bergen, after having been chased by *Trident*. (E Skjold Collection)

Also in the Skagerrak, there were a substantial number of German ships that could be encountered. Close to dawn on 4 May, *Severn* intercepted the 1,786-ton Swedish *Monark*. As she was neutral, Lieutenant Commander Bertram Taylor decided to surface and stop her to give the crew a chance to escape, in spite of the risk to his submarine from aircraft. Closing from astern, the freighter eventually responded to the signals to stop. A boat was lowered after a while and the Swedish master came on board *Severn*. To the surprise of the British submariners, he informed them that he was actually sailing under German command. *Monark* had been at Stavanger when the Germans arrived, taking control of all ships in the harbour. The cargo of wood pulp was considered valuable and the Swedish ship was thus being sent to Germany with a prize crew in charge. Most of the original Swedish crew was also on board.

Taylor realised he had a legitimate target on his hands, but nevertheless had the Swedish master sign a declaration that his ship had been seized and was in German service. Thereafter, he made sure that the Swedish sailors were on board a motor boat, heading for land, before he proceeded to sink *Monark* with a torpedo. The five-man German prize crew were taken prisoners.[16]

In the afternoon of 8 May, *Taku* fired torpedoes against the transports *Palime* (2,863 tons) and *Pelikan* (3,264 tons) off Thyborøn in western Denmark. The firing was hasty, though, due to the proximity of one of the escorts and some aircraft, and again both transports escaped. Instead, one of the torpedoes hit the torpedo boat *Möwe* aft, tearing off her rudder and propellers. *Möwe* was towed to port and had to spend several years in the yards.[17] On this occasion, *Palime* and *Pelikan* were heading for Stavanger with, among other things, long-range naval guns for the defence of the

Approaching the Norwegian coast on board *Alstertor*. Note the deck-load of various vehicles and the floats ready on the canvas roofs, from where they would float freely if the worst should happen. (Author's Collection)

entrance to Stavanger harbour. Together with two other companion-ships, *Alstertor* and *Alsterufer*, they were veterans of the eastern Skagerrak, which they repeatedly crossed on a regular route between northern Denmark and south-western Norway during the summer of 1940.

After the failed attempt to nail the two companions, two of *Möwe*'s fellow escorts looked for revenge. Lieutenant Commander van der Byl took *Taku* deep. Later, he wrote:

> Lost trim and hit bottom involuntarily at 150 feet on the gauge. Bounced off and tried to hold trim at 120 feet, but hit bottom again and decided to lie stopped [. . .] At 17:40, all motors were stopped. Sperry [compass] was covered with a blanket [. . .] In the resulting silence, a slight leak from No.9 tube emergency cock draining into control room bilges appeared to make a devastating noise. A funnel and rubber pipes were eventually led from this leak to the Petty Officers' bath room and the silence was complete. The first ten or twelve charges were apparently dropped at random at the end of the torpedo tracks and possibly a discoloration of water from hitting the bottom. The first explosions may have included bombs dropped by escorting aircraft. Two surface craft were then heard hunting apparently using the usual procedure of one stopping while the other attacked. A sound like a sonic echo sounder was heard as ship approached and explosions were preceded each time by what appeared to be a light tap on the hull and in some cases by a sound as of gravel being dropped on the hull. Twelve charges were being dropped singly between 18:07 and 18:31, after which they became less frequent [. . .] The charges shook the submarine very considerably, but caused no [serious] damage [. . .] Leading Stoker W.G. Pearson, who was in *Spearfish* when she was depth charged described the explosions as 'not so bad, but nearly so'. The suspense of waiting for the next charge was found trying to the nerves. The ship's company remained remarkably calm and cheerful (with some exceptions) and the Third officer and Engineer Officer actually played draughts.[18]

Things eventually quietened down and *Taku* left the seabed just before midnight, surfacing an hour and a half later. She was back in Rosyth on 5 May.

Danish Fishermen

On 12 May 1940, *Tetrarch,* with Ronald Mills now promoted to lieutenant commander, departed Rosyth for her second war patrol, this time heading for the west coast of Denmark and the Skagerrak. The patrol was largely uneventful, and on 23 May Mills 'decided to stalk a pair of fishing vessels and capture same'. The reason for this decision is not noted. The first two that came into sight, west of Hanstholm, were the Danish 30-ton fishing-ketches *L61 Terje Viken* and *L100 Immanuel*. For some reason, *Terje Viken* and its crew aroused Mills's suspicion and in spite of the Danish captain volunteering a lot of information on life as a fisherman in German-occupied Denmark, Mills decided to treat the small ships as 'enemy merchant vessels'. The four men from *Terje Viken* were taken on board *Tetrarch* in order to be properly interrogated in Britain. The pumps were opened and the vessel left sinking as *Tetrarch* departed. Before it sank, however, it was found drifting by another ship and subsequently towed back to Thyborøn.

Sub-Lieutenant Fyfe and a few men were sent onboard *Immanuel* with orders to take her to Leith, crew included. En route, another Danish fishing vessel was sighted, the 33-ton *L156 Jens Hvas*. The enterprising Sub-Lieutenant Fyfe sent some of the prize crew from the *Immanuel* over with orders to ensure this second vessel followed also and proudly brought both his prizes to Leith.

Tetrarch arrived in Rosyth on 26 May.[19]

At 15:00 on 18 May, Lieutenant Commander John Forbes of *Spearfish* sighted three Danish fishing vessels halfway between Northumberland and Esbjerg. This was not so uncommon, but he added that he 'made plans to seize them in the evening', which was perhaps less common. Why it was necessary to seize the Danish boats is not elaborated. Before this could be carried out, though, the French submarine *Thétis* was sighted on the surface. Without exchanging signals, the *Thétis* dived and to avoid any misunderstandings, Forbes fired several yellow smoke flares and made underwater identification signals, while the entire time keeping stern on to the direction in which the asdic operator told him *Thétis* was. When the contact was finally lost after half an hour, *Spearfish* proceeded southwards on the surface at full speed to get well clear of the French submarine. Hence, the Danish fishing vessels were forgotten for the time being.

Two days later, however, at 01:15 on 20 May, the white lights of another trawler appeared. Forbes took *Spearfish* alongside what turned out to be the Danish fishing boat *S130* and ordered the two men and two boys on board into the submarine. Just as they were going down the hatch, one of the lookouts reported a periscope some 500 metres (550 yards) to port. Forbes took *Spearfish* quickly down but then with some embarrassment identified the 'periscope' as a dan-buoy from the fishing boat he had just seized. The day was not over yet, though, and after resurfacing, Forbes continued:

> Did not wish to risk compromising position by gunfire and attempted to sink boat by ramming at 1½ knots. Practically no shock, but bow stuck in vessels side. She could only be shaken off by going astern at speed for ten minutes when vessel slewed and bow tore clear. Picked up a dog (later known to be called Pluto) which had been left on the casing during previous dive. Finished off fishing boat with 5-pound rounds of HE from the gun.[20]

The thoughts of the Danish fishermen about all this racket as well as leaving their homeland are not recorded. A few hours later, at 04:50, another three men were taken off a second boat, the *S175*, which was also sunk. A further five Danish fishing boats sighted at dusk were left alone, due to a rising sea.[21]

In the Arctic

During May, the efforts of the German naval air force in the Skagerrak and the Kattegat were intensified and every available aircraft was used for patrols, convoy escort or A/S missions. Hence, the British and Allied submarines had to run increasingly greater risks to spend time on the surface or even at periscope depth attacking the German traffic to and from Norway.

Truant departing Rosyth for the Arctic on 20 May 1940. In the background, *Renown* is being towed out of the dock, having just completed repairs. (Author's Collection)

As a test of conditions in the far north, *Truant* was dispatched to operate alongside the two Norwegian submarines *B1* and *B3* off North Cape in the second half of May, supporting the northern flank of the Allied expeditionary corps operating against the Germans landed at Narvik. Lieutenant Commander Hugh Haggard had relieved Hutchinson as CO on board *Truant* shortly before this mission. Initially it was thought she could operate out of Harstad, where a British supply base had been established. Conditions were rather difficult there, however, with frequent German air attacks and there were so many naval ships around that there was always the risk of being mistaken for a U-boat. While underway, orders were received to head for Tromsø instead. After a quick briefing by British and Norwegian naval personnel in Tromsø, Haggard took *Truant* to sea on 20 May, to patrol off the Norwegian coast, east of North Cape. On board, in addition to her regular crew was a prize crew of eight men, though these remained idle.

In the morning of 23 May, *Truant* sighted the 8,514-ton *Alster* west of North Cape, en route from Kirkenes to Harstad with a load of iron ore, to join a convoy headed for Britain. Not really sure what ship she was, Lieutenant Commander Haggard stalked her for some time, while trying to signal Naval Command in Tromsø to ask for advice. Communication was difficult, but eventually receipt of his signal was acknowledged by Tromsø. There was no return signal, though.

The escort, the trawler *Ullswater* and the Norwegian auxiliary *Nordhav II*, could not be identified either. The merchant ship altered course and appeared to be making for the Porsanger Fjord; she was steering an erratic course, making her course and destination difficult to judge.

Haggard eventually fired two torpedoes at *Alster*, in spite of at least one officer providing information that she was under British command. Luckily, the torpedoes missed astern and exploded on the shore. *Alster* sailed for Britain from Harstad in the morning of 27 May.

Truant was back in Harstad on 26 May. On the 27th, Lieutenant Commander Haggard received orders to return for home and *Truant* departed Harstad for Rosyth the same day. She arrived there on 1 June, ending her eighth war patrol.[22]

The German supply ship *Alster* was captured in the morning of 11 April by destroyer *Icarus* and taken to the repair base at Skjelfjord. There, she was used for accommodation while her derricks were used for makeshift repair of Allied naval vessels damaged in the battles around Narvik. When her services were not needed, she was sent to Kirkenes in still-unoccupied Norway, to take on board a load of ore, before going to Britain. Here she is seen in Skjelfjord with the heavily damaged destroyer *Eskimo* alongside. (Briggs Collection)

German naval tanker *Dithmarschen* next to destroyers *Ihn* and *Galster* in Norway in June 1940. (Author's Collection)

*   *   *

In the early morning of 24 June, Lieutenant Commander Geoffrey Sladen of *Trident* fired four torpedoes at the 10,816-ton German naval supply ship and oiler *Dithmarschen* off Trondheim. She had been standing by off Lofoten during Operation Juno, refuelling the destroyer escort, and was now on her way home, escorted by the destroyers *Friedrich Ihn* and *Karl Galster*. *Dithmarschen* was a sister ship of *Altmark* and she was one of the most valuable targets any Allied submarine could encounter in this period. Unfortunately for Sladen, there was a miscommunication between him and the torpedo officer and all torpedoes missed.

Two of the torpedo tracks were sighted from an overhead aircraft passing behind *Dithmarschen* and the destroyers were notified. As the assailant was already aft of the fast-moving convoy, it was decided by the escort commander, Korvettenkapitän Günther Wachsmuth of *Friedrich Ihn*, to keep the two destroyers close to the tanker and not engage in a submarine hunt that would leave her unprotected. An hour or so later, the ships were turning into the Trondheimsfjord, behind a screen of minesweepers. It is notable that *Trident* was not detected by the destroyers, even if the nearest was less than 500 metres (550 yards) away.[23]

Trident ended her tenth war patrol at Rosyth on 3 July.

Submarine Mining Operations

FOR MANY SUBMARINE OFFICERS, Allied as well as German, mine-laying was a questionable use of their boats. The task of mine-laying was unpopular with the crews and gave no sense of success as few of the ships damaged or sunk by the mines were ever observed or even identified. Getting into shallow waters close to the shore restricted operational freedom and was seen as unnecessarily dangerous. Having laid their complement of mines, the U-boats resumed normal patrol routines, but a full load of mines often meant a reduced capacity for torpedoes.

Mine-laying by submarines was planned for by most European navies in the 1930s. Some navies, like the Polish and Dutch, had some boats where a moderate amount of mines could be carried outside the pressure hull without affecting regular operations too much. Others, like the Germans, developed mines that were carried inside the hull, instead of torpedoes, and were deployed through the torpedo tubes. This significantly reduced the torpedo-carrying capacity of the submarine, however, even if the mines could be maintained, adjusted and primed at any time up to the actual laying. The mines were also less vulnerable, should the submarine be attacked. The Royal Navy and the French Navy chose a third method: a separate class of mine-laying submarines, the French with the *Saphir*-class and the British the *Porpoise/Grampus*-class. In addition, three of the early T-class boats, *Tetrarch*, *Talisman* and *Torbay*, were equipped with mine-laying systems through vertical wells in the saddle tanks. After unsuccessful trials in December 1939, however, these were welded shut and the systems were never used operationally.[1]

The French-built Polish submarines, *Wilk*, *Ryś* and *Żbik*, had mine-laying capabilities. On 5 September, after the German invasion of their country, they laid some sixty mines in the waters around the Hela Peninsula. Each boat had the capacity to carry forty mines each, although the amount of suitable French mines in Poland at the time was limited and they could not be allocated more than about twenty each. The German minesweeper *M85* hit one of the mines laid by *Żbik* on 1 October, sinking with a huge loss of life – the only German naval ship sunk by Polish submarines during the campaign. At the end of the campaign in Poland, *Ryś* and *Żbik* were interned in Sweden. *Wilk* escaped to Britain, but, partly due to the lack of suitable mines, partly to her mediocre technological state, she was never used for mine-laying missions. The Dutch submarines *O19* and *O20* were equipped for mine-laying, but neither operated in Europe during 1940.

The British submarines usually carried fifty Mk XVI mines, while the French *Rubis* carried thirty-two SH4 mines.[2] None of the Allied navies had magnetic mines available for submarines in 1939. During the war, magnetic mines that could be launched through the torpedo tubes of a submarine were developed in Britain (M Mk II mines). On a handful of occasions some of these were laid by T-class boats late in the war, but never to any significant extent.[3] British and French mine-laying submarines both carried their mines outside the pressure hull. This made their deployment less complicated as it required no lock mechanism and it was easier to balance the boat during the laying as the weight of the mines in most cases did not need to be incorporated in the displacement calculations. On the other hand, adjusting the mines after leaving harbour was in most cases limited and the mines were vulnerable should the submarine be attacked before laying them.

With mines on board, the British minelayers lost part of their stability and found that operating on the surface with anything but full buoyancy was challenging. Surfacing was also more difficult, requiring more time – it was feared that should any of the external tanks be damaged with mines on board, the situation would become extremely serious.[4]

In the British Admiralty, as the prospect of war with Germany loomed in 1938, plans for offensive mine-laying were brought forward. Based on the experiences from the Great War, the Heligoland Bight appeared the primary area for such operations, this being the main route for warships to and from the German North Sea ports. At the time, the only surface ships available for such offensive missions were destroyers, of which there were two ready, *Express* and *Esk*, with four more I-class ships that could be converted. Hence, the mine-laying submarines were considered key elements in the first offensive steps against Germany, should a war become reality. For a number of reasons, however, by the time the war broke out, the submarines were positioned elsewhere and the C-in-C Home Fleet was left with the destroyers, not all of which were yet available.[5]

In late February 1940, it was decided in a meeting held in the Admiralty that all the mine-laying submarines should be employed in the North Sea area, laying mines. This

Narwhal loading mines at Immingham. Note the 'tram line' of mines in the casing tunnel and the compactness of the Mk. XVI self-mooring mine-anchor set when stowed. (Briggs Collection)

was now possible as the French had taken over most of the convoy-escort assignments on the Halifax route, where some of the large minelayers had been deployed, substituting for capital ships needed elsewhere.

VA(S) Horton was not very enthusiastic about using his submarines for mine-laying, though. By default, the mines would have to be laid in shallow water, where the sea lanes were narrow, focusing the traffic. The large mine-laying submarines were difficult to handle in shallow waters and Horton decided as a compromise that the boats should not lay mines in less than 15 fathoms of water, equal to 27.5 metres or 90 feet. The mines could be laid quickly and – with careful planning and a little luck – the boats would be back in deep waters before they were discovered.

Taking Turns

The first submarine-laid Allied minefield (FD1) was laid by *Narwhal* on the early morning of 4 April in the Heligoland Bight, near '*Sealion*'s buoy' some 60 miles north-west of Heligoland (see page 81). It was believed that the buoy was a focal point for traffic going through the Westwall and hence a good place for a minefield. Fifty Mk XVI mines were to be laid, although one mine was found to be defective when tested and so was set to sink. A few days later, the fishing trawler *Emden* may have been damaged when striking one of these mines.[6] It was intended that *Narwhal* should lay further minefields in relation to known or suspected passages through the Westwall, but within a week, Norway and Denmark had been invaded and the entire strategic picture changed. Consequently, on 13 April, *Narwhal* laid its second field of fifty mines north of Læsø Island, east of Skagen (FD5). Lieutenant Commander Ronald Burch wrote:

> Proceeded submerged to laying position. Kattegat was full of trawlers, fishing vessels and miscellaneous craft. Some were armed and kept station in divisions of three in line abreast, columns disposed astern or quarterly, probably minesweeping. Others were in line ahead. Some unarmed craft appeared to be ordinary fishing vessels. Laid mines exactly where ordered, but on course 315°. Fix was obtained from three shore light houses. No traffic was seen in Laeso Rende.[7]

Later, the German merchant *Togo* was damaged by these mines, while the minesweeper *M1302 Schwaben* was sunk. On her return passage Burch attacked two different convoys off Denmark but was both times put off by efficient escorts.[8]

At the end of the month, *Narwhal* was back again, this time laying the mines in the Læsø Rende, between the island and mainland Denmark (FD6). Having deployed all the mines during the afternoon of 1 May, Lieutenant Commander Burch encountered a convoy of large transports off Anholt, escorted by six minesweepers and a torpedo boat.[9] Unknown to Burch, this was one of the largest convoys heading for Oslo in a long time, carrying more than 3,000 men and almost 1,000 horses. Just before dusk *Narwhal* was in a good position and Burch fired a full salvo of six torpedoes at the convoy. Two ships were hit, the 6,097-ton *Buenos Aires*, which eventually sank, and the 8,570-ton *Bahia Castillo*, which was severely damaged but could be towed ashore.

Buenos Aires sinking off Anholt, Denmark. (E Skjold Collection)

Most of the minesweepers focused on saving the men from the damaged transports, while three of them were ordered to chase the assailant, assisted by some R-boats that had arrived at high speed from Frederikshavn. Lieutenant Commander Burch found the attack 'most amateurish':

> The enemy took turns to try to pass over me (like our own hunting procedures). There seemed to be three craft which each steered round in circles. [. . .] After firing the torpedoes, I increased to 6 knots and altered course to pass through washes of enemy and under starboard wing ship. [. . .] Then stopped at 70 feet [21 metres] under a convenient layer. Afterwards proceeded at slowest speed to north when hydrophone effect in that direction faded away. 75 depth charges were dropped in the course of three hours. None dangerously close, but harassing.[10]

The onslaught on such an important convoy created a large degree of panic and every available escort in the region was ordered to gather on the area. By the time they arrived, however, *Narwhal* was long gone. Most of the troops were taken off *Buenos Aires* before she sank and between fifteen and twenty men were lost; the 220 horses could not be saved though. *Bahia Castillo* was towed into Frederikshavn; too damaged to be repaired, however, she was eventually broken up.[11]

On 4 May, *Seal* laid yet another minefield just west of the Swedish island Vinga off Gothenburg (FD7), before suffering the humiliation of being captured (see chapter 21).

After the loss of *Seal*, no more minefields were laid in the Skagerrak, in spite of C-in-C Home Fleet's insistence they should continue. Horton diplomatically agreed they should 'when dark hours enable a [battery] charge to be obtained unobserved'. In Skagerrak, he considered, this was no longer possible and would not be so for a couple of months, as long distances would have to be covered while submerged to avoid air patrols and A/S vessels.[12]

The mine-laying continued along the coast of western Norway throughout the summer. Even though the nights here were almost non-existent, it was possible to stay offshore to charge the batteries during what nights there were, and lay the mines submerged in daylight. The Germans simply had insufficient resources available in western Norway at this time to cover every part of the Leads at all times.

The Norwegian waterways are littered with navigation and sailing marks and even if the lights of nearly all were turned off at night, they were usually well visible during daylight by periscope, making navigation and fixing of position relatively easy. Nevertheless, adverse weather, currents and inadequate maps made going in between the islands and skerries of the Norwegian Leads a risky undertaking. All the more so as this was alien territory where A/S patrols and aircraft could appear at any time.

The CO of a submarine was, in his operational orders, given substantial freedom as to how and when he was to perform the mine-laying. Weather, ship-traffic and above all enemy activity would to a large degree influence his decisions and there were usually one or two alternative areas where the mines could be laid if the first position was for some reason unsuitable. Laying a full load of fifty mines would take no more than ten to fifteen minutes doing 4–6 knots – either from the surface at night, or submerged during daytime. The mines were usually laid in one, two or three lines, 50 metres (55 yards) apart, starting from a fixed position and moving in a specified direction. Depending on the nature of the area where the minefield was intended, a range of accuracy related to the starting point would be specified, usually a few miles, as well as the last date by which it should have been completed.[13]

The deployment of the mines would always have priority, but once this was done the submarine would withdraw to a nearby patrol area where the commanding officer would have a free hand to use his torpedoes on any legitimate target. Before the mines were laid, most commanders would refrain from attacking all but the most tempting targets in order not to reveal his presence in the area. In addition, the mines of both British and French submarines were outside the pressure hull and would be more vulnerable in case of depth-charge attacks. In high seas, there was also a risk that the mines might come loose or be damaged, and most boats were kept deep and away from the weather if it was poor on the way to their target.

The first minefield in Norwegian waters was laid by the French submarine *Rubis* off Egersund on 10 May 1940, FD14 (see below and Appendix V). On the following day, 11 May, *Narwhal* laid fifty mines in the Leads off Molde (FD12), and on the 15th *Porpoise* laid minefield FD11 in the Leads off Bremanger between Florø and Måløy, north of Bergen. During this, she grounded no less than twice in the narrow, twisting waters. The crew of the huge, awkward submarine had a challenging time. Lieutenant Commander Philip Roberts wrote:

02:50: Overcast day with visibility very variable due to heavy rain squalls. Stood to coast and eventually recognised entrance to Frosjøen Fjord. Closed to within 5 miles of Kvanhovden Light trimmed down on the surface. Visibility 1-6 miles.

06:25: Dived and proceeded up Frosjøen Fjord. [. . .]

10:19: While turning into fjord, *Porpoise* grounded forward on the south side of the fjord. She came off astern at once and I consider little damage was done except for removal of the A/S dome which had, unfortunately, been left down in view of unreliable visibility.

10:48: First mine of line A laid (24 mines).

10:57: Line A completed.

11:38: Again grounded with 36 feet [11 metres] on the gauge in a position off western side of Rognene Island where chart shows least depth of 15 fathoms [27.5 metres]. This grounding felt very unpleasant as *Porpoise* appeared to be ashore right under the control room and it is feared some damage is likely to have been done to her keel. It was necessary to blow main ballast tanks before *Porpoise* came off and she came up to 10 feet on the gauge during the operation.

11:40: First mine of line C laid (9 mines).

11:46: Line C completed. Proceeded as requisite. Dived out of Frosjøen Fjord and round Hovden and proceeded down Helle Fjord.

14:49: First mine of Line B laid (15 mines).

14:55: Line B completed without incident. Proceeded out Helle Fjord and Frosjøen Fjord and proceeded to seaward.[14]

In all, forty-eight mines were laid. Laying the mines in different stripes like this made them more difficult to sweep as it would not be a matter of finding one and then take the rest in one go. It is not known that any ships were sunk or damaged by these mines.

Porpoise returning to port in May 1940, having laid mines north of Bergen. (Author's Collection)

Captain Menzies, in command of 2nd Flotilla at the time, considered that 'no blame is attributable to the commanding officer for either occasion of which the submarine touched the bottom'. Horton, with a more distant view, believed the first grounding to be 'an excusable error of judgement', as Roberts had already admitted in his report. As the demanding operation was otherwise well carried out though, he saw no reason why Roberts should not be duly commended.[15]

On 3 June, *Narwhal* laid fifty Mk XVI mines in three groups 2–3 miles off land, between Feistein Lighthouse and Jærens Reef (FD16). Two days later, a fast, northbound convoy of four large supply and repair ships approached Stavanger, This was a most valuable convoy consisting of the tanker *Samland,* the repair ship *Huascaran* and supply vessels A*lstertor* and *Palime* heading for Trondheim to assist *Gneisenau* and *Scharnhorst* after Operation Juno (see chapter 22). For such a valuable and fast convoy, the escort was considerable, consisting of seven minesweepers, *M2, M6, M9, M10, M11, M12* and *M13*.[16] Submarines had been sighted in the area and the ships were doing 14 knots, close to the maximum for most of the ships, to make things as difficult as possible for any potential assailants. This meant that the minesweepers could not deploy their sweeping gear. No mines had been reported and speed was considered most important. Shortly before 08:00 on 5 June, as the convoy neared Feistein Island, south of Stavanger, the bow of *Palime* was destroyed by a massive explosion. Her luck had run out.

The convoy was near the coast and, through quick reactions, the minesweeper *M6* managed to tow the 2,863-ton transport onto the sandy grounds off Jærens Reef, where she settled with parts of the superstructure above the water. *M2* joined *M6* in assisting the stricken *Palime* and moved in to pick up the crew, who were all saved in spite of some panic among them.[17] Meanwhile, a third minesweeper, *M11*, screened the area, using her S-Gerät, searching for submarines. None was found, but depth charges were thrown at irregular intervals to scare away any submarine lurking in the area. The other ships continued towards Stavanger.

After a while, a mine was actually seen from *M11* in the clear water at 3–5 metres (10–16 feet) depth with parts of its anchor-line, and it was realised that *Palime* had not been torpedoed, but had ventured into a minefield. Kapitänleutnant Wolfgang Dittmers immediately halted all non-routine anti-submarine efforts and ordered his crew to prepare the minesweeping gear instead. The main sweep of *M11* was set at 12 metres (39 feet) depth and bow-sweeping gear was set as well for extra protection, as she was on her own. *M2* and *M6* were attending *Palime* and the rest of the escort were following the convoy towards Stavanger. After a sweep southwards, preparing the gear, *M11* turned north, back into the area where *Palime* had triggered the mine and the other one had been seen in the water. All men not needed below deck were called up and ordered to gather aft, just in case.

Two mines were dealt with almost immediately by the main gear. Shortly after 10:20, however, a third mine was snagged by the bow-sweep. The anchor-line was not cut, but got pulled towards the minesweeper and detonated against its port bow. The explosion was violent and many sailors were thrown overboard. Five men were killed and eleven seriously wounded.

M6 instantly left *Palime* and came to the assistance of her sister-ship. Once the wounded had been transferred, a tow was rigged from *M6*, while the hull of *M11* was

Palime has been dragged stern-first by *M6* onto the shallow sandbanks off Jæren south of Stavanger and *M2* has moved in to pick up the crew. Photo was taken from *M6*. (E Skjold Collection)

Palime settled firmly on the sandbanks off Jæren. The high tide made her slide slightly off, and she eventually ended up with only the upper superstructure and masts above water. (T Ødemotland Collection and E Skjold Collection)

The minesweeper *M6*. (E Skjold Collection)

strengthened and leaks closed off as best possible. The damage was too severe though. and once stress was put on the cable, the minesweeper broke in two. Each piece sank rapidly, but there was no additional loss of life, although several of the survivors were in a critical state. Ninety-eight survivors were eventually brought to Stavanger by *M6*, thirty of them wounded, including Kapitänleutnant Dittmers.[18]

During further mine-sweeping in the area where *Palime* and *M11* had sunk, six mines altogether were cleared. Some of these were found to have special anchor-chains, which the German bow-sweeping gear could not cut, and therefore it pulled the mine towards the hull of the sweeping vessel. This created some anger towards the British among the minesweeper crews as it was seen to be unfair and the prime reason for the sinking of *M11*.[19]

On board *Palime* was a large amount of ammunition for the battleships, including a deck-load of torpedoes, and retrieval of this was considered vital. The salvage tug *Ula* was requisitioned and commenced work within a few days. On 10 July, however, after less than a dozen torpedoes had been retrieved, the work was halted, being too complicated due to strong currents.[20]

Rubis

The *Saphir*-class mine-laying submarine *Rubis* was one of the very few French submarine actively engaged in offensive operations together with British and other Allied forces in the early part of the war. At the outbreak of war, Lieutenant de Vaisseau Georges Cabanier was her commanding officer. Being due for a refit, *Rubis* was not active until after completion of that and a training period, when she was stationed at Brest with her sisters *Saphir* and *Nautilus* in January 1940. From there, the boats were meant to support operations providing help to Finland during the Winter War. This project never materialised. Instead, Germany invaded Norway and Denmark and the British Admiralty requested French assistance, pointing in particular to the submarine minelayers in Brest.[21] The French Admiral Staff were reluctant to put half their submarine mine-laying capacity under British control though, and after some consideration allowed *Rubis*, which was in the best technical condition due to her recent refit, to go. *Saphir* and *Nautilus* were sent back to the Mediterranean.

Rubis sailed for Britain in late April and, after some tests off Harwich, was stationed at Dundee, attached to the 9th Submarine Flotilla. Shortly after, the surface minelayer *Pollux* also arrived with a load of SH4 mines suitable for *Rubis*'s launch systems and to act as a tender for her while in harbour. Lieutenant Ernest Turner was assigned as liaison officer on board *Rubis*, along with a leading signalman and a radio operator.

Rubis sailed for her first patrol on 3 May 1940. The original intention was to lay mines at the entrance to Kristiansand harbour, but as Lieutenant Cabanier was making his way towards the diving location, a last-minute change of orders was received. The new orders were to lay the mines across the southern entrance of the fjord leading into Egersund. This was done without incident on 10 May (FD14), after which *Rubis* headed back to Dundee, as per revised orders, instead of taking up position in a patrol area. This was just after the news of *Seal* having been captured had reached the VA(S) (see below) and as it had not yet been confirmed that the signal book had been destroyed, it appears that Horton wanted his boats to return home until the situation had been clarified.[22]

In all, three Norwegian vessels were sunk by these mines and one damaged. The small coastal steamer *Vansø* (54 tons) struck one of the mines on 26 May and sank; one person perished. The Germans swept the area and recovered seven mines, recognised as French, and believed that the area was clear. Some weeks later, though, on 6 July, the 2,433-ton freighter *Almora*, which had been requisitioned and was under German command, was damaged by an explosion while crossing the area and set aground to prevent her from sinking. Presumably she had hit one of the mines laid by *Rubis*. On 24 July, the 1,705-ton freighter *Kem* was on its way from Danzig with a cargo of coal when she struck a mine in the same area and went down, without any fatalities. Four days later, on 28 July, the 412-ton *Argo* also struck a mine and sank, one person being killed. A new, thorough, round of sweeping was initiated during the first days of August, and no more ships were troubled.[23]

Back in Dundee, the crew of *Rubis* was pleasantly surprised when *Jules Verne* and the other French submarines arrived a few days later from Harwich, prompted by the German attack in the west. *Rubis*'s second operation was challenging: this time, the northern entrance to Haugesund was chosen, being a focus area for traffic travelling both north and south. Air activity over the North Sea was intense, however, at this stage, and the crossings back and forth from Dundee were rather hectic for the crew, with frequent crash-dives.

Including the approach, it was expected that up to thirty-six hours would have to be spent underwater on the day the mines were to be laid. To conserve batteries and air, cold food was prepared with hot drinks in thermos bottles, whereafter the galley was shut down and all men not needed on duty were instructed to restrict movement as much as possible. The thirty-two HS4 mines were laid on 27 May (FD15), the nearest some 300 metres (330 yards) from land, without any incidents. Within four days, two Norwegian vessels, the 174-ton barge *Blaamannen* and the 938-ton *Jadarland*, had been sunk, after

Rubis in Dundee. (Y Grangeon Collection)

which the area was swept by German minesweepers of the 5th R-boat Flotilla. *Jadarland* was chartered on the passenger route between Stavanger and Bergen and, as she sank very quickly, at least seven crew and twelve passengers were lost, including two women. Six people went down with *Blaamannen*.

Rubis's third operation in early June, FD17, was similar to the previous one, only this time the mines were laid in the Fedjeosen, the northern entrance to the fjord leading into Bergen harbour. Thirty-two mines were laid on 9 June, 12 miles inside the fjord. A daring venture, but again they were not detected and there was no incident, in spite of a patrol boat being very close to the submarine on several occasions while going into the fjord. The 1,081-ton coastal steamer *Sverre Sigurdsson* ventured into these mines the following day and sank, killing the Norwegian pilot Einar Toft.[24]

Returning to Dundee from the third mission, a message was waiting for *Rubis*, calling her home to France. *Jules Verne* and the other French submarines had already left (see chapter 17). There was also a signal from VA(S) Horton, however, dated 12 June 1940: 'On the successful completion of your third operation, may I express my admiration for the efficiency and skill which have invariably characterised your work. I shall be extremely sorry to lose the services of *Rubis*.'[25]

The French Admiral Staff wanted *Rubis* to depart no later than 18 June. Horton had the British Admiralty insist on her doing one more mine-laying mission before she returned, though, and the French yielded, provided that she would be recalled if an armistice was signed. This was accepted and Lieutenant Cabanier took his boat to sea once more on 20 June to lay mines deep inside the Leads off Kristiansund in the main sound leading towards Trondheim (FD20). In a display of skill and courage, Cabanier took *Rubis* into the Leads, past the trawler patrol at the entrance of the fjord and a picket destroyer. The thirty-two mines were laid on 26 June in groups of four and eight to cover a large area and make sweeping more difficult. *Rubis* returned to open sea without being discovered.[26]

The French armistice with Germany was signed on 22 June, but a curious 'difficulty of communications' prevented *Rubis* from receiving this news until she was back out of the Leads again. Returning to Dundee on 30 June, *Rubis* was in limbo for a few days until, on 3 July, the British instigated Operation Catapult. As soon as he was made aware of the operation, Admiral Horton sent another signal to Lieutenant Cabanier and had the commander of the 9th Flotilla, Captain James Roper, handle things in a quiet, discreet manner. The signal read:

> It is with great regret and pain that I must order some restrictions to be placed on the liberty of you, your officers and the ship's company; one and all most gallant men who have done unsurpassed work for the Allied cause in the North Sea. I am sure you will appreciate that where steps of this kind have been ordered generally, it is necessary and advisable to make no exceptions while the situation as a whole remains so complicated. [. . .] I trust these measures will only be brief. My sincerest sympathy is with you and the undeserved blow fate has dealt you and yours in recent days. Should you wish to communicate with me direct, please do so.[27]

Roper confined the French mariners to their quarters, without making them prisoners. After some consideration, Cabanier and his crew responded positively and, with the exception of one officer and four ratings, they all decided to remain on board *Rubis* and continue the war from Dundee. Shortly after, they all enlisted in the Forces Navale Françaises Libre (FNFL) and *Rubis* became one of the first ships to serve on the Allied side under the French flag. Soon after, Cabanier received the DSO, while several of his officers and men received other distinctions. *Rubis* herself received a citation from General de Gaulle.

Small Successes

Both *Narwhal* and *Porpoise* were back off the coast of Norway in June laying more mines. On the 9th, *Narwhal* embarked more mines at Immingham, after which Lieutenant Commander Ronald Burch took his boat back out to sea. They had only been home for four days. His orders this time were to lay field FD19 off Haugesund. The mines were laid on 12 June without incident, after which *Narwhal* patrolled off Utsira for a few days before returning to Blyth on 18 June.[28] These mines appear to have remained undiscovered for quite some time. During the night of 16/17 August, the requisitioned Norwegian auxiliary *Biene* hit what was probably one of these mines and sank. The area was closed off and ships ordered to go outside. When finally resources were available to sweep the mines of FD19, a number of things went wrong. One after another, the ex-Norwegian patrol boats

This somewhat strange photo shows the bow of *Gnom7* being towed by *Kobolt1*. The latter hit a mine herself only minutes later, leaving nothing more than firewood drifting in the currents. (T Eggan Collection)

Gnom7, Kobold1 and Kobold3 all hit the mines they were supposed to be sweeping, more or less disintegrating from the heavy explosions. Only eight men were pulled out of the water, five of them seriously wounded.

On 14 June, Commander Philip Roberts took *Porpoise* into Ramsøyfjorden, between the islands of Hitra and Smøla. There, he laid three lines of mines, two of sixteen and one of eighteen, across one of the main channels of traffic leading towards Trondheim (FD18). The distance between the mines was about 50 metres (55 yards).[29] In the early hours of 18 June, the minesweeper *M5* triggered two of these mines and sank rapidly – twenty-eight men perished.

There was not much rest for *Narwhal* and her crew either. Having picked up the mines at Immingham on 30 June, Lieutenant Commander Burch set course for the Norwegian Leads off Kristiansund. There, fifty mines were laid, west of the island Smøla, on 4 July (FD21).[30] Two days later, on the 6th, a small convoy consisting of the two A/S trawlers *UJB* and *UJC* escorting the freighter *Karpfanger*, was approaching the area, southbound from Trondheim. *UJB* was *Treff VIII*, originally named *UJD* when requisitioned but renamed *UJB* on 1 June after the original *UJB* had been torpedoed and sunk by *Tetrarch* in late April (see page 220). This complicated name change was not fully incorporated by the crews or the flotilla and there are mentions of either name in several contemporary documents. *UJB* hit one of the mines that had been laid by *Narwhal* shortly before and sank quickly – thirteen men perished, twenty-two survived.[31]

On 22 July, Burch took *Narwhal* to sea once more, this time to lay mines off Kristiansund (FD22). In the afternoon of the next day, Oberleutnant Karl Müller on patrol in the North Sea with his Dornier Do17 of 1./KFlGr 606 sighted a submarine on the surface. Brazenly, he dived his rather large bomber in an attack against what he recognised with certainty was an enemy vessel. The crew registered hits and, upon returning to base, Müller claimed

The minesweeper *M5* operating in the waters off Trondheim shortly before she was lost. (E Skjold Collection)

The rest of 1st Minesweeping Flotilla clearing the remaining mines of FD18 in the Leads between the island of Hitra and the mainland after *M5* had been lost. This was the main channel for northbound traffic to Trondheim. (E Skjold Collection)

one submarine sunk some 125 miles east of Aberdeen. *Narwhal* was never heard from again and as she would have been near this position at the time, it very likely that she was the submarine attacked and actually sunk. She was reported overdue on 1 August 1940.

After this, no more minefields were laid off Norway during this period. *Porpoise* was needed in the Bay of Biscay and *Rubis* was in the yards. One last minefield, FD23, was laid west of Denmark, off Ringkøbing, by *Porpoise* on 29 July, but no record of any ships lost in this field has been found. Thereafter, *Porpoise* made one more patrol, without laying any mines, before transferring to Rothesay for operations off south-west France.[32]

Rubis was back in service in September after a refit, but there were no more suitable mines as both *Pollux* and *Jules Verne* had returned to France. She was deployed on regular patrol missions, but this was not what she was built for, and her moderate speed and limited number of torpedo tubes were a severe handicap. Hence, *Rubis's* four patrols between September and December 1940 achieved little. Returning from the last patrol on 18 December, *Rubis* was ordered to the yards again for a complete overhaul and a rebuild to allow her to take British mines.[33]

From Skagen in Denmark to Kristiansund in Norway, some 600 mines were laid inshore or near-shore in fifteen missions by *Seal*, *Narwhal*, *Porpoise* and the French *Rubis* between 13 April and 29 July (see Appendix V). At least twenty-two ships were sunk in these fields, some 15,000–18,000 tons. This was perhaps not significant in terms of tonnage, as many of the ships were small, coastal vessels, but the minefields created fear and uncertainty, hampered the coastal traffic and required significant resources for sweeping and escort. The majority of the ships involved were German or in German service, though not all.

There is little doubt that had more mine-laying submarines been available for a dedicated campaign, the German Naval Command in Norway would have been faced with a challenge they could not easily have met. Small minefields laid at carefully selected places in or near strategic channels or focal points, besides actually sinking ships, could disrupt traffic, drain resources and force convoys into areas where they became vulnerable to torpedoes from other submarines, aircraft or surface vessels.

Two submarines, *Narwhal* and *Seal*, were lost in these operations.

Black, Filthy Water

IN THE SPRING OF 1940, *Seal* had been in constant operation for a year and was due for a trip to the Chatham yards. In particular, she had had a minor collision with the Estonian freighter *Otto*, resulting in some damage to her stern. Sister-ship *Cachalot* had been in a more severe collision, though, with the Italian freighter *Beppe*, and was given priority at the yard, while *Seal* was patched up at Blyth and ordered to prepare for another mine-laying sortie in the Kattegat, east of Denmark, Operation FD7.

Captain Jock Bethell, the commanding officer of the 6th Submarine Flotilla, believed these operations were becoming too dangerous for the large mine-laying submarines and argued with Admiral Horton for FD7 to be cancelled. It was not cancelled, however, and Lieutenant Commander Rupert Lonsdale took his boat to sea from Immingham on 29 April, having taken fifty mines on board. Before departure, he was given two alternative areas in which to lay the mines, should conditions in the primary target area for some reason be adverse.

The journey from Humber to Skagen (the Skaw) was uneventful, almost boring. At one stage, during a period of high seas, some of the mines came loose, but were quickly re-secured. Rounding Skagen during the night of the 3/4 May, *Seal* met sister-ship *Narwhal* going home from a very successful mission and they exchanged a few signals by asdic; *Narwhal* wished them luck, adding ominously that they would probably need it. Shortly after, the radio operator of *Seal* also picked up signals from *Narwhal* informing VA(S) that, in addition to having laid her mines, she had fired torpedoes and scored several hits. Fine as this news was, Lonsdale realised that the other boat's achievements were to his disadvantage, as the Germans would be alert and vengeful.

Seal in July 1939. (W&L)

Into the Kattegat

Staying on the surface when heading into the Kattegat, this would soon be proven beyond doubt. In order to utilise the short night to the maximum, Lonsdale decided to stay on the surface, running on the main engines, as long as possible. To minimise the risk of being sighted when the first light started to appear in the east, he trimmed the boat down until only the conning tower was above the surface. In this way the diesels could still be used, charging the batteries while proceeding at 8 knots. Dawn would break shortly after 02:30, and Lonsdale called from the bridge to the control room with instructions to let him know when that time was reached.

At 02:27, however, the sound of aircraft engines was heard by the starboard lookout. He alerted Lonsdale who immediately gave the order to dive. It was too late – the aircraft was flying at a height of about 100 metres (330 feet) and in spite of there being some darkness at sea level, the aircraft, the He115 of KüFlGr 706, sighted the conning tower and banked around as quickly as it could to make an attack. As *Seal* passed 10 metres (33 feet) she was rocked by a heavy explosion. The bombs dropped by the Heinkel were conventional, not depth charges, and hence not lethal unless scoring a direct hit. Nevertheless, at least one exploded when striking the sea. Some lamps were broken, men were thrown to their knees and there were one or two minor leaks, but nothing too grave. The most serious harm was done to the forward hydroplane motor, where the field coil needed to be changed. This took several hours, but when this was done, there was no question in Lonsdale's mind that the mission should continue. There was no doubt, though, that the Germans knew where they were. During repairs, *Seal* had continued south-eastwards at

The crew of *Seal*. (Author's Collection)

3.5 knots and now they were between the Danish island of Læsø and Gothenburg, in an area where abundant German shipping activity had been reported. They were still some way from the primary target area for the mines, but very close to one of the alternative sites.

Through the periscope, Lonsdale sighted a group of armed trawlers ahead of the boat. They were obviously searching the channel down which *Seal* would have to go if she were to lay the mines as primarily intended. The sea was glassy calm with nowhere to hide and the trawlers appeared competent, working together as a team, one ship stopping and listening through its hydrophones while its compatriots moved forward. Passing undetected through the picket seemed impossible and, having been given an alternative location, Lonsdale eventually laid the mines off the island of Vinga, west of Gothenburg, just outside Swedish territory, between 09:00 and 09:45 on 4 May.[1]

Once the mines had been laid, Lonsdale turned *Seal* around, keeping away from the trawlers, which were part of the 5.U-Jagd Gruppe under the command of Korvettenkapitän Günther Brandt, on his way back towards Skagen. This took the submarine slightly closer to Denmark than she had been on the way in. After a while, half a dozen S-boats were also sighted to the north-east. Able to travel much faster, these were considered more dangerous than the trawlers and, skirting their expected course, Lonsdale turned further west towards the Danish coast. Unbeknown to him, this brought *Seal* into a newly laid German anti-submarine minefield (Skagen UMA-Sperre), consisting of two layers of mines, one at 15 metres (49 feet) and one at 30 metres (98 feet) below the surface.

What then happened is not absolutely clear. Apparently, one of *Seal*'s aft hydroplanes caught the anchor-line of one of the mines, dragging it along for some time and pulling it towards the hull. For a moment there was a loss of trim, probably when the cable was snagged, but nobody seems to have thought much about it. Some of the crew later said they heard an odd scraping sound – as if something was dragged down the length of the hull. Nothing further happened though, and, as supper and shift change was approaching, few thought anymore about it. With *Seal* 'sitting' on a layer of salty water, which kept her at a stable depth with minimum effort, and no German vessels in the immediate vicinity, Lonsdale decided to shut down the submarine as much as possible and wait in total silence.

At 18:55, a shattering explosion aft shook the submarine. When the sound died down, it was clear that water was pouring into the boat; closing the watertight doors behind them, all men aft ran forward as the boat tilted appreciably, bows upward. Nobody was quite sure what had happened and many believed that they had been depth-charged. No further explosions came, though, and as the asdic operator reported that the propeller noises of both the trawlers and the S-boats indicated they were travelling away from them, it was concluded that a mine was the most likely cause of the explosion. When slowing down, the mine may have drifted forward until it came in contact with the hull and exploded. Ironically, had *Seal* not stopped, the mine would probably have continued to trail behind until eventually breaking loose. Surprisingly, the explosion was not noticed by any of the German vessels in the vicinity, which all vanished out of range.

The explosion caused severe damage to the submarine, forcing her to the bottom in 40 metres (130 feet) of water. 'It seemed as though a hot blast of air struck me in the face,' Lonsdale later said, adding that, '*Seal* went down by the stern while the crew endeavoured to shut the after door through which water was pouring.'[2] The situation was definitely serious, instantly recognised by all through the painful increase in air pressure: large amounts of water were entering the boat, compressing the air inside. Miraculously, nobody had been killed and the men were safely inside the watertight doors. When things settled down and Lonsdale asked for damage reports, it became clear that the mining compartment was flooded. The stoker's mess-deck, auxiliary machinery space and motor room were partly flooded. The watertight door at the after end of the mess-deck had come loose from the explosion and been closed shut by the flow of water, in all likelihood saving the boat. A group of men led by Chief Engineer Lieutenant 'Nobby' Clark went back through the closed doors as far as they could, ensuring all openings were closed and the water contained, before starting to pump out the water that had entered the motor and engine rooms. *Seal's* stern was duly settled on the bottom and the boat rested at an angle of 18 degrees, bow up. There were some 130 tons of water inside the hull, while *Seal's* main ballast tank capacity was 380 tons. Hence, Lonsdale and Clark assumed the submarine should have sufficient buoyancy to surface when her ballast tanks were blown. *Seal* was relatively safe where she was, but time was running out as she had been operating underwater for quite some time already and the batteries were low, as were the oxygen levels. Still, Lonsdale decided it was better to wait for darkness up above before attempting to surface. In the meantime, the crew was advised to rest and conserve the dwindling oxygen. One of the few men kept busy was Chief Stoker 'Spoff' Middleton. Responsible for the submarine's pumping system, his competence in coupling up connections and pumping capacity would be vital in the recovery of the boat. At 22:30 Lonsdale decided it was time. By now, several of the crew had started to feel the effects of the rising CO_2 levels and had breathing problems. Nevertheless, they all moved to their diving stations without delay.

Optimistically, Lonsdale ordered 'Stand by to surface', followed by orders to blow the ballast tanks and use the engines to assist moving forward. To no avail – the submarine was firmly mired in the mud. A second attempt, including emptying some of the oil-fuel tanks and freshwater tanks was no more successful. Not even releasing the 11-ton drop keel – meaning that *Seal* would be unable to dive again should she manage to reach the surface – helped, other than giving the boat an increased bow-up position. Yet another attempt produced no further results and the situation was getting desperate.

After an impromptu gathering for a brief prayer, Lonsdale sent as many of the crew as could be spared forward to try to help level the boat. To facilitate this, a rope was rigged and the exhausted men went forward hand-over-hand. Meanwhile the engineers once more tried to think through the pumping system, maximising it for one final attempt. If this did not succeed, they would most certainly all have succumbed by the morning. The high-pressure air was almost exhausted and there would be no further attempts.

'Full ahead both' was the order from Lonsdale, without knowing if the propellers were free to move in the mud. Every possible valve was opened and the last reserves of compressed air hissed into the tanks. At first nothing happened. Suddenly the boat shuddered and all of a sudden it was level, sending water from the aft compartments forward. A few seconds later, this was followed by Lonsdale's voice: 'We have surfaced. Everybody will stay where he is until I call down my instructions from the bridge.' It was 01:30 and *Seal* had returned from the realm of the dead, having been submerged for almost twenty-four hours.[3]

Lonsdale carefully opened the conning tower hatch and climbed onto the bridge. As fresh air rushed in, the effects of carbon-dioxide poisoning for many turned into severe headaches and violent vomiting. 'These efforts made ever increasing demands on the mental and physical capabilities of my crew,' Lonsdale later said. 'It was obvious that their efforts took a greater toll on them as time went on.' He held that he himself could not remember having had any headache or feeling of sickness, but admitted he had noticed an inability to cope with situations where things did not turn out as he fully expected them to, adding: 'I could best illustrate this when the ship would not turn after we got to the surface,' he told the court martial. 'I could not think literally what to do next, and it was another person who suggested that we might go astern.'[4]

When surfacing, *Seal* was five miles off the Skagen Lightship in an area under total German air and sea control. Her damage turned out to be significant and, though both engines eventually started, the lubricating system was not working well. It was cleaned repeatedly – to no avail – and within minutes, they seized up. Equally serious, the steering gear was inoperable, probably as the rudders were bent, and the only alternative in the growing light was to head for neutral Swedish waters, stern first, using the motors, and hoping the batteries would last. Chief Engineer Lieutenant Clark felt 'ghastly' when they surfaced and later wrote to his wife:

> I was unhurt [. . .] but was suffering acutely from lack of air and carbon dioxide poisoning. The last 4 hours down below make me shudder to think of them, particularly the last 2 hours when we had all secretly given up hope. No one could stand, and several were unconscious. They just fell where they were [. . .] I went twice into the flooded compartment to shut doors etc, so that water could be pumped out. Black, filthy water, no lights, 200 feet down. It was ghastly. My pulse was 145 then.[5]

Unable to dive, *Seal* was in a dire predicament. Lonsdale instructed the navigation officer, Lieutenant Trevor Beet, to destroy the codebooks and instructed First Officer Lieutenant Terence Butler to see to it that all secret equipment, including the asdic, was destroyed, lest it should fall into German hands.

At 02:10 a coded message was sent to VA(S), reporting *Seal*'s damaged condition and the intent to run for Sweden. A little over an hour later, Horton replied that the signal was 'understood and agreed with'. Half an hour later, he added: 'Safety of personnel should be your first consideration after destruction of asdics.' Neither of these signals, which supported Lonsdale's general decisions, was known to him as the radio equipment had been destroyed before they were sent.[6]

Seaplanes

In the early morning of 5 May, there was hectic activity at the newly established German seaplane base at Aalborg-See in Northern Denmark. Acting on reports from the previous day of British submarines in the Kattegat, station commander and Gruppenkommandeur of Küstenfliegergruppe 906 (KüFlGr 906), Oberstleutnant Hermann Lessing, sent two Arado Ar196 floatplanes from the subordinated 5./196 on search missions as dawn approached, a little after 02:00.[7] Shortly after, several He115 aircraft from KüFlGr 906's own 1st Staffel, 1./906, were dispatched in a comprehensive search pattern. KüFlGr 906, augmented by 5./196, was the main naval air force unit in the north-east at this time. Its main tasks were escort and A/S patrols in the northern Kattegat, the Skagerrak and eastern parts of the northern North Sea, covering the supply routes to Norway.

Some twenty-five minutes after take-off – by which time it was almost full daylight – the Arado 6W+IN, piloted by Unteroffizier Heinz Böttcher, with Leutnant Günther Mehrens as observer in the back seat, sighted *Seal*. Banking and losing height, Böttcher went straight for the submarine.

Two Lewis guns had been brought to the bridge shortly after surfacing. Now, Lonsdale ordered everybody except the signalman Waddington and Leading Seaman Mayes inside the tower or below. Remaining with the two ratings in the open conning tower, he prepared to fight the aircraft. They did not fire at the Arado during its first pass, hoping that the airmen might believe *Seal* was a Swedish submarine, returning to port. Leutnant Mehrens recognised *Seal* for what she was though, and ordered Böttcher to attack. This he did, firing the aircraft's machine guns at the bridge and hull of the submarine. The Arado was armed with two MG FF 20-mm cannons, one in each wing, and one 7.92-mm machine gun in front of the cockpit, fixed to fire forward. In addition, there was one 7.92-mm MG 15 on a pivot-mounting in the after part of the cockpit that could be used by the observer.

The 20-mm cannon shells in particular were highly dangerous, and very soon First Officer Lieutenant Butler and one rating were injured by shrapnel inside the tower. Both were carried down into the control room. It is unclear if Lonsdale realised that Lieutenant Butler was so injured that he was incapable of carrying on at this stage. Böttcher also dropped two small bombs, carried underwing, but these appear to have had limited effect. In between the attacks, Böttcher sent a 'submarine alarm' radio signal and a few minutes later a second Ar196, 6W+EN piloted by Unteroffizier Sackritz with Leutnant Karl Schmidt in the back seat also arrived, joining the attack. Running low on ammunition, Böttcher and Mehrens stood off, looking for the armed trawler *UJ128* that had been detached from the escort of a Norway-bound convoy in response to the alarm signal.[8]

Cannon fire from the second Arado kept hammering into *Seal*'s hull; after a while an He115 from 1./906, 8L+CH captained by Leutnant Nikolaus Broili, also arrived on the scene, providing further firepower to the attacks. On board *Seal*, Lonsdale started firing back from one of the Lewis guns, while Mayes manned the other. Waddington passed ammunition pans as they were brought up from below, while keeping an eye on the aircraft and warning the gunners as they approached. Miraculously, the men remained unscathed during the German attacks. Soon, however, both Lewis guns jammed – Mayes' first, then Lonsdale's. Several voices shouted up through the conning tower for Lonsdale to give up the fight – the bombs in particular were frightening, the sound of their explosions reverberating through the hull, even if they all missed. There is no doubt that the majority of the men were suffering severely from the after-effects of the CO_2 poisoning, having intense headaches, fatigue and nausea.

Considering the situation, Lonsdale realised that *Seal* was helpless and his entire crew was in jeopardy. A series of cannon shells had perforated the port main ballast tank and there were further leaks aft, giving the submarine a pronounced list. In addition, water was coming into the stern, rising slowly in the motor room, straining the structure of the boat and ensuring that there was no more power to steer or move. For all practical purposes, *Seal* was defenceless and her crew faced almost certain death. Reluctantly Lonsdale gave instructions for the wardroom tablecloth to be brought to the bridge. This was done and, waving it, he surrendered his boat at 03:00. Sometime during these events, Able Seaman Charles Smith went overboard and was never seen again.[9] Lonsdale later recounted:

> It never occurred to me that I should stop the engines and hoist the white flag, and the aeroplane, quite naturally, went on firing at us. This made me almost desperate. I ordered the signalman from the bridge and the Lewis guns to be brought into action. I fired the Lewis guns until one after the other was jammed. [Then] I told the signalman to flash 'S.O.S. and surrender' to the plane.[10]

Leutnant Schmidt ordered Sackritz to land the Arado, which slid to a halt some 50 metres (55 yards) from the submarine. Mehrens' Arado returned and circled the scene, as did the Heinkel. Training the observer's gun at the tower of the submarine, Schmidt shouted over in English for the submarine's captain to come on board the aircraft. Troubled, Lieutenant Beet and Coxswain Higgins both volunteered to go, but Lonsdale found he had no choice but to take on the task 'which was something more than unpleasant' himself. Beet and some of the others on the bridge at the time assured Lonsdale that everything would be all right and they would ascertain whether the boat would sink.[11] One may argue that Lonsdale should have ensured his submarine was sinking by actually scuttling her. For this purpose, there were two depth charges in the bilges, set to explode at a depth of 20 metres (65 feet) if the boat was flooded for any reason. The fact that there were no vessels in sight to rescue *Seal*'s crew apparently held Lonsdale back from actively initiating the flooding. With the men floating in the sea above the submarine when her depth charges exploded, there would be certain injury or death to many of them. She was already listing to port and was down by the stern. There is little doubt that, as he swam across to the floatplane, Lieutenant Commander Lonsdale was deeply worried, but believed he was leaving a ship that would soon go down, while he was giving his men the best possible odds for survival.

Meanwhile, Leutnant Broili had also landed his He115, with a view to sending the observer of the Arado, Leutnant Schmidt, onboard the submarine in the dinghy (which he had onboard the Heinkel) to prevent the crew from scuttling her. Schmidt was too busy with Lonsdale, though, and ignored Broili's light signals. Once the wet and miserable British captain was on board the Arado, a triumphant Schmidt ordered Sackritz to take off again and set course for Aalborg. Annoyed, Broili took off again too.[12]

As Lonsdale was swimming away from his submarine, Lieutenant Clark, the chief engineer, came up onto the bridge from below. He had seen the state of Lieutenant Butler below deck and, once he realised what was happening above, he turned to Lieutenant Beet, saying, 'Well, chum, you're the boss now.'[13]

At this stage, Mehrens, presumably having seen Schmidt pick up Lonsdale, also landed and shouted across to the submarine for a second hostage. Coxswain Marcus Cousins volunteered and prepared to swim across. Seeing the second Arado on the water, Broili again landed his He115 to order the observer of the Arado across to the submarine to try to prevent her from being scuttled. Mehrens was apparently no more interested in such a task than Schmidt had been: even if he acknowledged the signals from the Heinkel,

Seal, with a heavy list, is towed into Frederikshavn by the tug *Seeteufel*. (Author's Collection)

he did little to execute the orders. Instead he repeatedly beckoned for a second man to come over. While PO Cousins was swimming across, a Swedish Ju86 came to see what was going on and both aircraft took off – Schmidt's Arado heading for Aalborg, Broili's Heinkel to chase the Swede away.[14]

Prisoners

The officers remaining on board the submarine were all certain she was going to sink, and hesitated to take further decisive steps to make this happen while the crew, including the two wounded, were still on board. As much as possible of the specialised equipment on board was smashed up and those confidential papers that had not yet been dumped or burnt were now thrown overboard. In particular, the asdic was thoroughly broken up and the parts thrown overboard. Some of the men tried to launch the berthing boat, but a few machine-gun rounds from the He115, which remained overhead, swiftly halted them.[15]

By the time the A/S trawler *UJ128 Franken* under Kapitänleutnant Otto Lang hove to near *Seal*, at 06:30, the submarine was listing profoundly and it appeared that she was going down by the stern. Still, First Lieutenant Heinz Nolte, who spoke some English, came across with some men to see if it was possible to prevent the submarine from sinking. Bravely, he pulled his gun and entered down the ladder to the control room to assess the situation. All the British sailors, except Lieutenant Clark and a few ratings, were hurriedly ordered up above, including the wounded, and their transfer to *UJ128* commenced. There, they were given hot soup, some warm clothes and a chance to go to the toilet, if needed.[16]

In spite of the German orders, Lieutenant Beet and some of the engineering crew went forward, opening all the valves they could access, until they were stopped at gunpoint. At least one of the deck hatches was left ajar, in order to flood the hull should towing be attempted. No direct orders had been given – by anyone, including Lieutenant Beet – to actually sink the submarine after Lonsdale had left. Confident that *Seal* was going down, the British sailors had let themselves be taken off their boat. Lieutenant Clark was also convinced *Seal* was going down and thought it unnecessary do anything other than leave the engine-room hatch slightly ajar. This, however, was promptly closed by one of the German sailors accompanying Nolte; they inspected the boat thoroughly, closing all valves they could access in an attempt to keep her from sinking. While Kapitänleutnant Lang brought *UJ128* alongside *Seal*, preparing a tow, Nolte remained below in the control room, keeping Clark with him.

Seal did not sink. Although CPO Telegraphist Charles Futer cunningly managed to unclip the hatch once again, leaving it slightly ajar, the sea was flat calm and no water came in during the tow. With the help of the tug *Seeteufel* that arrived in the afternoon, Kapitänleutnant Lang managed to nurse the captured boat into the nearest Danish port, Frederikshavn. Near the entrance to the harbour, *Seal*'s list suddenly increased but the experienced salvager, Kapitän Funk of *Seeteufel*, brought *Seal* through the harbour channel and secured her alongside a seawall in a corner of the harbour around 18:00; to prevent *Seal* from sinking, he neatly secured his tug on the outside.

Next morning, salvage operations were initiated under the supervision of Kapitän Hans Rösing. The salvage men from *Seeteufel* patched up all damage to the hull, leaving the scuttling charges where they were for the time being. When all holes had been wedged and the larger cracks covered by collision mats, the water was pumped out, returning the submarine to her normal trim. As soon as she was safe, *Seal* was towed to Kiel, where she arrived on 11 May, welcomed by a large crowd of dignitaries and curious observers.

Having a genuine propaganda object in their hands, the German High Command ordered *Seal* to be reconditioned and made operational. In November 1940, *Seal* was commissioned into the Kriegsmarine as *UB* under the command of Fregattenkapitän Bruno Mahn, a 52-year-old WWI veteran. She had no military value for the Kriegsmarine, though, and was never seriously considered for active duty, particularly as the German

The captured *Seal* became quite an attraction and was heavily photographed. Note the holes from the aircraft machine guns penetrating the non-armoured sides of the mine casing. Note also that several of the officers have cameras. (Author's Collection)

Navy had no relevant torpedoes or mines that she could use operationally. *Seal*'s main value was propaganda. Decommissioned in 1941, she was finally scuttled off Kiel in 1945.

Overall, the German Navy learned little from *Seal*. The construction of the boat itself did not impress the German naval engineers much. Some of the specialised equipment she had might have done, but most of it, including the asdic and secret documents, had been destroyed or thrown overboard and there was little left. Still, there is no doubt that a close study of the British torpedoes led to improved design of German detonators, costing Allied lives.

The crew of *Seal* is marched through Frederikshavn. The metal shields around the necks of the two front guards signify that they are military policemen. (Author's Collection)

From Aalborg, Lonsdale was sent, with dispatch, to Kiel for interrogation.[17] After interrogation, Lieutenant Commander Lonsdale and his men spent the rest of the war in various German prisoner-of-war camps.[18] In April 1946, Lonsdale and Beet were tried before a court martial on charges of failing to take steps to ensure the sinking of the submarine when it appeared possible that she might fall into enemy hands. Both were honourably acquitted, but Lonsdale has the unhappy distinction of being the only British commander to surrender his ship to the enemy during WWII.[19] Horton wrote in a memorandum to the Admiralty, after interviewing the survivors in 1945:

> In considering the action of the Captain and officers it must be remembered that these events occurred in the opening months of the war at a time when little consideration had been given to the action necessary to prevent a submarine falling into enemy hands. Such an event had always seemed wildly improbable. Moreover, it must be remembered that officers and men must have been suffering from the mental after effects of their prolonged dive without the modern assistance of oxygen and CO_2 absorbent, which may well have clouded their judgment. In actual fact the task of sinking the submarine with all pressure gone in the telemotor system would have offered some difficulty to men in an exhausted condition.[20]

— 22 —

Deep-Sea Stalkers

FOR THE ROYAL NAVY'S Submarine Service, the early summer of 1940 changed everything. From being shackled by complicated engagement rules and uninspired tactical considerations, they were suddenly at the forefront of the European naval war. Things were not easy though. Bill King wrote:

> The sea was glassy calm, giving nightmare conditions for periscope work. A tell-tale feather followed the smallest tip that broke the surface. Never in my life have I seen the sea so unrippled. We slid around watching enemy ships and trying to calculate the position of their escorts while maintaining a good attacking position [. . .]. I tried to keep the periscope from breaking the mirror-like surface of the sea more than gave the appearance of a fish jumping. It was ticklish work. The big periscope with its high magnification, binocular vision and other refinements could seldom be raised within three miles of the enemy. [. . .] Throughout the long sunlit day, I stood glued to the big periscope, popping it up and down, trying to take in the whole seascape in quick flashes.[1]

On the few occasions that the submarines could get close enough to a target to fire torpedoes, they would be seen the second they broke the surface and, in most cases, could be evaded. The German invasion of Holland, Belgium and France actually created a relative lull in the North Sea as the Kriegsmarine was licking its wounds from Norway while aircraft, escorts and A/S vessels were busy elsewhere. Some of the British submarines were diverted to lines off the Dutch and French coasts to protect troop movements and later evacuations. For the Submarine Service, this meant that all boats were utilised to the maximum. Repairs and maintenance was limited to the bare necessities: periods in harbour were shortened and time on patrol was maximised.

Strain

For many submariners, including the COs, mental stress began to tell after the Norwegian campaign and the intensification of the war in general through the German victory in France. A number of the older, more-experienced COs started to experience sleeplessness, unease and other signs of nervous strain. Fortunately, several of them were brave enough to speak up about it and it was recognised by both Horton and the Admiralty as a real and, above all, permissable phenomenon. There had been significant losses, and many near escapes affecting both officers and ratings. Some ratings had already quietly been allowed to find another job ashore or on a surface vessel, but now the strain also began to show on the commanding officers. Hutchinson of *Truant* had already applied to be relieved and was on sick leave, before proceeding to a staff job. Following the end of the Norwegian campaign, others also asked for relief. Horton and his flotilla commanders realised there was nothing else to do other than accept this and during the summer of 1940 a number of the more experienced COs were transferred or moved to alternative positions where they continued to serve with sterling results. This was not really a problem, as there were a good number of experienced first officers ready for the perisher course and each flotilla already had one or more qualified COs standing by.

Bill King had also been feeling the strain and started going for long walks on his own:

> Something had happened to me. I felt I had fallen down a well inside myself. As the captain of a crew whose lives depended on my instant decisions and with whom I lived in very close quarters, I could not now relax with any of them. I was cosseting my own mental forces, trying to keep my brain taut for the violent battles which occurred on every patrol. I was too alone to talk to anyone. . . . My crew remained outwardly cheerful, but the strain showed in curious ways. I think the over-taxed mind gives itself little blackouts. Even the best trained hands began to make mistakes.[2]

One reason for the increased strain was the German knowledge of the whereabouts of many of the Allied submarines. It is obvious from several notes in the war diary of the SKL that, at times, the German B-Dienst had very precise information regarding the submarines. On 21 June, for instance, it is noted that: 'Regarding enemy submarines, the Funkbeobachtungsdienst (radio tracking service) reports *Severn* some 25 miles south west of Egerø and *Salmon* some 20 miles off Lista. Two more boats are also in the area. These boats are regularly informed by their C-in-C of the movements of own ships.'[3]

It is not difficult to imagine what Lieutenant Commander Bertram Taylor of *Severn* would have thought had he known that the Germans knew the position of his submarine with such detail. Later, with the increased German use of aircraft in the search for submarines, it became increasingly difficult to operate in the Skagerrak and the southern North Sea. Off the coast of Norway the sea's surface was generally less smooth and thus easier to hide beneath, but as summer approached the days would lengthen and there would be serious limitations on the time available to charge batteries and move on the surface.

Large Ships on Starboard Bow

The cumbersome size and relatively extensive time to dive of the River-class submarines had in general made them unsuited for deployment in the North Sea. Nevertheless, in the second half of April, VA(S) Horton decided that they could be used in the periphery of the areas where 'intense A/S activity was to be expected'.[4] With *Thames* in the yards for a refit, *Severn* and *Clyde* were therefore, as much as possible, sent into the quieter parts of the central North Sea or north along the coast of Norway, where neither the Kriegsmarine nor Luftwaffe had the resources to keep standing patrols. It is clear from the war diary of the SKL that they knew well that there were submarines off central and northern Norway – even to the extent of which boats were there at any one time – but that they had few means to act upon this information, other than trying to keep a reasonable number of aircraft patrolling the area and to divert merchant vessels and transports to other routes.[5]

Clyde. (W&L)

On 3 May, *Clyde* was on her way to a billet off Trondheim. This was at the height of the Allied evacuation from Norway and operations were ongoing, both to the south (Molde–Åndalsnes area) and to the north (Namsos). Shortly after midday Lieutenant Commander David Ingram sighted a small fishing craft. At the time, they were more than 50 miles due west of Stadtlandet; finding it somewhat suspicious that a fishing craft should be so far from shore on a south-westerly course, Ingram closed and boarded her.

To his surprise, he learned that the vessel, *Jåbæk*, had nineteen people on board, two of whom were Norwegian naval officers.[6] The most surprising thing, though, was that there were British and Norwegian women on board as well. *Jåbæk* had been under Norwegian naval command for several weeks during the campaign and had left Ålesund by order of the naval commander there the previous night, endeavouring to reach a British port before their provisions ran out. This was a completely new situation for Ingram. Norway was the first European country to be occupied by the Germans where those who wanted to get away and take part in the fight to free their country again could escape by sea. Later, this would become quite normal – though punishable by death if caught. For now the British submariners were uncertain what to do.

As it turned out, one of the officers, Lieutenant Thorleif Pettersen, was wounded. The other, Lieutenant Jan Erik Haave spoke fluent English and German and volunteered to stay on board *Clyde* as a pilot, being very familiar with this part of the Norwegian coast. Ingram thought this was a good idea, and, taking the young Norwegian lieutenant on board, he continued northwards after having resupplied the fishing vessel with provisions and given the skipper, Peter Godø, sailing directions to Lerwick on the Shetland Islands.[7]

But the day was not yet over. At 16:24, some 15 miles further north, another larger ship came into view. By now *Clyde* was submerged, as three German flyingboats had been sighted earlier. The aircraft were not to be seen any more, though, so Ingram surfaced and stopped the ship, which was identified as the Norwegian 1,116-ton freighter *Bomma*.

To Ingram's surprise and amusement, the entire crew of the freighter took to the lifeboats as fast as they could and started to row away. One of the boats was ordered alongside the submarine, and the first officer came on board. With the help of Lieutenant Haave he had an interesting story to tell. *Bomma* had been southbound off Romsdal when the Germans attacked on 9 April. The master, Henry Johannessen, did not wish to be captured by the invaders and anchored in a fjord near Molde, behind Norwegian lines. Meanwhile, things did not work out well for the Norwegians and their British allies, and in the evening of 2 May, when the evacuation commenced, *Bomma* took on board a dozen refugees in Molde, including women and children, and set out to sea. There were ample provisions on board, but an almost complete lack of relevant maps. Ingram gave them what he could spare from his own sets and instructed them to head for Lerwick at their best speed. This they did and arrived safely the next day.[8]

For *Clyde*, a rather uneventful period ensued. The designated patrol area off Trondheim, known as Frohavet, was calm and there was little to observe during the days. The nights were spent offshore charging the batteries. A few aircraft were seen, but these appeared to be on specific searches, as they flew high and fast, just passing over the area. In the afternoon of 11 May, a signal was received with instructions to head during the night for Smøla, an island south of Frohavet, where a German transport had been reported. Nothing was found, but another signal on the 12th gave orders to continue south towards Stadtlandet as other ships had been reported there. At 13:02 on the 13th, due west of Ålesund, a ship was sighted, hull down, near the coast, on a northerly course. Ingram surfaced and gave chase at full speed. Some fifteen minutes later, they were sighted themselves and the transport turned towards the coast in haste. *Clyde* opened fire from the deck gun, but the distance was too large and the shots fell short. By now, the transport had worked up a considerable speed too, and even at 21 knots, *Clyde* was hardly gaining at all. In addition, it turned out that the transport was well armed and started firing back. Although the shots were rather erratic, it made Ingram careful not to get too close too fast. By 14.30 the ship vanished in a rainsquall and, seriously annoyed, Ingram had to give up the chase. He had only an approximate knowledge of his own position due to the rapidly deteriorating weather and heading blindly for a dangerous coast, where there would be many hiding places for the German vessel, seemed pointless.[9]

The ship that *Clyde* had brushed with was the 7,851-ton auxiliary cruiser *Schiff 21 Widder* which Korvettenkapitän Hellmuth von Ruckteschell had taken to sea from the Elbe estuary as one of the first wave of merchant raiders on 5 May. On the way, she was attacked by *Snapper* on 6 May; *Snapper* fired two torpedoes, both of which missed, before being driven off by an escorting torpedo boat. The next day, another submarine was sighted and also chased away.[10]

After a pause in Bergen, *Widder* continued northwards on the 8th, Ruckteschell being extremely cautious, keeping everyone on board at action stations. British air attacks made him seek refuge in one of the fjords north of Bergen, though, where he repainted the ship and disguised her as the Swedish ore-freighter *Narvik*. This helped: when continuing once more on the 12th, she was not attacked again – until, that is, *Clyde* appeared over the horizon at full speed off Ålesund. At that time, the weather had deteriorated so much that the assigned air escort had turned back and, as she was about to leave the Norwegian coast that night, there was no naval escort. Changing course towards land, *Widder* tried to escape, but the submarine gave chase and after a while opened fire. Attempting to maintain his neutral disguise, Ruckteschell hesitated as he initially took the fire to be only warning shots. However, when it became clear that the submarine was gaining slowly on them and intensifying her fire, he eventually revealed his stern gun and returned fire, entering a gunfight that lasted for about half an hour. When eventually a new rainsquall hid his ship, Ruckteschell took *Widder* inside the fjords north of Stadtlandet.

The following morning *Widder* continued. Once more she was sighted by *Clyde*, lurking outside, but again the weather was on Ruckteschell's side. The escorting aircraft returned, keeping *Clyde* submerged, and as Ingram did not realise the German would be heading offshore, he waited in the wrong position and did not see the raider again. *Widder* eventually slipped through the Denmark Strait and over the next six months went on to sink or capture ten ships, totalling almost 60,000 tons, before returning to occupied France in October.

After a few more fruitless days off Stadtlandet, Ingram set course for Dundee, where *Clyde* arrived in the early morning of 17 May. From Dundee, Løytnant Haave was sent to the director of naval intelligence at the Admiralty, where he had a lot of important information to convey.[11]

By mid-May, the Kriegsmarine surface units that had survived Operation Weserübung started coming back into service and SKL believed that it would be appropriate to initiate naval operations off northern Norway to relieve the pressure on Narvik. Primary targets would be Allied naval forces and transports and the operation could be launched as soon as *Scharnhorst* and *Gneisenau* were ready. The ambitious operation was codenamed Juno and the battleships *Gneisenau* and *Scharnhorst*, the cruiser *Admiral Hipper* and four destroyers were eventually cleared for the operation. Trondheim, which would be the main base for the operation, had been fortified, and ammunition, fuel and stores had been brought in. One of the supply convoys was that of *Alstertor*, *Samland*, *Huascaran*

Trondheim harbour in June 1940. The battleship on the left is *Gneisenau*; *Scharnhorst* is to the right and the cruiser *Admiral Hipper* is at the back. Several destroyers and supply ships are seen to the right. (Author's Collection)

and *Palime*, of which the latter never arrived, having struck a mine laid by *Narwhal* off Jæren (see chapter 20). Numerous R-boats and minesweepers, including captured Norwegian vessels, had also been sent to Trondheim in order to enhance the mine and anti-submarine defences.

At 08:00 on 4 June, Admiral Wilhelm Marschall took his fleet to sea from Kiel through the Danish Belts. Dawn on the 6th found the German ships 100 miles off Stadtlandet: heading north at 24 knots, still undetected, in light rain and variable visibility. The events that followed are beyond this account, but over the next few days the carrier *Glorious*, the destroyers *Ardent* and *Acasta*, the naval tanker *Oil Pioneer*, the trawler *Juniper* and the troop transport *Orama* were sunk. By nightfall on 9 June, the German ships had dropped anchor in Trondheim harbour, *Scharnhorst* with damage from a torpedo fired from *Acasta* as she was being sunk. *Scharnhorst*'s damage was severe, but could be patched up sufficiently within a few days for a safe return to German dockyards.[12]

Meanwhile, it had become clear to the German High Command that the Allies were in fact evacuating Norway and there was little time to lose. After refuelling, the fleet was ordered to resume operations against convoys reported off Lofoten. *Gneisenau*, *Admiral Hipper* and the destroyers *Hans Lody*, *Karl Galster*, *Hermann Schoemann* and *Erich Steinbrinck* pulled anchor at 09:00 on 10 June. After clearing Frohavet in the early afternoon, the ships worked up to 27 knots. Shortly after, some of the lookouts on *Hipper* reported a brief sighting of a submarine on the surface. It was only visible for few moments and all those who saw it were certain it had its periscope up. Hence, it seems the submarine had broken the surface involuntarily when coming up to periscope depth. Nevertheless, the departure had been compromised and with superior British forces reported by reconnaissance aircraft further offshore, Admiral Marschall chose to abort the sortie with the consent of Gruppe West. The ships turned back towards Trondheim at 20:10.[13]

The submarine sighted from *Hipper* was *Clyde*. Lieutenant Commander Ingram had sailed from Rosyth on 4 June for a second patrol off central Norway, virtually at the same time that Marschall was leaving Kiel. On the way north, there had been far more aircraft than last time, and the going was slower as he had to stay submerged for longer periods. Two fruitless days were spent off Stadtlandet, until at 12:30 on the 9th, a signal was received from VA(S) with orders to proceed to Frohavet off Trondheim again, as fast as possible. The presence of the German capital ships off Norway had become known to the Admiralty just hours before.[14] On the other hand, the German SKL knew that *Clyde* was operating off Trondheim the minute she arrived.[15]

At first *Clyde* was kept down by numerous aircraft sightings, but eventually the sky cleared and Ingram surfaced, increasing speed to 18 knots. At 18:55, while still west of Frøøyene, heading for the northern entry to Frohavet, *Clyde* was surprised by an He111 bomber diving out of the low clouds. No bombs were dropped, but the bridge was heavily machine-gunned as the boat crash dived. The aircraft remained in the vicinity for some time. Several other aircraft were also sighted and Ingram found it impossible to surface again. Something was definitely going on.[16]

The entrance to Frohavet was reached at 04:00 on 10 June. Aircraft were still continuously sighted above and reluctantly Ingram had to turn seawards a few hours later to try to find a quieter place offshore to charge the batteries. Surfacing close to land was not possible and during the morning less than one-third of the charge remained in the batteries.

Just after midday on the 10th, *Clyde* was some 13 miles north of Halten Lighthouse, still submerged and batteries very low, when Ingram sighted the masts of a 'pocket battleship and a *Hipper*-class cruiser' on a northerly course. They were well out of torpedo range and *Clyde* was not fast enough, even on the surface, to maintain contact. Annoyed, Ingram sent a sighting report and reduced speed to charge the batteries. With a few interruptions, having to dive for aircraft, the batteries were fully charged by 22:00, by which time course was once again set for Frohavet. At this time of the year at these latitudes, the night is very short, with less than four hours between sunset and sunrise.[17]

On receipt of Ingram's report, a Sunderland of 204 Squadron was flown off from Sullom Voe in the Shetland Islands with orders to search an area on either side of the reported course. As the ships had turned back, however, there was nothing to find. During the night, *Gneisenau*, *Hipper* and the destroyers re-entered Frohavet, once again sighted by *Clyde* at a distance. While Ingram had positioned *Clyde* in the central parts of northern Frohavet, the Germans chose the Inner Leads, hugging land behind Husøya.[18]

Lieutenant Commander Ingram and *Clyde* remained off Trondheim, but moved further north, on instructions from VA(S), towards Kya Lighthouse, where the German ships, should they attempt another sortie northwards, would have to leave the coast to pass round the Vikna Peninsula. Nothing much had happened during the week, except a few aircraft alerts and the usual charging routine, heading offshore during the few hours of darkness. The only ships sighted were a few fishing vessels and some coastal steamers close to land. Acting on a signal from VA(S) on the 18th, Ingram was hoping to intercept 'one cruiser and four destroyers' that had left Narvik a few days earlier on a southerly course, but these were not seen.[19] Instead, on the 19th, *Clyde* was attacked by an aircraft and had to make an emergency dive. This was one of *Gneisenau*'s own Arado reconnaissance aircraft. The pilot reported somewhat enthusiastically that he had sunk a large British submarine about 30 miles south of Halten.[20] This was not the case, though, and not long after the aircraft had gone *Clyde* was back on patrol.

By the evening of 20 June, *Scharnhorst* was sufficiently patched up and departed Trondheim for Germany, escorted by destroyers, torpedo boats and minesweepers.[21] At the same time, *Gneisenau*, *Hipper* and the destroyer *Karl Galster* also took to sea in order to make a diversionary attack on the Northern Patrol south of Iceland. As before, they stayed close to land through Frohavet before turning north-west towards open sea between Kya Lighthouse and Halten Island. Leaving sheltered waters, the three ships spread out, with *Gneisenau* and *Hipper* 2,000 metres (2,200 yards) apart and *Galster* in the centre, somewhat ahead, screening for submarines. One aircraft was overhead. Off land, they met a heavy swell, limiting speed to 18 knots and preventing initiation of a zigzag pattern. It almost beggars belief that the German C-in-C at the time, Vizeadmiral Günther Lütjens, found the A/S arrangements adequate. The presence of a submarine in the area had been reported repeatedly by SKL in the days preceding the sortie and had been confirmed by aircraft sightings.[22] The Seekriegsleitung had ordered all A/S forces on the Norwegian west coast to focus on the sea off Trondheim, but for some reason this had not been followed up. The poor weather was in the German's favour, but the total lack of A/S escort, except for one destroyer and one aircraft, is hard to endorse.[23] Even the cunning Kapitän zur See Hellmuth Heye of *Hipper* seems to have found the arrangement adequate as he made no comments about the A/S measures at departure in his otherwise detailed and analytical diary.[24]

Admiral Hipper with *Gneisenau* ahead taking to sea from Trondheim in the evening of 20 June. The photo is taken from the destroyer *Karl Galster*. (Author's Collection)

At 21:50 on the 20th, on the surface in rough seas off Kya Lighthouse, another aircraft was sighted to the south and Ingram took *Clyde* routinely down. Some twenty minutes later, his moment had come:

> At 22:09 two large ships were sighted on the Starboard bow steering towards, about 2 miles apart and 9 miles distant apparently in line abreast. *Clyde* was fine on the Port bow of the Starboard wing ship. The mast of a third ship, thought to be a destroyer, was between the two. Clyde altered course to cross the bow of the Port wing ship and avoid the destroyer. Periscope observations were extremely difficult in the steep sea and the southern horizon was black and indistinct. It was several minutes before the three ships were identified as capital ships with a destroyer forming a screen ahead. Depth keeping presented great difficulty. Continuous high speed had to be used and the submarine trimmed eight tons heavy to prevent breaking surface while periscope observations were being taken, it being impossible to see clearly unless the periscope standards were awash.[25]

Range-taking was difficult, as the hull and waterline of the ships were not clearly seen in the high seas and drifting spray. In addition, due to the seas running, the men operating the hydroplanes had a tough job controlling *Clyde*'s depth and angle. Ingram ordered '28 feet', higher than normal periscope depth to have as clear a sight as possible, but did not risk taking too long over his observations from fear of breaking the surface. Coxswain Tom Moore held the boat steady at the right depth, though, and surfacing was narrowly avoided several times. Ingram also had invaluable support from his asdic operator, who, after some time, managed to pick up the German ships in his earphones.

Eventually *Clyde* was in the desired position relative to the target. At 22:32 BrT, Ingram fired the first torpedo, followed by five more at nine-second intervals, staggered for depth between 4 and 5.5 metres (13 and 16 feet). The aim-point was one ship's length ahead of the target, allowing for a speed of 20 knots. The distance to *Gneisenau* was around 3,600 metres (3,900 yards) with a track angle of 70 degrees (almost beam on).

Just after 23:30, one of *Hipper's* lookouts reported something to the north-east. It turned out to be nothing more than some rocks in the Vikna area, but while Heye and the whole watch were busy scanning the coast, an explosion was heard from the direction of the flagship. At first there was some confusion on the bridge of the cruiser, but when a torpedo track was reported between her and *Gneisenau*, Heye ordered 'full ahead' and 'hard-a-port', initiating a series of violent evasive actions.

After he had fired his torpedoes, Ingram altered course 60 degrees to the west and dived deep, expecting a heavy retaliation. About three minutes later one loud explosion was heard, indicating at least one hit. *Clyde* was trimmed heavy due to the high swell on the surface and in his eagerness to get away, Ingram took his submarine far deeper than intended, passing 75 metres (250 feet) before control was regained. The stern went even deeper, below 90 metres (295 feet) at one point, resulting in damage to the structure of the submarine. In his report, Ingram wrote that 'to the accompaniment of loud groaning noises, a 4" steel stay pillar in the after mess deck started bending visibly', adding that 'it is satisfactory to be now aware of the limiting depth to which a River-class submarine can be taken.' Truly a terrifying moment for all on board. Control was regained, however, and as the counter-attack was half-hearted, with only one pattern of eight depth charges being dropped, none of them close, Ingram was able to steer a steady course to seaward on one motor at dead slow. Some two hours later, at 01:00 on the 21st, *Clyde* surfaced to send an enemy report.[26]

Porpoise, further south, was on the surface at the time, charging her batteries, and picked up the signal. When an hour later, the Admiralty asked Ingram to repeat his message and received nothing, *Clyde* having been put down by an aircraft, *Porpoise* retransmitted the signal at 02:05. Hence, the departure of the German capital ships from Trondheim was not known in the Admiralty until almost 02:10 on 21 June.[27]

To Ingram's disappointment, just one detonation had been heard. The target's speed had probably been slightly overestimated and by aiming ahead, instead of the accepted centre, and firing at nine-second intervals instead of thirteen, as the target size should have required, the forward salvo had almost missed altogether. Only the last torpedo fired had struck the bow of *Gneisenau* – just. Vice Admiral Horton, although undoubtedly satisfied that one of his submarines had scored a hit on a German capital ship, found reason to issue a signal to all flotilla captains to inform the COs of their submarines that he was concerned over the non-compliance with the instructions for salvo firing. He added that 'it is to be most strongly stressed that the governing principle of any salvo, be it concentrated or dispersed, is that the centre of the spread must be on the centre of the target to be covered.'[28]

Due to the rough sea, *Gneisenau's* lookouts did not see the torpedo tracks until 23:35 German time, when the nearest was less than 300 metres (330 yards) astern to starboard. Two further tracks were seen to pass ahead. The submarine alarm was sounded and orders were given for an emergency turn to port. But it was far too late and one torpedo

Gneisenau alongside the repair ship *Huascaran* being patched up for the journey home. The temporary plating over the huge hole in the bow from *Clyde*'s torpedo can clearly be seen. (Author's Collection)

struck just aft of the starboard anchor, even before the rudders had begun to take effect from the helm. The 365 kg of Torpex in the torpedo warhead threw up a column of water when it exploded, but only a minor shock was felt aboard the ship. Few that did not directly see the torpedo and its impact realised what had happened. Eventually responding to the port rudder, the battleship turned through 90 degrees and continued away from the submarine with a minor loss of speed. Hardly any damage could be seen, even if a significant amount of plating had been ripped open. There were no casualties.

Karl Galster searched for the submarine without success until ordered to return to the flag and stand by to assist. *Gneisenau* had taken on quite a lot of water, and the two forward compartments were flooded. The magazines of 'A' turret just aft were unharmed though. Damage-control parties shored up the bulkhead, allowing for 19 knots as long as a course was held which prevented a heavy swell breaking over the bows. Once control was regained at 00:05 the course was set back towards Trondheim, where the ships dropped anchor once more at 10:05 on 21 June. More than 1,000 cubic metres of water had entered the bow of *Gneisenau* and she was markedly bow-down. At this point, Germany's operational surface naval strength was reduced to less than a dozen cruisers and destroyers.[29]

As the German ships dropped anchor in Trondheim, *Clyde* set course for home, in response to a signal from VA(S). She arrived in Dundee without incident on 24 June.

Loss of Thames

In Trondheim, the repair ship *Huascaran* came alongside *Gneisenau* and makeshift repairs were initiated, enabling transfer back to Germany – there were no docks in Norway large enough to accommodate her. These took longer than at first anticipated and not until 25 July could *Gneisenau* head for home. *Hipper* also left with the battleship, but she was detached at midnight for a diversionary operation towards the north.

Scouting ahead, *Hipper's* Arado, flown by Leutnant Frendenthal with Unteroffizier Koch in the back seat, sighted a submarine at 02:25 on the 26th, east of Nordøyan Lighthouse. Two 50-kg bombs dropped from 300 metres (1,000 feet) straddled the boat and, during a second pass, several hits were recorded from the 20-mm cannon. The submarine dived with an apparent list, leaving air bubbles and an oil slick. The claim for a sunken submarine was accepted and Admiral Marschall awarded the Iron Cross, First Class to the crew. The submarine in question was *Triton*, on patrol at the northern entrance to the Frohavet. Lieutenant Commander Watkins reported the attack, but also that he took his boat down to 70 metres (250 feet) and escaped unharmed.[30]

A string of Allied submarines had been deployed along the Norwegian coast, anticipating that the battleship would attempt to move home. *Trident* was just south of Trondheim, *Tribune* off Stadtlandet, *Severn* off Utsira, *Salmon* off Egersund, south of Lista and *Sunfish* off the entrance to Heligoland Bight. In fact, several of these boats were known about and a signal was sent from Gruppe West with warnings – one of which mentioned *Porpoise*, which was suspected of having laid mines off Grip.

Gneisenau's departure from Trondheim with four destroyers at first went unnoticed by the British and nothing untoward happened during the first day of the journey, except a few false submarine alarms that resulted in nothing. On approaching south-western Norway in the morning of the 26th, *Luchs* and *Iltis* came out from Stavanger to meet the battleship and her escort and fell in with the fleet at 12:45. They took up positions slightly ahead of *Gneisenau* and the cruiser *Nürnberg*, which had come up from Germany to take charge of the escort operation. The two large ships steered in line-ahead, the cruiser aft. *Iltis* was on the starboard or seaward side, *Luchs* on the port or landward side. Off Jæren, at 15:49, an explosion shook *Luchs*, which broke in two and sank in minutes without any signals being sent.

Near the time of the explosion, a torpedo track was reported by *Gneisenau's* lookouts and shortly after, *Nürnberg* reported having seen a periscope to seaward. It is therefore quite possible that *Luchs* ventured into the path of torpedoes intended for *Gneisenau*, even if Kapitän zur See Harald Netzbrand concluded that it must have been a mine that sank the torpedo boat.[31] Naval Command in Stavanger, where the survivors were brought in, was clear that, in its opinion, *Luchs* had definitely been torpedoed – partly due to the water depth at the site of the sinking, partly due to the accounts of the survivors. A brief anti-submarine search was initiated by the other torpedo boats but nothing was found and the ships were ordered to proceed after picking up survivors: 102 men perished and most of those rescued were wounded. None of them could shed much light over what had caused the explosion and, as floating mines had been reported in the area, the loss of *Luchs* was ascribed to one such at the time.[32]

Luchs being hit by the torpedo from *Thames. Gneisenau* is on the horizon. (Royal Navy Submarine Museum Collection)

None of the submarines deployed to search for the battleship reported anything that might match these events upon their return to base. The only possible culprit is *Thames*: she is officially listed as 'missing, believed mined' on the 23rd, though the date is highly uncertain. If she were still operational on the 25th, she would have responded to an order from Submarine Command received over the radio to proceed from her initial billet towards a position further north, which could have brought her into the path of the German squadron.

Lieutenant Commander William Dunkerley had taken her to sea from Dundee on 22 July to patrol in the North Sea, south of Stavanger. During the following days, several new orders were sent to *Thames*, sending her across the northern North Sea, partly to intercept what was probably one of the screening forces for *Gneisenau*'s squadron.

Assuming it was *Thames* that torpedoed *Luchs*, it is somewhat surprising that Dunkerley never sent a sighting report as he would have realised the importance of passing information of German battleships at sea to the Admiralty. As Dunkerley in all likelihood would have aimed his torpedoes at *Gneisenau*, it is possible that he did not realise how close *Luchs* actually was and that she unexpectedly ventured into the torpedo tracks. If so, perhaps *Thames* was damaged by the violent explosion too. Or perhaps she was damaged or even sunk in the counter-attack and had no time to transmit. Since the counter-attack appears to have been ineffective, it is perhaps most likely that Dunkerley managed to get his boat safely away on this occasion, only to venture into a minefield on his way back to base. If she was not sunk near the site where *Luchs* went down, it is

Thames. (Royal Navy Submarine Museum Collection)

perhaps more probable that *Thames* also became a victim of the German minefield 17 (see below).

Gneisenau reached Kiel on 28 July. Both battleships were now in Kiel and both were crippled, excluded from further sorties for most of the rest of 1940. *Hipper* eventually arrived at Wilhelmshaven on 9 August and was taken into the yard for a much-needed overhaul.[33]

Unknown Minefields

The long Norwegian campaign was over. The Allied submarines had, between 8 April and the end of July sunk well over thirty ships, including those mined, and damaged at least a dozen more. The largest of the transport ships sunk included the 8,036-ton *Stedingen*, the 8,579-ton *Bahia Castillo*, the 8,320-ton *Preussen* and half a dozen more ships over 5,000 tons. The largest warships sunk were the cruiser *Karlsruhe*, the Q-ship *Oldenburg* and the gunnery training-ship *Brummer.* Equally important, though, the heavy cruiser *Lützow* and the battleship *Gneisenau* were both severely damaged and would require lengthy time in the yards. In addition, A/S trawlers, minesweepers and torpedo boats had been sunk, decimating the already weakened Kriegsmarine further and spreading their resources critically thin.

The Allied Submarines truly earned the signal sent them by the former First Lord, now Prime Minister Winston Churchill: 'Please convey to all ranks and ratings engaged in these brilliant and fruitful submarine operations, the admiration and regard with which their fellow countrymen follow their exploits.'[34]

The success had not been gained without injury, though. Twelve Allied submarines were lost between 10 April and 31 July (see Appendix III). Numerically, this did not cripple the Royal Navy even if the Submarine Service itself was weakened. On a personal level, though, for the men remaining, it cast long shadows, adding a bitter taste to their own victories.

Almost immediately after the invasion of Norway and Denmark, the Kriegsmarine laid several minefields in the central North Sea and western Skagerrak to protect the inner areas of the sound. These fields consisted of a mix of surface mines and anti-submarine mines and would naturally affect British deployment of submarines – both through posing a direct threat before being discovered and by influencing transit routing and patrol areas after discovery.

The first of these minefields – actually a series of stripes, two or three rows deep, most containing both surface and anti-submarine mines – had already been laid in the early hours of 9 April: stripes I and II, in the area between Mandal in Norway and Hanstholm in Denmark. Two more stripes were laid during the night of 12/13 April: stripe III, west of Kristiansand in Norway, stripe IV off Hanstholm, south-east of stripe II. Within two weeks, these were augmented by a fifth stripe, stripe V, between stripes I and III. This meant that Skagerrak was closed except close to shore, in theory. Even if the stripes overlapped, it was quite possible, at a certain risk, to sail through them, especially as the knowledge of their whereabouts grew. The water was deep, the fields were far apart and there were gaps.

In the waters east of Skagen, towards the Swedish territorial limit, a rather denser minefield was laid, the so called Paternoster-Sperre. This field consisted largely of anti-submarine mines, 12–15 metres (40 to 50 feet) below the surface.[35]

There is no record of any Allied submarines triggering any of these mines in the period covered by this book. During the war thousands of mines were added to these first stripes, and by 1945 the entrance to the Skagerrak was pretty well closed to all traffic, with heavy guns having been added on both sides in addition to the minefields (see map on page 313.)

Further west, in the central and northern North Sea, another set of minefields was laid, which would be of far more consequence to the Allied submarines during 1940. For the Germans, this was seen as a north-westward extension of the Westwall, or 'declared area'.

Four main stripes were laid near the location 57°N, 5°E between April and July 1940. The first was Sperre 17, which was laid on the night of 29/30 April by the minelayers *Roland*, *Cobra*, *Preussen* and *Kaiser* covered by two destroyers and four torpedo boats.[36] The sea was quite rough at the time, but close to 500 EMD mines were laid, interspaced with around 1,000 *Sprengbojen* anti-sweeping devices.[37] Hence, this was not a dedicated anti-submarine minefield, but consisted of mines dangerous to all ships.

A week later, the same minelayers headed back into the North Sea, this time to lay Sperre 16, further to the south-west. This time they were screened by the destroyers *Richard Beitzen*, *Hermann Schoemann*, *Bruno Heinemann*, torpedo boat *Greif* and four S-boats. The mission became known to the British, and a British force of eight destroyers and the cruiser *Birmingham* was sent to intercept them. The S-boats spotted the enemy in time, though, and the minesweepers got away while the British destroyer *Kelly* was hit by a torpedo and seriously damaged.[38] The intended Sperre 16 was eventually laid by the minelayer *Grille*, escorted by the cruiser *Köln*, on the nights of 17/18 and 19/20 May, without incidents, resulting in two adjoining fields: 16A and 16B.

Later, in mid/late July, Sperre 19 and Sperre 18 were laid north and west of the first two stripes. Each of the latter stripes consisted of more than 600 mines and at least as many *Sprengbojen*.[39]

These minefields were to have a profound effect on the Allied submarines and their deployment off the Norwegian coast. It has not been possible to find specific evidence that the Admiralty or VA(S) knew the precise locations of the fields. In a document sent to the Dutch Naval authorities from the Royal Navy Historical Branch in 1951, related to the loss of *O13* and *O22* (see below), it is stated that 'German minelaying had been on a more extensive scale than was realised by the Allied Authorities and, from post-war research, it appears that [. . .] submarines were routed through recently laid axis minefields.' In the accompanying map, the two stripes of Sperre 16A and 16B are marked roughly in the correct place, as are 18 and 19. Sperre 17, however, is marked in the wrong location. Hence, it is safe to assume the knowledge was no better ten years earlier.[40] Accepting this, it is likely that these areas, in particular that of Sperre 17, may contain one or more as yet undiscovered submarine wrecks. *Thames, Orzeł, O13, Narwhal* and *Salmon* have not yet been found and at least the first three may well be discovered in the area of Sperre 17. Sperre 16A and 16B have both been thoroughly searched by the Dutch and Polish navies and no submarine wrecks have been found there.[41]

— 23 —

Allied Submarines

EARLY IN THE WAR, the British military was, in principle, reluctant to host foreign military personnel. Above all, it was believed that security would be an issue as well as the different organisational and training matters, along with language and culture. Legal questions were also raised, as well as financial concerns.[1] After the defeats in Norway, France and the Low Countries, however, this changed as Britain needed any ship, sailor, airman or soldier that the exiled Allies could contribute. Severe losses at sea in particular made the situation challenging as the emergency shipbuilding programme was a long way from providing the necessary replacements.

A handful of Polish ships – destroyers and submarines – that had escaped the German onslaught, had been integrated into the Royal Navy after September 1939. The results had largely been positive, and when the situation became more urgent, concerns were put aside. Agreements were concluded with each exiled government and the attention turned to the practical issues. On 18 November 1939 an Anglo-Polish naval agreement was signed in London, setting the terms and conditions under which Polish naval vessels should operate, subordinated to the British, including organisational and technical details. The Polish ships were to remain under free Polish sovereignty, manned by Polish officers and ratings wearing Polish uniforms. Subsequently, on 29 December the Polish Naval Command moved from Paris to London, where it would be headed by Kontr Admiral Jerzy Świrski. Similar agreements were later signed between the Royal Navy and the Dutch, Norwegian and Free French navies.[2]

For Allied submarines to operate as part of the Royal Navy, several challenges had to be met. The most obvious was armament. The torpedoes, mines and shells available were not necessarily of suitable dimensions and so, in many cases, the boats had to be rearmed. Communication, routines and tactics also had to be learned by the foreign crews, at least to the extent where dangerous situations did not arise. To facilitate this and secure uniform communication procedures, correct use of cyphers and codes, and ensure orders and signals in English were properly understood, a British liaison detachment was placed on board each foreign boat. The team usually consisted of a junior officer, a signalman and a telegraphist. Such liaison teams were subsequently placed on board all Allied submarines and surface ships operating with the Royal Navy. The officers were usually junior and not intended to interfere with the command structure or give operational advice. Many developed a good rapport with the Allied crews, however, and became an integral part of the ship's team. The task of the British naval liaison officer (BNLO) varied significantly in difficulty, depending as much on the officer himself and his diplomatic abilities as the commander and crew of the boat on which he served. Naturally the BNLO had to be fluent in the language of the crew he worked with. The reports from the BNLOs available show that, in addition to communication, they also observed and reported back to the flotilla commander on the boats' technical characteristics, the performance of the crew and, not least, the captain and his ability to operate under wartime conditions (see page 232).

Polish Submarines

Arriving in Britain during September 1939, the Polish submarines *Orzeł* and *Wilk* needed extensive refit and repairs before they could be used for further war patrols. The crews were more than eager to get back to sea and fight the Germans, but their boats were not quite as ready. With *Orzeł* having been built in Holland and *Wilk* in France, neither could utilise British mines, torpedoes or shells without some rebuilding. After deliberations it was decided that the refit could take place in Dundee, without sending the boats to France or Holland. The crews were given a well-earned rest ashore while their boats were seen to.

Orzeł could use Whitehead 21-inch torpedoes with minor adaptations and these were provided in addition to a batch of French torpedoes sent over from Cherbourg. On the other hand, there was no breech-block in the deck guns, as these had been removed in Tallinn. A new block for the main gun had been ordered from Sweden, but never arrived in time to be installed. There was no rush, though, as ammunition of the correct calibre was not available in Britain anyway at the time, had the gun been operational. *Orzeł*'s double Bofors 40-mm A/A gun could have been made operational in Britain and ammunition provided, but red tape also prevented this gun from being set in working order. To give some A/A protection, a Lewis gun was mounted on *Orzeł*'s bridge. *Wilk*'s Hotchkiss A/A gun was found to be useless in heavy weather and replaced with two Lewis guns from British stocks.

The Polish boats did not have asdic and it was considered whether to have the equipment installed, both for communication and detection, as their hydrophones were of a similar quality to the average British ones. This would have required extensive training of the Polish crew, however, or additional trained British personnel on board to operate them, and neither boat ended up being equipped with asdic.

Orzeł returning to Dundee in April 1940. Note the absence of a gun on the foredeck. (IWM HU 76130)

After a few weeks at the yards, including having her tubes adapted for British torpedoes, *Orzeł* was assigned to the 2nd Submarine Flotilla at Rosyth with the pennant *85A*. The British liaison detachment at first consisted of Lieutenant Commander David Fraser with Yeoman of Signals Walter Green and Petty Officer Telegraphist Leslie Jones. After a few patrols, Fraser was replaced by the more junior Lieutenant Keith d'Ombrain Nott.[3]

At first, *Orzeł* was deployed escorting convoys in British waters, as an adaptation, before joining one of the convoys across the North Sea to Bergen in December. Tedious work, with orders to remain on the surface unless attacking an enemy surface ship, but a good way of introducing officers and crew to operating under British command. In mid-January 1940, the Admiralty cleared *Orzeł* for independent patrols in the North Sea and off the coast of Norway. The first patrols, in January, February and March in the North Sea, were largely uneventful. *Orzeł's* fifth war patrol in Allied service, on the other hand, when she sank *Rio de Janeiro*, would be of a very different character and give her an eternal place in the submarine 'Hall of Fame' – see chapter 13.

After the highly successful patrol in April, *Orzeł's* sixth patrol from 28 April to 11 May off the Norwegian coast south of Stavanger was disappointing, without any tangible results. *Orzeł's* seventh patrol commenced in the evening of 23 May, when Jan Grudzinski took her to sea from Rosyth. At first, they were sent into area A3, just west of the Westwall minefield. Subsequent signals moved *Orzeł* north, into area A1, west of the northern part of the German Declared Area. On 1 and 2 June signals from Rosyth ordered her to continue further north. Three days later she was signalled to end her patrol on the 6th and return to base. *Orzeł* failed to acknowledge receipt of these signals and did not appear in Rosyth as expected. On 11 June, she was officially recognised as missing, presumed lost, by the Polish Navy. Lieutenant d'Ombrain Nott, Signalman Green and Telegraphist Jones perished with their Polish colleagues.

In 1962 the British Admiralty made it known that British warships had laid mines around 57.00°N 03.40°E in late May, and that it had not been possible to inform all of the Allied ships in time, including *Orzeł*, of the existence of that new minefield. Hence, *Orzeł* could have been lost to British mines around 25 May 1940. Alternatively, while heading back to Rosyth between 6 and 8 June, *Orzeł* might have ventured into the new German minefield Sperre 17, which, unknown to the Allies, had been laid in late April. In fact, it is possible that both *O13* and *Orzeł* fell victim to the mines of this field within a few weeks of each other.

A third option, suggested by several Polish authors, is that *Orzeł* suffered some kind of technical problem while patrolling west of the Westwall and, instead of heading for her new billet to the north, set course for Rosyth more or less due west sometime on the 2/3 June. This is based on a German intercept of a signal from an unidentified Allied submarine signalling that she was about to leave area A1, returning to base. The German intelligence would not have invented such an interception and it must be assumed it is real, even if no record of the signal has been found in British archives. Most likely it was never received in Britain and *Orzeł* may have been the submarine attacked and claimed sunk by a Hudson from 224 Squadron on 3 June, 125 miles east of Rosyth. The wreck of *Orzeł* has not been found, in spite of several Polish search expeditions over the last few years. Until she is found, her fate remains a mystery.[4]

*   *   *

Wilk followed *Orzeł* to the 2nd Flotilla in December, but it was recognised that she would have to go back to the yards for a more complete overhaul during 1940, possibly in France. *Wilk* had the capability to lay mines, but the Polish naval attaché and RA(S) agreed that for now she should not be tasked with such operations, as negotiations with the French Navy regarding purchase of suitable mines needed to be concluded first.[5]

Wilk made her first two war patrols in December 1939 and January 1940, to the entrance of Skagerrak and off the coast of Norway. Both patrols were uneventful. There was some uncertainty as to how the foreign submarines would function under overall British command, and at first a rather senior officer, Lieutenant Commander Ronald Burch, was appointed to act as liaison officer on board. As most subsequent liaison officers in Allied submarines did, he made a confidential report on his observations during the first mission to the respective flotilla commanders, from where it was forwarded to RA(S) and later VA(S).[6] In his report after *Wilk*'s first patrol, Lieutenant Commander Burch reported most favourably on the Polish officers and men. In particular, he made positive remarks on their abilities as submariners and the enthusiasm with which they went to war.

In late April, Kapitan Marynarki Borys Karnicki took temporary command of *Wilk* as Boguslaw Krawczyk was sent to Sweden to attempt to negotiate the release of the three Polish submarines interned there (see chapter 7). At the time, she was in the yards at Dundee for repairs to her electrical systems, including motors and batteries. She was back at Rosyth by 4 June, and in the afternoon of the 18th, *Wilk* headed out and set course for the coast of Norway on her third war patrol. On the night of 20/21 June, halfway to Lista, something happened that has been the source of much controversy since.

First Officer Boleslaw Romanowski was on watch in the conning tower that night and later wrote a rather comprehensive story of how he perceived events had happened:

Left: Kapitan Marynarki Boguslaw Krawczyk of *Wilk*. *Right*: Kapitan Marynarki Borys Karnicki of *Wilk* and later *Sokol*. (IWM A1724 and A3419)

I had the night watch [...] Suddenly the signalman cried out: '10 degrees, a ship!' [. . .] 'Full speed ahead!' I shouted without taking my eyes off the observed thing. The diesels suddenly roared loudly, slowly picking up speed. 'It's a U-boat!' shouted the signalman. At the same time, I saw the characteristic silhouette of a submarine. 'Increase speed quickly!' I shouted. [. . .] We could see the enemy boat desperately diving to avoid the imminent collision. After reaching a speed of only 9 knots, the collision occurred. Our bow hit the U-boat in front of her deck gun, just as her deck had disappeared under water and her conning tower was about to submerge. The impact was very powerful. [. . .] 'What happened?' shouted the captain, Borys Karnicki, who had rushed to the conning tower. 'We ran down a U-boat sir!'[7]

According to *Wilk*'s official report, which differs somewhat from Romanowski's account, she was in the middle of the North Sea (at 56° 50' N, 03° 37' E) on 20 June when the submarine at 00:25 hit something in the water that 'appeared to lift her stern bodily out of the water and checked her forward motion twice within three seconds'. The officer of the watch (Romanowski), reported that he 'thought he had seen a dark shape which disappeared before *Wilk* reached it'. No flash or upheaval of water had been observed and an exploding mine was ruled out. Ratings in the forward part of the boat reported hearing a wire scraping along the hull immediately before the collision. Kapitan Marynarki Karnicki concluded in his report that he considered they had struck a submerged submarine, but did not elaborate why he thought so.[8]

The propellers and after hydroplanes were damaged and the jolting of the hull put the Sperry compass out of action. Some leaks occurred, and about 10 tons of water entered the engine room before they could be located and stopped. One of the leaks, into the mine compensation tank, could not be stopped. The patrol was initially continued, but eventually it was decided it was not possible due to vibrations in the propeller shafts and

Wilk in Rosyth, 1940. Note how the censor has obscured the pennant number, A64. (IWM HU76136)

the inability of the pumps to contain the leaks. *Wilk* slugged her way back to Dundee at 6 knots, arriving in the morning of 25 June.

When the boat was docked, it was found, somewhat to the surprise of the crew, that the damage was not as severe as expected. One blade of the port propeller was missing, but the damage to the starboard propeller and the hydroplanes just aft of them was minor. Apart from some leaks around the hydroplanes, the hull was intact. No sign of impact could be seen on any part of the structure. The limited damage and, above all, the lack of damage to the rudder and rudder guards, which extended well below the propellers and hydroplanes, make it unlikely that she had rammed and scraped across another submarine.[9]

There is no doubt that *Wilk* hit *something*. What she hit remains unclear, though. First Officer Romanowski was later adamant that he had seen another submarine before the collision. If this is true, there are two potential candidates: the Dutch submarine *O13* and the German *U122*, both lost around the said date. *O13* failed to return to Dundee on 21 June as expected (see below). It is unlikely, however, that *Wilk* had anything to do with her disappearance, as *O13* in all likelihood had a mishap in a minefield more than a week earlier. *U122*, a type IXB U-boat commissioned less than two months earlier, also vanished around this time. She left Kiel on 13 June but what happened after that is unclear. It is unlikely that Korvettenkapitän Hans-Günther Loof would keep his boat in the North Sea for seven days after leaving Kiel, though. Furthermore, it is normally assumed that *U122* was responsible for the sinking of the freighter *Empire Conveyor* south of Barra Head in the Hebrides in the afternoon of 20 June and she cannot have been in the North Sea at the same time. Most likely, the object *Wilk* hit was a *Sprengboje* or anti-sweeping device that had come loose from the minefields Sperre 16A or 16B nearby. The fact that there was no explosion indicates that it had lost its anchor and was thus rendered safe. This is supported by the fact that the location given by Karnicki for the encounter is right between the two minefields.[10]

The damage to *Wilk* was quickly repaired and on 10 July, she left Rosyth for her fourth war patrol at the entrance to Skagerrak, south of Stavanger. The patrol was uneventful, except repeatedly having to dive for aircraft, some of which dropped bombs that were pretty close at times. On 21 July a large tanker was sighted, but there was a heavy escort, including aircraft, and *Wilk* could not get in position in time for an attack.

In early August, Boguslaw Krawczyk was back as commanding officer of *Wilk*, by now promoted to Komandor Podporucznik, equivalent to commander. Between then and January 1941, he took her out for five more patrols off southern Norway. These were largely uneventful, apart from the seventh patrol in October 1940. That time, numerous vessels were observed off Lista and Lindesnes. For a variety of reasons, though, *Wilk* could not get into a favourable position for an attack, except on 19 October when three torpedoes were fired at what was most likely the 2,439-ton Norwegian freighter *Betty* off Lista Lighthouse, without any result. Krawczyk was very disappointed and depressed after this failure, blaming his own lack of training and experience for missing his first real opportunity to inflict damage on the Germans.[11]

Technical defects were increasingly experienced on board during these missions, reflecting the age of the French-built submarine. In November 1940, she was transferred to the 9th Submarine Flotilla at Dundee, joining the Dutch submarines in the first truly

Allied naval unit of the war. At this time, many of the most experienced members of her crew had been transferred to man new Polish submarines being commissioned. Their replacements were often new to submarines and, in spite of their enthusiasm, the fact that *Wilk* was in need of increasing technical attention, coupled with the fact that the crew were less able to provide that, meant that she ended up needing more and more time in the hands of the depot staff between patrols. Hence her efficiency as a front-line unit was markedly reduced. After her ninth war patrol in January 1941, *Wilk* went to the yards for a major overhaul. She remained in the yards for almost a year and was thereafter used as a training submarine until put in reserve in May 1942.[12]

Dutch Submarines

De Koninklijke Marine or the Royal Netherlands Navy, had thirty submarines in commission in 1940, most of them large boats stationed in the Dutch East Indies. These overseas submarines had no names, but were prefixed with a 'K' followed by a Roman numeral. The home-water boats were smaller, suited for North Sea work and prefixed 'O' followed by an Arabic number.[13] In 1937, however, all Dutch submarines were renamed with 'O' prefixes and a more flexible practice started with regard to home or overseas deployment, largely as the Royal Netherlands Navy could ill-afford to build boats with geographic limitations of employment. The oldest submarine in commission was *O8*, which had been in service with the Royal Navy during WWI.[14] About two-thirds of the rest were built and taken into service between 1920 and 1935. These were sturdy boats with strong hulls but the oldest of them were rather outdated by 1940.

Two mine-laying submarines, originally designated *K XIX* and *K XX*, were eventually commissioned in July and August of 1939 as *O19* and *O20*, respectively. The mines were carried in ten external shafts amidships on each side, each containing two mines, one above the other, copying the French Normand-Fenaux system. They were also equipped with experimental ventilation air ducts known as the *snuiver*. This extended above the surface when the boats were submerged at periscope depth and allowed the diesel engines to be run while under water. The technology was further developed by the Kriegsmarine during the war as the *Schnorchel* and, after the war, eventually used by the Royal Navy as the 'snorkel' or 'snort'.[15] The final group of Dutch submarines built before the war, *O21* to *O27*, were basically similar: advanced, modern submarines, that were strong and well constructed. Not equipped for mine-laying, though, they were smaller and more suited for North Sea operations.[16]

O21, under Luitenant ter Zee 1ste Klasse[17] Johannes van Dulm, and *O22*, under Luitenant ter Zee 1ste Klasse Albertus Valkenburg, had just finished their trials and working-up periods when Germany attacked Holland on 10 May. The two boats, which were nearly complete – except there were no torpedoes or deck-gun ammunition on board – were hastily made ready to sail to Britain, once the news of the attack broke. It was soon clear that the brunt of the attack was coming overland or by air, and the contribution from the submarine arm in the defence of the country at this stage would be limited. Departing Vlissingen in the afternoon of 10 May, escorted by auxiliary patrol vessel *BV37*, they

Dutch submarine *K XVIII* nearing completion at the naval yard in Schiedam, Holland, in January 1934. She was the last of a series of five. Note the swung-out central torpedo tubes: a special feature of Dutch submarines. *K XVIII* did not see any action in the North Sea. She suffered extensive damage from depth charges and was scuttled by her own crew after the Japanese invasion in Surabaya. (Author's Collection)

Conditions were not particularly better in Dutch submarines than in any others at the time. This is the torpedo storage room of *O13*. (Traditiekamer Onderzeedienst)

Luitenant ter Zee 1ste Klasse Johannes van Dulm at the periscope of *O21*. (Traditiekamer Onderzeedienst)

arrived in the Downs the next morning, from where they were ordered to continue west towards Portsmouth.

On 10 May, the day of the attack, *O13* was on patrol off the Dutch coast under the command of Luitenant ter Zee 1ste Klasse Eduard Vorster. She was repeatedly attacked by German aircraft and it was decided to withdraw to British waters for safety. Escorted by the minesweeper *Jan van Gelder*, *O13* arrived in Portsmouth at midday on the 12th.

The still-incomplete *O23* and *O24* were transferred from the Rotterdam Droogdok yard to the nearby Lekhaven docks and then camouflaged in order to keep them out of the hands of German paratroopers who had been seen landing outside the town on 10 May. Both boats had been commissioned, but had not completed their test programmes and were still missing much of the equipment they should have had on board. *O24* had not even started her diving tests and had not been submerged yet. From the naval headquarters in The Hague came orders that the boats should not attempt to escape to Britain as German aircraft had been observed dropping mines in the Waterweg channel.

On the 13th, Luitenant ter Zee 1ste Klasse Gerhard Koudijs took command of *O23*, while Luitenant ter Zee 1ste Klasse Gerardus van Erkel took command of *O24*. Conferring between themselves and with any other officers who could be contacted in the chaos that currently reigned, it was decided to leave for Britain that same evening, in spite of orders to stay and the potential risks of crossing the Channel unarmed on the surface. None of the submarines had torpedoes, guns or ammunition on board. On the Nieuwen Waterweg they hugged the northern wall and got safely through, cutting a barrier at the mouth of the channel using their net cutters.

At sea, as dawn broke, the risk of being discovered by German aircraft was acute, and both submarines were taken down – even *O24*, in spite of never having been submerged before. As things turned out, the submarine was too heavy and she sank 'like a brick' and hit the sandy bottom heavily. Water depth was around 35 metres (115 feet) at the site, but as there was sufficient air and they had fully charged batteries, van Erkel coolly decided that they were at a good location for some rest and ordered the engineering officer to keep watch and everybody else to sleep for the rest of the day. After a while, however, the boat started leaking. Not dramatically, but enough to be worried as the pumps quickly stalled from sucking up junk from the uncleaned bilges. The compressed-air system was also leaking. Van Erkel had no choice but to surface again, while it was still possible. On the surface they were sighted by a lone German fighter, but, after some strafing, he gave up and left O24 to sail for Britain on the surface.[18] She arrived at the Downs during 14 May, as did O9, O10 and eventually O23 the following night. They were all hurried on to Portsmouth, from where O23 and O24 were transferred soon after to the Thornycroft shipyard in Southampton for completion. In all, seven Dutch submarines made it to Britain.

O14 and O15 were in the Caribbean in May 1940. There was no need for them there and, in August, O15 sailed to Halifax for repairs and overhaul before being taken into service with the 2nd Flotilla under British control; she was used in Canada for A/S training of the rapidly expanding Canadian Navy. O14 arrived in Halifax in late September. From there, she joined convoy HX-79 for Britain in early October. En route, the convoy was heavily attacked by U-boats, with twelve ships being sunk. Three torpedoes barely missed the Dutch submarine. In Britain, O14 was attached to the 7th Flotilla at Rothesay and used for A/S training before being taken to the yards for repairs and overhaul in late December.[19]

Back in Holland, O8, O25, O26 and O27 were captured at the Wilhelmsoord naval base at Den Helder on 14 May 1940 and eventually taken into service. O11 and O12 were scuttled but later raised.[20]

The first Dutch submarine to be declared operational was O13. After a brief patrol in the Channel during the evacuation from France and following communication trials, she was attached to the 9th Flotilla in Dundee under British operational control. On 12 June Ltz1 Vorster took his submarine to sea. The assigned billet was at the entrance to the Skagerrak, just north of the German Westwall. Nothing was heard of O13 after she departed and on 19 June a signal was sent, instructing her to return to Dundee. When she did not show up on the 21st, as expected, anxiety rose. A few days later, VA(S) Horton had to acknowledge with regret that the boat was lost. In addition to Ltz1 Vorster and his thirty Dutch submariners, there were three British men on board O13: Lieutenant Brian Greswell, Leading Telegraphist Hugh McDonald and Signalman James Spettigue.[21]

The circumstances related to the loss of the O13 so far have not been fully ascertained, as the wreck has not yet been located. Most likely, she was lost in a German minefield, but there are also other theories. Some sources hold that O13 may have been the submarine that was attacked by two Arado aircraft from *Scharnhorst* on the 16th, although this was in all likelihood *Porpoise*. In other sources, it is speculated that the Polish submarine *Wilk* may have hit and run down O13, but this is very unlikely, as *Wilk* probably hit a drifting *Sprengboje* on that occasion, not a submarine (see page 305).

The most likely cause for the loss of O13 is that she hit one or more of the mines in the German minefield Sperre 17 at approximately 57° 00' N, 03° 40' E, the existence of

O13: still on patrol. Here seen at the Binnenhaven in Vlissingen. (Traditiekamer Onderzeedienst)

which was not known to the Admiralty at the time. The same field could possibly be responsible for the loss of *Orzeł* as well (see page 302). There were also British mines in the area but these had been laid in late May. *O13* left Dundee on 12 June though and it is virtually unthinkable that Ltz1 Vorster would not have been informed that mines had been laid close to his billet more than two weeks earlier. *Should* this have happened, though, it would amount to gross negligence at a very high level. On the other hand, in trying to avoid the British minefield, Vorster may well have taken a route that passed

Left to right: Signalman James Spettigue, Leading Telegraphist Hugh McDonald, with his son Brian, and Lieutenant Brian Greswell. (Traditiekamer Onderzeedienst)

through the German minefield Sperre 17, of which he presumably had no knowlege.[22] Until the wreckage of *O13* is found, the causes for her disappearance remain speculative.

During the course of the summer, *O9* and *O10* were briefly transferred to 5th Flotilla, performing a few patrols in the Channel, before they were assigned to the 7th and 9th flotillas, respectively, as training boats.

During June, *O21* and *O22* completed their outfitting at Portsmouth, including adaptation to British Mk IV torpedoes. After trials and exercises at Portland, both were assigned to the 9th Submarine Flotilla in Dundee.[23] After some final adjustments at the navy yard at Rosyth, including measures to reduce noise from various machines on board, the two submarines were declared operational, under British control, during July. By this time, Luitenant ter Zee 1ste Klasse Johan Ort had taken command of *O22*, while Ltz1 van Dulm was still in command on board *O21*. In the evening of 30 July, the two Dutch boats departed Dundee for their first war patrols. Early next morning, they separated: *O21* heading for an area just north of Dogger Bank, with *O22* further north, between Dundee and Esbjerg.

At 16:02 on 1 August, a submarine was sighted on the surface by *O21*, which was still submerged. Identified as German, two torpedoes were fired at 16:15 from a distance of about 1,500 metres (1,650 yards). Both torpedoes missed – the submarine was most likely *U60*, which had left Kiel the day before – probably as she was going faster than estimated by van Dulm. A little later, *U60*, still on the surface, was also sighted by *O22*, patrolling

O22 making ready to depart from Dundee. (Netherlands Institute for Military History (NIMH))

further to the north. The distance was too great to chase, though, and all Luitenant Ort could do was submit a sighting signal. The next day, Oberleutnant Adalbert Schnee took *U60* into Bergen, probably without ever knowing that his boat had been sighted twice and fired at.[24]

In August, the North Sea appeared packed with U-boats: the next morning, another U-boat was sighted from *O22* at great distance, before finally, in the afternoon of 2 August, one was encountered close enough to risk an attack. Two torpedoes were fired at 16:20 from a distance of 4,000 metres (4,400 yards). To Ort's frustration, the torpedoes passed in front of the U-boat, obviously not going as fast as he had estimated, whereafter she altered course and sped away at maximum speed. The lucky opponent was most likely Kapitänleutnant Heinrich Liebe in *U38*. Both *O22* and *O21* returned to Dundee on 9 August. On both these occasions, it is quite possible that more success might have been achieved had four torpedoes been fired in a wider spread than just two.[25]

Between the end of August and beginning of October, *O21* made two patrols, each a fortnight long, off Korsfjorden, the southern entrance to the Bergen Leads. At this time, however, most German traffic was inside the Skagerrak, consolidating the forces in Norway, and no ships worth attacking were encountered, except on 6 October, when a U-boat was sighted briefly before it submerged. Two subsequent patrols between Utsira and Korsfjorden in December were also uneventful.[26]

O22 also had some uneventful patrols off the Norwegian coast near Bergen in August, September and October. Luitenant Ort received orders for a fifth patrol in early November. This time, the station was to be off Skudeneshavn, north of Stavanger, and *O22* departed Dundee in the afternoon of the 5th. On the 6th, a signal was sent to *O22* detailing a new patrol area 18 miles off Lindesnes. This signal was not acknowledged, however, and nothing more was ever heard from the Dutch submarine. On 22 November, *O22* was declared lost with all forty-six men on board. In addition to Luitenant Ort and his forty-two Dutch submariners, there were three British liaison personnel on board: Sub-Lieutenant Michael Jackson, Leading Telegraphist Joseph Carruthers and Signalman John Hancock.[27]

As with *O13*, the cause of the loss of *O22* has never been ascertained. On 8 November, close to the Norwegian coast off Lista, the German A/S vessels *UJ177* and *M1104* attacked a hydrophone contact that was moving slowly and leaving a trace of bubbles. Thirty depth charges were dropped in several attacks. No oil or debris was seen at the surface, but the submarine was presumed sunk as the contact and bubbles all but disappeared. If this was *O22*, however, she was not sunk on this occasion, but she might have been damaged.

On 13 November at 20:30 GeT, *U28*, homebound for Germany after her last operational war patrol (she was to be subsequently used as a training boat), reported a torpedo attack south of Egersund. In the logbook of *U28* Kapitänleutnant Günter Kuhnke recounted that:

> two heavy explosions were heard, quite near the boat. No explosions were seen, but most likely we were attacked by a submarine. The torpedoes must have passed behind us and exploded at the end of their run or on hitting the bottom. The attacking submarine was probably submerged, as there was a very clear moon.[28]

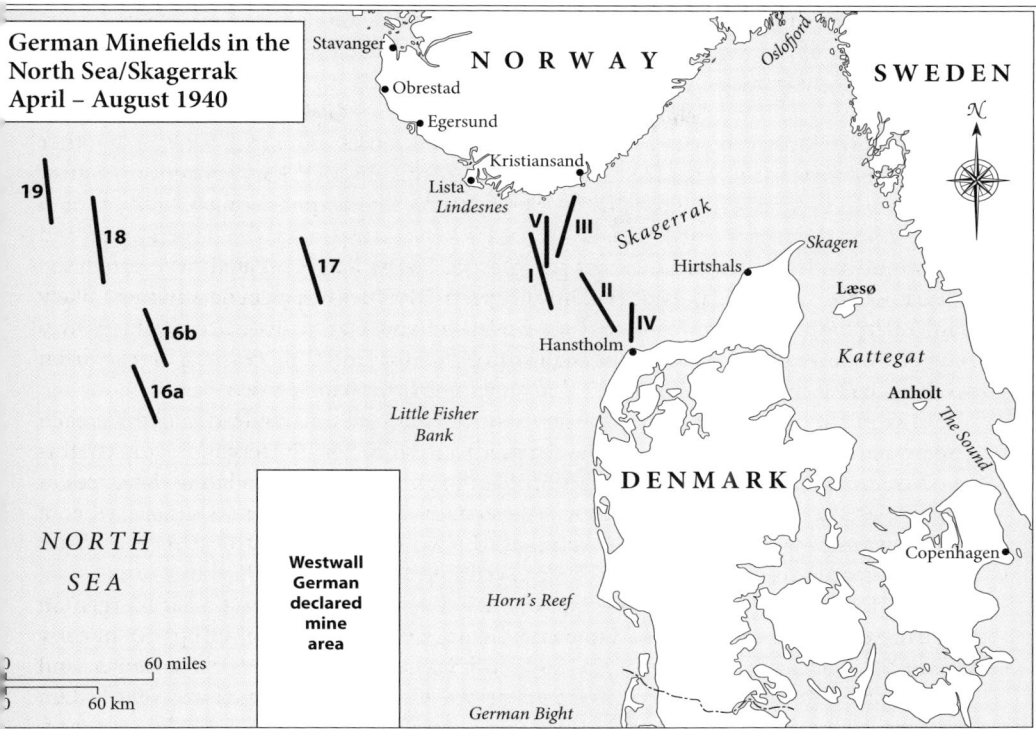

German Minefields in the
North Sea/Skagerrak
April – August 1940

Stavanger

Obrestad

Egersund

NORWAY

Oslofjord

SWEDEN

N

Kristiansand

Lista
Lindesnes

V III

I

II

Skagerrak

Skagen

Hirtshals

Læsø

IV

19

18

17

16b

16a

Hanstholm

Little Fisher
Bank

Kattegat

Anholt

The Sound

NORTH
SEA

Westwall
German
declared
mine
area

DENMARK

Copenhagen

Horn's Reef

60 miles

60 km

German Bight

Left: The last photo of *O22* and her crew before they left for their ultimate patrol. *Right*:
Luitenant ter Zee 1ste Klasse Johan Ort. (Traditiekamer Onderzeedienst)

If this was a torpedo attack, it may well have been *O22*, as no other Allied submarine was operating in this area at the time. If so, *O22* was therefore still operational on the evening of 13 November. It is quite possible that something went wrong during this attack, resulting in the loss of *O22*. Another possibility is that *O22* struck a drifting mine that had come loose from one of the many minefields to the west of her billet. The wreck of *O22* was found in 1993; the fact that the structure of the wreck does not appear to show any severe damage would imply that the drifting mine option is unlikely.[29]

In the yard at Thornycroft, Luitenant ter Zee 1ste Klasse Otto de Booij took command of *O24* in June while Ltz1 van Erkel transferred to *O23*. Completed in July, *O23* was transferred to the Scottish west coast for final trials and work-up. In early August, she was ready for operations and transferred to the 9th Flotilla at Dundee. *O24* took longer, being on the Scottish west coast in August, and only joined the 9th Flotilla in mid-September. The reason for the delay of *O24* was her hydrophones: the installation was of German design and was incomplete when she arrived in Britain. The Submarine Signal Co. in London supplied valves and other parts needed to complete the installation, but it never worked satisfactorily, in spite of a great deal of time and resources being spent on it, including numerous trials and adjustments.[30]

After two uneventful patrols with *O23* in the North Sea in August and September, van Erkel fell sick for a while and Luitenant Valkenburg took command of the boat. A further two patrols under his command were not very eventful either, in spite of patrolling what had been one of the hot-spots earlier in the summer, the Norwegian coast off Bergen and Stavanger, even going inside the fjords at times. The German coastal traffic was limited and well protected. South of Stavanger in November, *O23* was chased by A/S trawlers on a few occasions but Valkenburg had few problems outsmarting them. Van Erkel was back in late November, but *O23*'s last patrol of the year was as quiet as the four first.[31]

O24 was not much more successful in her first war patrols. Luitenant de Booij fired two torpedoes at a small merchant vessel and its escort off Bergen on 29 October, but both missed in the heavy seas. In December, after a third war patrol south of Stavanger, *O24* was taken into the Grangemouth dockyard for a refit.[32]

Norwegian Submarines

When the German invasion commenced on 9 April, the Norwegian Navy had nine submarines, eight of which were in service. The obsolete *A2*, *A3* and *A4* were on patrol in the Oslofjord. These submarines were of pre-WWI vintage, and were considered at least as dangerous to their own crews as to anything that might venture in front of their torpedo tubes. Running into German R-boats that were landing troops to capture the forts of the fjord, *A2* was depth charged and forced to surface, where she surrendered to avoid loss of life. The crew was taken on board the R-boats at gunpoint and *A2* was eventually towed to shore. The damage to her hull from the depth charges was significant and she was left as a wreck. *A2* is supposedly the oldest submarine ever to have been in battle. *A3* and *A4* remained submerged all day due to 'intense aircraft activity' and

Norwegian submarine *A2* captured by German R-boat *R21* at Melsomvik naval depot in the Oslofjord, 14 April 1940. (E Skjold Collection)

returned to base by nightfall, having achieved nothing. They were both scuttled on the night of 15/16 April.[33]

The slightly more modern *B2* and *B5* in Kristiansand and *B6* in Bergen achieved nothing and were eventually taken into German service as training boats.

In the far north, the submarines *B1* and *B3* were part of the so-called Ofoten Division guarding the strategically important ore-shipment facilities at Narvik. In the morning of 9 April, along with the depot ship *Lyngen*, *B1* and *B3* were deployed some 20 kilometres down the fjord from the entrance to Narvik on the northern side. In the darkness and the prevailing driving snow, the German destroyers attacking Narvik passed unseen. Later, when Narvik was taken, *B1* and *B3* were moved to Tromsø to operate off the coast of Finnmark where they would be out of harm's way from attacks by Allied ships.[34]

In June, the Allies decided to give up the fight for Norway and evacuate their forces. Many Norwegian officers and sailors wanted to continue the fight, however, and a large number of the naval vessels and auxiliaries still in service, including the submarines *B1* and *B3*, sailed for England. *B3* suffered an explosion in her battery compartment and had to turn back. She was eventually sunk, after equipment and provisions had been taken ashore. *B1* continued on to Britain, where she was used as a training vessel until 1944.[35]

Many of the Norwegian sailors who assembled in Britain volunteered for submarine duty – later in the war, three Norwegian-manned V-class submarines, *Ula*, *Uredd* and *Utsira*, operated out of Dundee as part of the 9th Submarine Flotilla, attacking German convoys on the Norwegian coast as well as landing saboteurs and intelligence groups. *Uredd* was lost with all hands in a minefield in February 1943.

Danish Submarines

In 1940, Denmark had a fleet of twelve coastal submarines. Eight of them were of WWI vintage and only the four H-Class boats from 1938–40, *Havmanden*, *Havfruen*, *Havkalen* and *Havhesten*, had any fighting value. These were 320/420-ton boats capable of 15/7 knots with five torpedo tubes, three bow and two stern. None of them saw any action during the occupation in April 1940.

All the Danish submarines were scuttled on 29 August 1943. As the Danish armed forces, including the navy, remained largely intact under German control, no vessels and few men escaped to Britain up until that point. Only after the disbandment in 1943 was a small Danish exile navy established, consisting largely of minesweepers.

— 24 —

A Summer of Grief

THE PERIOD OVER THE summer and early autumn of 1940 was to become the acid test for the British Submarine Service. After a slow and tedious start to the war, the occupation of Norway and Denmark, followed by the invasion of Holland, Belgium and France changed the situation completely.

Ben Bryant later wrote:

> The weather throughout the whole of that 1940 summer was glorious – but not for submarines. For us it was a terrible summer. It claimed half of our flotilla. But somehow through all my recollections of that grim time, the sheer beauty of the Norwegian coast remains the dominant memory. Yet every card was stacking against our submarines. The translucent seas had never a ripple to hide us from our foes above; the cloudless skies seldom darkened in those northern latitudes to give us the blessed shield of invisibility we craved to charge our batteries. There was the everlasting anxiety as to when we could venture up to change the foul air in the boat; the men panting like dogs in the carbon-dioxide-laden stench we breathed; the plaintively repeated signals from our base, asking for one of our flotilla mates to report their position – the sign that yet another was overdue. But all these things are unreal memories. The beauty remains.[1]

In a memorandum to his subordinates, the German Admiral der Norwegische Westküste, C-in-C Norwegian West Coast, Vizeadmiral Otto von Schrader, wrote on 26 May 1940:

> The British are deploying most of their submarines in Skagerrak and the German Bight. Some submarines are nevertheless observed from time to time in the areas off Feistein, Skudenes, Utsira, Bjørnefjorden, Korsfjorden, Sognesjøen Stadtlandet and Frohavet. At these points, no freighter shall travel unescorted. Inside the fjords or in the Leads, unarmed vessels shall act decisively if a submarine is sighted and try to ram if possible. Armed ships shall open fire and also attempt to ram. Fire shall first be aimed at the submarine's gun, then amidships at the waterline and the tower. 2 cm cannons are very effective against gun-crew and men on the bridge of a submarine.
>
> Active A/S measures against submerged submarines is not possible with the resources at hand; only in cases where a submarine has been positively identified through sightings of periscopes or boats on surface. If so, the use of depth charges <u>shall not be restricted</u>. Plaster the entire area. The opportunity will not return. Stay with the submarine as long as possible. Sometimes, oil traces will emerge or the boat will have to surface. If there are several vessels around, let them search the area thoroughly spread out, at low speed. Then remain stopped for ½ an hour to an hour. Continue the search for several hours.[2]

H49 in June 1935. (W&L)

No Restrictions

The German attack on France and the subsequent withdrawal of the majority of the French submarines from Allied service led to the almost immediate return of several of the ancient H-class boats from training to active service. *H28*, *H44*, *H50* and *H49* left Portland for Harwich on 10 May, with *H31* and *H34* following shortly after.

It was intended that these ancient boats would supplement *Ursula*, *Spearfish*, *Swordfish* and *Sturgeon*, operating from Blyth, off the Dutch islands south of the German Declared Area. A location that was challenging at the best of times due to sandbanks and currents, there were now German aircraft to look out for as well. Being close to land, where hectic activity was often going on, explosions, flares and various lights were observed during the night and the hydrophone operators kept those on duty busy reporting all kinds of sounds and echoes, both night and day. This made the patrols even more demanding, particularly as the atmosphere inside the small boats became foul towards the end of the day, reducing efficiency during the latter half of the submerged daytime. Fortunately for the men on these patrols, the Kriegsmarine still kept the majority of their naval A/S forces in the Kattegat and the Skagerrak, not off the Dutch and German west coasts.

In Britain, at the end of May 1940, following a conference between Horton and the Admiralty on the 22nd, several changes were made to the organisation and disposition of the Allied submarines. Two days earlier, German armoured columns had reached the Channel at Abbeville, thus severing communication between the British Expeditionary Force (BEF) in the north and the main French army in the south. Churchill was already considering withdrawal of the BEF, but few others were, and the capitulation of France with German-held ports south of the Channel was not even a scenario that had been contemplated.

Rosyth had become the main submarine base in Britain with the 2nd and 3rd flotillas operating from there. The 2nd Flotilla had eight T-class boats there in addition to

Porpoise, *Orzeł* and *Wilk*. Of these, *Triumph* and *Wilk* were refitting. Also at Rosyth was the 3rd Flotilla with six S-class boats and the French 10th Flotilla with six submarines, of which one was refitting. Supplying these units were *Forth*, *Maidstone* and *Jules Verne*, respectively. In addition, the 9th Flotilla operated out of Dundee, with *Clyde*, *Severn*, *Rubis* and three other French submarines. Many of these boats were kept almost constantly at sea during this period. The French boats, with the exception of *Rubis*, would all return to France in early June, following the events there. A further four T-class boats were under commission and would soon be ready for service. Several S-class and U-class boats were also under construction, but few of these would become operational until late 1940.[3]

At Blyth, the 6th Flotilla operated three S-class submarines and *Narwhal*, with *Ursula* refitting. At Harwich, three L-class boats remained under 3rd Flotilla. Later, a further five H-class submarines were mobilised from training duties at Portland and Plymouth and sent to Harwich to do anti-invasion patrols off Holland. At Portsmouth, a total of fifteen submarines were stationed under Captain(S) 5th, of which four were H-class and two O-class.

Lieutenant David Wanklyn took *H31* and *H32* on several North Sea patrols from Blyth in 1940 before he was appointed to *Upholder* in August 1940 and went to Barrow shipyard to see her completed. On 18 July, on his last patrol with *H31* before transferring to *Upholder*, Wanklyn was off the Dutch island of Terschelling, when, at 06:33, three trawlers were sighted to the west about 3 miles away. The vessels were steering a south-westerly course in line-abreast about 1 mile apart. It was not obvious to Wanklyn what they were doing. Assuming they were not mine-sweeping as they did not fly any signals, he thought they were either an A/S patrol or a small convoy. Either way, he decided they were worth a torpedo. There was a rapidly rising sea, and he assumed it would be 'a good prospect of escaping the surviving trawlers'.[4]

In fact, Wanklyn had sighted a group of three vessels from 12.U-Jagdflotille, *UJ125*, *UJ126* and *UJ 128*. They were on a sweep off the Dutch coast doing 5 knots, the normal speed for a submarine search. The lead boat *UJ126* was slightly ahead, using its active

H31. (Author's Collection)

S-Gerät, while the two other boats were line-abreast slightly behind and about 1,000 metres (1,100 yards) to each side, using only the passive Horchgerät listening device. The ships were on a routine war patrol, and somewhat surprisingly they had no idea that the British submarine was near. Kapitänleutnant Peters of *UJ126* was not even on the bridge, but in his cabin doing paperwork. The hydrophone operator of *H31* reported that he could clearly hear the trawler's echo-sounder transmissions, but as they appeared not to be in active contact with his submarine, Wanklyn chose to ignore the information.

About an hour after he had first sighted them, the nearest trawler was estimated to be about 800 metres (875 yards) away and Wanklyn fired one torpedo from number four tube. He choose an attack angle of 125 degrees, which would bring the three trawlers nearly in line, and aimed at the bridge of the nearest. Some two minutes after firing the torpedo, an explosion was heard on board *H31*, which by that time was below periscope depth and Wanklyn could not ascertain whether a ship had been hit. Only two vessels were identified in the subsequent chase, though, and it was assumed that the third was at least seriously damaged, if not sunk.

The trawler closest to *H31* was *UJ125* and it is obvious from a drawing in Wanklyn's report that he had aimed for her. On board *UJ125*, however, the surge from the firing of the torpedo was seen an estimated 200–300 metres (220–320 yards) away to port and orders for 'full ahead' and 'hard-a-port' brought the trawler out of harm's way. Before the other boats could be alerted by radio or semaphore signal, *UJ126* was hit forward on the port side. The torpedo broke the surface and was seen from the bridge of the trawler, but too late for any manoeuvring. As the torpedo hit *UJ126*, which was about 1,300–1,500 metres (1,400–1,600 yards) away, while Wanklyn had actually aimed at *UJ125*, which he believed was 800 metres (875 yards) away, he most likely overestimated the speed of the trawlers, missing his intended target and hitting the lead vessel instead.[5]

On board *UJ126*, a secondary, smaller explosion was felt shortly after the torpedo hit and it was believed to be a second torpedo. As only one was fired from *H31*, however, this must have been an internal detonation. A tilt to starboard developed and the foreship started to sink. It took about fifteen minutes for the trawler to go down and, except for four men killed outright, the remaining forty-two men had ample time to don life-vests and launch the floats before they went into the water. Eventually, thirty-seven of the crew from *UJ126* were picked up by the two other boats, including Kapitänleutnant Peters. Marinegruppenkommando West was later very critical of the fact that both trawlers had engaged in the rescue work and held that one would have sufficed while the other should have started hunting for the submarine. Only after most men had been rescued by the two companion trawlers did they start looking for the submarine. Wanklyn wrote:

> The enemy A/S frequency was 10.75 kc/s, having a fairly clear note. [. . .] It was easy to tell by the volume and quality of the note when contact was gained or lost. Transmissions were automatic at 4 second intervals. The enemy appeared to use the 'directing ship' method of attack. On one side an asdic would be heard, then H.E. (hydrophone effects) would start on the other side as the second ship came in to attack. Contact was lost as soon as *H.31* pointed towards the asdic, and the attack was either harmless or given up. The first charges were probably dropped indiscriminately. [. . .] The enemy retired to the eastward at 118 revs, two hours after the torpedo had been fired.[6]

12th A/S Flotilla. *UJ126* is nearest. (Author's Collection)

It soon became obvious that the old H- and L-class submarines were not up to the rigours of the North Sea. In particular, the batteries of these old boats needed a minimum of six hours for a full charge, which turned out to be far from easy when operating in an area with so much traffic at sea and in the air, even at night. In an emergency, both engines could be used for charging – this shortened the time needed, but required the submarine to be at anchor, or drifting. Also the telemotor pumps of the H- and L-class boats were very noisy, which among other measures made some commanders keep the periscope raised at most times, and brought it above or below surface by changing the depth of the submarine. The engines were well worn and were troublesome at times.[7]

In June, before going on patrol, *H44* had four pistons on the starboard engine replaced, with new piston rings fitted. During the subsequent patrol, the whole of the port engine as well as the remaining four cylinders of the starboard engine showed similar defects, progressively worsening every time the engines were used. In the end, it was only possible to obtain two-thirds power from the engines and the batteries were never more than half charged, in spite of the engine-room personnel working round the clock to make the boat serviceable. During this patrol, on 21 June, Lieutenant Edward Norman fired two torpedoes at the 844-ton Danish merchant *Alfa* off Texel, from a distance of 3,000 metres (3,300 yards). One torpedo hit amidships and the ship sank in three minutes; four of the Danish crew were killed.[8] On that occasion, there had been no escort as the ship was sailing alone, but otherwise the risks were as high, if not higher, for these old boats compared to the sturdier, modern ones, should anything happen.

On 30 August, submerged at 15 metres (45 feet), doing 1.5 knots halfway between Den Helder and Lowestoft, a wire was heard to scrape down the port side of *H44*. Lieutenant Norman wrote:

Increased depth to 65ft. Scrapings and bumps heard forward, abreast port plane. Shafting of foreplanes commenced to jerk and bumps and scrapes continued to be heard forward. It was evident that there was some obstruction though the trim was not affected. Worked fore planes through full limits and noise ceased. Decided to surface to see if there was anything hung up on the foreplanes. Altered course slowly to 180° to avoid heavy rolling and the increased possibility of exploding a mine on surface due to swell. . . . Commenced slowly to surface, being careful to keep boat on even keel. . . . At periscope depth a mine was observed apparently being towed about 4ft clear of stern by the starboard after plane or rudder. After surfacing, increased speed and put helm over and mine broke adrift. Stopped for a few minutes and endeavoured unsuccessfully to sink mine with Lewis gun fire.[9]

The mine had numerous horns that were not visibly damaged, so the shaken crew were lucky that this was one of the mines where the self-disarming mechanism actually worked as the mine broke loose. There is no doubt that, had the mine exploded, it would have been the end for *H44* and most men on board. These old hulls could not sustain the type of damage that an exploding mine would cause. Less than an hour later, two more mines were observed one on each bow. These mines were obviously still attached to their anchors and fully armed.[10]

On 16 September, Lieutenant Michael Langley of *H49* fired four torpedoes at a large convoy. Two explosions were heard and it was assumed that two torpedoes had hit one of the ships as disintegrating noises were heard shortly after. The torpedoes had actually hit the tanker *Ill*, but she was in ballast and able to absorb the damage and limp to port. Otherwise, these anti-invasion patrols were rather uneventful. Nevertheless, the patrols allowed the flow of new officers and men, who were to man the boats being built as fast as the capacity of the yards permitted, invaluable experience and 'on the job training'.

Following the losses of submarines to suspected German minefields in May and June, VA(S) adjusted the submarines' transit routes through the eastern part of the northern North Sea. This caused some confusion and at least one near-disaster. On 22 July, *Clyde* was on her way back from a relatively uneventful patrol off Stadtlandet, between Bergen and Trondheim. At the beginning of the patrol, both *Taku* and *Triad* had been sighted, challenged and recognised. But on the way home, things almost went wrong. At 23:36, having just surfaced some 100 kilometres west-southwest of Stavanger to charge the batteries, another submarine was sighted to the north-west, in the aft sector of the port lookout. The information available to Commander Ingram led him justifiably to believe any other Allied submarines in the area would have left by the time he approached. Quite the contrary, the signals he had received made him believe there was a high chance of encountering U-boats. Hence, when the other submarine was sighted, he dived quickly without attempting any identification or signalling and altered course to intercept. The other boat could not be seen through the periscope though and he resurfaced, trimming *Clyde* down instead, with only the tower above the surface.

In this way, the other submarine could be seen again and a few minutes before midnight, from about a mile away, six torpedoes were fired. For once, though, Ingram had got his estimates wrong, and the fruit machine gave his torpedo officer the wrong feedback, so they all missed. This was fortunate, as the other submarine was none other than *Truant*. Lieutenant Commander Haggard was supposed to have vacated the area earlier that day but had been delayed in setting course for home and had no appreciation of the danger of the situation. With things calmed down, sub-sea contact was established between the two submarines by asdic. Shortly after, both surfaced, exchanged signals to verify their identities and proceeded in different directions in order to use the few remaining hours of semi-darkness to charge their respective batteries.

It had been far too close for comfort and only a few miscalculated knots from another *Oxley*-type disaster. Ingram was completely exonerated as *Clyde*, according to Horton, was in an area where he had 'every expectation of sighting a U-boat and was therefore keenly anticipating it'. Nevertheless, VA(S) issued instructions to his flotilla commanders and senior officers to discuss with their COs 'the importance of withholding attack until the target is definitely identified on occasions on which there is any possibility of a friendly submarine being in the vicinity' – though it was hoped this would not conflict with the necessity to act with determination and haste if it indeed was an enemy submarine that was encountered.[11]

Slender Contours

On 31 July, *Spearfish*, under Lieutenant Commander John Forbes, put to sea from Rosyth for another patrol off the Norwegian coast. In the afternoon of the next day, 1 August, they were some 180 miles west of Stavanger, approximately midway between Norway and the Orkneys. Unknown to Forbes, the German U-boat *U34* was also approaching the same area from the north on its way back to base in Wilhelmshaven, completing a remarkably successful patrol.

The Commander of *U34*, Kapitänleutnant Wilhelm Rollmann, was four days away from his 33rd birthday and must have been in an extraordinarily exultant state of mind. Since leaving Germany over a month earlier, he had sunk twelve ships, totalling over 50,000 tons, including the British destroyer *Whirlwind*, and he knew he was returning to a hero's welcome. The patrol had included a brief docking at Lorient to take on fresh torpedoes, but now there was only one torpedo left in one of the bow tubes. The course for the last three days had been homeward bound, from Rockall Bank, north of Shetland and into the North Sea. During the 1 August, Shetland had been left behind to the west and in the afternoon, they were level with the Orkneys.

At 18:17, a 'slender object' was sighted on the horizon by the lookouts of *U34*, which was on the surface at the time. Rollmann dived and gave chase:

> Discern a submarine sailing straight towards us. The slender contours first seen over the horizon, can now be recognised as the two tall periscope casings. Gradually, the conning tower of the submarine comes into sight. Enemy course is 30°. Difficult to make out which type it is. Decide to position myself for an attack. Can see that it is a *Sterlet*-type submarine. Course and speed are difficult to determine. At 19:04, I fire a bow-shot after first having closed at high speed and maximum speed for a while to reduce the distance. Torpedo set to run at 2 metres. Opponent is doing 9 knots. Hit forward, 20 m from the bow. Running time one minute, 46 seconds, which means

The type VIIA boat *U34*. In seven war patrols under Kapitänleutnant Wilhelm Rollmann during the first twelve months of the war, she sank nineteen ships, accounting for 92,000 tons. (Author's Collection)

he was 1,610 metres away. Huge explosion which is felt inside our boat despite the distance. Assume the submarine's own torpedoes must have detonated as well. The boat sinks within 2–3 seconds. Large pieces of wreckage fly through the air.[12]

As what remained of *Spearfish* took its last dive, Rollmann took *U34* to the surface and approached the area of the explosion. Unbelievably, one man was found swimming among a few pieces of debris and brought on board. The sole survivor of *Spearfish*'s forty-two-man crew was Able Seaman William Pester. It was his first war patrol and he was a last minute 'pier-head jump' replacement, coming on board literally as Forbes cast off from Blyth, heading towards Rosyth to load torpedoes. At the time of the explosion, Pester was on duty as a lookout on the bridge together with Lieutenant Commander Forbes and another officer. The strap of his binoculars caught on the gyro repeater travel bar and he was dragged down with the wreckage, but managed to free himself at the last moment, drifting up to the surface, to be picked up by *U34*.[13]

In Wilhelmshaven, two days later, an excited C-in-C U-boats Konteradmiral Karl Dönitz waited with the Knight's Cross for Rollmann in recognition of outstanding achievements. His recent experience was considered so valuable that he was ordered ashore to a position as instructor at the 2.ULD, a training and tactical operations unit.[14]

At 22:18 on 3 August, *Triad* was on the last day of an uneventful patrol north of Bergen. Commander Eric Oddie had just taken his boat down, when loud diesel engines were picked up on the hydrophones from another submarine on the surface. The night was dark, and through the periscope Oddie could only see the dim outline of the other boat, so he decided to give chase on the surface. That seemed to work well and he called the gun crew to come on deck and man the 4-inch gun. Three rounds were fired at a range of some 3,000 metres (3,300 yards) before the U-boat was lost to sight as she dived. No hits were observed.

The quarry was the type VIIB boat *U46* under the command of the 29-year-old Oberleutnant Engelbert Endrass. *U46* was Endrass's first command and this was the start of his second patrol as CO.[15] They had left Kiel two days earlier and, after passing through the Kaiser Wilhelm Kanal and a brief stop at Heligoland, were now heading for the Atlantic. During the day, the radio had stopped working and Endrass was already contemplating entering the newly established U-boat base in Bergen, should it not be possible to repair it while at sea.

The gunfire came as a great surprise onboard *U46*, which had been on the surface charging for about an hour and a half. An emergency dive put *U46* out of harm's way, however, after the third round from *Triad*. Oddie took *Triad* down too, to pursue the U-boat and avoid becoming a target himself. Contact with the U-boat was obtained by asdic and Oddie gave orders to prepare to fire torpedoes and stand by to ram. Before any of these actions could be carried out, though, contact was lost and no more heard from the opponent.

Propeller noise and asdic impulses from the stalker were heard on board *U46*, but when Endrass brought his boat to periscope depth and surfaced a quarter of an hour later, there was nothing to be seen: *Triad* had lost contact. At this time, the radio operator reported that he could not repair the radio and *U46* turned north-eastward, heading for Bergen and repairs.

Triad was back in Rosyth at 19:45 on 4 August.[16]

The type VIIB boats *U45* and *U46* in the locks at Brunsbüttel. *U45* was sunk south-west of Ireland with all hands in October 1939 by British destroyers *Inglefield*, *Ivanhoe* and *Intrepid*. *U46* made thirteen patrols, sinking twenty ships for 85,792 tons before being retired as a training boat in September 1941. (Author's Collection)

Regrouping

When Mussolini finally found the time opportune to enter the war on 10 June 1940, the strategic situation for Britain and the Royal Navy changed totally. Overnight, some 110 Regia Marina submarines became alien in the Mediterranean, threatening vital French and British supply convoys.[17] During July and August, the naval war in the Mediterranean slowly commenced. At the time, there were twelve British submarines in the Mediterranean, four operational at Malta (plus two refitting) and six in Alexandria. Two were minelayers, *Grampus* and *Rorqual*, the rest O- and P-class boats transferred from the Far East.

These were not suited or trained for coastal operations and within three weeks three of the four Malta-based boats were lost off Italy: *Grampus*, *Odin* and *Orpheus*, all on their first war patrol. Within another month, two more boats, *Phoenix* and *Oswald*, had also been lost. This required a rethinking and reprioritisation of the resources and, for a while, British submarines were instructed to stay away from the Italian coastline, unless pursuing obvious targets, to avoid minefields and near-shore patrols.[18] In July/August, five T-class submarines, *Triad*, *Tetrarch*, *Triton*, *Truant* and *Triumph*, were sent to reinforce the 1st Flotilla in the Mediterranean. Matters in home waters still needed priority, though, and it would take some time until the immediate danger of a German invasion had receded and the transfer of submarines to the Mediterranean could commence in earnest. By the end of 1940, *Triad* and *Triton* had been lost with all hands, as had *Rainbow* and *Regulus*, transferred from Singapore in July and August. The total loss of British submarines in the Mediterranean in 1940 was thus nine, compared to the North Sea and the Atlantic where the number was fifteen, plus four Allied boats.

Following the Franco-German ceasefire in the early morning of 25 June, the Kriegsmarine established bases at Cherbourg, Brest, Lorient, Saint-Nazaire and La Rochelle among others. This naturally changed the whole strategic situation in the Atlantic, giving the U-boats far less transit distance to their hunting grounds. Almost instantly, it also created a new situation as it increased fear of a German invasion of Britain further, putting anti-invasion reconnaissance and defence as two of the most prioritised tasks for the RAF as well as the Royal Navy. For both, there was the added challenge of German bombing of ports and bases in the south and west, rendering the Channel area unsafe for the extensive training needed to cope with the expansion of the British armed forces. Until the summer of 1940, training of submariners and new-built boats had largely taken place out of Portsmouth, while the A/S training had focused on Portland, combining the two as much as practicable.

Based on suggestions from VA(S), it was decided in early July 1940 to move the A/S training to the Clyde, together with torpedo trials and working-up practices of new submarines, including the sea-training part of the qualifying courses for submarine commanders. For this purpose, the 7th Submarine Flotilla was set up at Rothesay on the Clyde in June/July, with Captain Roderick Edwards in command.[19]

C-in-C Home Fleet, Admiral Forbes, wanted submarines to operate in northern British waters against German U-boats passing through into the Atlantic. The Admiralty rejected this, however, partly as they considered the larger British boats at a disadvantage against the nimbler German boats, and partly as the presence of Allied submarines in the area would restrict the effectiveness of the A/S forces due to the difficulties of identification.

Instead, to keep German A/S resources busy and spread out as much as possible, a number of boats were sent to patrol various areas off Norway in late June and early July, in spite of the still limited hours of darkness for charging the batteries.

On 25 June, attacking a small convoy off Skudeneshavn, *Snapper* sank one of the escorts, the 286-ton trawler *V1107 Portland* of 11.Vorpostenflottille. The resulting explosion was huge, probably setting off the trawler's own ammunition and she went down very fast. Only two men were rescued, both seriously wounded. One of the other ships of the convoy later reported being missed by a torpedo by no more than a metre.[20]

As one of the most experienced submariners, Lieutenant Commander Bryant was ordered to take *Sealion* in to check the conditions in the Skagerrak and 'reveal his presence to ensure that enemy A/S forces would be maintained in this area'.[21] Although he had not sunk many ships, Bryant was considered a veteran with a reputation for being a survivor, having wrestled his boat out of many dangerous situations. Nonetheless, conditions in the Skagerrak were extreme. There was virtually no darkness and air and surface patrols were active around the clock. It was scarcely possible to surface to charge the batteries and refresh the air inside the boat at all. After a while it was simply a matter of survival and trying to get back out into the North Sea alive. 'On the 30th June', Bryant wrote, 'a very jaded and ineffective submarine sneaked out of the Skagerrak on the surface.'[22] Conditions were somewhat better west of Lindesnes, but not much.

— 25 —

Cygnus's *Convoy*

As June turned to July, conditions off southern Norway had become extremely challenging for the Allied submarines. No boat was expected to patrol for more than four days in the area before being relieved.

For the Germans, passing through the area required significant protective measures, draining scarce resources, and the convoys were operated in a very controlled manner. From late June to early July the waters between Kristiansand and Stavanger were actually closed for German non-naval vessels outside the organised convoys. The German Naval Command in Stavanger considered running larger convoys protected by several escorts as more efficient than taking smaller groups with less protection through the danger zone. To avoid mines, the convoys usually stayed 25–30 miles from land, where the water was too deep for Allied mines. This made them more vulnerable to submarine attacks, but it was believed that a heavy escort, including aircraft, would minimise the risk.[1]

At this time, the area off Stavanger was considered the most dangerous part of the Norwegian coast by the newly established German Naval Command in Norway. Here, there were no islands to hide behind, while the proximity to British bases in Scotland made air, mine and submarine attack likely. In the second half of June, the German naval commanders in the area became progressively more worried as there was an observed increase in the presence of submarines coinciding with a general increase in the convoy traffic and strong requests for additional escorts were submitted. Supplies needed to go north, to the German garrisons establishing themselves along the vast Norwegian coastline, and iron ore, fish, timber and other raw materials needed to go south to Germany. Throughout the summer of 1940, most days there was at least one convoy passing through the waters off Stavanger, requiring significant resources for protection. In addition there was copious Norwegian coastal traffic, necessary to maintain and difficult to restrict as there were few alternatives. After several requests for additional resources, Admiral der Südküste Norwegen (C-in-C Norwegian South Coast), Konteradmiral Schenk, was able by early July to provide a reasonable number of escorts – consisting of trawlers, R-boats, S-boats and minesweepers – for any one convoy, provided he was given full control of their movement up and down the coast, including when to wait and when to move. Inevitably this led to larger convoys, which were easier to defend, but also more tempting, and potentially more rewarding, targets for a lurking submarine.[2]

Among other measures, two naval *Seeflieger* units were stationed at Stavanger at the end of May 1940: 3./406 and 2./906. As usual with improvised units, they were named after their C-in-C Major Walter Schwarz, and thus were known as 'Gruppe Schwarz'. The units, flying out of Stavanger harbour or the seaplane base at Sola airfield, were equipped with Dornier Do18 flyingboats and used for maritime reconnaissance, convoy escort and A/S work. The Do18s were supplemented by a handful of Do17Z land-based aircraft of 3./606, flying back and forth over the Skagerrak between Sola airfield and bases in Denmark on daytime reconnaissance missions, weather permitting. In early June, the seaplane tender *Hans Rolshoven* was assigned to Gruppe Schwartz as support ship for the Do18s operating out of Stavanger harbour. Due to her powerful radios and trained staff, she also acted as general communication centre for all the naval aircraft operations off the south-western coast of Norway. In mid-June, Major Karl Stockmann replaced Major Schwarz, who returned to Germany, and the unit was redesignated Küstenfliegergruppe Stavanger. Shortly after, it was reinforced by a group of Arado 196s of 1./196. Operating from the seaplane base at Sola airfield as well as Stavanger harbour, these aircraft would be making life difficult for the British submariners off south-western Norway throughout the summer.[3] In August, the war moved further north and *Rolshoven* was relocated to Trondheim.

Sealion

In the morning of 3 July, a large convoy of fifteen ships prepared to depart from Stavanger. Five of the ships were German, the other ten were Norwegian vessels under German control with armed prize crews on board. Korvettenkapitän Hans Fuchs, commander of 11.Vorpostenflottille, on board *V1101*, was in charge of the escort. In addition to the three other vessels of his own group, *V1102*, *V1103* and *V1106*, he had the minesweepers *M1803*, *M1805*, *M1806*, and *M1807* of 18.Minensuchflottille and the A/S trawlers *UJ127*,

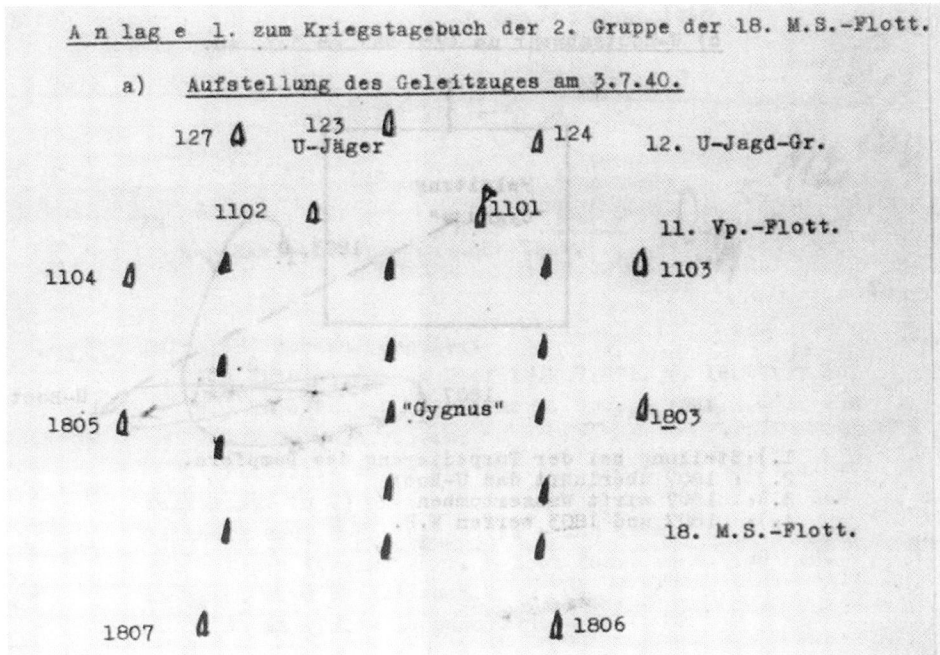

Cygnus's convoy. A map of the basic plan as described in the war diary, or KTB, of 18th Minesweeping Flotilla. (NARA T1022-32014-72459)

UJ123 and *UJ124* of 12.U-Jagd Gruppe under his command, totalling eleven escorts. The three *U-Jäger* would be sweeping a mile ahead of the convoy; the other boats would stay closer to the merchantmen, two in front and three on each side. In addition, two Do18 flyingboats were allocated to the convoy as submarine protection, as well as four Bf109 fighter aircraft from JG77 to cover against air attack.

The ships left Stavanger harbour individually during the morning and fourteen of them congregated offshore, north of Kvitsøy. Here they were organised in three columns, 500 metres (550 yards) apart – two columns of five and one of four – before turning south-east, towards the Skagerrak. Keeping them in tight columns, with 400 metres (440 yards) between each vessel, it was believed they would be a difficult target to intercept.[4]

The first submarine alarm came in the early afternoon, about five hours after leaving Stavanger harbour. At this time, the convoy was off Jæren. Two torpedo tracks were observed coming from portside aft and the alarm was sounded.

The submarine was *Sealion* and Bryant had sighted the heavily escorted, southbound convoy west of Håsteinen Island, off Stavanger, as a rainsquall lifted, leaving the sea glassy calm. He also saw there were flyingboats low overhead, but decided it was too good an opportunity to miss and manoeuvred to achieve a position from which to attack. Around 15:40, six torpedoes were fired at a range of some 5,000 metres (5,500 yards). Bryant wrote:

> we got within range and lined up for a shot from outside the screen. It was right in the orbit of the Dornier. As I gave the order to fire, I saw a sobering sight; first the nose, then the wings and finally the tail passed a few feet above the periscope.[5]

The Dornier had seen the submarine through the water, and frantic signalling from the aircraft made the convoy turn away from the torpedo tracks, while the two escorts

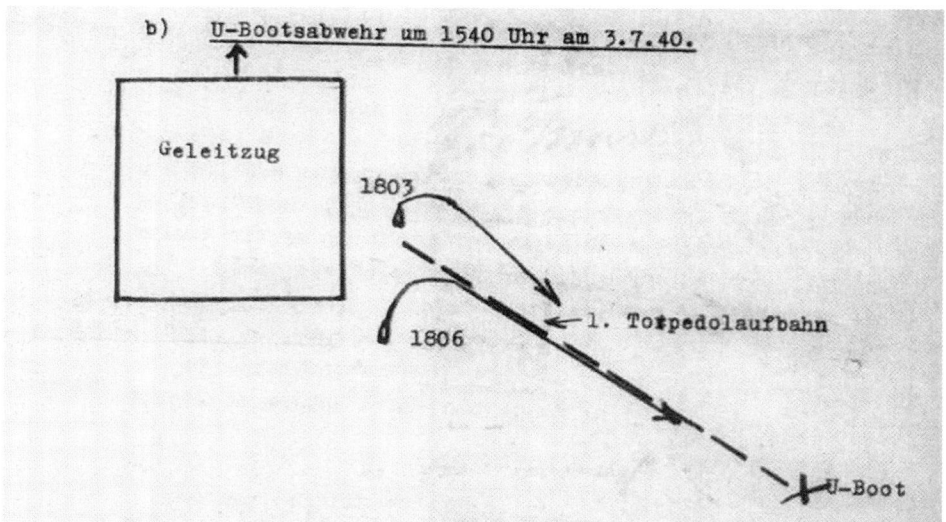

Another map from the same KTB showing *Sealion*'s unsuccessful attack and the response of *M1803* and *M1806*. *Geleitzug* means convoy. (NARA T1022-32014-72459)

nearest to where the torpedoes appeared to have come from, the minesweepers *M1803* and *M1806*, turned down the tracks. Two of the last torpedoes from Sealion came close to *M1806*, but she steered between them and headed for where they were clearly seen to originate. The Do18 aircraft came in first, but as it was only armed with two conventional SC 50 bombs, released by the observer, its accuracy was poor even at the best of times. The concussions of the bombs exploding were felt inside *Sealion* but did no real harm. Shortly after, though, *M1803* and *M1806* were on top of the submarine and these had real depth charges: twenty-five in all were dropped, according to German reports, in groups of six or seven.[6]

On board *Sealion*, thirty-four charges would be counted in all over the next hour, presumably including the bombs from the aircraft. Some were uncomfortably close, exploding underneath the submarine, forcing her bow upwards.

> Hugo Newton, our No. 1, was flooding everything he could, but still the boat rocketed upwards out of control and we could hear the escorts pounding in. If we broke surface we had had it – and at first it seemed [nothing] would stop her. Then Hugo caught her with five feet to spare. The next moment we were hurtling down, terribly heavy, and the hunt was overhead. We were going at high speed to try to regain control; our noise must have been nearly deafening to the sensitive German hydrophones.[7]

The lights went out, depth gauges failed and the asdic ceased to function. The emergency depth gauge was turned on and showed the boat was down to about 75 metres (240 feet), well past the maximum depth specified by the shipbuilders.

> Biddiscombe and Denzey, the Coxswain and Second Coxswain, wrestled with their planes, the shafting binding in its bearings as the hull distorted under the pressure. The air hissed as we blew the main ballast tank. Depth charges reverberated and all was noise and blackness except for the wavering pencils of light where the emergency flashlights pierced the dark gloom.[8]

The descent was checked in time – just. It was difficult to gauge what the trawlers were up to as the starboard hydrophones were out of action. To gain some height in the water, Bryant risked blowing some of the tanks, hoping the bubbles would not be seen in the choppy seas. The gamble paid off. With the hull creaking from the pressure of the water, *Sealion* porpoised a few times before settling down under control once more. Water was coming in through a leaking stern gland and a number of men were busy making a human chain, shifting the water from the after bilge to the engine room by means of buckets as quietly as possible. Those still in the control room started a discussion of the possible effects of the curfew, recently announced in the press, on sporting facilities on Brighton beach. A few more series of depth charges followed, but getting further and further distant, doing little more than creating layers of disturbed sea, under which Bryant could steer his boat away.

By 18:00, the hydrophones that were still working indicated that the hunt had moved elsewhere and Bryant let *Sealion* come to periscope depth to verify that the trawlers had left. They had indeed, and instead, to his immense surprise, Bryant sighted what he believed was an unescorted, northbound tanker coming his way. An immediate reload

Sealion in August 1935. (NPC)

of the torpedo tubes was ordered while he started to move his boat into position for an attack. This was most likely the tanker *Adria*, which had left Kristiansand two days earlier, in the company of the minesweepers *M17* and *M18*, though the minesweepers were obviously not seen by Bryant. Before he could get close enough to fire, however, a heavy rainsquall hid the ship; when it had passed, the sea was empty.[9]

The reason for the escort giving up the chase of *Sealion* just when they had her in their grip was twofold. Firstly, the convoy had come upon the next submarine to the south and a new alarm had been raised. Secondly, oil and bubbles were observed on the surface and the captains of *M1803* and *M1806* firmly believed that they had sunk the British submarine. So much so that, based on their reports, Seekommandant Stavanger (Sea Commander Stavanger) reported to his superiors that a submarine had been sunk in his area of responsibility.[10]

Having escaped the vengeance of *M1803* and *M1806*, *Sealion* withdrew to the north-west to charge her batteries, closing the southern tip of Karmøy at daybreak on 4 July. No further ships were sighted during the day and at nightfall Bryant surfaced again and set course south-westward to charge the batteries again. Almost as soon as they had settled down to the charging routine, however, an aircraft appeared from behind the clouds. Bryant managed to get his boat down before the bombs hit, but their explosions temporarily disabled the steering gear, hydrophones and compasses, as well as breaking just about every light bulb in the boat. Just after midnight, when things had been cleared up and the instruments were working again, *Sealion* was brought to the surface again. Again a low-flying aircraft bore down on them and Bryant retired to a safe depth. This time no bombs were dropped, or at least none that exploded. Conditions were obviously not healthy above and *Sealion* stayed submerged, using what was left in the batteries to steer west. The Sperry compass only worked intermittently, though, and it later became apparent that they had in fact been heading quite a way south of due west.

The rest of the night and all of the next day, 5 July, was spent underwater conserving what was left of the charge in the batteries. Cold food and lime juice were served but few ate as most were plagued by intense headaches, and when the conning tower hatch was opened, just before midnight, most of the crew became sick, endangering the safety of the boat. Apart from a period of less than ten minutes the previous night, *Sealion* had been submerged for forty-five hours. Interestingly, just before surfacing in the late evening of the 5th, the crew of *Sealion* could hear distant explosions, and upon surfacing, a 'firework display' was seen to the east, 'indicating air activity in that direction'. Unknown to Lieutenant Commander Bryant and his men, they were actually observing the last struggle of their fellow submariners in the sister-boat *Shark* – at the time probably no more than 3–4 miles away.[11]

Bryant found the conditions off the coast of Norway a bit too dangerous for comfort. For a while on the 6th, what was believed to have been a U-boat was chased, but never located with certainty. Otherwise, the traffic seen or heard was inshore or heavily escorted by surface ships and aircraft. In the afternoon of the 7th, *Sealion* was ordered to check the beached wreck of the German freighter *Palime* near Obrestad (see page 265). The ship was obviously a total loss, aground and deep in the water. Two small vessels were alongside or near the wreck, apparently salvaging cargo, and Bryant reckoned it was worth a torpedo to stop this. One was fired, but did not run properly – possibly as it was deflected by a shoal. Closing further, there was little sign of life on board the vessels and Bryant decided not to waste another torpedo. Somewhat frustrated, he turned back into deeper water and headed for home in response to a signal received shortly after.[12]

Snapper

Meanwhile, the large convoy continued south-eastwards into the billet of the next British submarine, *Snapper*. Lieutenant King:

> tightened in anticipation. Through the periscope I watched the nest of masts resolve into a convoy of a dozen small supply ships escorted by the same number of trawlers, indulging in leap-frog tactics. Half the party steamed ahead and then stopped to listen with hydrophones while the others caught them up with the convoy carefully surrounded. Then the other lot steamed ahead while the first party milled round the flanks of the supply ships.[13]

King believed the ships of the convoy to be rather small, but as they were so well protected, they probably had valuable cargo and he decided an attack was worth the risk. The merchant ships were very close together and having crept inside the screen, he fired a full salvo of six into the midst of them. Just before 19:00 (18:00 BrT), off Egersund, a torpedo struck the Norwegian freighter *Cygnus* in the foreship. She was in the middle of the convoy and the explosion caused a lot of confusion among the other ships. The 1,333-ton *Cygnus*, now under German command, was en route from Trondheim to Hamburg with timber. In addition she had picked up 537 tons of aluminium in Bergen, and 450 tons of ferro-chrome and ferro-silica in Ålvik before joining the convoy in Stavanger.

Cygnus in Trondheim, just before departure on her last voyage. (E Skjold Collection)

Cygnus at Ålvik in Hardangerfjord, east of Bergen. (Author's Collection)

Master Harry Evensen later told that he saw the torpedo just before it struck, coming in from starboard side, slightly from aft. Like most of the crew, he registered two explosions a few seconds apart, but saw only one torpedo track and did not know what the second explosion resulted from. Lieutenant King reckoned that he had hit three ships as he heard three explosions, but one of the others probably exploded as they hit land, unless there were two hits on *Cygnus*. The ship immediately dipped its bow, but remained afloat for some time due to the timber in the holds. Some men were thrown overboard by the explosion, the rest had plenty of time to take to the boats and there were no casualties. The minesweeper *M1805* picked up the nineteen-man Norwegian crew, the pilot, a German control officer and two German sailors. Around fifteen minutes after being hit, *Cygnus* went down, some 39 miles south-west of Eigerøy.[14]

Immediately the explosion onboard *Cygnus* was seen, the minesweeper *M1807* turned towards the reported direction where the torpedoes had come from. She was joined by *M1803* as soon as the latter could arrive from the aborted hunt for *Sealion*. The rest of the escorts stayed with the convoy, which continued southwards and reached Kristiansand without further mishaps.

The German minesweepers were slow and King found he could stay at periscope depth observing them as they approached and dodge them by visual contact. Depth charges were dropped in large numbers, but none dangerously close. Ironically, the minesweepers seem to have disturbed each other by dropping too many depth charges too frequently.[15]

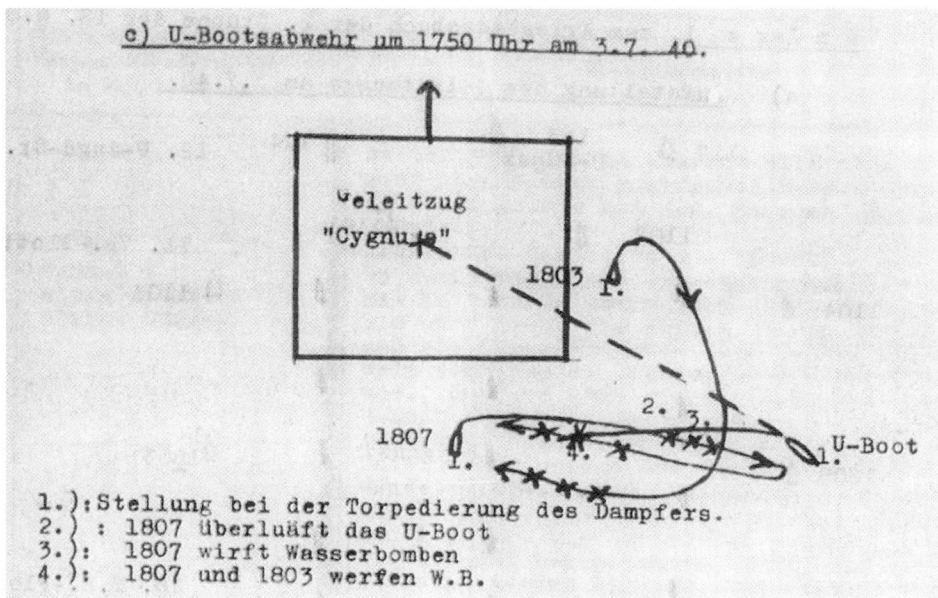

From the KTB of 18th Minesweeping Flotilla, showing the depth-charge attacks of *M1807* and *M1803* on *Snapper* after she had fired the torpedoes that sank *Cygnus*. (NARA T1022-32014-72459)

Cygnus going down, seen from *M1805*. (E Skjold Collection)

In King's mind, the most dangerous adversary was the Dornier aircraft that remained circling above, dropping bombs at times. It appears that the British submariners were unaware that the bombs were relatively small, 50 kg, and only dangerous if they actually hit the submarine hull at shallow depth. Some of the bombs probably exploded when hitting the sea surface, appearing more dangerous than they actually were. Eventually, King realised he would not be able to launch another attack and *Snapper* stole away. [16]

Somewhat amusingly, both parties were quite satisfied with the events of the day. The British believed they had successfully intercepted the convoy as the number of submarines had saturated the German escort. This was not quite true, although it had been a busy day for Korvettenkapitän Fuchs and his men. The Germans, on the other hand, believed that they had sunk a submarine for the loss of a captured Norwegian merchantman.

This was definitely not the case – at least, not quite yet. [17]

Loss of Shark

SHARK LEFT ROSYTH IN the evening of 3 July, heading east to relieve *Sealion* off south-west Norway. The 31-year-old Lieutenant Commander Peter Buckley had been in command of *Shark* since January 1939. It was his first command and, though respected by crew and colleagues, his commanding officer, Captain Philip Ruck-Keene of the 3rd Flotilla, had commented that he showed a lack of initiative on earlier patrols by not going deep enough into the Kattegat looking for targets.[1] No ships had been sunk, but a small convoy escorted by the depot ship *Saar* had been unsuccessfully attacked in April.

On 5 July, *Shark* was some 30 miles south-west of Skudeneshavn. Weather had been rough during the day and nothing had been seen or heard. Having spent the day submerged, the batteries were getting low, and Buckley took *Shark* to the surface around 22:00 BrT to get a good charge before he would try to enter the fjord leading to Stavanger harbour the next day.[2] A week after midsummer, the nights did not really get dark off southern Norway, but the next few hours would be the darkest and Buckley felt comparatively safe. On the surface, the starboard engine was started, making speed on a southerly course, passing west of Kvitsøy Island. Settling for 8 knots, he gave orders to change course 60 degrees every five minutes and make a full 180-degree turn every ten. The port engine should have been shunted to provide a charge of the batteries, but a delay occurred due to a leaking air connection, which the engineers set to work on. Buckley, Signals Officer Lieutenant David Wheeler, the officer of the watch, and one lookout entered the bridge.

Shark in January 1935. (W&L)

Before the charge could be started, at 22:15 the after lookout shouted a warning. A small seaplane was approaching from astern. Orders were given to dive and the bridge was cleared. There was no panic, just a fast, methodical routine practised many times before. *Shark* was slow in going down, though, as she was head on to a heavy swell. After the war, Buckley wrote:

> The control room depth gauge was reading (something) between 15 and 20 ft. Two or three bombs fell very close to the stern, followed immediately by two or three more, which shook the boat violently. Considerable damage was done by these explosions – lights were put out, Sperry went off the board and both hydroplanes and steering failed. The starboard main motor was also out of action and an electric fire started behind it. [. . .] There was a leak behind the port main motor switchboard and water was coming in in this place. The after planes were jammed 'hard-a-rise' and could not be moved either by power or by hand. The boat now took up an angle of about 35° bow-up and the bow broke surface in spite of having filled all possible tanks and attempting to lighten the boat aft. The port main motor was worked at full speed. As soon as the bow broke surface, a hail of machine gun bullets was heard on the hull and bombs were dropped around us. After what seemed an incredibly long period – it was probably not more than a minute or two – the boat at last began to gain depth, although at the same angle by the stern.[3]

The attacking aircraft was an Arado Ar196A of Bordfliegergruppe 1./196, temporarily assigned to Küstenfliegergruppe Stavanger. In the afternoon of 5 July, orders had been issued to KüFlGr Stavanger to send two aircraft on patrol during the night to search the area off Stavanger and down the coast towards Lista and Ryvingen Lighthouse. A second pair would take over later in the morning. It was emphasised that British submarines were in the area and special vigilance was required. The night before, a submarine had been sighted and attacked and, although oil had been seen on the surface, it was not believed to have been sunk. The nimble Ar196, originally designed for ship-based reconnaissance, was well suited for the A/S work. Easy to handle, they could fly low and slow when necessary and could stay up for hours due to large fuel tanks. Most important, though, their crews were trained naval fliers and observers.

The first two Arados took off from Sola seaplane base at 22:00. Less than fifteen minutes later, *Shark* was sighted off Feistein Island by Leutnant zur See Gottschalk flying aircraft T3+LH. In the back seat was Unteroffizier Manjok.[4] Gottschalk wrote:

> At 22:18, I dived from 800 metres and released the first bomb from 400 metres; approaching the submarine from astern. The bomb hit amidships, just behind the tower. The submarine vanished, but shortly after the stern reappeared and I attacked again. The boat vanished before I was in position to release the bomb, though. Again the stern appeared and this time I dropped the bomb from 400 metres. It detonated on the starboard side of the tower, three metres off and somewhat aft. The submarine was lifted slightly out of the water, sank quickly and then came back up, stern down and with a severe list. It slowly righted itself, but the stern remained deep in the water. The fore-end of the submarine was strafed by cannon and machinegun fire. Eventually the submarine vanished, leaving a large oil patch. The whole episode lasted less than ten minutes. I set course back to Sola where I landed at 22:45.[5]

The versatile Arado Ar196 aircraft played an integral role in the loss of both *Seal* and *Shark* (see chapter 21). It has been difficult to find photos of the exact aircraft involved in these episodes, partly as their *Staffel* codes changed as they were moved around between units. This aircraft, 6W+CN, being made ready onshore before taking off from Sola seaplane base outside Stavanger, comes from 5./196. It carries no bombs on this occasion and it is probably a practice or test flight. (MHFR)

Interestingly, the two accounts differ somewhat, most significantly in the number of bombs dropped. Buckley's report was written from memory more than five years later, but Gottschalk – who wrote his account only hours after the event – was elated and full of adrenalin and, as seen below, his ability to observe details in the semi-darkness was not always perfect.

Whatever the number and sequence, the two 50-kg bombs dropped by Gottschalk caused considerable damage on board *Shark*. Finally submerged, Buckley gave orders to stop the descent and trim the boat level by the main ballast tank – with no result. *Shark* continued down, rapidly, in spite of all efforts to control the descent. When he tried to reduce the speed of the port motor, the only one left working, this resulted in an even greater stern-down angle so he had to let the motor run at full speed, disregarding the drain on the batteries for now. With the lights out and the stern down, the inside of the boat was a mess, all the more so as everybody and everything not tightly secured slid uncontrollably aft. The after ballast tanks were blown to reduce the angle off and restore some trim. *Shark* responded by a violent 'porpoise' movement, sometimes up, but most of the time down. There was no alternative for Buckley but to use the remaining high-pressure air reserves to blow all the main tanks in a desperate attempt to get the boat to the surface before it was too late and hope for the best. It worked. By the time the descent stopped, the control room depth gauge showed 256 feet (78 metres), the one aft 300 feet (91 metres).

Shark reached the surface at an awkward angle and took time to right herself; this resulted in a large amount of acid being spilt from the batteries – one of the least-wanted things on board a submarine. Once the boat was stable, the starboard engine was started and, assisted by the port motor on half-ahead, a westerly course was set, away from the coast. There were no aircraft to be seen and things did not look completely hopeless at first, although Buckley already knew they would not be able to dive again. It was about 22:45, half an hour after the Arado had first been sighted. Orders were given for damage to be assessed and reported. The reports were not good. Even when running at full, the ballast pump was not keeping up with the leaks and, when back on the surface, it was seen that there was severe damage to the after end of the boat, including a hole in one of the after trimming tanks, a large dent in the pressure hull and several leaks. As soon as an aerial could be rigged to replace the one abaft the bridge, which had been blown away, a signal was sent, requesting assistance.

Eventually, the port engine was also started, but it could only be run at moderate speeds as the bearings aft of the engine room had been damaged and the shaft was misaligned. To his dismay, Buckley also found that the rudder was jammed at 'hard-a-port'. Attempts to free the rudder came to nought and steering by the engines turned out to be impossible as the damaged port engine was unable to counteract the rudder, even when slowing down the starboard engine. *Shark* could only move in circles to port. With full daylight approaching and unable to either dive or progress on a reasonable course, Buckley and his crew were in dire straits. Anticipating the worst, the main gun and the Lewis gun on the bridge were manned and ammunition brought on deck. Below, demolition charges were rigged and all secret papers were either thrown overboard or torn to minute pieces.[6]

Gottschalk's return to Sola created a flurry of activity, with all available aircraft in the region being made ready to fly. Having given a quick verbal report, he soon after took off again with further bombs and cannon shells, aiming for the oil patch. At 23:15, the submarine was sighted again. At the time, Gottschalk believed that it was a second submarine, as it appeared bigger and painted with light stripes. It was undoubtedly *Shark* both times, however, so the difference must have been in the pilot's mind. Encouraged by his first success, Gottschalk attacked again, this time dropping one bomb at a time. Both bombs missed, by a few metres astern. This time there was return fire from the submarine; after being hit twice while strafing, Gottschalk pulled back to observe. The submarine certainly had problems: it was going in circles and was obviously unable to dive. Believing he had bagged his second submarine of the day, Gottschalk again returned elated to Sola.

Meanwhile, the second Arado, T3+DK flown by Leutnant Eberhard Stelter with Unteroffizier Stamp in the backseat, also found *Shark*. They had initially been searching further south and were on their way back to Sola when the submarine appeared below. Dropping both bombs in the same attack, one exploded in the water near the stern.[7]

These were bombs number five and six that were dropped on *Shark* and, as Buckley admits, his recollection of the sequence of events was probably somewhat garbled five years later. He remembered more bombs being dropped in the first attack, which was not the case as the Arados carried only two. During one of the latter attacks, two men, Leading Signalman Eric Eaton and Leading Seaman Gerald Paine, were thrown over the side by the explosion, probably from one of the bombs dropped by Gottschalk. Fragments from this bomb holed no. 4 starboard main ballast tank, but the two men were unharmed. A little later, after Stelter had dropped his bombs as well, shouts were heard from the water and, against the odds, Eaton and Paine were pulled safely back onboard – wet and tired, but happy to be alive.[8]

At 00:37 Gottschalk took off for the third time, now with a new machine, T3+KH, as his original Arado had received some damage. *Shark* was more or less where she had been seen last time and was quickly found. A few strafing rounds showed that the guns of the submarines were manned and after dropping one bomb from relatively high, which missed by some 15 metres (50 feet), Gottschalk settled down at a safe distance to observe, firing a few shots at the submarine from time to time. During this, the main gun of *Shark* fired occasionally as well, showing she could still bite. The Lewis gun was used only when the aircraft attacked. Eventually, at 03:00, fuel was getting low and after dropping his last bomb in the sea off *Shark*'s stern, Gottschalk set course for Sola, content with his night's work.

By now, however, other aircraft had arrived and *Shark* was more or less continuously strafed and occasionally bombed by Arados throughout the morning. In the command centre at Sola there was great excitement over the events at sea, particularly when the reports confirmed that there was a submarine going in circles just off the coast, apparently unable to dive. A suggestion to send *Hans Rolshoven* from Stavanger harbour to capture her was dismissed as too dangerous in case there were other submarines around. Instead, a flotilla of mine-sweeping trawlers on their way to Stavanger from Kristiansand was diverted towards the scene with all dispatch. A large number of aircraft were standing by at Sola airfield, ready to attack the submarine should she gain control of her steering and attempt to escape before the trawlers arrived. Do18 flying boats of 2/KüFlGr 106 observed from a safe distance.[9]

Unable to dive and steer properly, *Shark* was a sitting duck when the German sighted her again before midnight. Buckley believed that his first signal might have been misleading, as it could have given the impression that they had made good their escape and so prevented VA(S) or the Home Fleet from putting any further effort into a rescue mission. By now, however, any further signalling was impossible as the breakers in the W/T room were all distorted.[10]

Conditions inside *Shark* were rapidly becoming very unpleasant. The wardroom and engine room were filling up with smoke and fumes from the batteries and water levels in the engine room were rising. Some of the water could be contained by the bulkhead doors, but it was necessary to have the pumps continuously operating at full capacity. The ammunition was stored in the wardroom and in order to get everything on deck where it was needed, First Lieutenant Denis Barrett put on a DSEA set and worked for a considerable time inside this area, under extremely unpleasant conditions. Other men still below, including the engine-room staff, all had to take occasional 'breathers' – short breaks under the conning tower hatch – to be able to continue. Throughout the ordeal, Warrant Engineer Cyril Loder and his men managed to keep the engines running, in spite of the extremely challenging conditions.[11]

On deck, those not needed below kept up a spirited fight. Some manned the deck gun, others the Lewis gun and a few even used rifles to fire at the aircraft.[12] Some were employed to pass the ammunition as it came up from below, filling the pans of the Lewis gun as they became empty. Among those showing calm determination that night was Able Seaman Ivor Clark. His deck position was on the 3-inch gun and when the high-angle ammunition for this was expended, he moved up to the bridge and took over the Lewis gun. He remained behind this throughout the ensuing action and was probably responsible for most of the damage to several of the German aircraft, though none were directly shot down. The aircraft could also bite back, however, and being up top was not safe. Many, including Clark, were injured; sometime around 03:00, Petty Officer James Gibson went overboard, probably hit by a German bullet.[13]

Meanwhile, four Messerschmitt Bf109s appeared, having taken off from Sola at first indications of daylight. These were armed with machine guns and 20-mm cannons and started a series of devastating attacks, aggressively raking the bridge and gun crews. Coming in low from astern – in the zone where the Lewis gun was partly blocked by the periscope standards – these attacks sealed the fate of the submarine. Several on board *Shark* were hit, including Lieutenant Commander Buckley, who sustained serious wounds to his leg as well as to his head. Stoker James Walsh was killed outright. The gunners on board the submarine fought back as best they could, defiantly replacing the wounded as they fell. By now, however, they were running out of ammunition.

One of the Arados, T3+BH, with Pilot Oberleutnant Schreck and observer Oberleutnant Junker, approached *Shark* carefully, signalling in English: 'Stop at once – take course to Stavanger'. According to Oberleutnant Junker, after some time the submarine answered back with something interpreted as: 'No machine, no engine, no steering'.[14] Lieutenant Commander Buckley later wrote:

> One of the seaplanes now signalled us by light to 'stop or steer to Stavanger'. No notice was taken of this signal but about a quarter of an hour later, after continuous attacks from the 109's, our ammunition being expended and having many wounded or dead (I could not tell which), I reluctantly decided to capitulate. Sometime after, the 'fighter' attacks had commenced, I called the First Lieutenant on to the bridge as I was feeling particularly shaky and, from this time on, I have only a vague recollection as to what actually happened.[15]

After a repeated series of attacks from the Bf109s, Oberleutnant Junker noticed that the fire from the submarine had ceased. Instead there was some light-signalling, interpreted as 'a-a' and eventually he also saw some men on the deck of the submarine raising their hands in what he interpreted as a sign of surrender. To stop further attacks from the Messerschmitts, Junker landed close to *Shark*, hoping to be able to take the British captain into captivity. While he approached after having landed, some of the British submariners remained with their hands raised, while others threw weapons and other equipment overboard. As the Arado came up next to *Shark*, it suddenly keeled over to port: the left-hand float was leaking, probably from multiple hits from *Shark*'s Lewis gun, and was taking water fast. Somewhat undignified, Junker and Schreck jumped on board the submarine while their aircraft drifted away and capsized.[16]

The situation on board *Shark* was tense, but with half a dozen aircraft circling overhead, the British submariners remained calm, with both Junker and Schreck having pulled out their Lugers. In the conning tower, Junker found several men heavily wounded, including Lieutenant Commander Buckley, with whom he spoke briefly. Neither of the German airmen was eager to go below, and when Lieutenant Barrett went down to make sure everything of interest had been thoroughly destroyed and the boat was fully rigged for scuttling, they did not try to stop him. Instead, with a signal lamp, Junker managed to contact one of the Do18s from 2./106, which landed to retrieve the two airmen. Lieutenant Commander Buckley and Sub-Lieutenant Robert Barnes were also taken on board the aircraft. The four extra passengers made the Dornier heavy, but in the calm sea it managed to take off safely, heading for Stavanger. *Shark* was now low in the water, stern down – when being transferred to the Dornier, Buckley was certain she would sink soon. With Buckley gone, First Lieutenant Barrett organised the wounded on deck and in the tower, sharing what dressings and cushions could be found. Rum and cigarettes were issued to those without head or stomach wounds.

At about 07:40 the mine-sweeping trawlers *M1803*, *M1805*, *M1806* and *M1807* arrived, with Kapitänleutnant Karl Föhner of *M1807* taking control of the scene. They had been on a return journey from Kristiansand to Stavanger, after delivering the rest of *Cygnus*'s convoy, when a radio signal from Naval Command in Stavanger at 04:10 instructed them to head for *Shark*'s position at utmost speed. Two hours later, they sighted a Do18 flying boat, beckoning them in the right direction. Kapitänleutnant Föhner wrote:

> The submarine lay with the afterdeck awash. Forwards, around the gun, most of the crew had gathered, many covered in woollen blankets, taking care of the wounded. Our boats launched their cutters and lifeboats while *M1803* and *M1805* went alongside. I lay *M1807* outside *M1805* and the wounded were forwarded to us, as we had a doctor on board. The senior officer and engineer were also sent over, on my request. It turned out that a bomb had hit the stern, and that water was now coming into the submarine both fore and aft, the English officers expecting she would sink in less than an hour. Only the Central was dry, the watertight doors being closed fore and aft. The Commander and the Chief had both been taken on board an aircraft during the night and flown to Stavanger. Due to the exceptionally heavy swell, the submarine was being tossed around and several steel wires broke, attempting to secure her. It also made the transfer of the wounded difficult, in particular the stretcher-cases.[17]

Of the forty-four men originally on board *Shark*, forty-two were rescued: PO Gibson was missing and Stoker Walsh was dead. According to the German sources, sixteen men

The trawlers of 18th Minesweeping Flotilla have arrived and are carefully approaching *Shark*, guns and depth charges ready. The crew may still be ready for a last-stand fight to the end. (Author's Collection)

M1805 Wesermünde coming alongside. (Author's Collection)

And eventually *Shark* is boxed in, with *M1803 Mulsum* on her starboard and *M1805 Wesermünde* on her port side. (Author's Collection)

Miserable, shaken and demoralised, the crew of *Shark* lines up to be taken on board the German trawlers. (Author's Collection)

were wounded; six of them seriously. Once these had been transferred to *M1807*, Föhner set course for Stavanger to get the most serious cases to hospital. The trawler arrived in Stavanger at 13:55 and the casualties were taken to the local hospital where they were given the necessary treatment. Stoker Eric Foster died, nevertheless, on 10 August, making the number of fatalities from *Shark* three.

Back at the site, a tow-line was rigged up and *M1806* moved in to start towing *Shark* once all the men were off. Before Buckley was taken off, he, Barrett and Wheeler had agreed that, due to the large number of wounded on board, they should not initiate scuttling until as many as possible of the men were safe. Wheeler later wrote:

> We had already worked out a ploy for this. When everyone else had been evacuated, an ERA would remain in the Control Room At an order from the Bridge, he would open by hand the hydraulic control valves to the vents of the main ballast tanks which would therefore gradually open without the characteristic 'phut' of escaping air which would undoubtedly be noticed and probably countered by the Germans. [. . .] Everything worked smoothly from our point of view. The Germans made the mistake of not setting an armed guard on board before the evacuation and I was able, in spite of threats and gestures, to remain at the bridge voicepipe until everyone else had left except the ERA and at the right time I was able to say the key words, 'you can come up now Hammond', down to the control room. After a short delay, Hammond appeared, gave me the faintest of nods and together we scrambled into captivity.[18]

Some German sailors risked going down the conning tower hatch when all the British submariners had been evacuated and returned shortly after with the draft of the engine log, a German ship-recognition book, maps and some private papers. Before returning

The last view of *Shark* going down. The next time she was seen was sixty years later as an echo-sounder image on the screen of a survey vessel. (Author's Collection)

to the trawlers, the British flag was hauled down and replaced by a German one. As the tow got underway at 09:20, *Shark* quickly began to sink, stern first. All vents had been left opened and all pumps shut down, ensuring that there would be no rescue for the stricken submarine once the water started pouring in, thanks to the efforts of ERA Frederick Hammond. The tow-line from *M1806* was cut and *Shark* sank about 25 nautical miles west-south-west of Egersund.[19] During this, the propeller of *M1805* was damaged and she had to be taken in tow back to Stavanger by *M1803*.

Some time after the submarine had gone down, *M1803* sighted what looked like torpedo tracks and, having *M1805* in tow, Kapitänleutnant Koch turned away. The brazen Kapitänleutnant Witting of *M1806*, however, gave chase down the tracks, towards where they appeared to have come from. The war diary accounts:

> At 11:03, *M1803* saw torpedo tracks to starboard. She and *M1805* turned away to avoid them. *M1806* attacked the submarine with 7 depth Charges. Following the 2nd and 3rd charge, oil patches were seen on the surface as well as strong air vortexes. Based on these, it is considered that the boat was destroyed.[20]

There are no matching reports for this episode from any Allied submarine. The sighting of the torpedo tracks and the results of the depth charges are difficult to disregard, though. Assuming there was a submarine in this area, it was in all likelihood *Salmon*.

Commander Bickford had taken *Salmon* to sea from Blyth on 4 July for a patrol off south-western Norway. This would be *Salmon's* ninth war patrol. The initial order put *Salmon* on a billet at 57° 20' N, 05° 00' E, north of the Westwall minefield. On the 9th, there were orders to move to a new position off Skudeneshavn (58° 20' N, 04° 30' E). Two days later, she was ordered to move an additional 20 miles north before being called home the next day. There was no answer from *Salmon* to any of these signals, nor did she show up in Blyth as expected.[21] Her wreck has never been found.

In the morning of 6 July, *Salmon* should have been some 50 nautical miles to the south of the events described above. At midnight she would most likely have been on the surface charging and it is very likely that Bickford's radio operator intercepted the distress signals from *Shark*. Bickford and Buckley were friends. They had been together for years in the Mediterranean under 'Ruckers' and it is very likely that they had a drink or two together only a few days earlier in Blyth before going on patrol. Most of the crew of the two boats would also have known each other well. Hence, a distress signal from *Shark* might well have prompted Bickford to head north without too much consideration for orders and billet limits. If so, he would have covered the 50 miles partly on the surface, and then partly submerged after dawn, just in time to be at the place where the torpedoes aimed at the minesweepers came from. If so, the air bubbles and the oil observed from *M1806*, may have been the last signs of life ever given by *Salmon*. It is therefore not unlikely that the wreck of *Salmon* may one day be found in the vicinity of 58° 49.5' N, 04° 43.0' E, the position given for the torpedo attack.[22]

The alternative explanation for *Salmon*'s disappearance is that she remained in her first billet until the 9th and only headed north in response to the orders from VA(S). If so, she might have ventured into the recently laid German minefield Sperre 17 (see page 298). This is a very plausible explanation, but if so, who fired the torpedoes and which boat was attacked by *M1806*?

In Britain, a sizeable rescue operation was mounted to see if *Shark* could be extricated. The 18th Cruiser Squadron was instructed by C-in-C Home Fleet at 00:45 on the 6th to send two cruisers and four destroyers to look for her and the second-in-command, Rear Admiral Marshal Clarke, took *Southampton* and *Sheffield* to sea from Scapa Flow within two hours,

The men from *Shark* being taken ashore from *M1805 Wesermünde*. (E. Ettrup Collection)

The next day the lightly wounded men were taken on a truck to the railway station; the others had to walk. (MHFR)

followed by *Cossack*, *Maori*, *Fame* and *Fortune*. The four destroyers kept some distance from the cruisers and during the morning they were sighted and eventually attacked by German aircraft. The attacks were quite intense, and Rear Admiral Clarke steered his cruisers to close the destroyers, which were actively searching along the expected route that *Shark* would take on her way home. By this time, though, *Shark* had already been lost. At 12:40, *Fame* was hit aft by a bomb, reducing her speed somewhat, killing four and seriously wounding as many again. As nothing more was heard from *Shark*, it was assumed she had been sunk and the rescue force was recalled at about 15:00.[23]

The reports of the approaching destroyers created panic in the command centre in Stavanger as it would mean certain destruction of the minesweepers should they be found. At one stage a request was submitted to Sola airfield to prepare to bomb and sink the submarine should the destroyers get too close, but by then *Shark* was already gone and the destroyers had turned back.

When the other three trawlers arrived in Stavanger at 15:40, the British submariners that did not need medical attention, twenty-four men and two officers, were marched ashore and taken to the German Naval Command offices to be interrogated, in spite of their exhausted condition. The following day, the unwounded officers and ratings were marched down to the railway station and placed on board a train for Oslo. Buckley and the other wounded were sent to Oslo for interrogation as soon as they were considered fit to travel. All of them eventually ended up in POW camps in Germany for the rest of the war.[24]

Brushes

TETRARCH, UNDER LIEUTENANT COMMANDER Mills, departed Rosyth for her third war patrol on 5 June, heading for the south coast of Norway. Nine days later, on the 14th, the 5,978-ton tanker *Samland* left Trondheim with two other ships, heading south after having replenished the *Scharnhorst* and *Gneisenau*.[1] On the way, one of the accompanying ships grounded, while the other docked in Bergen. *Samland* therefore continued south alone at high speed, escorted by 3rd R-boat Flotilla. In the evening of the 15th, in Karmsundet, just south of Haugesund, two magnetic mines exploded aft of the tanker. She was not seriously damaged, but speed was apparently somewhat reduced.[2]

Very early the next morning, south of Egersund, off Jøssingfjord, the small convoy was sighted from *Tetrarch*. Mills wrote in his war diary on 16 June:

> **04:40:** Sighted large freighter (or oil tanker) bearing 295 – 4 miles. Target screened by 'E' boats, each zigzagging independently. Sea glassy calm. Ran out 400 yards and commenced turn on to firing course. Chose a broad track to minimise the risk of screen sighting tracks. Was able to use so little periscope that my estimations were largely guess-work. . . . Passed the port wing screen about 200 yards range and fired unseen.
>
> **05:08:** Fired four torpedoes. Two hits. Hunt commenced. I went deep to 60 feet to adjust trim. Changed over planes and steering to telemotor. Kept under way on one motor, grouper-down, at 60 feet where there was a pronounced density

Tanker *Samland* replenishing German torpedo boats off El Ferrol during the Spanish Civil War. (Author's Collection)

layer. Attempted to keep end on. Four minutes after firing, the enemy dropped two charges . . . close astern but too far to do any damage . . . these were the only charges.[3]

The R-boats returned to *Samland*, picking up sixty-six survivors. *Tetrarch* was back at Rosyth on 20 June. The sinking of *Samland* made Commanding Admiral Norway, Generaladmiral Hermann Boehm, inform the SKL that unless he had a significantly increased A/S capacity immediately, he could not guarantee the safety of the battleships in Trondheim as well as the coastal traffic. The SKL had little to offer, however, as there were demands also from other recently subjugated coastal areas, particularly in Holland. Even the few Allied submarines that were active at any time off the coasts of occupied Europe were straining the German navy beyond their available resources.[4]

Slim Silhouettes

Tetrarch's fourth patrol was to be rather an odd one. She left Rosyth on 3 July, heading for a billet off Bergen. In the evening of the next day, between Stavanger and Aberdeen, a submarine was encountered.

2200 hours – Sighted a submarine on bearing 330°, distance 2 nautical miles. Visibility was deteriorating and as this was believed to be a U-boat, commenced attack.
2220 hours – After steering a most erratic course the submarine altered course 360° and disappeared.[5]

The sighted submarine was most likely *Shark*, which had left Rosyth the previous day. Later on that same day, no less than half a dozen bi-planes appeared and Lieutenant Commander Mills took *Tetrarch* down as fast as he possibly could. Giving the approaching planes a last glance as he dropped down the tower, closing the hatch, he recognised them as British Swordfish aircraft. Not sure that they had properly recognised his boat as friendly, Mills altered course 90 degrees to starboard and continued down past 30 metres (100 feet). A good thing he did, as soon after a loud explosion was heard towards port, where his boat would have been had he continued straight ahead. The Swordfish aircraft of 823 Squadron were out looking for an allegedly damaged merchant ship off Norway, and not finding anything there, they believed what they considered to be a German U-boat was an appropriate target on the way home. They had apparently not been briefed as to the risk of encountering one of their own submarines. Unknown to Mills, five torpedoes had been launched at his boat, but the prompt dive and his timely change of course saved the day.[6]

Arriving at the billet off Bergen, things were rather quiet at first, patrolling some 8 miles offshore, withdrawing seawards at night to charge the batteries. In fact, there was, as Mills anticipated, seeing smoke from time to time, quite significant German traffic to and from Bergen, including large tankers and supply ships. These were passing inshore, however, behind the chain of islands and well protected against the Allied submarines outside.[7]

Just after midnight on 11 July a submarine was sighted. Mills took this to be friendly and steered away. In all likelihood though, this was *U58* (Oberleutnant Heinrich Schonder), which had left Bergen a few hours earlier after a brief stop for some minor repairs, now heading for Lorient.

A few days later, on the 15th, *Tetrarch* was off the island of Sotra, probing Korsfjorden, the largest entry to the Leads south of Bergen. There was a large swell, but a calm surface and Mills used the periscope sparingly for occasional quick looks. At 18:40, he saw what he at first believed to be a small sailing boat coming out of the fjord. Five minutes later, though:

> the sailing boat was identified as a U-boat on coarse 260 deg, range about 4,000 yards. Carried out a 'snap' attack, lasting six minutes of which 4 minutes was full speed turning and closing at 50 feet and 2 minutes regaining control, stem to swell. At 18:46, on 105 deg track fired 3 torpedoes at about 2,500 yards range. Quite incorrectly I had assumed I had this 'on a plate', expecting to be inside 1,000 yards from my first sighting estimation. Seeing that my target was further away than anticipated . . . I fired ½ a length ahead using 8 seconds intervals, hoping thereby to cover a speed of 14 knots.[8]

The U-boat was *U57*, a type IIC boat under the command of Oberleutnant Erich Topp. He had been IWO (first officer) onboard *U46* under Herbert Sohler and this was his first patrol with his own command. *U57* had taken to sea from Bergen harbour a few hours earlier, after repairs. Luckily for Topp, his watch-keepers sighted one of the

The type IIC U-boat *U57*. She made eleven war patrols between the outbreak of war and being sunk in September 1940 in a collision with the Norwegian freighter *Rona* off Brunsbüttel. *U57* was raised and returned to service, but only used as a training boat. (Author's Collection)

torpedoes, which ran shallow in the high swell, and, turning towards where the tracks came from, he took his boat down. Onboard *Tetrarch*, Mills saw his opponent turn and gave orders to surface, adding 'ready for gun action'. Before *Tetrarch* could surface, however, *U57* had submerged. Mills went down again and started an underwater search, with no result.⁹ Without fully realising it at the time, Mills had stumbled across an important exit route for U-boats leaving for patrols in the North Sea or the Atlantic. He attempted to chase his opponent westwards during the night and sighted him twice, but lost contact at daybreak. It was time to depart the billet and on 18 July *Tetrarch* was back at Rosyth. After another, far less eventful patrol off Denmark in August, *Tetrarch* spent a couple of weeks in the yard in Newcastle before being ordered to join the Mediterranean Fleet.¹⁰

On 27 July, *Sealion* sailed from Rosyth for her eighth war patrol. By this time, Bryant had sunk only one German merchant ship, *August Leonhardt*, in April. All other torpedoes fired on merchantmen and U-boats had missed and Bryant was probably not in particularly high spirits when he left Inchkeith Island behind.

In the afternoon of the 29th, the Norwegian coast off Egersund came into sight and Bryant took *Sealion* down when the first A/S air patrols could be seen towards land. Shortly after, with Lieutenant Bowker on watch and Bryant trying to catch some sleep, the alarm rang out and warnings were shouted that there was a U-boat on the surface close by. While Bryant ran to the control room the helm was put hard over and the outer screw given full ahead to assist the turn. Meanwhile, there was frantic activity in the bow, ensuring all torpedoes were ready to fire.

The U-boat, which was the 250-ton type IIC *U62* under Oberleutnant Hans-Bernhard Michalowski, was heading for Kiel on the last leg of her fifth and final operational patrol. Upon arrival, she was to be re-commissioned as a training boat. At the time, her batteries were nearly exhausted after having been submerged the whole day. In addition, the GHG and S-Gerät were both down and she was out of torpedoes.¹¹ Bryant wrote:

> She was only about 300 yards away; it was a lucky day for her crew. Through the periscope I could see the men on her bridge as she slid by, every second rendering her safer; laboriously and maddeningly slowly the degrees clicked past the lubbers line, nearly 180 of these degrees had to go past before the boat would be turned enough to bring our tubes to bear. If only we had had a stern tube . . . When at last we did get round there was little more than her slim stern, rapidly drawing away, at which to aim.¹²

The chance was too good to miss though and Bryant let off three torpedoes. By now, however, the distance had increased to over 2,000 metres (2,200 yards) and *Sealion's* periscope had been seen. Hence, the salvo was easily avoided, the nearest torpedo passing some 100 metres (330 feet) away from *U62*. Realising his torpedoes had missed, Bryant took *Sealion* to the surface. The gun crew at first were very effective and in less than a minute the first shell went off. In the excitement though, the sight-setter got his settings wrong, resulting in a complete miss. Two more shots were fired, but the slim silhouette of *U62* submerged before the British gunners – undoubtedly stressed by Bryant's opinion of their abilities being shouted from the bridge – could get the settings right. There is no mention in *U62*'s Kriegstagebuch (KTB: German war diary) of having registered being fired at, so the shells must have missed by a good margin. *Sealion* followed quickly below, but was unable to make contact. Unknown to those on board the British submarine, *U62* had less than half an hour's worth of battery life left, but as she was not detected this was sufficient to get away – just.[13]

Collision

A week after her brush with *U62*, *Sealion* was to get even closer to an enemy ship – too close for comfort. But first there was a success, as on 4 August, *Sealion* torpedoed and sank the Norwegian merchant *Toran* (3,318 tons) east of Kristiansand, just inside the Skagerrak.[14]

Two days later, Bryant had taken *Sealion* back into the North Sea and was off Ryvingen Lighthouse outside Mandal when masts appeared over the horizon. This turned out to be the German tug *Steinbock* towing the damaged freighter *Cläre Hugo Stinnes I*, now under tow from Bergen to Germany, covered by a sizeable escort (see page 252).

At 14:30, *Sealion* was in a good position a few miles ahead of the convoy, preparing to go deep and thread its way through the escort screen. Half an hour later, they were through and on the inside when the convoy changed course, probably as a routine zig-zag. This put *Sealion* in an awkward position with one of the escorts approaching fast overhead. Bryant wrote:

> The port column, whose bows we had just crossed, had altered course to port and we were in a good position for a short-range attack if we could turn round in time; we were now stern on to them. There was very little time to turn and barely room between the columns. If we speeded up much, that unfriendly escort was bound to spot us; on the other hand if we turned right around to get the bow tubes to bear on the port column, it would be from an unfavourable angle on the quarter; they would be nearly past by the time we got round. All the same, at this short range we had an excellent chance of hitting. It was a pretty strenuous business at any time, being mixed up in the middle of a convoy making violent alterations of course.[15]

Contrary to German and American torpedoes, the British torpedoes at the start of the war could only travel straight ahead after being fired. There was no mechanism that would allow them to be fired at an angle to the target and steer onto the correct course by themselves. A few months into the war Royal Navy engineers came up with a device called the 'ninety bender' which allowed torpedoes to turn 90 degrees after leaving the tubes, no more, no less. Commander Bryant had been reluctant to use it earlier, in spite of orders to do so if there was an opportunity. Now he was in a situation that looked ideal and in order to avoid waiting for his boat to turn the full quarter-circle, decided to fire with the device turned on. The sights came on the leading ship of the port column and he ordered 'fire' with the torpedoes angled 90 degrees left. Unsure that the devices would work, Bryant kept turning *Sealion* around so the he could get another salvo off, if necessary, with normal settings. Meanwhile, he ordered the boat deeper down, just in case.[16]

A heavy influx of freshwater from rivers draining the snowy mountains of Norway makes this part of the North Sea and Skagerrak treacherous at the best of times. Alternating layers of salt- and freshwater made depth-keeping challenging and sometimes a significant excess of ballast water was needed to go from one layer to the other, delaying response in an emergency. On this day, there was a low-density freshwater layer on top, with a heavy saltwater layer just below periscope depth. Hence, *Sealion* stayed there, a few metres below periscope depth, in order not to take additional water in, which would have to be pumped out to get her back up.

When, after a few minutes, it was clear that none of the torpedoes had hit, Bryant went up again to have another look in the periscope. Unknown to him, the torpedo tracks had been sighted and, having cut the tow, the tug *Steinbock* was heading straight for *Sealion*'s position. Bryant wrote:

> A quick sweep round to take in the picture and all thought of attack disappeared. The small ship, second in the port column, had swung out to starboard and here she was bearing down almost on top of us. We were very fine on her starboard bow and swinging into her. We must go deep at once to get under her, but to go deep, we had to get through the layer of heavy salt water. [First Officer] John Bromage started flooding everything he could, while I put the helm hard-a-starboard [. . .]. We nearly succeeded, but through the periscope I saw a great rusty red sheet of iron coming at us.[17]

Seconds later, the periscope went black and a grinding, scraping sound filled the boat as it heeled alarmingly to starboard. Taken totally by surprise the submariners grabbed

The bridge of *Sealion* in August 1940 after being hit by *Steinbock*. (A Wilmar Collection)

anything they could find in order not be thrown into the filthy bilges. The scraping stopped and slowly the boat righted herself as propellers were heard to rush by, unbelievably close. For a little while *Sealion* was thrown about in the wake, her tower visible above the surface. Lieutenant Bromage's efforts started to take effect, and the submarine descended swiftly, straight into the saltwater layer.

Now *Sealion* became too heavy, dropping like a brick. Fortunately, the pressure hull had not been damaged and the descent was halted at 70 metres (230 feet), before any leaks occurred. A few depth charges followed, tossing the boat around, but the heavy layer probably also disturbed the German hydrophones, as the counter-attack was rather confused. To the relief of Bryant and his men, the escort seemed not to be able to follow as they crept away at depth.

Surfacing some hours later, after nightfall, Bryant found his bridge a shambles. Both bronze periscope standards had snapped off and the periscopes proper were bent beyond recovery. In addition, the jumping wire had parted forward of the bridge and the top of the bridge casing was damaged. It had been very close, but *Sealion* had been lucky. Everything that was loose was secured and course was set for home. Without periscopes little could be done. *Sealion* was in for a lengthy repair.[18]

On 23 August, Lieutenant Edward Balston took *Tribune* to sea from Rosyth for her fifth patrol. Two weeks later, at 06:00 on 6 September, *Tribune* was submerged some 8 miles north of St Kilda, when the sonar operator reported hydrophone effects that he believed was another submarine crossing ahead from port. Range was about 1,400 yards (1,280 metres), but nothing could be seen through the periscope. Balston took *Tribune* deep while trying to understand what was going on. The target made hydrophone effects that appeared to be a motor, stopping and restarting at intervals, changing bearing and range as if turning towards *Tribune*. At 06:33, noises were heard which the asdic operator described as 'similar to that heard on firing torpedoes'. Nothing more was registered, however, and it is doubtful if there were any torpedoes fired at all.

A few minutes later *Tribune* was back up at 20 metres (65 feet) depth, with the target about 900 metres (980 yards) dead ahead, and Balston gave the order to fire two torpedoes set to run at 38 and 44 feet – 11.5 and 13.5 metres, respectively – aiming at the centre of the asdic echo. After twenty-five seconds, there was a violent explosion, after which all hydrophone effects ceased. The second torpedo was heard to continue and explode at the end of its run, eight minutes later.

This was a daring new tactic that had not been tested before. At this time, firing torpedoes under water at another target also under water was considered risky at best, and success would rely more on pure luck than any skills or available technologies. Balston took *Tribune* to the surface just before 07:00 to find an extensive oil slick and some debris, which convinced him he had sunk a German U-boat. German records show that the only U-boat passing through the area on this day was *U56* under Oberleutnant Otto Harms. There is no report of any attack in this boat's KTB, though.[19]

On 30 August, Lieutenant Commander Maurice Cavenagh-Mainwaring took *Tuna* to sea from Rosyth for his first war patrol. This was a work-up patrol for the brand new submarine and not really intended for any specific actions. Two days into the patrol, though, while about 175 miles east of Dundee, on the surface charging batteries at 01:47 on 1 September, a submarine identified as German was sighted. The relative position of *Tuna* was good, and only three minutes after sighting the U-boat, four torpedoes had been fired from about 2,500 metres (2,750 yards). Shortly after firing the last torpedo, Cavenagh-Mainwaring ordered *Tuna* down and, while descending, one loud explosion was heard. Eight to ten minutes later three more muffled explosions were heard, taken to be the remaining torpedoes hitting the seabed at the end of their run. At 03:21 *Tuna* surfaced. Nothing was seen, but the crew on the bridge later reported a distinct smell of fuel oil. No German U-boat was in the area at the time and it is not known what *Tuna* attacked, if anything at all.[20]

On 5 September, Cavenagh-Mainwaring fired three torpedoes at a suspected U-boat contact, which appeared to be firing torpedoes back at *Tuna* in return. At 02:51 it was noted in *Tuna*'s patrol report that: 'it was now thought that there were two U-boats in the vicinity, one ahead and one astern. Accordingly, I decided it was too dangerous to remain and withdrew.' By next nightfall, *Tuna* was alongside *Forth* at Rosyth. No equivalent German reports have been found, and it is not clear what *Tuna* attacked or was attacked by on this day. On 6 September *Tuna* departed for Holy Loch to join the Bay of Biscay Patrol.[21]

Out of Luck

Successes in Norwegian and Danish waters were rather rare in late August, September and October 1940. Not for want of trying, but with few German ships moving in waters patrolled by Allied submarines it took a fair bit of serendipity to encounter any targets and then hit them afterwards as well. Similarly, while in the war diary of the German Sea Commander in Stavanger June and July the pages are covered with entries of Allied submarines and measures taken against them, August is much quieter, largely reporting air attacks on ships in harbour or at anchor. Most of the Kriegsmarine's large naval ships had left Norway; the occupation troops were in place, and the personnel traffic was slowing down, more and more limited to exchange and leave traffic over to Oslo and then by train to Bergen and Trondheim to avoid the dangerous south-western coast past Stavanger.

On 2 September 1940, the luck of the 3,285-ton German transport *Pionier* ran out. She had been crossing the Skagerrak repeatedly since the invasion of Norway in April, bringing troops, supplies and guns to the garrisons there.

On this occasion – her first trip for a few weeks, as she had been in the yards – *Pionier* had 753 soldiers on board. These had embarked in Frederikshavn, Denmark, earlier in the day and among them were Austrians from the Mountain Ranger Division to relieve their comrades at Narvik who had fought so hard during the invasion. Most of these men had never been to sea before. The rest of the passengers were Luftwaffe personnel, naval officers and a large group of medical personnel, including nurses. There was a crew of forty on board as well. As darkness started to fall, *Pionier* headed out of the port of Frederikshavn. Emphasis was on speed and the escort consisted of the T-class torpedo boat *T4* supported by aircraft, while the minesweepers *M1901*,

Troops waiting to embark *Pionier* (*left*) and *Peter Wessel* (*right*) in Frederikshavn, Denmark. *Peter Wessel* was a regular ferry operating in the pre-war Skagerrak and vehicles and equipment could be easily loaded into her bow-port. In Larvik there was a similar dock for easy disembarkation and off-loading. (Author's Collection)

Pionier being helped to sea by a Danish tug, hours before her demise. (Author's Collection)

M1904, *M1905* and *M1907* of the 19th Minesweeping Flotilla were in the area, covering several southbound ships, assisted by a number of auxiliaries. The weather was foul with strong winds and a high sea.[22]

At 19:30 BrT, the asdic operator of *Sturgeon* informed his CO, Lieutenant George Gregory, that he was picking up a faint echo. The alarm was sounded and some nine to ten minutes later, a large transport appeared in the growing darkness. They were about 15 nautical miles due north of Skagen and the sun was long gone, 'nautical twilight' prevailing. The general outlines of the transport could be distinguished, as could the silhouettes of 'two torpedo boats', one on each stern, as well as four or five 'smaller vessels' behind and two aircraft above. Gregory noted in his diary that the target was a '10,000 ton twin screw diesel transport', exaggerating the size of his target somewhat.[23] This may have been deliberate, as *Sturgeon* at this stage was a good bit further east than he was supposed to have been and Gregory may have been looking for an excuse to explain why he had surpassed his orders. There were several ships in the area, including the freighter *Utlandshörn*, which Gregory probably mistook for a second torpedo boat. The 'smaller vessels' were undoubtedly the minesweepers.

Gregory decided to fire two torpedoes at the transport and the remainder of the salvo at the concentration of smaller ships. The two first torpedoes were fired at 19:53. However, as speed was increased and course altered to aim for the smaller ships, two floatplanes were seen coming up the tracks and Gregory took his boat down. While descending, an explosion was heard. Coming to periscope depth a little later, when sufficiently distant from the tracks and the aircraft, now the sea was dark, dense columns of black smoke could be seen rising from the freighter, which was clearly on fire. The smaller vessels had scattered quickly and no longer constituted any target, so no further torpedoes were fired. Satisfied, Gregory took *Sturgeon* deep to reload.

The explosion onboard *Pionier* caused widespread panic, resulting in added loss of life. It was not recognised as a torpedo hit and therefore no search for *Sturgeon* was initiated by the escort. The aircraft had not seen the torpedo tracks, as Gregory believed. At the time, a mine or a boiler explosion was believed to be the most likely cause. At least 338 men perished, many horribly, during the fire that followed the explosion. As no torpedo tracks had been sighted, the minesweepers and auxiliaries, as well as *Utlandshörn* which was close by, used their searchlights to help rescue as many men as they could, some directly from the sinking ship, others from the sea. This

Pionier escorted by an He115 aircraft and the torpedo boat *Falke*. This photo is from a previous crossing, but very much like what Lieutenant Gregory must have seen through his periscope. (Author's Collection)

rather risky procedure undoubtedly reduced the losses significantly, but would hardly have been allowed had the men in command at the scene realised there was a British submarine in the vicinity.[24]

Coming back up to periscope depth at 22:30, there was nothing to be seen except the smaller ships picking up survivors, in the light of their searchlights. Gregory decided to leave them to it and headed off. *Pionier* had sunk in about an hour.[25]

In Germany, the sinking of *Pionier* created confusion and perplexity. It was some time since the Allied submarines had been dangerous this far into the Skagerrak. Now, the Oberkommando des Heeres (OKH, Army Supreme Command), demanded that all troop transports to Norway should be routed via Sassnitz in the German Baltic to Trälleborg in neutral Sweden and from there by train to Norway. Only supplies and equipment should be on board the ships leaving Frederikshavn and Aalborg. Even if this could not be fully adhered to, the personnel traffic across the Skagerrak was significantly reduced. The majority of the forces that were to be sent to Norway were now in place and those going back and forth could easily be disguised as being 'on leave' and hence be sent lightly armed through Sweden while their equipment and heavy weapons were still taken by transport vessels.[26] If possible, ships should only cross the Skagerrak in daylight when it was expected that the British submarines would not risk surfacing due to German air superiority. By mid-October, 130,702 soldiers had travelled north from Germany or Denmark to the Oslo region by ship since the invasion in April. At the same time, 20,773 had gone the other way, on leave, wounded, or because they were needed on other fronts. During the transports to and from Norway, several thousand men had been lost – distressing this early in the war, but nevertheless only a few per cent.[27]

On 10 September, just before turning for home a week after having sunk *Pionier*, Gregory fired six torpedoes at *U43*, south of Egersund. The distance was over 4,000 metres (4,400 yards) though, and all torpedoes missed, even though one torpedo was heard to explode.[28] Also on *Sturgeon*'s next patrol, on 14 October, midway between Kristiansand and Hirtshals, Gregory fired torpedoes at a U-boat. A 'small one' this time, but with the same unconfirmed result.[29] Coming home from this patrol on 21 October, he was informed that he had been promoted to lieutenant commander, in spite of some misgivings from the Admiralty regarding the fact that in September he had clearly sailed further east than the orders originally allowed.

Gregory had been in command of *Sturgeon* since her first war patrol more than a year earlier and was now one of the most experienced commanding officers of the 6th Flotilla. Hence, it was decided to send him into the Skagerrak again, to test conditions east of 8° E – after all, he had some experience in the area. This patrol, which would be his fifteenth and last one on board *Sturgeon*, would be a busy one. To start with, *Sturgeon* must literally have crossed the tracks of *Admiral Scheer* on the night of 27/28 October in the Skagerrak when the heavy cruiser came out of the Baltic heading for an Atlantic sortie, and the submarine was on her way into the Skagerrak. At this stage, the area inside Skagen–Lindesnes had not been frequented by submarines, since *Sturgeon* had been there last, sinking *Pionier*, seven weeks earlier. Nevertheless, the German escorts were vigilant, running strict routines involving speed alterations and zigzagging, each convoy being no larger than two or maximum three transports. Numerous vessels were sighted

Mass grave at Frederikshavn with the recovered bodies from *Pionier*. Vizeadmiral Raul Mewis Marinebefehlshaber Dänemark (Naval C-in-C Denmark) and Generalleutnant Schünemann, C-in-C of 160th Division attended. Their reports hastened the agreement with neutral Sweden to allow overland transit of soldiers to and from Norway. (Author's Collection)

at a distance, but Gregory could not get *Sturgeon* in position for an attack before a course change by the target or one of the frequent autumn rainsqualls of the area forced him to abort. Conditions were on his side though. After being hunted by three A/S trawlers on 31 October he wrote:

> It was noticed that there was a dense layer of water at 38 feet, so, with the hope of another and an asdic baffling one at that, the boat was taken down to 150 feet. A layer was noticed at 85 feet. On passing through it, a marked change took place in the conduct of the hunt. The trawlers found it difficult to maintain contact with the submarine end-on, and contact was never firm for any length of time. Eventually, about two hours after the start of the hunt, all trawlers lost contact, never to regain it.[30]

Finally, in the morning of 3 November, a 1,000-ton lone merchantman remained in sight long enough for Gregory to fire three torpedoes at her about 10 miles east of Larvik. The range was about 2 miles, but none of the torpedoes hit, and they were heard to explode further away after seven or eight minutes. Frustration was running high and no orders were given to reload the empty torpedo tubes. This must have created some anxious moments for Lieutenant Gregory when a few minutes later a second merchant ship was sighted on a similar course, also running alone. The attack was a mirror image of the first and the three remaining torpedoes were fired, again aiming half a ship's length ahead of the stem of the target from a distance of 2 miles. This time one torpedo was heard to hit and when observing through the periscope, the vessel, the 1,337-ton Danish merchant *Sigrun*, was seen to be on fire, sinking by the bows.

Two escorting A/S trawlers took up the hunt, but apparently having no active sonar, they seemed not to obtain a firm contact as Gregory was good at sneaking silently away at low speed. Thirty-two depth charges were dropped, but in an indiscriminate manner – the closest was some 250 metres (275 yards) away, but most were much further than that. 'Avoidance was not difficult,' Gregory wrote and after a little over an hour he had extricated his boat from their search area.[31]

As only one torpedo hit the Danish ship, far forward, it is likely that Gregory overestimated both size and speed of his prey. *Sigrun* was old and slow with a maximum speed of 8 knots, probably travelling at less than that. The torpedoes had a travelling time of about two and a half to three minutes. This is equivalent to an error of well over 50 metres (55 yards) per knot by which the target's speed was miscalculated. Gregory notes that he reckoned *Sigrun* was moving at 8 knots and that he used '1/2 ship's length ahead of stem' as point of aim. Hence, if the target was doing 6 knots instead of 8, the torpedoes would miss well ahead of such a small vessel.

The next day, 4 November, three more torpedoes missed the 938-ton Norwegian steamer *Ulv* in a similar situation further south, off Risør. On the 6th, however, fortune again smiled on Gregory. By now he had taken *Sturgeon* west of Kristiansand and she was off Jæren, close to the village of Varhaug. In the afternoon, the 1,293-ton Norwegian steamer *Delfinus* came in sight. Having been routed around Western Europe after the outbreak of the war, including trips to France and the UK, she was in Norway on 9 April and ended up in the German-controlled 'Home Fleet' after the invasion. On this autumn day, she was travelling alone and unescorted from northern Norway with a mixed cargo, including canned fish, fish products and cod-liver oil intended for Hamburg. There were seventeen men on board

The 1,294-ton *Delfinus* was built in Bergen in 1912. (MHFR)

Delfinus, including the pilot, but no German guards or passengers. She had left Stavanger just before midday, after taking on board the final quantities of cargo, and was hugging the coast, about a mile and a half off, doing 10 knots. There was ample rescue equipment on board, including several rafts on deck. As usual, the lifeboats were swung out and lowered to deck-level for easy access and rapid lowering.[32]

At 14:55 BrT, *Sturgeon* was no more than half a nautical mile away from the small freighter and Lieutenant Gregory fired two torpedoes. This time his point of aim was only some 12 metres (39 yards), or about a quarter of a ship's length abaft the stern. One torpedo hit aft, wrecking the stern. The other torpedo detonated on the beach a minute or two later. Nothing was seen by anybody on board *Delfinus* – neither torpedo tracks nor *Sturgeon*'s periscope. *Delfinus* went down in a little over ten minutes. The local coast guard came to the rescue though, towing the steamer's lifeboats to Egersund. There were no casualties.[33]

Later that day, Gregory set course for home, tying up alongside in Blyth on the 8th. He reported to his superiors that a submarine operating in the Skagerrak could easily make a nuisance of itself as there was still a significant amount of German ships moving about. On the other hand, his presence had already been noticed on the first day and he had been actively chased by both aircraft as well as A/S hunter groups. The merchant ships travelled very close to the coast, making use of every inshore channel, compelling the submarines to take many risks in shallow waters to get at them. He added that he hoped 'the morale effect of *Sturgeon*'s activities against shipping off this enemy coast may be greater than the material damage inflicted.' With hindsight, there is very little doubt that it indeed was, even if halting the German traffic across the inner Skagerrak would have required resources far beyond those available to the Allied submarine commands at that stage – and resulted in stark losses. In December, Lieutenant Commander Drummond Ford relieved Gregory as CO of *Sturgeon*.[34]

*   *   *

The next submarine to try its luck in the area between Skagen and Lindesnes, was the ill-fated Dutch submarine *O22* (see page 314). Her sister ship *O23* was patrolling between Bergen and Stavanger under Luitenant Valkenburg in October and November, but results were few and far between in spite of bold and sometimes aggressive attempts. Ships were largely moving in escorted convoys with ample air escort and were difficult to get at. Mine-laying was actually producing more results than stalking and torpedoing (see Appendices IV and V). It was also obvious that the German A/S forces were becoming very professional and had a far better grip on their job than earlier. Many started to question the use of valuable submarines in dangerous waters for little gain.

VA(S) Horton agreed and wrote on 29 November in a letter to the senior officer of Dutch submarines at Dundee, Captain C Hellingman, and commander of the 9th Flotilla, Captain James Roper:

> Submarines operating off the south west coast of Norway have in the past been employed on various duties such as attack on coastal shipping, attack on U-boats etc. At present however, I wish to consider that their primary duty is the attack of main units of the enemy fleet. Naturally I do not intend to put any restrictions on attacking merchant ships or small enemy naval units should favourable opportunities present themselves and subject to any risk entailed being considered justifiable, observing the value of the target.[35]

For all practical purposes this would inevitably reduce activities off the Norwegian coast for the time to come.

— 28 —

Autumnsong

Extending the naval war into the Bay of Biscay and the Mediterranean during the summer of 1940 meant fewer submarines were operating in the North Sea and off Norway. For those that did, conditions were every bit as challenging although in a different way. As summer gave way to autumn, perpetual daylight started to change to endless nights, longer the further north, plus heavy weather and few targets. More uncomfortable than unsafe, the patrols nevertheless wore down both men and boats at an alarming rate. As the winter approached, the really effective period of each patrol diminished. Shipping hugged the coast and was difficult to detect against the backdrop of dark, snow-streaked rocks. Keeping well away from the coastline at night, the Allied submarines steered towards land at dawn, utilising the few hours of daylight to the maximum. To have any chance of sighting any prey, it was necessary to get into the Leads, where openings permitted. With shore lights and lighthouses turned off, except when needed by a passing ship or convoy, this was challenging. All the more so as being in amongst rocks and layers of alternating water density rendered the sounding devices unreliable too. More often than not, patrols off Norway during the autumn and winter came back with no results to show.

The anti-invasion and anti-U-boat focus of the Allied submarine operation continued into the autumn of 1940. Neither was particularly successful – the anti-invasion measures because there was no invasion, and the U-boat hunting because it was based on qualified serendipity. Fifteen submarine attacks on U-boats were recorded during the summer of 1940, several of them considered successful at the time, but a careful study of German archives show that only one U-boat was sunk by a submarine in 1940: *U51* by *Cachalot* in the Bay of Biscay in August, in addition to the Italian *Tarantini* sunk by *Thunderbolt*, off the Gironde in December (see below).

Overall, considering the number of U-boats passing through the North Sea at this time, the results were minimal. The harassment and added risk to the U-boats, slowing down their transit and restricting their operational times in shipping lanes, may count for something, though.

Part of the reason for the relatively meagre results could have been Horton's unwillingness to send his large boats, which he considered to be at a disadvantage against the nimbler German boats. It is not explicit in the records, but it would not go against his character to discreetly avoid forwarding orders for missions he did not approve of, as much as he could.

On 10 August 1940, the new First Lord of the Admiralty, Albert Alexander, proposed that the Channel, east of a line from Bishops Rock Lighthouse on the Isles of Scilly to the Chaussée de Seine off Brittany and all waters of the Bay of Biscay east of a line from the Chaussée de Seine to the La Socca lighthouse in Spain should be areas of 'sink-on-sight' and mine-laying for the Allied submarines. This was approved by the War Cabinet on 13 August. In particular, it was considered critical to hunt U-boats in these areas.

On 17 September, the Admiralty issued further instructions clarifying that submarines and surface vessels could attack any ship in the North Sea, the Channel, and Bay of Biscay, whether at anchor, under way or alongside, from any of the countries now occupied by German forces. Spanish and Swedish waters were to be avoided, and restrictions were specified regarding attacks on neutral vessels under German charter, where these were identified as such.[1]

After a considerable amount of discussion and consideration during the summer, it was decided in a conference between the C-in-C Home Fleet and VA(S) on 25 September, with the concurrence of the Admiralty, to focus submarine operations during the autumn and coming winter in three main areas:

- In the Bay of Biscay, off southern Brittany, where several U-boat bases were located
- Off the Norwegian south-west coast
- North of the Shetlands.

Submarine presence would also be maintained in the Channel, between the Westwall and the Dutch coast and off Bordeaux. In addition, occasional patrols would be made along the western edge of the Westwall, to the west of the Hebrides and into the Skagerrak. Increased German traffic along the French coast in September led to a reinforcement of the Channel patrols until the end of October when this traffic appeared to have been reduced again.[2]

As the naval war extended into the Mediterranean, the first British submarines were transferred back to the Mediterranean: *Truant*, *Triad*, *Tetrarch* and *Triton* first, followed by *Triumph*. Later *Upright* and *Utmost* were also transferred from their brief Channel assignments. During the autumn, *Unique*, *Usk*, *Upholder*, *Unbeaten*, *Urge* and *Undaunted* were commissioned and commenced working-up in home waters before transferring to the Mediterranean. For expedience and practical reasons, this was often done by sending the new submarines into areas of the Channel or Bay of Biscay that were expected to be quieter, before heading past Gibraltar.

At the end of June, VA(S) ordered *Cyclops* to leave Rosyth and take up an anchorage in the Rothesay Bay off the Firth of Clyde. She would make up the core of the 7th Submarine Flotilla, which, besides training the many new submarines and their crews, was to provide submarines for A/S training and combined-operations exercises of surface units. During the summer, the level of activity increased and the 2nd Flotilla with the depot ships *Forth* and *White Bear* moved west, residing in Holy Loch a bit further north, across the Firth from Greenock. Eventually the 3rd Flotilla with *Titania* also settled in Holy Loch. The result of all this was a concentration of the submarines remaining in home waters on the west coast of Scotland, while only the 9th Flotilla remained on the North Sea coast, operating out of Dundee. By the beginning of September, priorities and requirements once again had to be balanced against resources, and the Allied submarines under British command in home waters were organised as follows (also see Appendix II):

- 2nd Flotilla at Holy Loch operating T-class boats and minelayers in the Bay of Biscay and the Atlantic area as well as being responsible for submarines on trials or working-up

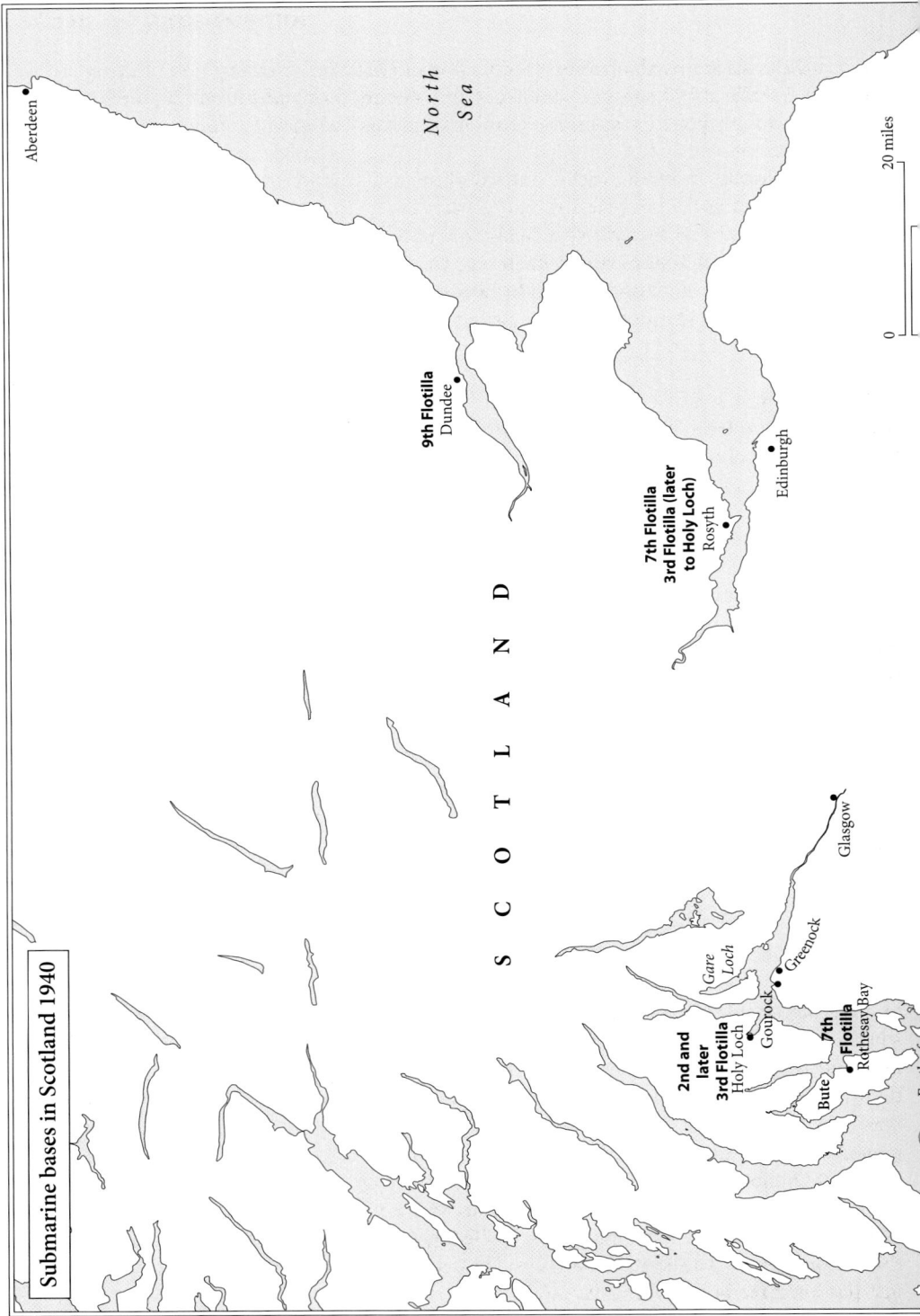

Submarine bases in Scotland 1940

20 miles

Aberdeen

North Sea

9th Flotilla
Dundee

7th Flotilla
3rd Flotilla (later
to Holy Loch)
Rosyth

Edinburgh

S C O T L A N D

Glasgow

Gare Loch

Greenock

2nd and
later
3rd Flotilla
Holy Loch

Gourock

7th
Flotilla
Rothesay Bay

Bute

- 3rd Flotilla at Rosyth operating S-class boats in the North Sea; moved to Holy Loch
- 5th Flotilla at Portsmouth running training courses and administering the building and acceptance trials for new submarines, as well as Free French submarines in reserve
- 6th Flotilla at Blyth, with mixed S-class and U-class boats operating in the North Sea and administering new U-class boats during working-up and gaining operational experience before being sent to the Mediterranean
- 7th Flotilla at Rothesay administering training of submariners and A/S vessels mainly using older boats not fit for war service
- 9th Flotilla at Dundee operating British, Polish, French and Dutch submarines in the North Sea and providing A/S training for the Home Fleet.

Later, the 2nd and 3rd flotillas would be merged at Holy Loch and all sea training would be moved from Portsmouth to Blyth. Otherwise, this overall organisation would be kept for the remainder of the war, although the composition and strength of each flotilla would vary significantly as requirements and available resources changed.[3]

Dundee in Scotland was the home port of the 2nd Submarine Flotilla during the autumn of 1939. From 18 April 1940, however, until the end of the war, 9th Submarine Flotilla made Dundee's dockyard basin its home. The 9th Flotilla was to become quite unique. During 1940 and 1941, it developed into an international unit that included boats and men from Poland, France, the Netherlands and Norway as these countries were occupied by Germany and developed their own exile navies. The first C-in-C, Captain James Roper, had the special task of integrating boats and personalities from several different backgrounds – a task he mastered with admirable skill. 'I know of no one but Roper who could have so successfully cemented us all together,' wrote Dutch submariner Lieutenant Pim Kiepe.[4] In a remarkably short time, Roper made a working unit of men and boats from six nations, Britain included, in spite of the different languages, traditions and routines. Many of the boats had very different equipment and weapon systems and, above all, the newcomers all used the metric system.

The Channel

Still fearing an invasion, a patrol of one or two H-class submarines was kept west and south of the Westwall minefield and off the Frisian Islands long into the autumn. *H28*, *H44* and *H49* shared this task among themselves, operating out of Harwich. In reality there was limited activity in the area and most of the patrols were largely uneventful. Nevertheless, German A/S forces were kept alert and many young submarine officers gained their first experiences on board these old boats.[5]

On 18 October, luck ran out for Lieutenant Richard Coltart and *H49*. Having put to sea from Harwich the day before, the submarine was sighted off Texel by three trawlers of the 11th A/S Flotilla. Kapitänleutnant Wolfgang Kaden on board the trawler *UJ116* was the senior captain. The weather had cleared up after a couple of stormy days and he had just put his three boats in line-abreast, moving slowly for a GHG search, when, around

16:00, one of the lookouts saw something he believed might have been a sail, fine on the starboard bow. The officer of the watch managed to get a glimpse of it through his binoculars as it appeared to vanish under the surface and was certain that it had been the tower of a submarine. Kaden sounded the alarm and ordered his three boats 'full ahead' in the direction of the sighting. Later, he wrote:

> We had only seen the tower for a few seconds and it had been difficult to judge the distance to it. After some 2,000 metres at 'Full Ahead', I slowed down and ordered the GHG operator to start listening again. There was nothing to see on the surface. All depended on him now. [. . .] Ten minutes passed. Still searching. Doubts emerged; had they indeed seen something? There are no German U-boats in the area, and if there is a submarine, it must be the enemy. Ten minutes more passed. An eternity for us all. Finally from the GHG operator: 'Submarine sounds in direction 305!'[6]

Coltart had in all likelihood seen the trawlers and taken *H49* down to 20 metres (65 feet). There, it seems he moved slowly eastwards, out of the way of the onrushing trawlers. They, however, had the scent and the situation was getting dangerous. Kaden steered *UJ116* across the track of *H49* to get a good bearing and approached the submarine from behind. With his GHG operator and helmsman, Kaden had taken the lead in the hunt. The two other trawlers followed on each side ready to intervene should the prey attempt to escape. After some time Kaden ordered full ahead and when they were right over where he believed the submarine was, he ordered five depth charges to be launched overboard: one on each side by the throwers and three to be dropped over the stern at short intervals. There was no obvious result, other than the GHG operator reporting that due to the shuddering their hydrophones had stopped working and needed to be reset. This took about twenty minutes. Even though the other trawlers screened the area, it was not until all three boats could line up for a systematic search that the submarine was found again. This took half an hour, and by now nightfall was approaching. Kaden changed tactics this

H49. (W&L)

time and the trawlers took turns in coming in for the attack, while the others kept *H49* under observation of their GHG receivers. The charges were well placed, shattering the nimble submarine, creating leaks and probably damaging the rudders and motors.

At around 18:50, there was a cry: 'Oil on the surface!' A large oil slick, growing by the minute, was sighted. Kaden took *UJ116* in to drop his charges right in the middle of the slick. More oil and a huge volume of air bubbles followed the explosions. There was no doubt that the submarine had been mortally hit. Still, a final attack was made, this time without the throwers, just rolling the depth charges off the stern, right into the stream of air bubbles. Then, the trawlers held back, waiting to see what would happen next.

To everybody's surprise, what looked like three oranges appeared and, more astonishing, a naked man was seen swimming among them. He was obviously alive and all further attacks were halted. Bleeding and covered in oil the freezing survivor was brought onboard *UJ116* where he was wrapped in blankets, given a large schnapps and taken to tell his story to Kaden.

The man was Leading Stoker George Oliver. He told Kaden that as the decisive depth charges from the trawlers ripped open the hull, he believed he had been sucked through the engine-room hatch in a rush of escaping air.[7] In spite of his experience, Oliver was not really any worse for wear despite some heavy breathing and pains in the chest; after a few more schnapps, he was put to rest in a bed below. The trawlers searched until it was too dark to see any more, but there were no other survivors.[8] Later, Kaden wrote:

> We remained at the site the whole night, keeping a watch with the GHG-set constantly manned. We could hear thudding and banging sounds from the wreck at times. Apparently, there were survivors attempting to get out. Unfortunately, there was nothing we could do to help. At dawn, we heard two shots from below – then all was quiet, the sea serenely masking the tragedy that had taken place in the deep. [. . .] Divers later found that the submarine lay on its side, the tower into the sand and the stern somewhat raised. There was no way the surviving men inside could have escaped.[9]

George Oliver was taken to port and would spend the rest of the war as a POW. Kaden received the Knight's Cross in recognition of his achievement, only the second to be awarded to a reserve officer of the Kriegsmarine.[10]

Further south, British anti-invasion patrols were organised under the direction of C-in-C Portsmouth. In mid-September, as the invasion alerts heightened, *Talisman*, *Swordfish*, *H43* and *L27* were temporarily transferred to 5th Flotilla. In November, *Seawolf* was also added to this patrol. In addition, several of the new U-class boats, including *Utmost*, *Upright*, *Ursula*, *Usk* and *Unique*, had one or two missions out of Portsmouth to allow the crews to become familiar with their boats. The patrols were focused in two areas to avoid interference with their own surface A/S forces: between Dieppe and Cap d'Antifer, and off Cherbourg, between Cape de la Hague and Cape Barfleur.[11]

In the patrol orders for these missions, issued to the submarine commanders through 5th Flotilla, it was stated that reporting was their most important objective and, if at all possible, they should send a sighting report immediately and attack afterwards. Enemy naval forces and shipping that appeared to be heading across the Channel were to be given absolute priority. Coast-wise traffic should only be attacked if 'considered of sufficient

German *Raubvogel*-class torpedo boats. Left *Möwe,* right *Kondor* with minesweeper *M1* in Stavanger, 6 May 1940. After the conquest of France, most of the surviving torpedo boats were moved to the French channel coast. (Author's Collection)

importance to justify the risk of the submarine's position being compromised.' With this in mind, Lieutenant Commander Philip Francis of *Talisman* did not fire his torpedoes on a large tanker, escorted by two trawlers sighted off Cape Barfleur on 26 September, which made the Admiralty revise the instructions so that coastal traffic could be attacked if it was 'considered of sufficient importance to justify the expenditure of torpedoes'.[12]

On 15 October, Lieutenant Robert Campbell fired three torpedoes from *L27* at a large camouflaged merchant vessel screened by seven trawlers off Cape Barfleur. The distance to the nearest escort was about 400 metres (440 yards) when firing and all three torpedoes appeared to hit a minute later. *L27* was thoroughly shaken by the explosions, which broke several lights in the boat and disabled instruments. Some of the escorts followed the torpedo tracks back towards *L27* and twenty depth charges were dropped, a few of them quite close. Campbell had little room to manoeuvre as land was close, but after an hour he had taken his boat out of immediate danger and an hour after that he proceeded northwards at maximum speed to clear the area.[13] The German ship, *Sperrbrecher III*, was damaged, but managed to reach harbour.

At 09:35 on 1 October, Lieutenant Patrick Cowell of *Swordfish* sighted four German torpedo boats off Cape Barfleur. These were *Falke, Kondor, Greif* and *Seeadler*, which were returning from Operation Werner, laying mines off Dover. When Cowell saw them, they were line-ahead in two columns, heading south-east, about 5,000 metres (5,500 yards) away. *Swordfish* was in an almost perfect position and less than ten minutes after initially seeing them, Cowell fired four torpedoes at the rear ship of the nearest column, which he estimated to be a little over 1,200 metres (1,300 yards) away, doing 18 knots. One violent explosion was heard sixty-nine seconds after firing the first torpedo, indicating a hit. The other three torpedoes were heard to explode six minutes later, some distance away. None of the torpedo boats was hit, however, and they all returned safely to their temporary base in Barfleur.

Content that he had hit the target, Lieutenant Cowell took his boat deep after the first explosion. To avoid breaking surface in the rough sea when firing the torpedoes, a larger than normal amount of water had been taken in forward and the boat was heavy. Remarkably, both the fore and after hydroplane connectors came off their brackets due to the concussion from the exploding torpedo, and could not be replaced in time to prevent the laden boat from hitting the seabed hard at 70 metres (230 feet). The crew were shaken, but damage was slight, except for the two remaining torpedoes, which had got stuck in their tubes, and the asdic dome, which had been torn off. As neither the German torpedo boats nor any other A/S forces were searching for them, *Swordfish* remained on the bottom for an hour before rising to 20 metres (65 feet), withdrawing northwards to repair the damage.[14]

Towards the end of October, *Swordfish*, which Lieutenant Michael Langley had taken over as CO with Lieutenant Harry Stacey as first officer, was back off Cherbourg. On the 27th, a convoy of eight merchant ships was sighted. Two torpedoes were fired at the extreme range of 8,000 metres (8,750 yards), but Langley reckoned that he had hit the target as two loud explosions were heard and a plume of black smoke was seen at sea level just aft of the after mast before he took *Swordfish* down and retired to the north.[15] Once again, the German ship was merely damaged.

On 7 November *Swordfish* took to sea from Fort Blockhouse once more, this time to relieve *Usk* off Brest. Nothing was ever heard from her again and it was believed she had been sunk by German destroyers. In 1983, however, the wreckage of *Swordfish* was discovered by divers some 12 miles south of St Catherine's Point, Isle of Wight. The boat is split in two just forward of the gun and most likely she struck a mine laid by German

Swordfish. (Author's Collection)

S-boats the night before, whilst carrying out a trim dive. Forty-one British submariners were lost.[16]

The results of the patrols off the French Channel coast were meagre, in spite of the amended instructions, and as demands from the Mediterranean and other theatres increased, the patrols were terminated in late November 1940, following the loss of *Swordfish*. C-in-C Portsmouth, Admiral William James, wrote:

> The Channel guerrilla warfare has assumed certain characteristics. All the evidence points to the enemy coast-hopping by day under air and shore gun protection, but little activity at night. [. . .] Occasional sweeps by our destroyers may, one night, produce an encounter, but in the present conditions submarines maintaining a patrol are the only certain means of taking a toll of enemy vessels. The toll will not be heavy as there is no great volume of shipping along the French coast, but if submarines again become available, they would be welcome in the Portsmouth command.[17]

Bay of Biscay

Shortly after the fall of France, the importance of the new naval bases in the Bay of Biscay to the Kriegsmarine's U-boat and surface units became obvious. Hence British submarine patrols in the Biscay were increased as much as resources allowed. The number of T-class and other long-range boats was limited, though, resulting in the Bay of Biscay patrols rarely consisting of more than one or two boats at a time. On some days, there was not a single Allied submarine in the Bay of Biscay.[18]

Operating the Bay of Biscay patrol out of Holy Loch had the advantage that the base was out of harm's way and the boats could be used in the Atlantic on convoy escort as well if necessary. The disadvantage was that almost a week was spent travelling back and forth, significantly reducing the patrol time on the billet. To avoid misunderstandings and reduce risk, escort was also needed from Land's End northwards through the Irish Sea, further draining resources that could have been used elsewhere.

The waters off the south-west coast of France are most unwelcoming to a submarine. Treacherous currents, shallow rocks and endless Atlantic swells make for miserable, strenuous patrols. The number of fishing vessels in the area in 1940 was remarkable, adding extra challenges. Sightings of U-boats were frequent in the Bay of Biscay, but there were few successes trying to sink them – not for want of trying, more due to a combination of efficient German escort routines and first-rate watch-keeping, coupled with a lack of luck on the British side. This probably reflected the large number of new young British submarine COs, who were aggressive and eager to perform, but lacked the experience and tenacity gained through years of standing at the periscope.

In the morning of 26 September, *Tribune* was at periscope depth about 10 miles south-west of Île de Groix. This was not long after it had become known that a German U-boat base had been established at Lorient, and most of the British submarines in the area were eager to see if this was the case and if they could catch some of them on the way in or out of the base.

The excitement of Lieutenant Edward Balston when he sighted two type VII U-boats on the surface must have been quite high. Especially after the failure off St Kilda three weeks earlier (see page 355). The two U-boats were *U138*, under Oberleutnant Wolfgang Lüth, and *U47*, under Kapitänleutnant Günther Prien. They had just been met by the A/S trawlers *UJ122*, *UJ128* and *UJE* and were now being escorted back to port. Balston got his boat in position and fired five torpedoes at the nearest adversary, *U138*, but all missed. In spite of being under the wings of the escort, Lüth maintained a vigilant lookout, which spotted the tracks, and he managed to steer away by initiating a feverish zigzag. One of the torpedoes ran under the U-boat and one missed, passing just ahead. Balston's thoughts when he realised that he had missed again are not recorded.[19]

Three minefields were laid by submarines in the Bay of Biscay during the autumn of 1940, two by *Cachalot* and one by *Porpoise*. The first minefield was laid in August. *Cachalot*, under Lieutenant Commander John Luce, departed Rothesay on the 5th with orders to lay the mines off the Gironde and thereafter patrol further offshore. The field FD24 was laid on 19 August, west of the Gironde estuary, off Belle-Île, in what was expected to be the departure route for U-boats from Saint-Nazaire. The fifty mines were laid in five groups of ten, scattered around a circle of radius 1.5 miles. This took one hour and fifteen minutes, after which *Cachalot* settled down on a patrol routine. The next day, 20 August, Luce wrote in *Cachalot*'s war diary:

> At 01:11, *Cachalot* was steaming down wind and sea and towards the moon. Sighted small object about 25° on starboard bow about 4 miles away. Brought all tubes to the ready. Object was identified as a submarine. Visibility five miles, bright moonlight. At 01:17, fired six torpedoes, staggered at 8 feet and 12 feet. First torpedo fired from the surface, remainder as submarine dived. Range about 1500 yards. One minute ten seconds later, an explosion was heard. [. . .] At 12:18, surfaced and proceeded to estimated position of enemy submarine, when torpedo hit. [. . .] Found an area about ½ mile across thickly covered with oil which smelt strongly of diesel fuel. [. . .] There were no indications that the submarine was still afloat.[20]

The U-boat had indeed gone down. Kapitänleutnant Dietrich Knorr had taken command of the type VIIB boat *U51* in January 1940 and during three patrols had sunk five ships, for a total of some 25,000 tons. On his fourth patrol, Knorr had taken *U51* out from Kiel on 9 August. During a sweep west of the British Isles the 5,709-ton British tanker *Sylvafield*, a straggler from convoy HX-52, had been sunk north-west of Ireland on 15 August. The following day, *U51* was caught on the surface by a Sunderland flying boat of 210 Squadron Coastal Command and seriously damaged. Knorr made a damage report and communicated with U-boat Command, obtaining permission to set course for France.[21] On 20 August *U51* was west of Saint-Nazaire, heading for the newly opened base at Lorient. It is not known if they saw the torpedoes coming, as there were no survivors. The R-boats sent out to escort Knorr and his boat to port returned empty-handed, and aircraft sent out to look for them found nothing either. *Cachalot* was back at Rothesay at midday on 4 September.[22]

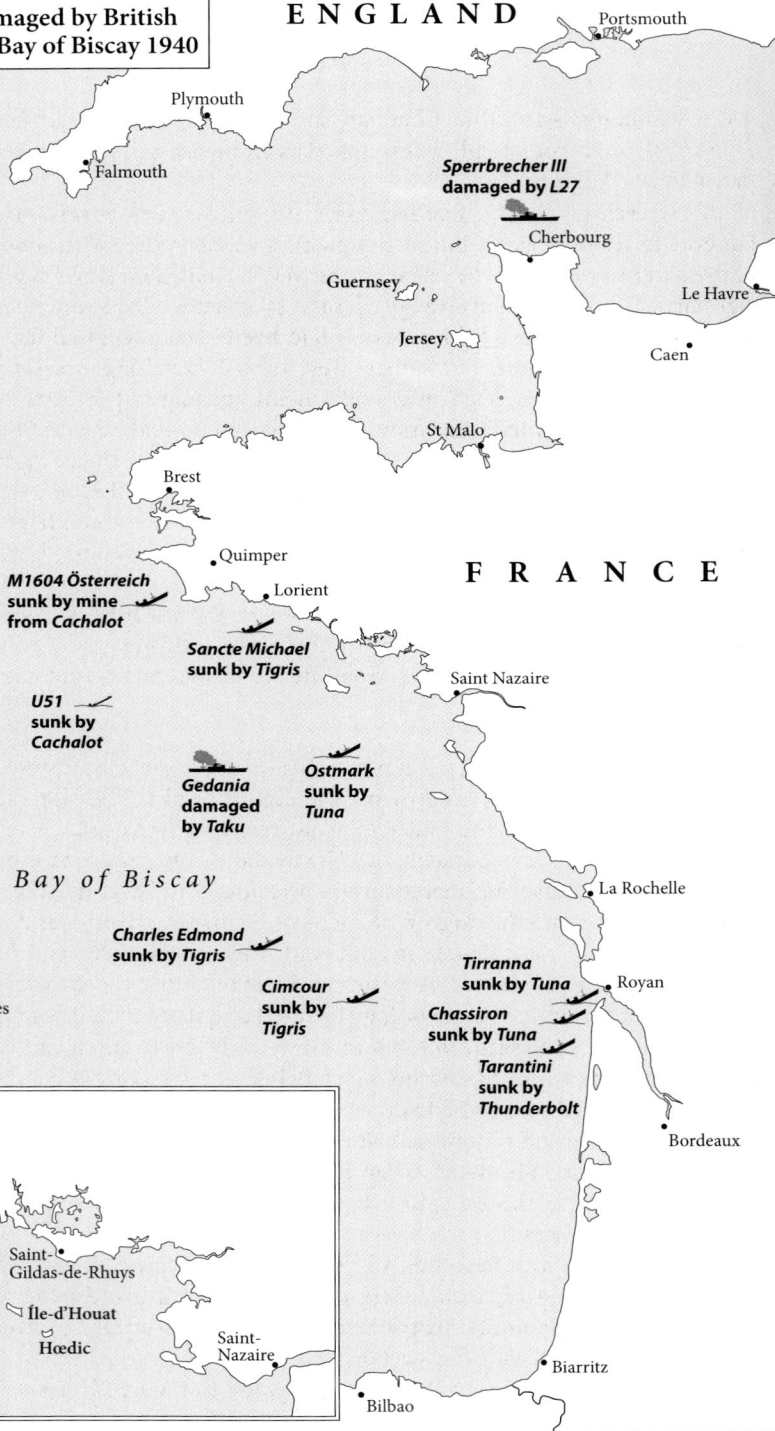

Ships sunk and damaged by British submarines in the Bay of Biscay 1940

ENGLAND

Portsmouth

Plymouth

Falmouth

Sperrbrecher III
damaged by *L27*

Cherbourg

Guernsey

Le Havre

Jersey

Caen

ATLANTIC
OCEAN

St Malo

Brest

Tropic Sea
sunk by
Truant

Quimper

FRANCE

M1604 Österreich
sunk by mine
from *Cachalot*

Lorient

Sancte Michael
sunk by *Tigris*

Saint Nazaire

U51
sunk by
Cachalot

Gedania
damaged
by *Taku*

Ostmark
sunk by
Tuna

Bay of Biscay

La Rochelle

Charles Edmond
sunk by *Tigris*

Cimcour
sunk by
Tigris

Tirranna
sunk by *Tuna*

Royan

Chassiron
sunk by *Tuna*

Tarantini
sunk by
Thunderbolt

0   50 miles

0   50 km

Bordeaux

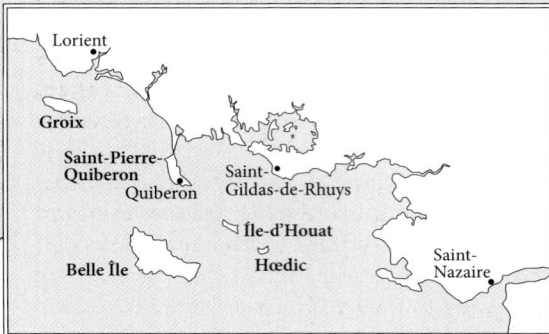

Lorient

Groix

Saint-Pierre-
Quiberon

Quiberon

Saint-
Gildas-de-Rhuys

Île-d'Houat

Belle Île

Hœdic

Saint-
Nazaire

Biarritz

Bilbao

September

Tigris was commissioned at Chatham on 20 June 1940, with Lieutenant Commander Howard Bone in command. Following trials and work-up, she joined the Bay of Biscay patrol in late August.

In the evening of 2 September, *Tigris* was on the surface off Lorient, charging her batteries in almost glassy-calm seas. A patchy haze alternated with good visibility, in spite of the darkness. At 22:31, the officer of the watch, Lieutenant Leslie Bennington, reported sighting a U-boat ahead at a range of some 450 metres (1,500 yards), steering from port to starboard. Numerous fishing vessels had been encountered all day, 'making passage both difficult and devious'. Now, there were at least six fishing vessels nearby. At the time of sighting the U-boat, *Tigris* was under helm, turning to port. Arriving at the bridge, Lieutenant Commander Bone immediately took command, reversed the rudder to hard-a-starboard and ordered 'action stations'. *Tigris* started to swing back, but the U-boat seemed to be diving so Bone fired the starboard mid-ship tube, which was at an angle to the centre-line and roughly in the right direction. Twelve seconds later, before *Tigris* had swung sufficiently to bring the bow tubes to bear, there was a bright flash followed by a tremendous explosion, which shook *Tigris* noticeably.

The U-boat, *U58*, got away, but the French 168-ton fishing vessel *Sancte Michael* existed no more. The five other boats that were with her searched for survivors but found none. *Tigris* hastened away from the scene, everybody on board convinced they had sunk a U-boat.[23]

In April 1940, the British 5,207-ton merchantman *Haxby* was captured by the German auxiliary cruiser *Orion* (*Schiff36*) off the Grand Banks. The ship was sunk, but the crew was kept onboard the raider to avoid revealing her existence. Two months later, in June, north of New Zealand, the Norwegian *Tropic Sea* was one of several ships intercepted. The 8,750-ton merchantman was found to be under charter to the British Ministry of Food and the cargo, 8,000 tons of Australian wheat, was destined for Britain. Such a cargo was too valuable to sink, and it was decided to send her independently to German-occupied France. A twenty-eight-man German prize crew under Leutnant Fritz Steinkrauss was put on board, while the thirty-three-man Norwegian crew – under Captain Henry Nicolaysen, with his wife part of the crew, sailing as a stewardess – were locked up below deck. The twenty or so British prisoners from *Haxby*, led by Captain Cornelius Arundell, were also transferred to *Tropic Sea* before she set course for Europe. The trip was uneventful until just after dawn on 3 September, about 235 nautical miles north-west of Cape Finisterre, when a submarine was sighted, coming up from astern some 5 miles off. At this time, the *Tropic Sea* was less than twenty-four hours from her destination, Bordeaux.

The submarine was *Truant* en route to the Mediterranean, under Lieutenant Commander Hugh Haggard, with orders to hang around a few days in the Bay of Biscay looking for an opportunity. Haggard signalled for the freighter to stop, not to transmit and to send a boat with the captain and the ship's papers. While the engines were stopped, and *Tropic Sea* came to a halt, Haggard positioned *Truant* on her port quarter. The submarine's gun was manned and trained on the bridge of *Tropic Sea*. To Haggard's surprise, a large number of men appeared on deck and it soon became evident that the ship was being abandoned. This took quite some time, but eventually all boats had been lowered and started to move away. None of them seemed to come in the direction of *Truant*, though, and Haggard gave chase to find the master. Before he could be located, two explosions were heard from aboard the ship, although she showed no signs of going down. Meanwhile, Leutnant Steinkrauss had been identified and ordered on board *Truant* to explain the history of *Tropic Sea* and the men she carried.

Faced with such an unexpected situation, Haggard eventually took the twenty-three survivors from *Haxby* on board *Truant*, as well as Captain Nicolaysen and his wife, who had hurt herself when abandoning the ship. Mrs Nicolaysen therefore most likely became the first woman to sail in a British submarine on a war patrol. The other Norwegians were left in the lifeboats together with the German prize crews.[24]

At first, *Tropic Sea* made no signs of sinking, but, while deliberating what to do with her, she suddenly took a list, bow down to port, and was gone in a couple of minutes. *Truant* sent a signal to VA(S) and headed off to land the rescued sailors in Gibraltar as soon as possible. Of the Norwegian sailors, ten were picked up from their lifeboat by a Sunderland flyingboat and taken to Plymouth. The rest of the Norwegians and the Germans landed in Spain over the next couple of days. As Spain was neutral and did not want responsibility for the care of a large number of sailors, the authorities gave them a free choice of where they wanted to go. Some of the Norwegians opted for home, but the majority joined their mates in Britain and from there rejoined the Norwegian merchant fleet now sailing under Norwegian flag in Allied service. The German prize crew was quickly repatriated to Germany.[25]

The second submarine-laid minefield in the Bay of Biscay, FD26 (forty-eight mines), was put in place on 13 September off the Île d'Yeu, north-west of La Rochelle, by *Porpoise* under Lieutenant Commander Jack Hopkins.

On 16 September, Lieutenant Commander Luce took *Cachalot* to sea from Rothesay once more, for her fifth war patrol. His orders were to lay a third minefield in the Bay of Biscay and thereafter to patrol the area. The passage south through the Irish Sea was made in the company of *Tribune* and *Utmost*, escorted by the armed yacht *Cutty Sark*.

On 23 September, fifty mines were laid off Pointe de Penmarch, field FD27. This time, the mines were scattered inside a 1.5-mile-radius circle centered on position 47° 48' N, 04° 33' W. The first mine was laid at 14:12 and the last at 15:26. Ten minutes later, three loud explosions were heard. Luce took *Cachalot* to periscope depth where he sighted four A/S trawlers, apparently hunting for him. He was at a safe distance, though, and retired quietly to the west. What Luce did not know at the time was that the explosions came from the 494-ton minesweeper *M1604 Österreich*, which sank after setting off two of the mines which *Cachalot* had laid shortly before.

The next day, *Cachalot* received instructions to head northwards to intercept a U-boat on its way to Lorient. An aircraft had sighted the enemy boat and was, for the first time, able to send its report directly to the nearest submarine. Five hours later, close to nightfall, the asdic operator reported echoes and *Cachalot* was brought to periscope depth. Luce was in a difficult position and could only see the conning tower of his opponent, but decided to fire anyway. He later wrote:

At 19:30, sighted conning tower of a submarine bearing 170°. Altered course to 140°. Proceeded at full speed. At 19:36, unable to see U-boat at 30 feet. Came up to 20 feet. Could just see U-boat's conning tower again. Visibility variable but fairly good in the direction of the enemy. At 19:43, fired 6 torpedoes on estimated track angle of 145°, three Mark VIII and three Mark VIII*. Enemy course 90° speed 12½. Two explosions were heard in quick succession about five minutes after firing. Two torpedoes were heard to pass very close. One down each side of *Cachalot*.[26]

At the time, Luce believed that, not only had he sunk one more U-boat, but before being hit, it had fired back at him. *Cachalot* surfaced at 21:10 and when approaching the area of the attack, there was a distinct smell of diesel fuel over a wide area, but nothing to be seen. *U37* and *U61* left Lorient earlier that day, and if there was a U-boat there at all it must have been one of them. There is no mention in either boat's KTB, however, of being attacked or attacking anything, nor of steering a south-easterly course at any time. The torpedoes heard passing *Cachalot* could have been one or two of her own that malfunctioned and turned back. Why two of the others apparently exploded after five minutes is unclear. The water depth in that area is over 3,500 metres (11,500 feet) and, having run their course, the torpedoes would likely have imploded before reaching the bottom, which would have taken a lot longer than five minutes. *Cachalot* was back at base in Rothesay on 27 September.[27]

In the second half of September, it was *Tuna*'s turn to take up a billet in the Bay of Biscay. Lieutenant Commander Maurice Cavenagh-Mainwaring took her to sea from Holy Loch on the 15th and was at the billet off the Gironde on the 19th. Things were quiet for a few days until, on the 22nd, a large merchant ship was sighted at midday. The ship was dark grey, flew no flag and had no neutrality markings painted on her side. Cavenagh-Mainwaring believed the vessel to be 'of a German type with cruiser bow and a high stern', possibly an armed merchant cruiser or raider. After about an hour *Tuna* was in position and four torpedoes were fired. Three hits were observed, two resulting in large explosions, and the ship started going down. Cavenagh-Mainwaring was quite content and turned to seaward, reloading his tubes. After a while, two trawlers were seen in the periscope and a few explosions heard astern, but no serious hunt was initiated. Having compromised *Tuna*'s billet, course was set for the area off Île d'Yeu, between La Rochelle and Saint-Nazaire.

Unknown to Cavenagh-Mainwaring at the time, he had just sunk the 7,230-ton Norwegian *Tirranna*, which had been captured by the German armed merchant cruiser *Atlantis* (*Schiff 16*) in the Indian Ocean in June 1940. She carried large quantities of food, wool and military vehicles for the Middle East and it was decided to send her as a prize to German-occupied France. Some 260 prisoners from other captured ships were transferred onboard, together with a prize crew of sixteen. Including most of the original Norwegian crew, there were almost 300 men on board *Tirranna* when she was intercepted by *Tuna*. Of these, eighty-seven died (seventy-one Indians, nine British, one German and six Norwegians). The survivors spent several hours in the water before being saved by German vessels coming to the rescue.[28]

Happily unaware of this, however, the men of *Tuna* continued their patrol to the north. In the early hours of the 24th, off Saint-Nazaire, three dark objects came in sight

Lieutenant Commander Maurice Cavenagh-Mainwaring bringing *Tuna* safely back to Holy Loch after a war patrol in the Bay of Biscay. (IWM A18930)

on the port bow at a significant distance. This turned out to be the 1,281-ton catapult ship *Ostmark* screened by the minesweepers *M6* and *M12*.

The *Ostmark* was one of three vessels used as floating bases for flyingboats on the pre-war route to South America. The two others, *Westfalen* and *Schwabenland*, were rebuilt merchantmen, while *Ostmark* was purpose-built, commissioned in April 1936. In addition to a large crane, there was a catapult aft to re-launch the flying boats after they had been serviced and fuelled. The outbreak of war found the *Ostmark* in the Atlantic and it sought refuge in the Spanish Canary Islands until ordered to France by the Luftwaffe in September 1940. The first part of this trip went well and on 19 September, *Ostmark* reached Le Verdon at the mouth of the Gironde. After a few days there, she continued towards her intended base at Brest, under escort, from where it was intended she should support long-range flyingboat reconnaissance missions.

At the time, *Ostmark* was identified as a merchant vessel escorted by two destroyers. Six torpedoes were fired from about 4 miles away, after which *Tuna* went deep. One of the escorts was heard to come chasing the submarine, most likely running down the torpedo tracks. Shortly after, an explosion was heard, but no counter-attack materialised, possibly as the escort returned to assist the stricken ship. *Ostmark* took two and a half hours to sink, and all but one of the fifty-man crew was saved.[29]

Tuna ended her successful second war patrol at Holy Loch on 3 October.

October

October 1940 was fairly bleak in the Bay of Biscay, both in terms of weather and successes. Some of the T-class boats had a few interesting encounters, though.

On 29 September, Lieutenant Commander Geoffrey Sladen took *Trident* to sea from Holy Loch on the submarine's thirteenth war patrol, with orders to patrol the U-boat lanes off Lorient. Sladen had taken command of *Trident* in late April, and had long since proven himself as an able submariner, even if he had not yet sunk any enemy ships. This was his sixth patrol as CO.

During the night of 6/7 October, Sladen took *Trident* across the billet, close to Île de Groix on a northerly course. It was known that many U-boats preferred to make their final approach to base during darkness, to avoid air attacks. German trawlers were also about, though, forcing *Trident* to the southward, and eventually she ended up west of Pointe des Poulains, Belle-Île. The next morning, at 05:04 on the 8th, *Trident* was submerged, moving very slowly at 25 metres (82 feet) depth when an echo was picked up, identified as a U-boat close by. This was *U31*, a type VIIA U-boat under the command of Kapitänleutnant Wilfrid Prellberg. They were on the last leg of a twenty-three-day patrol west of the British Isles, now approaching their new base at Lorient. Prellberg had sunk two ships: the Faeroese sailing schooner *Union Jack* and the 4,319-ton Norwegian motor transport *Vestvard*.

With no knowledge of this, Sladen took *Trident* to the surface, proceeding in the direction of the contact on both engines. Within a few minutes, the port lookout sighted *U31*. Sladen went to full ahead and, expecting *Trident* to have been sighted as well, gave instructions to swing on to a firing course. At 05:31, five torpedoes were fired from about 1,400 metres (1,500 yards). Number four tube misfired, though, so only four torpedoes went off. No results were observed, and four minutes later, a further two torpedoes were fired, this time from less than 400 metres (440 yards). Both these also missed. After a further two minutes, at 05:37, one more torpedo was fired – this was seen to pass just clear of the U-boat's stern. Number four tube was also fired at this stage, but, as *Trident* was turning to avoid getting too close, this torpedo went wide.

Onboard *U31*, the shadow of *Trident* was at first believed to be a fishing boat by one lookout and a cliff by the other and was not identified as a submarine until just before the first torpedoes were fired.[30] Once it was clear they were being stalked, Prellberg ordered two torpedo tubes to be made ready, as what was undoubtedly a British submarine was approaching fast from behind. The submarine was some 1,500 metres (1,650 yards) behind, close to the U-boat's wake, and Prellberg did not believe it would fire at such a tight angle until it had closed to less than 500 metres (550 yards). Suddenly however, his opponent pulled to the side to give himself a broader target and fired several torpedoes. These were avoided, even if they were close – the nearest being only a few metres to port. Shortly after, the British submarine crossed the U-boat's wake from port to starboard and a further two torpedoes were seen in the water. Again these were avoided and, rather than diving to get away, Prellberg chose to stay on the surface, hoping to get a chance to fire back.

The two boats were now very close, less than 100 metres (110 yards) apart. Sladen took *Trident* past his opponent's stern, steadied on a parallel course to port and opened fire with the deck gun. The muzzle-flash from the first round blinded the gun layer for a moment, but he soon recovered and the second round was seen to hit the target at the base of the conning tower. Sparks flew from the impact, but the shell bounced off and no explosion occurred. By the time the eyes of the men at the gun and on the bridge had adjusted, the U-boat was seen to be diving. Prellberg had finally had enough and opted to get out of the escalating situation.

Sladen took *Trident* down too. No echoes were heard, although a contact was obtained on what was thought to be the wreck of the submarine. Hence, Sladen claimed that the U-boat had been sunk. This was not the case, though: *U31* actually grounded at 70 metres (230 feet) and remained there for some time. Eventually, things grew quiet and Prellberg took *U31* back to the surface, continuing towards Lorient, where they docked in the afternoon. His last comment in the U-boat's war diary was: 'The main task for the boat on this patrol appears to have been as a target for British submarines. We were fired at three times and avoided altogether seven torpedoes.'[31]

Trident ended her thirteenth war patrol at Holy Loch on 16 October, without further events.[32]

In the last days of September, *Tigris*, heading into the Bay of Biscay on her second war patrol, ran into a new type of enemy.

Naval collaboration had already been discussed between the Kriegsmarine and Regia Marina in June 1939, including a commitment from the Italian side to a presence in the Atlantic. Little happened, though, until hostilities with Britain commenced in June 1940 – particularly as Franco denied Italy use of Spanish ports, and patrolling the Atlantic from bases in Italy, having to negotiate the Strait of Gibraltar both ways, was unfeasible. The fall of France and subsequent Axis access to French ports completely changed this picture. Referring to the earlier agreement, the Kriegsmarine now requested Italian submarines to take responsibility for the area south of Lisbon in Portugal. This was at a critical time, when the new strategic situation that had emerged through the occupation of France could not be fully utilised by Dönitz, as he simply did not have enough U-boats. Alternative base facilities were offered and, after inspection by a naval commission, the choice fell on Bordeaux. Though quite some way up the Gironde, the port facilities were suitable and, above all, there was a navigable system of canals connecting it to the Mediterranean. The base was officially opened on 30 August with the liners *De Grasse* and *Usaramo* acting as support vessels. A secondary base, with easy access to the sea, was set up at La Pallice, near La Rochelle.

The three first Italian submarines sent to the Atlantic, the *Alessandro Malaspina*, *Barbarigo* and *Dandolo*, crossed the Strait of Gibraltar during August without incident. *Malaspina* and *Dandolo* sank one British vessel each and damaged a few others, before they headed for Bordeaux, all in need of repair to some degree. In the subsequent weeks, a further twenty-four Italian submarines crossed the strait, with only one vessel, the *Bianchi*, being damaged by a British A/S patrol.[33] Before entering the Gironde, most of the submarines patrolled billets west of the Strait of Gibraltar for some time, achieving minor results. The Italian boats were larger, slower and less rugged than the German ones, and they were generally manned by experienced older officers, who were not as committed or prepared for the dangers and hardships of the Atlantic. Younger, dedicated officers were emerging, but in 1940 few of these had yet obtained the rank of CO. Technical failures would plague the Italian submarines throughout the war, in particular engines and pumps, while their torpedoes in general were quite reliable.[34]

In mid-September, the second group of half a dozen Italian submarines headed for Bordeaux via a sweep into the Atlantic, including the *Reginaldo Giuliani* and the *Maggiore Baracca*. In the morning of 5 October these two boats met up with their escorts *M9* and *M13* off the mouth of the Gironde to make the final approach up the river to Bordeaux together, when they were sighted by *Tigris*. For some reason Lieutenant Commander Bone believed he saw three submarines, but Italian and German reports only mention *Giuliani* and *Baracca*. Bone let *Tigris* approach the group of ships and, in spite of seeing the two escort vessels approaching through the periscope, he fired four torpedoes at one of the submarines from about 2,500 metres (2,750 yards). Three of the torpedoes were seen by the lookouts of *Giuliani* and she managed to steer away. On board *Tigris*, two explosions were heard after about two minutes. When looking through the periscope shortly afterwards, Bone saw only two escorts and two submarines and, as he believed he had seen three previously, he erroneously claimed one sunk.

The two minesweepers searched for *Tigris* for about half an hour, dropping eleven depth charges, but none of them were close. Both Italian submarines docked in Bordeaux in the early hours of the next day.[35]

Tigris continued the patrol off the Gironde. No more Italian submarines were encountered, though, but on the 16th the French 250-ton coaster *Cimcour* was sunk by gunfire as Bone believed she was attempting to ram his submarine. When fire was opened, the crew of the French boat turned on their lights, blew the ship's whistle and shouted. Nevertheless, two rounds hit *Cimcour* amidships and she started to settle before the fire was checked. Apparently somewhat embarrassed, even though the vessel was under German flag and therefore a legitimate target, Bone turned westwards, leaving it to a nearby trawler to pick up the survivors. *Tigris* ended her third war patrol at Holy Loch on 19 October.[36]

Tigris's sister ship *Talisman* was on her fourth war patrol in October. From the 18th to the 22nd, she was patrolling her billet off the Gironde River in calm seas and moderate winds with little happening, except having to avoid a few fishing vessels and on one occasion an A/S patrol consisting of four armed trawlers. At 06:30 on the 22nd, however, just as it was starting to get light, a black object was sighted to the west. Lieutenant Commander Francis wrote:

> Object was identified as a submarine. Course was altered as necessary to close the range and keep on a track. At 06:44 fired 6 torpedoes using night sight at lowest speed (10 kts) on an estimated track of 120°. Firing interval 7 seconds. Range 3000 yards approx. Point of aim half a length ahead. About 10 seconds after giving the order to fire, there was a violent explosion close ahead of *Talisman*. This explosion was undoubtedly one of our own torpedoes, either exploding on the bottom or the air vessel blowing up. The explosion seemed hardly violent enough for the former. The Torpedo Gunner's Mate was knocked off his seat by the explosion, so there was a gap of 15 seconds before the 3rd torpedo was fired. On observing the enemy after firing, it was apparent he was going at a speed considerably less than 10 knots and in all probability torpedoes missed ahead.[37]

The submarine fired at was the Italian *Enrico Tazzoli* and she was indeed not hit on this occasion. There is no doubt, however, that at least one torpedo exploded prematurely.

Water depth at the given location is around 50 metres (165 feet) and the torpedo might have reached that depth quickly if it had headed down just after leaving the tube due to a gyroscope fault, for example. Francis's second explanation is perhaps more likely, though, considering the apparent violence of the explosion. If this was really the case – that something went wrong with the hot air/gas mixture of the Mk VIII** torpedo's burner-cycle engine and it blew up shortly after leaving the tube – this could well have happened on other occasions too, explaining some of the difficulties correlating apparent hits reported by the submarine COs with actual results.

Having seen the tracks of at least four of his torpedoes missing his opponent, Francis took *Talisman* down. There was flooding in the fore-end, however, due to the automatic inboard venting (AIV) tank of one of the external tubes not being properly closed, and the weight of the excess water moving about made the submarine unstable. Fearing that there was an uncontrollable leak due to the explosion, Francis surfaced again, having bottomed briefly. There was also intense pressure building up inside the boat as one of the reload torpedoes had come loose due to the explosion and smashed a high-pressure air pipe. On opening the conning tower hatch, therefore, it slammed open with great force, damaging both clips and becoming distorted.

Coming onto the bridge, *Enrico Tazzoli* was still in sight, about two miles to the south-south-west. It did not appear that they were in any way preparing to attack *Talisman* and Francis decided to man his gun. It was not clear at this stage what was causing the leak, and even if there were two torpedoes left forward he did not want to risk firing them, but would rather try to damage the Italian boat to at least prevent her from diving. No hits were scored, though, before she dived. On diving, a recognition signal of three white flares was fired from *Tazzoli*, indicating that she might have believed it was a German

Italian submarine *Enrico Tazzoli* entering Bordeaux after having just escaped the attack from *Talisman*. (Author's Collection)

U-boat attacking her. *Enrico Tazzoli* had passed the Strait of Gibraltar two weeks earlier and was now on her way towards Bordeaux after a patrol in the Atlantic where she had sunk the 5,135-ton Yugoslav freighter *Orao*.[38]

Talisman withdrew hastily towards the west to get out of harm's way, repair the defects and continue her patrol. Nothing more happened; four days later, Lieutenant Commander Francis left the patrol area, starting the long passage back to Holy Loch.[39]

The presence of the Italian submarines in western France was duly registered by VA(S) and the Admiralty, and British bomber attacks on Bordeaux commenced in mid-October. Prior to that, British and French agents, landed clandestinely from *Talisman* as early as 2 August near Hourtin Lighthouse, had already surveyed the base, confirming what was going on.[40]

Tuna's third war patrol, from 23 October to 15 November, was uneventful except for an almost continuous gale blowing with heavy swell. No vessels, except fishing boats, were seen.[41]

On 20 October 1940, *Ursula*, with Lieutenant Alexander Mackenzie in command, departed Portsmouth for Gibraltar to join the Mediterranean Fleet. She was to be based at Malta to operate against Italian traffic towards North Africa. In the afternoon of 26 October, far into the western area of Biscay, *Ursula* was at periscope depth when a submarine was observed at the surface, quite close, less than 100 metres (110 yards) away. Mackenzie surfaced to attempt using the gun, but the weather was too rough to send the gunners on deck and the submarine disappeared from view. Most likely, this was an Italian submarine, possibly *Maggiore Barraca* or *Alpino Bagnolini*, both of which were taking to sea for patrols in the Atlantic at that time. Neither reported the encounter. On 30 October, *Ursula* arrived at Gibraltar with various problems and required several weeks of repairs before she could proceed to Malta. After ten weeks of repairs and trials, she eventually arrived in Malta mid-January 1941.

November

As the autumn of 1940 carried on into November, the British submarine presence in the Bay of Biscay turned into long, eventless patrols in poor weather interrupted by a few episodes of intense activity.

Lieutenant John Brown was an experienced submarine CO by the time he took *Taku* to sea from Holy Loch on 18 October. His first command, *Unity*, which he had commanded since the outbreak of the war and taken on nine war patrols, had been lost in a collision in April while he was on sick leave (see chapter 16). Having spent the summer recovering and retraining, Brown had taken command of *Taku* only a few days earlier and presumably had some familiarisation to do with his new command, which was no less a veteran, having been on six war patrols before this one.

The billet assigned to *Taku* was in northern Biscay, off Lorient–Saint-Nazaire. The first few days were rather routine, patrolling between Belle-Île and Penmarch during the day, looking for inbound U-boats, and retiring seaward to charge the batteries during the night. Nothing was sighted except trawlers, until in the early hours of 2 November, while on the surface charging, some 30 miles south-west of Belle-Île, a large tanker was sighted less than a mile away.

Within a few minutes, the ship was within firing range and eight Mk VIII* torpedoes were fired from no more than 750 metres (820 yards) distance. After thirty seconds, there were three heavy explosions in quick succession, which shook *Taku* severely, causing some minor damage. No escort had been observed, but Brown turned away nevertheless, eventually diving. Strangely, there had been no sign of any of the torpedoes having hit the tanker while the watch had remained on the bridge. Having heard the remaining five torpedoes explode on the seabed some way away, *Taku* surfaced again. There was no sign of the tanker but a 'pronounced smell of oil fuel' and the violence of the explosions made Brown confident that he had definitely hit the target and most probably sunk her. Quite satisfied, he turned westwards again to clear the area and finish the charging of the batteries.[42]

In spite of Brown's belief, however, the tanker, which was the 9,923-ton *Gedania*, had not been sunk. Apparently, one torpedo hit the ship, but did not explode properly, resulting in only superficial damage. What happened to the other two, and why *Taku* was rocked by what appeared to be three explosions, is less obvious. On the 4th, *Taku* met up with *Clyde* and *Cachalot* in Mount's Bay and was escorted towards Holy Loch by a trawler.

The next boats to take up billets in Biscay were *Tigris* accompanied by the newly re-commissioned *Triumph*. They both left Holy Loch on 6 November, escorted by the armed yacht *Cutty Sark*. En route, *Tigris* developed engine problems and diverted to Milford Haven for repairs, while *Triumph* continued towards Gibraltar and the Mediterranean. The repairs took a few days, but on 8 November *Tigris* headed to sea again to resume her fourth war patrol.

Things were largely quiet until, just before midnight on the night of the 12th/13th, a ship was sighted about 70 nautical miles west of the Gironde estuary and Lieutenant Commander Bone decided to have a look. This turned out to be the French 300-ton, three-mast schooner *Charles Edmond*, carrying 300 tons of cod from Saint Pierre and Miquelon off Canada. To Bone, there appeared to be a small vessel following astern. *Tigris* had been warned of a damaged U-boat that might attempt to pass through the area and he suspected this might be what he believed he had seen. Moving closer though, no vessel following the schooner could be seen any longer.

The weather was too rough to use the gun, so one torpedo was fired from about 750 metres. To their surprise, it passed underneath the schooner without exploding. Bone steered downwind for a while and ordered the gun to be manned after all. A 'slow and deliberate fire' was then opened with high-explosive shells. The crew was seen to abandon ship. As Bone had expected, the rough sea meant that there were few hits, in spite of the close range. Annoyed, he pulled back again and fired a second torpedo from 500 metres (550 yards) with minimum depth setting at the stationary ship. It exploded at the expected time, but 'nothing was seen of it and it certainly did not hit the target.'[43] Closing the ship again, it was seen to be on fire below and it was decided not to waste any more ammunition. Nothing more was seen of the unfortunate crew of *Charles Edmond*, nor of any U-boat emerging in her wake. According to French sources the second torpedo did hit the schooner, sinking her. Most of the crew apparently managed to get into the lifeboats and eventually reached land, with several of them wounded. Two men were missing. Little else happened on this patrol, and *Tigris* was back at Holy Loch on the 29th.[44]

Talisman also had a lengthy November patrol in the Bay of Biscay. This time, she had seven extra men onboard: a team of six French agents led by the RNVR officer Lieutenant Merlin Minshall of the Admiralty's Naval Intelligence Division (NID). They were to implement Operation Shamrock, using captured French fishing boats for reconnaissance of how and where U-boats were operating from French Atlantic ports.[45]

Arriving at her billet off Lorient, *Talisman* was met by an A/S trawler patrol, but managed to keep them at arm's length until they finally withdrew. These patrols were observed daily between Penmarch, Île de Groix and Belle-Île, keeping a screen outside the entrance to Lorient. Three torpedo boats were also sighted at a distance on one occasion, though these did not appear to be on an active submarine hunt. At night, powerful searchlights were actively sweeping to seaward, forcing Lieutenant Commander Francis to stay far to the west when charging *Talisman*'s batteries.

On 25 November, six torpedoes were fired from over 5,000 metres (5,500 yards) away at a tanker escorted by three trawlers, without any apparent results, apart from the tanker stopping for a while. Again, though, there appeared to be a premature explosion similar to that experienced on the previous patrol (see page 382). The water depth at this location was almost 100 metres (330 feet) though, and it is perhaps more likely that there was something wrong with the torpedo itself or that there was a problem with one of the tubes, making the torpedo detonate prematurely.

Compared to earlier in the autumn, the number of fishing vessels around was considerably reduced. In the evening of 26 November, though, the French fishing ketch *Le Clipper* was sighted west of Île de Groix. Minshall and Francis decided she was suitable for the purpose and surfaced to capture her. The agents were transferred to the ketch while the skipper and three of his crew were taken on board *Talisman*. The rest of the crew remained onboard with the agents. By daylight, *Talisman* dived and headed away, leaving the men on board *Le Clipper* to themselves. Whether the ketch was actually used for much reconnaissance of the U-boat lanes is unclear, but it made fast in Falmouth on 5 December. The French skipper and his crew had much to tell, however, as they had observed the German military build-up for quite some time. Among other things, they warned of mines off Penmarch and A/S trawlers in Lorient. As for the U-boats, they said that there were rarely more than four at a time alongside in Lorient, as the rest of about a dozen apparently stationed there were usually out on patrol. The French fishermen had limited information on the inward and outward routes that the U-boats used to and from Lorient as they largely travelled at night or submerged during daylight. For *Talisman*, the rest of the patrol was uneventful and she was back in Holy Loch on 5 December.[46]

In November 1940, the armed merchant cruiser *Jervis Bay* was lost in an attempt to keep the German heavy cruiser *Admiral Scheer* away from convoy HX-84 south of Iceland.[47] Following this, VA(S) Horton reluctantly agreed to a request from the Admiralty and sent a few submarines to Halifax to supplement limited escort forces and act as deterrent for further German raiders in the northern Atlantic. Submarines had been used as convoy escort before, both in the Atlantic and the North Sea, but it was a controversial and challenging task for the assigned boats.

The tactical advantage of a submarine is best utilised in offensive operations operating alone or in concert with other boats. Having been freed from the operational shackles of fleet operations, acting as convoy escorts was a setback, but one that could be understood to some extent. The best position for an escorting submarine would normally be ahead of the convoy where she would have some room to manoeuvre and a fair chance to attack approaching heavy surface ships. There would always be the risk, however, of being overrun by the convoy or other surface escorts and mistaken for a U-boat. Positioned astern of the convoy, the submarine would in theory be well placed to intercept U-boats pursuing the convoy or trying to sneak up from behind. Stragglers could be a problem, though, and should an attack develop there would be a substantial risk of being taken for an enemy, especially at night.

Horton was thus very reluctant to use his submarines as convoy escorts and flatly refused to let them operate as such in the Western Approaches or north of Ireland, where the risk of surface attacks were rather slim and where aircraft and naval anti-submarine forces should be able to attack any submarine encountered without running the risk of it being Allied.[48]

It was feared for a while that the Germans might attempt to establish a U-boat and surface-raider base on the Azores and in November 1940 a patrol was established off Ponta Delgada by three submarines withdrawn from the Mediterranean, *Otus*, *Pandora* and *Olympus*, based at Gibraltar. These were designated the 8th Submarine Flotilla, subordinated to Flag Officer Commanding, North Atlantic and later briefly reinforced by the Dutch boats *O21*, *O23* and *O24*. No German forces materialised, however, and in February 1941 the Azores patrol was withdrawn.

December

If anything, patrols in the Bay of Biscay were even drearier for the British submarines in December. Weather was generally foul and the legitimate targets were few and far between.

Lieutenant Commander Cavenagh-Mainwaring took *Tuna* to sea from Holy Loch on 12 December for her fourth war patrol. Again, she was hampered by an engine defect. This time, however, it could be repaired while submerged and slowly underway on the motors – after 30 hours' hard work by the engineering crew, the patrol was resumed.

In the early morning of the 18th the Italian submarine *Brin* was sighted and attacked with torpedoes and gunfire some 55 miles off the Gironde estuary, but again the Regia Marina submariners had luck on their side and she escaped unharmed. As she drew away – faster than *Tuna* due to her engine problems – *Brin* fired two torpedoes at *Tuna* from her stern tubes, but both missed. Shortly after, the escort *Brin* had been waiting for arrived and Cavenagh-Mainwaring gave up the chase while the going was good.[49]

The following night, another darkened shadow was sighted. Two torpedoes were fired: one missed ahead and one took off on its own. Annoyed, Cavenagh-Mainwaring ordered the gun crew to action stations for what he assumed was an A/S vessel looking for him. In fact, it was the 172-ton French tug *Chassiron* used by the German harbour commander at

La Pallice. The gun crew's shooting was good, weather considering, and soon the tug was ablaze. The fire was bound to attract attention and *Tuna* turned away once it was clear the tug was beyond rescue. *Chassiron* went down half an hour later, some 25 miles west-south-west of the Gironde estuary.

Tuna's port engine continued to cause problems, but as there were few ships around except the odd trawler, Cavenagh-Mainwaring remained in the billet between Bordeaux and Gijón until 27 December. On that day, several trawlers, minesweepers and aircraft were around, presumably as one or more U-boats were expected back, but none were intercepted as the activity above kept *Tuna* below, using her periscope sparingly. Two days later, Cavenagh-Mainwaring set course for home.[50]

Lieutenant Balston with *Tribune* was also on patrol in the Bay of Biscay in December, but further north than *Tuna*. On 16 December six torpedoes were fired at the 6,864-ton German tanker *Karibisches Meer* east of Île de Yeu. All torpedoes missed. The escort, minesweeper *M13* and patrol boats *V406* and *V411*, chased the submarine for half an hour, dropping thirty depth charges. Balston went deep, however, and skilfully managed to extract his boat from the situation.

Three days later, an attack on the merchant ship *Birkenfels* was equally unsuccessful.[51]

In December 1940 *Thunderbolt*, under the command of Lieutenant Cecil Crouch, was on her very first war patrol in the Bay of Biscay. From the recovered wreck of *Thetis*, a brand-new submarine had been built. She had been commissioned on 26 October and, after a period of trials and exercises at Greenock, was now ready for war. Lieutenant Crouch, like every submariner onboard *Thunderbolt*, knew the story of their boat – and every one of them had volunteered to serve on board her. *Thunderbolt* slipped and headed to sea on 3 December 1940.

Capitano Raffaele Tarantini was one of four submarines built at the Tosi shipyard of Taranto in the late 1930s. She displaced 1,166 tons on the surface, 1,484 tons submerged, and could dive to 100 metres (330 feet); she had a maximum speed of 18 knots on the surface, reduced to 9 knots underwater. The boats of the *Liuzzi*-class, to which *Tarantini* belonged, had eight torpedo tubes, four in the bow, four aft. On deck, there was one 100-mm gun and two twin 13.2-mm machine guns. *Tarantini* was commissioned in early 1940, and had operated in the Mediterranean since Italy joined the war. The CO was Capitano di Corvetta Alfredo Iaschi and with him he had six more officers and fifty men.

On 10 September Iaschi took his boat past the Strait of Gibraltar, arriving at Bordeaux on 5 October after a fruitless patrol off the Azores. In November *Tarantini* had been on patrol in the Atlantic, encountering little more than foul weather. When finally a convoy was sighted on 2 December, *Tarantini* was detected by the escort before she could launch her torpedoes, resulting in a lengthy chase, involving over 100 depth charges. A week later *Tarantini* was heading back for Bordeaux.[52]

The Admiralty had somehow gathered intelligence that one or more submarines were heading for Bordeaux and the three U-class submarines *Unique*, *Upholder* and *Usk*, on their way towards Gibraltar and the Mediterranean, were ordered to halt in the southern Bay of Biscay to make a patrol line together with *Thunderbolt* to intercept the incoming Italian.

Lieutenant Cecil Crouch (*right*) with his first lieutenant, John Stevens, on board the depot ship after returning from their first mission in the Bay of Biscay with *Thunderbolt*. (IWM A2584)

During the morning of 15 December, some 12 miles south-south-west of the Gironde estuary, Lieutenant Crouch saw something through his periscope he thought might be the conning tower of a U-boat. Closing to investigate, he also discerned three trawlers, apparently on the same course. Crouch assumed he had come across an alien submarine under escort towards Bordeaux. At 09:20, six torpedoes were fired at twelve-second intervals from 2 miles away. Four minutes later an explosion was heard and Crouch could see through the periscope a tall column of water rising into the air. For a short while, he could also see what he believed to be either the bow or the stern of the other submarine protruding out of the water, before it was all gone.

More than a dozen explosions followed, some probably the rest of the torpedoes exploding on the seabed, some probably depth charges. The three 'trawlers', which were the patrol boats *V401*, *V407* and *V409*, were actually escorting a French coaster not seen by Crouch and do not seem to have been too concerned about what happened to

Thunderbolt returning to Holy Loch from the Bay of Biscay. First Lieutenant Stevens is on the bridge. (IWM A2581)

the *Tarantini* – possibly as they might not have realised that the submarine had been torpedoed, but believed she had hit a mine.

As Lieutenant Crouch had observed, *Tarantini* sank almost immediately. Only five men were later rescued, the first officer, Teniente di Vascello Attilio Frattura, and four ratings – presumably those on the bridge when the torpedo hit.

Thunderbolt was back at Holy Loch on 21 December. *Unique, Upholder* and *Usk* sighted nothing and eventually received orders to continue towards Gibraltar and the Mediterranean.[53]

Legacy

The legacy of *Thetis* would always sail with *Thunderbolt*. Even so, under her new CO Cecil Crouch, who was promoted to lieutenant commander in June 1941, she was to have a fine series of successes in the Mediterranean until she was sent to the bottom for good off Sicily by depth charges from the Italian corvette *Cicogna* in March 1943.

At the end of 1940, however, *Thunderbolt* represented the conversion of the British Submarine Service from a poorly understood, strategically and tactically misused part of the Royal Navy to a versatile weapon of choice. Still, there was a long way to go – particularly by those who did not go to war in them – but the lessons learned from the sub-surface war off Norway, in the Skagerrak, the North Sea and the Bay of Biscay during the first sixteen months of the war made a solid foundation on which to build.

To sea once again. *Thunderbolt* casting off for another patrol from Holy Loch. (IWM A2577)

Many of the original submariners from September 1939 were no longer around. Losses had been substantial and many were 'still on patrol'. Others had reached their own personal limit, serving out the rest of the war in other parts of the navy instead. New officers and men were ready to take over, though, including Polish, Dutch, Norwegian and French sailors in exile.

There is no doubt that the vast majority of the British and Allied submarine commanders sent on patrol in 1940 were every bit as competent and aggressive as their German counterparts – Horton saw to that. But they had less aggressive orders. Time and again, the submarines were used for reconnaissance and patrol lines, limiting their tactical and operational capacity. When the Allied submarines were given a specific task, and their COs the freedom to solve it in the best way they could, given the particular circumstances at the time, they obtained spectacular results.

The design and construction of British submarines had improved significantly and those coming from the yards in a steady stream were better than ever, most flaws having been ironed out. At this point of the war, the Allied submarines had sunk less tonnage of shipping per patrol than their German counterparts, largely because there were far fewer targets for them, but also because their prevailing tactic was to fire large salvos from a great distance. This meant that even if one or even two torpedoes hit, the rest of the salvo was wasted. U-boats were notoriously difficult targets to hit under any circumstances, being agile and small with a shallow draught, and the orders from the Admiralty to prioritise hunting them was not good for the statistics either.

Furthermore, the British 'fruit machines' were not as reliable and simple to use as the German equivalent, the *Vorhaltsrechner* and the theory for its use, the so-called *Auswanderungsverfahren*. Hence, all conditions being equal, it appears that a German torpedo had a greater likelihood of hitting its target than a British one, provided they were not duds or exploded prematurely, as was often the case with German torpedoes at the time. Any calculation of percentage hits from torpedoes fired is greatly hampered by the German torpedo problems of this period; nevertheless, any in-depth study allowing for this will almost certainly come up with a positive bias towards the U-boats.

The British torpedoes were in general very reliable, but the Mk VIII and the Mk VIII** had their problems too. The number of reports where torpedoes were heard to explode without any corresponding result being available in the German archives are numerous. Perhaps the British triggers were oversensitive, setting themselves off by hitting some debris in the water, or a freak wave, or perhaps they had some built-in flaw not fully recognised at the time. In any case it appears that a number of torpedoes headed straight to the bottom when fired rather than towards the target.

In general, the British Submarine Service and the foreign units incorporated within it stood up well to their task in the first year and a half of WWII. The move to the Mediterranean during the second half of 1940 meant not only a shift of theatre of war, but also a shift towards a more versatile, strategically correct use of the submarines. As with *Thetis*, lessons were learned the hard way and many of those involved in those first lessons did not return to tell their fellow submarines of their experience. In this way legends emerged of boats and men. 'In a submarine', according to Max Horton, 'there is no room for mistakes. You are either alive or dead.'

Appendices

— Appendix I —
Key Data for British Submarines

	O-Class	River -Class	Porpoise -Class	Seahorse S-Class, Group I	Triton T-Class Group I	Ursula U-class Group I
Length overall	283 ft 6 in	345 ft	293 ft	217 ft	276 ft 6 in	190 ft 7 in
Displacement tons						
Surface	1,781	1,850	1,520	640	1,090	540
Submerged	2,038	2,723	2,117	935	1,575	730
Power						
Diesel	4,400 bhp	10,000 bhp	3,300 bhp	1,550 bhp	2,500 bhp	615 bhp
Electric	1,320 shp	2,500 shp	1,630 shp	1,300 shp	1,450 shp	825 shp
Speed knots						
Surface	17.5	22.5	16	14	15.5	11.5
Submerged	9	10	9	9	9	9
Torpedoes						
Internal	6 bow; 2 aft	6 bow	6 bow	6 bow; 1 aft	6 bow	4 bow
External	-	-	-	-	4	2
Reloads	8	6	6	6	6	4
Guns	4 in	4 in	4 in	3 in	4 in	3 in
Complement	53–55	61	59	38	62	31
Diving depth	500 ft	300 ft	300 ft	350 ft	300 ft	200 ft

Pertinent data, British submarines.

— Appendix II —
Home Water Submarine Flotillas, 1939–1940

Flotilla	2nd	3rd	5th	6th	7th	9th
CO	Captain W D Stephens Feb 1940: Captain G C Menzies	Captain P Ruck-Keene Aug 1940: Captain H M Ionides	Captain C Coltart Dec 1939: Rear Adm R B Darke	Captain J Bethell May 1940: Captain G Voelcker	Captain R L Edwards	Captain J G Roper
Base	Dundee In Oct 1939 to Rosyth In Jul 1940 to Holy Loch	Harwich (+ Sheerness) In May 1940 to Rosyth	Portsmouth	Blyth	Rothesay	Dundee
Depot ship	*Forth* later plus *White Bear*	*Cyclops* later *Maidstone*, and *Titania*	*Alecto* later shore based	*Titania* later *Maidstone* and shore based	*Cyclops*	Shore based
Submarines September 1940	*Seahorse, Starfish, Sturgeon, Swordfish, Spearfish, Sterlet, Seawolf, Sunfish, Triumph, Triton, Thistle, Oxley*	-	*H28, H31, H50, H33, H34, H44, H49, Oberon* Refitting *H43, H50, L23, Thames*	*Undine, Ursula, Unity, L26, L27, H32*	-	-

Flotilla	2nd	3rd	5th	6th	7th	9th
November 1939	*Triton, Triumph, Trident, Thistle, Triad, Orzeł, Wilk,* Under RA3BS *Narwhal, Cachalot, Seal*	*Swordfish, Seawolf, Shark, Sealion, Salmon, Snapper, Sterlet, Sunfish, Spearfish*	*H28, H31, H32, H33, H34, H43, H44, H49, H50, L26, L27 Oberon, Tribune, Truant* Refitting *Thames, Porpoise*	*Undine, Unity, Ursula, Sturgeon, Seahorse, Starfish, L23* Later also *Severn* and *Clyde*	-	-
April 1940	*Seal, Porpoise, Thistle, Triad, Trident, Triton, Truant, Tribune, Triumph, Taku, Tarpon, Tetrarch Orzeł, Wilk*	*Sealion, Seawolf, Shark, Snapper, Sterlet, Sunfish, Salmon*		*Spearfish Swordfish, Severn, Sturgeon, Clyde, Ursula, Unity, Narwhal*	-	-
September 1940	*Trident, Tribune, Tuna, Tigris, Talisman, Taku, Porpoise, Cachalot, Orzeł, Wilk*	*Sealion, Snapper, Sunfish, Seawolf*	*H43, L27, H32,*	*Swordfish, Sturgeon, Ursula*	*Oberon, Otway,* H28, H31, H33, H34, H44, H49, H50 L23, L26, O9, O10 O14 (in Oct) B1	*Clyde, Severn, Rubis,* O21, O22 O23, O24,

NA-ADM 234/380; NA_ADM-199/279; and www.dutchsubmarines.com.

— Appendix III —
British and Allied Submarines Lost in 1939–1940 in Home Waters, North Sea and Bay of Biscay

Submarine		Date	Cause	Location	Depth (m)
Oxley	Br	10.09.39	Off Position. Torpedoed by *Triton* Lieutenant Commander Harold Bowerman	Off Stavanger 58°36'N, 05°20'E	255
Seahorse	Br	07.01.40	Most likely minefield Lieutenant Dennis Massy-Dawson	West of Horns Rev (possibly near 55°27'N, 07°05'E)	25–30
Undine	Br	07.01.40	A/S trawlers *M1203*, *M1204* and *M1201* Lieutenant Commander Alan Jackson	Heligoland Bay 54°08'N, 07°33'E	37
Starfish	Br	09.01.40	Minesweeper *M7*, assisted by *M5* Lieutenant Thomas Turner	Heligoland Bay 54°45'N, 07°10'E	30
Thistle	Br	10.04.40	Torpedoed by *U4* Lieutenant Commander Wilfrid Haselfoot	Off Skudeneshavn 59°07'N, 05°16'E	200
Tarpon	Br	10.04.40	Most likely depth charges from *Schiff40* – *Schürbeck*. Lieutenant Commander Herbert Caldwell	North Sea (possibly near 56°43'N, 06°33'E)	
Sterlet	Br	18.04.40	Depth charges from *UJ 125*, *UJ 126* and *UJ 128* or possible minefield Lieutenant Commander Gerard Haward	Off Swedish coast (possibly near 58°55'N, 10°10'E)	
Unity	Br	29.04.40	Collision with *Atle Jarl* Lieutenant Francis Brooks	Off Blyth 55°13'N, 01°19'W	50
Seal	Br	05.05.40	Captured Lieutenant Commander Rupert Lonsdale	Off Skagen	
Doris	Fr	09.05.40	Torpedoed by *U9* Capitaine de Corvette Jean Favreul	Off Texel 52°47'N, 03°49'E	25–30
Orzeł	Pl	06.40	Minefield? Kapitan Marynarki Jan Grudzinski	North Sea	
O13	Du	20.06.40	Minefield? Luitenant ter Zee 1ste Klasse Eduard Vorster	North Sea	

Submarine		Date	Cause	Location	Depth (m)
Shark	Br	06.07.40	Damaged by aircraft, scuttled Lieutenant Commander Peter Buckley	Off Stavanger 58°46'N, 04°21'E	251
Salmon	Br	09.07.40	Sunk by *M1806* or minefield? Commander Edward Bickford	North Sea	
Thames	Br	07.40	German torpedo boats or minefield? Lieutenant Commander William Dunkerley	North Sea	
Narwhal	Br	23.07.40?	Aircraft or Minefield ? Lieutenant Commander Ronald Burch	North Sea	
Spearfish	Br	01.08.40	Torpedoed by *U34* Lieutenant Commander John Forbes	North Sea 58°07'N, 01°32'E	
H49	Br	18.10.40	Depth-charged by *UJ116* and *UJ118* Lieutenant Richard Coltart	Off Texel 52°33'N, 00°22'E	26
Swordfish	Br	07.11.40	German minefield, probably laid by S-boats Lieutenant Michael Langley	Off Isle of Wight 50°28'N, 01°22'W	40
O22	Du	19.11.40	Unclear. Luitenant ter Zee 1ste Klasse Johannes van Dulm	North Sea 57°55'N, 05°31'E	180

— Appendix IV —
Ships Attacked by Allied Submarines in 1939–1940

Date	Submarine	Target	Status	Location
20.11.39	*Sturgeon*	*Gauleiter Telschow, V209* – 428 tons	Sunk	North Sea
04.12.39	*Salmon*	*U36* – 626 tons	Sunk	SW Lindesnes
13.12.39	*Salmon*	*Leipzig* – 6,310 tons *Nürnberg* – 6,980 tons	Damaged Damaged	North Sea
14.12.39	*Ursula*	*F9* – 825 tons	Sunk	Heligoland Bight
25.02.40	*Narwhal**	*U63* – 291 tons	Sunk	South of Shetland
21.03.40	*Ursula*	*Heddernheim* – 4,947 grt	Sunk	Off Skagen
23.03.40	*Truant*	*Edmund Hugo Stinnes IV* – 2,189 grt	Sunk	Off Jutland
04.04.40	*Narwhal*	*Emden* – 709 grt	Damaged (m)	Off Heligoland
08.04.40	*Orzeł*	*Rio de Janeiro* – 5,261 grt	Sunk	Off Lillesand
08.04.40	*Trident*	*Stedingen* (ex *Posidonia*) – 8,036 grt	Sunk	Oslofjord
09.04.40	*Truant*	*Karlsruhe* – 6,650 tons	Sunk	Off Kristiansand
09.04.40	*Sunfish*	*Amasis* – 7,129 grt	Sunk	Off Lysekil
10.04.40	*Triton*	*Friedenau* – 5,219 grt *Wigbert* – 3,648 grt *V1507 Rau VI* – 354 grt	Sunk	Off Lysekil
10.04.40	*Sunfish*	*Antares* – 2,593 grt	Sunk	Off Lysekil
11.04.40	*Sealion*	*August Leonhardt* – 2,593 grt	Sunk	Off Anholt, Kattegat
11.04.40	*Spearfish*	*Lützow* – 10,600 tons	Damaged	NE Skagen
11.04.40	*Triad*	*Ionia* – 3,102 grt	Sunk	Off Larvik
12.04.40	*Snapper*	*Moonsund* – 322 grt	Sunk (g)	Off Larvik
13.04.40	*Sunfish*	*Schiff40 Schürbek*	Damaged	Kattegat, off Tjörn
14.04.40	*Sunfish*	*Schiff35 Oldenburg* – 2,312 grt	Sunk	E Skagen
14.04.40	*Snapper*	*Florida* – 6,148 grt	Sunk	Off Lysekil
15.04.40	*Snapper*	*M1701 H.M.Behrens* – 525 grt *M1702 Carsten Janssen* – 472 grt	Sunk Sunk	NE Skagen
15.04.40	*Sterlet*	*Brummer* – 3,010 tons	Sunk	Off Larvik
18.04.40	*Seawolf*	*Hamm* – 5,874 grt	Sunk	Off Strømstad
21.04.40	*Narwhal*	*Togo* – 5,042 grt	Damaged (m)	Off Skagen

Date	Submarine	Target	Status	Location
23.04.40	*Tetrarch*	*UJB Treff V* – 330 grt	Sunk	Inner Skagerrak
23.04.40	*Narwhal*	*M1302 Schwaben* – 436 grt	Sunk (m)	Off Skagen
01.05.40	*Narwhal*	*Haga* – 1,296 grt, Swedish	Sunk (m)	Off Skagen
01.05.40	*Narwhal*	*Bahia Castillo* – 8,579 grt	Total Loss	Off Skagen
		Buenos Aires – 6,079 grt	Sunk	
02.05.40	*Trident*	*Cläre Hugo Stinnes I*	Damaged	Bjørnefjorden
03.05.40	*Narwhal*	*M1102 H.A.W.Müller* – 460 grt	Damaged (m)	Off Skagen
04.05.40	*Severn*	*Monark* – 1,785 grt, Swedish, German prize.	Sunk	North Sea
04.05.40	*Seal*	*Almy* – 46 grt, Swedish	Sunk (m)	Kattegat, off Vinga
06.05.40	*Seal*	*Vogesen* – 4,240 grt	Sunk (m)	Kattegat, off Vinga
20.05.40	*Spearfish*	*S130 Orkney* – 25 grt and *S175 Söstjernen* – 19 grt, Danish	Sunk (g)	Central North Sea
25.05.40	*Tetrarch*	*L61 Terje Viken* – 26 grt, Danish	Damaged	North Sea
26.05.40	*Rubis*	*Vansö* – 54 grt, Norwegian	Sunk (m)	Off Egersund
28.05.40	*Seal*	*Torsten* – 1,206 grt, Swedish	Sunk (m)	Kattegat, off Vinga
28.05.40	*Rubis*	*Blaamannen* – 174, Norwegian	Sunk (m)	Off Haugesund
30.05.40	*Narwhal*	*V1109 Antares* – 291 grt	Sunk (m)	Off Molde
31.05.40	*Rubis*	*Jadarland* – 938 grt, Norwegian	Sunk (m)	Off Haugesund
31.05.40	*Seal*	*GG5 Mode* – 20 grt, Swedish	Sunk (m)	Kattegat
05.06.40	*Seal*	*Skandia* – 183 grt, Danish	Sunk (m)	Kattegat, off Vinga
05.06.40	*Narwhal*	*Palime* – 2,863 grt, Norwegian	Sunk (m)	Off Feistein
05.06.40	*Narwhal*	*M11* – 874 tons	Sunk (m)	Off Feistein
10.06.40	*Rubis*	*Sverre Siggurdsson* – 1,081 grt, Norwegian	Sunk (m)	Off Bergen
10.06.40	*Porpoise*	*Sonja* – 1,828 grt, Swedish	Sunk (m)	Off Bremanger
14.06.40	*Porpoise*	*M5* – 874 tons	Sunk (m)	Off Hitra
16.06.40	*Tetrarch*	*Samland* – 5,978 grt	Sunk	Off Obrestad
20.06.40	*Clyde*	*Gneisenau* – 26,000 tons	Damaged	Off Trondheim
21.06.40	*H44*	*Alfa* – 844 grt, Danish	Sunk	Off Texel
25.06.40	*Snapper*	*V-1107 Portland* – 295 grt	Sunk	Off Stavanger
03.07.40	*Snapper*	*Cygnus* – 1,334 grt, Norwegian	Sunk	South of Egersund
04.07.40	*Narwhal*	*UJB, Treff VIII* – 356 grt	Sunk (m)	Off Kristiansund
06.07.40	*Rubis*	*Almora* – 2,433 grt, Norwegian	Damaged (m)	Off Egersund

Date	Submarine	Target	Status	Location
16.07.40	*Clyde*	*SF-52-SV Fredheim* – 15 grt, Norwegian	Sunk (rammed)	Off Stad
18.07.40	*H31*	*UJ 126 Steiermark* – 446 grt	Sunk	Off Terschelling
24.07.40	*Rubis*	*Kem* – 1,705 grt, Norwegian	Sunk (m)	Off Egersund
26.07.40	*Thames*	*Luchs* – 933 tons	Sunk	Off Stavanger
28.07.40	*Rubis*	*Argo* – 412 grt	Sunk (m)	Off Egersund
04.08.40	*Sealion*	*Toran* – 3,318 grt, Norwegian	Sunk	East of Kristiansand
16.08.40	*Narwhal*	*NB15 Biene* – 173 grt	Sunk (m)	Off Haugesund
20.08.40	*Cachalot*	*U51* – 753 tons	Sunk	Bay of Biscay
02.09.40	*Tigris*	*Sancte Michael* – 168 grt, French	Sunk (g)	Bay of Biscay
02.09.40	*Sturgeon*	*Pionier* – 3,285 grt	Sunk	Skagerrak
07.09.40	*Truant*	*Tropic Sea* 5,781 grt, Norwegian, German prize	Scuttled	Bay of Biscay
22.09.40	*Tuna*	*Tirranna* – 7,320 grt, Norwegian, German Prize	Sunk	Bay of Biscay
23.09.40	*Cachalot*	*M1604 Österreich* – 494 grt	Sunk (m)	Off Penmarch
24.09.40	*Tuna*	*Ostmark* – 1,280 grt	Sunk	Bay of Biscay
13.10.40	*Narwhal*	Minesweepers, *Gnom7 M5207* – 49 grt, *Kobold1* – 23 grt and *Kobold3* – 47 grt	Sunk (m)	Off Haugesund
15.10.40	*L27*	*Sperrbrecher III*	Damage	Off Cherbourg
16.10.40	*Tigris*	*Cimcour* – 250 grt, French	Sunk (g)	Off Gironde
03.11.40	*Sturgeon*	*Sigrun* – 1,337 grt, Danish	Sunk	Off Obrestad
06.11.40	*Sturgeon*	*Delfinus* – 1,293 grt, Norwegian	Sunk	Off Obrestad
02.11.40	*Taku*	*Gedania* – 8,923 grt	Damaged	Bay of Biscay
13.11.40	*Tigris*	*Charles Edmond* – 301 grt, French	Sunk	Bay of Biscay
05.12.40	*Sunfish*	*Oscar Midling* – 2,182 grt, Finnish	Sunk	Off Stad
07.12.40	*Sunfish*	*Dixie* – 1,571 grt, Norwegian	Damaged	Off Stadtlandet, Norway
15.12.40	*Thunderbolt*	*Tarantini*, – 1,031 tons, Italian	Sunk	Bay of Biscay
18.12.40	*Tuna*	*Chassiron* – 172 grt, French	Sunk (g)	Bay of Biscay

* With destroyers *Escort*, *Inglefield* and *Imogen*
g: gunfire, m: mine, otherwise torpedo.

— Appendix V —
Minefields Laid by Allied Submarines, 1940

Date/Submarine/ Minefield	Number	Position	Losses
04.04.40, *Narwhal*, FD1	49	57° 37' N, 06° 35' E Heligoland Bight	D: Ger *Emden* (709 grt)
13.04.40, *Narwhal*, FD5	50	57° 26' N, 10° 45' E off Skagen	D: Ger *Togo* (5,042 grt), 21.04 S: Ger *M1302 Schwaben*, (436 grt), 23.04
01.05.40, *Narwhal*, FD6	50	57° 30' N, 10° 43' E off Skagen	S: Swe *Haga* (1,296 grt), 01.05 D: Ger *M1102 H.A.W.Müller*, 03.05
04.05.40, *Seal*, FD7	50	57° 33' N, 11° 35' E off Vinga	S: Swe *Almy* (46 grt), 04.05 S: Ger *Vogesen* (4,240 grt), 06.05 S: Swe *Torsten* (1,206 grt), 28.05 S: Dan *Skandia* (183 grt), 05.06
10.05.40, *Rubis*, FD14	32	58° 21' N, 06° 01' E off Egersund	S: Nor *Vansö* (54 grt), 26.05 D: Nor *Almora* (2,433 grt) 06.07 S: Nor *Kem* (1,705 grt), 24.07 S: Nor *Argo* (412 grt), 28.07
11.05.40, *Narwhal*, FD12	50	62° 58' N, 06° 48' E off Molde	S: Ger *V1109 Antares* (291 grt), 30.05
15.05.40, *Porpoise*, FD11	48	61° 46' N, 04° 54' E off Bremanger	S: Swe *Sonja* (1,828 grt), 10.06
27.05.40, *Rubis*, FD15	32	59° 28' N, 05° 12' E off Haugesund	S: Nor *Blaamannen* (174 grt), 28.05 S: Nor *Jadarland* (938 grt), 31.05
03.06.40, *Narwhal*, FD16	50	58° 46' N, 05° 25' E off Feistein	S: Ger *M11*, (874 grt) 05.06 S: Ger *Palime* (2,863 grt) 05.06
09.06.40, *Rubis*, FD17	32	60° 36' N, 04° 55' E off Bergen	S: Nor *Sverre Siggurdsson* (1,081 grt), 10.06
12.06.40, *Narwhal*, FD19	50	59° 26' N, 05° 10' E off Haugesund	S: Ger *NB 15 Biene* (ex *Øyulf*) (173 grt) 16.08 S: Ger *Gnom7*, 13.10 S: Ger *Kobold1*, 13.10 S: Ger *Kobold3*, 13.10
14.06.40, *Porpoise*, FD18	50	63° 30' N, 08° 12' E off Hitra	S: Ger *M5*, 18.06
26.06.40, *Rubis*, FD20	32	62° 28' N, 05° 20' E off Kristiansund	-
04.07.40, *Narwhal*, FD21	50	63° 15' N, 07° 34' E off Kristiansund	S: Ger *UJ B* (ex *UJ D*) (356 grt) 06.07

Date/Submarine/ Minefield	Number	Position	Losses
27.07.40, *Narwhal*, FD22	*	63° 16′ N, 07° 13′ E off Smola	?
29.07.40, *Porpoise*, FD23	50	West of Ringkøbing	?

S: Sunk, D: Damaged; Dan: Danish, Swe: Swedish, Nor: Norwegian, Ger: German or under German command at time of striking the mine. *Narwhal* probably did not lay her mines before being sunk.

Modified from NA-ADM 199/1827; NA-ADM 199/1877; NA-AADM 199/294; NA-ADM 199/300; www.wlb-stuttgart.de/seekrieg; www.warsailors.com; and www.uboat.net.

— Appendix VI —
French Submarine Patrols out of Harwich and Dundee in April and May 1940

Submarine	Out	In	Events
Antiope	04.04	12.04	North of Terschelling. Uneventful.
	12.04	19.04	Off Terschelling. Uneventful
	28.04	08.05	Off Terschelling to off Egersund. Uneventful
	10.05	11.05	Called back to Harwich. Uneventful.
	16.05	20.05	Off Terschelling. Fired torpedoes on *La Sibylle*. Otherwise largely uneventful. Returned to Rosyth
La Sibylle	31.03	05.04	Off Terschelling. Uneventful.
	09.04	18.04	Inside German Declared Area. Uneventful.
	27.04	08.05	North of Declared Area. Uneventful.
	16.05	24.05	Off Terschelling. Largely uneventful, except avoiding torpedoes from *Antiope*. Returned to Rosyth
Amazone	04.04	12.04	Off Terschelling. Uneventful.
	16.04	28.04	Off Terschelling. Uneventful.
	07.05	20.05	Off Den Helder. Attacked by and fired torpedoes on unknown submarines on both 11 and 12 May. Probably *U7* and *Shark*. No hits. Returned to Rosyth
Orphée	19.04	23.04	NW Ringkøbing. Fired two torpedoes on *U51*. Both missed
Doris	19.04	25.04	In Central North Sea. Defect in port engine air compressor.
	08.05	-	Off Texel. Lost.
Circé	20.04	23.04	Off Den Helder. Uneventful.
	29.04	06.05	North of Terschelling. Uneventful.
	16.05	19.05	Off Terschelling. Uneventful. Returned to Rosyth
Thétis	25.04	07.05	Off Den Helder to west of Westwall. Uneventful.
	10.05	11.05	Called back to Harwich. Uneventful.
	16.05	25.05	Off Terschelling to west of Westwall. Uneventful.
Calypso	29.04	10.05	Off Den Helder. Sighted torpedoes passing close. Otherwise largely uneventful.
Sfax	18.04	01.05	Off Egersund–Flekkefjord. Several sightings. Fired torpedoes but no results. Returned to Dundee.
	10.05	23.05	Sailed from Dundee. Off SW Norway. Several sightings. Fired no torpedoes. Returned to Dundee.
Achille	18.04	28.04	Off Stavanger. Uneventful. Returned to Dundee.

Submarine	Out	In	Events
	07.05	20.05	Sailed from Dundee to west of Lindesnes. Uneventful. Many aircraft. Bombed by British aircraft upon returning to Dundee.
Casabianca	18.04	28.04	Sailed from Dundee. Off and inside Selbjørnsfjorden – Korsfjorden, south of Bergen. Uneventful. Returned to Dundee.
	09.05	21.05	Sailed from Dundee to off Lindesnes. Chased and depth-charged by German vessels. Otherwise uneventful. Returned to Dundee.

Abbreviations

Abbreviations

A/A	Anti Aircraft
Aldis lamp	Hand-held lamp for signalling
A/S	Anti Submarine, Royal Navy usage
ASDIC or asdic	Anti-submarine detection equipment, now known as sonar
A/U	Anti U-boat, RAF usage
B-Dienst	Beobachtungsdienst ('observation service') – German shipboard cryptanalyst service.
Billet	Patrol area assigned to a submarine
C-in-C	Commander-in-Chief
DCNS	Deputy Chief of Naval Staff
ERA	Engine Room Artificer
FAA	Fleet Air Arm
Fix – take a fix	Calculate the position of a ship by means of cross-referencing directions to two or more fixed positions or by help of stars on the open sea.
HA	High Angle
Hydrophone	Microphone mounted outside the hull of vessel to record the sound of other vessels, in particular submarines.
Hydroplane	Horizontal rudder on submarines, allowing the boat to dive or rise.
Kriegsmarine	German Navy
KTB Kriegstagebuch	German War Diary
MIR	Military Intelligence Research, Intelligence section of the War Office formed in 1939.
MTB	Motor Torpedo Boat
NCO	Non Commissioned Officer
OOW	Officer of the Watch
ORP	*Okret Rzeczypospolitej Polskiej* – Ship of the Polish navy
PO	Petty Officer
POW	Prisoner of War
R-Boot, Raumboot	German light minesweeper
RN	Royal Navy, British Navy
RNR	Royal Naval Reserve
RNVR	Royal Naval Volunteer Reserve

S-Boot, Schnellboot	German motor torpedo boat, MTB (also known as E-boat later in the war)
SKL Seekriegsleitung	German Naval High Command
Sigint	Signals Intelligence. Assessment of intercepted radio traffic
VC	Victoria Cross
VHF	Very High Frequency
W/T	Wireless Telegraphy
Zerstörer	German Destroyer

Equivalent Naval Ranks

Marine Nationale	**Royal Navy**	*Kriegsmarine*
Matelot breveté	Seaman	Matrose
Quartier-maître de deuxième classe	Able Seaman	Matrosen-Gefreiter
Quartier-maître de première classe	Leading Seaman	Matrosen-Obergefreiter
	Leading Seaman (4½ years)	Matrosen-Hauptgefreiter
Second-maître	Senior Leading Seaman	Matrosen-Stabsgefreiter
		Matrosen-Stabsobergefreiter
Maître	Petty Officer	-maat*
Premier maître	Chief Petty Officer	Ober-maat
Maître principal	Boatswain	Bootsmann
	Senior Boatswain	Stabsbootsmann
Major	Chief Boatswain	Oberbootsmann
	Senior Chief Boatswain	Stabsoberbootsmann
Aspirant	Midshipman/Cadet	Fähnrich zur See
Enseigne de vaisseau	Sub-Lieutenant	Oberfähnrich zur See
Lieutenant de vaisseau	Lieutenant (Junior)	Leutnant zur See
	Lieutenant (Senior)	Oberleutnant zur See
Capitaine de corvette	Lieutenant Commander	Kapitänleutnant
Capitaine de frégate	Commander	Korvettenkapitän
		Fregattenkapitän
Capitaine de vaisseau	Captain	Kapitän zur See

Marine Nationale	Royal Navy	Kriegsmarine
Contre-amiral	Commodore	Kommodore
Vice-amiral	Rear Admiral	Konteradmiral
Vice-amiral d'escadre	Vice Admiral	Vizeadmiral
Amiral	Admiral	Admiral
		Generaladmiral
	Admiral of the Fleet	Grossadmiral

* A man's trade would prefix the word -maat such as Funkermaat for a Radio Petty Officer or a Bootsmannsmaat for a Deck Petty Officer.

Notes

Introduction

1. Allegedly phrased by Rear Admiral A K Wilson, VC, regarding submarines in general.
2. ADM 116/3164
3. RNSM-A1934/5; RNSM-A1993/117; NA-ADM 116/164; NA-ADM 234/380.
4. www.rnsubs.co.uk.
5. The tonnage was to be measured as standard surface displacement.
6. Japan withdrew from the conference, Italy never signed the treaty and Germany was not invited.
7. Roskill, *Naval Policy Between the Wars*; and Kemp, *The T-class Submarine*.
8. Meeting on 1 May 1935, NA-ADM 1/9378; Kemp, *The T-class Submarine*.

Chapter 1

1. Booth, *Thetis Down* and Warren and Benson, *The Admiralty Regrets*. This inspection was later to be the subject of much controversy, and it was never fully ascertained how or when it had actually been performed.
2. NA-ADM 116/3817; NA-ADM 1/10234; and Harris, *The Rouge's Yarn*.
3. NA-ADM 116/3817. Among those on board were also Lieutenant Commanders Garnett and Lloyd, the COs of submarines *Taku* and *Trident* respectively, which were also being built at Cammell Laird at the time.
4. Harris, *The Rouge's Yarn*.
5. Warren and Benson, *The Admiralty Regrets*.
6. The 'trim chit', or trim chart, containing the status of the tanks (and hence the draft and the stability of the submarine) would have been provided by the Cammell Laird representatives on board and made available for the CO through the first officer.
7. NA-ADM 116/3817.
8. NA-ADM 116/3817; and *Glasgow Herald*, 6 July 1939.
9. *Glasgow Herald*, 6 July 1939.
10. *Glasgow Herald*, 6 July 1939. In addition to the mechanical indicators, there was a set of electro-hydraulic indicators, but these were not considered as it was known from previous tests at Cammell Laird's wet basin that they were not working properly and there had been no time to fix them yet , so Woods did not trust them. NA-ADM 116/3817.
11. *Glasgow Herald,* 6 July 1939.
12. NA-ADM 116/3817; and *Glasgow Herald*, 5 July 1939.
13. To allow the torpedoes to be loaded into the tubes, the opening in the watertight bulkhead between the tube space and the torpedo stowage compartment consisted of four doors. Three of these were usually kept shut when preparing to dive.
14. NA-ADM 116/3817. There is some uncertainty as to whether the clips were actually blocking the door or not, but the fact remains that the door was not properly shut due to a complicated mechanism, unsuitable for an emergency.
15. NA-ADM 116/3817; Harris, *The Rouge's Yarn*; Warren and Benson, *The Admiralty Regrets*; and Booth, *Thetis Down*.
16. NA-ADM 1116/3817.
17. There was no direct teleprinter line installed at Fort Blockhouse until well into 1940.
18. There are some discrepancies in the reports as to exactly when these arrangements with L & G Salvage Co. were made – during the evening of the 1st or morning of the 2nd. Very little was done, though, until normal work hours started on the 2nd as the real urgency of the matter was not stressed until then.
19. NA-ADM 116/3817.
20. NA-ADM 116/3817. *Winchelsea* arrived in Liverpool Bay around 16:15 on 2 June.
21. For a description of the Davis Submerged Escape Apparatus, DSEA, see page 46. Working inside the submarine, breathing oxygen from the DSEA apparatus under high pressure, would give a man about fifteen minutes before losing consciousness and most likely succumbing.
22. NA-ADM 116/3817; Harris, *The Rouge's Yarn*; Warren and Benson, *The Admiralty Regrets*; and Booth, *Thetis Down*. Even if blowing the water back out of the forward end of *Thetis* had been successful, it

would have required a skilled and delicate balancing of the other tanks to prevent the submarine from becoming dangerously unstable and it may not have been a successful operation after all.

23 Harris, *The Rouge's Yarn*; and NA-ADM 116/3817.

24 There was no technology available that allowed the rescuers to communicate directly with the people inside the submarine and it seems that nobody really considered the hammering of Morse Code signals on the hull as useful.

25 NA-ADM 116/3819.

26 NA-ADM 116/3817; and NA-ADM 116/3819.

27 NA-ADM 116/3812; Harris, *The Rouge's Yarn*; Warren and Benson, *The Admiralty Regrets*; and Booth, *Thetis Down*.

28 NA-ADM 116/3817. Glenn is Engineering Officer Roy Glenn, Jamison is Lieutenant Anthony Jamison of *Trident*, one of the observing officers.

29 Roberts, *HMS Thetis: Secrets and Scandal*. Leading Stoker Arnold was taken on board the destroyer *Brazen* and later to hospital in Portsmouth. Not once was he asked to give his opinion on what would be the best way to rescue his fellow submariners.

30 NA-ADM 1/10234.

31 Booth, *Thetis Down*.

32 NA-ADM 116/3812.

33 Armstrong and Young, *Silent Warriors, Vol. III*.

34 Oram sent several confusing signals around this time, largely related to the plan he had brought up from *Thetis*.

35 NA-ADM 116/3812.

36 NA-ADM 199/286. Four months later, in September 1939, when sister-ship *Triumph*'s rudder became disconnected abaft the after bulkhead, the Z-tank was emptied and repairs effectuated by going through the manhole door into the tank while submerged. Hence, this was possible, even if space was very confined.

37 NA-ADM 116/3812.

38 NA-ADM 116/3812; NA-ADM 116/3817; Booth, *Thetis Down*; and Armstrong and Young, *Silent Warriors, Vol. III*.

39 NA-ADM 116/3817. The three-man board, appointed by C-in-C Portsmouth Admiral William James, consisted of Captain Claude Barry and Rear Admiral William Wake-Walker in addition to Vice Admiral Raikes. Rear Admiral Bertram Watson had taken over as RA(S) from Raikes in December 1938.

40 The Right Honourable Sir Alfred Bucknill presided over the tribunal when it opened in London on 3 July 1939.

41 Most were buried at Maes Hyfryd Cemetery near Holyhead. Lieutenant Commander Bolus was buried at sea.

42 NA-TS 32/112, NA-ADM 1/10234 and NA-ADM 116/3817

43 NA-ADM 1/10234, NA-ADM 116/3817; Booth, *Thetis Down*; and Roberts, *HMS Thetis: Secrets and Scandal*.

44 Roberts, *HMS Thetis: Secrets and Scandal*. Some years after the war, Arnold left the navy and took a quiet civilian job.

45 For details of this and the stories of those left behind, see Roberts, *HMS Thetis: Secrets and Scandal*.

46 Booth, *Thetis Down*; and Roberts, *HMS Thetis: Secrets and Scandal*.

47 NA-ADM 1/10234; NA-ADM 116/3812; and NA-ADM 116/3817.

48 IWM soundfile 12571.

Chapter 2

1 In giving the tonnage of a submarine, the first number (891 tons) refers to the weight on the surface, while the second (1,074 tons) refers to the weight submerged.

2 Vickers Shipbuilding and Engineering Ltd, *Barrow Built Submarines, Vol. 8: 1916–1945 L, H and R Class Submarines*

3 RNSM-A.1934/5.

4 After four years' service with the Australian Navy, *Oxley* and *Otway* were transferred back to the Royal Navy in 1931.

5 RNSM-A.1934/5; and www.rnsubs.co.uk.

6 RNSM A1993/117; King, *The Stick and the Stars*; Simpson, *Periscope View*; Mackenzie, *The Sword of Damocles*; and McCartney, *British Submarines 1939–45*. For an account and analysis of the German torpedo crisis, see Haarr, *The Gathering Storm* and Haarr, *The Battle for Norway*.

7   RNSM-A.1934/5; and Vickers Shipbuilding and Engineering Limited, *Barrow Built Submarines, Vol. 10: 1929–1945 The River Class Submarines.*

8   NA-ADM 199/1827.

9   Vickers Shipbuilding and Engineering Limited, *Barrow Built Submarines, Vol. 11: 1930–1946 The Minelaying Submarines.* In the Mediterranean, the surviving minelayers had an additional career running emergency cargoes to Malta in 1941 and 1942, their mine-decks filled with ammunition, lubricants and other supplies.

10   *Cyclops* was in reserve at Malta as the war started, but returned to home waters where she served through the conflict.

11   Hart, *Discharged Dead.*

12   *Medway* was sunk off Port Said in June 1942 by *U372* while evacuating Alexandria for Lebanon.

13   Anscomb, *Submariner.*

14   www.rnsubs.co.uk; Poolman, *Allied Submarines of World War Two*; and McCartney, *British Submarines 1939–45.* Of the sixty-two S-class submarines built, seventeen were lost during the war: nine in the North Sea and Atlantic; six in the Mediterranean; and two in the Pacific and Indian oceans.

15   See chapters 13, 14 and 15.

16   NA-ADM 199/286; Kemp, *The T-class Submarine*; Vickers Shipbuilding and Engineering Limited, *Barrow Built Submarines, Vol. 12: 1935–1970 T Class Submarines*; www.rnsubs.co.uk; and McCartney, *British Submarines 1939–45.*

17   RNSM-box 5 *Records of Warship Construction: The History of DNC Department*; and Kemp, *The T-class Submarine.* The unfinished *Trooper* was knocked off her blocks during an air raid, setting back her completion several months. In all, twenty-nine of the fifty-three T-class boats were built at Vickers-Armstrongs.

18   During the war, several U-class boats went significantly deeper than this – and surfaced to tell the tale.

19   NA-ADM 199/1814.

20   Hart, *Discharged Dead.*

21   Hart, *Discharged Dead.*

22   The Mk VIII torpedo was still in service with the Royal Navy in the 1980s.

23   For the early part of WWII this set-up coped with requirements. In 1943 though, the Torpedo Experimental Establishment (TEE) was established at Greenock to focus on development, while production was gradually transferred to Alexandria. By 1947, Greenock was purely dedicated to research and development.

24   During the war, experiments were conducted using captured German G7e torpedoes, but the war ended before British-produced versions were in service.

25   A replacement was only developed in 1943 and did not become standard on submarine torpedoes until 1945.

26   Torpex is a mixture of 37–41% TNT, 41–45% RDX (cyclonite, cyclomethylene trinitramine) and 18% aluminium.

27   A 'fruit machine' is another name for a slot machine or 'one-armed bandit'.

28   The fruit machine could be set up for a 90-degree-angle shot by turning a handle, but this was very rarely done. It required adjusting the torpedo to make a 90-degree turn to one side or the other and required the boat to be running more or less parallel to its target and was, in most situations, as cumbersome as pointing the bow in the right direction.

29   IWM-94/6/1.

30   IWM-94/6/1.

31   IWM soundfile 11745.

32   For an account of the German torpedo-failure issue see Haarr, *The Gathering Storm.*

33   Bryant, *One Man Band.*

34   Clayton, *Sea Wolves.*

35   Kemp, *The T-class Submarine.*

36   Asdic is allegedly an acronym for the Anti-Submarine Detection Investigation Committee fostering it, but it is unclear if such a committee ever existed.

37   NA-ADM 1/17659; NA-ADM 1/9501; Grove, *The Defeat of the Enemy Attack on Shipping 1939–45*; and Haarr, *The Gathering Storm.*

38   The VLF station at Rugby came into service in January 1926, transmitting telegraph messages to the Commonwealth as part of the Imperial Wireless Chain. During WWII Rugby was also used for communication with submarines.

39   NA-ADM 199/1840.

40   If deflated, the bag could be topped-up by blowing through the mouthpiece or in later versions by opening a small oxygen cylinder on the front of the bag.

41   Clewlow, *HMS Ursula.*

Chapter 3

1   However frustrating for the submariners, the safety measures were justified as collisions did occur, mostly with fatal consequences for the submarine.
2   Bryant, *One Man Band*. In September 1939, *Courageous* was torpedoed by *U29*. See Haarr, *The Gathering Storm*.
3   Mackenzie, *The Sword of Damocles*.
4   IWM soundfile 11745.
5   Bryant, *One Man Band*; Simpson, *Periscope View*; and Clayton, *Sea Wolves*.
6   Allaway, *Hero of the Upholder*.
7   Simpson, *Periscope View*.
8   Clayton, *Sea Wolves*.
9   Evans, *Beneath the Waves*.
10 Clayton, *Sea Wolves*.
11 Bryant, *One Man Band*.
12 Bryant, *One Man Band*.
13 Bryant, *One Man Band*.
14 Bryant, *One Man Band*; Simpson, *Periscope View*; King, *The Stick and the Stars*; and Allaway, *Hero of the Upholder*.
15 King, *Adventure in Depth*; and King, *The Stick and the Stars*. Lieutenant Francis Ruck-Keene, Rucker's son, was onboard *Upholder* with Lieutenant Commander Wanklyn when the boat was lost with all hands in the Mediterranean in April 1942.
16 HMS *Dolphin* took its name from the hulk that was used for accommodation and lectures.
17 Bryant, *One Man Band*.
18 King, *The Stick and the Stars*
19 King, *The Stick and the Stars*
20 Harris, *The Rouge's Yarn*.
21 King, *Adventure in Depth*.
22 Hart, *Discharged Dead*
23 NA-ADM 199/294.
24 NA-ADM 178/194. German U-boats on war patrol usually had four lookouts, each responsible for a 90° sector.
25 Brighton, *Life on the Porpoise*.
26 King, *The Stick and the Stars*.
27 RNSM-A1994/95.
28 RNSM-A1995/75.
29 RNSM-A1995/75 .
30 NA-ADM 199/286; King, *Adventure in Depth*; and Bryant, *One Man Band*.
31 Bryant, *One Man Band*.
32 When this happened, it was immediately known all over the boat that the unlucky submariner 'got his own back'.
33 NA-ADM 199/288; and Bryant, *One Man Band*. The galleys were electric and could be used when submerged, providing the charge of the batteries allowed.
34 Bryant, *One Man Band*.
35 IWM soundfile 9137.

Chapter 4

1   In the Elizabethan naval prayer still read at Sunday Service in most British ships at the outbreak of war, it was asked for protection from '. . . the dangers of the sea and the violence of the enemy'.
2   Later in the war, a few naval trawlers were built from scratch, but these programmes were also largely cancelled.
3   Depth-charge throwers were added over time to boats where space and structural strength allowed.
4   Sondergerät für Aktive Schallortung literally translates as 'special device for active sound location'. It was also known as Schallwellengerät, which translates as 'acoustic wave device'.
5   NA-ADM 199/1925; NARA T1022-3798-82156; NARA T1022-3505-73562; and NARA T1022-3683-82186. A shipwreck in shallow waters makes noises audible on a passive listening apparatus when currents flow along or through it.
6   There was normally no direct radio contact between the aircraft and the A/S vessels and communication was by light signals or rockets of various colours and shapes.

7   NARA T1022-3798-82156.
8   BA-RM 92/5267.
9   NA-ADM 199/1877.
10 NA-ADM 199/1877.
11 NA-ADM 199/294.
12 Hart, *Discharged Dead.*
13 Brighton, *Life on the Porpoise.*
14 NA-DM 199/288; and NA-ADM 199/1843.
15 NA-ADM 199/294.
16 NARA T1022-3505-73575.
17 NA-ADM 199/288.
18 Bryant, *One Man Band.*
19 IWM 91/38/1.
20 UMA and UMB are short for *U-Boot-Abwehrmine A* and *B* (U-boat anti-submarine mine A and B).
21 *Sprengbojen* were explosive devices dispersed among the mines. When hit by the wire or any other parts of the sweep, they would explode to destroy the equipment and prevent further sweeping.
22 NA-ADM199/1827; NA-ADM 234/380; Kutzleben et al., *Minenschiffe 1939–1945*; and Kurowski, *MS Hansestadt Danzig.*
23 Thiele, *Luftwaffe Aerial Torpedo Aircraft and Operations*; and Kurowski, *Seekrieg aus der Luft.*
24 Kurowski, *Seekrieg aus der Luft.*

Chapter 5

1   From the naval prayer asking for protection from '. . . the dangers of the sea and the violence of the enemy'.
2   IWM-90/24/1; and RNSM-A1988/032. The signal was intercepted by the German B-Dienst.
3   RNMS-A1993/117. Three of the twelve WWI boats were L-class and nine H-class.
4   Four O-class boats were sent to Colombo in late October to search for German raiders in the Indian Ocean.
5   These were *Sunfish, Thistle, Triad, Trident, Taku, Tarpon, Tribune* and *Truant.*
6   IWM soundfile 12571.
7   NA–ADM 234/380.
8   NA-ADM 199/277.
9   RNSM A1993/117; NA-ADM 199/373; and NA-ADM 199/277
10 NA-ADM 199/2063.
11 RNSM A1993/117.
12 RNSM A1993/117; and NA-ADM 234/380.
13 NA-ADM 234/380.
14 NA-ADM 234/380; RNSM-A1993/117; Hezlet, *British and Allied Submarine Operations in WWII*; and Poolman, *Allied Submarines of World War Two.* The supplementary signal adding that German merchant ships should be sent to Kirkwall with a prize crew or the crew taken on board the submarine was simply ignored.
15 Hessler, *The U-boat War in the Atlantic*; Haarr, *The German Invasion of Norway*; and Haarr, *The Battle for Norway.*
16 Coastal Command had been allocated 183 aircraft at the outbreak of the war, of which 135 were Ansons.
17 *Starfish* had to return home with an injured man on 3 September.
18 NA-ADM 178/194; NA-ADM 199/278; and NA-ADM 199/279
19 King, *The Stick and the Stars.*
20 NA-ADM 199/1921; and NA-ADM 199/1837.
21 NA-ADM 199/373; and NA-ADM 199/277.
22 NA-ADM 234/380.
23 NA-ADM 199/1827. See Chapter 12.
24 NA-ADM 199/277; RNSM-A1993/117; and Clayton, *Sea Wolves.* The 2nd and 6th flotillas were briefly withdrawn to Rosyth while A/A defences were established at Dundee and Blyth.
25 NA-ADM 234/380; and NA-ADM 199/1921. *Titania* had to be towed and, delayed by U-boat sightings off Blyth, took a week to arrive at Rosyth.
26 NA-ADM 234/380; and Simpson, *Periscope View.*
27 NA-ADM 199/279; NA-ADM 234/380; and RNSM-A1993/117.

Chapter 6

1 NA-ADM 199/278; and NA-ADM 173/16115.
2 IIWO is the German term for second watch officer on a U-boat.
3 NA-ADM 199/1819; and KTB *U35*.
4 KTB *U35*, KTB *U21* and KTB *U23*. *U23* reported having seen three torpedo tracks, even if *Ursula* only fired one in the second salvo. *U21* also reported observing multiple torpedo tracks. None of them mentions actually sighting *Ursula*. *U35* was sunk on 29 November on her second war patrol by British destroyers *Kingston*, *Kashmir* and *Icarus* in the northern North Sea. All men on board were rescued, to spend the rest of the war as POWs.
5 NA-ADM 178/194. The communication between *Triton* and *Oxley* was via asdic through underwater Morse.
6 NA-ADM 178/194. Lieutenant Stacey could later recall only two challenges being made before the rifle grenade was fired, but Signalman Cavanaugh maintained that he made three. Everybody on the bridge confirmed the grenade exploded properly and was very visible.
7 NA-ADM 178/194.
8 NA-ADM 178/194.
9 NA-ADM 234/380; NA-ADM 178/194; NA-ADM 199/2063; and Clayton, *Sea Wolves*.
10 NA-ADM 199/1921.
11 NA-ADM 199/1921.
12 NA-ADM 199/278.
13 NA-ADM 199/1830.
14 IWM soundfile 12571.
15 NA-ADM 199/192; and NA-ADM 199/1828.
16 NA-ADM 199/278; and NA-ADM 199/292.
17 NA-ADM 199/277.
18 NA-ADM 199/277.
19 NA-ADM 199/277.
20 For an account of these events, see Haarr, *The Gathering Storm*.
21 NA-ADM 199/286.
22 KTB *U23*.
23 NA-ADM 234/380.
24 KTB *U21*.

Chapter 7

1 Peszke, *Poland's Navy 1918–1945*. PMW stands for Polska Marynarka Wojenna, 'The Polish Navy', an unofficial name frequently used instead of the formal Marynarka Wojenna Rzeczypospolitej Polskiej (MWRP). Polish naval ships had the prefix ORP: Okręt Rzeczypospolitej Polskiej, or Ship of the Polish Republic.
2 Bachmann, *Die Polnische U-boot Division im September* 1939.
3 NA-ADM 199/277; NA-ADM 199/1921; Bachmann, *Die Polnische U-boot Division im September 1939*; Harnack, *Zerstörer unter Deutscher Flagge 1939 bis 1945*; and www.polishnavy.pl.
4 The ancient battleship *Schleswig-Holstein* fired the opening shots of WWII on the Polish Westerplatte depot outside Danzig in the early morning of 1 September. She did not leave the town for some time, so it did not matter that *Orzeł* did not pick up the warning to look out for her. For a detailed account, see Haarr, *The Gathering Storm*.
5 Henryk Kloczkowski stayed three days in hospital in Tallinn. He eventually ended up in Britain, where he was tried and convicted for cowardice and negligence of orders by a military court. Having served his sentence, he went to Canada where he died in 1962.
6 Grudzinski was reserved, almost shy and, though highly respected for his strong character and discipline, he was known to his men as 'Panienka', meaning 'girlie' or 'lassie' in English.
7 Two Estonian guards ended up on board and were landed on the Swedish island of Gotland with money and food.
8 To justify the hunt for *Orzeł*, Germany and Russia launched a propaganda campaign where the submarine was blamed for firing indiscriminately at any ship in the Baltic that was sunk or damaged whether by mine or other means.
9 NA-ADM 199/1925; NA-ADM 199/1853; RNSM-A1995/303; Sopocko, *Orzeł's Patrol*; and http://crolick. wbsite.pl. In November, Grudzinski was awarded the Silver Cross of the Polish Virturi Militari order. In December he was also awarded the Distinguished Service Order (DSO) by the British.

10 Later, the three submarines were moved into Lake Mälaren inside Stockholm. Twenty-nine of the 135 interned men were eventually allowed to transfer to Britain to join the Polish Navy there. The submarines were handed back to Poland in 1945, but over half of the men chose to stay in Sweden or go elsewhere, other than Poland.

11 The OKW mistakenly reported two Polish submarines sunk on the 4th, one on the 6th and one on the 8th.

Chapter 8

1   NA-ADM 199/278 and RNSM A1993/117

2   NA-ADM 199/1843

3   B-Dienst, short for Beobachtungs-Dienst was the German radio monitoring service which included direction-finding, interpretation and analysis. At the outbreak of the war, the B-Dienst could read and decypher a significant amount of the encrypted Allied radio communication, including the most widely used code of the Royal Navy. The B-Dienst operators could routinely monitor the positions of most British warships as well as read a large share of the signals they sent.

4   NA-ADM 199/1843; NA-ADM 199/278; NA-ADM 199/2063; NA-173/16115; NA-ADM 267/89; and BA-RM 7/123.

5   John Eaden was transferred to the brand-new *Utmost* as her first commander until January 1941. After that he spent the rest of the war on the surface, mostly commanding destroyers. In July 1943, the German U-boat *U409* was sunk north-east of Algiers by British destroyer *Inconstant* with Lieutenant Commander Eaden in command. A year later *U767* suffered the same fate off Guernsey by depth charges from *Fame*, *Havelock* and *Inconstant*, still with Eaden on board.

6   NA-ADM 199/278; and NA-ADM 199/1921.

7   The cruisers and destroyers of the Home Fleet were at sea searching for German battleships in the Norwegian Sea after the sinking of *Rawalpindi*.

8   NA-ADM 199/278.

9   NA-ADM 199/1848.

10 NA-ADM 199/278.

11 RA-Boks1600 – 2B06234.

12 RA-Sjøforsvaret før 1940 – Boks1600 – 2B06234; and NA-ADM 199/278. Røren later wrote that he and Dahl had the 'best impressions' of the British destroyer, her crew and Captain Todd.

13 RA-Sjøforsvaret før 1940 – Boks1600 – 2B06234; NA-ADM 199/1921; and NA-ADM 199/278. *Taku* experienced a similar failure in the Atlantic in February 1941 and had to be towed home. Interference by the Admiralty in on-going operations at sea would be a major issue during the campaign in Norway, see Haarr, *The German Invasion of Norway* and Haarr, *The Battle for Norway*.

14 NA-ADM 199/1830.

15 NA-ADM 199/1830.

16 King, *The Stick and the Stars*

17 Most of the men, that is – but Seaman Wood slept through the incident, in spite of being only 30 feet from the explosion. He was later known as 'Sleepy' Wood.

18 RNSM-A1988/032; NA-ADM 199/286; and NA-ADM 199/278.

Chapter 9

1   King, *The Stick and the Stars*

2   NA-ADM 199/288

3   Bickford had actually crossed the Atlantic to America and back in *Bremen* in 1933.

4   NA-ADM 199/288.

5   NA-ADM 199/288; and King, *Adventure in Depth*.

6   NA-ADM 199/288; and NA-ADM 199/1839.

7   The torpedo boats were either in the yards or on shake-down cruises in the Baltic. It had been attempted to make two additional destroyers, not already part of the mine-laying force, ready to join the cruisers as escort, but this had not been possible. For a detailed account of these minelaying operations, see Haarr, *The Gathering Storm*.

8   This triangular formation had been tested during pre-war exercises and found to give the least possible target for attacking submarines, while still being advantageous for mutual anti-aircraft protection.

9   NARA T1022-2794/48204. German time was one hour ahead of British time. 10:30 German time is hence 09:30 British time.

10 NA-ADM 199/288. There is a ten- to fifteen-minute time discrepancy between the war diaries of *Leipzig* and *Salmon*.
11 NARA T1022-2794/48204. The second aircraft saw no periscope and when trying to bomb the end of the torpedo track, its bombs did not release.
12 NARA T1022-2794/48204.
13 NARA T1022-2794/48204.
14 NA-ADM 199/288; and NA-ADM 199/1839. The radio report from *Salmon* was intercepted by German radio stations and Lütjens learned early who the attacker was. 'Splice the mainbrace' signifies that an extra tot of rum would be served.
15 NARA T1022-2793/48188.
16 NA-ADM 199/1819.
17 NARA T1022-2793/48188. The underlinings are in the original text.
18 KTB SKL; RNSM-A1994/95; NA-ADM 199/1819; NA-ADM 199/1925; and Clewlow, *HMS Ursula*.
19 NA-ADM 199/288.
20 In his early thirties, Bickford was the youngest commander in the Royal Navy since Beatty.
21 At the meeting, Bickford suggested that two crews should share one submarine to increase the use of the boats without over-straining the crews. Churchill liked the concept, but Horton dismissed it as completely unrealistic.
22 *Ursula* was transferred to the Russian Navy in May 1944. She was returned in 1949 to be scrapped the following year. George Phillips retired from the Royal Navy in 1947. He died at the age of 90 in 1995.

Chapter 10

1 Chalmers, *Max Horton and the Western Approaches*.
2 Chalmers, *Max Horton and the Western Approaches*.
3 Of the eleven boats, *E13* was lost during transit and *E11* was sighted and damaged in the subsequent pursuit, having to return to England. *E18* struck a mine in May 1916 and *C32* went aground in October 1917. The rest, *E1*, *E8*, *E9*, *E19*, *C26*, *C27* and *C35*, were scuttled outside Helsinki in 1918 to prevent capture by advancing German troops.
4 Chalmers, *Max Horton and the Western Approaches*. For an account of the Northern Patrol in the early part of the war, see Haarr, *The Gathering Storm*.
5 Chalmers, *Max Horton and the Western Approaches*
6 NA-ADM 199/1827
7 Rayner, *Escort*
8 Chalmers, *Max Horton and the Western Approache*s
9 Rumour had it that the real reason for the move was that Northways was near some of Horton's favourite golf courses.
10 Chalmers, *Max Horton and the Western Approaches*.
11 Chalmers, *Max Horton and the Western Approaches*; Clayton, *Sea Wolves*; and Broome, *Convoy is to Scatter*.
12 Chalmers, *Max Horton and the Western Approaches*.
13 When the war ended, Horton stepped down voluntarily. In 1948, he was 'granted unrestricted permission to wear the Grand Cross of the Royal Order of St Olav, bestowed by the King of Norway for service to the Royal Norwegian Navy during the war'. Max Horton died in 1951.

Chapter 11

1 NA-ADM 199/278.
2 NA-ADM 199/278.
3 NARA T1022-3142/72206.
4 NA-ADM 199/278. Commander Jackson filed his report on the sinking of his submarine to the Admiralty on 25 June 1945, following release from a POW camp.
5 NARA T1022-3142/72206. Some of the men from *M1201* appear to have still been inside when *Undine* went down.
6 NA-ADM 199/278; and NA-ADM 199/1925. As *Undine* sank the chief petty officer was unable to swim in the cold water. Lieutenant Harvey jumped back in and saved his life, for which he was subsequently awarded the Royal Humane Society Bronze Medal.
7 KTB SKL.
8 NHB-FDS 327/85.

9   NHB-FDS 327/85.
10 NHB-FDS 327/85; and Kutzleben et al, *Minenschiffe 1939–1945*. Stripe f was laid across 7°E and stripe d just west of it, but as these are closer to Heligoland and well into Zone B, it is likely that *Seahorse* would have crossed the median by the time she came this far south. Today, the area of stripe b is marked on the Danish sea maps as a zone where fishing, anchoring and seabed operations are prohibited.
11 NA-ADM 199/1925; and NHB-FDS 327/85.
12 NARA T1022-3505-73575.
13 NA-ADM 199/278; NA-ADM 267/114; and NARA T1022-3505-73575. Oberleutnant Timm was awarded the Iron Cross First Class for the sinking of *Starfish* and actions during the invasion of Norway. Nevertheless he chose to transfer to the U-boat arm and qualified for command of *U251* in 1941. He eventually sank nine ships totalling some 54,000 tons and was awarded the Knight's Cross in 1944, before being interned by British forces in Singapore in 1945. He later served in the Bundesmarine and retired in 1966.
14 NA-ADM 234/380; and NA-ADM 199/278.

Chapter 12

1   NA-ADM 199/2063; NA-ADM 199/1921; and NA-ADM 199/286.
2   RNSM-A1995/75.
3   NA-ADM 199/286. H.E. stands for 'hydrophone effect'.
4   NA-ADM 234/380.
5   NA-ADM 199/286.
6   NA-ADM 199/286; and NA-ADM 199/1921. Upon returning from patrol, Lieutenant Commander Davies spent some time in hospital.
7   Four casualties are associated with the Scandinavian convoys. *Eskdene* was torpedoed by *U56* while a straggler from HN-3, but did not sink and was towed to the Tyne. *Svinta* hit a mine and was sunk while under tow, having been damaged by aircraft while in convoy ON-21. *Svartön* was torpedoed and sunk by *U58* while a straggler from HN-6. *Signe* was sunk by a torpedo from *U38* while a straggler from HN-23A.
8   Kretschmer, as part of the screen for Operation Nordmark, had been made aware of the convoy through a signal from BdU (Befehlshaber der Unterseeboote – C-in-C Submarines) the day before and during the night, he had been guided towards it by a signal from *U19*.
9   NA-ADM 1/10667.
10 RNSM A 1995/75.
11 RNSM A1995/75.
12 NA-ADM 1/10667; RNSM A1995/75; and *The War Illustrated*, Vol. II, pp. 220–1.
13 KTB *U23*.
14 There is some uncertainty as to the actual number of merchant ships in HN-14. More than half of the thirty-seven ships originally leaving Bergen could not find the escort due to fog and turned back.
15 NA-ADM 234/380; and NA-AIR 15/16.
16 NA-ADM 234/380.
17 NA-ADM 234/380; NA-ADM 199/1921; and Hessler, *The U-boat War in the Atlantic 1939–1945*.
18 NARA T1022-3505-73575; and NA-ADM 199/1830. The minesweepers were identified as 'two destroyers and a cruiser'. After this incident, the L-class submarines did not carry fuel in the external tanks unless needed.
19 For a full account of these events, see Haarr, *The Gathering Storm*.
20 NA-ADM 199/286.
21 IWM soundfile 9137.
22 NA-ADM 199/286. Place names have been modified to Norwegian style. According to Hutchinson's later account, the first lieutenant and second cox'n went into the water to help cut the ropes and free the propellers.
23 NA-ADM 199/286; NA-ADM 199/294; IWM soundfile 9137.
24 NA-ADM 234/380.
25 The detonators of magnetic mines react to the magnetic field of ships passing nearby. Reducing this field by sending electrical currents through cables wound around the hull was known as 'degaussing', after the unit of measurement of magnetic field strength, the 'gauss'. For an account of the mine war in 1939/40, see Haarr, *The Gathering Storm*.
26 NA-ADM 116/4471; NA-WO 193/772; NA-CAB 65/11; NA-CAB 65/12; NA-FO 371/24818; RNSM A1995/312; Churchill, *The Second World War*, vol. I; Butler, *Grand Strategy*; Haarr, *The German Invasion of Norway*; and Haarr, *The Gathering Storm*.

27 Simpson, *Periscope View*. For a full account of the Allied plans to assist Finland, see Haarr, *The German Invasion of Norway*; and Haarr, *The Gathering Storm*.
28 For an account of these political events, see Haarr, *The German Invasion of Norway*.
29 BA-RM 35 II/35; BA-RM 7/180; RNSM A1995/312; and KTB SKL A March40.
30 KTB SKL.
31 NA-ADM 199/1940; and Walters, *The History of the British U-Class Submarine*. There is some uncertainty of the date of the attack on *Protinus*. The 18th, 19th and 20th are all given in various accounts, but the 20th seems to be the correct date.
32 Within less than an hour, all men from *Heddernheim* were safely on board a Danish pilot cruiser from Skagen.
33 NA-ADM 199/1819; NA-ADM 199/294; NA-ADM 234/380; KTB SKL; and Staatsarchiv Bremen, *Kriegsschädenamt*, A608/43.
34 NA-ADM 199/286.
35 IWM Soundfile 9167/1. Hutchinson called Weiss a 'very quiet, dear old boy'.
36 NA-ADM 199/286; NA-ADM 234/380; and *Betænkning til Folketinget*, Bilag 1.
37 BA-RM 7/180; BA-RM 7/124; BA-RM 7/92; BA-RM 35 I/32; KTB SKL A March40; Generaloberst Halder, *Kriegstagebuch*, and *Lagevorträge des Oberbefehlshabers der Kriegsmarine vor Hitler 1939–1945*; and Haarr, *The German Invasion of Norway*.
38 NA-WO 106/1969; NA-CAB 66/6; NA-WO 193/773; Butler, *Grand Strategy*; Auphan and Mordal, *The French Navy in WWII*; and Churchill, *The Second World War*, Vol. 1. The minelaying of the Rhine was quickly abandoned.

Chapter 13

1 Bryant, *One Man Band*.
2 NA-ADM 199/288. Underlining in original report.
3 Bryant, *One Man Band*.
4 NA-ADM 199/1814. *Unity* fired three torpedoes at *U2* in rough seas off the west of Ringkøbing. All missed, although two loud explosions shaking the boat are noted in *U2*'s war diary with an addition: 'detonation of missing torpedoes from a British submarine?'
5 NA-ADM 234/380; BA-RM 7/11; and BA-RM 35/II-35.
6 NA-ADM 199/288.
7 NA-ADM 199/1840. By coincidence, *Seal* had stopped *Otto* on 23 March east of Kristiansand when she was travelling from Copenhagen to Bergen in ballast. All papers had been in order, and she was allowed to sail on at the time.
8 There were 163 soldiers from I/IR159 and pioneers from 169th Pioneer Battalion. The rest were Luftwaffe A/A gunners and administrative personnel.
9 There are several times given for the firing of the first torpedo, between 11:45 and 12:05. *Orzeł*'s log book gives 11:45.
10 Thirty-five of the dead from *Rio de Janeiro* were buried at Kristiansand churchyard on 12 April, with another fifteen on the 13th. The wreckage was found in 2014 at a depth of 135 metres.
11 NA-ADM 199/285; NA-ADM 199/1853; Sopocko, *Orzeł's Patrol*; and Steen, *Norges Sjøkrig 1940–45, Vol. II*.
12 'Army this side. Navy this side'. Lieutenant Voss was from the Regimental Staff of IR 159.
13 RA II-C-11-52; and RA FKA Ec, 0125. For a full account of these events and the consequence of not reacting to Onsrud's information, see Haarr, *The German Invasion of Norway*.
14 NA-ADM 223/126; and NA-ADM 199/278. Reuter's News Agency reported the sinking at 20:30 and a low priority signal was sent to the Home Fleet at 22:55, received on board *Rodney* at 02:58 the next day.
15 NA-ADM 199/285; NA-ADM 234/52; NA-ADM 199/1843; SKL KTB; Sopocko, *Orzeł's Patrol*; Chalmers, *Max Horton and the Western Approaches*; and http://crolick.website.pl.
16 NA-ADM 199/286.
17 NA-ADM 199/286; and IWM soundfile 12571. There were no German speakers on board *Trident* and communication with the German prisoners was very limited until they were back at Rosyth.
18 NA-ADM 199/286.
19 NA-ADM 223/126; NA-ADM 199/288; NA-ADM 199/1847; NA-ADM 199/361;and NA-ADM 234/380. Larvik had good landing facilities, railway connections and no defences. Landings there would be a good alternative to facing the forts of the Oslofjord.

Chapter 14

1   NA-ADM 199/288; NA-ADM 234/380; NA-ADM 234/52; NA-ADM 199/1843; SKL KTB; Haarr, *The German Invasion of Norway*; and Haarr, *The Battle for Norway*.
2   NA-ADM 199/288.
3   RA-II-C-11/52; RA-FKA-II-C-11/1103; RA II-C-11-1100; AE 2958/41; RM 35/II-35 NA-ADM 199/892; NA-ADM 199/288; and NA-ADM 234/380. For a complete account of these events, see Haarr, *The German Invasion of Norway*.
4   ADM 199/288
5   NA-ADM 199/1814.
6   BA-RM 102/3742.
7   For a full account of the events, see Haarr, *The German Invasion of Norway*.
8   Haarr, *The German Invasion of Norway*.
9   BA-RM 57/93; and IWM 91/38/1.
10 Haarr, *The German Invasion of Norway*.
11 NA-ADM 199/1861; IWM 91/38/1; and IWM soundfile 9137. Hutchinson later admitted he learned a lesson on this occasion and would next time break 90 degrees away from the tracks as soon as the torpedoes were fired.
12 BA-RM 92/5257; and BA-RM 57/93.
13 IWM 91/38/1.
14 IWM Soundfile 9167/1, transcribed in Hood, *Submarine* (slightly modified).
15 BA-RM 92/5257; BA-RM 57/93; and IWM 91/38/1.
16 BA-RM 92/5257; BA-RM 57/93; and IWM 91/38/1.
17 IWM 91/38/1; IWM soundfile 9137; NA-ADM 173/16665; and NA-ADM 199/1861. According to an officer visiting *Truant*, Hutchinson was 'a dark, sallow-complexioned, slightly built man who spoke very little'.
18 RNSM A1993/117.
19 Of the four (*Roda*, *Mendoza*, *Tijuca* and *Tübingen*), *Roda* was sunk by the Norwegian destroyer *Æger*.
20 NA-ADM 116/4471; NA-ADM 199/1848; and RNSM A1993/117.
21 NA-ADM 199/1848.
22 The German radio message, which was completely erroneous, was that a submarine had been sunk by a seaplane off the south-west coast of Norway. The radio message was in English and may well have been a deliberate hoax. A later German report held that 'a small German U-boat had torpedoed and sunk a large British submarine which had previously attacked the U-boat.' NA-ADM 199/1848.
23 DUBM-*U4* file.
24 KTB *U4*. Not long after, *U4* was returned to training duties. Hinsch went on as commander of two more U-boats, *U140* and *U569*, with moderate success. He survived the war and died in 1967.
25 NA-ADM 199/1848; ADM 116/4471; DUBM-U4 file; and BA-RM 98/4. *Thistle* sank south-west of Karmøy in 200 metres (650 feet) of water in position 59° 06'N, 05° 05'E. Fifty-three men died. For a detailed account of the invasion of Norway, see Haarr, *The German Invasion of Norway*; and Haarr, *The Battle for Norway*.

Chapter 15

1   NA-ADM 186/798.
2   NA-ADM 199/285; NA-ADM 199/1853; Sopocko, *Orzeł's Patrol*; and *The Polish Navy: A Short Story*. In some sources, *Orzeł* is credited with sinking the trawler *Ozbrojeny Rybarsky* on this patrol, but this is incorrect.
3   Bech, *Søkrig i Danske Farvande*.
4   NA-ADM 199/1847; NA-ADM 199/286; and BA-RM 72/169. *Triton* was lost with all hands in the Adriatic in December 1940, by then under the command of Lieutenant Commander G C Watkins.
5   NA-ADM 199/288; and Kaden, *Auf Ubootjagd gegen England*.
6   NARA T1022-267/39582.
7   Thiele had red hair: being nicknamed 'Curry' is equivalent to 'Ginger' in English.
8   *Lützow* was one of the German raiders built in the early 1930s. She was originally named *Deutschland*, but Hitler ordered it changed to *Lützow* after *Graf Spee* had been sunk, for fear of losing a ship with such a prestigious name. The need for repairs was related to the auxiliary engine, where some loose bolts had been discovered, as well as damage to the forward gun turret by the Norwegian batteries at Drøbak. For a complete account of these events, see Haarr, *The German Invasion of Norway*.
9   RM 92/5223
10 NA-ADM 199/1843

11 RNSM A1994/95.
12 Four days later, the upper conning tower hatch fell back after opening, hitting Forbes hard on the head. The counterweight had fallen off, probably as a result of the hatch slamming open on 10 April.
13 *Lützow's* sister ship was actually in dock.
14 RNSM A1994/95; ADM 199/1843; and ADM 199/294. Lieutenant Commander John Forbes perished when *Spearfish* was torpedoed by *U34* off Stavanger in August.
15 The starboard propeller was gone. The port was still attached to the shaft but all bearings and gears were destroyed
16 BA-RM 92/5223.
17 BA-RM 57/93. *Kondor* had damaged a propeller on wreckage from *Blücher* and, capable of only 20 knots, lagged behind. *Jaguar* and *Falke* were eventually ordered back to Kristiansand.
18 BA-RM 48/176; BA-RM 6/87; and BA-RM 92/5223.
19 NA-ADM 199/288.
20 NA-ADM 199/1874.
21 Bryant, *One Man Band*.
22 The signal did not indicate any hits on the heavy cruiser and Bryant was not aware she had been disabled.
23 NA-ADM 199/288. The moon was new, but unusually bright in Kattegat during these nights.
24 NA-ADM 199/288; and NA-ADM 199/1847.
25 NA-ADM 199/1847.
26 NA-ADM 199/288.
27 King, *The Stick and the Stars*. Ten men perished when *Moonsund* sank, including the two who died on board *Snapper*.
28 NA-ADM 199/1847. The 'destroyers' were probably a group of torpedoboats, escorts or minesweepers.
29 KTB SKL
30 NA-ADM 199/1840.
31 NA-ADM 199/1847.
32 NA-ADM 199/288.
33 NA-ADM 199/288.
34 NA-ADM 199/288.
35 NA-ADM 199/288; BA-RM 102/3742; and BA-RM 74/7.
36 In his report, King felt obliged to justify this waste of a good torpedo, holding that he at the time feared a stranded forward periscope wire would not last the patrol, and he 'decided to take whatever opportunity' he could while the wire was still functioning.
37 ND-ADM 199/288.
38 NA-ADM 199/288.
39 The two torpedo boats had left Kristiansand on the 13th for Frederikshavn where each embarked some 150 soldiers. *F5* had about 100 men on board.
40 BA-RM 57/93; and BA-RM 102/3622.
41 BA-RM69/30; and BA-RM 69/7.
42 NA-ADM 199/1847.
43 King, *The Stick and the Stars*.
44 NA-ADM 199/288; and King, *The Stick and the Stars*. Throughout these events, the German survivors from *Moonsund* were kept in some corner of the boat, enduring the same ordeal as the crew. Any POW camp would presumably have been preferable, in spite of King's words that they were 'in good heart'.
45 NA-ADM 199/1840.
46 NA-ADM 199/1877.
47 www.uboat.net; and www.ubotarchive.net – *Report of Interrogation of Crew of U95*. In August, Schreiber was given command of *U95*. She was sunk in November 1941 in the Mediterranean by *O21*. Schreiber was one of twelve survivors.
48 DUBM-U3-file; and NA-ADM 199/1877.
49 www.uboat.net; and www.wrakkenmuseum.nl. The wreck of *U1* was located by divers in 2007 confirming that she was lost in the British minefield no. 7.
50 For an account of Operation Duck, see Haarr, *The German Invasion of Norway*.
51 NA-ADM 199/1840; Warren and Benson, *Will Not We Fear*; and Wiggins, *Fatal Ascent*. In his report from the patrol, Lonsdale asked for *Seal* to be allowed to go back to Ogna, south of Stavanger where the railway line to Egersund ran near the coast, and destroy it by gunfire or landing party. This was dismissed by VA(S) Horton, however, as he had already decided that *Seal* should be transferred to 6th Flotilla and start doing what she was built for – mine-laying operations.
52 Voltelin van der Byl was a South African. He entered the Royal Navy as a cadet in the early 1920s and had his first experience of submarines in 1929 when he was assigned to *Odin* in Chinese waters.

53 NA-ADM 199/285, NA-ADM 234/380 and NA-ADM 199/1846
54 NA-ADM 199/288; and NA-ADM 199/1836.
55 NA-ADM 199/1847.
56 In September 1940, he was one of those killed when his lead boat *UJ121* hit a mine and sank off Ostend. He was replaced by Korvettenkapitän Günther Brandt.
57 *Brommy* was an old WWI minesweeper rebuilt to tender for R-boats.
58 NARA T1022-3798-82156. The *U-Jägers* were also known by their German phonetical names, *UJA* for *Anton*, *B* for *Bruno*, *C* for *Cäsar*, *D* for *Dora* and so on.
59 NARA T1022-3798-82156.
60 NA-ADM 199/1843.
61 NA-ADM 199/1843.
62 RNSM A1994/95; NA-ADM 199/1843; BA-RM 74/7; NA-ADM 199/1840; and NA-ADM 199/1877.
63 NA-ADM 199/1847.
64 NA-ADM 199/285.
65 In fact, they received two alarm calls within half an hour, but chose to steer for the one that turned out to be *Tetrarch* as this was the nearer. The other one was further to the north. The four trawlers involved from 12.U-Jagdflotille included *UJ125*, *UJ126* and *UJ128*.
66 NA-ADM 199/285.
67 NARA T1022-3798-82156.
68 NARA T1022-3798-82156.
69 NA-ADM 199/285.
70 NA-ADM 199/285; and NARA T1022-3798-82156.
71 NARA T1022-3798-82156.
72 KTB SKL April40. The SKL had ambitions to initiate operations in the North Sea and decided to keep 2nd S-boat Flotilla in the west, for the time being, with the depot ship *Tsingtao* stationed in Kristiansand.
73 Hart, *Discharged Dead*.
74 NA-ADM 199/288; and NA-ADM 199/1847. Lieutenant Commander Oddie was awarded a DSO for the sinking of *Ionia*.

Chapter 16

1 For the commander of a surface ship, the naval expression 'with dispatch' would mean to proceed at three-fifths power. For a submarine commander, it would also imply that the submarine was to proceed on the surface during daytime, unless compelled to dive for some safety reason. The board of inquiry later concluded that, considering circumstances, *Unity* should have been proceeding at no more than 6 knots and should have been making foghorn signals. The signalman claimed no knowledge of the signal, nor one referring to it, but the board found this difficult to believe. NA-ADM 1/12025.
2 Hunt was about to relieve Trickey as watch officer, but due to the events, this was never formally done.
3 NA-ADM 1/12025.
4 NA-ADM 1/12025. Low and Miller were originally awarded the Empire Gallantry Medal, but in September 1940 this was exchanged for the George Cross when this was instigated by King George.
5 Hood, *Submarine*
6 Hood, *Submarine*
7 NA-ADM 1/12025; Dornan, *Diving Stations*; Hood, *Submarine*; and Walters, *The History of the British U-Class Submarine*. In November 1942, the Admiralty agreed to pay the owners of *Atle Jarl* the sum of £1,200 plus interest as a settlement for repair of the damages sustained by the Norwegian freighter.

Chapter 17

1 The French sailors were a mix of volunteers and enlisted men, drawn on a rotational basis from the merchant and fishing fleets, where a sailor usually served a full year in the navy every five years. Almost three-quarters of them came from Brittany, the rest largely from the Mediterranean coastal districts.
2 Auphan and Mordal, *The French Navy in WWII*; and Hood, *Royal Republicans*.
3 Ocean-going submarines were restricted to 1,500-ton surface displacement, coastal submarines to 600 tons, though there were few limits placed on the numbers of these vessels that could be built.
4 The further improved and enlarged *Phenix*-class were ordered but never built, due to France's defeat in 1940.
5 *Saphir* and *Turquoise* in 1930, *Nautilus* in 1931, *Rubis* in 1932, *Diamant* in 1933, *Perle* in 1937.
6 Rousselot, *Rubis Free French Submarine*.

7 Including ten reloads for the four internal tubes.
8 The large 1,500-ton French submarines were considered suitable for transatlantic convoy escort as defence against German surface raiders.
9 NA-ADM 199/277; and Auphan and Mordal, *French Navy in World War II*.
10 NA-ADM 199/1857.
11 NA-ADM 199/1858.
12 NA-ADM 199/1858.
13 NA-ADM 199/1858. *La Sibylle* was lost in November 1942 off Casablanca under uncertain circumstances.
14 KTB *U51*. Tirpitzmole is the Tirpitz Pier.
15 NA-ADM 199/1858. *U51* had been at Narvik during the invasion of Norway. Two days earlier, on his way home, Knorr had himself fired two torpedoes at the French cruiser *Emile Bertin* off Namsos, but missed. *U51* was lost with all hands in the Bay of Biscay in August 1940 when torpedoed by *Cachalot*, see page 373.
16 NA-ADM 199/1858.
17 www.taucher.net and Sluijs, *Discovery of Doris*. The British boats involved in this mission were *Sturgeon*, *Snapper*, *Seawolf*, *Shark* and *Triad*. The French were *Doris*, *La Sibylle*, *Calypso*, *Amazone*, *Circé*, *Antiope* and *Thétis*.
18 NA-ADM 358/88; NA-ADM 199/1858; KTB *U9*; and NARA T1022-1057-30007. The wreck of *Doris* was discovered by Dutch divers Hans van Leeuwen and Ton van der Sluijs in 2003. Due to the time difference, *Doris* is recorded by German logs as having been sunk just after midnight on 9 May, whereas British and French time-keeping sets her loss at 23:15 on the 8th.
19 NA-ADM 199/1858. *Sfax* was sunk in error by the German U-boat *U37* on 19 December 1940 off Cap Juby, Morocco. At the time, *Sfax* was under Vichy French control and, as such, no legal prey for Kapitänleutnant Clausen.
20 NA-ADM 199/1857.
21 NA-ADM 199/1857.
22 NA-ADM 199/1857; and NA-ADM 199/285.
23 NA-ADM 199/1857.
24 The difference between 'believed' and actual position for the Hudson was as much as 64 miles at the end of a five-hour patrol.
25 NA-ADM 199/1857.
26 NA-ADM 199/1857
27 The armistice between France and Italy was signed two days later, on the evening of 24 June, and hostilities ceased the next day.
28 Sixteen submarines were destroyed by their crews in Toulon in November 1942, together with a large part of the remaining French surface fleet, lest they should be captured by the Germans: *Redoutable*, *Eurydice*, *Diamant*, *Thétis*, *Sirène*, *Vénus*, *Vengeur*, *Naïade*, *Pascal*, *Espoir*, *Achéron*, *Fresnel*, *Caïman*, *Henri Poincaré* and *Galatée*.
29 Auphan and Mordal, *French Navy in World War II*.
30 NA-ADM 358/184. The British officers killed were Commander Denis Sprague, commanding officer of *Thames*, and Lieutenant Patrick Griffiths of *Rorqual*, acting liaison officer for the French submarines. The third Briton killed was Leading Seaman Albert Webb. The French officer killed was Lieutenant Yves Daniel.
31 Auphan and Mordal, *French Navy in World War II*.
32 Damage to *Resolution* was severe and she had to be towed to Freetown for temporary repairs before going to the US where she remained in the yards until August 1941.
33 *Surcouf* was lost with all hands under unclear circumstances in February 1942. Most likely she was run into by the US freighter *Thompson Lykes*.

Chapter 18

1 BA-RM 102/3679.
2 NA-ADM 199/277; and NA-ADM 199/288.
3 KTB SKL. Cynically, most of the goods and supplies for the garrisons between Kristiansand and Trondheim, that could not be taken over land, were loaded onto Norwegian or neutral ships.
4 NA-ADM 234/380, see page 236.
5 NA-ADM 199/277; and NA-ADM 199/1921.
6 KTB SKL; and www.wlb-stuttgart.de.
7 KTB SKL; and www.wlb-stuttgart.de.
8 NA-ADM 199/277.
9 King, *The Stick and the Stars*.

10   Macleod and Kelly (eds), *The Ironside Diaries 1937–1940*.
11   NA-CAB 80/15.
12   NA-ADM 234/380; and NA-ADM 199/277.
13   NA-ADM 199/277; NA-ADM 234/380; and RNSM A1994/3. Reconnaissance could arguably have been performed at least as well by aircraft, giving the added advantage of being able to observe what was going on inside the harbours proper. There were few aircraft available for such missions, however, and even fewer cameras.
14   Clayton, *Sea Wolves*.

Chapter 19

1   MIR, Military Intelligence Research, was a small department of the War Office, also known as 'Churchill's Toyshop'. It was primarily set up to develop and test new weapons and techniques for irregular warfare, but its members were sent into the field at times. David Stirling and Jim Gavin of later special operations fame, were both involved with MIR.
2   Having landed the soldiers, *Truant* was to escort the Norwegian submarine *B1*, hiding on the coast, to Britain.
3   Kemp, *No Colours or Crest*.
4   Kemp, *No Colours or Crest*.
5   Kemp, *No Colours or Crest*.
6   IWM soundfile 9137; NA-ADM 173/16665; and NA-ADM 234/380.
7   IWM soundfile 9137.
8   The radio station was discovered by the Germans in May 1941, and the five operators were executed.
9   NA-ADM 199/1836. Admiral Horton was rather sceptical afterwards at firing three torpedoes on such a small target. Danielsen rejoined the Norwegian Admiral Staff in London and became instrumental in rebuilding the Norwegian Navy. Voltersvik later served as captain of several Norwegian escort vessels and destroyers. Brinch flew anti-submarine missions from the Allied airbases in Iceland, eventually becoming CO of the Norwegian unit there.
10   NA-ADM 234/380.
11   NA-ADM 199/300.
12   NA-ADM 199/300.
13   Ulstein, *Englandsfarten*, vol. II. At least some of the officers had been involved with the early resistance groups in the Arendal area and they had brought codebooks that were to be given to British intelligence. The resistance group was uncovered not long afterwards and several of its members arrested. This early in the war, however, they were not executed but sent to a prison camp.
14   RA II-C-11-1200; RA II-C-11-1240,0; BB A.2848.002/y/0052/04; BB A.2848.002/y/0002/01; RM 8/1152;and Steen, *Norges Sjokrig 1940–45*, vol. 3.
15   NA-ADM 234/380; NA-ADM 199/286; and Mars, *British Submarines at War 1939–1945*. *Cläre Hugo Stinnes I* was pulled afloat and towed to Bergen for repairs. She was sunk in 1944 by a mine laid by French submarine *Rubis*.
16   NA-ADM 199/1878; NA-ADM 199/300; and NA-ADM 199/1921. Two members of the prize crew came from the cruiser *Königsberg* and could confirm that she had been sunk by Skua dive bombers in Bergen harbour on 10 April.
17   Due to lack of resources and priority, *Möwe* was not operational again until the spring of 1943.
18   NA-ADM 199/285.
19   NA-ADM 199/285; and www.uboat.net. Lieutenant Fyfe later served with distinction throughout the war as CO of *Unruly*, *Trusty*, *Uther*, *Tribune* and *Tally-Ho*.
20   RNSM A1994/95.
21   RNSM A1994/95. The crews of the two Danish boats were: Niels Erik Kragh (master of *S175*), C P Kragh (master of *S130* and brother of Niels Kragh) J P Kragh (son of C P Kragh), Johannes Andersen, Viggo Nielsen, Torin Hansen (aged 16) and Viggo Nielsen (aged 15). They were, according to Forbes, very pro-British and, although concerned about their families left behind, willingly gave the information they could about the Germans in Denmark. Among other things, they said that the cruiser that had been hit by a torpedo off Skagen on the night of 10/11 April was *Lützow*, but maintained she had been sunk.
22   NA-ADM 199/474; and NA-ADM 199/278. The German merchant *Alster* was a German transport vessel captured in Vestfjorden, outside Narvik on 10 April 1940 by the British destroyer *Icarus*. After a period assisting in the naval repair base at Skjelfjord, *Alster* was taken into British service. Later, she was renamed *Empire Endurance* before being sunk south-east of Rockall on 20 April 1941 by *U73*.
23   NA-ADM 1/19910; BA-RM 7/888; and NARA T1022-3292/74308.

Chapter 20

1 Kemp, *The T-class Submarine*.
2 The Mk XVI mines were tailor-made for the submarines and had an explosive charge of 160 kg.
3 Kemp, *The T-class Submarine*.
4 RNSM-A.1934/5.
5 NA-ADM 234/560. For an account of the surface mine-laying operations in the early part of the war, see Haarr, *The Gathering Storm*.
6 www.historisches-marinearchiv.de. It has been difficult to find solid evidence of *Emden* being damaged in this minefield.
7 NA-ADM 199/1827. FD2, FD3 and FD4 were planned minefields, the laying of which were cancelled.
8 NA-ADM 199/294; and NA-ADM 199/1827.
9 Burch estimated the convoy to consist of '9 or 10 merchants' but according to German sources there were only four: *Kreta, Buenos Aires, Bahia Castillo* and *Wiegand*.
10 NA-ADM 199/294.
11 ADM 199/294; ADM 199/892; ADM 199/1827; and NARA T1022-2607/39582.
12 NA-ADM 199/1827; and NA-ADM 234/560.
13 NA-ADM 199/1827.
14 NA-ADM 199/1877.
15 NA-ADM 199/1877.
16 For a full account of Operation Juno, see Haarr, *The Battle for Norway*.
17 At one stage, the angered captain of *M6* had to threaten to open fire in order for the crew of *Palime* to assist in securing the tow-line and not just focus on getting into the lifeboats.
18 NARA T1022-3505- 73578. Kapitänleutnant Dittmers was made C-in-C of Stavanger Harbour Flotilla.
19 NARA T1022-3505-73578; and NARA T1022-3505-73574.
20 Erling Skjold, *Norsk Skipsvrakarkiv*. Numerous salvage attempts were made during and after the war and several divers have perished on the wreck.
21 For a full account of these events, see Haarr, *The German Invasion of Norway*; and Haarr, *The Gathering Storm*.
22 NA-ADM 199/300.
23 KTB SKL; and KTB *Seekommandant Stavanger*.
24 NA-ADM 199/300; KHFR 1940-file; and Rousselot, *Rubis Free French Submarine*. There is some uncertainty as to the number of casualties from *Jadarland*, which some sources hold to be as high as twenty-four.
25 Rousselot, *Rubis Free French Submarine*.
26 NA-ADM 199/300.
27 Rousselot, *Rubis Free French Submarine*.
28 NA-ADM 199/1827.
29 NA-ADM 199/1877.
30 NA-ADM 199/1827.
31 KTB 12th UJ-Flottille. The new *UJD* (ex *Rau IX*) was transferred to the flotilla on 16 June.
32 NA-ADM 199/1877.
33 NA-ADM 199/300; Rousselot, *Rubis Free French Submarine*; Auphan and Mordal, *French Navy in World War II*; and Jones, *Experiment at Dundee*. Back in service during the summer of 1941, *Rubis* would continue to serve with distinction to the end of the war. In all, she was to lay 683 mines during twenty-eight wartime patrols. These would be responsible for sinking at least fourteen merchant ships, almost 21,500 tons, and seven minesweepers or A/S vessels. In addition, one transport was sunk by torpedo. From 1946 *Rubis* was deployed as a training ship in Toulon before she was decommissioned in October 1949 and eventually sunk off Saint-Tropez to be used as a sonar target.

Chapter 21

1 Warren and Benson, *Will Not We Fear*. The mines eventually resulted in the sinking of one German freighter (*Vogesen*, 4,241 tons), two Swedish ships (*Almy, Torsten*) and one Danish ship (*Skandia*) during May and early June.
2 *The Evening News and Southern Daily Mail*, 9 April 1946.
3 Warren and Benson, *Will Not We Fear*.
4 *The Evening News and Southern Daily Mail*, 9 April 1946.
5 NA-ADM 199/1840.
6 NA-ADM 156/283.

7   The two Ar196 aircraft belonged to Bordfliegergruppe 5/196, intended as reconnaissance aircraft on board cruisers and battleships. As there were few capital ships in service, this meant they were also used for other tasks and 5/196 had temporarily been stationed at Aalborg-See for A/S missions.

8   Though fully qualified pilots, Schmidt and Mehrens sat in the backseat of the Arados, acting as observers and flight captains, as they were senior to their pilots Sackritz and Böttcher respectively. This was quite normal in German naval aircraft at this stage of the war.

9   Warren and Benson, *Will Not We Fear*. Smith was most likely hit by a bullet from one of the aircraft.

10 *The Evening News and Southern Daily Mail*, 11 April 1946

11 At the court martial, there was some uncertainty as to the exact wording of this assurance – whether it was in the form of 'it will sink' or more actively that they would ensure it actually sank.

12 Kurowski, *Seekrieg aus der Luft*.

13 *The Evening News and Southern Daily Mail*, 9 April 1946

14 Kurowski, *Seekrieg aus der Luft*.

15 Most of the airmen involved received the Iron Cross, First Class. Leutnant Günther Mehrens was killed with his pilot Unteroffizier Böttcher when their Ar196 crashed in the Kattegat on 17 May 1940. Leutnant Karl Schmidt was killed a year later, on 19 May 1941, when his aircraft was shot down by Hurricanes over the Channel. Oberleutnant Nikolaus Broili, first watch officer on board *U207*, was killed when she was sunk off Iceland in September 1941.

16 IWM soundfile 11730.

17 The SKL found it completely unbelievable (*völlig unverständlich*) that the crew had not scuttled the boat before abandoning her.

18 Petty Officer Maurice Barnes was killed in September 1940 by Russian border guards after having escaped from a prison camp and been taken care of for a while by a Polish underground group.

19 ADM 156/283; ADM 234/380. Warren and Benson, *Will Not We Fear*; Kurowski, *Seekrieg aus der Luft*; and Wiggins, *Fatal Ascent*. Lonsdale resigned from the Royal Navy shortly after the court martial. After taking theological training, he served as a minister in the Church of England for the rest of his working life. Rupert Lonsdale died in April 1999 at the age of 93.

20 ADM 156/283.

Chapter 22

1   King, *The Stick and the Stars*.

2   King, *The Stick and the Stars*.

3   KTB SKL.

4   NA-ADM 199/1877.

5   KTB SKL.

6   *Jåbæk* is only referred to in the British reports by her registration number M-85-G, probably as her real name would be rather difficult to write – and pronounce – in English.

7   NA-ADM 199/1877. Lieutenant Jan Erik Haave was killed on 19 August 1941, when the Norwegian destroyer *Bath* was sunk after being hit by a torpedo from *U204*. Another of the men on board *Jåbæk* was the British/Norwegian engineer John Turner. He later became an active SIS officer, but his military associations at this time are uncertain.

8   NA-ADM 199/300; and Ulstein, *Englandsfarten, vol. I*.

9   NA-ADM 199/300.

10 NA-ADM 199/288.

11 NA-ADM 199/1877; NA-ADM 199/300; and www.bismarck-class.dk. *Widder* was known to the Royal Navy as *Raider D*. In spite of her success, she was found unsuitable as a raider, converted to a repair ship and renamed *Neumark*. After the war she was for a while taken into British service as *Ulysses*.

12 For a full account of these events, see Haarr, *The Battle for Norway*.

13 BA-RM 92/5267.

14 The hospital ship *Atlantis* had been accompanying the troop ship *Orama*, which was sunk by *Hipper*, but was allowed to proceed unmolested under the rules of the Geneva Convention, provided that she did not use her wireless. This was observed by her captain and it was not until the morning of 9 June, when *Atlantis* met the battleship *Valiant* coming north to meet the retiring convoys, that the presence of the German fleet become known to the Admiralty.

15 KTB SKL.

16 Three holes were found in the bridge plating in addition to some other minor damage.

17 With only three weeks to midsummer night, 24 June, sunset at Frohavet is half an hour before midnight and sunrise shortly after 03:00. The average duration of diving for this patrol was 19.5 hours, the longest 25 hours.

18   BA-RM 92/5178; BA-RM 7/888; KTB SKL; NA-ADM 199/294; NA-ADM 1/19910; and NA-ADM 199/1877.
19   ADM 199/1877. This was the cruiser *Nürnberg* returning from the Narvik area, having transported soldiers and equipment northwards (Operation Nora). She was escorted by the minesweepers *M9*, *M10*, *M12* and *M13*.
20   KTB SKL.
21   In spite of extensive air attacks on the way, *Scharnhorst* reached Kiel on 23 June.
22   KTB SKL.
23   KTB SKL. Admiral Marschall was relieved of his command as Flottenchef and replaced by Vizeadmiral Lütjens on 18 June.
24   BA-RM 92/5267; and BA-RM 92/5245.
25   NA-ADM 199/1877
26   NA-ADM 199/300; and NA-ADM 199/1877.
27   NA-ADM 199/450.
28   NA-ADM 199/1877; and NA-ADM 199/300.
29   BA-RM 92/5245, and KTB SKL. When anchoring, *Gneisenau* had to use her stern anchors as those in the bow were unusable.
30   Whitley, *German Cruisers of World War Two*.
31   BA-RM 92/5245; and BA-RM 57/126. Netzbrand's conclusion was mainly based on the fact that no radio intercepts from any British submarine had been made in the area.
32   BA-RM 45/III-136.
33   NA-ADM 234/380; BA-RM 92/5267; BA-RM 92/5245; and Haarr, *The Battle for Norway*.
34   ADM 234/380.
35   Kutzleben et al., *Minenschiffe 1939–1945*; and Bech, *Søkrig i Danske Farvande*.
36   On this mission, the escorting torpedo boat *Leopard* lost her steering and careened in front of the minelayer *Preussen*. The two ships collided and *Leopard* eventually sank. The only casualty from this incident was Sub-Lieutenant Marschall, the son of the fleet commander at the time, Admiral Wilhelm Marschall.
37   EMD – *Einheitsmine D* – is a moored contact mine. Spherical shape, 100 centimetres in diameter, charge 150 kilograms, total weight 900 kilograms. Five horns on the upper half. Could be moored in 100–200 metres of water.
38   For a full account of this event, see Haarr, *The Battle for Norway*.
39   Kutzleben et al., *Mineschiffe 1939–1945*.
40   TO-O13 file. The document is dated May 1951 and signed by a commander of the Royal Navy.
41   Andrzej Bartelski and Jouke Spoelstra, personal communication.

Chapter 23

1   Brown, *Airmen in Exile*.
2   Jones, *Experiment at Dundee*. Belgium had for all practical purposes abolished their navy between the wars and the Danish Navy remained in Denmark, under German control.
3   NA-ADM 116/4121. Lieutenant Commander Fraser was given command of the Submarine *Oswald*. Telegraphist Leslie Jones, known as 'John', was popular on board *Orzel* as he happily translated letters between the Polish sailors and their British girlfriends.
4   NA-AIR 2/2925; NA-ADM 199/1925; NA-ADM 199/285; NA-ADM 199/1853; www.orzelsearch.com and www.bartelski.pl.
5   NA-ADM 199/277.
6   Burch was replaced by a more junior officer in February 1940, after which he had a spell at *Forth* in Rosyth before being appointed commanding officer of *Narwhal*.
7   Varvounis, *The Wilk Case*. Boleslaw Romanowski later became one of the most successful Polish submarine captains, being in command of *Jastrzab*, *Dzik* and *Sokol*.
8   NA-ADM 199/1853. The report is slightly anomalous as it is neither addressed to the flotilla captain nor signed, as was usual. It is nevertheless the official document and bears the mark of having been written jointly by Kapitan Marynarki Karnicki and the British liaison officer.
9   NA-ADM 199/1853.
10   NA-ADM 199/1853; ADM 234/380; and Varvounis, *The Wilk Case*.
11   Komandor Podporucznik Krawczyk committed suicide in July 1941.
12   NA-ADM 199/1853. By this time, the rebuild of the Polish Navy had started and many of the submariners that had escaped from the Germans in 1939 now served on board one of the three submarines to sail under the Polish flag in the second half of WWII: *Jastrzab*, *Dzik* and *Sokol*. The hulk of *Wilk* was towed back to Poland after the war and finally scrapped in 1954.

13 The prefix 'K' was short for *Kolonien* or colonies, O was simply for *Onderzeeboot* or underwater boat. Initially, the 'K' boats were paid for by the Ministry of Colonies while the 'O' boats were paid for by the Ministry of Defence.

14 *O8* was the former British submarine *H6* that had been wrecked on the Dutch coast in January 1916. She was salvaged and eventually purchased for the Dutch Navy. In May 1940, *O8* was captured by the Germans at Den Helder and used for training by the Kriegsmarine, thus also becoming the oldest U-boat in German service.

15 When the Dutch submarines came to Britain, the ventilation system was removed before the boats were declared operational in 1940 and the technology was not pursued by the Royal Navy until after the war.

16 www.dutchsubmarines.com.

17 Luitenant ter Zee 1ste Klasse (Ltz1) is equivalent to lieutenant commander.

18 To achieve ballast, *O24* had taken on board a number of copper weights when leaving Holland. These were later sold in Britain where the metal was used for making propellers.

19 TO-O14 file; and TO-O15 file.

20 Van Beers et al, *Periscoop Op*. The incomplete *O25*, *O26* and *O27* were eventually rebuilt and completed and taken into German service as supply boats, named *UD3*, *UD4* and *UD5*, respectively.

21 NA-ADM 199/1856; and NA-ADM 116/4121.

22 NA-ADM 234/380; TO-O13 file; and www.dutchsubmarines.com.

23 From late 1940, a Mk X torpedo was also produced in British factories for use in the Dutch submarines.

24 DUBM-*U60* file; and KTB *U60*.

25 NA-ADM 199/1856; NA-ADM 199/1880; and www.uboat.net. On 17 August, the Dutch naval commander, Vice-Admiraal Fürstner, visited Dundee and decorated van Dulm and Ort for having taken their boats to Britain.

26 NA-ADM 199/1880.

27 NA-ADM 199/1856; and Ort, *Hr,Ms, O22*.

28 DUBM-*U28*; and KTB *U28*.

29 TO-O22 file; and www.uboat.net. In August 1993, a survey vessel of the Norwegian Petroleum Directorate located the wreck of *O22* in 180 metres (590 feet) depth 40 miles off the Norwegian coast at 57° 55' N, 05° 31' E. ROV video images identified the boat, but revealed no damage to the hull, which is upright on the seabed. In November 1996, a ceremony was held at the site.

30 NA-ADM 199/1879; and www.dutchsubmarines.com.

31 NA-ADM 199/1879.

32 NA-ADM 199/1879.

33 BA-RM 70/1; and RA II-C-11-1100. The Norwegian Military Investigation Committee of 1946 found the conduct of the two commanders at fault and recommended that they were charged with neglect of duty.

34 RA II-C-11-1350; and RA II-C-11-1360.

35 RA II-C-11-1350.

Chapter 24

1 *The Sydney Morning Herald*, 27 December, 1958.

2 BA-RM 45/III-124. Underlining is in the original.

3 NA-ADM 234/380.

4 NA-ADM 199/1828.

5 NA-ADM 199/1828; and NARA T1022-3683-82186. *UJ126* was a 446-ton trawler built in 1938. She was originally ordered by the Nordsee Deutsche Hochseefischerei Company of Cuxhaven, but requisitioned in 1939 by the Kriegsmarine and armed and equipped as a submarine hunter.

6 NA-ADM 199/1828. Upon returning to Blyth, Lieutenant Wanklyn transferred to the brand new U-class submarine *Upholder* which was to become one of the most legendary submarines of all time. As her commanding officer, Wanklyn was awarded the Victoria Cross in December 1941. *Upholder* was lost with all hands on her twenty-eighth war patrol in April 1942. *H31* was lost with all hands to unknown causes in the Bay of Biscay in late December 1941, probably hitting a mine. At the time, Lieutenant Frank Gibbs was commanding officer.

7 NA-ADM 199/1828; and NA-ADM 199/1829. *H28* is the only British submarine known to have been on active patrol in both wars.

8 NA-ADM 199/1829.

9 ND-ADM 199/1829.

10 ND-ADM 199/1829.

11 NA-ADM 199/300.

12 KTB *U34*.

13 Morgan and Taylor, *U-boat Attack Logs*.
14 2.Unterseeboot-Lehrdivision (2.ULD) was established in November 1940 and several 'older' commanders with successful operational experience were posted there for a period. A 'Lehr' unit was a concept used both in the German navy and air force, being like an academy where tactics, techniques and drills were discussed, tested and trained by men who had proven their skills, made into best practices and communicated to those with less experience. In February 1943, Rollmann commissioned *U848*, a large type IX boat, which was sunk with all hands by depth charges from long-range US aircraft south of Ascension Island in November of that year. As far as is known, Able Seaman Pester spent the rest of the war in German POW camps only to be killed in a motorcycle accident shortly after repatriation in 1945.
15 Endrass was Prien's first officer aboard *U47* when they infiltrated Scapa Flow and sank the battleship *Royal Oak* in 1939. During his first patrol with *U46*, in June 1940, Endrass sank five ships, totalling 35,347 tons, and damaged a sixth.
16 DUBM-*U46*-file; and NA-ADM 199/285. Engelbert Endrass was killed on 21 December 1941 when *U567* was sunk with all hands by British A/S vessels *Deptford* and *Samphire* off the Azores. At that time, he had been awarded the Knight's Cross with Oak Leaves, having sunk twenty-two ships, 118,528 tons, and damaged a further four. For Oddie, this would be the last patrol with *Triad*. Lieutenant Commander George Salt would take over the boat and head for the Mediterranean three weeks later. *Triad* was sunk in the Ionian Sea on 15 October 1940 by the Italian submarine *Enrico Toti*. There were no survivors.
17 On 10 June 1940, Regia Marina had 117 submarines in commission, of which less than 10 were older models.
18 NA-ADM 199/1115.
19 NA-ADM 234/380; and NA-ADM 199/277.
20 BA-RM 45/III-136.
21 NA-ADM 199/1921.
22 Bryant, *One Man Band*. On the same day, 30 June 1940, Ben Bryant was promoted to commander. Later, after the war, Bryant would eventually become Flag Officer Submarines.

Chapter 25

1   BA-RM 45/III-136.
2   BA-RM 45/III-100. The danger zone was generally from Kristiansand, inside the Skagerrak, to Bergen, but the most precarious stretch was the open waters west of Lista, off Obrestad and north to Stavanger.
3   In late July, the group was reduced and reformed as Küstenfliegergruppe (stab) 706. From mid-September, the A/S patrols off the coast of south-western Norway were tactically organized by KüFlGr 706, using He115s and a few AR196s.
4   BA-RM 45/III-136. The ex-Estonian prize vessel *Taat* developed engine defects and never left Stavanger.
5   Bryant, *One Man Band*.
6   NARA T1022-3204-72459.
7   Bryant, *One Man Band*.
8   Bryant, *One Man Band*.
9   NA-ADM 267/114; and Bryant, *One Man Band*.
10 BA-RM 45/III-100; BA-RM 45/III-209; BA-RM 45/III-136; and NARA T1022-3204-72459.
11 NA-ADM 267/114.
12 NA-ADM 267/114.
13 King, *The Stick and the Stars*.
14 BA-RM 69/133; BA-RM 45/III-136; and Bergen Byrett, Sjøforklaring, Sak B144/1940, Eske 33.
15 NARA T1022-3204-72459.
16 BA-RM 45/III-136; NARA T1022-3204-72459; and King, *The Stick and the Stars*.
17 BA-RM 45/III-136; and King, *The Stick and the Stars*.

Chapter 26

1   NA-ADM 199/1840
2   At this time of the year, the Germans (and Norwegians) were on summer time which is one hour ahead of the British. All times in this chapter, including those in the German accounts, have been adjusted to British time for consistency.
3   NA-ADM 199/278; RNSM's *Shark* file.

4   *Unteroffizier* is equivalent to non-commissioned officer (NCO).
5   KTB Küstenfliegergruppe Stavanger.
6   NA-ADM 199/278; and Wheeler's account RNSM's *Shark* file.
7   KTB Küstenfliegergruppe Stavanger.
8   NA-ADM 199/278; and RNSM's *Shark* file.
9   KTB Küstenfliegergruppe Stavanger.
10 The signal at 22:50 was received and air and surface searches initiated, failing to find her. NA-ADM 199/1115.
11 Both Barrett and Loder received a DSC for their efforts in 1945 after they had returned to Britain.
12 A few rifles had also been brought up and were used at times, probably bolstering the morale of the submariners more than damaging the Arados.
13 NA-ADM 199/278; and RNSM's *Shark* file.
14 KTB Küstenfliegergruppe Stavanger. On board German aircraft, the pilot was not necessarily in command and in this case Schreck was the pilot while Junker decided where he should fly and what he should do.
15 NA-ADM 199/278; and RNSM's *Shark* file.
16 The aircraft did not sink and was later towed back to Stavanger and recovered.
17 BA-RM 45/III-136.
18 Wheeler's account, RNSM's *Shark* file.
19 The wreck of *Shark* was found by a survey vessel, while it was surveying a cable route in April 2008, at 251 metres (823 feet) depth. Sonar pictures showed that she was upright on the seabed and appeared to be in a good condition. The position where she was found is some 7.5 kilometres north-north-east of the position given by the Kriegsmarine as where she had been bombed and captured.
20 BA-RM 45/III-136.
21 Evans, *Beneath the Waves*.
22 BA-RM 45/III-136. This position is 24 kilometres or 13 nautical miles north-east of where the wreck of *Shark* was found, and 50 kilometres or 27 nautical miles due west of where the author lives.
23 NA-ADM 199/278.
24 BA-RM 45/III-136; NA-ADM 199/1925; NA-ADM 199/278; NARA T1022-3204-72459; RNSM's *Shark* file; and KTB Küstenfliegergruppe Stavanger. As Lieutenant Commander Buckley succeeded in ensuring his boat was not captured, contrary to Lieutenant Commander Lonsdale of *Seal*, Buckley was not court-martialled. In fact, he received a DSO in 1945 and had a notable post-war career in the navy until retiring as rear admiral in 1965. James Walsh is buried at Eiganes churchyard in Stavanger and Eric Foster at Sola churchyard, respectively.

Chapter 27

1   Part of the fuel had been polluted by salt water on the way to Trondheim, and this was still on board to be cleaned back in Germany.
2   These mines had most likely been dropped by aircraft.
3   NA-ADM 199/285.
4   KTB SKL; and BA-RM 45/III-124.
5   NA-ADM 199/285.
6   NA-ADM 199/285.
7   BA-RM 45/III-124.
8   NA-ADM 199/285.
9   *U57* had a brief patrol lasting five days north of Scotland, before returning to Bergen. After a few more days there, she headed for Lorient, west of the British Isles. *U57* was sunk after a collision with a Norwegian freighter in September; she was raised and re-commissioned as a training boat. Erich Topp survived the war, having sunk thirty-six ships, almost 200,000 tons. He served in the post-war German Navy and died in 2005, 91 years old.
10 NA-ADM 199/285.
11 On previous patrols with *U62*, Michalowski had sunk the British destroyer *Grafton* off Ostend during Operation Dynamo. Earlier on this patrol, the 4,581-ton steam merchant *Pearlmoor* had been sunk off Malin Head on 19 July.
12 Bryant, *One Man Band*.
13 Bryant, *One Man Band*; and http://uboat.net.
14 Ironically, *Toran* had sailed in at least three of the convoys between Norway and Britain earlier in 1940 under British protection. On this voyage, *Toran* was heading for Thamshavn near Trondheim to load pyrite. Three men died when she was sunk; twenty-seven were rescued.

15 Bryant, *One Man Band*

16 On 5 May 1940, Lieutenant Commander Philip Roberts of *Porpoise* was in a similar situation and fired with 'a wonderful target of 9 ships in approximate line-abreast' to starboard and ordered '90 right'. Not one of the six torpedoes fired hit any of the ships, which most likely were in a convoy that included the transports *Alstertor, Alsterufer, Mendoza, Tijuca* and *Tübingen*, escorted by torpedoboats *Kondor* and *Möwe* and others. (ADM 199/294).

17 Bryant, *One Man Band*; and *The Sydney Morning Herald*, 27 December 1958.

18 Bryant, *One Man Band*.

19 NA-ADM 199/1921; and www.uboat.net.

20 NA-ADM 199/1844; and NA-ADM 199/1921.

21 NA-ADM 199/1844; and NA-ADM 199/1921.

22 Rumour has it that there also was a number of German scientists on board and several crates of equipment that were to be sent to the factories at Rjukan where the production of heavy water was to be intensified, needed in Germany's atomic research programmes. This has been difficult to verify.

23 NA-ADM 199/285. Nautical twilight is defined to start when the sun is 12 degrees below the horizon. Under clear conditions general outlines of objects may be distinguishable at sea, but the horizon is indistinct.

24 NARA T1022-2607/39582.

25 NA-ADM 199/1837l; and BA-RM102/3679.

26 After the Norwegian campaign had ended, the Swedish government held that its obligations as a neutral would not be violated if it granted the incessant German requests for transit privileges. On 5 July 1940, it was officially announced in Stockholm that an agreement had been concluded with Germany under which German officers and men, 'principally on leave', would be allowed to travel unarmed using the Swedish railway system. This so-called 'leave traffic' was severely criticised both in Sweden and abroad as incompatible with the obligations of neutrality. The Hague Convention explicitly forbids a neutral state to allow a belligerent to move troops, munitions or supplies across its territory. Sweden's contention that war in Norway had ended was scarcely sound, for Britain and Germany were still at war and the Germans were preparing quite openly to attack Britain from Norway. The exact nature and extent of the 'leave traffic' is still very much a matter of dispute and there are allegations that the Germans flouted the agreement forbidding them to carry arms on the Swedish trains by loading the troops in one train and their weapons in another following immediately behind. These charges have always been denied, but there is no doubt that soldiers travelled relatively freely through Sweden to Oslo, Trondheim and Narvik over the Swedish railway network. Officers, travelling in special compartments, were allowed to carry their pistols – soldiers, only their bayonets, other arms not being allowed on the trains. Above is adapted from an article published by the Swedish Foreign Office on their website www.foreignaffairs.com/articles/70405. See also Haarr, *The German Invasion of Norway* and Haarr, *The Battle for Norway* for more information on this issue.

27 NARA T1022-2607/39582.

28 NA-ADM 199/1837.

29 NA-ADM 199/285.

30 NA-ADM 199/1837.

31 NA-ADM 199/1837.

32 RA/S-1643/D/Dd/L0003/0005.

33 RA/S-1643/D/Dd/L0003/0005; and NA-ADM 199/1837

34 NA-ADM 199/1837. Vice Admiral Gregory retired from the Royal Navy in 1966, his last posting being as Flag Officer Scotland and Northern Ireland. He died in 1975, at the age of 64.

35 NA-ADM 199/1879.

Chapter 28

1 NA-ADM 234/380. The instructions were followed by detailed geographical specifications, generally giving the submarine commanders a free hand in the areas they were sent to patrol.

2 NA-ADM 234/380.

3 NA-ADM 23-380.

4 www.dundee-at-war.net.

5 NA-ADM 199/292

6 Kaden, *Auf Ubootjagd gegen England*.

7 In his book, Kaden adds that Oliver later told interrogators onshore that he and two others had attempted to get out through the after escape hatch. He managed to get out, but the other two, both wearing DSEA equipment, did not – possibly as they became entangled. It has not been possible to verify this.

8   *The Mail*, 16 January 1997, www.uboat.net and www.rnsubs.co.uk.

9   Kaden, *Auf Ubootjagd gegen England*.

10   Wolfgang Kaden was killed on 9 July 1942 when his new trawler, *UJ1110*, struck a mine off Hammerfest, Norway. By then, he had also with certainty sunk the Russian submarine *K23*. Attempts to raise the wreck of *H49* were unsuccessful as it was too quickly covered by sand. Lieutenant Richard Coltart was the man on board the *Grebe Cock* during the *Thetis* event in June 1939 (see chapter 1). He served as first lieutenant on board *Taku* before being appointed CO of the *H31* after Wanklyn. Coltart had been transferred to *H49* just days before she was sunk.

11   NA-ADM 199/292; and NA-ADM 199/1836.

12   NA-ADM 234/380; and NA-ADM 199/292. No blame was attached to Lieutenant Commander Francis. He merely followed the instructions given to him at the time.

13   NA-ADM 199/292; and NA-ADM 199/1830.

14   NA-ADM 199/292.

15   NA-ADM 199/292.

16   Young and Armstrong, *Silent Warriors, Vol. II*.

17   NA-ADM 234/380. The after escape hatch was open when the wreckage was found, so it is possible that some men escaped, only to be carried away by the tide as there was nobody on the surface to rescue them.

18   NA-ADM 234/380. *Clyde*, also assigned to 3rd Flotilla, was refitting.

19   DUBM-U138-file; and www.warsailor.com

20   NA-ADM 199/1827; quote is compiled from two entries in *Cachalot*'s report.

21   DUBM-*U51* file.

22   NA-ADM 199/1827; and DUBM-*U51* file. U51 sank in position 47° 06' N, 04° 51' W.

23   NA-ADM 199/285 and NA-ADM 199/1921

24   Captain Nicolaysen was very concerned about the safety of his crew and was reluctant to leave them. As his wife was hurt, though, he eventually opted to stay with her as Haggard assured him that 'something' would be sent to the rescue of the rest.

25   NA-ADM 234/380; www.uboat.net; and www.warsailors.com. Among the 'Norwegian' crew of *Tropic Sea* were at least three from other Scandinavian countries. In most cases, these men chose to follow their colleagues onto other Norwegian ships and continue to fight the Germans alongside them, rather than go home.

26   NA-ADM 199/1827; quote is compiled from two entries in *Cachalot*'s report.

27   NA-ADM 199/1827; and monthly anti-submarine reports September/October 1940.

28   www.warsailors.com.

29   BA-RM 7/84; BA-RM 7/91; and NA-ADM 199/1844.

30   After the event, Prellberg gave both men, who had neither identified, nor reported the shadow, a few lessons.

31   DUBM-*U31*-file. Prellberg believed torpedoes had been fired at him by British submarines before on this patrol, west of Ireland, but there is no obviously matching attack report. *U31* was sunk on 2 November north-west of Ireland by depth charges from British destroyer *Antelope*. Forty-four men survived, including Prellberg.

32   NA-ADM 199/1864.

33   In all, five groups of six boats were sent from Italy to Bordeaux. At least three turned back with technical problems.

34   D'Adamo, *Regia Marina Italiana*.

35   NA-ADM 199/285; and D'Adamo, *Regia Marina Italiana*.

36   NA-ADM 199/285. It appears there were three casualties onboard the *Cimcour*.

37   NA-ADM 199/285.

38   *Enrico Tazzoli* would become one of the most successful Italian submarines, sinking almost 100,000 tons of Allied shipping, before being sunk herself by aircraft in the Bay of Biscay in May 1943.

39   NA-ADM 199/285.

40   NA-ADM 199/300.

41   NA-ADM 199 1844.

42   NA-ADM 199/285. Brown had intended to fire only four torpedoes, but due to snappy, imprecise orders, the torpedo officer let off the full salvo. Brown took the full blame himself for what he considered a waste of four torpedoes.

43   NA-ADM 199/285.

44   NA-ADM 199/285.

45   Richards, *Secret Flotillas*.

46   NA-ADM 199/285; and Richards, *Secret Flotillas*. The mines off Penmarch were likely those laid by *Cachalot* on 23 September. According to the French fishermen, three French trawlers and a German merchantmen had been sunk by these mines.

47   *Jervis Bay* was hopelessly outgunned and ruthlessly sunk. *Scheer* went on to sink five ships of the convoy, but the convoy had managed to scatter and the remaining ships escaped. Sixty-five survivors from *Jervis Bay* were picked up by the Swedish ship *Stureholm*. Captain Edward Fegen was not among them and received a posthumous Victoria Cross.

48   Chalmers, *Max Horton and the Western Approaches.*

49   NA-ADM 199/1844.

50   NA-ADM 199/1844.

51   NA-ADM 199/286.

52   www.regiamarina.net.

53   NA-ADM 199/1846; and www.regiamarina.net.

References

Published

D'Adamo, *Regia Marina Italian, see* Websites.

Auphan, P, and Mordal, J, *The French Navy in WWII*, US Naval Institute, Annapolis, MD, 1959.

Allaway, J, *Hero of the Upholder*, Airlife Publishing, Shrewsbury, 1991.

Anscomb, C, *Submariner*, Kimber, London, 1957.

Barclay, G, *If Hitler Comes*, Birlinn, Edinburgh, 2013.

Bech, P, *Søkrig i Danske Farvande*, Schønberg, København, 2008.

Beers, A C van, Dulm, J F van and Geijs, J H, *Periscoop Op: De Oologsgeschiedenis van den Onderzeedienst der Koninklijke Marine*, Netherland Publishing Company, London, 1945.

Betænkning til Folketinget, Bilag 1, J H Schultz, Copenhagen, 1945.

Booth, T, *Thetis Down: The Slow Death of a Submarine*, Pen and Sword, Barnsley, 2008.

Broome, J, *Convoy is to Scatter,* Kimber, London, 1972.

Brown, A C, *Airmen in Exile: The Allied Air Forces in the Second World War*, Sutton Publishing, Phoenix Mill, 2000.

Bryant, B, *One Man Band*, Kimber, London, 1958.

Chalmers, W S, *Max Horton and the Western Approaches*, Hodder & Stoughton, London, 1954.

Churchill, W, *The Second World War Vol 1,* Cassell, London 1948.

Clayton, T, *Sea Wolves*, Little Brown, London, 2011.

Clewlow, S, *HMS Ursula: The Chorley and District Submarine*, Chorley, 2010.

Dornan, P, *Diving Stations*, Pen & Sword Maritime, Barnsley, 2010.

Evans, A S, *Beneath the Waves*, Pen & Sword, Barnsley, 2010.

Haarr, G H, *The German Invasion of Norway, April 1940,* Seaforth, London, 2009.

Haarr, G H, *The Battle for Norway, April–June 1940,* Seaforth, London, 2010.

Haarr, G H, *The Gathering Storm: The Naval War in Northern Europe, September 1939–April 1940,* Seaforth, London, 2013.

Harris, W, *The Rouge's Yarn: The Sea-going Life of Captain 'Joe' Oram*, Leo Cooper, London, 1993.

Hart, S, *Discharged Dead: A True Story of Britain's Submarine War*, Odham's Press, London, 1956.

Hezlet, A, *British and Allied Submarine Operations in WWII*, Gosport, Royal Navy Submarine Museum, 2001.

Hood, J, *Submarine: An Anthology of First-hand Accounts of the War under the Sea, 1939–1945*, Conway Publishing, London, 2007.

Jones, 'Experiment at Dundee', *Journal of Military History*, vol. 72, no. 4, October 2008.

Kaden, W, *Auf Ubootjagd gegen England*, Hase & Koehler, Leipzig, 1941.

Kemp, P, *No Colours or Crest*, Cassell & Co., London, 1958.

Kemp, P J, *The T-Class Submarine: The Classic British Design*, Arms & Armour, London, 1990.

King, W, *Adventure in Depth,* Nautical Publishing, Wallop, 1975.

King, W, *The Stick and the Stars*, Hutchinson, London, 1958.

Kurowski, F, *Seekrieg aus der Luft,* Verlag E S Mittler, Herford, 1979.

Kutzleben, K, Schroeder, W and Brennecke, J, *Minenschiffe 1939–1945*, Koehler, Herford, 1974.

McCartney, I, *British Submarines 1939–45*, Osprey Publishing, Oxford, 2006.

Mackenzie, H, *The Sword of Damocles*, Sutton, Penzance, 1995.

Macleod, R and Kelly, D (eds), *The Ironside Diaries 1937–1940*, Constable, London, 1962.

Morgan and Taylor, *U-boat Attack Logs,* Seaforth, Barnsley, 2011.

Ort, H M, *Hr.Ms. O22*, Van Soeren & Co., Amsterdam, 1995.

Poolman, *Allied Submarines of World War Two,* Arms and Armour Press, London 1990.

Richards, B, *Secret Flotillas, Vol. I: Clandestine Sea Operations to Brittany, 1940–1944*, Frank Cass Publishers, London, 2004.

Roberts, D, *HMS Thetis, Secrets and Scandal: Aftermath of a Disaster*, Avid Publications, Merseyside, 1999.

Roskill, S, *Naval Policy Between the Wars, Vol. 2*, Collins, London, 1976.

Rousselot, H L G, *Rubis Free French Submarine*, Profile Warship 26, Profile Publications, Windsor, 1972.

Simpson, G, *Periscope View*, Macmillan, London, 1972.

Sopocko, E, *Orzel's Patrol*, Methuen & Co., London, 1942.

Steen, *Norges Sjøkrig 1940–45, vol II*, Gyldendal Norske Forlag, Oslo, 1954.

Ulstein R, *Englandsfarten, Vol. I: Alarm i Ålesund*, Det Norske Samlaget, Oslo, 1965.

Ulstein R, *Englandsfarten, Vol. II: Søkelys mot Bergen*, Det Norske Samlaget, Oslo, 1967.

Walters, D, *The History of the British U-Class Submarine*, Pen & Sword, Barnsley, 2004.

Warren, C E T and Benson, J, *The Admiralty Regrets*, Popular Book Club, Watford, 1959.

Warren, C E T and Benson, J, *Will Not We Fear*, Harrap & Co., London, 1961.

Whitley, *German Cruisers of World War Two*, Naval Institute Press, Annapolis, MD, 1985.

Wiggins, M., *Fatal Ascent: HMS Seal 1940*, Spellmount, Stroud, 2006.

Young, R and Armstrong, P, *Silent Warriors: Submarine Wrecks of the United Kingdom, Vol. II*, History Press, Briscombe, 2009.

Young, R and Armstrong, P, *Silent Warriors: Submarine Wrecks of the United Kingdom, Vol. III*, History Press, Briscombe, 2010.

Lagevorträge des Oberbefehlshabers der Kriegsmarine vor Hitler 1939–1945

Archive Material

Bergen Byarkiv, Bergen
Bergen Byrett, *Sjøforklaring,* Sak B144/1940, Eske 33, BB A.2848.002/y/0002/01, BB A.2848.002/y/0052/04

Riksarkivet, Oslo
RA FKA Ec, 0125, RA II-C-11-1100, RA II-C-11-1200, RA II-C-11-1240, RA II-C-11-1350, RA II-C-11-1360, RA II-C-11-52, RA-Boks1600 – 2B06234, RA-FKA-II-C-11/1103, RA-II-C-11/52, RA-Sjøforsvaret før 1940 – Boks1600 – 2B06234, RA/S-1643/D/Dd/L0003/0005

Staatsarchiv, Bremen,
Kriegsschädenamt, A608/43

Traditionsarchiv Unterseeboote (Deutsches U-Boot-Museum), Cuxhaven-Altenbruch
DUBM-U3-file, DUBM-*U4* file, DUBM-*U28,* DUBM-*U31*-file, DUBM-*U46*-file, DUBM-*U51* file, DUBM-*U60* file, DUBM-*U138*-file

Bundesarchiv, Freiburg
BA-RM 35 I/32, BA-RM 35 II/35, BA-RM 45/III-100, BA-RM 45/III-124, BA-RM 45/III-136, BA-RM 45/III-209, BA-RM 48/176, BA-RM 57/126, BA-RM 57/93, BA-RM 6/87, BA-RM 69/133, BA-RM 7/11, BA-RM 7/123, BA-RM 7/124, BA-RM 7/180, BA-RM 7/84, BA-RM 7/888, BA-RM 7/91, BA-RM 7/92, BA-RM 70/1, BA-RM 72/169, BA-RM 74/7, BA-RM 8/1152, BA-RM 92/5178, BA-RM

92/5223, BA-RM 92/5245, BA-RM 92/5257, BA-RM 92/5267, BA-RM 98/4, BA-RM 102/3679, BA-RM 102/3742, BA-RM 102/3622, BA-RM 69/7, BA-RM 69/30

The National Archives, Kew
NA-ADM 1/10234, NA-ADM 1/10667, NA-ADM 1/12025, NA-ADM 1/19910, NA-ADM 1/9378, A-ADM 116/3164, NA-ADM 116/3812, NA-ADM 116/3817, NA-ADM 116/3819, NA-ADM 116/4121, NA-ADM 116/4471, NA-ADM 156/283, NA-ADM 173/16115, NA-ADM 173/16665, NA-ADM 178/194, NA-ADM 186/798, NA-ADM 199 1844, NA-ADM 199/1115, NA-ADM 199/1814, NA-ADM 199/1819, NA-ADM 199/1827, NA-ADM 199/1828, NA-ADM 199/1829, NA-ADM 199/1830, NA-ADM 199/1836, NA-ADM 199/1837, NA-ADM 199/1839, NA-ADM 199/1840, NA-ADM 199/1843, NA-ADM 199/1844, NA-ADM 199/1846, NA-ADM 199/1847, NA-ADM 199/1848, NA-ADM 199/1853, NA-ADM 199/1856, NA-ADM 199/1857, NA-ADM 199/1858, NA-ADM 199/1861, NA-ADM 199/1864, NA-ADM 199/1874, NA-ADM 199/1877, NA-ADM 199/1878, NA-ADM 199/1879, NA-ADM 199/1880, NA-ADM 199/1921, NA-ADM 199/1925, NA-ADM 199/1940, NA-ADM 199/2063, NA-ADM 199/277, NA-ADM 199/278, NA-ADM 199/285, NA-ADM 199/286, NA-ADM 199/288, NA-ADM 199/292, NA-ADM 199/294, NA-ADM 199/300, NA-ADM 199/361, NA-ADM 199/373, NA-ADM 199/450, NA-ADM 199/474, NA-ADM 199/892, NA-ADM 223/126, NA-ADM 234/380, NA-ADM 234/52, NA-ADM 234/560, NA-ADM 267/114, NA-ADM 267/89, NA-ADM 358/184, NA-ADM 358/88, NA-ADM199/1827, NA-AIR 15/16, NA-AIR 2/2925, NA-CAB 65/11, NA-CAB 65/12, NA-CAB 66/6, NA-CAB 80/15, NA-FO 371/24818, NA-TS 32/112, NA-WO 106/1969, NA-WO 193/772, NA-WO 193/773, NA–ADM 234/380

Imperial War Museum, London
IWM 90/24/1, IWM 91/38/1, IWM 94/6/1, IWM soundfile 11730, IWM soundfile 11745, IWM soundfile 12571, IWM soundfile 9137, IWM Soundfile 9167/1,

Royal Navy Submarine Museum, Gosport
RNSM A1993/117, RNSM A1994/95, RNSM A1995/312, RNSM A1995/75, RNSM-A1934/5, RNSM-A1988/032, RNSM-A1993/117, RNSM-A1994/95, RNSM-A1994/95, RNSM-A1995/303, RNSM-A1995/75, RNSM-box 5 *Records of Warship Construction: The History of DNC Department,* RNSMrds *Shark* file

The US National Archives and Records Administration
NARA T1022-1057-30007, NARA T1022-2607-39582, NARA T1022-2793-48188, NARA T1022-2794-48204, NARA T1022-3142-2206, NARA T1022-3204-72459, NARA T1022-3292-74308, NARA T1022-3505-73562, NARA T1022-3505-73574, NARA T1022-3505-73575, NARA T1022-3505-73578, NARA T1022-3683-82186, NARA T1022-3798-82156

Traditiekamer Onterzeedienst, den Helder
TO-O13 file, TO-O14 file, TO-O15 file, TO-O22 file

German War Diaries (Kriegstagebücher KTB)
These come from several sources, Deutsches U-Boot-Museum in Cuxhaven-Altenbruch, NARA and various books are the most important. As they often vary in quality, parts of each document have been taken from different sources.

KTB 12th UJ-Flottille, KTB Küstenfliegergruppe Stavanger, KTB Seekommandant Stavanger, KTB SKL, KTB *U4*, KTB *U9*, KTB *U21*, KTB *U23*, KTB *U28*, KTB *U34*, KTB *U35*, KTB *U51*, KTB *U60*

Unpublished or published on the web

Brighton, J, 'Life on the Porpoise', unpublished verbal account at Diss Museum, Norfolk.
Schwarz, E R, *Submarine vs Submarine*, available at www.dutchsubmarines.com.
Skjold, E, *Norsk Skipsvrakarkiv*, Norwegian Shipwreck Register
Varvounis, M, *The Wilk Case*, available at www.dutchsubmarines.com.
Slujis, T van der, *Discovery of Doris*, available at www.uboat.net.
D'Adamo, C, *Regia Marina Italiana*, available at www.regiamarina.net.

Newspapers or periodicals

The War Illustrated, Vol 2, Dec 1939
Glasgow Herald, 5 July 1939.
Glasgow Herald, 6 July 1939.
Sydney Morning Herald, 27 December 1958.
The Evening News and Southern Daily Mail, 9 April 1946 (www.cavillconnections.co.uk/seal.htm)
The Evening News and Southern Daily Mail, 11 April 1946 (www.cavillconnections.co.uk/seal.htm)
Jones, M C, 'Experiment at Dundee: The Royal Navy's 9th Submarine Flotilla and Multinational Naval Co-operation during WW II', *Journal of Military History* 72 (October 2008), pp. 1179–212.
Vickers Shipbuilding and Engineering Ltd, *Barrow Built Submarines*
    Vol. 8: *1916–1945 L, H and R Class Submarines*
    Vol. 10: *1929–1945 The River Class Submarines*
    Vol. 11: *1930–1946 The Minelaying Submarines*
    Vol. 12: *1935–1970 T Class Submarines*
    Vol. 14: *1936–1958 U and V Class Submarines*

Websites

Information on the web is notoriously unreliable and often just repeats from a book or another website. It must be used with caution. The following websites have been found reliable and are recommended.

www.polishnavy.pl
www.rnsubs.co.uk
www.uboat.net
www.ubotarchive.net
www.dutchsubmarines.com
www.regiamarina.net
www.wrakenmuseum.nl
www.wlb-stuttgart.de
www.historisches-marinearchiv.de
www.dundee-at-war.net
www.warsailor.com
www.foreignaffairs.com/articles
ww.taucher.net
www.bismarck-class-dk

Index

People

Vorster, Eduard Herbert; Luitenant ter Zee 1ste Klasse 308–10

Voss; Lieutenant 172

Wachsmuth, Günther; Korvettenkapitän 258

Waddington; Signalman 279

Walsh, James Joseph; Stoker 342, 343

Wanklyn, Malcom David; Lieutenant 319, 320

Watkins, Guy Claire Ian St Barbe Sladen; Lieutenant 95, 295

Watson, Bertram Chalmers; Rear Admiral (Submarines) 9, 84, 133, 140

Weiss, Albert; Kapitän 164

Westmacot, Richard Evelyn; Lieutenant 237

Wheeler, David Edward; Lieutenant 337, 345

Wilson, Harry C; Yeoman of Signals 237

Witting, Kapitänleutnant 346

Woods, Frederick Grenville; Lieutenant 1, 4, 5, 7, 10–13, 15, 17–21, *21*

Wykeham-Martin, Maurice Fairfax; Lieutenant 120, 124, 132

Yorke, George J D; Pilot Officer 88

Young, Edward Preston, Sub-Lieutenant 55

Ytterlid, Reidar; Captain (Master) 251

Ships

Ships with no country designator are British

Dk: Danish

D: Dutch

Est: Estonian

Fr: French

G: German

N: Norwegian

Pl: Polish

Sw: Swedish